The International Handbook of

CORPORATE FINANCE

Third Edition

Brian J. Terry
Editor

Glenlake Publishing Company, Ltd.
Chicago • London • New Delhi

Fitzroy Dearborn Publishers
Chicago and London

©1997 The Chartered Institute of Bankers

ISBN: 1-888998-30-X

Library Edition: Fitzroy Dearborn Publishers, Chicago and London
ISBN: 1-884964-85-0

Printed in the United States of America

GPCo
1261 West Glenlake
Chicago, Illinois 60660
glenlake@ix.netcom.com
www.glenlake.com

Contents

CONTENTS

Contributors

Alby Cator is an Executive Director and Head of Syndications for NatWest Capital Markets.

Graham Allatt is Head of Credit Rating for NatWest Markets, where he is responsible for assessing the credit quality of multinational corporates worldwide.

Francis D'Souza is Head of Swaps Trading and Sales in Citicorp Investment Bank, London.

Patrick Donlea is a partner at Cazenove & Co., where he is a member of the Corporate Finance Department.

David Hager is a partner at Bacon & Woodrow, consulting actuaries, where he specializes in investment consulting.

Andrew Higgins specializes in the provision of financial engineering techniques and treasury management advice at National Westminster Bank.

Allen Hing is an Associate Director within the Structures Finance area of NatWest Markets.

J. Gordon McKechnie is a Vice President with J.P. Morgan.

Chris Mitchell is an Assistant Director examining and marketing hedging strategies at NatWest Markets.

Chris Porter is a member of NatWest's Primary Syndication team in Hong Kong.

Sarah Scarlett has worked at Credit Suisse First Boston Limited, principally on negotiation and execution of international securities transactions.

Philippa Skinner is an Assistant Director in UBS Philips and Drew in the Derivative Products Sector.

Michael Stocks is Head of the Country Risk Economics Unit at Midland Bank.

Brian J. Terry is Chief Examiner, Multinational Corporate Finance, The Chartered Institute of Bankers.

Eric Warner is a Vice President at First Chicago.

David Wells is a director of Barclays de Zoete Wedd Capital Markets Limited, where he is responsible for marketing within the commercial paper and medium-term note product areas.

John Willingham is Vice President, Marketing in Asia, at Sumishin Capital Group in Seattle, USA, an American-Japanese joint venture specializing in asset based finance, leasing and technical services for the airline industry.

Max Ziff is Director in charge of the Financial Structuring and Advisory Group at Warburg Securities.

CHAPTER 1

Principles of Lending–Part I

- THE ART OF CREDIT ASSESSMENT AND
  TRANSACTION DESIGN – A FRAMEWORK

by
John Willingham

"A Banker is a person who will lend you an umbrella when the sun is shining and will want it back the moment it starts to rain." This indictment, attributable, I believe, to Mark Twain has become a jibe often levelled (not always tongue-in-cheek) at the banking community by those unable to borrow from it on terms they believe they need or deserve. A similar conflict has, furthermore, developed within individual international banks themselves as, in response to increasing worldwide competition, they have attempted to become marketing orientated and aimed for a pro-active approach to their customers. Many a frustrated Account Officer has been heard to complain that his Credit Committee will allow him to lend money only to those who have no need for it, or that he is being forced by that same Committee to attempt to negotiate terms which his borrower will not accept and which are apparently not being sought by other banks bidding for the business.

This chapter, which represents the introduction to the credit section of the book, will explore briefly why these tensions implicit in the role of a lending bank are inevitable and then try to indicate how a thorough understanding of credit, fundamental to anyone involved in putting a bank's capital at risk, can help to alleviate the problems and misunderstandings. We shall then look at a framework for analysing the creditworthiness of a customer or potential customer in the context of a specific financing requirement and the principles involved in designing a transaction to suit the circumstances.

In this and other chapters I shall be focusing on what might be labelled the traditional financing activities of commerical banks in the international market viz. corporate and sovereign lending. The principles discussed, however, relate not only to lending but to any financial product which entails taking a credit risk on a customer. They, therefore, have relevance to, for example, swap transactions and forward foreign exchange facilities. To the extent that investment banking seeks to package and arrange finance where others will have to be persuaded to take the credit risk through the bond, note and commercial banking markets, credit assessment again plays a key role.

Most specific references in these chapters will be to issues arising with respect to industrial corporate customers. Consideration of other types of borrower will be by comparison to this core banking client.

1. THE PURPOSE OF CREDIT ASSESSMENT

1.1 Bank Vulnerability
I shall probably be accused of over-simplification in this section. I make no apology as I trust that the message arising from the analysis, *i.e.* "credit is crucial" is what is important for my purposes!

Banks as financial intermediaries are vulnerable institutions by their nature. Their primary source of funds tends to be short-term or on-demand deposits from a mix of private customers, companies and other banks. These deposits will total between 12 and 40 times the risk capital provided by shareholders depending on a bank's location, internal policy and regulatory environment. Such deposits are, of course, legally repayable in full to the depositors on their due dates whether or not the bank is successful in reinvesting the money received at a profit.

The primary use to which banks put the funds received from depositors is in lending to governments, other banks, companies and personal customers. The term of such lending will range from on-demand or "call" to periods in excess of 10 years. The balance varies from institution to institution, but it would not be untypical to see 70–80% of a bank's "total assets" absorbed by loans to various customers with repayment periods in excess of one month; within this loan portfolio 40% of total assets might

2

be loans with maturities in excess of one year and 20% with maturities over five years. This ignores any off-balance-sheet commitments.

A core role of a bank can, therefore, be seen as the conversion of short-term, risk-averse money into committed investment in the world economy for considerably longer periods. By doing so, it adds value to the raw materials of banking (deposits) and thereby seeks to make a profit. This creates two potential problems: *liquidity* and *creditworthiness.* Both require active central management.

1.2   Liquidity and Portfolio Management
Liquidity management will seek to ensure that the bank has at all times adequate liquid resources (cash, on-demand placings, government bills etc.) to ensure that it can satisfy any realistic demand for cash arising from withdrawal of deposits by customers. Failure to manage this area may result in an inability to repay depositors when due, notwithstanding a loan portfolio which might be paying interest and repaying principal on time. The result would be liquidation or, more likely, an approach to a Central Bank as lender of last resort. An over-liquid or short-term portfolio, on the other hand, will not earn the returns usually demanded by bank shareholders.

The management of bank creditworthiness ("Portfolio Management") will attempt to ensure that a bank does not expose itself to a risk of loss material enough to endanger its ability to satisfy its obligations to its depositors while, at the same time, attempting to achieve a portfolio balance which will provide an adequate return to its investors, the shareholders. If, for example, a bank has "Total Liabilities" which comprise (simplistically) 6% equity capital and 94% loan capital/deposits and a loan portfolio comprising 80% of "Total Assets", it does not take an accountant to appreciate that only 7.5% of that loan portfolio needs to default and fail to repay to result in that bank being unable to satisfy its obligations to its lenders/depositors.

1.3   Confidence
The practical result of this vulnerability is that a bank must seek at all times to maintain the confidence of its depositors to ensure that there is no unanticipated withdrawal of funds or "run on the bank". This confidence

is absolutely critical and requires a bank to maintain a reputation as a virtually risk-free home in which to place money. The maintenance of this confidence in personal customers is often helped by implicit government-backed guarantees of repayment (e.g. the Federal Deposit Insurance Corporation in the USA). Large corporate and inter-bank deposits are, by contrast, usually unprotected and sudden removal of money by these depositors can, because of the amounts involved, be catastrophic as demonstrated in the 1980s most graphically by well-publicised examples in the USA.

In practice, loss of this crucial confidence is likely to arise if major depositors become uneasy about a bank's ability to accommodate potential losses arising from exposure to one or more industrial or market sectors, countries or major customers. In the USA, for example, banks which have faced problems have in several cases been those with established bad-debt problems and perceived high exposure both to customers suffering from the weakness in oil prices and to customers with problems in the agricultural market.

The illiquid loans of many banks worldwide to developing countries are a major threat to confidence.

1.4 Implications for Bank Policy and Lending Practice

At the policy level, those charged with portfolio management at any bank must direct and monitor credit exposure to the various customer segments with which that bank is, or wishes to be, involved. Segmentation may include companies, industries, countries, regions and the various credit products offered by the institution (especially high risk products such as leveraged buy-outs). Effective communication and two-way formulation of policy guidelines in this area will assist the bank's customer relationship managers to seek and structure business compatible with the goals outlined. Such communication will also prevent the waste of resources represented by an enthusiastic marketing officer or team chasing business which will be summarily declined in the credit assessment process.

At the level of specific transactions, the nature of a bank and its business entails that those engaged in marketing, negotiating or approving new credit-related business must all have a thorough appreciation both of their banks' policies and objectives and of the principles of credit assessment. This should not be taken to imply a negative or reactive

4

approach. In the highly competitive market in which international banks now operate, success and market leadership will not come to those who rely on new business walking in the door of its own accord and being accepted or turned aside at will. As we see major banks selling off loan assets because of a change in emphasis from a desire for ever-larger balance sheets to a desire for stronger capital ratios and higher returns on investment, business may well be offered to those equipped only to react. Such business, however, will tend to be thinly priced and unrewarding.

Those who will establish and maintain themselves as leaders will do so by a pro-active and positive approach to the needs of the market. Potential credit problems can provide opportunities to those equipped with the imagination, experience and knowledge to devise structures to mitigate the risks. It is the credit problems which are not understood or which are ignored in a desire to do business which are the dangerous ones. Even where a whole market segment becomes depressed (as shipping and oil have become, for example), all banks do not suffer equally – much depends on the quality of the individual transactions in that part of a bank's portfolio.

Credit assessment, therefore, is neither a specialist role nor a policeman function; it is a fundamental banking skill acquired partly by a study of the principles but, more importantly, by experience of putting those principles into action in the real world. The rest of this chapter will establish the basic framework for a credit-orientated approach to specific customers and requirements. Following chapters will then seek to fill out some of the details. After that, there is no substitute for practical involvement and further reading, particularly of the quality financial press.

2. A FRAMEWORK FOR CREDIT ASSESSMENT AND TRANSACTION DESIGN

With hindsight, it is usually possible to recognise a successful transaction. It has **four** characteristics:

(a) *repayment* – the facility was serviced and repaid when due;

(b) *remuneration* – a reasonable return was earned for the bank in the context of the risk assumed and the administration/management time required;

5

(c) *relationship* – the relationship with the customer was enhanced producing opportunities for other banking business with that customer whether it be risk business or pure service business;

(d) *reputation* – the bank's reputation in the market was enhanced by the transaction, leading to opportunities with other customers.

Of the four characteristics, the first must be regarded as the most important. In the current market where banks will typically earn a pre-tax margin on funds lent in the international market of well under 1% p.a., it requires a large volume of successful business to overcome one US$10 million write-off! The primary focus of the following credit indicators is, therefore, how a facility will be repaid, what threats to successful repayment are there and how might these be mitigated.

Devising answers to these simple questions can be a complex process. It involves not only, or even mainly, financial analysis but rather a combination of analysis, judgement and problem solving based on critically directed research and questioning; the process is not scientific albeit that it is not an intuitive "look at his eyes and ignore the figures" either. For this reason, I prefer the term "credit assessment" to "credit analysis" as, to me at least, it conveys a more subjective and less number-crunching approach. If this appears to be underplaying the importance of financial analysis, may I say at this stage simply that the context in which that financial analysis is done is crucial to a sensible conclusion on any specific credit requirement. Numbers alone mean very little.

A framework for arriving at a conclusion as to the creditworthiness of a specific customer and the principles behind designing a transaction to suit the financing requirement of a customer in the context of that creditworthiness are described in the following sections and the next four chapters. The features are set out and explained primarily with reference to industrial corporate customers, the core international banking client – the different characteristics of other types of borrower are summarised in Chapter 2. I shall make no attempt in this general account to go into detail about lending to specialised industries such as commodity traders, insurance underwriters and oil producers. Those of you who are or who become involved in taking credit risks in those areas should, however, be able to adapt the basic principles to suit the specific circumstances, by combining them with the specialist knowledge you develop of the relevant industry.

In this context, the key elements of the methodology are as follows:

2.1 Assessing Creditworthiness – The Context

2.1.1 *Industry*
You cannot judge the creditworthiness of a company, or expect to produce a transaction which is likely to work both for the borrower and the bank, unless you understand the business the company is in and the opportunities and risks associated with it. This, together with the country analysis described below provides the context for the rest of the credit assessment.

2.1.2 *Country*
Companies do not, however, operate only in the context of an industry; they may be affected by developments in countries where they:

* trade;
* manufacture;
* have their headquarters;
* are owned.

Such country risks are both economic and political and are investigated in detail in Chapter 12.

2.2 Assessing Creditworthiness – Who Runs the Business?
Chapter 3 goes on from industry and country analysis to describe the principles of financial analysis. There are, however, further important related considerations for determining corporate creditworthiness which we shall examine in a little detail here.

2.2.1 *Management*
Standard and Poors in their Credit Overview summarise, aggressively but fairly, the role of management in the success or failure of a business: "According to many annual reports, corporate managements are innocent victims of "depressed" market conditions, "unprecedented" interest rates or "irresponsible" competition. Yet in the final analysis management can, should and will be held fully responsible for the corporation's results.

This is because at some point management made all the basic decisions as to what business to be in, chose competitive strategies and determined how the business should be financed. Successful companies are constantly rethinking these issues". Of fundamental importance, therefore, is a management's balance of experience, sensitivity and responsiveness to change in its environment, together with its philosophy towards business and financial risk.

2.2.1.1 *Contacts*

The judgement by a banker of a company's management is necessarily subjective and requires the devotion of time and resources. Clearly, meeting key figures in the management structure both in business and social settings enables a banker to investigate the thought processes, personalities and motives influencing the strategies which are being devised and implemented. These strategies will be crucial determinants of a business's success or failure in the future.

Often effective contact will be achieved by setting up relationships at several different levels (e.g. Account Officer – Treasurer/Assistant Treasurer; Section Head-Finance Director; General Manager – Chief Executive), a process which works well as long as the individual bank officers communicate effectively! In addition, plant tours and the like enable the observant and experienced account officer to judge morale and efficiency in the workplace.

The danger in this process is for a bank to become too close and thereby to lose the ability to make judgements about a company in a detached manner.

2.2.1.2 *Annual Reports*

Outside these contacts, it is possible to learn a significant amount about the quality of management from annual reports and accounts. Firstly, familiarise yourself with the company's core activities by means of the industry analysis and then examine the accounting policies and notes for signs of either an overly cautious or "creative" accounting approach to presenting the results of the business (the latter in particular sometimes being symptomatic of an inability to address or unwillingness to recognise underlying problems).

Secondly, analyse the track record in terms of profitability and cash flow (see Financial Analysis below) and, by comparison with the performance of the competition and by viewing the track record in the context of economic and market conditions, make a judgement on both the track record and management's role in achieving it. Was an improved level of profitability simply the result of lower oil prices and interest costs or has management shown an ability to improve the aspects of the business within its control (higher sales volume; greater productivity; new products etc)?

Finally, look at how the company presents and explains the track record in the narrative section. Are successes advertised and failures ignored? Are promises and expectations fulfilled? Are explanations coherent?

If, after the research, you have detailed questions (you should have), then ask the company representative with whom you are acquainted. Properly handled, he/she will not be offended but impressed that you have done your homework.

Possible signs of danger to be investigated are:

(i)   those which may imply willingness to assume an undue degree of business or financial risk. Examples include an aggressive dividend policy out of line with profit increases and cash flow generation perhaps to protect the share price in view of takeover fears; major acquisitions, especially diversification into unrelated areas of activity, financed mainly by debt; and the undertaking of a major project out of scale with the size of the company, the failure of which might endanger the business as a whole;

(ii)   those which may imply stagnation or loss of direction such as an ageing management team, no obvious path of succession and low new investment;

(iii)   those which may imply discord such as high management turnover;

(iv)   those which imply either possible failure to identify and tackle problems as they arise or a desire to disguise financial risk being assumed; such signs include the adoption of new accounting principles

9

or accounting-driven financing techniques to make the figures look better (some, but by no means all, sale and leaseback transactions, factoring arrangements and operating lease deals would fall into this latter category).

2.2.2 *Organisation*

As we come to understand a business better, we can come to conclusions as to whether the management and business organisation are suitable for the company in question.

- Is there a team with a breadth of experience, expertise and age at the top or is there undue reliance on one figure, perhaps a founder chairman/ chief executive?

- Is the executive management balanced by non-executive directors and, if so, are those non-executives individuals with the expertise, influence and experience to benefit the company or nominal figureheads brought in to appease shareholders?

- Are subsidiary managements given autonomy to act? There are advantages and disadvantages inherent in both centralised and decentralised management – both can work in suitable situations, an issue dealt with in the Nature of Management syllabus and in more detail in Human Aspects of Management in the F.S.D. Visiting subsidiary companies will help in making judgements here but, in addition, it is important to determine individual subsidiaries' powers in the financing area to establish whether they, or perhaps a central group treasury only, are empowered to take financing decisions.

- Does the way in which the business's activities are split make sense? An element of industry specialisation within a bank here as elsewhere can help to spot positive and negative signs through comparison with other industry participants. For example, businesses built from a series of inadequately integrated acquisitions can result in intra-group tensions and a parochial approach by individual operating units. Furthermore, companies which go through radical reorganisations once every few years may simply be demonstrating an inability to grapple with the fundamental business challenges facing the organisation, rather than an effective response to changes in its environment.

2.2.3 *Ownership*

There are four main types of ownership typically found in international banking transactions:

- state-owned;

- company-owned (usually in a parent-subsidiary relationship);

- privately-owned or controlled;

- publicly quoted on a Stock Exchange or Bourse.

Various combinations of the above are also not unusual. Owners both place restraints on a company and provide to varying degrees financial, managerial and trading resources. The restraints can be beneficial in keeping a company management focused on (hopefully long-term) profitability and prosperity rather than glamour or empire-building; they can also be stifling of enterprise and demoralising, one of the common arguments for privatisation. Resources provided can be a source of considerable strength (the Canadian aircraft manufacturing company De Havilland, for example, showed signs of considerable benefit following its sale by the Canadian Government to The Boeing Company in the USA); the transfer of resources can, alternatively, be negative with a struggling corporate parent or government draining a strongly-performing subsidiary of cash in an attempt to satisfy its own needs.

A public quotation is no less of a two-edged sword. A 'star' of a major stock market such as New York or Canada, with a market capitalisation well in excess of the net worth shown in its accounts and a price-earnings ratio which is high by the standards of its industrial sector can be relatively sure of raising equity capital in the market to fund its activities; in normal times it can usually also be sure of shareholder support against a hostile takeover (the "arbitraging" mid-80s were not normal times!).

A market capitalisation, by contrast, standing at a discount to net worth may reflect:

- market disenchantment with a sector (in which case the market capitalisation of other companies in that sector will also stand at a discount);

- market disenchantment with a company's management and earnings prospects.

11

Such companies may find new equity difficult to place economically or be forced into high dividend payments to protect the share price from further weakness. They may also be vulnerable to a hostile takeover.

The danger is that excessive preoccupation by management with its share price in the context of an active stock market may cause that management to act in ways detrimental to the interests of creditors of the business by, for example, over-borrowing in an attempt to boost return on equity or concentrating on short-term accounting profitability at the expense of longer-term investment. The most dramatic example of such a preoccupation, however, is the process of a company using debt to buy in its own shares in a deliberate attempt to reduce its equity base. There were some dramatic examples of this during the '80s in attempts by company managements to avoid being taken over, particularly in the USA.

Brokers' or analysts' reports, together with the financial press, can often be of significant help in understanding what factors are underlying an individual company's share price performance. In assessing what such reports say, it is worth remembering that the interests of ordinary shareholders whose rights on a liquidation are subordinate to the rights of all creditors, but whose return is not limited to a pre-determined interest rate, are not necessarily the same as the interests of a company's creditors. A share price swelled, for example, by takeover speculation or a generous dividend policy is not usually a recommendation to lend.

In assessing the impact of a public quotation on a company, it is also important to understand the stock market in which its shares are quoted. In the USA and UK, the major lending banks do not have shareholdings in their customers – the roles of lender and shareholder are (in general) rigidly separated. By contrast, 'establishment' banks in Japan and Germany often control large blocks of shares in major companies to which they are also significant lenders. There are strong arguments in favour of each system which it would not be appropriate to rehearse here; suffice it to say that bank shareholdings in German and Japanese companies appear to contribute to a more stable industrial environment where hostile takeover activity is rare and where long-term investment by various industries has proved highly successful in world markets. This is not to say that I recommend a shift in a bank's corporate lending emphasis from the USA and UK to Japan and Germany, but rather an indication of the need to understand as fully as possible the environment or context in which a company operates.

2.3 Assessing Creditworthiness – Financial Capacity

As stated in the introduction to this Section 2, the dominant consideration in assessing a financing transaction is how the bank is to be repaid. Financial statements are a key tool in assessing the ability to repay in as much as they attempt to portray the performance of the business in monetary terms. Properly handled, therefore, they enable conclusions to be drawn as to the borrower's, or potential borrower's, ability to service its financial obligations in accordance with their terms; they also enable an assessment to be made of what protections are available if something goes wrong. In other words the focus is on (i) the company's ability to generate CASH from its trading activities to continue in business and pay its debts on time and in the last resort, (ii) its ability to generate CASH from sales of assets, and investments or from other sources to pay creditors should its trading performance be inadequate.

In particular, I should like to emphasise the following points here:

- the need to appreciate the CONTEXT in which the results have been achieved; the importance in this regard of the industry and country analysis has already been mentioned;

- the need to understand the implications for a lender of CORPORATE STRUCTURE in the context of the limited liability of shareholders for the performance of the companies they own; the way a group of companies is structured can have a profound impact on the quality and priority of your recourse for repayment to the cash flow and cash flow generating assets of that group;

- the need to be familiar with the rules and conventions of the language of accounting and to appreciate the strengths and limitations of accounts in presenting the true health of the business;

- the need to remember that accounts are historic and out-of-date; they are useful to us only in acting as a guide for the future; we therefore need to focus on TRENDS over a period of years and, where possible, on MANAGEMENT PROJECTIONS;

13

- the need to recognise that, notwithstanding good historic results, the company's ability to prosper in the future will be largely determined by the QUALITY OF MANAGEMENT in shaping events and responding to challenges presented by the industrial environment and countries in which it operates.

Financial analysis is thus important but not all-embracing; it requires both an appreciation of its purpose and knowledge of its limitations; it is not synonymous with, but nevertheless a key part of, credit assessment.

Against this background, we shall examine how to extract the necessary information from accounts in terms of:

- PROFITABILITY: the measure of trading performance, to be analysed both in terms of quantity of earnings and the quaility or reliability of those earnings;

- CASH FLOW: the measure of the business's ability to convert reported profits to cash available both to finance trading and growth and to service obligations to creditors and shareholders;

- CAPITAL: the measure of the protection available to creditors in the value of a business's assets should trading performance be disappointing;

- LIQUIDITY: the measure of the availability to the business of ready sources of cash to enable it to satisfy obligations maturing over the short-term; this includes assessment of the adequacy of committed but unutilised sources of finance.

Completion of the above three stages of assessment should enable you to draw conclusions about the overall creditworthiness of a customer or potential customer. Some banks will, on the basis of the assessment, assign internally a "RISK RATING" as a readily understood indication of the attractiveness of credit exposure to a company, and thus a useful guide to marketing officers responsible for developing business with suitable clients.

3. TRANSACTION DESIGN
If new facilities are under consideration, then the analysis of creditworthiness needs to be supplemented by a detailed examination of

14

the terms of the exposure to be assumed by the bank. To take an example, the fact that a medium-sized, industrial company based in Germany has a creditable track record and apparently encouraging prospects does not of itself make a US $100m five-year unsecured loan facility a safe credit risk!

We, therefore, need to look closely at the specific FINANCING PROPOSAL OR PROPOSITION. The phrasing of that statement rather implies a situation where you have been presented with a ready-packaged deal and simply asked to react. Nevertheless, understanding of the principles works equally well, if not better, in cases where there is a need for a positive and pro-active approach as it should ensure that a proposal is drawn up which both takes into account the risks involved and seeks to mitigate them.

As with the discussion on creditworthiness above, in this chapter we are setting the scene for a further discussion later in the book. Chapter 4 will look in detail at SITUATION, PURPOSE, AMOUNT, TERM AND REPAYMENT. Chapter 5 will then go on to examine issues related to SECURITY, QUASI SECURITY, CONTROL AND MONITORING AND PRICING.

The following is a summary of the key issues discussed in those chapters.

3.1 Situation
This is the context in which the proposition is presented to you or you identify an opportunity to do business:

- To what extent is your flexibility to act limited?
- What are your options?
- What are you trying to achieve?

3.2 Purpose
The purpose of the financing sets the main parameters for designing the transaction structure because, inter alia, it affects the safety of repayment and attractiveness of the business and largely determines the type of financing required.

Chapter 2, Sections 2 and 3, look at different needs or purposes for finance which typical borrowers have and at the range of banking products available to meet those needs.

Chapter 4, Section 2 takes the purposes identified and relates them to the following issues:

- compliance with the bank's internal policy in extending finance (financing of arms sales or hostile takeovers are examples of where controversy may arise);

- the commercial and economic logic of the purpose to be financed;

- the ability and experience of the management to handle the proposed venture;

- compliance with the bank's legal constraints;

- legal complications arising from the purpose of the financing which may impair the creditworthiness of the transaction.

3.3 Amount

The amount of the total financing requirement and the amount you are prepared to contribute merit close consideration from the following perspectives:

- Adequacy: is it adequate for the purpose? A bank which lends £500,000 when £1m is needed and fails to satisfy itself that the balance can be financed elsewhere does neither itself nor its customer any favours.

- Cushion and Contribution: in project lending or transactions secured by fixed assets, a cash contribution from the shareholders or company itself acts as evidence of commitment and a cushion to the lenders against failure of the project or failure of the secured assets to generate repayment; in unsecured transactions the same principles apply but here we are focusing on the extent to which a company is, in general, financing itself by debt rather than equity capital.

16

- Portfolio Considerations: how does the proposed exposure affect the bank's limits on exposure to the relevant Corporate Group, industry and country?

- Transaction Risk and Term: banks will wish to limit their exposure to individual high risk and longer term transactions more tightly than to lower risk and short-term deals.

- Yield: increasingly banks are concerned to maximise yield from the use of their balance sheet and the amount "taken" in the transaction can be a significant determinant of the overall return from the deal.

- Legal Considerations: is it legal for the borrower to borrow such an amount and is it legal for a bank to lend it?

3.4 Term
The length of time for which you will be exposed must be consistent with the borrower's ability to repay; longer term, however, generally implies higher risk because of the greater uncertainty associated with looking further into the future.

3.5 Repayment
The key issue: how are we to be repaid and what is the margin of error if trading conditions deteriorate? We shall be looking at:

- The TYPE of repayment source;
- The QUALITY of repayment source;
- The CURRENCY of income from the repayment source (i.e. the margin of error);
- CASH FLOW protection;
- FINANCIAL FLEXIBILITY (i.e. alternative sources of cash to cover shortages);
- ASSET PROTECTION to cover you if cash flow is inadequate;
- COUNTRY RISKS associated with payments to be made by the borrower;
- The need for good DOCUMENTATION.

We shall also examine various repayment structures in terms of their suitability for different types of transaction.

3.6 Security and Quasi-Security

Security is your protection against non-payment from the primary repayment source - it is your insurance against failure and takes the form of a legally enforceable claim on tangible assets or a third party. Quasi-security attempts to fulfil the same role either indirectly or by means of a moral not a legal claim.

Such additional protection is not necessary in all cases; unsecured transactions are quite acceptable where cash flow protection is generous and reliable and adequate asset cover is available through the recourse available for creditors generally to a company's assets.

Lending without security

It is quite common for lending to large quoted companies to be made without security. Lenders are willing to do this partly because of competitive pressures, but also because they believe the size, diversity and financial health of the company mean that it is unlikely to collapse suddenly. However, lenders still need to protect themselves against each of the following:

(i)   gradual deterioration over time;

(ii)   sudden deterioration due to a significant event which increases the company's level of debt, such as a takeover of, or a major acquisition by, the group. This is often referred to as "event risk".

Protection against both of these circumstances is provided by covenants in loan documentation. Protection against gradual deterioration is provided by financial ratios which the borrower covenants to meet ("ratio covenants"). These also provide protection against "event risk", but additional protection may be provided by:

(i)   Change of ownership clauses. These may give the lender additional rights if ownership of the borrower changes;

(ii)   Material Adverse Change clauses. These will give the lender certain rights if the borrower's financial position is subject to "material adverse change". This procedure has limitations as there is no watertight legal definition of what constitutes "material adverse change".

18

The rights which accrue to the lender when a covenant is breached may vary, and have to be defined in the documentation. They may include the right to receive security, to call an event of default, or to obtain immediate repayment.

Where additional protection is required, however, then we need to assess it to determine whether it:

- has a stable or rising value;
- is cheap and simple to:
    - take;
    - realise;
    - monitor and control.

3.7   Control and Monitoring
The ability to take control of a lending situation before a deterioration in the borrower's condition becomes terminal is crucial. It is achieved by insertion in the documentation of "triggers" or provisions which, if breached, will enable you to convert a committed facility into one immediately repayable on demand. Such provisions and how compliance by the borrower can be monitored are discussed in detail in Chapter 5, Section 2.

3.8   Structuring
Structuring is the process of designing the details of a transaction within the broad parameters above to maximise the benefits for the borrower and the protection and remuneration for the bank. We shall look at issues which commonly occur viz:

- priority of recourse (the dangers of holding companies and the use of subordinated debt);
- the impact of taxation;
- the choice of debt market;
- the balance between flexibility, cost and simplicity;
- the need to sell transactions to other banks.

3.9 **Pricing**

Finally, we shall examine the complex issues associated with achieving satisfactory remuneration in a competitive market including:

* the risk-reward ratio;
* the costs of administration and overheads;
* reserve asset costs;
* capital adequacy "costs";
* techniques to optimise yield.

4. CONCLUSIONS ON THE FRAMEWORK

At first sight, the framework may appear to involve a formidable list of considerations. In any given situation, however, not all of the issues will require detailed consideration; it is the cases which involve previously unknown customers, marginal propositions or complex commercial or legal issues which absorb the greatest time. Efficient credit assessment and transaction design will require you to use judgement and common sense in applying the principles described. Sensible conclusions will always be easier to reach if you ensure that your assessment and design focus closely on the following fundamental questions:

* "If I lend this money, how and when will I be repaid?"
* "What can go wrong and what protections do I have if it does?"
* "What advantages are in this transaction for the bank and how can they be safely maximised?"

This focus should prevent any tendency to go off unproductively at a tangent.

5. INFORMATION SOURCES

Never be afraid to use all the sources of information available to you. As a member of an international bank, these will include:

* The customer (you don't know until you ask!);

* The customer's competitors and other industry participants (what do they think of their rival? Take great care, however, about your duty of confidentiality);

20

- Annual Reports and Accounts plus interim statements;

- International Financial Press especially   – *Financial Times*
    – *The Banker*
    – *Wall Street Journal*
    – *Euromoney*
    – *Economist*
    – *Euromarket*
    – *Business Week*

- Local Quality Press;

- Industry Press;

- Trends in Stock Market Price and Market Capitalisation supplemented by brokers'/analysts' reports;

- Credit Rating Agency Reports and ratings e.g. Standard and Poors and Moodys where available (mostly major companies); Dunn and Bradstreet is useful for middle-market companies in the USA & UK;

- The Economic Analysis and Country Analysis sections of your bank which will tend to have access not only to press data but also to the publications of e.g. the Organisation for Economic Co-operation and Development, the International Monetary Fund, the World Bank and various Central Banks;

- Country Reports and Surveys in the International Press;

- Lawyers and Accountants, both of individual borrowers for specific legal and financial information subject to the consent of the borrower, and those in general practice for information on legal, tax and accounting issues in the country in which they are based;

- Again taking great care about the need for confidentiality and bearing in mind also your own competitive position, other banks.

6. CREDIT COMMITTEES

Finally, a word about those internal tensions within banks which I touched on in the introduction to this chapter. I have heard it argued that a bank which employs the right people to deal with borrowing customers and trains them properly should simply give them high personal lending discretions and allow them to "get on with it". Banks, however, as discussed earlier, have a duty not to place their depositors' money unduly at risk and, indeed, are highly vulnerable should they be perceived to have done so. There needs, therefore, to be a set of checks and balances both to prevent problems occuring and, where nevertheless problems arise, to see that these are promptly identified and tackled.

Furthermore, in situations where a customer relationship officer (whose performance will often be assessed, at least in part, by the volume of business he transacts) is involved in detailed negotiations with a company, pressure to "get a deal done" can sometimes detract from the detachment with which a banker needs to assess credit-related issues. An approval process forces a detached look to be taken before an irrevocable decision is made.

Banks handle the approvals process in different ways. At least one major and highly respected commercial bank leaves the approval process to "calling officers" – the higher the amount or longer the term, the higher the number and level of seniority of signatories required. Others have a separation of marketing and credit functions, each with independent reporting lines to Executive General Management. Banks will usually refer to either approval chain as a "Credit Committee".

Each system has its advantages and disadvantages seen in the context of the twin requirements to earn a return for shareholders and to maintain credit quality. For either system to work, however, requires both those involved in the approvals process and those involved in marketing or relationship management to understand the principles of credit assessment, and to be able to apply them in a disciplined but (increasingly) creative manner. When this situation is achieved, key issues can be identified, summarised accurately and addressed enabling responses to customers to be fast and comprehensive. Disagreements will not be eradicated – much of credit assessment is, after all, a question of individual judgement –

but understanding of the issues should reduce the incidence of frustrated account officers bleating unconvincingly to dissatisfied customers that the nebulous "Credit Committee" will not allow them to do what they regard as perfectly sensible and reasonable.

CHAPTER 2

Principles of Lending–Part II

- MATCHING PRODUCTS TO NEEDS
  – BORROWERS, FINANCING REQUIREMENTS,
  FACILITIES AND TAXATION

by
John Willingham

Chapter 1 looked at the nature of the business of banking and the key role of credit assessment within that business. We then discussed a framework for carrying out a credit assessment in any given situation with specific reference to lending to companies.

This chapter will compare the different types of borrower commonly found in international finance by reference (1) to their main characteristics and (2) to their typical needs for financing. We shall then (3) match these needs to the facilities or financing products which have been offered by banks for some time, and continue to be offered, to satisfy these needs. In Section 4 we briefly look at the issue of taxation. Other contributors to this book will look in detail at the alternatives to these products which have been developed both as evolution of markets has taken place (e.g. Commercial Paper, MTNs and the range and variety of bond and equity issues) and as sophisticated risk management techniques have been devised (e.g. currency and interest rate swaps, futures and options, caps, floors and collars). I hope, however, that the principles involved in matching a financing product to the customer's needs will become clear enough from this chapter to enable you to draw your own conclusions about suitable alternatives or enhancements which may be available in what we can loosely refer to as the capital markets arena.

1. CHARACTERISTICS

1.1 Corporates

1.1.1 *Legal*

Let us recap some of the legal characteristics of companies, the most common type of borrower internationally and the implications of these characteristics when things go wrong.

A company is a legal personality separate from its owners. In other words, a company may act in its own name and (in the absence of fraud or other special circumstances related to the laws of individual countries) neither a company's owners nor its managers have any personal liability should that company be unable to fulfil its obligations. True, the owners of such a company may lose their investment and control of its activities and the managers may lose their jobs, but failure of the company in general gives creditors no recourse to the owners or managers as individuals.

This separate legal personality has two consequences:

(a) *Authorisation*: A company's right to act (including its right to borrow money, guarantee etc) is limited by the rules by which it is established; these rules are contained in the corporate rule-book which, depending on location, may be referred to as the Memorandum and Articles of Association, the Bylaws or Corporate Statutes.

A lender who knows, or should have known because the rule book is public, that a company is not empowered to borrow from it on the terms agreed with management (i.e. the transaction is "ultra vires" or "beyond the powers" of the company) may find it has no legal redress to the company for recovery of monies lent. Great care, therefore, needs to be taken to ensure all obligations undertaken by a company are duly authorised under its own rules through close inspection of those rules and/or legal opinions.

(b) *Recourse*: If a company fails to fulfil its obligations to creditors, its assets may become generally available to those creditors under the provisions of the bankruptcy or liquidation laws applicable to the company. Creditors will then be repaid from the proceeds of sale of those assets according to the priorities established by security previously granted by the company and the relative preferences established under the law. Only the assets owned by the company itself will be available to its creditors in the absence of guarantees or other undertakings given by third parties. If, therefore, you are lending to a holding company whose assets comprise solely shares in its subsidiaries, you will have recourse only to those shares; any direct lenders to those subsidiaries will thus be repaid out of the assets of the respective borrowing subsidiaries before those assets become available to you. Beware, therefore, situations where you are asked to lend to a holding company particularly where only consolidated figures are available.

1.1.2 *Creditworthiness*

The range and variety of companies are enormous. As a lender, you need to understand fully the implications for a borrowing company of the industry in which it operates, the competition it faces and the location/locations in which it is based and to which it trades. See Chapter 3.

1.2 **Sovereigns**

"Sovereigns" constitute borrowers who represent the full faith and credit of the government of the borrowing country. Such borrowers will, therefore, usually be the government itself or a Ministry of that government or a borrower whose obligations are indemnified by that government.

1.2.1 *Legal*

(a) *Authorisation*: Due authorisation is essential; local legal advice will be required to ensure that the official signing any document is empowered to bind the government at the time he/she signs.

(b) *Governing Law*: A government which borrows under a loan agreement drawn up under the law of that country may, in theory, make the agreement null and void simply by subsequently and retroactively changing its law. For the implications for creditworthiness of what, it should be emphasised, is an extremely rare occurrence, see below.

(c) *Sovereign Immunity*: A government which borrows under the law of another country (usually English as the primary law of international commerce) will, as long as the obligation was duly authorised, have a binding obligation under that foreign law. In a default, however, that government may be able to claim exemption from legal proceedings under the concept of sovereign immunity so that the binding obligation becomes unenforceable. Under English law, this problem can be mitigated for commercial transactions by requiring from the borrowing government in the loan documentation the following explicit assurances:

(i) a waiver of sovereign immunity;

(ii) a submission to the jurisdiction of the English courts;

(iii) an agreement that the assets of the government may be seized after a default to pay any debt due.

In practice, this would permit the freezing of e.g. bank accounts held by the government abroad but would give no effective recourse to a government's assets in its own country.

1.2.2 *Creditworthiness*

As a result of the above, a sovereign's creditworthiness is determined by two factors:

(a) *Ability to Pay*: The economic factors which govern a country's ability to service debt are fully discussed in Chapter 12, on Country Risk. In summary, the ability to pay is dependent on the extent to which (i) the economy can be taxed to raise money for the government and (ii) on the ability of that economy to generate

28

foreign exchange to which the government can gain access by obliging its citizens to repatriate, and exchange for local currency, foreign currency received.

(b) *Willingness to Pay*: If a government were to decide to renege on its debts, its creditors would not have the remedy which is usually available to creditors lending to companies i.e. that of forcing a liquidation. Action would have to be in the form of a cut-off of further credit, trade embargoes and other political and commercial pressures. To date, the only celebrated formal refusals to acknowledge debt of which I am aware are those by the newly installed communist governments of Russia and China after the revolutions which brought them to power, when they refused to acknowledge debts incurred by the previous non-communist regimes.

In more modern times, many countries have faced an inability to pay debts when due and have taken the route of renegotiation and rescheduling, with most agreements including the provision of some new money by creditors in proportion to their existing commitments. Unilateral actions by debtors have been limited to moratoria on debt or interest payments, while negotiations take place on a rescheduling, and to the imposition by a limited number of countries of a restriction on debt service payments tied to a percentage of exports. In what is now a highly integrated world, for a country to renege would entail such damage to its national reputation and such damage to its commercial activities that there is little attraction in this alternative as a solution to economic problems while reschedulings can be negotiated. Continued successful management of what has become known as the 'Debt Crisis' will require that all parties retain and develop further a constructive and broad approach to the problems.

The results for lenders are:

(i) *New Money*: if you find yourself lending to a country which hits problems, you will almost certainly not be able to cut your losses and refuse further credit unless you are able to find another institution willing to buy you out at a discount. Most likely will be a requirement

29

upon you as a lender, reinforced by pressure from other commercial banks plus your government and Central Bank, to lend more money. Such pressure may indeed also prevent you exercising your rights over any security held by you outside or inside the country if to do so would cross-default the country's other loan agreements including perhaps, ones in which your bank is also a participant.

(ii) *Control and Monitoring*: the effectiveness of the sort of documentary protection discussed in Chapter 5 (covenants and events of default) is minimal, except as a trigger for renegotiation, and a lender's ability to have any influence on the way a country conducts its affairs is, in general, slight. True, the International Monetary Fund (IMF) may be able to exert influence once a rescheduling has become necessary but, by then, the situation may already have deteriorated beyond redemption at least in the short to medium term. Furthermore, sufficiently accurate, timely and comprehensive information may not be available to enable developing problems to be promptly identified even if monitoring mechanisms are in place.

(iii) *General*: the above points should be looked at in the context they are made i.e. what happens if something goes wrong – they are, therefore, addressing the worst case and are, inevitably, rather negative in tone. Do not forget, however, that:

• in the absence of security held outside the country on terms which insulate it from a country's general debt, transactions with a Government will probably be the strongest transactions available in that country;

• reneging on debt is not a rational alternative except for a country which has the *desire*, for political reasons, and *ability*, owing to domestic resources, to become isolationist; and

• problems of taking control when a loan encounters problems are not entirely restricted to sovereign transactions because, notwithstanding the technical option for a creditor to go for liquidation, a major

30

corporation with a multitude of line banks may be able to use political pressure to force a rescheduling of its obligations if it hits trouble – the story of Chrysler in the early 80s (now, of course, re-established as a successful corporation) is instructive in this regard.

The moral is that, just as in lending to companies, you need to understand sufficient about a potential sovereign customer and its environment to enable you to make a reasoned judgement about the risks involved in any lending proposal. Do not be tempted to go in simply because major banks are involved and "that is the market" – the market can be wrong!

1.3   Quasi-Sovereigns

"Quasi-Sovereign" borrowers are those owned by, but not legally an integral part of, a government. The commonest examples are state-owned corporations and state-owned authorities.

1.3.1   *Legal*

The extent to which loan obligations of such entities equate to credit obligations of the host government depends on the legal constitution of those entities. In theory, a government which owns a company as 100% shareholder has no legal obligation to bail that company out should it become unable to fulfil its obligations.

This legal separation of shareholder and company may be over-ridden by laws in a host country which commit the government to support its state-owned organisations, or by formal undertakings given by a government to the same effect.

1.3.2   *Creditworthiness*

The creditworthiness of any quasi-sovereign organisation will depend on the same factors as those discussed in Section 1.2.2 together with the extent and quality of committed or implied government support for the organisation.

In the absence of legally committed support by way of guarantee or a

31

binding commitment to support given for the benefit of creditors generally, there may nevertheless be significant implied sovereign support (or *willingness* to pay) arising from the role played by the organisation in the host economy (e.g. a monopoly telephone company) or from the need of a government for reasons of pride and commercial standing not to be seen to allow one of its owned or controlled organisations to fail.

Of course, extensive implied support for a loss-making state-owned organisation is useful only to the extent that the host government has other resources which are adequate to enable it to provide the tangible support if it becomes required (i.e. *ability* to pay). The quality of the support is thus, of course, equally crucial and dependent on the issues discussed in Chapter 12.

1.4 Supra-Nationals
"Supra-national" borrowers are those which are owned and supported by more than one government. Examples include the International Bank for Reconstruction and Development (more commonly known as the World Bank) and the African Development Bank.

1.4.1 *Legal*
As with many "quasi-sovereigns", supra-national borrowers will usually be independent legal entities. Their capital is, in general, provided by the participating governments in proportions agreed in the treaty or other instrument which provides for the establishment and operation of the organisation. The participating governments may also be legally liable under the terms of the treaty or capital issue to make further contributions of capital if required by the organisation to enable it to function. The terms of such obligations to provide additional funds thus determine the extent to which the participating governments can be regarded as being "on the hook" for the obligations of the supra-national borrower.

1.4.2 *Creditworthiness*
As with "quasi-sovereigns", the creditworthiness of supra-nationals should be assessed both in terms of their ability to pay from their own resources and in terms of the extent and quality of the sovereign support behind them. Again, it may be possible to infer from the role the organisation

plays in the world economy or in the economies and politics of the participating nations, and from the need of these nations to protect their own reputations in the banking markets, a level of sovereign support in excess of the legal obligations of those nations to provide additional support. Again, also, any clearly apparent willingness to support needs to be matched by a demonstrable ability to pay in case of need.

I should emphasise that the strength of implied support should be closely analysed in each individual situation. It is not sufficient to assume that part-ownership by, or participation of, one or more highly creditworthy countries will ensure that any lenders to a particular organisation will be paid off if that organisation fails. Where the role of the relevant organisation is, or becomes, unpopular with some or all of the participating governments and disagreements arise between the participants over the desirability of continuing support, then lenders to the organisation may face the prospect of losses if the organisation ceases to be able to fulfil obligations from its own resources. The failure during 1985 of the Tin Council and the consequent problems for lenders is an instructive example.

1.5 Other Borrowers

International bankers may also find themselves with opportunities to finance other types of borrowers such as joint ventures, limited partnerships and various forms of trusts and vehicle companies set up for a variety of tax and other reasons. In each of these situations, legal advice will probably be required to determine the legal consequences and effectiveness of the arrangements proposed, whilst the creditworthiness of the borrower will depend both on its quality as a stand-alone entity and the extent and quality of committed and implied recourse to the individuals, companies and other organisations participating in the transaction.

The form of such arrangements tends to be complicated and tailor-made to fit the individual circumstances. It would, therefore, neither be possible nor desirable to attempt to go into detail in this book.

We can, however, simply enumerate a few key factors in looking at any complex borrowing structure:

(i)   Why is the structure necessary?

(ii) Does the answer to (i) produce any risks not present in a straightforward transaction? If, for example, a complicated structure is required to exploit a tax advantage, is it possible that the tax efficiency of the arrangements might be challenged by the relevant authorities? If so, who is responsible for meeting any additional financing costs and the costs of any litigation, management time and expense in resolving a dispute and the cost to terminate the arrangements if they are finally decided to be disadvantageous?

If you as a lender are indemnified by another party for any such costs, will that party be able and willing to pay if called upon and to what extent will you be able to control the way any problems are handled? Risks identified in this type of transaction may, therefore, include not only credit risks but also risks of burdensome administration and risks to the bank's reputation.

Such deals are often attractive to bankers because they are interesting, and produce a reputation for creativity and innovation. Badly handled, however, they can simply be a catalyst for expense and acrimony – do not allow yourself to be blinded by the science which goes into the structure so that you lose sight of the underlying important credit, administrative and policy considerations.

2. FINANCING NEEDS
Each of the above categories of borrower have typical needs for finance which can be satisfied (at least in part) by bank loan facilities.

2.1 Corporates
The typical needs of industrial companies are summarised below. They exclude specialised needs of various types of company including those engaged in banking, insurance, commodity trading, broking etc. which are outside the scope of a general study such as this.

2.1.1 *Working Capital/Net Working Assets*

Most industrial companies will have a requirement to fund a portion of their stock and trade debtors which is not funded by trade creditors. The extent of this requirement will usually vary according to production and seasonal cycles, being at its highest when stocks are being built up, sold and invoiced and at its lowest (or negative) as invoices are paid by customers and stocks run down.

Most companies will have a more-or-less permanent need to have finance for working capital available as it is unusual for industrial companies to hold sufficient surplus cash to enable them both to hold adequate stocks and allow the credit required by customers without recourse to borrowing at some stage of their production and/or seasonal cycle.

Companies which are expanding their sales and production quickly will find the most pressing need for such finance as they will usually need both to invest in the additional stock required to enable them to service growing demand efficiently and to allow new customers the extent of trade credit accepted in the industry *before* cash from the increased sales flows in as invoices are paid.

See Chapter 3, Section 5.4.3 for further explanation of working capital/ net working assets.

2.1.2 *Trade Finance*

Closely related to the above is trade finance and the financial products which have been designed particularly to facilitate cross-border trade. The difference is simply that working capital finance is usually required to fund the general excess of trading assets over liabilities whilst trade finance products are usually tailored for specific sales or sets of sales. Examples of the latter include both acceptance credit facilities drawn by means of bills of exchange endorsed with the details of specific trade transactions and finance supported by the export finance agencies of individual countries to encourage exports (e.g. EXIMBANK in the USA, COFACE in France, HERMES in Germany and ECGD in the UK).

We shall not concern ourselves in this book with specific trade finance products as they are outside the scope of the International Finance and

Investment examination, and are discussed in detail by Alasdair Watson in *Finance of International Trade*. They can, however, be an advantageous way for companies, especially those engaged in exporting, to finance their trading as an alternative to borrowing under more general facilities.

2.1.3 *Capital Expenditure*

In addition to their need to fund trading assets or working capital, companies will usually require funds to invest in production facilities (factories and equipment) and offices, with repayment tailored to some extent to the working lives of the capital assets built or acquired.

2.1.4 *Project Finance*

Certain types of company will require finance tailored to suit the cash flow requirement of specific projects, often with the lender agreeing to take some portion of the project risk through the acceptance of limited recourse to the company or companies running the project (see Chapter 8). Such finance is common e.g. in the oil industry to finance the development of oil fields and in the property/real estate industry to finance commercial building.

2.1.5 *Acquisition Finance*

The '80s saw major acquisitions of companies by other companies financed by bank loan facilities. Repayment was usually tailored to the cash flow surpluses expected to be generated by the combined entity.

Within this category of financial requirement comes the 'Leveraged Buy Out', fashionable especially in the USA, whereby an acquirer of a company (either an existing management in a management buy-out or another corporation or the company itself by buying in a portion of its own shares) uses a high proportion of bank debt in relation to its equity stake to finance the purchase. In this situation, the lenders will look primarily at the acquired company's ability to generate the cash for repayment from a combination of asset sales and trading. The relation of debt to equity in a company emerging from an acquisition financed in this way (even after the book value of fixed assets has been revalued) can be as high as 10:1. For particularly leveraged transactions, however, there will usually be three "layers" of finance: "pure" equity or common shares; preference shares or debt subordinated to the rights of bank lenders and bank debt often secured on the assets of the acquired company. The subordinated debt will often be in the form of "junk bonds", i.e. bonds rated by rating agencies such as Moodys and Standard & Poors below "investment grade" and therefore considered "speculative". These are usually placed by investment banks with a variety of institutional and individual investors at an attractively high interest rate. Such subordinated debt effectively increases the equity cushion available to the bank lenders – but see Chapter 5, for key considerations to make this subordination effective.

2.1.6 *Contingency Cover*

Companies will often seek a committed source of bank finance at a pre-arranged pricing which they can use at their option at any time when either additional funds are required over and above those currently in use or the bank pricing becomes attractive compared to the available alternatives. In this way, a company can be certain of having financial resources available to it should an investment opportunity arise (i.e. a "standby commitment") and of having an alternative source of cash should funds cease to be available in the various (usually cheaper) short-term markets e.g. US and Euro Commercial Paper (a "back-up commitment"). Because of the fact that lenders will usually have little control under arrangements designed to give this contingency cover over the purpose to which funds lent are put, beyond perhaps an undertaking not to use them for hostile takeovers or purposes which might breach regulations affecting the lenders, the types of facility meeting this need will usually be available only to the highest quality borrowers.

2.1.7 *Exposure Management and Debt Mix*

Through a combination of the above financial requirements, a company will attempt to form a mix of debt suitable for its business activities. In looking at the type of debt assumed, a company will also be looking at (i) its exposure to economic factors outside its control, particularly changes in currency exchange rates and interest rates, (ii) the possible impact on its access to funds should either its performance deteriorate or the availability of credit become generally restricted through an economic downturn or the imposition by governments of tight monetary policies, (iii) the consequences for its tax bill of borrowing in different locations and in different forms and (iv) its flexibility to expand and invest confidently as opportunities are created or occur.

Companies, therefore, have a need for bank facilities which:

(i)   match the currency of debt to the currency of a company's income.

(ii)   hedge a company's exposure to changes both in the level of interest rates generally and to changes in the relative levels of interest rates between countries.

(iii)   guarantee that funds will be available to it in case of need notwithstanding that they may not be needed at present or may not be needed if business is buoyant.

(iv)   in the case of a group of companies, match the location of lending centres and the borrowing entity or entities to the group's tax position and local needs in its various locations.

(v)   match the form of lending to a group's tax position (see below under Tax Considerations for instances where banks able to provide tax based lending or lending-equivalent products will be at an advantage).

2.2   **Sovereigns**

Sovereign borrowers also have requirements related to trading and the need to invest:

2.2.1   *Balance of Payments/Rescheduling*

A country will have to fund, through its banking system, any deficit in receipts from abroad in comparison to expenditures abroad. Such imbalances can arise through the cost of imports exceeding receipts from exports, capital investment out of the country exceeding investment coming in from abroad, changes in the levels of foreign holdings of a country's currency (e.g. withdrawal of bank balances by non-residents) and changes in a government's or central bank's holdings of foreign currency and gold reserves.

The economic impact of balance of payments imbalances is discussed in the Recommended Reading for the Monetary Economics examination and need not be repeated here. Suffice it to say that a government which requires its residents to exchange all foreign currency holdings for domestic currency and which restricts the ability of residents to purchase foreign currency will thereby take control of, and assume responsibility for, funding any balance of payments deficit incurred by its country.

In the late 1970s and early 1980s, it was fashionable for banks to lend to developing countries to fund balance of payments imbalances as part of the "recycling" of OPEC balance of payments surpluses which materialised largely as eurodollar deposits within the international banking system. Such lending was and is sensible and creditworthy if the proceeds are being applied to the import of goods and services required to enable the country to develop its economic base and thereby generate revenues through exports and import substitution to repay the debt. If, however, the proceeds eventually flow through to residents who, by fair means or foul, use them to build up deposits in foreign banks or to import e.g. luxury cars or are applied to prestigious but non-income producing projects, then debt is being assumed without development of the means to repay. Unfortunately, in the absence of a loan directed to, and tied to, a specific project it is extremely difficult for a lender to assert control over the application of proceeds from balance of payments lending.

As a result of the debt crisis, which arose through a complex interaction of economic factors, easy money and mismanagement within many debtor countries, bankers have focused closely on the need for highly competent economic and political management within countries requiring balance of payments finance. Voluntary lending for this purpose has thus become highly selective.

By contrast, countries which have become overburdened with foreign currency debt for whatever combination of reasons have been able to access new funds and to refinance maturing debt only through complex and lengthy rescheduling negotiations, usually involving the International Monetary Fund in a role as policeman of the economic strategy and practices of the rescheduling government.

This is not the place to discuss the possible "solutions" to the debt crisis which have been propounded by various parties. For our purposes it will be sufficient to recognise that voluntary balance of payments lending to any country relies fundamentally for its creditworthiness on the quality of economic and political management within that country and the resources available to that management to develop productive capacity to provide for repayment. Selectivity must, therefore, remain the key.

"Involuntary" lending under rescheduling arrangements will require satisfaction that steps are being taken within the debtor nation to provide a prospect that the nation might grow sufficiently as an economy eventually to be able to service its debt comfortably. If and when the corner is turned, there is no reason to doubt that the country which has thereby re-established commercial credibility will be able both to resume voluntary borrowing in banking and bond markets and to attract equity investment to finance further growth. The intervening period will be difficult and there is no guarantee of success – "involuntary" new money will thus continue to be at least as much a product of political deal-making as credit assessment.

2.2.2   Trade Finance

Governments which cause their countries to carry out foreign trade through government agencies effectively assume responsibility for raising trade finance on behalf of their residents. Usually finance is required through the international banking system for specific imports and, because of both the tie-in to specific contracts for often crucially-needed imports and (in some cases) an ability to control the movement of the underlying goods, this represents a safer form of lending for banks even without export agency credit support than "blanket" balance of payments finance.

2.2.3   Reserves

Countries will occasionally borrow specifically to fund holdings of foreign exchange reserves for use, if required, to defend the domestic currency against speculative pressures. Such borrowing is creditworthy if the lender is confident that the borrowing country has the resources and economic management to generate adequate hard currency to pay its foreign obligations and thereby remain an attractive home for overseas money, so avoiding the long-term deterioration of its domestic currency which might put repayment of the loan in jeopardy. In the absence of this ability to succeed economically, a country which borrows foreign currencies to purchase its own will simply be pouring the money down an unproductive black hole.

2.2.4 *Project Finance and Capital Expenditure*
Countries need to invest in infrastructure to allow their economies to develop. Such infrastructure includes directly and indirectly productive investment in electricity generation, roads, telecommunications and oil production. It also includes investment in the population through provision of efficient education and healthcare.

The dangers are that too much is spent on the wrong projects or that projects are inefficiently carried out for reasons of misjudgement, mismanagement or bad luck. The dangers can be averted (i) through tying finance specifically to stages of development of projects, which have been approved by the financing bank or banks and the economics of which have been commercially demonstrated, and (ii) through the involvement of the highly influential World Bank as a joint financier and project monitor ("co-financing").

2.3 **Quasi-Sovereigns**
Borrowing needs depend on the role or business of the borrower but will involve some combination of those decribed under the two preceding sections.

2.4 **Supra-Nationals**
Borrowing needs are usually for long-term funds to finance a portfolio of investments in developing projects. As such, 10-year plus bond financings linked to swaps to reduce cost and hedge currency/interest rate exposures are the most common funding instruments.

3. **TYPES OF FACILITIES**
Bank loan facilities are usually differentiated by reference to various characteristics which can be combined and tailored to suit individual requirements. The major characteristics are:

3.1 **Maturity Date and Term**
The maturity date is the date on which or by which the facility must be repaid. The period between the first date on which funds are available for

the borrower to use (or "draw") and the maturity date is usually referred to as the "Term" of the facility. The Term can be:

3.1.1   Short-Term

Short-term facilities are those with a maturity of under one year. In many cases, the maturity may in fact be two years as a company may be allowed one year in which to draw the facility and may have the option to choose a 12-month "interest-period" or "fixture period" i.e. to borrow funds for a 12-month period from drawdown at an interest rate set at the beginning of that period; there is then the possibility that a company may draw the funds 364 days after they first become available for a further twelve months.

Short-term facilities are appropriate for:

- *working capital finance* where debts or stocks financed will be converted to cash for repayment in under one year;

- *trade finance* where the transactions financed will generate cash for repayment in under one year;

- *exposure management* where, e.g. as a protection against currency movements, funds are borrowed to match the currency of, and to be repayable on the due date of, a debt owed to the company. Occasionally there are also arbitrage opportunities where a borrowing in one currency switched through the foreign exchange market into another can produce below-market funding in that second currency – a common example in the early-mid 80s was UK companies raising cheap 3-month or 6-month US Dollars (i.e. below the aggregate of LIBOR and whatever margin they would have been charged in London) in the US Commercial Paper market, changing the dollars into sterling at the spot rate and then taking out a forward foreign exchange contract to reconvert the proceeds plus accrued interest into US Dollars for settlement of the Commercial Paper at its maturity; because forward foreign exchange rates tend to follow differences in relative LIBOR rates and the companies were borrowing US Dollars at below a LIBOR-based cost, the foreign exchange contract enabled them to convert cheap US Dollar funding (which they did not require) into cheap sterling, which was of benefit;

- *bridging finance* where temporary funding is required pending the drawdown of long-term finance e.g. to permit the swift completion of an acquisition. Beware the refinancing risk here – bridging finance is only effective if there is an assured take-out or source of refinance for when the term of the bridging finance expires; in the absence of this, the lender could find itself effectively tied into a long-term commitment it did not envisage at the start of the transaction because of a borrower's inability to refinance or repay;

- *reserves financing* where a country wishes to make interventions in the foreign exchange markets as a weapon against speculators, by using foreign currency borrowed to purchase its domestic currency.

3.1.2 *Medium-Term*
Maturity for medium-term facilities, for my purposes, is 2-5 years (some banks categorise medium-term as 2-7 years). Such periods are suitable for:

- *working capital finance* where, notwithstanding that stock and debtors "turn over" (i.e. are converted into cash) every three months, a guaranteed source of finance is required to give the company the comfort that funding will be available to fund trading activities as required over an extended period;

- *capital expenditure* where finance is required for the purchase of equipment with an estimated useful life, and direct or indirect cash flow generating ability, of several years;

- *exposure management* where e.g. a company wishes to fix an interest rate for a period of up to 5 years to hedge its exposure to interest rate rises, or a company wishes to hedge its exposure to fluctuations in the value of its foreign currency investments by matching the currency of its investment with a liability in the same currency;

- *balance of payments/rescheduling* to finance the development of the productive base of the economy of a country whereby the import purchased or substituted should produce a return in the form of net generation of hard currency over the loan period. Perhaps the most realistic approach to the needs of developing countries is one which recognises that such financing needs to be extended as a combination of equity and long-term lending (see debt for equity swap schemes, for example).

3.1.3 Long-Term

Any facility with a term of in excess of 5 years. Common uses for such financings are:

- *acquisitions*: in the absence of sales shortly after an acquisition of previously under-valued fixed assets or subsidiaries it is unlikely that an acquired business can pay off its cost in under five years. Long-term finance is therefore usually required, repayable in instalments perhaps after an initial period (a "grace period") during which the operations of the acquired company are integrated into the acquirer.

  Leveraged buy-outs, by contrast, may be structured as medium-term loans with a sizeable lump sum ("balloon") due at maturity. The assumption or implication here is that either the company will have progressed sufficiently profitably to enable it to refinance the buy-out more cheaply well before maturity, or that it will, if business has not gone as anticipated, either be in default before maturity or be forced into default by the balloon payment due so that the facility will therefore be up for renegotiation.

- *capital expenditure*: where assets purchased or built have a long life cycle (certain machine tools, factories, aircraft, ships, cranes etc.), and thereby a long-term ability to generate net cash flow, then long-term finance to pay for such assets may be appropriate depending, of course, on the creditworthiness of the borrower. For how the asset financed may be used by a lender to enable it to assume an apparently greater risk than might be contemplated under conventional criteria, see Chapter 6 on Asset Finance;

- *project finance:* as with acquisitions, a major project is unlikely to be completed and paid off in under five years. Such transactions therefore usually require the lender to take a long-term view;

44

- *rescheduling/development finance*: the development of a country's economic resources and infrastructure is a long process and, once funds are committed by lenders, there are few means whereby they can pull out early if things do not transpire as anticipated. For this reason, development finance which does not benefit from a close link into a well-managed, specific project is risky and the lender must have great confidence in the management ability of those running the economy.

As any futures or option trader will tell you, life is much more uncertain (or, to use the jargon, "volatile") the longer the view you are required to take. Who, for example, in 1980 forecast that a barrel of oil would cost in 1986 under $15? Longer term facilities are, thus in general, inherently more risky as there is simply a greater timespan for what can go wrong to do so. As a principle, therefore, the longer a facility the greater the protection and return to the lender required. In this context, beware short or medium term facilities with large "balloon" or "bullet" repayments (the latter term refers to a loan which is repayable in one amount at maturity, the former to a loan where the last scheduled repayment is larger than previous scheduled repayments). Where is it envisaged that such an amount of money will come from if not from a successful refinancing? What are the alternative sources of repayment if such refinancing cannot be achieved? Why is such a "back-loading" of payments necessary – can not the discipline of staged repayments be more suitably substituted?

3.2 Commitment to Lend

3.2.1 *Committed*
A "committed" facility is one where a bank has an obligation to lend for a predetermined period of time (the term) on condition that the borrower complies with its obligations under the relevant loan agreement or contract signed by both parties. This provides the borrower with a largely guaranteed source of funds and commits the resources of the bank to the borrower for the term agreed notwithstanding a deterioration, up to agreed limits, in the market or in the borrower's performance.

In a period when the capital resources of banks are under pressure, a commitment to lend is a serious obligation precluding the undertaking of other business and thus requires remuneration. During the period when the borrower is borrowing under the facility, the lender usually gains his return from the margin he charges over his cost of funds. During periods where either:

(a) the lender is currently committed to lend if required but the borrower is not actually borrowing (as often occurs, for example, under revolving credit facilities for working capital purposes),

or

(b) the lender has agreed to lend on a specific date in the future (e.g. to fund the purchase of a fixed asset on delivery) but drawdown has not yet occurred,

then the borrower will usually be required to pay a "Commitment Fee" on the amount of the facility undrawn. Typical levels for such fees extend from 0.05% p.a. to 0.5% p.a. depending on the borrower's creditworthiness (and thus the risk the bank is undertaking in committing its resources) and the transaction structure.

An alternative fee structure to the above is the "Facility Fee". This fee will be charged on a per annum basis on the total amount of the facility whether or not it is drawn. The margin the lender will charge on amounts drawn will then take into account the fact that it is already receiving a return on the amount borrowed in the form of the Facility Fee.

For example, let us assume you decide to grant a committed revolving credit facility and wish to receive 0.25% p.a. on amounts committed but not drawn and a total return of 0.5% p.a. on amounts drawn. You could achieve this by charging either:

(i)   Commitment Fee on Undrawn Amounts   :   0.25% p.a.
      Margin on Amounts Drawn   :   0.5% p.a.
      or
(ii) Facility Fee on the Total Facility Amount :   0.25% p.a.
      Margin on Amounts Drawn   :   0.25% p.a.

The latter fee structure clearly distinguishes the price being charged for the *commitment* to lend for an extended period (say 5 years) and the price

46

being charged for a given lending within the committed period or term (say a 3-month interest period). A bank in the committed facility may then be able to sell to another bank individual loan drawings when they occur at a margin of 0.25% p.a. without surrendering his Facility Fee. As a presentational matter this may prove easier than trying to sell loan drawings yielding 0.5% p.a. to another bank to yield that bank only 0.25% p.a.

3.2.2 *Uncommitted*

Banks will also grant good borrowers uncommitted facilities. In this case, "in principle" approval will be put in place within the bank to extend credit to a specific borrower for a maximum amount and period (usually short-term) and the approval will be communicated to the borrower formally in a loan agreement, or informally by letter, depending on local law and practice. If, however, the borrower wishes to drawdown at anytime, the lender may refuse to lend if either he considers that the borrower's creditworthiness has deteriorated or that his own funding and liquidity position is such that further lending is unattractive. The borrower thus does not have a guaranteed or committed source of funds under such a facility.

There is a technical question. If a bank lends money under an *uncommitted* facility for a period of six months at, say, 6 month LIBOR plus 0.25% p.a., can it demand repayment should it wish to do so before the 6-month period expires? The answer is that it depends on the law and practice of the jurisdiction in which you are lending and the terms of your loan agreement (if any). If in doubt, take legal advice – if the answer is that once funds are lent you would be committed for the loan period, then you will need a formal loan agreement for the reasons discussed in Chapter 5. In any case, if you grant a loan for six months, even if it is technically "on demand" (see below), as a matter of practice you are unlikely to risk harming your relationship with a customer by demanding repayment before scheduled maturity unless there is a severe deterioration in the circumstances of the borrower.

3.2.3 *On Demand*

Money lent "on demand" is repayable by the borrower immediately the lender requests repayment. The borrower thus has no legal right by which it can require an unwilling lender to continue a loan. English overdrafts are, by definition, repayable "on demand". Many US loans extended for, say, three-month periods are evidenced by "demand notes" which thereby give the lender the right to call in the loan before maturity. Although the courts (especially in the USA) have tended to look unsympathetically at any apparently capricious use by the lenders of this "on demand" power, a borrower of such money leaves itself wholly exposed to any deterioration (temporary or not) of its perceived creditworthiness or any reduction in the availability of funds in the financial markets.

The advantage of uncommitted and on demand facilities for borrowers is that they tend to be cheaper than committed facilities as borrowers are not paying a commitment fee nor a facility fee nor an element in the loan pricing or margin to compensate the lender for the commitment of his resources. The disadvantage is, of course, the uncertainty over whether the funds will remain available.

3.2.4 *Evergreens*

As an alternative to a committed fixed term, a lender may also agree to an "Evergreen" facility. Evergreen arrangements and attitudes towards them differ markedly between financial institutions but the principle is that there is no fixed date for repayment. Instead, when the lender decides that he wishes to be repaid, he gives notice to the borrower to that effect. In the absence of such notice, the facility will remain in place indefinitely unless the borrower repays or cancels voluntarily. Notice periods, or "the evergreen element", under these facilities vary from one year (or one year and a day to ensure that the facility remains, for accounting purposes, a non-current liability of the borrower) to, rarely, four or five years. The lender may have the ability to give the notice at anytime or, more usually, only on annual or six-monthly review dates. These notice periods may be designed so that they come into play after an initial fixed term: for example, a lender may commit to lend for 4 years initially with the provision that, if he is unwilling to continue the facility for a further year beyond that date, he will be able to give notice at the end of year 3 that he will require repayment at the end of year 4. You may find this arrangement described as a "four-year evergreen"; you may also find a facility where money is made available, with the lender required from day one to give four years' notice to obtain repayment, described in the same way – it pays to check the definitions!

In seeking an evergreen facility, a borrower will be looking thereby to achieve:

- maximum repayment flexibility; in a borrower's market, it is unlikely that a bank will give notice to demand repayment unless the borrower's or market circumstances deteriorate markedly; in the absence of such developments, the borrower will have a source of quasi-permanent capital and no discipline of a repayment schedule; if, however, the unlikely happens, the length of notice gives the borrower time to make alternative arrangements;

- attractive pricing; notwithstanding the above, the evergreen provision means that the lender has in theory a committed period of exposure limited to the time remaining to the expiry date of the notice period; the borrower may, therefore, be able to negotiate pricing based on that period rather than pricing appropriate to a long-term facility.

For a lender, there are attractions in structuring what appears likely to be a long-term facility as an evergreen particularly now that the Federal Reserve in the USA and the Bank of England have indicated that they intend to determine banks' capital adequacy by reference, in the case of standby commitments at least, to the term of those commitments. The reason is that shorter committed periods will require less capital than longer periods (cf. Chapter 5).

Nevertheless, the absence of a defined repayment schedule, the need for the lender to make a formal request (which will not endear him to his customer) to obtain his usual right to obtain repayment and the length of the notice period, make those facilities in general appropriate only for restricted purposes (working capital) and stronger borrowers. The lender must ensure that review dates chosen are appropriate (i.e. to coincide with the availability of up-to-date accounts) and that control procedures are in place to ensure that adequate and timely reviews are indeed carried out.

3.3 Repayment and Prepayment Flexibility

Within committed facilities there are two basic types of repayment profile, "revolving" and "non-revolving".

3.3.1 *Non-revolving*

This is the term loan with a fixed repayment schedule. Any amount voluntarily repaid early by a borrower (a "prepayment") will, depending on the terms of the loan agreement, be set against future instalments either in their order of maturity or in their reverse order of maturity and may not be redrawn. For example, a prepayment of US$1,000,000 by a borrower under a 5-year loan of $5,000,000, repayable in ten instalments of US$500,000 each, will either result in the borrower being relieved of the obligation to make the first two scheduled repayments or the last two. The latter alternative shortens the effective term of the loan to four years and, because it thus shortens a lender's "risk horizon", is the treatment of prepayments lenders usually seek to negotiate.

Non-revolving term loans are, for many banks, attractive assets to hold because, in the absence of credit problems, they can be expected to produce a steady stream of income at predetermined levels. For the borrower to have an unrestricted prepayment option is not, therefore, to the lender's advantage as that attractive earning asset could suddenly disappear. Lenders, therefore, will sometimes seek either to limit a borrower's prepayment flexibility or to impose a penalty fee for early repayment on the grounds that a term commitment *by* the lender should be matched by a degree of term commitment *to* the lender on the other side.

Non-revolving loans are suitable for situations where repayment is to come from an identified source which can be expected to generate a reasonably predictable cash flow over a given period. For example, a loan extended to assist a borrower to purchase a machine tool will usually be structured on this basis as the tool can be expected to generate a regular stream of cash for repayment over its useful life through sale of the items it produces. The same is true for any lending to finance the purchase of assets which are expected to produce pay back of the investment required in a given period of time, whether those assets be equipment, property, companies or trademarks.

3.3.2 *Revolving*

"Revolving" loans are those where, during the term, the borrower has the ability to repay amounts borrowed and subsequently to reborrow them. Because, unlike non-revolving facilities, amounts repaid may be redrawn

50

by the borrower under the provisions of the loan agreement, a commitment fee or facility fee is usually payable by the borrower on undrawn amounts. For example, a borrower who has a revolving credit facility of DM 5,000,000 of which he is currently borrowing DM 3,000,000 will be paying interest on the DM 3,000,000 and a commitment fee of, perhaps, 0.25% per annum quarterly in arrears on the undrawn DM 2,000,000.

These facilities are appropriate as committed financing for working capital needs because, as we discussed when looking at the needs of industrial companies earlier in this chapter, borrowing requirements to fund debtors and stocks/inventory typically fluctuate according to season and/or production cycle. Such facilities thus give flexibility similar to that of the overdraft whilst giving the borrower the benefit of a committed term. As most industrial companies will have a more-or-less permanent requirement for working capital finance to be available to them for use on a cyclical basis, it is usual for revolving credits for working capital purposes to be repayable in one lump sum (a "bullet") at maturity. Lenders should therefore focus closely, in extending such facilities, on a borrower's likely ability to refinance at the expiry of the term.

For major borrowers of high quality, banks are often prepared to grant revolving credit facilities for periods of 5–10 years for "general corporate purposes". In doing so, banks thereby relinquish control over the purposes to which drawings under such loans are put (albeit the extent to which they can be drawn in ways which significantly undermine a borrower's creditworthiness, e.g. to buy-in a company's own shares or to engage in highly-leveraged takeovers, can to some extent, be controlled by financial covenants – see Chapter 5). Provisions can also be included in documentation to prevent a company borrowing to finance a hostile takeover or activities which contravene regulations governing the lenders.

These "general corporate purposes" may include "standby" and "back-up" as previously discussed under the heading "Contingency Cover". If, in the latter case, a company can draw on the loan only after it has attempted to raise the required money from alternative uncommitted sources at a cheaper rate (e.g. in the US or Euro Commerical Paper Markets or by seeking quotes from banks for short-term advances or acceptance credits), then the facility may be defined as a Revolving Underwriting Facility or "RUF" rather than a revolving credit. RUFs, when first devised, were arranged at a lower commitment or facility fee than traditional revolving credits as it was argued that the chances of their being drawn, given the linked arrangements whereby the borrower would first attempt to raise money in the (probably cheaper) uncommitted markets, were slight. From a credit perspective, however, I see no difference between a RUF and revolving credit – it will be used in either case when cheaper money is unavailable conveniently elsewhere.

3.4 Interest Rate Determination

At this point, it may be helpful to distinguish between the "committed term" and "interest" or "fixture" periods (the latter two terms being synonymous). The "committed term" defines the period for which a lender is obliged to allow the borrower to borrow subject to compliance by the borrower with the terms of the loan agreement. An "interest period" describes the length of time for which the borrower can lock-in his interest rate during the term. For example, a borrower may be granted a five year committed term loan, with funds to be drawn in 3 or 6 month interest periods. At the end of any given period, the borrower will pay the interest accrued during that period and the lender will "roll-over" (i.e. continue lending) the outstanding principal amount for a further 3 or 6 months at a new interest rate. The rate will usually be set out at a margin over the cost to the Bank of borrowing for such three or six months periods in the inter-bank market.

Where the borrower has the option to fix his interest rate for periods up to 12 months, the loan will be described as "floating rate". Where a given interest period exceeds twelve months, the loan will usually be described as "fixed rate". A borrower may negotiate a mixture by requiring the option to borrow on e.g. 3, 6, 12, 24 and 36 months interest periods within, say, a five year facility. The supply however, of fixed rate funds through the inter-bank market for in excess of 5 years is limited, even in the major currencies.

The choice of whether to "go fixed or floating" is a question of exposure management. Fixed rate funding removes a borrower's exposure to rises in market rates over the relevant interest period but gives it no benefit if interest rates fall.

Floating rate borrowing, by contrast, gives no protection against rises but all the benefit of falls. It will usually be more expensive to take fixed rate funds, because of the phenomenon known as the "yield curve" whereby long-term interest rates tend to be higher than shorter-term rates.

A borrower will determine its preferred choice based on its expectations as to the direction of interest rates and its perception of the relative impact of any material rise or fall in market rates. From a credit perspective as a lender, a borrower taking fixed rate funds when interest rates generally appear low may be making a wise choice. If, however, a default occurs after rates have fallen further, the bank's exposure will be increased as it will need to recover from the borrower, in addition to principal and accrued interest, the amount of the loss the bank will take in redeploying funds recovered for the remainder of the committed period. Such "redeployment costs" will be the present value of the difference between the interest earned on any new deposit and the interest payable for the remainder of the interest period by the bank to the person or institution funding it.

3.5 Availability

A consideration for a borrower once it has decided to arrange a committed facility is the extent to which it needs that facility to be "available" at various points during the term. The available portion of a loan is that which the borrower may draw immediately; an unavailable portion is that which requires some predetermined event to occur before drawdown is permitted.

The scope for use of this distinction occurs typically in two situations:

(a) *Project or real estate construction*
   Drawdown of a loan to be used to develop a project or to construct a building will usually be controlled by the lender through his permitting drawing of individual tranches only after the previous stage of construction has been satisfactorily completed. The amount agreed for the stage of development in progress will thus be available for drawing by the borrower; amounts which should become needed only after completion of that stage will be, as yet, unavailable.

(b) *Working Capital/Standby transactions*
   A borrower may wish to ensure that funds will be at its disposal to finance working capital for a period of, say, five years. It may know, however, that cash flow is such that, for twelve months at least, it will have a need for a maximum of perhaps 50% of the total

facility. The borrower may, therefore, request that the balance be designated "unavailable" for a specific period.

The advantage to the borrower is that it will be charged less in the way of commitment fee (perhaps 50% less) on an unavailable portion than on a portion of loan which the lender is immediately committed to lend. The theory is that, although the lender has committed himself and his resources to lend the unavailable portion at some stage in the future, if the borrower were to go into default before those funds become available then the lender will not be exposed for the unavailable portion as, by definition, it cannot have been drawn.

Be careful, however, of how individual arrangements define "unavailable". In some cases, a borrower will be granted the option to convert the unavailable portion into available simply by giving a predetermined period of notice. There may then be some "clawback" whereby the borrower will be obliged to pay the higher commitment fee on the amount converted. For example, the notice required may be thirty days and the borrower be obliged to pay the higher fee in respect of the ninety days period before the conversion comes into effect. In the absence of a material clawback provision combined with a restriction on the number of times it may be used, there is no real difference between available and unavailable portions from a risk point of view as the supposedly unavailable portion is, in effect, always available in case of need. Without doubt, it will always be fully drawn when a default occurs!

3.6 Choice of Borrower

Most loans will be to a specified single borrower. Occasionally, however, lenders will be asked to make a facility available to *"alternative borrowers"* whereby the loan may be drawn in whole or in part by one or more borrowers, perhaps a parent company and a subsidiary. Each borrower will be liable for only the portion of the loan it borrows unless the loan agreement specifically provides for joint and several liability or for each borrower to guarantee the other. Such flexibility enables a customer which controls a group of companies to borrow through whichever company is most efficient from a commercial, tax or accounting viewpoint.

An advance on the alternative borrower concept which takes the flexibility still further is the *"umbrella"* facility. In such facilities, a lender agrees with a company (usually a holding or parent company) a total borrowing limit available to it and its nominated subsidiaries or affiliates. Individual companies within the group then may borrow up to certain sub-limits within this overall "umbrella".

Key issues are:

- recourse: for any given loan, do you have recourse only to the individual borrower or is there a parent guarantee or arrangement whereby each eligible borrower guarantees the others? ("cross guarantees" cf. Chapter 5, Section 1.1).

- control: what are the procedures for the parent company to nominate companies to be borrowers under the facility – to what extent does the bank have the right and opportunity to vet and approve nominations?

- administration: administering an umbrella facility can be time consuming, particularly when it involves many borrowers in a variety of countries perhaps borrowing from a variety of branches of your bank; are you being adequately remunerated?

3.7   The "Multis"

As the international banking markets have become more integrated and sophisticated, the number of characteristics in facilities which allow a corporate borrower flexibility has burgeoned. Many such characteristics are described by the prefix "multi-".

3.7.1   *Multi-Currency*

The borrower is given the right to borrow in a variety of currencies at its option subject to them being available to the bank in the inter-bank market. This assists a borrower considerably in the management of exposure to currency risk. Care needs to be taken to determine proper procedures for dealing with changes in currency parities during the course of a loan. For example, a company has a multi-currency loan with a limit of equivalent US$5,000,000 and draws down at the beginning of a 6-month interest period in Swiss Francs when the US$ equals Swiss Francs 1.6. The borrowing is thus Swiss Francs 8,000,000. If, at the end of the

6-month interest period, the rate has moved to US$1 = Sw.Fc. 1.45, then the Sw.Fc.8,000,000 will now be equivalent to US$5,517,241. Borrowers will usually be required to repay the loan down to the equivalent US$ limit at the end of each interest period, subject perhaps to some element of grace such as 10%. This can be an onerous requirement unless the borrower has adequate net *cash* income in the currency in which it chooses to draw down (perhaps from a currency receivable) to enable it to make the additional payment on the due date.

3.7.2 *Multi-Centre*
The borrower is given the right to borrow from a variety of the bank's branches (e.g. London and New York). This will provide it with the ability to access the cheaper centre for the finance required. The customer may also be able to avoid withholding tax (see Section 4.2) which might be levied on payments to lenders abroad from some countries if the loan to a given borrower can be made from one of the bank's branches in the borrower's country.

In considering such facilities, check:

• administration: do time differences or variations in notice periods required for drawdown in different markets make rate fixing and switching between centres a problem?

• capacity: is each branch chosen of a size, type and capacity to accommodate the size and type of lending which it may be required to produce?

3.7.3 *Multi-Option*
The "MOF" or Multi-Option Facility is perhaps the ultimate "multi" – the seductive all-singing, all-dancing transaction.

Such facilities are usually designed to combine a committed back-up loan with options to access as many different banking and non-banking sources of finance as can be practically accommodated.

"Multi-option" may, at its narrowest, simply give access during the committed period to a variety of funding bases on which to determine interest rates on roll-over dates (e.g. LIBOR, New York CDs, Prime etc.) or may provide for, perhaps, a variety of "tender panels" of banks which will make competitive bids to provide short-term advances, sell short-term notes to investors, provide interest rate and currency swaps etc.

The flexibility implicit for the borrower enables it to access the cheapest sources of finance in a desired currency from the widest possible number of sources. Many such sources are available only for "household" names whilst administrative considerations make such a complex facility uneconomic for small transactions. An MOF will probably, therefore, be successful only for borrowers rated at least Single A for a total amount in excess of US$100,000,000.

The following example on pp 58–59 is an MOF although the selection of options shown are by no means definitive. The specific options included in any facility will depend upon the requirements of the borrower and the capabilities of the banks constituting the syndicate.

The facilities available as uncommitted options are described as being available at "market rates" for the very good reason that banks which are prepared to make these particular options available at the specific request of the borrower may do so at prices not agreed by the syndicate as a whole. The facilities are made available by way of banks tendering in a competitive environment. From time to time it may suit the books of certain banks to lend at rates lower than those available under the committed element of the MOF. However, banks are not obliged to bid and, therefore, the borrower cannot rely on getting funds under the "uncommitted" section of the facility.

Few, if any, new MOFs are written now (1994) but some are still in existence. It seems unlikely they will be extended at maturity.

4. TAX CONSIDERATIONS FOR BORROWERS

Tax planning in multi-national (or even single-national) companies can be a complex process. The rules of the game change frequently as governments around the world change their fiscal strategies, either giving tax "breaks" or "benefits" to those engaged in certain types of activity or restricting the scope of, or abolishing, those already in place. Because of the often haphazard way in which tax regulations have evolved, seemingly straightforward transactions can have apparently bizarre consequences for a company's tax bill.

A Typical Multi-Option Facility (MOF)

Banks' Funding Centres & Drawdown Arrangements	Facility & Purpose	Interest, Yields, Fees & Commission	Amount
	7-year, multi-option facility fully under-written and lead managed by XYZ Bank *Purpose:* General corporate finance including acquisitions and back up for US$ Commercial Paper programme.	*Facility Fees:* 0.50% pa *Underwriting Fee:* 0.09% flat (Arranger to take 0.03%) *Utilisation Fees:* 0-50% - Nil 51-100% - 0.025% pa	Full amount US$250m (Arranger to syndicate and to selldown and retain US$25m for self).
London Offices/ Branches 1,2,3,6 or 12 months rollovers	*Committed Options* US$ loans (3 days' notice) Pounds sterling loans (same day) Multicurrency loans (3 days' notice)	*LIBOR + 0.50% pa (plus MLA costs for sterling loans)	

New York Offices/ Branches – up to 7 days	US$ swingline (same day funds)	*NYIBOR + 0.75% pa or PRIME (borrower's option)
London Offices/ Branches – bills 1,3,6 months	Sterling Bankers Acceptance Credits	*Reference Bank rates. Acceptance Commission 50 b.p.
New York Offices/ Branches – bills up to 6 months	US$ Bankers' Acceptance Credits	
London Offices/ Branches – 7 days & 1,2,3, and 6 months rollovers	*Uncommitted Options* Via a Tender Panel US$, DMs, FFs & Sterling short term loans	Market rates.
London Offices/ Branches 1,2,3, and 6 months rollovers	Sterling Bankers Acceptances	Market rates.

This is not the place to attempt to go into great detail on international tax issues – only a specialist lawyer or accountant with contacts in similar professions around the World would be competent to do so. Some basics of particular relevance to banking can, however, be discussed:

4.1 Tax Deductibility

Interest on loans will usually be regarded as a business expense for companies and, therefore deducted from their operating profits to arrive at the taxable profit figure. Equally, interest received is usually treated as taxable income. A company, therefore, which has taxable profits will reduce its tax bill through borrowing by the following amount:

$$\text{Interest Paid} \times \text{Tax Rate}$$

Thus, the after-tax cost of borrowing for a company, were it to borrow at 10% p.a. and pay tax at 30% p.a., would be 7% p.a. Dividends, by contrast, are paid out of after-tax income.

A multi-national company looking to fund a subsidiary will, therefore, look at the most tax efficient manner to accomplish its objective. Should the subsidiary borrow directly from banks (perhaps, with the guarantee of the parent company) or should the parent company borrow itself and fund the subsidiary by an equity injection or inter-company loan?

All other things being equal (they usually are not!), if the subsidiary has, and can be expected to continue to have, taxable profits which are taxed at a higher rate than those of the parent company, then it will be cheaper, in after-tax terms, for the subsidiary to borrow rather than raise equity. The precise impact will also depend on the extent to which the parent can offset taxes paid by its foreign subsidiaries against its own domestic tax bill: i.e. are there double taxation agreements between the two countries?

4.2 Withholding Tax

Payments of interest, dividends, royalties, etc. by a company in Country X to a lender in Country Y may be subject to "withholding tax". This tax is usually deducted by the taxing authorities of Country X as a means to ensure that it receives a share of business profits which have been generated by a company operating in or from its country, before those profits are remitted abroad. The Withholding Tax rate can vary from 0% to 30% or higher.

Under bilateral tax treaties between individual countries, borrowers may be granted relief from such taxes or lenders may be permitted to offset against their own tax bill in whole or in part the amount of tax thereby deducted (see Chapter 9).

The position needs to be checked carefully before any cross-border lending is agreed. It will be usual for the borrower to indemnify the lender against any change in regulations after the loan is put in place (with the lender perhaps agreeing to take steps to mitigate the impact of any such change), but it will be unusual for a borrower to find a loan proposal attractive which would require it from day one to "gross up" all payments by an amount of withholding tax to enable the lender to receive the net return anticipated. Occasionally, there is no alternative.

4.3 Tax Allowances

As incentives for investment in productive equipment, governments will often offer companies undertaking such investment a reduction in their tax bill or delay in tax payments. The most common such incentive is "accelerated depreciation".

In the absence of tax incentives, one would expect a company purchasing a piece of equipment to be able to depreciate it (i.e. set the cost against its taxable profits) over its estimated life as happens usually in published financial statements. An asset with an anticipated life of 10 years might thus be depreciated by one tenth of its cost per year.

"Accelerated depreciation" allows the company to set off against its taxable profits greater amounts in the early years after purchase. For example, the UK allows such an asset to be depreciated for tax purposes by 25% of depreciated cost per year. In Year 1, the company's taxable profits would be reduced by 100% of cost x 25%. In Year 2 the reduction would be 75% cost $\times$ 25% etc.

The effect of accelerated depreciation is to delay payment of tax. Taking a simple example of an item of equipment costing $1,000, accounting depreciation of 10% p.a. and accelerated depreciation of 30% p.a. of cost, the delay works as follows producing, in effect, an interest-free loan from the tax man.

	1	2	3	4	5	6	7	8	9	10
Book Dep'n ($)	100	100	100	100	100	100	100	100	100	100
Accelerated Dep'n ($)	300	300	300	100	–	–	–	–	–	–
Taxable Profit Reduction/(Increase)($)	200	200	200	–	(100)	(100)	(100)	(100)	(100)	(100)
Cumulative	200	400	600	600	500	400	300	200	100	–

The value of this delay depends on both the rate of corporation tax and prevailing interest rates. The higher they are, the greater the benefit of the tax delay.

Notwithstanding high tax and interest rates, a company will not gain the full benefit of the allowances unless it has adequate taxable profits to absorb immediately the benefits available. In the previous example, a company with taxable profits of only $100 p.a. for the ten-year period would gain little benefit from the accelerated depreciation as it could offset only a maximum of $100 p.a.

Leasing can sometimes overcome this problem. A company (often a subsidiary of a bank) with adequate taxable profits to absorb the allowances will buy the equipment and "rent" it to the company needing it. The latter will usually then be able to use the equipment as if it were the owner. The lease rentals payable by the company under a typical finance lease will repay the cost of the equipment to the lessor over the lease period and give it a return which will enable it to pay interest on the cost and make a profit. Factored into the equation will be the value of the accelerated depreciation to the lessor (the interest free loan) producing an effective cost to the lessee below the cost of normal borrowing.

The precise mechanics will, however, depend on the leasing rules and regulations in the country or countries in which the lessor and lessee operate. See also Asset Finance, Chapter 6.

4.4   **Conclusion**

This, I should re-emphasise, no more than scratches the surface of a wide and complex subject. "Tax-driven" lending should be handled with care both because, if not properly structured, the tax benefits on which the transaction relied may not, in the event, be available and because the authorities around the world are increasingly seeking to preclude "tax aggressive" deals which use loopholes in regulations to gain tax benefits for transactions for which the legislation was not designed. An awareness of tax issues, however, will help you to recognise opportunities and to understand and discuss requests from borrowers for specific financing structures.

CHAPTER 3

Principles of Lending–Part III

● EXAMINING AND ANALYSING THE ACCOUNTS

by
Graham J. Allatt

1. THE ISSUES

When assessing whether a facility should be extended to a corporate borrower, you should address the following issues:

Non-Financial Factors

(i) The borrower and its relationship to the group of which it forms a part (Section 2);

(ii) The industry/market background to both the group and the borrowing company (Section 3.2);

(iii) The quality of management (Section 3.1.4);

(iv) Country risk (Chapter 12);

Financial Factors

(v) The background to the group's financial statements, particularly its accounting policies (Section 4);

(vi) The strength of the group's financial position, based on ratio analysis (Section 5.4);

and finally

(vii) based on all the above, but particularly (ii), (iii) and (vi), an estimate of the likely future financial health of the borrower and the group.

2. The Borrower and the Corporate Structure

When lending to a large group of companies, a bank may be asked to provide a facility to any of the following:

(a)   the ultimate holding company (the "top" company)

(b)   a single nominated subsidiary

(c)   several named companies within the group, any of which may draw on the facility (an "umbrella" facility)

(d)   an intermediate holding company and its subsidiaries, which together form a sub-group of the main group.

Lending to a "top" company is sometimes considered the most secure kind of facility, because if problems arise in servicing the borrowing, the top company should be able to obtain cash from its subsidiaries by means of management charges, dividends or, ultimately, the sale of its shares in the subsidiary. This can be further assisted by key subsidiaries guaranteeing the parent's borrowing ("upstream guarantees"). However, you should bear in mind that exchange control, taxation considerations, and legal or regulatory restrictions on payment of dividends may inhibit this access to subsidiaries' assets. Furthermore, lenders to strong subsidiaries may have prior claims on their assets, and may therefore be in a better position than lenders to the top company.

When lending to a subsidiary or sub-group, the banker will wish to assess the financial strength of the borrower. However, it is unwise to take comfort from a strong borrower if the group it belongs to is financially weak. There is a danger that cash will be transferred to the weaker parts of the group. Covenants in loan documentation which require bankers' approval for such transfers may provide some protection, but the banker is ultimately dependent on the morality of management, who may be under pressure to ignore legal and other restrictions – be very cautious about relying on a strong subsidiary in a weak group.

In normal circumstances the borrowing subsidiary is weaker than the overall group, if only because the group is larger and takes strength from the diversity and geographic spread of its activities. It is usual to seek the benefit of the group's strength by obtaining one of the following, in descending order of value to the bank:

66

(a) full cross-guarantee – a legal arrangement in which the parent and all its participating subsidiaries guarantee each others' liabilities to the bank;

(b) top company guarantee ("downstream guarantee");

(c) Letter of Comfort – a letter to the bank from the "top company" stating that it will support its subsidiary. The legal status of such a letter, and its precise wording, varies from country to country and from company to company. It is usually intended not to have legal force, but to be a moral commitment by the parent, so that its reputation in the world's financial markets would be destroyed if the undertaking were not honoured;

(d) Letter of Awareness – a letter from the "top company" stating that it is aware of its subsidiary's obligations to the bank. This never has legal status, but represents a moral commitment not to reduce the subsidiary's ability to repay its borrowing by, for example, extracting heavy dividend payments (often called "upstreaming").

After considering all of the above, the lender must decide whether to rely on the financial strength of the group, or the borrowing subsidiary, or both. This will indicate whether it is appropriate to analyse the consolidated accounts alone, or the accounts of the sub-group/subsidiary as well: normally both should be reviewed. You should never analyse a sub-group or subsidiary without considering the strength of the overall group.

In analysing a subsidiary's accounts one needs to have a full appreciation of its role within the overall group of which it is a part. In particular, "transfer pricing" between group companies can have a major impact on performance, this being the process by which companies within the same group price sales of goods and services to each other. Supplies priced "below market" act as an effective subsidy and thereby flatter the results presented by the purchasing subsidiary. "Above market" purchases or "below market" sales by the same subsidiary, of course, have the opposite effect.

Before drawing conclusions about the accounts, therefore, it is important to realise the extent to which the company cannot be looked at as a "stand alone" entity and to carry out the analysis in the context of that information.

Trading margins above or below industry average often act as an indicator of "off-market" pricing. The company itself can also be questioned about its customer base, sources of supply and pricing practices.

This chapter concentrates on reviewing the group, but identical considerations apply to reviewing an individual subsidiary.

3. Non-Financial Analysis

3.1 The Purposes of Non-Financial Analysis

The purposes of non-financial analysis are as follows:

(a)   obtaining the background necessary to understand the realities behind the historical financial accounts;

(b)   identifying future general trends in the industries and economies in which a group operates;

(c)   identifying volatility in the industry/business;

(d)   getting a feel for management quality and style.

Each of these is considered in more detail below.

3.1.1   *The Background to Historic Financials*

The areas we are trying to cover are:

• Obtaining an understanding of the mix of businesses to appreciate the factors which affect them.

• Relating this to the figures in the accounts. Are we looking at a low volume, high margin business or vice versa?

• Deciding whether the business is capital or labour intensive. In the former, depreciation charges form a large percentage of total costs, whereas in the latter, wages and salaries are a substantial proportion of the total.

• Understanding the critical factors for success. Does the group have any competitive advantages in these areas?

• Identifying which markets and products are important actual or potential contributors to turnover and profits/losses.

- Knowing the company/sector averages with which you should compare the business.

3.1.2 Identifying Future General Trends
The first objective here is to identify whether the industry is likely to grow or decline. You should look at:

- industry surveys, which will give an idea of both past and future trends in the business.

- the aspects of demographics and the impact of technological development, etc.

- general economic forecasts for the countries in which the group's customers are based.

Secondly, identify whether the group is better or worse than the industry as a whole. You should look at:

- whether the corporate's segment of the market is growing, mature or declining.

- the industry structure, particularly the size and number of companies in it and the barriers which face new entrants.

- where the group stands in the market – what is its market share and the current rate of growth of that share? Does it have product differentiation, either because of its marketing image or for technological reasons? Alternatively, does it have to compete largely on price? Is it a price-taker or a price-setter? Is it a high cost or a low cost producer?

3.1.3 Identify Volatility in Future Trends
Volatility depends on:

(i) The nature of the goods sold. For example capital goods, or those which depend on "discretionary" spending by consumers or industry, experience drastic declines in a recession. Necessities such as food are more stable.

(ii) Dependence on a volatile factor, either because of the market or the inputs to production, e.g. oil price, exchange rate.

69

(iii)　The capital intensity or fixed cost intensity of the group. This is considered further in Section 3.5.

(iv)　Other factors which may dislocate smooth trends in market size. Are there governmental, regulatory or environmental issues at work? Of particular concern to banks is whether the group has activities which might have adverse environmental consequences, e.g. responsibility for oil spills or toxic wastes. There is already legislation in the USA which can make banks responsible for clean-up costs in the event of their customers' insolvency, and similar statutes may be enacted elsewhere as environmental concerns increase.

If the group is a conglomerate, are the constituent businesses such that they will experience downturns at different points in the economic cycle, providing a measure of protection against a recession?

3.1.4　*Management Quality and Style*
Key issues which need to be considered are:

- Have the group's strategies been successful compared with those of its competitors?

- Is it building on its area of competitive advantage and taking steps to eliminate disadvantages?

- Is the management essentially by one person or by a team? If heavily dependent on one person, will the succession be smooth?

- Is the person a dominant personality? This would create problems if he does not listen and respond to other people's opinions and advice.

- Does he combine the role of Chairman/Chief Executive? Bankers and institutional investors generally consider it to be undesirable to have so much power vested in one person.

- Is the overall management style risk seeking or risk averse? A risk averse management will have gearing (see Section 5.4.4) which is low for its industry, and will finance takeovers by equity issues rather than an increase in debt.

3.2 Method and Sources

Suggested procedures for non-financial analysis are as follows:

- Start by reading the Notes to the Accounts which show the proportion of turnover, profit and capital employed in each of the major activities of the business. It is important to gain this perspective before carrying out the rest of the work, or too much importance may be attached to a high profile, but financially unimportant, part of the business.

- Then read the Annual Report. In particular, note what is not said! Poorly performing parts of the business are frequently glossed over.

- Obtain any major reviews by analysts – not the one page updating of opinions, but the occasional "ten page plus" detailed analysis of the group's activities.

- If relatively recent, obtain any flotation or capital market issue prospectuses – these are always very detailed.

- In the USA, do not be content with the Annual Report, but obtain the Form 10-K filed with SEC. This contains much more detailed background on the business than the published accounts. Non-US companies with US share listings file a similar document called a 20-F. (In addition, all companies listed in the USA file quarterly accounts – the Form 10-Q.)

- Obtain industry information. Principal sources are:

(i)   government statistics (e.g. in the UK, the publications of the Central Statistical Office)

(ii)   the national and trade press

(iii)   the trade association of the industry concerned

(iv)   commercially produced industry reports by organisations such as the Economist Intelligence Unit, Mintel and Inter-Company Comparisons.

- Review press cutting services, especially on any on-line database to which you may have access.

In all of this work try to understand:

(i) the relative financial importance (present and future) of each activity in the overall context of the group;

(ii) not only the broad market, but whether the group has identified any niches or sub-niches. It is frequently possible to find a small profitable sector, despite the market as a whole being over-supplied;

(iii) the underlying factors which affect the pattern of growth in the group's main markets.

- Are they demographic, general economic, or related to the specifics of particular industries?

- Do they depend on consumer spending, government expenditure, or investment by industry and commerce?

- Are the markets related to other factors outside the group's control?

- What is the rate of technological change in the industry, and is the group's research, design and development effort adequate to keep it in the forefront?

3.3 Country Considerations

Chapter 12 on Country Risk Assessment, deals with the aspects a banker must consider when lending cross-border to a borrower in the country being assessed. However, even for a UK bank lending to a UK company, country considerations may apply.

Economic and political factors could impact on the group's export markets, or on its ability to extract cash from its customers or investments overseas.

Where the borrower is heavily dependent on any one country for these reasons, the economic and political questions posed in Chapter 12 must be considered, and the impact of adverse answers on the group assessed.

3.4 Summarising the Results

The following questions need to be answered:

(i)   Is the industry's market increasing or declining?

(ii)   Is the industry more volatile or less volatile than average?

(iii)   Are there special factors of concern which may be unpredictable, e.g. environmental, regulatory?

(iv)   Is the group a strong or a weak player in its markets?

(v)   Can the group withstand likely fluctuations in its turnover, estimated on the basis of (ii) to (iv) above? (This will depend on its fixed/variable cost ratio – again this links into the financial analysis.)

4. FINANCIAL STATEMENTS – TRUTH OR FICTION?

4.1 The Terminology

Before beginning an examination of financial statements, it is important to understand some of the key terms used. Among the most important terms are accounting concepts, bases and policies, accounting standards and financial statements. Each of these terms is explained below.

4.1.1 Concepts

Accounting concepts are the broad basic assumptions which underlie the production of financial statements. There are four fundamental concepts which are recognised worldwide, even though there are considerable variations in their application. These are:

(i)   **The 'going concern' concept.** The assumption is that the business enterprise will continue to operate for the foreseeable future. This enables assets and liabilities to be carried at an historical cost or valuation figure, rather than the figure that they would fetch on an immediate break-up.

(ii)   **The accruals concept,** which means that income and expenditure should be recognised when incurred rather than when payment is

73

received or made. This enables the income and related expenditure of the business to be matched with each other on a consistent basis, so that the reported profit of the business is not distorted by the timing of the settlement of invoices.

(iii) **The consistency concept**, which means that financial statements are prepared using consistent bases, methods and policies from one period to another.

(iv) **The prudence concept**, which means that whilst foreseeable losses are recorded as soon as they are identified, profits are not anticipated and are only recorded when a sale has been completed. Completed means that either they have been realised by the receipt of cash or that the ultimate cash realisation can be assessed with reasonable certainty.

4.1.2 *Bases*
Accounting bases are the methods developed for applying accounting concepts to items in preparing financial statements. Bases are the theoretical techniques from which accounting policies are selected. For example, for stock valuation the common bases are First In First Out (FIFO), Last In First Out (LIFO) and average cost.

4.1.3 *Policies*
Accounting policies are the specific accounting bases selected by the group for preparing its accounts. These are usually set out in a note immediately adjacent to the principal financial statements (see below) in published accounts.

4.1.4 *Standards*
Accounting Standards are statements issued by formally constituted bodies which define or limit the accounting bases which may be used by companies. They also lay down minimum levels of disclosure in the published accounts.

4.1.5 *Financial Statements*
Financial statements consist of the key formats for a group's accounts, together with the associated notes. The term is also used to refer to the

key formats alone, i.e. profit and loss account, balance sheet, funds flow statement and statement of movements in either shareholders' funds or retained earnings.

4.2 Accounting Regimes

Accounting regimes differ from one country to the next, but there are a number of common principles:

(i)   Most countries have statute law covering the accounts to be produced by corporates, although for small, unquoted companies, the requirements are frequently minimal. Statute law usually prescribes the layout of the principal statements (balance sheet, profit and loss account and sometimes cash flow statement) and the content of some limited notes. Statute law may also limit options for accounting policies in a generalised way in certain key areas, e.g. carrying values for fixed assets, stock.

(ii)   Accounting standards usually limit options for corporates' choice of policies, requiring certain policies and prohibiting others. Occasionally alternatives are given (rarely in the USA, but commonly in Australia and the UK). Standards usually prescribe much more detailed disclosure in notes to the accounts than is required by statute. In some countries, accounting standards may have statutory force for quoted and/or large companies.

(iii) Statements of Recommended Practice (SORPS). These are a UK innovation and are usually industry specific. They lay down best accounting practice in a number of areas and are not mandatory.

Non-compliance with statute law or accounting standards will normally produce a qualified audit report. Non-compliance with a SORP will normally be highlighted in the notes to the accounts, but the audit report will not be qualified.

It should be noted that in the USA, UK and British Commonwealth countries, the tax calculations prepared for the revenue authorities are on a completely different basis from the figures in the accounts. Reported profit in the accounts is normally a starting point, but such matters as depreciation rates and provisions for doubtful debts are effectively recalculated on totally different bases for the tax computations.

In most of Europe and in Japan, the opposite is true; the figures in the tax computation must be identical to those in the accounts, and therefore such items as depreciation are determined by tax allowances rather than considering the useful life of an asset. To this extent, accounts in most European countries do not show a "true and fair view".

It should be noted that in most areas of the world the regimes for quoted companies are much stricter than those for unquoted. An extreme example is in the USA where unquoted companies (unless specially regulated, such as banks) are not required to file audited accounts, and their accounts for shareholders can be prepared on any basis whatsoever.

4.3 Accounting Standards

Accounting Standards are statements issued by a formally constituted body which usually contains representatives of the accounting profession, preparers of accounts (i.e. companies), the National Stock Exchange and other interested parties (such as government, university accounting bodies, banks, etc.). From time to time, the governing bodies in each country may be reconstituted and renamed (this has happened both in the USA and more recently the UK, where the Accounting Standards Committee (ASC) has been replaced by the Accounting Standards Board (ASB)). When this happens, the terminology of the standards themselves usually changes. In the UK, the ASC had issued Statements of Standard Accounting Practice SSAP1 to SSAP25 before being replaced by the ASB, which now issues Financial Reporting Statements (FRSs).

Compliance with standards is usually effectively mandated by any or all of the following:

(a) Statute law.

(b) The Stock Exchange for quoted companies.

(c) A review body. The powerful Securities and Exchange Commission (SEC) in the USA acts as a review body for quoted companies. In the UK, the Financial Reporting Review Panel has been established for this purpose by the ASB.

(d) The requirements of auditors.

Standards are usually issued as a consultative document first: in the UK this is called a FRED (Financial Reporting Exposure Draft). It should be noted that the nature of standards varies widely from country to country. In the USA, there are far more standards (Statements of Financial Accounting Standards (SFASs) exceed 100) and the individual standards are longer, more legalistic and present fewer choices. In the UK and the Commonwealth, standards tend to restrict options but still allow choices: they are far less detailed.

There is also an international body called the International Accounting Standards Committee (IASC). This has issued a series of accounting standards called International Accounting Standards (IAS). Unfortunately, it has proved difficult to reach agreement between the various parties worldwide on the contents of these standards, and therefore, in order to reach agreement, standards have often reflected a wide range of choices. The weakness of this approach has been recognised, and in 1989 the IASC issued an exposure draft E32 called "Comparability of Financial Statements". This set down proposals to limit the options provided by IAS, over a period of time, in order to make International Accounting Standards worthwhile. Progress in this area is likely to be very slow.

Compliance with International Accounting Standards is not mandatory in any country throughout the world. However, listing particulars often contain a reconciliation of the figures therein to figures calculated on the bases in International Accounting Standards. It is also fairly common for major companies in the smaller economies, which seek stock market listings in the major centres – Tokyo, New York or London – to prepare financial statements on the basis of International Accounting Standards.

4.4 Auditors' Report

4.4.1 *Unqualified Report*
Here is an example of a UK unqualified auditors' report.

AUDITORS' REPORT TO THE MEMBERS OF ABC LIMITED

We have audited the financial statements on pages 00 to 00 which have been prepared under the historical cost convention and the accounting policies set out on page 00.

(There then follows a standard paragraph setting out the "Respective responsibilities of directors and auditors" and two standard paragraphs setting out the "Basis of Opinion". This is followed by *Opinion.*)

In our opinion the financial statements give a true and fair view of the state of affairs of the company and the group at 31 December 19XX, and of the profit and source and application of funds of the group for the year then ended, and have been properly prepared in accordance with the Companies Act 1985.

Registered Auditors
Date

A US unqualified report is similar, but the opinion merely states that the accounts comply with Generally Accepted Accounting Principles ("US GAAP"): this statement is shorthand for saying that the statements comply with US accounting standards and relevant US statutes.

The UK report is rather different. It refers specifically to the relevant Companies' Act with which the statements are required to comply. More importantly, it expresses the opinion that the statements "give a true and fair view of the state of affairs of the company and the group".

What does this statement about "true and fair view" mean?

(a)   First of all, it obviously places great importance on the judgment of the auditor.

(b)   It also means that the fundamental accounting concepts described in Section 4.1.1 have been followed.

It is fundamental that the auditors have expressed an opinion – hence their statement should always be described as an Audit Report or Auditors' Report, never as a certificate. This is significant because users of accounts must recognise that there is no "correct" profit figure for the year. Indeed, the words "true and fair" were originally chosen for the UK audit report to avoid the implications of the original suggestion of "true and correct". In even the most straightforward company, there are a substantial number of areas of judgment where there is no right answer. The most obvious area is that of provisions, where an estimate has to be made of the amount of receivables which will subsequently prove uncollectable, and the amount of stock, which, because it is slow moving, obsolescent, or has been costly to produce, will not be subsequently sold at a profit.

An unqualified audit report provides considerable comfort to a banker because it means an independent firm has reviewed the accounts and is satisfied that they reflect the performance of the business. It is not an absolute safeguard – companies have failed in circumstances which have indicated that the previous year's accounts were a gross misrepresentation, even though they received a "clean" (i.e. unqualified) audit report.

4.4.2   Qualified Audit Report
A qualified audit report has two features. There is an additional paragraph in the "Opinion" section which states the nature of the qualification. The opinion section will contain either some reservation, such as "except for", or, worse still, may say that the accounts do not show a true and fair view or do not comply with the relevant legislation.

A qualified report of this nature should immediately put the banker on his guard. It means there is disagreement between the directors and auditors about the accuracy of the accounts, and the scope and impact must be fully understood if any reliance is to be placed on the figures.

There is another type of audit report which is not technically 'qualified', but which requires careful consideration. There may be substantial figures in the accounts which are subject to considerable uncertainty, and which, despite the best efforts of both the directors and auditors, cannot be estimated with reasonable certainty. In these circumstances, the "Basis of Opinion" section contains a paragraph headed "Fundamental Uncertainty".

A report of this nature is not necessarily a cause for concern, unless the uncertainty has arisen from the failure of the corporate to keep adequate records. Provided the banker understands the worst possible impact of the uncertainty on his financial assessment, the figures in the accounts can still be used in his assessment.

4.5   Accounting Policies

4.5.1   *Choice of Accounting Policies*

Most companies have choices in preparing their accounts. These choices are much more restricted in the USA, where not only are the accounting standards more prescriptive, but the standards are rigidly enforced by the Securities and Exchange Commission. Even in Europe, where tax accounting determines, for example, depreciation rates for fixed assets, companies still have significant choices. For companies in British Commonwealth countries, which follow the UK regime, choices can be very wide and in the past enforcement has often been weak – some spectacular company failures in Australia (e.g. Bond Corporation) are frequently cited as an example of the problems which may ensue. There has recently been a dramatic tightening up of enforcement of Accounting Standards in the UK, with the introduction of a Review Body.

Choices reflect either areas where existing Accounting Standards are in force but permit more than one basis, or areas which standards do not currently cover. Some of these areas have only modest impact on overall reported profit or net assets, but others are fundamental. Amongst the fundamental areas are:

(i)   Revenue recognition. For example, if a service is delivered over a prolonged period, such as leasing an asset or providing repair and maintenance services, how is profit calculated and spread over the service lifetime?

(ii)   Treating items as extraordinary "below the line" or exceptional "above the line". If costs are regarded as relating to the closure of an activity, in some regimes they can be treated as extraordinary. This means they appear in the profit and loss account below the line on which pre-tax profit is struck, thus flattering the all-important profit figure.

(iii)   Deferring revenue expenditure by carrying it forward as an asset. For example, the costs of launching a product might be deferred and matched to subsequent income from sales. Other items which may be deferred are research and development expenditure. Deferring expenditure increases profits in the year of deferral: profits in subsequent years are reduced by the amortisation charge.

(iv) Revaluing tangible assets. There is nothing wrong with revaluing assets in regimes which permit this (e.g. the UK, but not the USA). It increases shareholders' funds and reduces gearing ratios, thereby flattering the balance sheet of a company which revalues, compared with one which does not.

(v) Depreciating fixed assets. Different companies, even within the same industry, may depreciate similar assets over widely differing asset lives. The longer the lives used, the lower the charge against profits in the initial years.

(vi) The inclusion of goodwill. If one company acquires another, and pays more in total for its assets than the sum of their individual market values, the additional value is called goodwill. Some companies write off all goodwill as soon as they acquire it, thus reducing shareholders' funds. Others carry it forward and depreciate it each year (in the USA, this is compulsory) which reduces profits instead.

(vii) The inclusion of other intangible assets. Items such as brand names, newspaper titles and even the value of customer lists may appear in the balance sheet, boosting shareholders' funds.

(viii) The use of provisions. European companies make substantial use of provisions to reduce reported profits in good years, and flatter profits in bad ones. Scandinavian companies are permitted to set aside certain amounts out of pre-tax profits: analysts should really treat such charges as appropriations of profit rather than expenses.

(ix) The treatment of pension charges and refunds from pension funds. If the pension fund is in surplus, the employer may take an immediate refund, giving a one-time boost to this year's profits.

(x) The sale of fixed assets or investments. Profits from these sales may be included in trading profit, although their exceptional nature will usually be shown in the notes to the accounts.

(xi) Sale of subsidiary companies. As with fixed assets, profits from this source may provide an unrepeatable source of income if included in 'normal' profit.

(xii) Stock valuation. Whilst it is widespread practice to value stock and work-in-progress at the lower of cost and net realisable value, there are a variety of ways of calculating cost. The most usual are first-in first-out (FIFO), last-in first-out (LIFO), and average cost. FIFO is the most widely used. Where prices do not fluctuate widely, it is the closest to replacement cost. Companies carrying stocks on a LIFO basis may have artificially low stock/sales ratios

4.5.2 *Change of Accounting Policies*

There are four reasons why a company or group changes its accounting policies:

(i) Changes in company law: a new statute may forbid a previous policy.

(ii) Changes in accounting standards, which may also disallow a previous policy.

(iii) Significant changes in the nature or mix of its activities. A group accounting policy which may have been satisfactory when an activity was negligible in a group context may have to change if an acquisition means it is now a major segment of the group.

(iv) "To present a truer and fairer view", i.e. an optional change.

The first two changes are totally innocuous, and the third usually so. The change in the fourth category is much more significant as it is entirely voluntary. It would be extremely unusual for a voluntary change to reduce reported profit for the year, and it usually produces a significant enhancement. The inference is obvious – companies make voluntary changes in accounting policies in order to enhance their reported results.

Companies are normally required to state the effect of a change, but usually do this by stating what effect the new policy would have had on last year's results. This is frequently uninformative and uninteresting; what the reader really needs to know is what last year's policy would have produced as a reported profit this year, in order to see the effect of the "creative accounting".

Most developed accounting systems require accounts prepared by a company from year to year to be on a consistent set of principles. Where an accounting treatment or "basis" is changed, then a company will usually be required to quantify and disclose the effects of the change. Consistent treatment between years will, for example, eventually iron out distortions caused by stock over-valuation in one year albeit that the *trend* in a company's performance may be obscured. A company would not, for instance, be able to change backwards and forwards between LIFO and FIFO from year to year.

4.5.3   *Window Dressing*
Apart from the selection of, and change in, accounting policies, there are other ways in which companies can improve the appearance of their financial statements. These are often referred to as "window dressing".

They are generally designed to enhance the appearance of the balance sheet. The techniques fall into two categories:

(1)   Arrangements which take advantage of the fact that the balance sheet is only a snapshot at one point in time, so that very short term measures can produce a different picture at the balance sheet date from the norm during the year. An example would be selling a large quantity of inventory to a third party on the last day of the year, but buying it back the next day. The balance sheet would show much lower levels of both borrowing and stock than was typical during the year.

(2)   The long-term removal of assets (and the borrowing to fund them) from the balance sheet, using an "off-balance sheet" vehicle, such as a trust, associated company or partnership.

Accounting standard-setters and legislators are gradually outlawing these and similar devices, but opportunities still exist for those seeking ways of flattering their financial performance.

4.5.4   *Off Balance Sheet Activities*
Consolidated Accounts are generally prepared on the basis of ownership, not on the basis of recourse for creditors. Where ownership and recourse are similar, removing assets and liabilities from the group balance sheet causes few problems. An example of this might be a stand-alone project financed on a non-recourse basis.

Problems arise where liabilities are not shown in the consolidated balance sheet, but where the creditors have some recourse to "group" assets.

Subsidiaries are always consolidated in group accounts where the immediate parent company owns a majority of the subsidiaries' equity. This fairly narrow criterion creates obvious opportunities to exclude a subsidiary from consolidation using different classes of shares, different voting rights, or controlling its activities by other means than shareholdings (e.g. by contracts and agreements). In the UK these loopholes were blocked by the Companies Act 1989 and by FRS2, which defines a subsidiary on the basis of control rather than ownership of its shares. However, in other jurisdictions these opportunities may still be available to groups wishing to reduce the gearing levels shown in their consolidated balance sheets.

Even where these avenues are blocked a number of options for removing borrowings from the balance sheet remain open:

(i) **Investments in Associated Companies**
These may represent genuine minority stakes. However, the majority shareholder could be a "sleeping partner", particularly if it is a bank, which acts in accordance with the wishes of the minority but dominant partner. Associated companies where the group's interest is 40% or more should always be examined carefully.

(ii) **Non-consolidated Subsidiaries**
Some regimes permit subsidiaries to be excluded on a variety of grounds, such as:

- because its activities are fundamentally different, e.g. a bank or insurance company owned by an industrial company

- because it is to be sold

- because the parent's control of its activities is restricted.

These exceptions have been exploited: some loss-making subsidiaries were conveniently held for sale for several years. In the USA and UK these loopholes have largely been closed.

(iii) **Partnerships and Trusts**
Similar considerations apply to partnerships and trusts as to associated companies. Particularly important in a partnership is the responsibility of the various partners for liabilities – does the partner effectively underwrite all the risks of the partnership and guarantee payment of creditors and lenders?

(iv) **Sale and Repurchase of Assets**
Assets, and the liabilities used to fund them, may be removed from the balance sheet by selling them prior to the period end but repurchasing them later. The temporary owner will be protected from any fall in asset value by a repurchase agreement, put option or similar device. Such schemes have the character of a secured loan: accounting standards are beginning to address this issue and, in the future, accounting for such schemes may have to follow the commercial substance of the transaction.

(v) **Securitisation of Assets**
Assets may be sold to a stand alone special purpose vehicle company which has non-recourse funding. Such assets can validly be excluded from consolidation provided there is no recourse to the original group if the assets realise less than anticipated.

(vi) **Leases**
Many accounting regimes now require a distinction to be drawn between finance and operating leases. The boundary is usually drawn based on the proportion of an asset's life/value for which it is used by the lessee. Assets where lease payments represent a high proportion of the asset's value are characterised as finance leases. For these, the asset is capitalised and recorded in the lessee's balance sheet, together with the associated liability. Inevitably, leases are often designed to fall just outside these criteria, so that they can be accounted for as operating leases.

4.5.5 *Identifying and Analysing Off-Balance Sheet Finance*
Apart from the note on accounting policies, the most important notes to the accounts are those on contingent liabilities and investments. Almost

as many company failures have arisen from problems with contingent liabilities as have been caused by inability to meet on-balance sheet liabilities.

Scrutiny of the notes on contingent liabilities should reveal:

(a) Borrowings of associated companies and other entities guaranteed by the parent

(b) Other commitments to associates

(c) Obligations to repurchase assets or fulfil contracts at prices below market price

(d) Lease commitments

(e) Commitments to insulate third parties from any fall in value of assets sold to them by the group.

A review of the notes on investments should reveal the nature and extent of investment in associated companies, joint ventures and partnerships.

4.6   Consolidated Accounts

Consolidated Accounts are the most useful source of information about a group's financial position, because they bring together all the activities of a group, and summarise its trading results, financial position and cash flow. However, before basing decisions on this information, a number of limitations in consolidated accounts needs to be recognised:

(a) Consolidated accounts are based on assets the group legally owns or (for limited classes of assets such as those under finance leases) where it has the risks and rewards of ownership. Ownership does not necessarily mean access or control.

(b) Access to assets overseas may be restricted by exchange controls or other local regulations. Payment of dividends may be restricted for the same reasons.

86

(c)   The holding company may not have unrestricted access to its subsidiaries' assets, even where those subsidiaries are in the same country.

Legal restrictions on the distribution of reserves, taxation or the fiduciary responsibilities of the subsidiaries' directors may reduce the scope for payment of dividends to the parent company.

Whilst consolidated accounts remain a vital source of information about the group, the possible impact of the limitations outlined above must be considered as part of lending decisions.

5.   RATIO ANALYSIS

5.1   Objectives

The overall objective in credit analysis, particularly in ratio analysis, is to decide whether a corporate appears to be in sufficient financial health, both now and in the future, to service the proposed borrrowing and repay the capital when due.

We need to translate this into specific objectives which a healthy corporate should meet. These can be categorised as:

(i)   Real sales growth

(ii)   Satisfactory profitability

(iii) Effective asset utilisation

(iv)   Strong cash flow

(v)   Conservative gearing, liquidity and capital structure.

5.2   What Statements Are Analysed?

5.2.1   Audited Financial Accounts

The usual starting point for ratio analysis is the published financial accounts for the last three to five years. This is because they are factual, rather than forecasts or estimates, and are audited independently. We have noted in Section 4 that there can still be problems with these figures because of the accounting policies employed. We also consider in Section 5.3 below other factors which may make them misleading. Nevertheless, they remain the most important starting point. They form a solid base against which management accounts, projections or pro forma accounts can be assessed.

5.2.2 *Management Accounts*
Management accounts are accounts produced for decision-making purposes within the business.

Analysis of management accounts can be very beneficial (if a corporate is prepared to make them available to a banker – many are not) because the format of the accounts is usually much more appropriate to the activities of the corporate. Statutory P&L accounts in particular are often ill-designed for the specifics of a particular business. All the various elements of cost are summarised in a few lines; it is impossible to identify those which vary in line with turnover and those which are fixed costs of the business. All kinds of unusual items may be hidden in the figures because of the need for a simplified format. Furthermore, in consolidated accounts many different businesses and products are added together. The individual unit company's accounts may make more sense, because they can be compared more readily with similar businesses elsewhere.

Management accounts are obviously usually more up-to-date than the most recent statutory accounts.

However, it is important to understand that, quite legitimately, management accounts may use different accounting policies from statutory accounts. Without the constraint of statutory requirements, and the need to comply with accounting standards, the directors of the business are free to determine the most appropriate way of measuring the performance of the underlying business.

Furthermore, the methods used to prepare the management accounts may be inherently less reliable than those used for annual accounts. This is because the annual accounts have to meet a high standard of precision to satisfy the auditors: for example, physical stock will have to be carefully counted and evaluated. Such procedures may be very expensive and time consuming, and impossible to follow on a monthly basis. In the management accounts, management may therefore use reasonable estimates to arrive at certain figures, e.g. estimate cost of sales using a percentage of sales. These estimates will be revised periodically by the disciplines of a physical stock-taking and other detailed procedures.

Bankers should not rely substantially on management accounts unless they have taken steps to satisfy themselves that they are sufficiently reliable for their purposes. One way of gaining some comfort in this area is to examine the previous year-end reconciliation of the management and statutory accounts, which any company with strong financial controls will prepare.

5.2.3 *Projections*
In some circumstances, bankers will be provided with projections by a company or its advisers. These should always be treated with the greatest care. Where the business already has a track record, it is important that projections are compared with the historic figures. Differences in turnover levels, gross margin percentages, or fixed cost expenditure should be questioned. Simple sensitivity tests (see Chapter 8 – Project Finance) should then be applied to the projections, i.e. the banker should work out what the effect would be if certain events occur. Amongst the sensitivities which should be applied are:

(i) Certain figures, such as turnover and margin percentage, continue at historic levels rather than those shown in the projections

(ii) The impact of a (conservative) fall in turnover or margin percentages

(iii) Worst case movements in exchange rates, commodity prices, inflation, interest rates, etc.

In certain circumstances, projections are the only figures that are available, e.g. when a new business is being commenced. In these circumstances, independent reports will need to be commissioned on likely turnover levels, etc. Conservative sensitivities should then be applied to the base case.

5.3 Making the Figures Meaningful

As noted above, historical accounts are generally a reliable starting point. However, leaving aside the issue of accounting policies and window dressing, even thoroughly reliable and conservative accounts contain a number of distorting factors which the user may wish to eliminate in order to get a better appreciation of what is happening in the underlying business.

The principal distorting factors are:

(i)   Acquisitions and disposals

(ii)   Extraordinary/exceptional items

(iii) Impact of exchange rates

In such circumstances it may be appropriate to adjust the historical figures and create pro forma figures for analysis.

5.3.1 *Acquisitions and Disposals*

Generally the acquisition or disposal of businesses gives rise to a change of mix in activities which affects margins and other ratios in the business. However, it is not always appreciated that an acquisition or disposal has an even more powerful effect, which is very distorting in the actual year when the acquisition or disposal is made.

Under the most commonly applied accounting policy for acquisitions (acquisition accounting), in the group's consolidated accounts the acquired subsidiary has only its turnover and profit included for that part of the year in which it is in ownership. However, whatever date it is acquired during the year, the full effect of ownership is reflected in the closing balance sheet. This means that for a group with a December year end, an acquisition at the end of January will have an identical balance sheet impact to an acquisition at the end of November.

Consider the following example of Group A acquiring Company B. Both have stable turnover and operating profits, which do not vary from year to year.

90

Annual Figures

	Group A	Company B
Turnover	200	60
PBIT	20	12
Net Interest	(6)	(4)
PBT	14	8
Net Assets	150	40

Suppose both companies have a 31 December year end, and A acquires B on 30 September 19X2. The consideration is £40m cash and there is no goodwill. Published results for the A Group for the year to 31 December 19X2 will be as follows:

£m	A	B	Impact of Acquisition	A Consolidated
Turnover	200	15		215
PBIT	20	3		23
Interest	(6)	(1)	(1)	(8)
PBT	14	2		15
Net Assets	150	40	(40)	150

and in the year to 31 December 19X3, assuming no growth, will be:

£m	A	B	Impact of Acquisition	A Consolidated
Turnover	200	60		260
PBIT	20	12		32
Interest	(6)	(4)	(4)	(14)
PBT	14	8		18
Net Assets	150	40	(40)	150

The entries in the column "Impact of Acquisition" reflect the replacement of B's shareholders' funds by borrowing, and the interest charge arising from this.

The return on net assets appears to be $15/150 = 10\%$ in 19X2 and $18/150 = 12\%$ in 19X3: in fact the performance of the business is identical. The published accounts in 19X2 are not comparing like with like; the profit and loss account should be adjusted to provide a fair basis of comparison:

(a) when comparing 19X2 with 19X1, the acquisition should be completely excluded;

(b) when comparing 19X2 with 19X3, the acquisition should be included for 12 months.

The adjustments to be made for forward comparison are as follows:

(a) Adjust turnover and operating profit to include the acquisition for 12 months

(b) Adjust interest on B's pre-acquisition debt to reflect a 12 month charge

(c) Include interest charges on the non-equity portion of the purchase consideration for 12 months

(d) Include a full year's dividend on any shares issued to fund the takeover.

Similar adjustments (to exclude B for the whole year) must be made for backward comparison.

In most accounts, there is sufficient information to arrive at reasonable estimates for the adjustments which should be made. If the accounts themselves do not contain the figures, they will be included in the documents issued at the time of the takeover.

5.3.2 Extraordinary/Exceptional Items

In the USA, there are virtually no items which are treated as extraordinary. Therefore the reported profit for the year may contain all kinds of large exceptional items, such as profit on sale of subsidiaries, profit/losses on sale of investments, reorganisation and rationalisation provisions, etc. In the UK, and elsewhere in the British Commonwealth, it has been possible to treat many of these items as extraordinary, thus boosting the reported profit figure. This practice was reviewed in 1991 and, from 1992 onwards, following the implementation of FRS 3, the situation in the UK is similar to that in the USA.

Whilst this prevents companies boosting their reported profits by putting items "below the line" (i.e. after Profit Before Taxation), it does not necessarily help the analyst to understand the underlying profitability of the business, which he needs to know to estimate future years' profits. It may therefore be appropriate to take out of reported profits items such as:

(i)   Profit/loss on disposal of business

(ii)   Profit/loss on disposal of investments

(iii)   Sometimes profit/loss on disposal of *major* fixed assets.

5.3.3   *The Impact of Exchange Rates*

Many groups will have a significant proportion of their sales and/or production overseas. When one year is compared with another, figures in the accounts will reflect differences in exchange rates between the reporting currency and the currency in which the transactions are conducted. For example, if a UK company makes half its sales in the USA, and sterling weakens by 10% against the dollar, then, other things being equal:

(a)   US sales as reported in £ sterling will increase by 10%, and therefore total group sales by 5%

(b)   If the US sales are of goods produced in the USA, then US trading profits will increase by 10% in £ terms. If they are produced in the UK, then the cost of sales will be the same as in the previous year and the whole of the increase in sales will flow through to trading profits

(c)   US domiciled trading assets and liabilities will increase by 10% in the £ denominated balance sheet. The net movement will be taken to reserves

(d) US$ denominated debt will increase by 10% in sterling terms. If the debt has been used to fund non-UK assets, the increase in liabilities can be offset against reserves. If it has been used to fund UK assets, the group has a problem – the charge has to be taken through the profit and loss account.

For an international group, significant movements in exchange rates may have a substantial impact on its accounts. This aspect has to be considered carefully in any analysis (see Chapter 10 on Currency Exposure Management).

5.4   Key Ratios

As noted in Section 5.1, bankers are looking for their borrowers to satisfy five key objectives in terms of financial performance. It is helpful to identify ideally one, or, if necessary, a small number of key ratios for each objective in order to decide whether it is met. Focusing on key objectives avoids the common failing of computing a large number of ratios with no disciplined way of drawing these together to reach an overall decision.

Objective	*Key Ratio*	*Target*
Real Sales Growth	Real Sales Growth	Greater than zero
Profitability	PBIT / Net Assets	Greater than cost of funds + 2 to 5%
Asset Utilisation	Sales/Net Assets	Compare with other corporates
Cash Flow – Actual	OCF/Sales	Greater than 3 to 5%
– Sustainable	Debt divided by Sustainable Cash Flow	Less than 10 years
Gearing & Liquidity	Gross Gearing	Depends on accounting regime
	Interest Cover	3.0 times

Key ratios should be interpreted as follows after calculation:

(i) Compare with the "pass mark" suggested above, or with one determined by the banker

94

(ii) Compare with other similar companies or the sector average

(iii) Compare for the group under review from one year to the next

(iv) Where the same ratios have been identified in covenants, compare with "trigger" levels.

If the tests above are applied and no problems are met, the objective has been satisfactorily achieved. If there are any problems, the banker should go down to the subsidiary ratios which underlie the key ratio or the figures which make up the calculation of the key ratio. For example, the ratios which make up PBIT/Funds are described in the section on Profitability below, and the "pyramid" of ratios underlying Sales/Total Net Assets is described in the section on Asset Utilisation.

Each of the key ratios are considered further in the section below. To illustrate the ratios, we will examine the accounts of X Group PLC. Its consolidated balance sheet and profit and loss account are set out below: the cash flow statement is shown in Section 5.4.5.

PROFIT AND LOSS ACCOUNT
X GROUP PLC

	19X2 £m	19X1 £m
Turnover	100	80
Cost of sales	(80)	(65)
Gross profit	20	15
Distribution & administration costs	(10)	(8)
PBIT	10	7
Net interest payable*	(4)	(4)
PBT	6	3
Taxation	(2)	(1)
Profit after taxation	4	2
Dividends	(1)	(1)
Retained profit	3	1

*Payable 5, Receivable 1

BALANCE SHEET
X GROUP PLC

	£m 31/12/ 19X2		£m 31/12/ 19X1	
Goodwill		30		30
Fixed Assets				
Property	20		20	
Plant & Machinery	20		14	
		40		34
Current Assets				
Stock	30		24	
Debtors	25		20	
Cash	5		10	
	60		54	
Current Liabilities				
Borrowings	(10)		(10)	
Creditors & Accruals	(20)		(16)	
	(30)		(26)	
Net Current Assets		30		28
Total Assets				
less Current Liabilities		100		92
Creditors due after more than one year		(20)		(20)
Total Net Assets		80		72
Funded by Shareholders' Funds		80		72

5.4.1 *Sales Growth*

Sales growth is calculated by determining the percentage increase in turnover from one year to the next, i.e.:

$$\text{Apparent growth} = \frac{\text{this year's turnover} - \text{last year's turnover}}{\text{last year's turnover}} \times \frac{100}{1}$$

For X Group PLC

$$\text{Apparent growth} = \frac{(100 - 80)}{80} \times \frac{100}{1}$$

$$= 25\%$$

From this apparent growth figure we then subtract the amount of growth which is caused by inflation, acquisitions or disposals, and movements in exchange rates. When each of these is deducted, we derive the real growth. If this is not positive, then the company is seeing volume shrinkage in its continuing businesses.

Suppose for X Group, inflation in its principal areas of operation was 5%, and exchange rate movements had added 2% to total turnover, and new subsidiaries had added 14%. Real growth would be approximately 4% (25% – 5% – 2% – 14%).

Real growth is important because it is what economists call a lead indicator. It gives us an early warning of things going wrong. If turnover is declining this year, the market is likely to see a price war in subsequent years, with an inevitable effect on margins and profits. It is important that we understand the reasons why real growth is declining. Is the overall market shrinking or is our group suffering a decline in market share? Negative real growth is not always a cause for concern: our group may have taken a decision to withdraw deliberately from less profitable segments of the market.

One important consideration when calculating real growth is the inflation figure. Usually it is simplest to use the retail price index. However, in companies where commodity prices (such as copper, lead) are a significant part of the final selling price, you may need to use more specific inflation factors.

5.4.2 *Profitability*
The key ratio is

$$\text{Return on Total Funding (ROTF)} = \frac{\text{Profit before Interest \& Tax (PBIT)}}{\text{Total Funds Employed}}$$

Total funds employed consists of equity, minority interests plus all forms of debt (net of cash), less intangible assets.

The target should be the average cost of funds in the group's funding markets, together with an appropriate premium for risk. This premium should be a minimum of 2 – 5%, depending on the industry and countries of operation.

If a company is not making returns at this level, the shareholders would be better off investing elsewhere. They may be unwilling to subscribe for rights issues, and any funding requirements are likely to fall on banks.

Note that we have deducted intangibles (goodwill) in our calculation. This is because we are examining the return on operating assets. If as an alternative we wished to assess management's performance in earning a return on both operating assets and the amounts they had expended on acquisitions we would leave intangibles in the asset base, which would reduce the overall return to $10/105 = 9.5\%$.

The reason for using ROTF rather than the more commonly used Return on Shareholders' Funds (ROSF), is that it is totally independent of the method of funding the business. The return on shareholders' funds, i.e.

$$\text{ROSF} = \frac{\text{Profit Before Tax}}{\text{Shareholders' Funds}}$$

can be dramatically altered by increasing gearing or taking other financial measures. ROTF measures the performance of the underlying business rather than its funding structure.

Profitability can be analysed into two components, because:

98

$$\frac{PBIT}{Total\ Funds\ Employed} = \frac{PBIT}{Turnover} \times \frac{Turnover}{Total\ Funds\ Employed}$$

$$= Sales\ Margin \times Asset\ Utilisation$$

In our example, for X Group PLC in 19X2:

$$13.3\% = 10.0\% \times 1.33$$

The asset utilisation ratio is considered further in Section 5.4.3. below. The (PBIT/Turnover) ratio is called the sales margin (or operating margin).

Whilst all industries should be seeking a similar ROTF, it is important to recognise that they aim to achieve it by different combinations of sales margin and asset utilisation. For example, a housebuilder should have a high margin (say, 20%), but will have a low asset turnover (say, 1.0 times) because it has to carry a land bank and substantial work-in-progress in its balance sheet. A construction company, on the other hand, receives progress payments from customers to cover its work-in-progress, and often has very low funds employed and a high asset turnover (say, 5.0 times). It can therefore afford to have low margins (say, 4%).

It must not be assumed that, even in the short term, the sales margin is a fixed percentage of turnover, because some of the operating costs will be fixed. For example, consider a company with £100m turnover and a 10% sales margin where variable costs are 30% of turnover:

	Current £m	If turnover rises by 20% £m	If turnover falls by 20% £m
Turnover	100	120	80
Variable costs (30% of turnover)	30	36	24
Contribution to fixed costs	70	84	56
Fixed costs	60	60	60
PBIT	10	24	(4)
PBIT/Turnover	10%	20%	–5%

When analysing corporates, it is very important to understand the proportions of variable costs and the amount of fixed costs. Companies with high material, direct labour and sub-contracted elements of costs will tend to have high variable costs, whereas capital intensive industries, such as chemical manufacturing, will have high fixed costs.

5.4.3 *Asset Utilisation*

The key ratio here is turnover/total net assets employed in the business. The net assets employed in the business can be calculated as:

net assets in business = (total assets except cash)
                                          minus
                                          (total liabilities except debt and equity)

In a simple business with only basic trading assets and liabilities:

net assets in business = (fixed assets + current assets − cash)
                                          minus
                                          (trade creditors + accruals + taxation + provisions)

There is no target for asset utilisation. Some businesses have high asset turnover and low margins, whilst businesses with low asset turnover compensate with very high margins. The asset utilisation ratio should be compared with the industry average and with other businesses in the same sector. Even more important is to look at trends in the ratio over time.

The asset utilisation ratio is important for two reasons:

(i) Movements in the ratio, and comparisons with similar businesses, tell you a lot about the business, its stockholding level, debtor collection, etc.

(ii) Mathematically, asset utilisation is a component of profitability because:-

ROTF = sales margin × asset utilisation

Taking the balance sheet of ABC Company:

Liabilities	£m	£m	Assets	£m
Capital & Reserves	80		Fixed Assets	40
Less goodwill	30	50		
Long term borrowing		20	Stock	20
Short term borrowing		10	Debtors	35
Creditors		20	Cash	5
		100		100

This balance sheet can be re-analysed:

Business assets and liabilities	£m	Funding	£m
Net working assets		Borrowings	
		-short term	10
Stock	20	-long term	20
Debtors	35		30
	55	Less cash	(5)
Creditors	(20)	Net borrowing	25
	35		
Fixed assets	40	Shareholders' funds	80
		Less goodwill	(30)
Assets employed	75	Funds employed	75

Then, using either side of our balance sheet, assets employed or funds employed:

$$\text{Asset turnover} = 100/75$$
$$= 1.33 \text{ times}$$

Suppose the asset turnover of the group shows a declining trend, or is lower than industry averages. For further investigation, we can analyse the asset turnover into its component parts. The first step is to invert the ratio, i.e. calculate

$$\text{Net assets/sales} = 75/100$$
$$= 75\%$$

This is done to make all the components capable of addition or subtraction, for example:

$$\text{Net assets/sales} = \frac{\text{Fixed assets}}{\text{Sales}} + \frac{\text{Net working assets}}{\text{Sales}}$$

i.e. for X Group PLC

$$75\% = \frac{40}{100} + \frac{35}{100}$$

$$= 40\% + 35\%$$

We have used the term net working assets throughout this section to refer to (stock plus debtors less creditors). The more widely-used term working capital can be confusing. Some commentators use it as a synonym for net working assets: others include, in addition, overdrafts, cash balances and other current assets and liabilities. In either definition working capital can be positive or negative.

If the net asset/sales ratio is worse (i.e. higher) than the industry average, we can then establish whether the problem lies with the fixed assets/sales ratio or with net working assets/sales. If the problem lies with the latter, then we can analyse further:

$$\frac{\text{Net working assets}}{\text{Sales}} = \frac{\text{Debtors}}{\text{Sales}} + \frac{\text{Stock}}{\text{Sales}} - \frac{\text{Creditors}}{\text{Sales}}$$

Each of the three component ratios above actually has a meaning in business terms. First, we convert each of them into a period rather than a percentage, for example:

$$\text{Period of credit allowed} = \frac{\text{Debtors}}{\text{Sales}} \times 12 \text{ months}$$

In our example of X Group PLC:

$$\text{period of credit allowed} = \frac{25}{100} \times 12 \text{ months} = 3 \text{ months}$$

The stock/sales ratio can also be converted into a period called the stock turnover: the creditor/sales period is called the credit taken. In the case of these last two ratios, strictly speaking it would be better to compute the ratio of the asset compared with cost of sales rather than with sales. However, this would damage the consistency of our investigation into the total assets/sales ratio. Furthermore, since we are investigating trends in the ratio, or comparisons with similar companies, the substitution of sales for purchases will usually be acceptable.

Trends in credit allowed, stock turnover and credit taken can tell us a lot about changes in the business.

Suppose there is an increase in credit allowed. This immediately puts the banker upon enquiry because it may indicate weaker credit control procedures, which in turn may imply that the group may have to write off some uncollectable debts in the future. However, there may be a more satisfactory explanation for the trend. Perhaps the business is making an increasing proportion of export sales, where credit periods may be longer. Alternatively, perhaps the product or customer mix is changing towards parts of the market which expect longer periods of credit. It can be seen how a proper understanding of the underlying business is vital in order to interpret trends in financial accounts.

It should be remembered that a reduction in the debtors/sales ratio is not always a favourable trend. It may indicate, for example, that the company is under cash flow pressures and is factoring a proportion of its debtors. This, in turn, will give rise to higher finance charges in the profit and loss account.

Similar considerations apply to the stock/turnover ratio. Increasing stock levels may be a sign that production is running ahead of sales, with possible future problems of obsolescent or slow moving stocks. However, it could equally be that the group is building up for the launch of a new product range. Alternatively, perhaps the group is moving from selling via wholesalers to selling direct to the retail trade, with a consequent need to carry larger stocks in order to respond rapidly to retailers' demands. Of course, if this is the explanation, by virtue of cutting out the wholesaler, we would expect the group to achieve higher sales margins, thereby compensating it for the financial costs of holding larger stocks. It is

103

always important to ensure that any explanation for changes in a ratio are consistent with the other figures in the accounts. Generally speaking, if a group voluntarily makes a change which worsens one financial ratio, there should be some compensating benefit elsewhere.

Like the two previous ratios, trends in the creditor/sales ratio can reflect underlying changes in the business, such as new channels of supply. Alternatively, it may reflect changes in financial policy, such as paying creditors more quickly in order to receive prompt payment discounts. Here the loss of free finance from creditors is compensated for by reductions in the cost of purchases.

An increase in the creditor/sales ratio is, on the face of it, favourable to a corporate because it provides it with additional free credit. It may indicate strong negotiating by the company's buyers. However, it should be monitored carefully because it may be one of the early warning signs that the company is under sharp cash flow pressures and is unable to pay creditors in its usual timescale. If borrowing levels are high, and the banker knows that a company is using all its facilities, rises in the creditor/sales ratio should be treated with concern.

5.4.4 *Gearing and Liquidity*
Gearing is a widely used term, as is its US counterpart of leverage. However, there is no universally acknowledged definition of either. We shall use the definitions shown below, but in discussion with corporates and other banks you will always need to agree the definition you are using.

The key ratios for gearing are:

$$\text{interest cover (gross)} = \frac{\text{profit before interest and taxation}}{\text{gross interest payable}}$$

$$\text{gross gearing} = \frac{\text{total debt}}{\text{net worth}}$$

or, alternatively:

$$\text{leverage} = \frac{\text{total liabilities}}{\text{net worth}}$$

For our example, X Group PLC:

Interest Cover = 10/5 : 2.0 times

$$\text{Gross Gearing} = \frac{(20 + 10)}{(80 - 30)} = 60\%$$

$$\text{and Leverage} = \frac{(30 + 20)}{(80 - 30)} = 100\%$$

In the calculations above, net worth is shareholders' funds (plus any equity element of minority interests) less any intangibles such as goodwill which a banker may wish to discount. It is a matter of opinion whether you should also deduct intangibles such as newspaper titles, brand names, etc.

The gearing ratio is heavily dependent on what assets are included in the balance sheet, and whether they are carried at cost or revalued. In the USA, where fixed assets are not permitted to be revalued, acceptable gearing levels may be quite high. In the UK, where fixed assets are usually revalued, a target of below 60% is reasonable.

For interest cover, a figure of at least three times is considered prudent.

It is important to remember why we are looking at gearing levels. Although bankers should always have some feeling for the level of asset backing for their lending, this is not the prime reason for looking at the gearing ratio. It must be recognised that the figures at which assets are carried in accounts are very different from that which they would realise on a break-up, and therefore low gearing does not necessarily give us comfort that banks would be repaid on the break-up of a business. The main reason why gearing is of concern is that, where assets are financed by debt, sufficient earnings must be generated to repay interest on that debt. Where assets are financed by equity, there is no compulsion to pay dividends, and therefore a group can survive difficult times by reducing or eliminating payments. Companies with high gearing are therefore much more vulnerable to a recession or other setbacks to their business.

In addition, high gearing indicates a management strategy which not only likes to take risks, but prefers to risk banks' money rather than their own or their shareholders' money. If profits grow, the shareholders get

105

more benefit with high gearing than with low gearing, and if the corporate fails, the banks take a greater share of the loss.

In some industries, gearing ratios are of questionable value. In businesses such as advertising and employment agencies, particularly when the intangible assets of the business are not carried in the balance sheet, it is common to see a business with negligible net assets. The key issues therefore are not the level of gearing, but whether the profits and cash flows comfortably cover interest outgoings. In these businesses, interest cover is particularly important.

In calculating interest cover, it is usually appropriate to add back to the interest charge any element which has been capitalised in the accounts. The capitalisation of interest is quite legitimate: indeed in the USA it is mandatory in certain circumstances. However, there is no correlation between a corporate's capitalising of interest and its being allowed to "roll it up" by lenders: most capitalised interest still has to be paid as it accrues. It is therefore prudent to calculate "cash interest cover" which includes capitalised interest.

Interest capitalised will be shown in the Profit and Loss Account. This is interest expenditure which has been classified as "capital expenditure" and thus charged to the Profit and Loss Account and treated as an "Application of Funds". It usually relates to specific fixed assets developments or purchases (as described in the company's accounting policies) where interest payments on the money borrowed during the construction or delivery period are treated as an integral part of the cost of the asset. As explained above, in analysing cash flow strength such amounts should be deducted from the capital expenditure and added to interest paid.

Other costs, e.g. maintenance and repairs, are sometimes capitalised. If they are then adjustments need to be made to capital expenditure and pre-tax profit when calculating ratios.

As well as considering gearing and its impact on interest cover, you must also consider liquidity. This is the availability of cash to meet liabilities. Of course, not all liabilities have to be met immediately: in assessing liquidity short-term liabilities have much greater significance than longer-term ones. Furthermore, corporates do not usually hold cash balances large enough to meet all their liabilities: they rely on their ability to turn current assets into cash or to generate cash from operations.

In the past it was common to focus on two ratios to assess liquidity as follows:

$$\text{Current Ratio} = \frac{\text{Current Assets}}{\text{Current Liabilities}}$$

$$\text{Quick or Acid Ratio} = \frac{(\text{Current Assets} - \text{Stock})}{\text{Current Liabilities}}$$

In our view these ratios have very limited value. They are not very good indicators of potential problems because:

(1)   they depend on the industries concerned. For example, efficient retailers have low stocks, negligible debtors and substantial creditors. Their current and quick ratios will probably be very low. This does not mean they have a liquidity problem, it simply demonstrates that they are "cash" businesses;

(2)   they can be changed simply by changing the funding mix. Replacing overdrafts and short-term loans with, for example, two year facilities will dramatically improve both ratios, because the borrowing will no longer be included in current liabilities.

We prefer to focus on cash generation and debt/cash flow ratios, which are considered in the sections below.

5.4.5   *Cash Flow*

Whilst profit is important, cash flow is vital. Profit is a "paper" figure essential for monitoring by creditors and shareholders: cash flow is real money which pays bills and repays debt.

Cash is different from retained profit for a variety of reasons, the principal ones being:

(1)   The absorption or generation of cash by increases/decreases in working capital;

(2)   Capital expenditure (i.e. cash out) being different from the depreciation of existing assets charged against profits;

(3)   Taxation and dividend payments having timing differences from the related charges in the accounts;

(4)   Deferred taxation having no cash impact;

(5)   The impact of acquisitions and disposals of business;

(6)   The impact of the sale of fixed assets and investments, where the whole of the proceeds goes into the cash flow statement;

(7)   Provisions are often established (e.g. for re-organisation) to meet cash outflows in future years.

A typical format for a UK cash flow statement is set out below:

X GROUP PLC
Cash flow statement for the year ended 31 December 19XX

	£m	£m
Operating activities		
Operating profit	10	
Depreciation charges	4	
Profit on sale of tangible fixed assets	(1)	
Increase in net working assets	(3)	
Cash flow from operating activities		10
Returns on investments and servicing of finance		
Interest received	1	
Interest paid	(5)	
Dividends paid	(1)	
Cash flow from returns on investments and servicing of finance		(5)

Taxation	£m	£m
UK corporation tax paid	(1)	
Overseas tax paid	–	
Tax paid		(1)
Investing activities		
Purchase/sale of tangible fixed assets	(6)	
Purchase/sale of subsidiary undertakings	(10)	
(net of cash acquired)		
Cash flow from investing activities		(16)
Cash flow before financing		(12)
Financing		
Issue of ordinary share capital	5	
New loans	5	
Repayment of amounts borrowed	(3)	
Capital element of finance		
lease rental payments	–	
Net cash inflow from financing		7
Decrease in cash and cash equivalents		5
Net financing		12

(a) **Operating Activities**
These are the cash effects of transactions and other events relating to operating or trading activities.

(b) **Returns on Investment and Servicing of Finance**
These are receipts resulting from the ownership of an investment and payments to providers of finance.

(c) **Taxation**
These are cash flows to taxation authorities in respect of the corporate's revenue and capital profits. They do not include payments and receipts in respect of VAT, sales or property taxes.

(d) **Investing Activities**
These are flows related to the acquisition or disposal of any asset held as a fixed asset or a current asset investment.

(e) **Financing**
These consist of receipts of, or repayments of, principal to external providers of finance.

In US cash flow statements, the activities are classified as operational, investment or financing. Interest and taxation are classified under operating activities and dividends paid under financing activities.

The example in the cash flow statement for X Group PLC shows it in the UK format. It is important to appreciate that all items in the statement are cash flow items, not charges to profit. For instance, taxation will be the amount *paid in a year*, which may represent the amount due for the preceding year's profits.

5.4.6 *Cash Flow Actual*
For analysis purposes, it is necessary to recast our cash flow statement in the following way:

	£m
Cash flow from operating activities	10
Interest paid (net)	(4)
Dividends paid	(1)
Taxes Paid	(1)
Retained operating cash flow	4
Net capital expenditure	(6)
Free cash flow	(2)
Acquisition/disposal of subsidiaries	(10)
Financing requirement	(12)
Financed by:	
Equity	5
Net increase in debt	7
Net financing	12

We then look at two key areas:

110

$$\frac{\text{Retained operating flow}}{\text{Sales}} \left\{ \begin{array}{l} \text{should be greater than } 3 - 5\%, \text{depending on} \\ \text{the capital intensity of the business.} \end{array} \right.$$

Free cash flow should be positive or neutral. If net capital investment is *much* greater than depreciation, then a negative figure is acceptable in years of particularly high capital expenditure.

If retained operating flow is small or negative, this points to one or more of the following problems:

(a)   Profits before interest and taxation are too low. Review profitability ratios to see if this is the case.

(b)   A substantial increase in net working assets. If turnover is rising, some increase is expected in line with turnover. Review the asset utilisation ratios, i.e. stock/sales, debtor/sales and creditor/sales. Have these percentages worsened significantly? Consider the possible explanations suggested in Section 5.4.3.

(c)   Interest paid is very high. This could either reflect a peak in interest rates or excessive borrowing. Review the interest cover and gearing ratios (see Section 5.4.3).

(d)   Dividend policy is too generous. Check the dividend cover ratio which is defined as:

$$\text{Dividend cover} = \frac{\text{profit after taxation and before dividends}}{\text{dividends}}$$

(e)   Taxation is high. Review the tax charge in the profit and loss account and calculate it as a percentage of reported profits. Is it in line with corporation tax rates? If not, review the taxation notes to the accounts – it may be that the corporate is making losses in some activities/ countries which cannot be offset for tax purposes against profits in other areas.

In our example, X Group PLC, we have seen that profitability is adequate at 13.3%, but not strong, gearing is fairly high at 60%, and interest cover is quite weak at 2.0x. In addition capital expenditure is substantial at 1.5x depreciation. All these factors have contributed to the cash deficiency.

Weak cash flow ratios are the most serious signs of possible problems for bankers. If a company's cash flow ratios are poor, it is usually a symptom of problems elsewhere. Bear in mind that, whilst virtually all areas of the accounts can be window dressed, it is much harder to conceal an adverse situation in the cash flow statement.

5.4.7 Cash Flow – Sustainable

Examining actual cash flow alone may not be sufficient. For example, cash flow may temporarily be enhanced by squeezing stock levels or cutting back on capital expenditure. It may, therefore, be necessary to estimate sustainable cash flow, by making the following adjustments to actual cash flow:

(1)   Eliminating non-recurring items from profits;

(2)   Replacing actual capital expenditure with an amount sufficient to replace existing assets as they wear out;

(3)   Allowing working capital to grow in line with turnover;

(4)   Reflecting the impact of acquisitions for a full year.

It is useful to divide sustainable cash flow into outstanding debt to provide a notional repayment period. Ideally, this should not exceed ten years: greater than twenty years is usually a cause for concern. However, it is not sufficient for a group to have a notional repayment period of less than 10 years. Ideally, the debt maturity profile should be compatible with the ability to generate cash, i.e. debt repayable in each of years two to five should not be substantially greater than sustainable cash flow (year one is excluded because it includes such facilities as overdrafts).

5.4.8 Net Working Assets and Growth Companies

A company with a consistent or gradually expanding volume of sales should generate adequate operational cash flow to cover increases in net working assets with a generous margin. In this situation, furthermore, the ratio of Net Working Assets to Turnover should be consistent if management control of stocks and debtors is adequate.

112

The quick check on this is:

$$\frac{\text{Net Working Assets}}{\text{Turnover}}\ \%$$

A company which experiences a period of fast growth in turnover will usually find it has to maintain (or even marginally increase) this ratio during the expansionary period. When this occurs, it is likely that the additional investment required in stocks and debtors (net of creditors) will absorb a significant proportion of operating cash flow. Let us take an example.

Growth Inc. achieves in Year X the following figures:

Turnover:	$10,000,000
Profits Pre-Tax, Depreciation & Interest:	$1,500,000 (15% of Turnover)
Net Working Assets:	$2,000,000 (20% of Turnover)
Operating Cash Flow Pre-Interest:	$1,400,000 ($1,500,000 minus an increase in NWA of $100,000)

In Year X + 1, growth burgeons and turnover rises by 50% with operating margins maintained causing the following to occur:

Turnover:	$15,000,000
Profits Pre-Tax, Depreciation & Interest:	$2,250,000 (15% of Turnover)
Net Working Assets:	$3,000,000 (20% of Turnover; up $1,000,000)
Operating Cash Flow Pre-Interest:	$1,250,000 ($2,250,000 minus increase in NWA of $1,000,000)

Thus, notwithstanding a markedly improved sales performance, Operating Pre-Interest Cash Flow has fallen and pressure on cash flow will be exacerbated by increased tax obligations, dividend expectations and interest costs to fund the additional net working assets.

Assuming you are content that the expansion is being properly managed, then it is justifiable to treat part of the increase in Net Working Assets as a discretionary investment designed to expand the business. In this situation, therefore, one could strip out the increase associated with growth in excess of, say, 10% (i.e. $800,000) and add it to Capital Expenditure. The adequacy of the resulting Retained Operating Cash Flow in contributing to the financing of the business can then be assessed as discussed above.

Material differences over time in the Net Working Asset ratio can be further investigated by looking at individual ratios for stocks, debtors and creditors.

5.4.9 *Retained Operating Cash Flow (ROCF)*

This is the amount of cash available to the business after adjustment for net changes in Net Working Assets and payment of those who expect a return from the profit earned by the company, viz, lenders, the tax man and shareholders. It represents the extent to which the company has the capability to service existing levels of debt and to finance replacement and expansion of its operating capacity without recourse to external sources of capital.

Assessment of the adequacy of this figure requires, therefore, comparison with:

(a)   the size and maturity profile of the company's debt and

(b)   the extent of capital expenditure requirements both in the context of the volatility and risk associated with the business.

The first of these comparisons can be made using the following.

5.4.10 *Long-term Debt Service Capacity*

$$\frac{\text{Total Interest Bearing Debt}}{\text{ROCF}}$$

This indicates the number of years which the company would require to pay off its interest bearing debt on the (admittedly implausible) assumption that it could survive with no capital expenditure during that time. This should be considered in the light of the anticipated life cycle of the company's products and fixed assets. Companies in a relatively mature industry with modern facilities and a stable product line which does not demand large commitment for research and development (e.g. food companies; departmental stores) can live with a high multiple. Companies, by contrast, in a highly competitive environment with short product life-cycles (e.g. computer manufacturing) may be vulnerable if this ratio exceeds, say, 3. Be careful to take into account distortions arising from any deconsolidation of debt.

5.4.11   *Short-Term Debt Service Capacity*

$$\frac{\text{Current Maturities of Long-Term Debt}}{\text{ROCF}}$$

If this ratio is in excess of 1, then the company will have to refinance its maturing debt unless operating cash flow improves in the following year. A company in this position is vulnerable and should cause close examination of its ability to raise and repay new external finance. I exclude overdrafts and other debt with an original maturity of under one year, on the grounds that such funds will usually be on a revolving basis to fund trading balances and will not usually be finally repaid in any one year. If, however, analysis of liquidity (see 5.4.3 above) reveals that the long-term capital requirements of the business are being funded in this manner, then again close attention should be paid to a company's ability to refinance.

This ratio can also be used in conjunction with the debt maturity profile to check whether current annual ROCF appears likely to be adequate to service the stated scheduled maturities.

A second comparison can be made, on a rough basis, by using Replacement Cost Depreciation, or, if this is unavailable, a multiple of Historic Cost Depreciation. The relevant multiple can be derived by assessing the age of fixed assets, and the stage in their life cycle they have reached, from the extent to which cost has been depreciated. This should be revealed by the note detailing fixed assets in the accounts and the note revealing depreciation periods used. Where plant appears relatively modern, then a multiple of 1.2 may be appropriate; where it appears to be nearing the end of its useful life, then a multiple of 2 may be more appropriate.

ROCF, if the company's turnover is growing no faster than inflation, can be expected to be, as a minimum, equal to the Replacement Cost Depreciation figure or the Historic Cost figure adjusted as above.

Neither of the above approximations is as valuable as a knowledge of a company's expenditure needs, should you be able to derive this both from the company's management and a close understanding of the company's industry and its relative position within it. They should, however, give you an insight on which to base further discussions and questions.

Companies with aggressive expansion or acquisition plans need to demonstrate strong Retained Operating Cash Flow (well in excess of Replacement Cost Depreciation) to enable them to contribute sufficiently to capital expenditure requirements, and provide for increased net working asset requirements without assuming unsupportable levels of debt. Alternatively (or additionally) they will need an ability to reinforce operational cash flow by raising equity. "Growth" companies, however, often demonstrate neither.

Companies which demonstrate a strong position with respect to Long-Term Debt service capacity will also have more flexibility to supplement ROCF with debt to fund productive capital investment than those already in a stretched situation.

6. CREDIT DECISION

Finally, the bank has to reach a decision whether or not to do business with the corporate. Is the decision a yes, a no or a qualified yes? It is now necessary to summarise the results of all previous analysis and reach conclusions as to whether the bank is satisfied about the following:

(i)   Management and its strategy

(ii)   The current financial health of the business

(iii) The best estimate of future financial health

(iv) The volatility in the business and any special risks, such as environmental hazards

(v)   The position of the borrowing entity in relation to the group as a whole, and whether there is adequate protection for the banker.

CHAPTER 4

Principles of Lending – Part IV

- THE TRANSACTION (1): TAILORING TO FIT
  –SITUATION, PURPOSE, AMOUNT, TERM AND
  REPAYMENT

by
John Willingham

Chapter 1 (Section 2), Chapter 2 (Section 1) and Chapter 3 considered general issues of creditworthiness, focusing on means of assessing both a borrower's ability to survive and prosper in its environment and its resilience to shocks and difficulties.

The general assessment thus provides the background against which to formulate ideas on what type of banking business can be contemplated for a customer (or potential customer) in the context of its needs, activities and creditworthiness. Business transacted, however, must not only be tailored to the requirements of the customer but must also be tailored to the bank's responsibilities to its depositors and shareholders. This latter constraint dictates the targeting and structuring of facilities which (i) give the bank the maximum protection possible against the possibility of non-repayment, consistent with the need to do business, (ii) are at a price which provides a reasonable return to the bank and its shareholders and (iii) enhance the bank's relationship with the customer and its reputation in the market, thereby providing opportunities for further business.

At this point, therefore, a banker should combine his knowledge of the borrower's strengths, weaknesses and requirements with the capabilities of his bank to provide financial and other services to arrive at the optimum facility consistent with the needs of both the customer and the bank. The key issues will usually be the following:

1. SITUATION

Lending proposals can usually not be considered in isolation. Notwithstanding suggestions over recent years that banking is now a transaction-orientated business rather than a relationship-orientated one, it remains a business where personal contacts, relationships and reputation play a crucial role. Major companies may no longer give all their business to one bank, but they will usually restrict their dealings to banks which they are confident can deliver what is required quickly and efficiently. Such confidence has to be earned by establishment of a market presence and reputation in chosen areas through engaging in transactions which foster the bank's objectives. This does not mean that money should be placed unnecessarily at risk nor priced unrealistically to 'buy' market presence – indeed, the herd instinct can be particularly dangerous when combined with inexperience in transacting the business contemplated – but it does mean that transactions have to be done from time to time which include unattractive elements to achieve wider objectives.

Equally, when the bank has considerable facilities to a borrower which encounters financial trouble, it will not usually be a viable option simply to refuse further credit and demand repayment. The bank may find that its only chance to recover the investment put in to date is to advance more under close surveillance and a planned strategy and hope that the borrower will be able to recover viability. In these situations, the only choice is to act pragmatically and protect your interests as best you can.

When considering a proposal, therefore, look at what your options are and who is "calling the shots". Can you realistically expect to achieve a secured transaction at a generous pricing level? Or do competitive conditions or other factors dictate that you offer an unsecured transaction at the minimum pricing level you can accept, structured perhaps to enable you to sell off part of your exposure to other suitable banks at a profit? What are the consequences for your other business with the borrower if you say "No"? What are the consequences for the bank's market and public reputation? Is it realistic, for example, to refuse to accept a rescheduling proposal for a major developing country when other banks have agreed

120

and your government and Central Bank are committed to the "rescheduling solution"?

A full awareness of the options open to you will save both time and possible embarrassment compared to the alternative of acting in actual or pretended ignorance of the situation in which an opportunity or problem arises.

2. PURPOSE
The purpose to which a borrower intends to put borrowed money plays a key role in determining:

● the safety of repayment

● the adequacy of remuneration

● the optimum transaction structure (particularly term, repayment arrangements, control and security)

● the attractiveness of the business to the bank in terms of its compliance with policy guidelines, legal and regulatory requirements and its likely effect on the bank's reputation.

We have already looked at various purposes for which companies require financing (Chapter 2, Section 2) and the bank facilities available to match those needs (Section 3). Let us look again at the purposes identified, this time from the standpoint of policy and creditworthiness.

2.1 Working Capital
A request for working capital finance is unlikely to cause policy controversies – it is the traditional business of banks.

From a credit standpoint, it is necessary to focus closely on the quality and liquidity of the working assets to be financed and the production/seasonal cycles which will determine utilisation. Commodity-type stocks (e.g. grain, basic consumer products) allied to debtors with a fast turnover (3–4 weeks), inasmuch as they generate cash inflow quickly and reliably, will justify a relatively high level of borrowing against levels of stock and debtors held from time to time. Slower moving stocks (e.g. jewellery, automobiles) and debtors with less reliable values and longer delays before cash inflows arrive, will demand lower levels of debt and a consequently higher contribution to the financing of net working assets from equity and debt capital (see Amount, Section 3).

Notwithstanding that working capital finance may be sensibly arranged under a medium-term facility, one will expect considerable swings in utilisation consistent with production and seasonal cycles (see also Section 5.9.2 below and Chapter 5, Section 2, Monitoring and Control).

Occasionally, one sees proposals for "working capital finance" from companies with no or minimal apparent need for such finance (e.g. service companies). The true purpose may either be unclear or disguised and should be closely investigated.

2.2 Trade Finance
Policy controversies here will arise only where the related trade obligation is with a country with which the bank has a policy not to do business, or where the underlying transaction is of a type with which the bank does not wish to be associated (e.g. perhaps, arms sales).

The credit issues specifically related to such finance are explored in Alasdair Watson's *Finance of International Trade,* published by The Chartered Institute of Bankers, and can be related also to the general issues discussed in Chapters 1–3 of the book.

2.3 Capital Expenditure
Policy considerations may arise in connection with the industry involved. Some banks have been reluctant to finance construction of nuclear power stations, for example. Occasionally, banks with a close relationship with a major manufacturer may show reluctance to finance the purchase of equipment sold by a rival.

A full appreciation of the risks being run will require an understanding of the commercial reasons for the capital expenditure being undertaken and of the management's ability to control and manage the assets. Where the expenditure relates to the starting of a new business, rather than the replacement or expansion of existing facilities, then the same credit considerations will apply as those discussed below under "Acquisitions".

Credit issues will then centre on the cash generating potential of the assets purchased or developed and the financial cushion over debt service requirements this can provide, together with the quality of recourse available for the bank to the cash flow and assets of the company generally should the development not be self-financing (See Repayment). Such financing will often require careful structuring and secured asset backing. (See also Asset Finance, Chapter 6).

2.4 Acquisitions
Acquisition-related proposals can give rise to major policy, credit and legal issues.

2.4.1 *Hostile Acquisitions*
The major issue of policy arises in connection with hostile takeover bids. If you have followed the progress of any of the major contested bids which have occurred particularly in the USA and UK over the last few years, together with the investigations into alleged insider-dealing and other practices which have gained wide publicity, then you will realise that this area of corporate activity is highly controversial. This is not to imply that hostile takeover activity is per se undesirable – it can be a means to achieve more efficient allocation and utilisation of resources within an economy – but such bids are highly public transactions and usually give rise, as a minimum, to heated debate both between the direct combatants and a variety of other interested parties (politicians, unions, competitors etc.).

Certain bank managements have, therefore, taken a view that they will finance only "friendly" or agreed mergers. Others have refused to join standby acquisition facilities (i.e. ones which are put together before a specific acquisition target has been decided) because of a concern that they may find themselves through such a facility financing a hostile bid for one of their other customers. Not only might this damage the bank's relationship with that customer, it might also cause other companies to question what the loyalty of that bank might be if they find themselves the subject of an unwelcome bid.

When presented with, or looking for, opportunities to transact acquisition finance transactions, you must be closely aware of the circumstances surrounding the bid and the policy of your bank in the context of those circumstances.

2.4.2 *Credit Considerations* centre on the impact of the acquisition on the borrower. Acquisitions, whether friendly or not, inevitably bring tensions, uncertainties and problems because of the need to integrate one business into another. This involves the need to integrate often incompatible management styles, philosophies and structures, personnel policies and practices, market strategies and images and customer portfolios. The process is complex and requires high levels of management competence and resources.

Prima facie the task is easier if the acquisition or merger is friendly and the two managements have agreed to work together; in practice, this may not prove to be the case as difficult decisions may be postponed or shirked and necessary conflicts avoided to appease established vested interests.

Major acquisitions will also have a considerable effect on the financial condition of the borrower. The precise impact will depend on whether the acquisition is funded by the issue of shares or by debt. Take an example of Company A taking over Company B for a price of US$60m. Summary figures from the accounts are as follows:

		Company A ($m)	Company B ($m)
Equity	:	100.00	50.00
Interest Bearing Debt	:	50.00	50.00
Gearing	:	50%	100%
Other Liabilities	:	50.00	25.00
Leverage	:	100%	150%
Total Assets	:	200.00	125.00
Annual ROCF	:	20.00	10.00
Debt/ROCF	:	2.5	5.0

124

Netting out the $10m goodwill from equity, the consolidated figures will look as follows if (i) the acquisition is funded by an issue of shares and (ii) the acquisition is funded by debt.

		Company A Consolidated	
		(i)	(ii)
Equity	:	150.00	90.00
Interest Bearing Debt	:	100.00	160.00
Gearing	:	67%	178%
Other Liabilities	:	75.00	75.00
Leverage	:	117%	261%
Total Assets	:	325.00	325.00
Annual ROCF	:	30.00	30.00*
Debt/ROCF	:	3.3	5.3*

*minus additional interest on debt raised.

In the second case, additional debt has been raised without increasing the cash generating ability of the combined group and in consequence produced worse cash flow coverage, leverage and gearing. In the first case, the takeover has been effected by a merger of the equity bases and thus the debt burden of the combined group is not increased.

The creditworthiness of the combined group will have to be closely assessed in terms of the principles described in Chapter 3 and the specific factors described below.

2.4.2.1 *Commercial Logic*

How is the acquisition justified? What is its purpose? Are existing activities being expanded by purchase of a similar business? Is perhaps vertical integration being sought (i.e. the purchase of a company which might otherwise be a supplier or customer of the existing one) in order to smooth out cyclical trading variations or to increase control over, and reduce the costs of, the total production, selling and distribution process in which the acquirer is involved (e.g. an oil production company purchasing filling stations)? Or is diversification into an unrelated area being sought perhaps to reduce dependence on the current core business or businesses? Perhaps horizontal integration is desired (i.e. the purchase of a company which serves a different segment of the same market). Or perhaps the acquirer believes that the company for which it has bid might be worth more if broken down into constituent businesses and sold off, than the constituents are worth collectively as a combined whole.

Whatever the justification, quiz the reasoning. The decision to launch a takeover, just as any other commercial decision, is taken by people from a mixture of motives, not all of which will necessarily be coherent. Check the attitude of the financial and industry press and the opinions of stockbrokers/analysts where possible.

2.4.2.2 *Consistency with Management Experience*
As emphasised above, the management challenge to make an acquisition successful is a considerable one. Thus, one will usually have a higher level of confidence in the prospects when management has demonstrated experience and expertise in both the business of the company to be acquired, and the countries in which that business is transacted. It will need to demonstrate further, however, an ability to cope with an expanded scale of operations and consequently increased need for monitoring, administrative and control systems.

In saying this, I am not attempting to claim that expansion in the same or related businesses is necessarily preferable to diversification – there are many examples of success and failure of both strategies. Nevertheless, I would venture to claim that the burden of proof is higher for those wishing to enter new businesses or countries, both because the difficulty of knowing whether the initial acquisition deal is a good one is increased and the challenge of integration is heightened by the need to learn a new business.

Further credence will be given to the acquiring management's intentions if it can also demonstrate a track record of successful acquisition activity.

2.4.3 *Legal Issues*
When the purpose of a proposed financing is to be an acquisition which will have a major impact on the acquirer, certain legal issues should be flagged:

(a) *Company*

Does the legal system and acquisition structure permit the merging of the two businesses or will the acquirer have to rely only on dividend receipts to repay the acquisition debt? Restrictions in the UK, for example, on the provision by a company of financial assistance, including security, for the purchase of its own shares can cause severe problems in this respect. You will need good legal advice.

Do the statutes of the company permit acquisition of the type of business contemplated?

(b) *Bank*

The involvement of certain banks, notably US commercial banks, in financing acquisitions is regulated. Regulation U, for example, in the USA prevents US banks lending for a company to buy publicly quoted shares in the USA if those shares are pledged as security and, when purchased, are worth less than 200% of the related debt. You need to be familiar with the issues involved in the regulation of your bank to enable you to recognise possible problems and to have access to in-house or external legal expertise.

2.4.4   *Leveraged Buy-Outs (LBOs)*

Because, by definition, protection available to lenders if the business's performance declines will be relatively thin, the credit and legal issues are thrown into still sharper focus. Most banks involved in the business have, therefore, specific policy guidelines on LBO transactions detailing rules for producing projected cash flow figures, cash flow coverage ratios which should be sought, security cover required, maximum amount and term of exposure and minimum pricing levels. There may also be a maximum overall amount of such business the bank will accept in its portfolio. Transactions which do not comply with the guidelines will require specific policy exceptions from senior executive management. You should be aware of the constraints your bank imposes.

LBO financing is suitable only for companies in stable industries with highly reliable cash flows and/or for ones where a large portion of initial acquisition debt can be repaid quickly from the sale of certain assets or subsidiary businesses.

2.4.5   Management Buy-Outs (MBOs)

2.4.5.1   Background

During the 1980s there was considerable growth in the number of what have come to be known as Management Buy Outs or MBOs. An MBO may be defined as a transaction whereby the managers of a business acquire the ownership of that business. The transaction may involve the acquisition by the managers of the company itself or the assets that make up the business.

The majority of MBOs result from the wish, on the part of a large group of companies, to sell a subsidiary the activities of which are no longer regarded as part of the group's core business. Company takeovers and mergers have often led to the ownership, within a group, of several diverse subsidiaries. The management teams within such subsidiaries often welcome the opportunity to become independent of the group, particularly if the parent company has imposed constraints which have restricted investment and entrepreneurial development. A sale of the business to its existing managers gives the parent company the opportunity to dispose of the subsidiary as a going concern rather than face the possibility of closing the business down.

Disposal may, alternatively, be achieved by selling the business to a new management team when the transaction is known as a Management Buy In or MBI. This may be appropriate if the existing management team do not wish, or are unable, to undertake an MBO. MBIs are less common than MBOs due to the difficulty of matching a suitably experienced incoming management team to a given business.

Very recently, a new type of MBO has emerged where the management team of a publicly quoted company buys the shares held by the public.

2.4.5.2   Legal Developments

The growth of MBOs in, for instance, the UK has been fuelled by changes in UK company law. Of particular relevance are sections 151

128

to 158 of the 1985 Companies Act which provide exceptions to the long established prohibition of a subsidiary company giving financial assistance to its parent for the purchase of the subsidiary's shares.

MBO transactions usually involve the formation of a new company which is used as a vehicle to buy the shares or assets of the business being sold. The management team undertaking the MBO rarely have sufficient personal means to finance the transaction. Finance is, therefore, raised by way of equity and debt with reliance placed upon the assets and cash-generating ability of the company being acquired to repay, and provide security for, the debt. Without the use of the exceptions which allow the giving of such financial assistance in certain circumstances, many MBOs would not legally be possible.

2.4.5.3 *Is an MBO appropriate?*
MBOs are not appropriate in all cases. The underlying business must be capable of generating sufficient cash flow and profits to service the finance raised for the acquisition. The management team wishing to buy the business must be sufficiently capable and committed to the business to convince the banks and equity houses putting up the finance that they will run the business well. The price payable to the seller must be at a level that the post MBO business can expect to service.

2.4.5.4 *The MBO structure*
If a management team decides to undertake an MBO, it will usually seek guidance from a venture capital or equity house, such as a merchant or investment bank, as to how the transaction should be structured. The price may already have been set by the seller or it may be assessed by reference to the price being paid for similar businesses at that time. This assessment will usually base the price upon a multiple of current annual earnings.

Once the price has been established, it must be decided what proportion should be raised by way of equity capital, and what proportion by way of borrowing. Here, the ability of the business to generate cash flow to service and repay debt will be the most relevant factor. The investors providing equity capital will be reliant upon future profitability for dividend income and capital gain when the investment is realised.

A typical MBO structure may be as follows:

	£
Ordinary shares representing the management team's investment	0.5m
Ordinary shares) representing the	1.5m
Preference shares) institutions' investment	8.0m
	10.0m
Senior debt, ie bank loan	30.0m
Overdraft facility	5.0m
	45.0m

In addition to senior debt, there may be a layer of mezzanine finance. This is described more fully in the following section. Senior debt is so called because it ranks ahead of all other types of finance in the structure in terms of safety. It carries the lowest risk and as a result has the lowest reward. It has the first call on the income generated in order to service the debt and it has a first charge over any assets available as security. Mezzanine debt holders and shareholders stand to earn a higher reward but their investments carry higher risks.

The level of risk involved in financing MBOs is reflected in part by the invariably high levels of gearing seen. In the UK an MBO will typically have a 300% (or more) ratio of borrowing to surplus resources. This is because the purchase price, including any goodwill element, is structured and financed to maximise borrowing potential. A typical senior debt interest margin is $1^1/2\%$ to 2% above LIBOR.

2.4.5.5 Cash Flow Analysis

As mentioned above, MBOs typically involve high levels of borrowing, with a high level of dependence upon strong cash flows to service the debt. The assets of the business, excluding intangible assets, are often inadequate to provide lenders with full security cover.

This necessitates close examination by potential lenders of the future plans of the business, particularly its future cash flows and profit projections. These projections are subjected to the closest scrutiny to ensure they are both realistic and achievable.

Forecasts covering at least three years are normally required and lenders may amend the forecasts to make them more conservative if considered appropriate. The resulting figures are called the Base Case projections. Using specially designed software these projections will be extended beyond the three years forecast to the full term of the loan, usually a further three or four years. For the purposes of this extension of projections, a conservative view will be taken of sales and profit growth.

The Base Case figures are then subjected to various sensitivity tests to assess how robust the cash flow is to withstand possible eventualities. The tests may include increases in interest rates, reduced levels of turnover or failure to achieve projected cost savings and combinations of two or more of these possibilities.

Only if the business projections stand up well to such scrutiny and to an independent accountant's report on historical performance and the achievability of future projections will the MBO lender wish to proceed.

2.4.5.6   *Subsequent Monitoring*
The performance of the business post-MBO is monitored, sometimes as often as monthly, against management information to ensure that any deviation from projections is identified and acted upon promptly. A further check on performance is the use of financial covenants, whereby the lender sets certain targets based on Base Case projections which the business must meet periodically. The areas targetted will probably include operating profit levels, interest cover, minimum tangible net worth and gearing/leverage ratios.

2.4.5.7   *Flotation*
Most MBOs are structured with the intention of the business being sold or floated after three or four years. The proposed "exit route" and the timing thereof is an especially important consideration for equity investors when assessing their involvement in a transaction. This is because they are dependent upon achieving a capital gain on the realisation of their

investment to achieve the overall level of return they require. Dividend income alone is rarely sufficient to meet their long term criteria for returns of between 30% and 40% on funds invested.

Whilst the exit proposed is relevant to senior debt providers, they will wish to ensure that even in the absence of a sale or flotation (which normally provides the funds to repay all borrowing) the debt can be repaid from continued trading profits generated over the original six or seven year term. Their income or return for the risk they carry as lenders emanates entirely from the interest margin so they are not looking to the flotation for a capital gain, although a by-product of a flotation may be that senior debt is repaid before maturity.

2.4.6   Mezzanine Finance

2.4.6.1   Definition
In financing the acquisition of a company, two of the traditional sources of funds have been equity (where the shareholders take the risk that the company will be successful and if it is not then the value of their investment will decrease), and debt (where lending banks expect repayment of funds from an identified source). A development in acquisition financing, particularly in the field of management buy-outs and buy-ins, has been the creation of a layer of funding which is neither pure debt nor pure equity, but comes somewhere between the two – *the mezzanine layer.*

Mezzanine debt is usually *subordinated* to the ordinary, or 'senior' debt i.e. mezzanine will not normally be repaid until the senior debt lenders have been repaid in full, and where a borrowing company is in difficulties it may be required to repay senior debt even before interest is paid on the mezzanine. In addition, mezzanine debt will generally be unsecured lending, as the senior debt provider will probably have a charge over all the assets of the business.

In return for accepting this subordinated position, mezzanine lenders receive a higher interest margin over cost of funds than the senior debt providers. They may also receive equity warrants*, which convert

*Not in the same form as warrants linked to bonds which require the payment of an appropriate sum of money in order to acquire equity.

132

to equity when the borrowing company is floated on a stock exchange or sold. In this way, the mezzanine lenders share in the benefits of the borrowing company's success – i.e. there is 'upside' potential to the deal.

To clarify the structure, Fig. 1 below shows a typical management buy-out scheme, where mezzanine debt forms part of the financing package.

FIG. 1

	£ m
Cost of purchasing company	45.0
Fees incurred in purchase	1.5
	46.5

Funded by:

Senior debt	30.0
Mezzanine debt	6.0
Equity from institutions	10.0
Equity from management	0.5
	46.5

2.4.6.2 *Yield Calculation*

In calculating the return on mezzanine lending, there are two aspects to consider:

(i) Interest received over the period of the loan

(ii) The value of any equity warrants converted on flotation/sale of the company.

In the UK it is industry practice to express the return on mezzanine debt in the form of an Internal Rate of Return, which takes into account the above elements.

(i) In many deals the borrower is required to "fix" its interest rate obligation by means of fixed rate borrowing, an interest rate swap or a "cap". In calculating the interest element of their overall return on lending, mezzanine lenders must forecast the likely trend in future interest rates, and this is obviously made much easier if the rates have been fixed.

(ii)   The value of any equity warrants will be forecast bearing in mind:

   (a)   the likely date of flotation/sale;

   (b)   P/E ratios for the industry which will give some indication of the likely value of the company if forecast profits for the year of sale are realised.

Fig. 2 below gives a simplified example of the type of IRR calculation performed by a potential mezzanine lender. Whilst different lenders will have their own minimum lending criteria, an IRR of between 20% and 25% would be usual in a UK deal.

FIG. 2

Assumptions
An MBO is due to float at the end of 1994 with forecast profits after tax of £8.0m, in an industry with an average P/E of twelve.

The equity in the company is divided amongst the original shareholders as follows:

Management	30%
Institutional investors	60%
Mezzanine lenders	10%

The MBO involved a mezzanine loan of £50m, drawn down on 1st January 1992 for a period of up to 9 years, at a fixed interest rate of 15% p.a.

Calculation
To calculate the value of the mezzanine holders' equity stake on flotation, we first calculate the exit capitalisation of the company. This is calculated as:

profit after tax   x P/E
i.e. £8.0m   x 12 = £96m.

The mezzanine lenders, entitled to 10% of the equity of the company, can therefore expect to receive £9.6m on flotation. Thus the return on their initial outlay of £50m (which principal sum will be repaid from flotation proceeds) is:

> £7.5m interest in 1992
> £7.5m interest in 1993
> £7.5m interest in 1994 plus
> £9.6m flotation proceeds, also in 1994.

These cash flows, together with the movement in principal amounts, can be shown diagrammatically as:

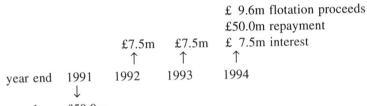

The Internal Rate of Return for the above cashflows can be calculated at 21% p.a. This calculation cannot easily be done manually. In the UK a sophisticated pocket calculator is used. The calculation is based on the mathematical concept of discounted cash flow. It should be borne in mind that the return of 21% p.a., whilst appearing high, does not take into account the cost to the lender of providing the funds, a cost which may fluctuate significantly over the life of the loan, if matched funding has not been arranged.

2.4.6.3 *The Mezzanine Market*

The United States was the first country to see mezzanine financing used in the funding of buy-outs and other types of acquisitions. Mezzanine can be structured in many ways, bearing in mind its rather vague definition as a funding instrument which is neither pure equity nor pure debt. In the US the issue of "Junk Bonds", which bear a fixed interest coupon but also form part of the capitalisation of a highly geared company, is often regarded as a type of tradeable mezzanine financing. The first mezzanine was used in the UK in 1984, on the buy-out of Evans Halshaw.

Mezzanine offers equity investors an opportunity to lend and earn interest income alongside their equity stake, whilst it is also attractive to banks which seek an additional return over and above the interest margin they can charge for senior debt, whether or not this is fully secured. In an environment where competition makes it increasingly difficult to justify the dedication of costly capital to finely-priced corporate lending business, the banks reason that they can increase returns by lending at a mezzanine level in addition to the senior debt they have provided traditionally.

The increased willingness of UK lenders and investors to provide mezzanine finance has broadened the borrowing base of acquisitive companies, illustrated by the appearance of bids such as those for the Magnet and Gateway Groups in the UK, both of which involved previously unseen levels of subordinated debt. These two deals underline the usefulness of mezzanine to borrowers involved in large acquisitions, where the financing required is beyond the limits set by equity and senior debt providers in their own lending criteria.

Equity investors also like to see mezzanine included in a deal structure because it can improve their own returns. This is because the inclusion of mezzanine debt allows a lower equity share as a percentage of the total funds provided than straight equity investment. It follows that where mezzanine is included in a deal, the amount of investment required from the equity investors is reduced by a greater proportion (say 30%) than the reduction in their ultimate share in the company (say 10%), and the overall return on investment is increased.

2.5 Project Finance

"Purpose" considerations are similar to those arising under Capital Expenditure proposals. Limited recourse financing of projects produce further considerations since such financing removes some of the economic risk of the investment from the company or project sponsor itself and places it directly on the banks. Such financing, therefore, requires significant expertise within participating banks to allow commercial and technical risks to be assessed and is generally suitable only for projects designed to produce commodity-type products (e.g. oil and coal) which can be readily traded. (See Chapter 8.) The concept has been expanded, however, to finance e.g. the co-generation of electricity in the USA and operating leasing of jet aircraft, where a combination of a perceived reliability of demand for the product, a relative cost advantage over competitors and perceived good security values have enabled certain banks to accept limited recourse risk.

2.6 Contingency Cover

The need for standby and back-up financing was explained in Chapter 2, Section 2.1.6. Facilities designed to satisfy this need have been subject to close review by banking regulators, particularly the Federal Reserve and Bank of England, because of the size of commitments to lend being built up by banks in a way which was not reflected on their balance sheets, and because of the low remuneration being accepted by banks for providing such facilities. Many banks, recognising the need to control the level of such exposure, have policies related to the total amount of such business they will accept in their portfolio, maximum amounts they will allow for specific customers and minimum acceptable pricing levels.

Because:

(i)   such facilities are designed to provide funding to a company simply in case of need, so that control for the banks over the purpose to which these funds are put is usually weak (albeit financial and other convenants, if they can be negotiated, may assist – see Chapter 5); and

(ii)   they are usually priced on the basis that they will not be drawn, on the assumption that the borrower will continue to be capable of raising cheaper funds in the short-term markets.

Such facilities are usually made available only for highly rated borrowers.

2.7 Exposure Management and Debt Mix

See Chapter 2, Section 2.1.7. Credit considerations here will usually centre on your assessment of the company's strategy in managing its funding mix, bearing in mind the reliability of its sources of cash income and the currencies of its income and expenditure. Of particular concern is that maturities of borrowings do not coincide and that there is a mix of short, medium and long-term funds appropriate to the type of business.

2.8 Balance of Payments and Rescheduling (Sovereign Borrowers)

Where rescheduling is required, the situation will often be the crucial issue as your options will usually be highly restricted. Balance of Payments lending in general suffers from difficulties of control and effective recourse if things go wrong – it should be done highly selectively. See Chapter 2, Section 2.2.1.

To summarise this Section, "purpose" considerations centre around:

- the policy issues (if any) they raise for the bank, whether they be issues of reputation, morality or portfolio exposure
- the commercial or economic logic of the purpose to be financed
- the ability and experience of the management, be it a company management or country's government, to handle the proposed venture
- the legal constraints (if any) on the undertaking of the relevant financing by certain banks
- legal complications associated with specific types of activity by companies, e.g. acquisitions, which may affect the creditworthiness of the relevant financing
- additionally, banks are becoming increasingly concerned that purposes are environmentally acceptable.

3. AMOUNT

The amount you will be prepared to lend will depend on the following factors:

3.1 Term and Repayment

The safety of repayment from the intended source. See below, Sections 3.4 and 3.5.

3.2 Adequacy

In an attempt to reduce the problems of obtaining finance for a relatively risky transaction, a borrower may be tempted to budget over-optimistically and omit to seek financing commitments for amounts to cover unforeseen delays, circumstances, costs, etc. In financing development of a factory site, for example, a bank or group of banks which agrees to lend $100,000,000 against an optimistically anticipated cost of $150,000,000, with the balance to be provided by other sources, will be severely exposed if the development finally costs $200,000,000 and no source of finance has been committed for the balance. Does the bank group fund the additional $50,000,000 to complete, or abandon the development and crystallise a heavy loss?

Additionally, has the need for financing of additional stocks and debtors related to sales from the factory been considered?

Similarly, an expanding business seeking working capital facilities will leave itself exposed to the problems of a liquidity crunch described in Chapter 3 if it does not secure adequate financing facilities to cover the possibility of slower than anticipated debt collection, bad debts, increased raw material costs etc.

3.3 Cushion and Contribution
The repayment analysis will determine the extent of cash flow coverage of debt servicing requirements. This will usually need to be reinforced by a level of asset cover to protect against the possibility that actual cash flow generated will not reach anticipated levels.

The extent of such cover is determined by:

3.3.1 The *leverage* and *liquidity* of the borrower after incurring the new borrowing (see Chapter 3); keep closely in mind the need to ensure that you have as far as possible direct recourse to the assets of a group of companies, not simply recourse to shares in subsidiaries owned by your borrower, and check carefully the extent to which other creditors have priority access over you to assets of the borrower because of security arrangements or legal preference.

3.3.2 *Security Cover*
If you finance e.g. the purchase of an item of equipment, you can obtain first priority access to surplus value in the equipment by lending only a proportion of the cost against a first priority mortgage over the equipment (see Asset Finance – Chapter 6). For working capital facilities to weaker borrowers, you may require a charge over the debtors and stock of the borrower and determine the loan amount you make available by reference

to the outstanding level of those debtors and stock at specific (e.g. monthly or quarterly) intervals (see Chapter 5, Section 1.5). The precise formula will depend on the liquidity and marketability of the stock and the quality of the debtor portfolio but a formula based on 50% of stock and 75% of debtors would not be unreasonable. For fast-moving commodity style stock which has a wide re-sale market, the figure may be higher, but slow-moving specialist inventory which includes a large proportion of work-in-progress may require a significantly more conservative approach.

Asset cover available from the borrower can also be supplemented by taking third party guarantees (see Chapter 5).

In addition to providing asset cover (the "cushion"), a material contribution from the borrower, in the form of the maintenance of low leverage and/or a cash contribution to the purchase price of an asset by which you are secured, reinforces the borrower's commitment to making the transaction work in order to ensure that its investment is not lost.

3.4 Portfolio Risk

As discussed in Chapter 1, banks usually impose limits on the amounts of credit risk they will have outstanding at any one time for individual countries, industries and companies to avoid exposing themselves to an excessively narrow range of risks. As a variety of surprise developments over the last few years have demonstrated, no borrower or group of borrowers can be regarded as wholly risk-free. The sharp reduction in oil prices, the dramatic decline of the shipping industry and the progress of the $10bn-plus Pennzoil litigation against Texaco are just a few examples of the unexpected.

A bank's portfolio should, therefore, contain a wide range of transactions and the size of its capital resources will determine the maximum amount which it is prudent to have at risk to the various business segments defined. This in turn will impact the amount which is available to lend for any given transaction. See also Transaction Risk below.

3.5 Transaction Risk

No lender will go into a transaction where he expects to lose money. Lenders have to accept, however, that some transactions have higher risk of failure than others and will attempt to structure them so that the risks are mitigated as far as possible and compensation for the additional risk being run is obtained in the price charged. Lenders from time to time will also wish to branch into new areas of business by participating in types of transactions with which they have little experience or for borrowers with whom they have not previously dealt. For the portfolio reasons referred to above, a bank will wish to spread its involvement in higher risk transactions thinly and, usually, to take a gradualist approach to involvement in unfamiliar areas. A bank, therefore, which may be content to advance $50,000,000 for three months to e.g. General Motors to fund working capital may wish to limit its exposure in a 7-year limited recourse project financing for a relatively small oil company to $5,000,000 because of the additional risks associated with the term, borrower and facility structure.

3.6 Yield
As pricing on transactions has become tighter over the years and, as many banks have faced both regulatory pressure to restrict the size of their balance sheets in comparison with the size of their capital resources and shareholder pressure to increase the returns on that capital, banks have increasingly sought ways of maximising the yield on assets (loans) held on the balance sheet.

One technique for achieving this is to underwrite and/or arrange large facilities which are subsequently sold-down or syndicated. A Management Fee is charged on the total facility at commencement (say 0.25% flat on $200,000,000 i.e. $500,000), the arranging bank takes a "praecipuum" or "skim" out of this fee (say 0.10% flat – $200,000) and brings in other banks to share the deal, which receive a participation fee of 0.15% flat on the amount they take. The arranging bank may, thus, be left with a final exposure of $20,000,000 in the transaction on which it has earned a total fee of $200,000 (0.10% flat praecipuum) plus $30,000 (0.15% flat participation fee). This $230,000 represents 1.15% flat on the $20,000,000 which spread over, say, a five-year term facility with a bullet payment, at a discount rate of 10% p.a., is equivalent to an additional margin, over and above the lending margin, of 0.33% p.a.

Thus, although syndication of bank facilities was originally developed primarily as a risk-sharing mechanism, it is increasingly being seen as a yield-maximisation tool with final "takes" being targeted accordingly. See also Chapter 5, Section 4 on pricing and Chapter 7 on Syndication.

3.7 Legal and Regulatory Considerations

The regulatory authorities may impose a maximum amount which can be lent to an individual borrower (US banks, for example, are permitted to lend a maximum of 15% of their Primary Capital to any one company or consolidated group of companies); UK banks have to report exposures to individual borrowers in excess of 10% of Primary Capital to the Bank of England and to consult before any individual exposure rises above 25% of Primary Capital.

4. TERM

"A week is a long time in politics" once commented Harold Wilson when he was Prime Minister in the UK. In banking, situations rarely change fundamentally in quite such a timescale but events can occur over the term of a facility to change the creditworthiness of that facility dramatically. Of course, the longer the term of any facility, the greater the possibility that such a change may occur and, thereby, the greater the risk of non-payment associated with the transaction.

The term required for a facility will largely be determined by the source of repayment. A trade finance transaction may mature in three months if that is the date on which the trade debt is due for payment; a jet aircraft finance loan, by contrast, may have a term of 12–20 years to link into the expected economic life of the asset concerned. There is generally no point in imposing a term on a facility which a borrower is unlikely to be able to meet, because (a) a subsequent default will be burdensome on both the borrower and the bank from an administrative viewpoint as discussions on a solution to the problem take place, and (b) the bank may eventually become committed to longer term repayment arrangements whatever its initial reservations because it may find it has little option other than to refinance the maturing obligation. In other words, if the borrower cannot realistically be expected to repay in under 10 years, it is of little use either to the bank or to the borrower to impose a 5-year term and hope for miracles. Either structure the transaction to make it palatable for a 10-year period, locate an additional source of repayment, or (if possible) decline the deal. In saying this, I am not arguing against 'tight' repayment terms – these can be a valuable discipline – simply unrealistic ones.

For qualifications to the above which do not, however, affect the thrust of the argument, see Section 5.9.3 below on bullet, balloon, evergreen and 'on-demand' forms of repayment.

5. REPAYMENT

The crucial issue in any lending transaction is how the bank is to be repaid. In the first part of Chapter 1 we looked briefly at the business of banking and the key role credit quality plays in determining whether a bank can continue to be viable. As highly leveraged institutions themselves, reliant on the continuing confidence of their depositors, banks cannot afford to be reckless in extending facilities which involve credit risk.

This is not to say that a bank should not engage in business which involves a degree of risk – no bank can be very profitable by lending only to AAA-rated borrowers. Where a transaction, however, does involve a degree of uncertainty associated perhaps with one, or a combination of, a long term, volatile industry, an economically weak country and high leverage, then the focus on what can go wrong and what are the bank's protections should it do so, needs to be all the sharper.

We, therefore, need to focus on:

5.1 Repayment Source – Type

The intended source of repayment will usually be determined by the purpose of the financing and act as a guide to suitable repayment arrangements. For example:

(a)   A loan to finance the purchase of an item of equipment, where the equipment is intended to generate a net cash inflow from its use, will usually be repayable on a basis consistent with the anticipated net cash flow to be generated and the anticipated useful life of the equipment.

(b)   An oil production or mining project loan will be closely tailored to the cash flow generating potential of the project and the production life and capacity of the reserves being tapped.

(c)   An acquisition finance will usually be repayable on a basis consistent with the anticipated ability of the acquired company to generate net cash flow from operations and/or planned asset sales.

(d)   A loan to fund a specific trade transaction will be repayable on maturity of the underlying trade debt.

(e)   A working capital loan will be repaid and re-drawn over its term (i.e. it will "revolve") in accordance with the company's production and seasonal cycles.

(f)   The repayment of funding to substantial multinational companies may not be linked to the specific purpose of the loan (if there is one – lending is often for "general corporate purposes") but, rather, will be achieved from the general, diverse cash inflow to the company.

The various forms of debt and equity finance will be evaluated by a company primarily in terms of cost and flexibility against the background of the need to maintain the attractiveness of the company to a range of investors. Debt levels may, therefore, be set at a maximum level consistent with maintaining a desired rating with the Rating Agencies and maximising the published earnings available to shareholders. Equity may be raised when the share price is at a high level where the dividend cost makes equity financing a cheap alternative.

The term and repayment schedule of debt raised by such corporations will turn, therefore, not on the income generating potential of specific assets but on a combination of:

(a)   the need to stagger maturities over a period to avoid the need to refinance/repay an unduly large amount at any one time;

(b)   the relative cost of various maturities and repayment schedules, determined after funds raised have, perhaps, been swapped into other currencies or interest rate bases (e.g. 5-years fixed to 3-month LIBOR).

The banker to such a corporation is more likely, therefore, to see his facility refinanced before maturity than to be repaid in full over its term out of operational cash flow. The exception arises where, whether for reasons of increases in interest rates, penalties negotiated for early repayment, hardening market attitudes generally or a decline in a company's creditworthiness, such refinancing is not available on attractive terms. Nevertheless, if refinancing is not achieved, it is the borrower's operational cash flow which is the primary source of repayment and it is this which, therefore, merits closest attention.

5.2 Repayment Source – Quality

For a term facility to a corporate borrower, where the bank's recourse is firstly to the operational cash flow of the borrower, then the quality of the repayment source is determined primarily by the factors described in Chapters 1–3, tied together as suggested in Chapter 3.

You are looking at the potential reliability of the net cash flow available to service your debt as determined largely by

- the industry or industries in which the borrower is engaged
- the country or countries with which it is involved
- the demonstrated ability of management to create opportunities and respond to challenges
- the level of other claims on operational cash flow and their type (interest, dividends, tax and essential capital expenditure)

It is crucial to remember, in addition, the need to link directly into the cash flow producing assets to ensure that the bank does not suffer from being effectively subordinated to other creditors. Careful structuring may also enable you to gain priority recourse to key assets and, thereby, improve the quality of your primary source and the protection you have should the borrower not perform as expected.

For sovereign borrowers, considerations expressed in Section 1.2 of Chapter 2 and in Chapter 12 will be central in determining both the anticipated ability and the willingness of the borrower to pay on time. See Chapter 2 also for Quasi-Sovereign and Supra-National borrowers.

5.3 Repayment Source – Currency

The volatility of exchange rates has brought into ever sharper focus the need for an international company to manage its currency exposure, not simply as a matter of administrative efficiency but also as an important determinant of creditworthiness.

There have been instances in the past where companies, with income denominated only in US$ or £, have borrowed Swiss Francs or Yen because of their relatively low prevailing interest rates and been badly affected as the currency borrowed appreciated strongly against the currency of their income.

The basic principle is, therefore, that the currency or currencies borrowed should match the currency or currencies of the primary repayment source. This may be achieved either by direct borrowing or through the currency swap market. Where a proposal is made that this principle should not be adhered to, then the justification needs to be clearly spelt out and the additional risks of the currency mismatch factored into the analysis. It may be, for example, that an exposure may be assumed on the basis that it can be closed out through the forward exchange or currency option markets in case of need; such actions are legitimate but only to the extent you have confidence in the borrower's ability and willingness to effect the close-out if and when it becomes necessary.

See also Exposure Management, Chapter 10.

5.4 Cash Flow Protection

The quantity of cash flow protection for your debt can be calculated using the ratios discussed in Chapter 3, as calculated from the Cash Flow Statement projected forward.

When analysing this, again be careful to ensure that the cash flow you are looking at is one to which you will have direct access, and that you are not unwittingly subordinated to claims of other creditors.

The less reliable or more volatile you consider the operational cash flow to be, the greater will be the quantity of protection you will desire.

Where adequate protection is not available in the borrower itself for there to be minimal risk of failure, then additional protection will be required in the form of good asset cover arising through low leverage and/or security and/or third party support. Use of security and quasi-security to convert what may appear to be too risky a transaction on an unsecured basis into an acceptable one is discussed in Chapter 5.

146

It is impossible to be dogmatic about minimum levels of cash flow coverage which will make a transaction acceptable. Clearly, there is a trade-off between reliability of net cash flow and its quantity. In addition, cover ratios can be lower for short-term facilities than for long-term because of the increased uncertainties which taking, say, a 7-year view brings in comparison with a 6-month view. It is for this reason, of course, that the major Rating Agencies rate short-term commercial paper issued by companies on a different basis from that which they employ for long-term bond issues.

Nevertheless, at the risk of over-simplification, let me say that the highest quality companies in a competitive manufacturing environment (those which would be rated Single-A and above) will consistently display Long-Term Debt service capacity of under 3 and Short-Term Debt service capacity of under 0.20 without evidence of under-spending on capital assets. Interest cover as defined in Chapter 3 will be in excess of 4 and Interest and Rental Cover in excess of 3. Where, in a moderately competitive environment, such ratios start to be closer to 6, 0.5, 2.5 and 2 respectively then additional protection begins to look necessary.

Let me re-emphasise, however, that these are not figures set in tablets of stone. Confidence in a management's (or parent company's management) ability to achieve results and a favourable industrial environment may enable you to be less demanding. A short track record, non-availability of detailed information, an uncertain industrial outlook or the relative position of other creditors may, by contrast, cause you to require additional protection even for cases where the quantity of cash flow coverage appears generous.

5.5 Financial Flexibility

Temporary interruptions in efficient cash flow generation arising from e.g. a cyclical downturn, will not usually be a threat to the viability of repayment as a whole, unless such an interruption causes the company to run out of cash sources to pay to maturing obligations. Such a crisis may develop if there are delays in payment by debtors, stock turnover slows down and/or (if the company is using the short-term non-bank commercial paper markets) demand for its paper dries up for reasons associated either with developments in the commercial paper market generally or with the performance of the company specifically.

A company can avoid being caught out by such developments, unless they are symptomatic of a deeper underlying malaise, by arranging committed standby or working capital facilities which, while trading conditions remain satisfactory, are little utilised. Such facilities provide valuable flexibility to cushion shocks and give comfort to the term lender, who is providing, perhaps, a 7-year loan for a specific item of capital expenditure, that viability of repayment will not be affected by cyclical phenomena.

Similar comfort can also be derived if the company has access to strong equity markets and a variety of debt markets or, perhaps, to a strong parent or Government (if state-owned). It is, of course, true that access to such markets or parental support could become restricted for reasons associated with the performance of the company or circumstances affecting the investors themselves. Such access should, however, allow better and more flexible management of a company's finances over time and help to prevent a company being forced into panic-raising of funds after a crisis has been allowed to develop.

5.6 Asset Protection
See above, Section 3.3

5.7 Country Risk
We have considered the effects of country risks on the viability of a multinational company. We need also to relate it to a lending transaction to an individual borrower domiciled in a specific country.

Where a bank is lending "cross-border" i.e. to a borrower in a different country, then it faces the following risks:

5.7.1 *The transfer risks that:*
(a)   the country may restrict the access of the borrower to foreign exchange, thereby preventing it from servicing its foreign currency debt notwithstanding the strength of its own performance;

(b)   the country may impose an unanticipated withholding tax on interest payments made out of the country; the borrower will, in virtually all cases, indemnify the lender for this risk but, inasmuch as this requires the borrower to make additional payments to the lender to service its obligations, the lender's credit risk on that borrower is increased.

5.7.2 *The political risk that* the borrower may be forced by its Government to renege on its debts (unlikely) or that its viability may be affected by

148

actions such as nationalisation, new regulations which increase operating costs, etc.

5.7.3   *The economic risk that* the economy of the country of the borrower may deteriorate to an extent whereby the viability of the borrower may be affected through reduction in demand for its products, high domestic taxes and interest rates, labour problems, cost inflation and deterioration in the value of the domestic currency; if the borrower is able to survive these developments, it may find that its obligations are subject to rescheduling arrangements negotiated by the Government on behalf of all borrowers of foreign currency in its country.

Where such country risk is perceived to be high (see Chapter 12), then protection may be required in the form of one or more of:

- tangible security held outside the borrower's country;

- guarantees from third parties outside the country (e.g. a foreign parent company);

- political and/or commercial risk insurance, available in certain circumstances from either export credit agencies or commercial insurance brokers (see Alasdair Watson, *Finance of International Trade*, for e.g. buyer credit guarantees applicable to sales finance transactions; commercial markets may be able to provide coverage for nationalisation, confiscation of assets etc. but financial and transfer risks are usually not insurable in my experience).

5.8 Documentary Protection
Good documentation is critical to protect you if things go wrong. Poorly executed or administered agreements may not give you the right to take steps to recover your money before it becomes too late or may result in your not having the available security interest you thought you had. See Chapter 5, Section 2.

5.9 Repayment Schedules
The finally agreed repayment schedule will thus depend on the purpose for which the financing is extended, the term over which you are prepared to take a view, the quality and quantity of the net cash flow available for repayment, the quality of your asset cover and the anticipated useful life

of any asset over which you have security. Chapter 2, Section 3 went into detail on how different banking facilities with varying repayment arrangements can be available to suit different requirements for borrowing, so I shall confine myself here to some summarised comments:

5.9.1 *Amortising Term Loans*

Term loans to finance e.g. capital expenditure or acquisitions may be repayable over any period from 3 to 20 years. Where the asset or company purchased will commence to generate income immediately it is purchased, then it is good practice to impose the discipline of repayment from the beginning. For example, the loan may be reduced in equal monthly, quarterly, 6-monthly, or annual instalments of principal or, perhaps, by substantially equal aggregate payments of principal and interest (i.e. "mortgage" or "annuity" style). The latter equalises the total debt servicing costs of principal and interest over the term and reduces the borrower's initial cash flow – the corollary is that the lender's principal is reduced less quickly than under the former method as most of the initial payments are absorbed by interest costs.

Let us take an example of a $10,000,000 7-year loan at an assumed interest rate of 10% p.a. with quarterly repayments:

	Annuity			Level Principal		
($000)						
Quarter	Interest	Principal Repaid	Principal Outstanding	Interest	Principal Repaid	Principal Outstanding
1	250	251	9,749	250	357	9,643
2	244	257	9,492	241	357	9,286
3	237	264	9,228	232	357	8,929
4	231	270	8,958	223	357	8,571
5	224	277	8,681	214	357	8,214
6	217	284	8,397	205	357	7,857
7	210	291	8,106	196	357	7,500
8	203	298	7,808	187	357	7,143
9	195	306	7,502	179	357	6,786
10	188	313	7,189	170	357	6,429
etc.	2,199	2,811		2,097	3,570	

5,010   5,667

Monthly and quarterly instalments permit closer control through a more regular monitoring of promptness of payment. The lender's profit is also crystallised more quickly. Six monthly and annual payments are less administratively burdensome and may be easier to swap in the market should this be required.

Where the cash generation will not commence immediately, e.g. because there is a construction period and drawdown is staged over that construction period or because the acquisition of a company will involve significant reorganisation and initial costs, then a "grace" period may be appropriate before repayments commence. (e.g. a 7-year term loan, with two years' grace, and equal semi-annual repayments thereafter). Interest will invariably be covered during the grace period.

5.9.2 Revolving Term Loan

The repayment flexibility associated with "revolvers" is appropriate for working capital facilities which will be repaid and re-drawn over the term in accordance with the production/seasonal cycle. Where such facilities become fully drawn for an extended period, then the reasons should be investigated as it may indicate pressure on liquidity and the need to consider a refinancing by means of an amortising term loan. See also below 5.9.3.

Such repayment flexibility is also appropriate for back-up facilities as it will be envisaged that such facilities will be drawn only on occasions when cheaper short-term funding is unavailable. You may wish, however, to impose a reduction schedule on the underlying need for funds, by reducing the amount available for drawing over the term (i.e. a "reducing revolver"). Such a structure would enable a borrower to finance, for example, a purchase of capital equipment by commercial paper borrowings, with a back-up facility designed with the same reduction schedule as a term loan would have had.

For standby facilities, the borrower will usually seek maximum repayment flexibility in order that, for example, he can draw down for bridging purposes before refinancing in the bond or equity markets or so that he can fund build-up of stocks for an unusually large order etc. This is usually acceptable as long as the borrower is of the high credit standing required for such facilities.

5.9.3 *Balloon and Bullet Repayments*

Borrowers can reduce their ongoing debt service obligations for a period or raise debt in a manner attractive to non-bank investors and the swap markets by negotiating loans or standby/back-up facilities which incorporate one of the following features:

5.9.3.1 *A balloon* repayment whereby the borrower makes relatively low principal repayments during the term but then is obliged to make one larger repayment of principal (the "balloon") at maturity.

5.9.3.2 *A bullet* repayment whereby no principal repayments are made until maturity when the amount lent is repaid in one lump sum (the "bullet").

In both cases, the likely ability of the borrower to make that final payment must be closely examined. If the facility is one of a range of loans in its books, all of which mature at different times (see the debt maturity profile in the accounts) and if the balloon/bullet is comfortably accommodated by anticipated annual retained operating cash flow, then the source of repayment can genuinely be regarded as operational cash flow as usual.

Where these two conditions do not apply, then the bank has to consider the refinancing risk and decide whether it believes, looking forward, that (a) the company will be sufficiently creditworthy before the maturity date to obtain a refinancing on suitable terms (the credit risk) and (b) finance will be available in the market (the market risk). This is a dangerous game for all but the most creditworthy borrowers.

Working capital facilities will often incorporate a bullet repayment feature. This can be mitigated by:

(a)   setting the maturity date at a "low" point in the seasonal cycle i.e. just after the seasonal sales peak has passed and cash has been received

152

from debtors; monitoring of this cycle can be effected during the term by requiring a "clean up" period to coincide with each seasonal low as it occurs when, for a period of e.g. one month, no drawings are allowed – the value of such an ongoing monitoring device is, however, questionable for a multi-banked customer with a wide variety of funding sources;

(b)   negotiating, as an alternative to a bullet, a reduction schedule towards the end of the term (e.g. a 5-year facility with reductions after 2 years); this avoids the need for the company to seek to refinance the whole facility in one block and eases the adjustment process if refinancing transpires to be difficult, giving time to consider the alternative options of asset sales, seeking additional equity, sale and leasebacks etc.

5.9.4 *Evergreen Loans*

The credit aspects of evergreens are described in Chapter 2, Section 3.2.4. Where possible, I would recommend that such facilities be avoided for the reasons described. Where, however, a borrower is strong and the choice is to do business on an evergreen basis or miss the opportunity, then I would recommend that the notice period be set at one year (the minimum under which a refinancing can be negotiated without imposing counter-productive pressure) and that review dates be set as soon as possible after each set of accounts are produced. Covenant protection (see Chapter 5, Section 2.1.2.2) should be particularly carefully negotiated and the interest rate should be higher than would be acceptable for a conventional fixed term loan of comparable initial maturity.

5.9.5 *On Demand Loans and Uncommitted Loans* (c.f. Chapter 2, Sections 3.2.2 and 3.2.3)

In theory, "on demand" loans provide lenders with the maximum control lever, the right to demand repayment in full at anytime. They do not impose the discipline of a repayment schedule, however, and are thus similar to an evergreen with no notice period.

Such loans are, therefore, most appropriate for revolving working capital funding where individual drawings should be short-lived and the account will swing from debit to credit in accordance with the company's production/seasonal cycle. They are not suitable for funding of capital expenditure or other long-term assets.

Similarly, uncommitted loans will usually be for short-term periods for working capital purposes and one will not expect an uncommitted line of credit to be fully drawn for extended periods.

Some stronger borrowers will draw such short-term money to satisfy long-term requirements, with the exposure they have to an unexpected demand for repayment of such funds covered (at least in part) by a third party committed back-up facility. Short-term lenders in this situation have, therefore, a third party committed source of refinance – such lending to borrowers without a third party committed back-up leaves the short-term lender vulnerable to a withdrawal of alternative funding lines which would deprive the borrower of the ability to refinance. The short-term lender may then find himself locked into a longer-term lending.

Conclusion
At the end of this stage of the process, you should have the outline of a transaction which has been tailored to fit the circumstances i.e. one which, in the context of the then current situation, the purpose of the finance and the creditworthiness of the customer, has the best chance of success. Chapter 5 will look at protections available should, nevertheless, success prove elusive.

Principles of Lending–Part V

- THE TRANSACTION (2): PROTECTION AND PRICING –
  SECURITY, QUASI-SECURITY, CONTROL AND
  MONITORING, STRUCTURING AND PRICING

by
John Willingham

In Chapter 4, we looked at key considerations in designing a transaction which has the best chance of success. In other words, the amount financed, term and repayment profile in the context of the borrower's prospects and the purpose for borrowing should be such that the borrower can be anticipated to be able to service the borrowing in accordance with its terms, even if the business or project does not perform quite as anticipated. In looking at the criteria for a successful transaction (Chapter 1, Section 2) we, therefore, should be confident of satisfying the first criterion (repayment).

The second criterion, remuneration, will be discussed later in this chapter.

Accomplishment of the third criterion, enhancement of the relationship with the borrower, should be assisted by a transaction which has been constructed in the context of a thorough understanding of that borrower's business. The issues discussed in this chapter will also have a strong bearing on this aspect and are often the subject of heavy negotiation.

Negotiating practices and techniques are not, however, part of the scope of this book. For those interested in pursuing what is nevertheless a crucial determinant of a banker's ability to finalise a transaction in a competitive market without sacrificing his protection or his rewards, I would recommend a book which is a general discussion on the subject by Fisher and Ury, *Getting to Yes*, published by Hutchinson Business. Even in a competitive market, a banker will find people prepared to take his money; he may find, however, that they are not able or willing to repay or not prepared to pay him a reasonable return for the service provided. Good negotiating skills on the back of a solid understanding of credit and the business of banking should help to prevent him from succumbing to defeat.

The fourth criterion, enhancement (or, at minimum, protection) of the bank's reputation has also been considered in the context of the purpose of the transaction and the situation under which it is considered. Again, this can be only part of the story. The effects of a specific transaction on a bank's reputation will also depend on how the interaction is handled with the customer, market participants, press, other directly and indirectly associated parties (e.g. regulators and bureaucrats) and the public. Negotiation once more plays a key role.

Nevertheless, no individual has a perfect vision of the future. Repayment can be threatened by a multitude of factors and the viability of a transaction compromised. We need, therefore, to look at how we can protect the bank when what can go wrong does go wrong and how the risk of loss can be minimised. One has to accept, however, that there will always be a further danger that "what cannot go wrong", or "what was never contemplated", also goes wrong. Texaco being forced into Chapter 11 (bankruptcy) by a legal action over a disputed takeover has already been mentioned as an example of the inconceivable; the discovery of health problems related to asbestos and Union Carbide's accident at Bhopal are others.

Over-zealousness in trying to gain protection against this sort of disaster is likely to result simply in a transaction which is over-burdensome for the borrower – banking is a commercial business and transactions have to reflect commercial realities. Protection against the impact on the bank of losses arising from the totally unexpected can, therefore, best be gained by spreading risk over a variety of businesses, industries and

156

countries (see Chapter 1, Section 1). A credit-conscious approach to specific transactions thus does not preclude the need for disciplined portfolio management.

Protections are, nevertheless, available against possible dangers which might threaten repayment. All these protections are imperfect but are considerably better than nothing. Their role must always be to protect against, or prevent, the unlikely, not the inevitable or probable. By their nature, they involve pain to the protector when the remedies are called upon – he may, indeed, be fighting for survival as a result. It is, therefore, neither commercially sensible nor, perhaps, morally acceptable in most cases to enter a transaction where you are likely to be repaid only by realisation of security or by exercise of your rights under other protective provisions. Such protection must be secondary – your insurance against failure. As with insurance, you wish to ensure that the likelihood of your calling on it is as remote as possible but also that, should a call become necessary, the insurance coverage will fulfil its role. The main forms of protection in international banking transactions are considered below.

1. SECURITY AND QUASI-SECURITY

"Security" is a legally-enforceable claim on a person, company, government, other entity or organisation or a legally enforceable claim on items of property, which provides additional recourse for repayment for the bank to that which is available under the primary loan agreement. This additional recourse is usually available to the bank only when the borrower has breached the terms of the agreement.

"Quasi-security" is a claim which either is not legally enforceable or which does not constitute recourse for repayment as such, but which gives a bank either a moral claim on another party or a right to seek damages for non-performance of an undertaking.

Consideration of security in this chapter will not focus on the legal technicalities of perfecting an interest, filing or registering that interest, or the legal process of realisation. We shall be looking rather at the commercial considerations associated with the various types of security commonly seen in international banking transactions.

We shall, therefore, be concentrating on the quality of various types of security in terms of their value and factors relating to cost and administration. The ideal item of security in these terms is one which:

(a)   has (and can be anticipated to maintain) a stable or rising value; and

(b)   is easy (i.e. cheap and simple) to:

* take
* realise
* monitor and control

1.1 Guarantees

By far the most common form of security found in international financing transactions is the guarantee, particularly those given by one company (especially a parent) to support obligations undertaken by a related company and those given by a government or governmental agency (e.g. a central bank), usually to support a state-owned borrower. A cross guarantee structure is one in which each company in a group (i.e. the parent and each subsidiary) guarantees, and is itself guaranteed by, every other company in the group.

Let us examine the species by reference to the above criteria.

1.1.1 *Valuation*

You can value a guarantee as you value an equivalent type of borrower with one major caveat: a borrower expects to repay a borrowing it assumes; a guarantor, by contrast, does not expect to be called upon. A borrower is able to take the cash it borrows and put it to work in an attempt to generate repayment; in borrowing, a company, therefore, not only increases its liabilities but also its assets and (usually) its cash flow generating potential. A guarantor, in paying a guarantee demand, either borrows, sells assets or decreases his cash balances to do so and, in each case, the only benefit he receives is subrogation into the rights of the lender against a borrower which has defaulted and thereby demonstrated itself as not creditworthy to repay the loan in accordance with its terms.

A careful look is, therefore, required at the flexibility inherent in the guarantor's financial condition to determine its ability to absorb such a shock. Remember in doing so (a) that guarantees are off-balance-sheet

158

contingent liabilities, usually mentioned in a note to the accounts (it is necessary, for example, to consider whether a call by you under your guarantee will occur at the same time as other contingent liabilities to other lenders crystallise under cross-default provisions) and (b) a guarantee from a holding company does not give you a direct link into the assets of the rest of the group of companies under that holding company.

Recourse to a guarantor in international transactions will usually be limited in the guarantee document to a specific amount (few companies being prepared to give an unlimited guarantee). The current and estimated future ability of a guarantor to honour that obligation will depend on the credit assessment carried out in the context of the above caveat. Prima facie, the ability should increase as a company guarantor grows or as a government's country develops. The incurring by a guarantor, however, of other financial obligations or a deterioration in its business or economic prospects may invalidate this assumption.

Finally on this aspect, let me make the perhaps obvious comment that double-counting should be avoided. Where, for example, a guarantor has strong consolidated figures but most of this strength is represented by a subsidiary which is your borrower, then the guarantee may add little financial value. It may nevertheless, by committing the guarantor to the transaction, provide that guarantor with an important incentive to ensure that the loan is repaid by the borrower if at all possible. The "incentive" can, of course, be increased if the guarantee is backed by tangible security over assets of the guarantor.

1.1.2 *Taking*

A guarantee is simple to take. All that is required is a signature and evidence of sufficient power and authorisation to sign*. There is, however, one legal issue with specific reference to companies which can reduce or even negate the value of a guarantee and which relates to the commercial relationship between a guarantor and the company it guarantees rather than the legal technicalities of obtaining a properly executed guarantee document. This issue is "CONSIDERATION".

* Some corporate guarantees may need to be given under seal–take local legal advice if any doubt arises.

Companies are separate legal "persons" or entities. In the absence of a formal agreement to the contrary (e.g. a parental guarantee) creditors of a company, whether or not it is a subsidiary of another, have no recourse for repayment to any person or property except the assets of that company. Directors of a company have a fiduciary duty to act in the best interests of that company. A guarantee is a contract. A contract (in general) requires consideration to be received by a party for it to be legally binding on that party. "Consideration" means simply a benefit. Thus, in many legal jurisdictions, a guarantee given by a company will be enforceable against that company only to the extent that it has received benefit from giving that guarantee.

Let us look briefly at some implications of this in the context of the following corporate structure:

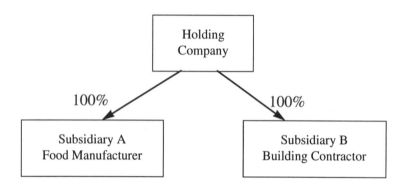

Thus we have a holding company, the assets of which are all the shares in two companies each engaged in distinct and unrelated businesses. The following examples indicate the difficulties:

(a) The holding company borrows $1,000,000 and on-lends it to Subsidiary A. The loan to the holding company is guaranteed by both Subsidiary A and Subsidiary B. The guarantee given by Subsidiary B will probably be unenforceable as it has received no benefit from giving it.

(b) The holding company borrows $1,000,000 and on-lends it to Subsidiary A ($500,000) and Subsidiary B ($500,000). Each subsidiary guarantees severally or jointly and severally the whole $1,000,000 loan to the holding company. Each guarantee will probably be enforceable against a liquidator only up to $500,000 – non-payment or a low payment under one could, therefore, not be compensated for by a higher payment under the other.

(c)   Subsidiary A borrows $1,000,000 for its own use. The holding company and Subsidiary B both guarantee the loan. The holding company guarantee will be enforceable because the loan has been used to benefit a company which it owns and thus to enhance the value of the holding company's investment in that subsidiary; the guarantee from Subsidiary B will probably be unenforceable as it, again, receives no benefit from the loan.

If we amend the company structure as follows, we obtain a different result under (c) above although (a) and (b) remain the same. The change is to make Subsidiary A a manufacturer of clothes whose main customer is Subsidiary B which is a chain of retail shops and whose main supplier is Subsidiary A. Here, each company has a major interest in supporting the other arising from their close commercial relationship and can give what should be enforceable guarantees in support of the other's borrowing.

Each case has to be carefully considered with legal advisors in the context of the corporate structure and commercial relationship between the parties in that structure.

1.1.3 *Realisation*

Realisation can be affected by two primary factors: the ability to pay and the willingness to pay. As discussed above, guarantors, when they sign a guarantee, do not usually expect to be called upon. Furthermore, should your guarantee crystallise at the same time as other contingent liabilities, or cross-default other obligations of the guarantor, a previously solvent guarantor may be unable to raise the cash to pay; it may, additionally, already have dedicated cash and resources to an attempt to preserve the solvency of the borrower and compromised its own solvency in doing so. In these circumstances, realisation of a guarantee, which itself is simply an unsecured claim on the guarantor, may prove extremely difficult.

Even where a guarantor is able to pay, it may be unwilling to do so because, for example, of a dispute over whether the borrower is indeed in default. Where a bank has acted in good faith in its relationship with a borrower, the risk of a court upholding such an objection is low. Nevertheless, there have been examples during the Debt Crisis where borrowers in certain countries have complied with local regulations in paying debts when due into the Central Bank in local currency; the Central Bank, however, has been unable to remit the equivalent hard currency to the lender. Certain lenders have, therefore, claimed on guarantees from companies outside the borrower's country on the grounds they have not received payment when due; some of these claims have been resisted, however, because the guarantor has been able to point to the payment which has been made on time by the borrower in accordance with local regulations, and the bank's loan document has not specified sufficiently clearly what constitutes "payment" to enable the validity of the local payment for the purposes of the loan to be successfully challenged.

Where a sovereign guarantor is involved, then the points made about governments as borrowers in Chapter 2, Section 1.2. hold true. If the borrower's problems are symptomatic of problems in the country generally, then you will probably find yourself sucked into a rescheduling rather than receiving payment. You should, however, as a consequence of the guarantee rank equally with unsecured direct lenders to the sovereign in the revised arrangements.

As a final point, a banker's ability to realise a guarantee will be affected by its type. There are two main types to be considered: the first is an obligation which is a primary obligation of the "guarantor" inasmuch as no claim on, or legal redress against, the borrower has to be pursued before the guarantees can be called upon; the second is a guarantee that the borrower will pay, but it can be crystallised only if all legal remedies against the borrower have first been exhausted. The first is referred to as an "indemnity" in England, a "guarantee of payment" in America and a "guarantee à première demande" by the French. The second is respectively a "guarantee", "guarantee of collection" and "caution". The latter gives much weaker protection as the obligation to pursue all legal remedies can be administratively burdensome, time-consuming and costly. Most banks insist on receiving the first type of document in virtually all cases.

1.1.4 *Monitoring and Control*

A banker can monitor the condition of a company guarantor as he would monitor a borrower through contact, press, audited and management accounts, reports of stock market analysts, etc.

From a control perspective, it is important that the underlying loan includes as an event of default a cross-default into direct obligations of the guarantor. In the absence of such a provision, the guarantor may go into liquidation without you being able to make a claim because, if the borrower itself continues to comply with its obligations, then you will not be able to crystallise a claim on the guarantor.

This cross-default provision can then be reinforced by direct covenants on the guarantor – see Section 2 of this chapter.

1.1.5 *Resistance to Giving Guarantees*

In many tax jurisdictions it is a requirement that the beneficiary ie company being guaranteed, must pay the guarantor a fee. This fee then becomes taxable income to the recipient and, in circumstances where a fee is not paid (but, technically, should have been) the tax authorities may deem that a fee has been paid and levy a tax charge on the guarantor.

Many parent companies put only minimum capital into foreign subsidiaries leaving such subsidiaries to borrow locally. If, in such circumstances, the parent then guarantees such loans the local authorities may invoke "thin capitalisation" regulations. This would prevent the interest being paid on the loans being set against local taxable income on the grounds that the loans are "quasi capital" and the interest thereon is, consequently, regarded as dividends.

It is often against this sort of background that parent companies may resist giving guarantees to support borrowing of subsidiaries.

1.2 **Guarantee Substitutes**

There are a few legally binding documents which come close to or equal the protection offered by a guarantee. They are popular in situations where a guarantee cannot be given either because obstructive regulations prevent the prospective guarantor giving such a commitment or because the prospective guarantor does not wish to record the obligation in the notes to its accounts. In the latter case, the popularity of the arrangements has been reduced as accountants around the world have tightened up their attitudes to structures designed to take an obligation off-balance-sheet and begun to record these guarantee substitutes as full contingent liabilities. The instruments include:

1.2.1 *Letters of Credit*
This is a documented obligation to pay usually on presentation by the beneficiary of a bill of exchange and a document certifying that payment is due. It is equivalent to an indemnity.

1.2.2 *"Put" Contract*
This is a document whereby a company which would otherwise be a guarantor grants the lender a right whereby, on a default by the borrower, the lender can sell its debt to the company granting the "put" at face value. This is often used where the underlying loan has been made in the form of a purchase of preference shares for tax reasons and a guarantee would compromise the standing of the preference shares as equity under applicable regulations.

1.2.3 *"Take or Pay" Contracts*
Often used in project financings, these are contracts whereby the would-be guarantor enters into a long-term contract under which it undertakes to purchase the relevant product from the borrower at a specified price which will enable the borrower to service its loan obligations. As both the product and the contract are assigned as security to the lender and as the take or pay contract commits the buyer to specific payments, the protection it offers is very close to that of a guarantee. The one problem which may arise is if the borrower fails to produce the goods which are required to be sold under the contract; legal advice will be required to provide a structure which ensures that the contracted amounts remain payable in this event.

164

1.3 Quasi-Guarantees

These are documents which come in two forms: one is a legally binding document (the "Financial Maintenance Undertaking") under which damages from non-compliance would have to be proved before a claim could succeed – this is at best, therefore, equivalent to a guarantee of collection; the second category is various forms of "comfort" document which, although not legally binding, provide a moral obligation on the issuer of the document to come to your aid if necessary.

1.3.1 The Financial Maintenance Undertaking

This will usually contain in some form statements which:

• acknowledge that the issuer is *aware* of the terms of the loan being provided to the borrower;

• *approve* of the terms of that loan;

• *undertake* that the borrower will remain a subsidiary of the issuer (where appropriate);

• *undertake* that the issuer will give the borrower the necessary financial and managerial support to enable the borrower to fulfil its obligations either in general or specifically to the lender during the term of the loan.

Drawn up in this form, such a letter is a litigable contract unless either a further clause is added to make it clear that it is not intended to be legally binding or local regulations do not give such documents legal standing. A litigation clause avoids any confusion by providing for the document to be construed in accordance with, say, English Law and for the issuer to agree to submit to the jurisdiction of the English courts. In the absence of the clause, the local law of the issuer will probably apply.

Its litigable nature, however, will not prevent dispute arising in difficult circumstances and, because it is not a direct promise to pay a specific amount, complex situations such as the ones outlined in 1.1.3 above and 1.3.2.3 below may cause realisation to be difficult.

1.3.2 *The Letter of Comfort*

This is the financial maintenance undertaking stripped of its legally binding nature. Thus the two undertakings described in 1.3.1 above are replaced by phrases which state that it is the "current intention" of the company to retain its majority interest in the borrower and the "policy" of the company that its subsidiaries should fulfil their obligations. Neither phrase gives any undertaking that such intentions or policies will remain applicable in the future.

The letter may also include a clause specifically declaring that it may not be construed as a legally binding undertaking.

Let us consider this document in the same way as we considered guarantees:

1.3.2.1 *Value*

A company which is *unwilling* to honour a letter of comfort simply will not do so and the bank will be left with no legal redress. There can, furthermore, be no recourse to a company which is *unable* to honour its obligation as you cannot claim in a liquidation for an amount which the company being liquidated is not legally bound to pay. A letter of comfort will have value, therefore, only if the issuer is of high integrity and significant financial strength.

1.3.2.2 *Taking*

Procedures for taking a letter of comfort should be as for a guarantee, including inspection of evidence of authorisation. The more senior the signatory to the document, the more likely it is that the letter will be honoured if at all possible. Consideration is rarely an issue, as letters of comfort are usually issued by parent companies and are not intended to be legally binding contracts.

1.3.2.3 *Realisation*

Realisation of a letter of comfort can be extremely difficult. For the reasons stated above, it is crucial that the issuer be not only able but willing to honour its commitment. Any dispute over whether the borrower is in default (c.f. the example in Section 1.1.3) will undoubtedly affect that willingness as will any perceived absence of good faith or

166

co-operation by the bank in dealing with problems being experienced by the borrower. There may, furthermore, be disputes over the risks the issuer was intending to cover by issuing its letter of comfort. An alternative twist to the example in 1.1.3 would be agreement between the parties that payment has not been made as due under the loan, notwithstanding the local payment by the borrower. The parent company may argue, however, that it has ensured that the local company has fulfilled its commercial obligations under local regulations and that the default arising under the loan is not one covered by the understanding in the letter of comfort; in other words, the argument may run that the political risk of lending to the borrower was taken by the bank. If the borrower is paying a margin higher than the parent pays for direct borrowing, this may be a difficult argument to refute as, presumably, the higher pricing was agreed because the bank was taking some risk not covered by the parent.

File notes and letters, written at the time a letter of comfort is issued, setting out the intention behind the letter can be most helpful in settling such arguments.

1.3.2.4 *Monitoring and Control*
A letter of comfort is not a promise to pay and, because the issuer will usually be keen to satisfy its auditors that the document is genuinely non-binding, it will usually prove difficult to negotiate direct covenants from the issuer.

The best protection you can realistically expect is a cross-default clause in the loan agreement with the borrower which triggers if the issuer defaults on any direct loan. This may be reinforced by a further clause which defaults the loan if the parent ceases to own a majority stake in the borrower.

Of the two clauses, the latter is perhaps most useful as it may enable you to prevent a sale of the borrower to a party with which you are not satisfied or to obtain repayment before it occurs. The former clause may, in the event, prove cosmetic as an issuer in trouble will not be able to honour its letter of comfort anyway, because creditors with legally binding claims will probably force it not to do so. At least, however, it gives you the opportunity to renegotiate in such a situation.

1.3.3 *The Letter of Awareness*

A letter of awareness is a letter of comfort stripped, as a minimum, of the reference to a policy to ensure that subsidiaries fulfil their obligations and, possibly, also stripped of any reference to an intention to retain a majority stake in the company.

Its bare bones, therefore, simply indicate an awareness of the terms of the loan being made to the borrower and, hopefully, approval of the terms. In receiving this, you at least have the comfort that the parent knows of, and agrees with, the act of its subsidiary in entering into the borrowing; the parent is agreeing that the borowing is a sensible one for the subsidiary to undertake and that the subsidiary should be able to repay. There is, therefore, some moral lever on the parent to support the borrower going forward and to ensure that the bank has been given all reasonable information to enable it to assess the creditworthiness of the borrower before the loan is drawn.

Any reliance you place on such a letter can arise only from a belief that the parent company will not allow one of its subsidiaries, which has been acting in accordance with parental approvals, to default because of the damage this would do to the parent's reputation in the banking markets and more generally. The only reinforcements to the moral lever you can apply are again file notes and letters, written at the time the letter was being negotiated, which set out the purpose the letter intends to serve, and insistence that the letter be signed by as senior an executive as possible under board authorisation.

1.4 **Capital Assets**

There are many different types of financing which are tailored to the cash flow generating capacity, economic life and re-sale capability of various capital assets. These assets include oil fields, mines, aircraft, ships, rigs, cars, computers, residential homes and commercial property. The principles behind looking at such assets as security are discussed in Chapter 6, Asset Financing with specific reference to aircraft finance; specific reference to oil fields and other project assets is made in Chapter 8.

I shall not, therefore, go into detail here. Suffice it to say that "know your asset" is the key theme. Knowledge both of the circumstances which affect the value of a specific capital asset taken as security and of the practicalities of perfecting an interest, controlling and monitoring that interest and realising the value in case of need is crucial to success in handling such transactions. Ignorance of such matters may either cause you to transact business without full consideration of the risks being run or to adopt, from apprehension, such a cautious approach that you are not competitive in the market and your credibility suffers.

Charges over assets may be "fixed" or "floating". When the charges are fixed specific, existing assets are identified and a formal document is signed (or sealed in certain instances) by the "chargor" in favour of the lender. A mortgage over a designated property is a good example of a fixed charge.

The alternative, a "floating" charge, allows the assets of the chargor to continue to be used in the normal course of business of the chargor (albeit the fixed charge would also allow, say, charged capital items to be used in the ordinary course of business – but not sold or exchanged) and this will include allowing, say, assets to be sold or exchanged. Thus, the floating charge potentially covers existing and future assets. Such a charge becomes fixed when an event such as a default occurs from which time all assets (i.e. including debtors, stock and cash) are subject to a fixed charge. Debentures, in addition to being secured by a fixed charge upon the company's property, may also be secured by a floating charge upon the stock, receivables, etc.

The realisation of security to achieve repayment of obligations is concerned with the "break-up" value or "forced sale" value of a company. This is in contrast with the 'going concern' principles described in Chapter 3 in which emphasis was placed on the ability of the borrower to generate cash in order to service borrowing.

1.5 Stocks and Debtors

Forfaiting is available as a means of financing debtors on an international scale and is a product discussed in Alasdair Watson's *Finance of International Trade,* 5th Edition, published by The Chartered Institute of Bankers. Those transacting the business have the experience and resources (both computers and personnel) to monitor the quality of debtors taken on and the collection of those debts. This close control enables advances of up to 80% of the value of such debtors to be made, often without recourse or with very limited recourse to the customer.

169

Various commodity stocks (grain, etc.) can be financed with moderately high leverage by produce loans (see Watson) and certain banks have developed specific expertise in financing the activities of commodity traders by this and other methods.

More generally, banks may find opportunities to finance the working capital needs of certain borrowers by loans secured on the circulating stocks and debtors of the borrower (c.f. Chapter 4, Section 3.3.2).

1.5.1 *Value*

Detailed valuation of this security can be a time-consuming process. The liquidity analysis discussed in Chapter 3 presents a reasonable picture of trends in the composition and likely quality of the relevant assets. If you are looking to advance a relatively large percentage of their value, however, and therefore require protection should the borrower's trading performance prove disappointing, a closer inspection will be required.

Valuation of debtors will embody consideration of:

- the number and variety of customers
- the quality of those customers
- the historic bad debt record
- the historic record of promptness in payment

Rather than analysis of each individual debtor, segmentation by country or other suitable grouping may be required with only individual debtors accounting for over, say, 5% of the total being separately identified.

Stock valuation can be very difficult and it may simply not be feasible to break it down by meaningful segments. The value in the accounts may have been determined on the FIFO basis (high), the LIFO basis (low) or another basis, the impact of which you should question. Nevertheless, work-in-progress is likely to have negligible value if ever you come to realise it and even finished manufactured goods will probably have to be sold at a significant discount. If this were not the case, then the company probably would not have gone under, whilst a forced sale tends to put potential buyers in a strong negotiating position. The value of raw materials will depend on their nature but they may, in the event, have no value as

170

security if there is a valid retention of title clause in the supply contract which means that they remain the property of the supplier until he is paid. The effectiveness of such a clause varies in different jurisdictions.

1.5.2 *Taking*

The procedure for taking a security interest in debtors and stocks varies considerably from jurisdiction to jurisdiction and can be costly and time-consuming especially in terms of legal filings and recordings. The "blanket lien" (USA) or "floating charge" (England) may work adequately but suffers from a ranking behind holders of any fixed assignment of a debt and certain other creditors preferred by law (salaries, wages, taxes etc.).

1.5.3 *Realisation*

Realisation of such security can also be costly, time-consuming and inefficient because:

(a)   on the date realisation becomes necessary, the security will almost certainly have minimum value as, otherwise, it is unlikely that a default would have occurred; losses, of course, hit working capital directly as, for example, reduced or discounted sales produce lower debtors, obsolescent stock, reduced cash and increased debt; the value of the security is thus closely tied in to the trading performance of the business;

(b)   debtors may have counter-claims and refuse to pay;

(c)   stock may be subject to retention of title clauses and dispute over who has priority entitlement;

(d)   a receiver or administrator may be able to prevent your realising the security in the manner you desire – this will depend on the relevant insolvency laws to which the borrower is subject.

1.5.4 *Monitoring and Control*

The security cover available in such transactions can be monitored and controlled as follows:

(a)   Make funds available on the basis of a prescribed formula such as:

• 75% of debtors (excluding any in pre-defined unacceptable countries and those more than, say, 15 days past due)

• 50% of stocks based on FIFO valuation (excluding work-in-progress and stock delivered under retention of title clauses) up to a maximum of, say, 30% of total drawings; this latter constraint will prevent unduly high financing of stocks which cannot be sold.

(b)   Monitor the formula by monthly or quarterly updates from the company in a prescribed format detailing the information required for the calculation to be made.

The company will have to adjust its borrowing levels monthly or quarterly to keep within the maximum specified.

Overall, this is a difficult and burdensome type of security to value, monitor and control in the detail required to make it genuinely effective. Do you have resources and is the remuneration adequate compensation for the administration involved?

1.6 Shares

Regulation U in the USA, as mentioned in Chapter 4, Section 2.4.3(b), restricts US commercial banks to lending a maximum of 50% of the acquisition value of quoted shares held as security for the loan. This was originally conceived to prevent a repeat of the result of the 1930 Stock Market crash, when certain banks were placed in great difficulties as stock prices collapsed and companies and people who had bought shares with large amounts of borrowed money went bankrupt.

Taking and realising quoted shares held as security is, in general, little problem; the bank usually holds the shares itself in a nominee name and has full power of sale. Monitoring of the value is also easy through electronic screens, press etc. Judging what value to place on those shares as security can, however, be difficult as stock markets, notwithstanding their bullish tone throughout the '80s, are increasingly volatile and prone to sudden withdrawals of large sums of capital by international banks and investors.

172

There may also be a problem in obtaining an expected value on a forced sale if the amount of shares involved represents a large portion of the issued capital of the company; the availability for sale of a large stake, in the absence of parties wishing to mount a takeover, can severely depress a price.

I have no specific recommendation on security values to be applied; much will depend on the size of the stake, the quality of the company whose shares are on offer, the volatility of its share price, the state of the market at the time of acquisition and the presence of any speculative factors affecting the price (e.g. expectation of a takeover bid), which might cause a sharp drop in value should the speculators' expectations not be realised.

If a top-up provision can be negotiated as a control mechanism (i.e. a provision to the effect that if the value of shares falls below, say, 120% of the amount lent, the bank has the right to demand additional security or partial repayment and, if such security is not provided, sell the shares) then a loan of 70–75% of value may be feasible for banks with no regulatory constraints. The specific trigger level required will depend on the factors mentioned in the above paragraph; 25% coverage may not be enough in a particularly speculative situation.

Unquoted shares require a different approach. Realisation may be difficult if there is no ready market and there may be restrictions in the company's statutes on who can hold its shares. Valuation can be carried out based, for example, on comparison with similar quoted companies but may be unreliable as there may, in the absence of a quotation, simply be no buyers. This is not, therefore, a form of security to be recommended.

1.7 Bonds
Quoted bonds are, like quoted shares, in principle easy to take and realise. Their value can also be readily checked. Factors affecting their value are:

- the *credit rating* of the issuer: any deterioration in this rating will tend to reduce the price of the bond;

- the *interest rate* basis applied: the value of fixed rate bonds will rise as interest rates fall but drop as interest rates rise; floating rate bonds should, in the absence of other factors, trade at around par;

- the *market appetite* for the type of bond in question: for example, problems during 1986/7 in the perpetuals sector of the eurobond market, arising mainly from fears about the effects of anticipated regulations governing the holding by Japanese banks of such investments, virtually caused trading in those bonds to cease.

As with quoted shares the "top up" clause is a useful control and protection mechanism.

1.8 Summary
1.8.1 *What are the assets?*

- Are they primarily fixed or trading (i.e. current)?

- To the extent they are fixed, do they comprise marketable assets with a potentially strong re-sale value (well-located land, office or hotel property; certain types of large, moveable equipment with wide application, e.g. aircraft)?

    Are they alternatively mainly factories in non-prime locations and specialised, largely immobile, plant and equipment?

- To the extent they are current, do they comprise largely a well-spread portfolio of debtors or are debtors concentrated in one country or narrow band of customers? Do you have a view on the quality of the customer base? Is there vulnerability to the loss of one customer?

- Alternatively, do current assets include large amounts of stock and work in progress? How liquid is such stock?

- If there are material other assets (e.g. "Investments" of various sorts or "Intangibles") assess them in the same way for liquidity and marketability.

- If the company is engaged in a variety of activities, might one or more of these businesses have a value as a going concern independent of the rest of the company in excess of the net book value of its assets in the company's accounts? If a group goes into liquidation, it will usually be more advantageous to creditors to sell the viable parts of the company as ongoing businesses as a better price can usually be obtained for a business with management, workforce and customer base in place than for the stock and fixed assets alone. Diversification in this context is a positive feature.

1.8.2 *How are assets valued?*

- Look at the accounting policies.

- Is the depreciation policy relatively conservative, liberal or neutral?

- Have fixed assets been revalued – if so, on what basis, when and by whom?

- Have exchange rate translation losses been capitalised into fixed asset values? This is a practice often encountered outside the USA and UK. If so, what is the impact? Such "losses" arise when assets located in one country and accounted for in the currency of that country are financed in the currency of another country, and the latter currency appreciates in value against the former. Where the assets concerned are, in fact, generators of income in a currency which matches the debt, then such treatment may be justified.

  For example, a Norwegian oil company may finance its oil exploration and production activities in US$ because that is the currency in which its sales will be denominated. A depreciation of the Norwegian Krone against the $ will thus cause translation "losses" in its accounts which have no bearing on the economic substance of the situation. In cases, however, where assets are not of this type, then capitalisation of translation losses may be misleading (e.g. a French property company financing itself for reasons of low interest rates in Japanese Yen).

- If there are significant intangible assets (either described as such or included in fixed assets), do these have value? Patents and trademarks for strong brands may merit capitalisation. Improvements to short leasehold properties may have no resale value. Interest capitalised into a new development may or may not cause the balance sheet value of the asset to be overstated – do you know or can you estimate the

175

development's true market value? Capitalised exploration costs will have value only if the exploration is successful in finding the relevant mineral.

- Would sale of certain assets at book value give rise to a tax bill not provided for on the balance sheet?

Consideration of these issues will usually not allow you to come to a definite conclusion about a precise value for the assets of a business.

It will, however, enable you:

- to identify possible areas where asset values may be overstated or where understatement may imply "hidden reserves" in the value of the company;

- to draw conclusions about whether you are financing a company with predominantly marketable and liquid assets whose value going forward looks reliable.

The conclusions will enable you to judge the extent to which the Cash Flow protection you have identified in the Profitability and Cash Flow analysis is reinforced by protection from Asset Quality. To the extent it is, you may be prepared to accept lower cash flow protection than in cases where, if trading performance goes awry, realisation of assets is unlikely to produce pay-out as there is little value in these assets independent of their value to that business.

1.8.3 *Level of asset protection*

Having assessed asset quality, we can move to draw some conclusions about the level of asset protection. Firstly, some definitions: "Net Worth" is most simply defined as the excess in value of a company's assets over its liabilities. In calculating "Net Worth", one will, therefore, deduct surplus asset values caused by inclusion of assets with no tangible value (i.e. intangibles such as capitalised interest costs) and, at least when comparing trends over a period of years, surpluses arising from revaluation of assets. The latter exclusion is carried out because a lender will primarily wish to examine over a period how Net Worth has been increased by retention in the business of realised profits and equity injections from shareholders. Revaluations, inasmuch as they represent unrealised profits

176

based on often optimistic valuation criteria, have no place in this primary analysis.

There are special cases where the calculation of "Net Worth" is not as straightforward as the simple calculation just explained. For companies involved in, say, publishing the major assets shown in their audited accounts may well be the titles and copyrights of the publications. Similarly food companies may attribute worth to their brand names. These types of assets are intangible but it may not be appropriate to discount them when calculating "Net Worth". Bankers must take guidance from the attitude of the companies' auditors and the manner in which such assets have been evaluated.

"Liabilities" here refer to amounts payable to third parties whether or not the business is successful and whether or not such amounts are interest bearing (i.e. they *exclude* shareholders' investment but remember that in many cases Preference Shares have more of the characteristics of debt (i.e. fixed servicing costs, may be redeemable) than shareholders' funds and may be included as liabilities). Remember also to include de-consolidated debt.

The "capital employed" by the business represents the extent to which assets are funded by sources other than trading balances.

1.9 Conclusion

In concluding this section, let me re-emphasise certain key factors in considering security protection:

- the realisation of security must always be your insurance against loss not your primary source of repayment;

- do not allow the availability of security to cloud your judgement of the viability of the underlying loan facility;

- understand the characteristics of the security offered in terms of what affects its value and how easily it may be:

  - taken
  - realised
  - monitored and controlled

177

- ensure you take good legal advice in perfecting your interest;

- ensure adequate control and monitoring procedures are in place to protect the value of, and your rights to, the security taken.

2. CONTROL AND MONITORING

The technicalities of documentation are not part of the scope of this book. Nevertheless, it may be helpful, before we discuss how a loan, once made, can be controlled and monitored, if we look at the role which documentation fulfils from a commercial perspective.

Documentation is required for most types of international banking facilities to define the following:

(i)   the *liabilities* to be undertaken by the bank and the *remuneration* to be paid in return for assuming those liabilities;

(ii)   the method of *operation* of the facility (including e.g. the number of days' notice required for drawings, documentation required before drawings are allowed, accounts to which payments are to be made etc.);

(iii) the *undertakings* to be given by the borrower and in certain cases the bank. These will include (i) *REPRESENTATIONS & WARRANTIES* relating to the status of the borrower, its powers to borrow and the accuracy of information provided to the bank on the basis of which the decision to extend the facility has, in whole or in part, been made and (ii) *COVENANTS* whereby the borrower agrees to do or not to do certain things throughout the term of the facility (e.g. to provide audited accounts, not to exceed a certain level of gearing etc.);

(iv)   events which will cause the facility to cease to be available and any amounts which have been lent to become immediately repayable on demand (*"EVENTS OF DEFAULT"*) e.g. receivership, bankruptcy, etc.;

(v)   details of any *security* agreed.

There are exceptions, common examples of which are the following:

(a) Domestic sterling overdrafts and Market Lines within the United Kingdom – market practice, backed by the courts, dictates that such liabilities are uncommitted and repayable on demand; mandate only is, therefore, required, detailing persons authorise to deal;

(b) Foreign exchange facilities – market practice generally accepts a mandate as adequate documentation.

With these exceptions, documentation will usually be required to cover points (i)–(v) above. For some facilities, a combination of the use of a standard clause manual and reference to in-house legal specialists will enable facilities to be documented "in house". For more complex or specialised deals (e.g. aerospace financing and project deals) external legal advice will be required, in which case it is important that lawyers are properly instructed so that documentation is drawn up with the necessary protection for the bank and/or that a legal opinion is obtained confirming the efficiency of the documents in achieving what is intended.

Much of the content of documentation is standard clauses derived from established practice and legal precedent. Certain variables will relate to funding and related issues on which the bank's treasury or dealing area will have a view (e.g. appropriate funding centres; definition of LIBOR etc.) whilst others will fall for comment by tax and accounting departments (e.g. tax sparing/withholding tax absorption provisions). Proposed non-standard practice should be referred to the relevant specialists. There are, however, certain other crucial variable areas with relevance to the monitoring and control of credit risk assumed.

2.1 Control

The ability to control arises from insertion in the documentation of provisions which confirm understandings on the basis of which a loan has been made and provisions whereby the company agrees to do, or not to do, certain things. These provisions should prevent the borrower, if at all possible, acting in a way which may be materially detrimental to your interests without your consent. Your remedy, if the provisions are breached, is to convert the term facility into an "on demand" loan under which you can demand repayment immediately and either renegotiate or commence legal proceedings for recovery.

The key provisions are:

2.1.1 *Representations and Warranties*

These are defined as *statements* of fact made by the borrower within the documentation as formal confirmation that assumptions being made by the bank about the borrower are correct. Sometimes the bank will also give similar statements for the benefit of the borrower. Most are standard and relate to the borrower's legal ability to borrow and perform its obligations, but other statements may be valuable.

Let us take two examples: (a) if the bank is lending and relying on information furnished by the borrower/guarantor which is unaudited or impossible to verify independently, a formal representation of its truth and accuracy is often required to give the ability to call a default and demand prepayment if that reliance has been misplaced; (b) when the last audited figures are old (e.g. 9 months out of date) a representation that since those accounts there has been no adverse change in the financial position of the borrower would be useful (and prompt questions if there is a refusal to give it!).

Additionally, a representation that any projections have been prepared in accordance with the accounting principles employed in the company's audited accounts and with due diligence by the company may prove valuable if, later, it transpires that the projections were prepared negligently or recklessly or with an intention to mislead.

None of these provisions is as satisfactory as establishing the facts before lending, but they may enable you to exercise control by demanding repayment quickly if your trust transpires not to have been merited. Companies will also be very careful about making such statements if they have any doubt about them, as the consequences of misleading the bank even accidentally can be very serious if these provisions are in the loan document.

2.1.2 *Covenants and Events of Default*

Covenants are defined as *promises* by the borrower to do or not to do certain things during the term of the facility. *Events of Default* are defined events which, if they occur, give the bank the right to demand immediate repayment notwithstanding the unexpired term of the facility. A breach of a covenant will always be documented to be an event of default.

Examples include:

2.1.2.1 *General*

(a) *Negative Pledge*

The borrower undertakes not to pledge its assets as security for   any other borrowing unless the bank is given a pro-rata share of   that security. Where lending to a holding company, then the undertaking should refer to consolidated assets.

Especially where you are lending unsecured, it is important to ensure that no other lender gains a priority recourse to the assets of the company. Mortgages on new assets, the purchase of which has been financed by new loans, are usually excluded on the basis that such "purchase money mortgages" do not dilute the recourse of existing lenders to existing assets.

(b) *Restriction on Asset Sales*

The borrower undertakes not to sell a material portion of its (consolidated) assets either without the consent of the lenders (preferable) or for below market value. "Material" is defined preferably as assets having a book value or market value (whichever is the higher) of X amount or greater.

This prevents, for example, transfers of assets between a group of companies which reduce the value of your borrower and sale and leaseback arrangements which, in substance, are exercises to raise new debt secured on existing assets.

(c) *Cross Default*

This is a clause which states that it is an event of default under this agreement if the borrower defaults in performance of *someone else's* agreement. It gives the Bank the protection of other lenders' events of

181

default and covenants and, depending on the wording, ensures that you can demand repayment either if another party is put in a position where it can do so (irrespective of any waiver given by that other party), or if another party actually declares an event of default (i.e. the cross default triggers only if no waiver is given by the other party).

(d) *Pari Passu Clause*

A reinforcement to the negative pledge. The borrower undertakes not to create any debt which, on a liquidation, will rank for payment ahead of the Bank and to treat all lenders equally.

(e) *Continuing Ownership*

This is either a covenant or, differently expressed, an Event of Default. It protects against a change in ownership by providing the right to renegotiate or demand repayment if a change in control of the borrower or a merger occurs. It is very useful when lending to a subsidiary or state owned company where there is a strong parent or Government but no guarantee from that parent or Government and should ensure that you are consulted before any such change occurs.

2.1.2.2 *Ratio Covenants*

Ratio covenants are designed to convert a term loan into an "on demand" facility if the financial condition of the borrower deteriorates *materially* (i.e. to the extent that safety of repayment is threatened). They can be designed to suit individual circumstances in the light of the ratios highlighted in Chapter 3.

Examples of ratio covenants are:

(a) *Debt Service Ratio*

Company undertakes that profits after tax and after adjusting for all material non-cash items will exceed a specified percentage (e.g. 150%) of term debt due within one year and/or will exceed a specified percentage, depending on the business, of Total Debt (e.g. 20%). This triggers if cash flow looks like becoming inadequate to make principal repayments when due.

If you can define cash flow to equate to Retained Operating Cash Flow, this can prove a most valuable trigger because the scope for creative accounting is minimised. The complexity of the accounting adjustments, however, often mean that borrowers will prefer to accept restrictions on TNW, gearing and interest cover.

(b)   *Minimum Tangible Net Worth (MTNW)*
      The borrower undertakes to maintain a minimum level of Tangible Net Worth.

      "Tangible Net Worth" should exclude intangible assets (but care re. copyrights, brand names, etc. which, in some instances, may be included in TNW) and any increases arising solely from revaluations of assets (this limits the scope for accounting creativity). Rather than have a simple figure which may soon become out of date, you may also choose to require that TNW shall not fall below eg. 85% of its previous high on any annual or six monthly accounting date.

      This should enable you to step in before your asset cover is dangerously eroded by losses or by acquisitions, funded by debt, which involve significant goodwill.

(c)   *Maximum Gearing*
      A company undertakes that its total borrowings will not exceed a specified proportion of its tangible net worth.

      "Borrowings" should include capitalised leases at balance sheet amount and committed rental payments under operating (or off balance sheet) leases discounted at a suitable interest rate. You may also wish to include guarantees given by the borrower in respect of debts not on its consolidated balance sheet.

      This should prevent a build up of unsupportable levels of debt by restricting increases to a proportion of increases in the equity cushion, tangible net worth.

(d)   *Minimum Liquidity*
      A company undertakes to maintain a certain level of working capital either expressed as a ratio or as a monetary amount by which Current Assets should exceed Current Liabilities. This attempts to allow you to take control before a liquidity crisis occurs.

183

(e)   *Interest Cover*
A company undertakes that the aggregate of Pre-tax Profits plus Interest Paid for any given period will not fall below e.g. 1.25 times interest paid. Where leases are not capitalised, one can add total rents to interest paid; where the accounting practice of equity-accounting of associates/subsidiaries has a material effect, this source of profit should be excluded except to the extent that dividends are received; where material costs are capitalised (such as interest, development costs and maintenance) these should be deducted from the profit figure in calculating the ratio. The covenant triggers immediately on the occurrence of losses and low levels of profitability which may put interest payments in danger.

(f)   *Dividend Cover*
Company undertakes that the aggregate of Retained Profits plus Dividends Paid for any given period will not fall below e.g. 2 times dividends paid. This should prevent excessive dividend payments either to public shareholders or by a subsidiary to a parent. In the latter case, the ability of the parent to strip cash from the subsidiary can be further restricted by controls over lending by the borrower to other companies in the group.

(g)   *Security Maintenance*
Where you are lending under a formula related to stocks and debtors such as that described in Chapter 4, Section 3.3.2. and 1.5.4. of this chapter, you will need a clause to require prepayment or provision of additional security if the value of stocks/debtors falls below prescribed levels.

Such a clause may also be possible to negotiate for loans secured by fixed assets, to be effective if the value of the security, based on e.g. a quarterly valuation, falls below a prescribed multiple of the loan (e.g. 120%).

This will enable you to renegotiate if your security cover begins to look inadequate and, in the last resort, to sell the security while it remains adequate to pay off the loan. In practice, you should not rely on automatic repossession simply if security cover falls below prescribed levels, but the right to renegotiate at a relatively early stage is a valuable tool to ensure your interests are considered if the borrower's fortunes are not transpiring as anticipated.

This list is not exhaustive and covenants may be designed to cover specific circumstances and types of borrower.

Covenant "protection" will not make a bad loan into a good one. The role of covenants is simply to act as a deterrent to loose or risk-orientated financial management and to convert, on occurrence of a breach, a term commitment into an "on demand" facility. This enables the lender to exercise control and thereby to force changes or to exercise any rights it may have to security at a stage when, hopefully, there are still assets to go for. If you have to wait until actual non-payment of sums due, the situation may be irretrievable.

Covenants should be included, where possible, in all term facilities – even highly-rated companies may sacrifice financial prudence to pursue acquisitions or major projects or to buy back shares to avoid a takeover, if wholly unrestrained. Where inclusion is not possible (e.g. a major borrower refuses to accept), the consequent risk must be addressed and an opinion made as to the philosophy of the company's management with respect to financial risk as well as its prospects and current financial position, together with the likelihood of imprudent policies being forced upon it e.g. by takeover activity.

2.2 Monitoring
Monitoring has two purposes:

(1) Ensuring that no breaches of covenants or events of default have occurred, or seem likely to occur in the foreseeable future.

(2) Identifying any material deterioration in the financial health of the borrower, even though this may not result in an immediate covenant breach.

It will normally be a condition, included in the loan documentation, that the borrower provides financial statements to enable monitoring to be carried out. Where covenanted ratios cannot be calculated directly from the accounts, it is usually a requirement that the auditors provide a statement of the ratios concerned, certifying that they have been properly calculated from figures incorporated in the accounts.

It can be seen that monitoring goes beyond mechanical checking of the covenanted ratios. There are several reasons for this:

(i)   It is important that lenders act as early as possible when a borrower begins to show signs of distress. Prompt action usually means that a turnaround is easier to achieve by, for example, encouraging changes in a corporate's strategy or even changes in its management.

(ii)   The covenants may include a "material adverse change" clause which allows the lender to initiate action following a general deterioration in the company's health, rather than the breach of a specific ratio.

(iii)   Even when the individual lender has no legal basis for taking action, the implications of cross-default must be considered. Other lenders may have stricter covenants and may be about to take action. Any lender who is not watchful may be disadvantaged.

(iv)   Even if none of the above apply, the borrower must still be carefully monitored. Breaches of covenants make resolving a group's problems more difficult, because cross-default may create a large number of lenders with conflicting legal claims on the group. It is better to anticipate such a situation, and avoid it by changes in strategy, asset disposals to reduce borrowings, etc.

For all the reasons above, lenders must not only check compliance with covenants on the due date, but should also have systems in place to keep a continued watch on borrowers. Such systems should include:

(1)   Keeping a diary of due dates for accounts to be received (usually required within 180 days of year end/within 60 days of half year end).

(2)   Analyse the accounts using the techniques described in Chapter 3.

(3)   Monitoring press and brokers' reports for profit warnings and major profit downgradings.

186

(4)   Monitoring trade press and economic research for a substantial deterioration in the outlook for the industry or companies within it.

(5)   Producing forecasts of the borrower's financial ratios in the future, following any substantial acquisition or disposal.

3.   STRUCTURING

Chapters 4 and 5 have looked at the fundamentals of why a borrowing is needed, how much will be advanced, the source and timing of repayment, cash flow and asset protection, "insurance" against failure (i.e. security/ quasi security) and control requirements.

"Structuring" is the process of designing a facility within those parameters so that, as far as is possible, it maximises the benefits to the borrower in the context of its objectives in negotiating the transaction and maximises the income, flexibility and credit protection available for the bank.

Key aspects in this context include the following:

3.1   Priority of Recourse

3.1.1   *Holding Companies*

The need to have direct recourse to the assets producing the cash flow has been emphasised before, together with the problems of lending to a holding company in this context. You will, therefore, usually be in a stronger position if you lend not to the holding company but to the operating subsidiary or subsidiaries which it is intended should use the proceeds, with a guarantee from the holding company. By this means, in a liquidation, you will be able to stake a claim in full both against the assets of the operating subsidiary, pari passu with other creditors of that subsidiary ranking equally with you, and against the guarantor.

This, therefore, gives you direct recourse both to the assets which are intended to be your primary source of repayment and, if the guarantor has investment of value in other businesses (e.g. other subsidiaries which may be going concerns), recourse to the value of those investments. As a simplistic calculation of the relative advantage of this structure, if the

187

subsidiary on liquidation is able to pay, perhaps, 60 cents per $1 of debt and the guarantor is able to pay, perhaps, 40 cents per $, you will be repaid in full. Had you lent to the holding company you may have been left with only a 40 per cent repayment.

Covenants on both the borrower and the guarantor will strengthen your ability to maintain your relative advantage, particularly ones on the subsidiary which limit (i) dividend payments, (ii) loans to affiliated companies and (iii) sales of assets for below market value, thereby restricting the extent to which cash and other assets can be stripped out of your borrower to the detriment of its creditworthiness. A cross default clause, which defaults the loan either if the guarantor defaults on any covenants imposed on it in the guarantee (minimum) or if the subsidiary or guarantor defaults on any other debt (preferable), is also important so as to ensure that you can crystallise a claim on the guarantor if its creditworthiness deteriorates. Of course, if you can take enforceable guarantees from other operating subsidiaries in addition to that of the parent, then your position is improved further. Consideration may, however, be a problem for the reasons discussed in Section 1.1.2. of this chapter.

There may, nevertheless, be occasions when you are left with no alternative but to lend to the holding company, perhaps because the holding company acts as banker to the group or wishes to use the funds borrowed in a variety of its operating companies. Guarantees from the various operating subsidiaries may be an option but again may suffer from the problem of consideration.

If you are satisfied that the creditworthiness of the operating subsidiaries is such that the danger of the holding company not being able to upstream adequate cash from their operations to service its obligations is remote, then you may be prepared to accept the position. You can, however, prevent other lenders who might otherwise gain a priority position over you by lending directly to strong operating subsidiaries from gaining that priority, if you negotiate a covenant with the holding company that all or most of the group's external borrowing be raised through the holding company pari passu with, or subordinate to, your debt.

Inevitably, however, trade creditors will deal directly with the subsidiaries themselves which limits the value of this protection – it is, nevertheless, considerably better than nothing.

188

3.1.2 *Subordinated Debt*

In considering certain transactions, particularly leveraged buy-outs, you may be requested to analyse the creditworthiness of the company on the basis that debt which is subordinated to you is equivalent to equity.

In structuring a transaction where you are to rank ahead of a subordinated lender, (i.e. you are to be a provider of "Senior Debt") you need to look for provisions in the subordinated debt to the effect that:

(i)   on a liquidation, no payment will be made on the subordinated debt until the senior debt is first paid in full

(ii)   if any event of default occurs under the terms of the senior debt and is not cured or waived, then no further payments of principal or interest will be made on the subordinated debt

(iii)   scheduled repayment of principal on the subordinated debt will occur after the scheduled maturity date of the senior debt and, ideally,

(iv)   an authorisation from the subordinated lenders to the Senior Lenders giving the latter the right on behalf of the former to demand repayment, take legal proceedings, lodge claims in a liquidation etc, while any amounts owing under the senior debt remain unpaid.

The subordinated debt agreement should not, furthermore, contain covenants on the borrower such as a negative pledge which might prevent the senior debtor negotiating security from the borrower in case of need.

Items (i) – (iii) above are the basis which ensure that your senior debt is repaid in priority to the subordinated debt. Item (iv) gives you control over actions of the subordinated debt holders after a default, so that you can ensure that the holders of such debt do not take action detrimental to your interests (e.g. waiving claims, voting against the senior debt in favour of a restructuring detrimental to the senior debt etc.).

With this latter provision included, subordinated debt gives the senior debt holder better protection in a liquidation than the same level of equity cushion. The reason is that the debt is subordinated, unlike shares, not to all creditors but only to the defined senior debt. The senior debt holder, therefore, is able effectively to prove for payment twice in a liquidation alongside the general creditors – once in respect of his own debt and once in respect of the lender of the debt subordinate to himself. If creditors each receive 50 cents per $ of debt and if the amount of subordinated debt is, say, 50% of the amount of senior debt, then the senior debt will receive 75 cents on the $ against 50 cents for other creditors. Had the subordinated debt been invested in the company as equity, the benefit of the "cushion" would have been spread equally over all creditors. Without the control provision, however, it is likely that the subordinate debt holders will do all they can do to force a rescheduling to enable themselves to have some chance, however remote, of ultimately receiving some repayment. Inevitably, of course, prospective subordinate debt holders will resist attempts to include item (iv), and item (ii) can also be difficult to negotiate; without them, you really lack the control to enable the subordination to be truly effective.

3.2 Impact of Taxation

The final section of Chapter 2 discussed various tax considerations for borrowers.

In the international arena where cross-border transactions are common, great care needs to be taken to ensure that the economics of a transaction are not adversely affected by the levying of a withholding tax on interest paid which, if the transaction were differently structured perhaps by lending out of an alternative location, could be legitimately avoided or mitigated.

Where the transaction proposed involves investment in plant, equipment or buildings for which tax incentives or grants are available, then consideration should be given to optimising the available benefits. In many cases, where the borrower is unable to take full advantage of the benefits on offer, leasing may provide a solution.

In analysing the most efficient borrower to use within a group of companies for any specific transaction, an analysis of relative *after-tax* borrowing costs can be important in ensuring that the cost to the group as a whole is minimised.

In structuring transactions, however, which involve any material risk that either an increase in income or corporation tax rates might significantly

190

affect the viability of a transaction (e.g. a tax-based lease) or where there is some uncertainty that anticipated tax allowances will, in the event, be made available (e.g. tax "aggressive" cross-border leases), then analyse closely who is taking the risk of such events occurring and whether they are able to support such risks.

3.3   The Choice of Debt Market
The rapid expansion of bond and note markets in recent years and the development of derivatives markets presents opportunities for good quality borrowers to reduce costs of borrowing considerably by use of the most advantageous debt market or combination of markets.

The Capital Markets chapters of this book will explain what is currently available and give you the basic tools with which to identify opportunities for satisfying the funding needs of borrowers most efficiently.

3.4   Flexibility, Cost and Simplicity
Borrowers differ considerably in the philosophies they employ in funding their activities. Some actively seek to be innovators and, often through sophisticated central treasury functions, seek opportunities to reduce costs, manage funding risks and minimise taxation by whatever means appear appropriate. Others are content to keep their finances as simple as possible and accept higher costs as the price of avoiding complexity. Some borrowers will deal with any reputable bank which can provide a competitive proposal; others prefer to develop closer relationships with a restricted panel of banks in the hope that those banks will develop a better understanding of the business and demonstrate greater loyalty in times of trouble.

Structuring of facilities must take account of these differing philosophies and the balance between flexiblity, cost and simplicity must be designed appropriately. A highly complex swap structure, for example, designed to reduce funding cost by, perhaps, 50 basis points per annum over comparable alternatives over five years and involving risks for the borrower on a range of counterparties, may simply not be appropriate for a borrower which lacks the sophistication and inclination to assess the risks and other spin-offs involved such as reduced flexibility to prepay, costs of monitoring etc.

3.5 Sales Appeal

Many banks today seek to originate transactions and arrange them so that other banks or investors fund most of the deal either immediately or after subsequent sell-down. In designing transactions, it is therefore crucial that a banker at such an institution plays close attention to what constitutes attractive business to others in the market and does not focus only on the abilities of his bank. Fully underwritten transactions which cannot easily be sold down may leave the originator either with a size of exposure he did not want or sizeable losses in selling at a discount. Non-underwritten transactions which fail may not cause immediate loss but can cause acute embarrassment, loss of reputation and wasteful absorption of valuable management time. Take care, therefore, about that final point you give way on to win the mandate!

Sale of a transaction usually occurs in one of three ways and careful thought needs to be given to the most appropriate mechanism in each case:

(a) *Syndication:* before drawdown, a group of banks is assembled to provide the facility, each of which funds its portion of the transaction and has a direct lending relationship with the borrower, albeit that day-to-day contact with that borrower may be carried out by an agent bank on behalf of the banks in the group.

(b) *Assignment:* a bank assigns its rights under the loan to another bank; such assignment will sometimes be subject to the consent of the borrower, not to be unreasonably withheld, and will usually involve the borrower agreeing that, following such assignment, it can look only to the assignee (or purchaser) to fulfil the obligations of the lender in the loan document; the assignee thus effectively assumes the previous lender's direct relationship with the borrower.

(c) *Sub-participation:* a vendor bank arranges for another bank, the participant, to fund the vendor to the extent of its loan commitment to the borrower, with recourse for repayment for the participant limited to receipts by the vendor from the borrower under the loan; the vendor thus retains the direct relationship with the borrower and its obligations to the borrower under the loan; the participant has a risk on both the vendor bank and the borrower for repayment as the borrower's payments are still passed through the vendor bank; this type of sell-down is thus less satisfactory in many ways than the other two but can be arranged without the formalities of assignments, consents etc.

3.6 Novation

Novation means that, there being a contract in existence, some new contract is substituted for it, either between the same parties or between different parties. The consideration mutually being the discharge of the old contract. An instance of novation could be found in a lending situation in which Bank B took over the lending of Bank A to Company X without the borrower having to repay one borrowing and redraw a new borrowing. The terms and conditions applicable to the original loan would normally be transferred to the new loan by way of a novation agreement between the borrower, the original lender and the new lender.

Thus, whereas an assignment would be an agreement between the two banks, a novation is an agreement in which the two banks and the borrower join so as to provide for the loan, thereafter, to be between Bank B and Company X.

4. PRICING

Although often not considered a credit issue per se, pricing is a crucial determinant of a successful transaction.

In theory, a moderately sophisticated computer programme should be able to specify a required yield for any given transaction based on:

- the quantity and quality of the risk(s) assumed;

- the costs of direct administration and overheads;

- the costs of compliance with regulations governing the maintenance of bank liquidity (reserve asset costs) and;

- the opportunity cost of absorbing the bank's capital (capital adequacy "costs").

An enhancement to that system should then, by using discounted cash flow techniques, be able to present alternative means of achieving the required yield through various combinations of margins charged over the cost of funds, front-end fees, commitment fees and other fees.

Unfortunately, it tends not to be that easy. Let us first examine each of the above factors individually.

4.1 Risk and Reward

A high risk transaction is simply one where it is anticipated that there is a relatively strong chance that the bank will lose money.

Such risks typically arise in the form of:

- credit risk: whereby loss will occur if a customer is unable to pay amounts owing (e.g. a company cannot repay a loan);

- market risk: whereby loss may occur if a transaction cannot be sold off to other banks or investors except at a discount (especially relevant in underwriting bonds or loans to be syndicated);

- interest rate/currency risk: whereby loss will occur if interest rates or currency exchange rates move adversely and no hedge is in place (particularly relevant in pricing currency and interest rate option contracts and fixed rate loans which are not to be "match funded", i.e. funded by fixed rate deposits).

Pricing of risk will usually be done both quantitatively and qualitatively. Reward will thus be assessed quantitatively in terms of a percentage yield per annum on the amount of risk assumed and qualitatively in that a relatively high percentage will usually be required for a transaction where the quality of the risk is perceived to be relatively low.

The need for relatively high reward for relatively high risk arises because, as a greater number of such transactions can be expected to fail, a smaller number and size of high risk transactions is needed to cover one such high risk transaction going wrong. If one in fifty of the type of transaction under consideration can be expected to cause loss, then the pricing should (other considerations aside) be such that a healthy profit

194

is made overall if only forty-nine perform; such pricing should (again other considerations aside) be doubled if one in twenty-five can be expected to fail.

In this context, it is worth emphasising that an average gross yield of 1% p.a. (i.e. *before* tax and any deductions for administration costs) would be regarded as highly attractive for assumption of credit risk in today's market. With this sort of return, recovery of each $1 million of principal lost through a failed transaction would absorb one year's gross earnings on $100 million of loans. If one were to factor in the administration costs of administering bad loans and the costs of funding a non-performing debt, then that figure could easily be increased to $120 million. It is thus extremely difficult to recover from material credit losses in today's market.

4.2 Direct Administration and Overheads

A large loan will usually require little more direct administration than a small one. Determinants of administration cost are, rather, complexity and risk because they increase the need for management time and expertise in documenting the transaction initially and in monitoring and controlling the facility thereafter. Each transaction will, of course, need to cover its direct administration costs and contribute adequately to overheads if the bank is to make a profit, albeit that some "loss-leading" can be accommodated if other established business is sufficiently remunerative to make up the difference.

Small, complex transactions are, therefore, the least cost-effective and need to be relatively highly priced. Large "vanilla" or straightforward deals are the most administratively efficient and, therefore, tend to be the most attractive to banks with limited human and administrative resources.

4.3 Reserve Asset Costs

Most Central Banks, both as a means of monetary control and as a means of supervising banks' abilities to meet anticipated levels of withdrawals of short-term deposits, require banks in their catchment area to maintain certain levels of cash in various high-quality, liquid instruments. Such instruments may be non-interest bearing demand deposits with the Central Bank itself or other relatively low-yielding deposits and marketable securities. The size of such required liquid balances will usually be determined by the size of the bank's deposit base.

195

A bank making a new loan will have to fund itself with a new deposit. Such a deposit may, depending on the liquidity requirements in force, produce a need for additional low yielding balances to be placed in the relevant instruments. The cost to the bank of making such additional placements will be the difference between the cost of raising such additional funds in the inter-bank market and the yield received from the placements made. It will, therefore, vary depending on the prevailing level of interest rates and the interest differential between inter-bank funds and the return on the placements.

To take the UK as an example, the Bank of England currently imposes liquidity requirements by reference to banks' domestic sterling deposits only; no requirements are set by reference to deposits denominated in other currencies. Banks lending domestic sterling will, therefore, either factor into their rate or, more usually in the corporate market, charge as a separate item a "Mandatory Liquid Asset" or "MLA" cost. At present, this adds approximately 0.034% p.a. to the cost of a sterling loan.

4.4 Capital Adequacy "Costs"

In July 1988, the Central Banks of the major banking nations agreed a series of guidelines to secure international convergence of supervisory regulations governing the capital adequacy of international banks. Let us look at the guidelines as implemented by the Bank of England to illustrate the principles.

The process is relatively simple. The various categories of bank assets (both on- and off-balance sheet) are assigned a factor or weighting according to their perceived level of risk (a "risk-weighting" of 0%, 10%, 20%, 50% or 100%).

For example:

- Commercial loans, in whatever currency, to the extent they are drawn down on any given date: 100%;

- Loans to individuals secured by a first legal mortgage: 50%;

- Loans to multilateral development banks: 20%;

- Loans to OECD central governments and central banks: 0%.

The above weightings are for fully drawn facilities; generally speaking undrawn facilities are weighted at half the drawn weighting. There is an exception for undrawn facilities for periods of up to 365 days which are nil weighted when undrawn. The pricing of the undrawn element of 365 day facilities can, therefore, be fine as there are no associated capital costs. However, the drawn margin must reflect the cost of capital which is required to support a 100% weighted asset.

The amounts under each category in a bank's statistical returns to the Bank of England are multiplied by their assigned weighting to arrive at a total figure for Risk-Weighted Assets.

This figure is then compared to the size of the Adjusted Capital Base, or the cushion against loss available to depositors. A bank's capital base is divided into two tiers according to its quality as such a cushion.

Tier 1 Capital comprises:

- Share Capital

- Disclosed Reserves

- Minority Interests

less

- Goodwill

Tier 2 Capital comprises:

- Undisclosed Reserves;

- Revaluation Reserves;

- General Provisions against bad debts (i.e., those not specifically linked to individual bad debts which are, unlike General Provisions, not available to absorb future losses);

- Subordinated Loan Capital, subject to restrictions as to type and the proportion of the capital base made up in this manner.

197

Tier 1 plus Tier 2 represents a bank's Total Capital and from this figure is deducted assets which should prudently be funded out of shareholders', not depositors', funds including:

- Connected lending of a capital nature;

- Holdings of other banks' and building societies' capital instruments.

The adjusted Tier 1 Capital Base and the adjusted Total Capital Base are then divided by the total figure for Risk-Weighted Assets to arrive at the two regulatory ratios required for capital adequacy by the Bank of England. The Tier 1 ratio may not drop below 4% and the Total Capital ratio may not drop below 8%. The ratios for each bank may be higher than this and are agreed in individual discussions between the bank and the Bank of England based on the range and depth of the bank's activities.

The objective is to ensure that banks maintain adequate capital resources on a sole and consolidated basis to absorb losses in their activities without affecting their ability to repay their depositors.

The guidelines are important because, for the first time, they take into account off-balance sheet activity and undrawn commitments to lend. Included in the calculation are risks assumed, for example, by way of swap transactions, and commitments to lend under e.g., revolving underwriting facilities. Differentiation is also made between various contingent liabilities in order to weight direct credit substitutes which have the same credit risk as loans (i.e., guarantees of actual liabilities such as loans or bonds) differently from genuinely contingent risks (i.e., ones where some separate event such as a failure to fulfil some separate contract has to occur before the liability crystallises).

The effect of such regulation on banks is to restrict the extent to which they can expand their risk-taking activities. It has caused them to focus more clearly on the opportunity cost to them of doing specific transactions inasmuch as it involves the allocation by them of a limited resource, their capital, which reduces their ability to transact other (perhaps more remunerative) business.

Let me explain the point in more detail. There is no *fixed* cost to a bank of allocating its Adjusted Capital Base. Returns to shareholders are paid as a distribution of profits not as a fixed, legally enforceable, charge; unlike interest, therefore, dividends can be reduced or withheld. The same, of course, is not applicable to subordinated loan capital, but this does not affect the validity of the general point.

Inasmuch, however, as a given transaction requires an allocation of the Adjusted Capital Base, an *opportunity* cost can be calculated based on a bank's targeted return on shareholders' funds. This would indicate what the average return for a transaction with a given weighting needs to be (net of direct expenses and overheads) on the theoretical assumptions that all the bank's income arises from risk transactions. Unfortunately, the calculation tends to produce a "required" average figure which in today's market is unrealistic. This, together with other factors, has resulted in many banks devoting resources both to earning fees and income from other activities which do not involve allocation of the bank's capital and to trading their loan assets to optimise yield and create capacity on their balance sheet for new transactions (see 4.6 below).

4.5 The Pricing Dilemma
Pricing transactions in the context of the above factors is, therefore, extremely difficult.

- Equating a given level of risk to a price is a highly subjective process; banks in general have not undertaken the research required to produce actuarial calculations for the probability of transaction failure and continuing innovation in transaction types would, in any case, make such calculations of doubtful accuracy.

- Allocating administration costs and overheads to an individual transaction is again problematic; most bank personnel and administration costs are, in the short to medium term at least, fixed not variable; any income-earning transaction will, therefore, make a contribution to overheads but the question is whether such contribution from a deal is adequate and, if not, whether alternative deals are available at a better return.

- Pricing for capital adequacy can be difficult and even dangerous; the setting of "hurdle" rates as minimum acceptable returns for given types of business can lead to a tendency to accept only higher risk deals,

199

thereby affecting the credit quality of a bank's portfolio; over-emphasising types of transaction (which, although they involve risk, for the time being are not included in the prudential calculations of capital adequacy), can lead a bank to under-price the real risk being assumed. Swaps have been an example of this.

These difficulties have been compounded by increasingly intense competition, as problems with loans to developing countries and the decline in the oil producing and shipping sectors have combined with reduced demand for foreign borrowing from more creditworthy countries and companies. The activity of selling in a buyers' market a product (i.e. money) which, like commodities such as oil and grain, is difficult to differentiate from a cost base which is largely fixed has resulted in the economist's classic progression of cheaper and cheaper pricing.

Pricing a transaction is, therefore, a process which is driven by competition – the price of the base commodity, the money, tends to be set on the basis of precedent. Such precedent can be established from the banks' own records and transactions published in e.g. *Euromoney, International Insider* and the quality international financial press such as the *Financial Times, Wall Street Journal* etc. Premium pricing can be achieved usually only if "added value" can be put into the transaction through an innovative structure which produces additional benefits to the borrower or a niche can be found where competition is less strong (specialist financing) or (increasingly rarely) if a borrower is prepared for relationship reasons to pay a modest premium to its selected panel of banks as a price for loyalty and service.

4.6 The Tools of Pricing and Yield Optimisation

The pricing of loan transactions typically includes a mix of the following:

- a per annum *margin* over the bank's cost of funds on amounts borrowed; this will often be expressed as e.g. x% p.a. over 3 or 6 month LIBOR, the London Inter-bank Offered Rate; depending on the perceived risk and complexity, x might be anything from 0.10% p.a. to 2% p.a.;

- a one-off or "flat" *"front-end"* fee on the total facility which may be broken down into various elements (see Chapter 7 on Syndicated Loans);

● a per annum *"commitment" fee* on amounts committed but undrawn (see Chapter 2, Sections 3.2.1. and 3.5).

● a *"facility"* fee payable throughout the term on the full amount of the loan.

All these percentage figures are equally commonly expressed as "basis points". One basis point equals one hundredth of one per cent: i.e. 0.10% p.a. is 10 basis points and one per cent is 100 basis points.

The "yield" is the return to the bank on a per annum basis of the combined pricing elements. The calculation of yields on complex repayment/amortisation schedules with a variety of pricing elements is most efficiently done on a computer. Nevertheless, a simple example will illustrate the role of discounted cash flow analysis in this calculation.

The facility is:

Amount	– $10,000,000
Term	– 5 years
Drawdown	– immediate
Repayment	– bullet
Margin	– 0.5% p.a. over 6-month LIBOR ($50,000 p.a.)
Fees ·	– front-end fee of 0.375% flat ($37,500)

In this example, the front-end fee can be converted to a per annum margin at a discount rate of 10% p.a. by using the formula:

$$M = \frac{F \times r}{1 - (1 + r)^{-n}}$$

Where:

M	=	the margin equivalent
F	=	the front-end fee
r	=	the discount rate per annum
n	=	the number of years

The result is 0.099% p.a. and the yield on the asset (combining the margin and the fee) is thus 0.599% p.a. This can be compared with yields available on transactions with different combinations of pricing elements.

If a yield on capital employed is required rather than a yield on the asset then the above annual income of US$59,892.41 (i.e. $50,000 margin and the front end fee annualised to give $9,892.41 p.a.) would give a return on capital employed (ROCE) of 7.4866% (assuming a capital adequacy ratio of 8%).

Yield can be optimised by increasing the amount of fees received on a transaction. The most common way for this to occur is through a bank arranging a facility which is syndicated to other banks and taking a higher portion of the total front-end fee for doing so. Let us look at a further simple example of a loan facility:

Amount	– $100,000,000
Arranging Bank "take"	– $10,000,000
Drawdown	– immediate
Repayment	– bullet
Margin	– 0.5% p.a. over 6-month LIBOR ($50,000 p.a.)
Fees	– 0.125% flat on total facility amount to Arranger ($125,000)
	– 0.25% flat on "take" of $10m to participants ($25,000 each)

In this facility, the arranging bank does not underwrite the $100,000,000 (i.e. promise to provide it in full itself if it cannot arrange a syndicate to do so) but arranges the deal on a best efforts basis, retaining $10,000,000 for its own book.

The arranger's yield on his $10,000,000 risk is thus:

the margin of 0.5% p.a.

plus

the per annum equivalent of 0.125% flat on $100,000,000 (i.e. the per annum equivalent of 1.25% flat on the $10,000,000 take)

plus

the per annum equivalent of 0.25% flat on $10,000,000.

Taken together, the two fees total the equivalent of 1.50% flat on the $10,000,000 risk and result in an overall yield of 0.896% p.a. based on the same formula as that used above. If the participation of the lead bank were reduced to $5,000,000 then the yield on the risk taken would increase to 1.22% p.a. because of the greater impact of the arrangement fee on the total facility amount (equivalent to 2.5% flat on $5,000,000).

Reducing the take to $5,000,000 would, of course, reduce the total undiscounted income on the facility from $400,000 ($(50,000 x 5) + 125,000 + 25,000) to $262,500 ($(25,000 x 5) + 125,000 + 12,500) and the question arises as to whether $5,000,000 is an efficient amount to hold on the bank's book from an administration point of view. Yield in percentage terms does, therefore, have to be balanced against total income and seen in the context of administration costs.

The bank may also agree to underwrite as well as arrange the transaction. This involves taking a market risk since, if the deal cannot be sold as anticipated, the bank may have to take a loss by selling at higher fees than it receives itself or retain an uncomfortably large exposure. Such underwriting should, therefore, attract an additional fee, i.e. an underwriting fee payable until such time as a syndicate is assembled.

Similarly, there are increasing attempts by banks to sell off, either by assignment or sub-participation, loans which they have on their books without yielding the full margin. If, for example, the lead bank in the above example could subsequently sub-participate its $10,000,000 take to another bank which is prepared to accept a margin of only 0.40% p.a., then the seller can keep the remaining 0.10% p.a. without retaining any lending on its balance sheet.

In summary, therefore, the yield on a given risk taken can be improved by means of fees received for arranging or underwriting the transaction and by surpluses arising from profitable sell off. It may also be improved by undertaking profitably remunerated administration and consulting roles associated with either specific transactions or the management of the borrower's finances generally, and by spin-off business such as foreign exchange, cash management etc.

5. CREDITWORTHINESS AND BANK FINANCE – CONCLUSIONS

To conclude the credit section of this book, let me summarise the key considerations I have attempted to convey which dictate a credit-orientated approach to international commercial banking and the main features of that approach.

Banks are highly leveraged institutions, dependent on the continuing confidence of their depositors. Major credit losses are the primary factor which can damage that confidence. Banks compete currently in a buyers' market mainly with a product, money, which is difficult to differentiate from the product being offered by competitors, with the result that the price charged for risks taken tends to be low. One major loss can, therefore, wipe out a considerable portion of earnings even if the solvency of the bank is not threatened. There is, thus, no alternative but to control closely the credit risks assumed both on a portfolio and individual transaction basis.

Nevertheless, banks must be prepared to engage in difficult transactions to have the opportunity to enhance the returns available to their shareholders from the competitive markets in which they operate. Creativity, both in terms of product and in the approach to credit issues, against a disciplined, credit-orientated background, is therefore a key criterion for business success. Such creativity requires a solid understanding of the principles of credit assessment and transaction design, backed by close familiarity with the needs of your customer and the capabilities, needs and objectives both of your bank and other banks and investors with whom co-operation might be necessary or desirable. All this can be learnt by a combination of normal teaching, reading and relevant work experience. A level of flair and interpersonal/negotiation skills are also required to make the creativity effective – banking is a marketing-orientated people business – but these skills are at best ineffectual and at worst dangerous without the technical competence.

Against this background, the basic framework of key considerations in assessing the creditworthiness of a customer and designing a transaction is as follows:

204

A. *Credit Assessment*
(a) The Context:

- Industry Factors
- Country Factors

(b) The Running of the Business:

- Management
- Organisation
- Ownership

(c) Financial Capacity:

Against an understanding of the language of accountancy and the corporate structure:

- Profitability
- Cash Flow
- Capital
- Liquidity

B. *Transaction Design*
(a) Situation
(b) Purpose
(c) Amount
(d) Term
(e) Repayment
(f) Security
(g) Control and Monitoring
(h) Structuring
(i) Pricing

The objective in applying this framework in the context of the business of banking can be summarised as the completion of a successful transaction, defined as one which produces:

- timely repayment
- adequate remuneration

- enhancement of the customer relationship
- enhancement of the bank's reputation

The task may not be easy but it provides scope for challenge and innovation.

CHAPTER 6

Principles of Lending-Part VI

● ASSET FINANCE (AIRLINES AND JET AIRCRAFT)

by
John Willingham

1. INTRODUCTION

It takes some courage to advocate in the early 1990s that bankers consider aircraft finance positively. The end of the 1980s signalled the end of the boom in aircraft values. The 1990s have tested the assumptions upon which many of those "boom" valuations were based and found them wanting. Many banks which undertook aircraft finance in the late 1980s are now facing write-offs because airlines or lessors, once considered reasonably creditworthy, are now restructuring their finances, in receivership or bankruptcy, or in liquidation and the values of the aircraft securing the loans are inadequate.

With 20/20 hindsight, perhaps it all seems so predictable. History has repeated itself – the downturn was simply more dramatic than usual. Strong economic growth worldwide in the mid to late 1980s increased demand for air travel. Manufacturers were unable to deliver new aircraft quickly enough to satisfy demand from airlines for additional capacity. Values for used aircraft increased sharply. Money was relatively easily available, enabling airlines to obtain finance on favourable terms for both new and used aircraft. Some leasing companies expanded rapidly on the back of speculative orders and others were willing to pay premium prices to win deals from airlines.

Then, in 1990/1, various interrelated factors combined to transform heady optimism into alarmed pessimism. The "bubble" economy in Japan burst, leaving Japanese banks with considerable problems domestically. The major source of aircraft finance thereby shrank dramatically. The economy of the USA and of several European countries entered recession, driving down the demand for travel. Saddam Hussein invaded Kuwait and threatened worldwide air terrorism: as a result, recession-induced travel reductions were exacerbated. In 1991, world air travel dropped by 2%, the first year-on-year drop since the beginning of the jet age. The manufacturers, having geared up to increase production in the boom years found themselves delivering aircraft into a weakening market. Many of these increased deliveries went to leasing companies who had ordered them speculatively and who were forced to lease them at lower and lower rents. New noise and safety regulations, much discussed in the 1980s, were finally enacted and accelerated the obsolescence of older aircraft.

The fallout has been spectacular. In the USA, Pan Am, Eastern, Midway and Braniff have all disappeared. TWA and America West are both operating in bankruptcy (Chapter 11). Continental has recently re-emerged from over two years of operating in bankruptcy. Northwest has to date succeeded in reorganising its finances without resorting to Chapter 11. Between them, these four airlines accounted for 28% of domestic traffic carried by the major US airlines in 1992. The "Big Three" (American, United and Delta) reported net losses totalling US$800m in aggregate in 1991 and US$1.5bn in aggregate in 1992. This excludes losses from adoption of a new accounting standard. Of the majors, only Southwest has been profitable throughout the 1990s. In Canada, Canadian Airlines is reorganising its finances and several small charter carriers have failed. Many lenders and lessors, dealing with bankrupt airlines in the USA, have found themselves unable to enforce their security and provisions contained in the related documentation because of the wide discretion given to bankruptcy judges. In other cases, they have had to resort to time consuming and expensive litigation to do so.

In Europe, the major flag carriers all survive but, in most cases, with severe bruises. In the UK, Air Europe, Dan Air, Paramount and British Island Airways have all disappeared. In Spain, Spantax, Hispania and others have folded. As a result, the European flag carriers have increased their grip on European air travel, a consolidation which may threaten the benefits to consumers which European liberalisation was supposed to bring.

In Asia, the situation is relatively bright, but expansion ambitions are now being tempered in many cases. Demand for air travel is expanding fast in some Asian countries (China, Hong Kong, Taiwan, Malaysia and Indonesia are examples) but so is transport capacity. By contrast, demand in Japan is weak which in turn impacts airlines in neighbouring countries such as Korea. Deregulation in Australia has had the ironic result of reducing the number of major Australian carriers to two from three, in less than two years.

The lessor community has seen a severe shakeout. Many second-tier lessors have been forced out of business or are being propped up by their bankers. Most notably, GPA, the world's largest lessor, is currently restructuring its finances and has been forced to cancel large numbers of speculative orders with the major manufacturers.

What are the bright spots?

- No major flag carrier has defaulted. Even flag carriers in weak countries have continued to service their obligations (e.g. Ethiopian Airlines). The one exception of note was Royal Jordanian. Both the airline and its home country were badly affected by the Gulf War.

- Lenders into well-structured transactions, secured by good aircraft, have been able to extricate themselves from an airline's bankruptcy without material loss: the syndicate which financed Boeing 757–200s and Boeing 737–400s for Air Europe appears to be a notable example.

- The manufacturers in 1993 sharply cut back production rates. For example, Boeing announced cuts totalling over 40%. This is a response to significant cuts in orders by airlines and lessors. This will gradually lead to the restoration of the supply/demand equation.

- Economic growth is slowly being restored in the major economies; this will increase the demand for travel.

- Because of the withdrawal of many lenders from the market and significant retrenchment by many others, returns available to those prepared to consider aircraft finance transactions have risen sharply.

- Many aircraft delivered in the delivery boom of the late 1960s are now finally reaching economic obsolescence and are being retired. This will further improve the supply/demand ratio for the modern jet aircraft needed to replace them.

The airline industry will take some years to recover fully from the traumas of 1991/2 and the leasing and finance industries still have significant problems to work through. Nevertheless, for banks which are prepared to risk not following the herd and which have some capacity for long-term lending of ten years or more, there are attractive financing opportunities available.

2. DEFINITIONS
Aircraft finance can be described as the provision of financial packages which include one or more of the following characteristics.

2.1 **Repayment Profile** is tailored to some extent towards the operating life and cash flow generating characteristics of a specific item or items of moveable capital equipment, e.g. an aircraft.

2.2 **Return Options** are incorporated whereby the operator can return the asset to the financier on a specified date or series of dates without payment of the full principal balance then outstanding under the financing, leaving the financier to recoup its remaining investment from selling or leasing the asset; the financier thus assumes an exposure to the "residual value" of the asset on a given date or series of dates.

2.3 **Tax Allowances or Credits** linked to the ownership of equipment minimise the effective borrowing cost for the operator, i.e. the financing is designed to enable tax incentives or other grants/subsidies available to purchasers and users of the relevant equipment to be claimed most cost-effectively and the benefit to be passed on to the operator in the form of a lower financing cost.

This chapter will explore these characteristics with specific reference to the financing of commercial jet aircraft, but the principles can also be applied to the financing of other items of moveable capital equipment once differences in the nature and marketability of those assets have been

210

taken into account. Such other assets include equipment with multi-million dollar values (e.g. ships and oil rigs), which are commonly referred to as "big ticket" items and medium/small ticket items such as cranes, turboprop aircraft, business jets, computers, railway wagons and cars.

3. ASSET FINANCE AND ASSET-BASED FINANCE

Whatever the assets in question, there is an important distinction to be drawn between "asset finance" and "asset-based finance".

3.1 **Asset Finance** is a broad term embracing all transactions where the purpose is to finance the acquisition or use of a capital asset, including transactions where the financier places no or little reliance on the value of the asset as security because:

(i)   the creditworthiness of the operator is such, based on the principles discussed in Chapters 1–5 and the specific considerations discussed below, that the financier can regard himself as covered on an unsecured basis; and

(ii)   the operator is committed to repay the financing in full, whether or not he uses the asset for the whole of its useful life, so that the financier has no residual value exposure.

3.2 **Asset-based Finance** is a narrower term and refers to types of asset finance transaction where:

(a)   (i)   the ability of the asset itself to generate the necessary revenues for repayment will be crucial to the operator's ability to repay; and

        (ii)   the quality of the asset as security or as your insurance against failure by the operator to perform is a key consideration; or

(b)   either in combination with the above two features or as part of a transaction where the operator can be judged to be good for its committed payment obligations on an unsecured basis, the financier is required to take an exposure to the residual value of the asset financed.

211

In engaging in an asset finance transaction which is not asset-based, the financier will concentrate on the nature of the asset only to ensure that:

(i) available tax incentives for investment in such an asset are most efficiently utilised;

(ii) provision is made in the documentation to require that the asset be maintained and insured by the operator so that the financier will not be exposed to any claim from a third party for damages arising from misuse of, defects in, or accidents involving the equipment;

(iii) provision is made in the documentation and the administration procedures of the financier to monitor compliance by the operator with maintenance and insurance provisions through rights to inspect the equipment periodically, to examine maintenance records and to check insurance certificates.

The considerations for an asset-based financier are much wider and will be discussed below. You will find similarities between some of the considerations described and those present in project finance (Chapter 8) inasmuch as a financing in each case is tailored around the characteristics of a revenue-generating capital asset. There are also similarities with property or real estate financing. The characteristics of these different classes of asset, however, each merit sufficiently different approaches for them most usefully to be considered separately.

4. LEASING – DEFINITION AND ROLE

We touched on leasing in Section 4.3 of Chapter 2 in the context of a discussion of the efficient use of accelerated depreciation allowances but, as its role in asset finance is broad and important, we need to focus more closely on the product here.

Leasing is an arrangement whereby one party (a"lessor") *purchases and owns* an item of equipment and allows another party (a "lessee") to use that equipment in consideration for a periodic payment usually described as a "rental" or "rent".

Such leases may be "capital" or "full payout" leases whereby the lessee over an initial term or "primary period" is committed to pay an adequate number of rentals to enable the lessor to recover substantially all the asset's purchase price, financing costs and a profit element. At the end of the lease term, the lessee may then be entitled under the lease (i) to purchase the equipment for a nominal price (i.e. the lease is in substance a hire-purchase, instalment sale or conditional sale transaction) or (ii) to continue to rent the equipment for a "secondary period" at a nominal rental or (iii) to receive from the lessor the majority of any proceeds received by the lessor from a sale of the equipment to a third party. In this situation, the lessee can be seen to have substantially all the rights and obligations of ownership notwithstanding that it does not have title to the asset, since it is both committed to pay the cost of the equipment just as it would be under a loan and is entitled to the value of the equipment at the end of the financing period. This type of transaction is often described as giving the lessor "legal ownership" and the lessee "economic ownership"; we shall discuss its uses below in considering asset-based repayment structures and tax enhanced packages.

Other leases may not commit the lessee to pay an adequate number of rentals to pay the lessor out in full. These are usually described as "operating leases" and they provide that, at the end of the committed lease term, the lessee will return the asset to the lessor in a prescribed condition. The lessor will then seek either to sell or re-lease the asset. Any profit or loss the lessor makes on sale or re-lease by reference to its remaining net investment in the asset will usually be for its own account and the lessor has no recourse to the lessee for any shortfall. Thus both legal and economic ownership remain with the lessor. We shall discuss the application of this form of leasing and its derivative, option leasing, in considering residual value or asset value exposure in Section 7 below.

In some circumstances, the risks can also be structured so that a transaction is a full payout lease for the lessor but an operating lease for the lessee. This occurs when a third party guarantees to the lessor a re-sale value for the asset at the end of the lease term. For example, a lessor may buy an aircraft for $10 million, lease it to an airline for five years during which its net investment will reduce to $6 million and be guaranteed a $6 million re-sale price by a third party, possibly a bank, residual value insurer or manufacturer. This dual structure will also be considered with residual value exposure below.

5. RISKS IN ASSET-BASED FINANCING

There are two major and distinct categories of risk to be considered in asset financing. Unfortunately, you will find both defined as "asset risk" depending on the context of a particular discussion which can lead to dangerous confusion. For my purposes, therefore, I shall differentiate between:

(a)   SECURED CREDIT RISK where the financier focuses primarily on the ability of the airline to generate repayment from operating cash flow and secondly on the asset as the bank's security or insurance against failure; and

(b)   ASSET VALUE RISK where the financier's recourse for recovery of its remaining net investment is to the value of the asset and thus the focus is on the financier's likely future ability, on a specific date or dates, to re-sell or re-lease the asset to recoup that investment.

In assessing these risks in the context of a commercial jet aircraft transaction for an airline, the following considerations apply.

6. SECURED CREDIT RISK

From the description of Secured Credit Risk above, it should be clear that a financier needs to be satisfied both that the airline has the qualities, resources and opportunities available to make the aircraft chosen work successfully and that the aircraft itself is of such a quality as an asset that its value should be adequate to pay off the outstanding debt if the airline nevertheless fails. The considerations are, therefore, those described in Chapters 1–5 overlaid with a detailed knowledge of the airline industry and the factors affecting both aircraft values and protection of those values.

The following is a summary of the issues which relate to airline finance in general with specific reference made to asset-based transactions where appropriate:

6.1   The Operator

6.1.1   The Airline Industry Context

This section constitutes but a brief introduction to the basic features of the commercial airline industry to set the context for the later discussion and does not attempt to be comprehensive.

214

Further information can be obtained by reading of annual reports and promotional literature from airlines and aircraft manufacturers together with the industry press including:

Aircraft Investors
Airfinance Journal
Airline Monitor
Aviation Daily
Aviation Week and Space Technology
Avmark Aviation Economist
Blue Print
Flight
Speednews

The airline industry has an easily comprehensible basic function: the transportation of passengers and freight between destinations. As such, the industry as a whole competes with other forms of commercial and recreational transportation including cars, trains and ships but, over distances between major towns and cities of 500 miles and above over land, and 200 miles and above over water, it is unrivalled except where speed of arrival is not a factor or the product to be carried is heavy and bulky. Indeed, in the USA, with its highly developed commuter and regional air transport market, airlines operate successfully even over significantly shorter distances. As such, the industry:

(i)   is a crucial one within the world economy with the result that it tends to be accorded particular strategic importance in most countries and particular economic importance, especially in developing countries, as a generator of foreign currency revenues;

(ii)   closely follows the fortunes of the world economy inasmuch as increased economic activity both implies higher levels of trade and business-related travel connected to such trade and increased leisure travel from those benefiting from greater levels of prosperity; economic recession equally implies the opposite effect.

Competition between airlines providing regular services to passengers and freight transporters would naturally focus on a combination of price, flight frequency, reliability of departure, comfort and quality of pre-, post- and in-flight service. But the strategic and economic importance of the industry has led many governments to control airline activities within, into and out of, their countries through state-owned or controlled airline companies. It is, therefore, important to understand the regulatory context in which a specific airline operates before you can judge its business prospects.

6.1.2 *International Scheduled Services*

Scheduled or timetabled international airline traffic and route allocation are closely controlled by bilateral treaties between countries; it is, therefore, simply not possible for a new entrant to operate scheduled flights between, say, Paris and Tokyo without obtaining approvals from both cities' national governments, which approvals will be considered (if at all) in the context of the dangers they pose to the established carriers on that route. Indeed, limitations on competition on international routes may extend further to regulation of prices charged and revenue-sharing or "interline" arrangements between airlines. These limit the extent to which airlines can benefit from increases in their individual market share on a given route because they provide that total revenues generated on the route by the airlines allowed to fly it are shared according to a pre-set formula. Notwithstanding the trend internationally towards privatisation of major international scheduled airlines, most governments prohibit foreign control of their major airlines and restrict foreign shareholdings to under 25%.

6.1.3 *International Charter Services*

International charter flights are, however, a different matter. Charter aircraft are booked in advance by tour operators mainly to transport holiday makers as part of a package holiday – seats on such flights tend to become available to the general public only when a particular flight has not been fully sold. These flights do not fall under the same regulatory constraints as scheduled operations because typical bi-lateral treaties provide that charter flights may be flown between the two countries, without restriction, by licensed airlines from each country. Subject to obtaining and maintaining its licence to operate as an airline and reservation of runway space (or "slots") for take-off and landing, an airline can usually freely operate charter flights between its own country and international destinations. It would be unusual, however, for say a British-based airline

216

to be permitted to operate charter flights between France and Greece. Charter airlines independent of the main national airlines have flourished in the UK over the past decade, are well established in The Netherlands, Scandinavia and West Germany and are developing in France and Spain. The market is highly competitive by comparison with most scheduled operations. As a result failures have occurred in recent years including Air Europe in the UK, Spantax and Hispania in Spain, and Air Holland in the Netherlands.

6.1.4 *European Services*

With the introduction of the "free" EC internal market in 1992, there are signs that competition among scheduled airlines in Europe will become less restricted. Any EC airline may now, in theory, fly from any EC country to any other. The practicality of this remains severely limited because the established carriers on the major routes continue to dominate the relevant airports. As a result, new contracts find difficulty obtaining suitable "slots" for landing and take-off. In addition, airlines are now free to set their own fares subject only to a "double disapproval" system. Under this system, both governments have to disapprove a given fare in order to prevent an airline offering it.

Nevertheless, airlines are actively forming strategic alliances designed to enhance their competitive position not only within Europe but also on international routes into Europe and elsewhere. Examples include the links between British Airways and Qantas, British Airways and US Air, SAS and British Midland, KLM and Northwest, KLM and Air UK and the links between Singapore Airlines, Swissair and Delta. SAS, Swissair, Austrian Airlines and KLM are in advanced negotiations about a full integration of their operations, although large complications remain to be solved.

Notwithstanding the above, most European governments continue to promote the interests of their flag carrier: British Airways was, for example, permitted to absorb the UK's former No. 2 flag carrier, British Caledonian in 1987 and Dan Air in 1992, whilst Air France absorbed UTA. Government regulation will continue to restrict the scope of cross-border alliances and, probably, also cross-border competition, even within Europe.

217

6.1.5 Deregulated Markets: USA and Australia

Besides international scheduled services and the European charter market, the other major commercial airline market, accounting for the world's largest airline fleets, is providing internal or domestic services in the USA. This market was deregulated in 1978 and since that time has gone through rapid change. Freedom for US carriers to compete on all US domestic routes resulted in the establishment of many small airlines attempting to satisfy a niche, but most have been squeezed out as intense competition between the major airlines on the most popular routes forced down prices, caused managements to take vigorous action to reduce costs and drove even some large airlines into bankruptcy or liquidation and others into mergers. The industry has now emerged into one dominated by a few large carriers based at major airports ("hubs") from which their route systems radiate like "spokes"; smaller airlines tend to prosper only to the extent that they (i) have a well established regional base and operate routes economically which are not of interest to the majors because of relatively low passenger demand and high costs of establishing suitable facilities at the relevant airports or (ii) are closely tied into a major carrier and use small aircraft to provide regional "feeder" services to a popular hub. Price competition on popular routes remains intense but, following the consolidation of the industry through merger and acquisition, has lessened considerably on routes where the number of competing airlines has been reduced or where direct competition no longer exists. Nevertheless, the losses of the Big Three continue to demonstrate that consolidation does not necessarily bring profitability, at least in a weak economic environment.

In 1991 Australia introduced a regime for domestic flights based on the US model. The most promising new entrant, Compass, raised A$65m in capital based on a plan to operate relatively large jets on the denser Australian trunk routes. Against severe price competition from the established carriers, Ansett and Australian, it was unable to generate adequate revenues and failed at the end of 1991. An effort to resuscitate it failed in 1993. Further rationalisation has followed with the merger of Qantas (previously restricted to international operations) and Australian. British Airways is taking a 25% stake in the merged entity and the remaining 75% is scheduled for sale to the public by the Australian government. Ansett, previously restricted to domestic services, will be able to commence international operations but lacks the capital to do so. At the time of writing, it is looking for strong international partners.

6.1.6 *The Country Context*
The country in which an airline is based is a further important factor affecting its ability to be commercially successful because:

(i)   it will be a major determinant of the popularity of the routes it operates. Clearly, British Airways is at an advantage in this respect being based in a country which (a) has an export-import orientated economy with well-established tourist traffic into and out of the country, (b) has one of the world's three major financial and business centres and (c) is situated conveniently as both a gateway for Europe and as a mid-point between the time zones of East and West; Air Malawi, by contrast, has few such advantages;

(ii) the philosophies and policies of the host government will influence the extent of competition to which airlines, operating within and into its country, will experience and their freedom to develop new routes and air transport facilities;

(iii) the resources of that government, its political stability, the strength of its economy and quality of its legal system will have a strong bearing on the airline's ability to finance development of its fleet efficiently.

Of importance also are the countries to which an airline flies inasmuch as they will play a significant role in determining popularity of services, the currency of revenues generated and the ease with which overseas earnings can be repatriated.

6.1.7 *The Specific Operator*
In assessing the creditworthiness of an airline in the context of the above considerations one, therefore, needs to focus on the following factors:

6.1.7.1 *Passenger/Cargo Base*
For scheduled airlines, their ability to generate profitable passenger and cargo volume (the former in most cases being by far the dominant

element) will depend firstly on the quality of their route network and the competition on those routes. Low levels of competition or heavily regulated competition on popular routes may enable premium pricing to be charged in comparison to routes of similar distances where competition is strong. London–Paris, for example, is one of the densest routes in the world but, on a cost per mile basis, also one of the most expensive. The longer New York–Washington route can be flown at a fraction of the price as can certain routes in Europe where restrictions on entry and price competition have been eased (London–Amsterdam and London–Dublin, for example).

For a charter airline, the reliability of its source of passengers in a competitive market is crucial. Those charter airlines which are subsidiaries of major tour operators have an advantage inasmuch as, if the tour market declines, the tourists to whom the parent company has sold holidays can be directed to the in-house airline to preserve cash flow and minimise losses. Independent charterers are, from this point of view, in a relatively vulnerable position and rely on relationships built up with a variety of tour operators to minimise exposure to the loss of, or reduction in, one source of revenue.

Charter airlines, and scheduled airlines which carry a significant amount of leisure travellers, will be subject to considerable seasonal swings in passenger volumes. Most European holidaymakers take their vacations in June – September and, despite the increasing popularity of ski-ing and winter breaks, charter airlines will lose money in the winter months.

6.1.7.2 *Cost and Efficiency*

An airline with a strong passenger base will be commercially successful only if it can serve that passenger base at a profit. Pressures on prices and yields tend to be strong where competition is prevalent, so that control over costs is a crucial determinant of an airline's ability to prosper.

The main cost inputs into an airline are:

(i)   fuel

(ii)   capital costs of aircraft used (interest plus depreciation/leasing charges)

(iii)   maintenance of the aircraft fleet

(iv)   flight and cabin staff

(v)   insurance

(vi)   administration and marketing.

These can be juggled in numerous ways in the attempt to achieve maximum efficiency. For example, the purchase of a new, efficient aircraft ideally suited for a part of an airline's route structure will produce lower costs in terms of maintenance, breakdowns, fuel and (probably) flight and cabin crew but result in higher capital costs. Taking aircraft on, say, a three-to-five year operating lease will produce probably lower capital costs than purchasing with loan finance. An operating lease will also allow flexibility for the airline to return the aircraft at the end of the period with no additional payment due; it will not usually, however, give the airline the benefit of any build-up in the value of the aircraft. Reduced marketing costs will cut expenditure but may result in a reduction in passenger demand.

The equations are further complicated by (i) the lead time required for aircraft purchases, which dictates detailed planning in advance, (ii) the fact that fuel prices and prevailing interest rates are outside airlines' control, (iii) the impact of the volatility of exchange rates on a business with income often denominated in a variety of currencies and (iv) uncertainties associated with regulations and proposed regulations designed to reduce aircraft noise and emissions for environmental reasons. All these may affect both the operational cash flow of airlines and the re-sale values of their aircraft.

6.1.7.3   *Track Record*
In analysing the track record in the context of the above, one will, therefore, focus particularly on trends in the following key areas. The necessary information can be obtained by a combination of:

●   airline annual reports

- statistics compiled by the International Air Transport Association (IATA), the Civil Aviation Authority in the UK, the Federal Aviation Administration in the USA and other aviation authorities

- publications from the major manufacturers

- information services offered by various organisations including Aviation Information Services, Airline Monitor and Avmark.

(a)   Revenue
Trend in turnover is clearly the first indicator of success in revenue generation but further useful indications are trends in:

- YIELD. This is an airline's unit price. For passenger operations it is the figure derived by dividing total passenger revenues (turnover) by Revenue Passenger Miles. RPM is a measure of capacity sold, defined as the figure derived from multiplying the total passengers carried by the distance flown. Thus an aircraft which carries one hundred passengers a distance of two hundred miles completes 20,000 RPM. Yield, therefore, gives a figure for revenue generated for one passenger carried over one mile as an airline's average unit price. The yield figure should be used with care as different types of airline will demonstrate very different yields. A predominantly short-haul scheduled airline with average route distance of e.g. 500 miles or below will usually require higher yields to survive than long-haul airlines (perhaps $0.18 against $0.13) because of the higher per mile cost of landing fees, high fuel burn on take-off and landing etc. The figure is useful, however, to indicate pricing performance over a period of years and for comparison purposes with similar or directly competing airlines.

- LOAD FACTORS, being capacity sold, defined as RPM for passenger activities, as a percentage of total capacity in use. Total Capacity in use is measured as Available Seat Miles (ASM) – the total number of seats in service multiplied by the total distance flown. Thus, if the aircraft carrying 100 passengers mentioned above has 120 seats, then the total ASMs on that 200 mile flight are 24,000 and the load factor is 20,000/24,000 or 83%. This indicates how successfully the capacity in use is being sold. Averages vary for different markets, 60% being a typical

222

figure on US domestic routes, 65% on European/Asian scheduled services and 80% plus for successful charter airlines. Clearly, there can be a trade-off between yield and load factor, as discount prices may bring higher loads but result in lower yields whereas premium prices will produce higher yields but may deter customers and reduce loads carried.

Both yield and load factors are often split between passenger, cargo and mail to allow further analysis of the major segments of an airline's activity. The cargo analysis may be done in terms of Revenue Tonne Miles (the number of tonnes flown multiplied by the distance over which they were flown) and Available Tonne Miles (the number of tonnes of capacity in service multiplied by the distance flown), in accordance with the principles discussed above.

- AIRCRAFT UTILISATION, being an indicator of the extent to which capacity is being used. The measure is the average number of hours in service (flight hours) achieved by aircraft in a given fleet. As an indicator, 2,000 hours per year per aircraft is relatively low whilst 4,000 hours is relatively high. An airline may demonstrate prima facie adequate yield figures (e.g., US$0.13) and reasonable load factors (62%) but perform poorly if its capacity made available (ASM) reflects an average aircraft utilisation of only 1,500 hours per year. Again, beware inter-airline comparisons as airlines flying longer routes should find it easier to achieve relatively high utilisation, whilst the relative flexibility of charter airlines in general enables them to achieve higher utilisation than their scheduled counterparts; nevertheless, comparison between competing airlines and of the trend over a period can provide useful insights.

(b)   Profitability
- operating profit margin (and trends in individual components of fuel, maintenance and labour); my preferred approach is to look at profits before depreciation, interest, leasing charges, exceptional items and tax and thus to look at operating profitability initially excluding capital costs; the adequacy of the operating margin in terms of capital costs can be assessed when looking at interest and rental cover and cash flow; the trend in an individual airline's performance is most useful –

inter-airline comparisons can be useful general indicators as long as one bears in mind the relative age and efficiency of the fleets being operated and uses consistent definitions.

- interest and rental cover.

- dividend cover.

(c)   Cash Flow

Difficulties of interpretation arise when financial obligations are incurred by a company in the form of leases. With leasing such a popular product in the airline industry, we need to focus on it particularly closely here. US and UK accounting practice treat full payout or capital leases as debt (FASB 13 and SSAP 21). The present value of the committed future lease payments is recorded on the balance sheet as debt and the aircraft is recorded as an asset. Only the interest element of the lease rentals are charged in the Profit and Loss Account. The aircraft is depreciated in the same way as an owned aircraft. This is not true of some other jurisdictions where all leases are off balance sheet and the profit and loss account simply deducts as expense items lease rental payments accrued. Leases which under the terms of FASB 13 and SSAP 21 are not full payout, i.e. operating leases, also are not treated as debt, but rental payments thereunder are deducted as expense items in the profit and loss account as above.

Operating leases for aircraft are, however, usually term obligations of three years and over (excluding some seasonal swapping arrangements between airlines themselves and short term leases granted recently by lessors to airlines because of the downturn in the market). Leases are thus a financial overhead in the same way as debt. The committed payments falling due in the future are usually disclosed in a note to the accounts.

Airlines need very little working capital – see (d) below. Loan and capital lease liabilities are thus usually related to aircraft acquisitions, are non-revolving in nature, carry original terms of 10-18 years and have prescribed, fixed repayment instalments. In the USA, major carriers have often been able to finance aircraft acquisitions using capital leases with terms in excess of 23 years. This compares with the flexible revolving facilities, with bullet repayments, which more commonly fund manufacturing industries (cf Chapter 2, Sections 2-3). Annual repayments for the following five years will usually be set out in the notes to the accounts. Reported depreciation often bears no resemblance to the repayment profile of the aircraft-related debt, with the same new aircraft depreciated by different airlines over 8 to 20 years.

All the above can make the assessment of an airline's viability a confusing exercise. Cash generated is, however, ultimately the key to continued viability and cash flow analysis attacks this issue directly. In particular, you need to focus on annual operating cash flow in comparison with both annual debt and lease servicing obligations and the airline's fleet replacement needs and related cost.

In assessing these relationships, let us revert to the Proforma Cash Flow Statement and alter it slightly.

PROFIT BEFORE INTEREST AND TAX _____

Add Adjustment for Depreciation and Amortisation _____
Add Adjustment for other non-cash items _____
Add Decrease/Deduct Increase in Net Working Assets _____
Add Lease Rentals Paid* _____

OPERATING CASH FLOW BEFORE FIXED CAPITAL CHARGES _____

FIXED CAPITAL CHARGES
Interest Paid _____
Lease Rentals Paid _____
Scheduled Reductions in Long-Term Debt** _____
Dividends Paid _____
TOTAL FIXED CAPITAL CHARGES _____

Tax Paid*** _____

RETAINED OPERATING CASH FLOW _____

DISCRETIONARY APPLICATIONS
Capital Expenditure****
Aircraft Acquired on Operating Lease****   _____
Net Increase in Long-term Investments   _____
Other   _____
Less: Proceeds from Disposals****   _____
TOTAL DISCRETIONARY APPLICATIONS   _____

NET CASH INFLOW/(OUTFLOW)   _____

FINANCED BY/(APPLIED TO):

Share Capital Issued   _____
Other   _____
Operating Lessor Financing****   _____
Increase/(Decrease) in Net Debt   _____
Analysis of Increase/(Decrease) in Net Debt   _____
(Increase)/Decrease in Cash and Cash Equivalents _____
Increase/(Decrease) in Short-Term Debt   _____
(Voluntary Prepayment) of Long-Term Debt   _____
New Long-Term Debt Raised   _____

*   As stated above, annual lease rentals are in substance a financial
       overhead in much the same way as debt. In arriving at Operating Cash
       Flow before Fixed Capital Charges, these amounts should therefore be
       added back.

**   Because of the non-revolving nature of typical airline debt, amortisation
       is not as flexible as is usual for some other industries and must be
       adhered to if the airline is not to be forced into refinancing arrangements,
       sales of assets or bankruptcy.

***   Some may object that I have placed tax paid in this position, because
       scheduled repayments of long-term debt are not pre-tax expenses,
       unlike interest and rent. My response is that depreciation is a pre-tax
       deduction which, in theory, provides funds for reduction of long-term
       debt associated with capital equipment. In addition, the availability of
       accelerated tax depreciation allowances (cf Chapter 2) in many

226

jurisdictions means that, in practice, airlines pay little tax. An acceptable, and more conservative alternative, would be to include tax paid as a Fixed Capital Charge.

**** The amount to be supplied here is the full cost or value of an aircraft taken on an operating lease. Information on the number, type and serial numbers of aircraft which have been taken on operating lease during the year should be available from the airline or the information services mentioned in (D) below. The information services will also be able to provide an estimated value of such aircraft. This figure is useful as it indicates the extent of capital expenditure being provided off-balance sheet for the airline by operating lessors (cf Section 7 below). Return of an aircraft to a lessor equally reduces the capital burden.

This statement can be created both for historic figures and, using the information on future obligations to be found in the notes to the accounts, on a projected basis for future years. Those of you with computer skills will be able to create spreadsheets with assumptions for yields, load factors, interest rates, aircraft acquisitions and disposals, which will enable you to examine a range of scenarios.

The key items are thus:

1.   The Debt Service Ratio, being:

$$\frac{\text{Operating Cash Flow before Fixed Capital Charges}}{\text{Fixed Capital Charges}}$$

This indicates the level of coverage for existing annual debt and quasi-debt obligations. A comfortable minimum for this ratio is 1.25:1 but, for the reasons set out below, should be significantly higher if the airline's fleet is ageing and replacement is required.

2. $$\frac{\text{ROCF plus Proceeds from Disposals}}{\text{Perceived Net Capital Expenditure Needs}}$$

Assessment of this second ratio will require evaluation of fleet quality and existing orders and discussions with management on fleet replacement and expansion options being considered. One will be looking for an

227

ability in an airline to generate from operations and sale of old equipment excess cash flow over its existing debt servicing obligations to enable it to contribute 20-30% towards fleet replacement and expansion.

(d)   Balance Sheet and owned fleet including that on capital leases
Airlines typically need very little working capital. Tickets are either sold for cash or prepaid by customers and stock needs relate in general not to trading but to spares for maintenance etc. A deficit of current assets over current liabilities is therefore usual and acceptable as long as the trend in the current ratio is steady. For a modest fee, appraisers such as Aviation Information Services, Avitas, Avmark and Boullion Aviation Services will provide a specific owned fleet valuation if more detail is required. You should note that i) such valuations will be based on transactions for individual aircraft currently taking place in the market under then current market conditions, not on the basis of a liquidation value and that ii) the valuation process is subjective, with the result that different valuers may reach materially different conclusions.

The key balance sheet item on the asset side is thus the owned fleet, including those on capital or full payment leases. With the help of publications such as *J.P. Airline Fleets*, which details the composition and age of individual commercial airline's equipment, and the *International Aircraft Price Guide*, the financier will be able to estimate the current value of a fleet to enable comparison to be drawn with its book value and the airline's debt levels. To make the estimate and comparisons as accurate as possible, you will need supplementary information from the airline or its accounts on (a) the split between aircraft reflected on the balance sheet and those operated under off-balance-sheet financing arrangements, (b) details of any such off-balance sheet arrangements, including lease rentals being paid and (c) details of any aircraft in which the airline has no equity interest and thus no interest in any surplus value (i.e. because they are used on pure operating leases).

Analysis of the fleet's age and type should, furthermore, enable the financier to judge whether the airline will be able to service its route structure efficiently going forward or whether increasing maintenance costs on old aircraft, the approach of noise-enforced obsolescence and undue exposure to increases in fuel prices will dictate a major re-equipment programme.

The key balance sheet item on the liability side is usually the term debt, adjusted to capitalise the committed portion of off-balance-sheet lease obligations. This needs to be examined in terms of:

- the cash flow available to service it and the relationship between this cash flow and scheduled maturities – see (c) above;

- the currency or currencies of the debt against the main currency or currencies of the airline's net income;

- the value and age of the fleet;

- the extent to which the interest rates on the debt are fixed or floating; fixed rates locked in which are higher than the prevailing market rates will be a competitive disadvantage and expensive to prepay because of the break costs involved (cf. Chapter 2, Section 3.4) whereas floating rates leave the airline exposed if interest rates rise; a balance between the two is usually preferable.

6.1.7.4   *Cyclicality, Volatility and Management*
As should be clear from the above, airlines operate with a customer base which:

(i)   fluctuates considerably with changes in economic conditions and with a cost base which is largely fixed, at least in the short-term, and

(ii)   to the extent it is not fixed, is subject to changes outside the airline's control (especially fuel prices, interest and exchange rates).

Once the breakeven load factor is reached, the marginal cost of carrying each additional passenger is negligible and thus a small percentage increase in turnover and improvement in load factor can have a major effect on profitability. Equally, a relatively small drop in passengers carried and deterioration in average load factor can cause an airline to fall into loss. Competitive pressures furthermore tend to encourage airlines to discount fares or offer free flight bonuses etc. where permitted to attract that valuable additional passenger. When demand is slack, this often has the effect of forcing other competing airlines to follow with the result that revenue per passenger is reduced, the breakeven load factor rises and the impact of either the drop in passenger demand, or increase in seat availability which caused the initial discounting, is exacerbated.

Inevitably, therefore, airline results are volatile and margins are tight so that a major task of airline managements is to ensure that costs are kept low, efficiency is maximised, exposures to exchange rate and interest rate movements are managed and fleet procurement and disposals are carefully planned to minimise the impact of downturns in the market. Airlines, therefore, need a well balanced management team including strong representation both by engineering and financial personnel – it is a dangerous game without this expertise.

6.1.7.5 *The Asset Based Approach to an Operator*

Many financiers have developed a willingness to overcome credit problems which the above analysis of an operator's creditworthiness may highlight by tailoring financial packages around specific assets and by developing specialised expertise to assess the viability of smaller airlines' development plans.

This has enabled state-owned airlines in developing countries to raise finance for aircraft acquisitions when general banking lines to those countries were closed. For, notwithstanding a relatively weak or short track record, such an airline may be able to demonstrate that, going forward:

(i)   there is a clear need for airline services between certain destinations from which hard-currency revenue can be generated;

(ii)   regulatory approvals and suitable landing rights (slots) at the relevant airports are in place or can be obtained to fly those routes;

(iii)   a specific aircraft or number of aircraft will, based on cost and technical factors, enable that need to be satisfied at a cost in hard currency well below the potential for revenue generation;

(iv)   the government is committed to a strategy to develop airline services to its country so that the airline will receive state support in arranging routes and financing;

(v)   it has the management competence to control the expansion.

The case is often made with the help of a detailed feasibility study prepared jointly by the airline and an aircraft manufacturer bidding to sell its product. Such studies are valuable as long as the assumptions underlying the figures are clearly set out to permit sensitivity analyses to be carried out and comparisons to be made with historic performance.

A similar analysis of demand, regulatory issues, aircraft compatibility and management competence has also enabled banks to assist many independent charter airlines to become strong competitive forces in developed countries.

6.2 Asset Values

With the credit risks analysed, the focus shifts to the quality of the asset as an item of security. In this section we shall focus on its value and remarketability; issues relating to taking and enforcing the security will be dealt with under REPOSSESSION AND LEGAL PROTECTION below and issues relating to monitoring and protecting the value of the security will be considered under ASSET VALUE PROTECTION.

6.2.1 *Jet Aircraft – General*

First, some general comments:

(i)   the fleets of all the commercial airlines in the world contain a total of approximately 11,000 jet aircraft (excluding Russian manufactured aircraft which are not freely traded) each of which can be expected to have a useful life in excess of 20 years from new;

(ii)   the annual production capacity of the manufacturers of jet aircraft in the western world is approximately 800 units and, between 1970 and 1992 *actual* production averaged under 400 units;

(iii)   three major companies dominate the manufacture of large commercial jet aircraft in the western world (Airbus, Boeing and McDonnell Douglas); British Aerospace and Fokker are important but smaller players; competition between these rivals is fierce but ultimately commercially- and profit-orientated;

(iv)   the enormous costs which would need to be incurred to develop a jet aircraft from scratch (perhaps $5 bn plus) and the power of the major companies established in the market means that there is unlikely to be a major competitor for the above manufacturers for the foreseeable future;

(v)   major advances in aircraft technology take years to develop; the Boeing 7J7, for example, was discussed seriously by Boeing in 1985 with availability scheduled for 1992 and has now been postponed indefinitely. The Boeing 777 concept was first mooted in 1989, launched in October 1990 and is scheduled to enter service in 1995. Improvements are consequently predictable over an adequate timescale to enable adjustments to be made by industry participants and are expensive; they currently focus on improving operating efficiency with the result that airlines continue to be able in many cases to choose between the higher operating costs but lower capital costs of old aircraft and the high capital costs but lower operating costs of new models;

(vi)   jet aircraft remain unrivalled as the most efficient method of international passenger transportation; many areas of the world are still poorly served by air so that even on a conservative assumption of economic growth rates, demand for transport by air looks fundamentally strong albeit subject to cyclicality.

This combination of (i) demonstrated need, (ii) long design lives, (iii) restricted sources of supply, and (iv) long lead-times for technological development indicates that values of well-maintained jet aircraft should hold firm going forward. Inevitably, there will be times when shocks hit the market like the second oil price rise in 1979 and the bankruptcy of a major airline such as Braniff, when prices will fall steeply for a time. In certain other industries, the depression in values caused by such shocks has been exacerbated because manufacturers have continued to produce even without orders thus reinforcing the problem of over-supply, placing further pressure on already-weak values and preventing a balance between supply and demand being re-established. This has occurred particularly where the industry is supplied by a variety of state-owned manufacturers, who have been under strong pressure to avoid politically unpopular plant closures and redundancies. In the airline industry, by contrast, the restricted number of major manufacturers and their primarily commercial orientation should ensure that the supply side of the market adjusts production levels to match reduced demand, enabling equilibrium to be restored. Any depression in values should, therefore, be followed by a recovery within a reasonable period.

For what it is worth, the track record of aircraft values bears out the above analysis. Re-sale studies of various major aircraft types tend to show cyclical variation but with the highs for re-sales of, say, 6 year old aircraft at around 120–130% of original cost and lows at between 50–60%. The relative decline in values experienced during the depression of 1980–2 was followed by a sharp recovery in 1983 onwards.

Be careful, however, about placing too much reliance on average historic re-sale prices – sales tend to be frequent in hard markets as airlines are keen to realise sale profits and purchasers have confidence to invest, but infrequent in soft markets as those who can hang on to existing aircraft do so. Furthermore, inflation helped to maintain $ re-sale values in the '70s; a low inflation environment will tend to make maintenance of such values more difficult. There is no exchange or market for selling aircraft; it can be a complex and time consuming activity.

Note also that my comments about the supply side are complicated by the impact in a weak market of the growth of the major operating lessors whose portfolios grew in the 1980s and who, by 1991, owned approximately 14% of the world fleet. These are not users of aircraft, but traders and financiers, and thus a sale to a lessor is not a sale to a user but a sale to a supplier. The leases they contract with airlines allow the airline to hand-back the aircraft after a pre-determined period (typically 3–9 years) and pay no more. In a depressed market, these lessors start to receive significant numbers of aircraft back from airlines which fail or which are trying to cut capacity to match reduced passenger and cargo demand without selling their owned aircraft. In addition, leasing aircraft which they have ordered from the manufacturers becomes extremely difficult at a reasonable price.

Overall, however, the fundamentals are good both on the demand and supply sides for a financier to have confidence in the strength of values of aircraft over time.

233

6.2.2 Jet Aircraft – Specifics

Within the overall picture described above, individual jet aircraft models will demonstrate markedly different performances in maintaining their values. Much will depend on:

- the breadth of the resale market for the specific aircraft;

- the specification of the aircraft (engine type in particular) and its compatability with specifications used by other operators;

- the extent of competition from other new and second-hand aircraft equipped to fulfil the purpose for which the specific aircraft was designed;

- the model's record and reputation for reliability;

- its relative fuel efficiency in the context of fuel price levels at the time of re-sale;

- proximity to any enforced obsolescence of the aircraft through technical factors and noise or other regulations.

The breadth of demand and impact of engine choice is largely demonstrated by the number of orders and deliveries achieved by the model and by the number and type of operators. A detailed analysis of commonality requires expert analysis of an individual aircraft's specifications. This analysis is important because even aircraft of the same model type, powered by the same engine, can have significantly different performance capabilities and maintenance characteristics. Reliability, of course, is easier to assess for models which have been in service for some time.

Factors relating to competition and enforced obsolescence are usually predictable because of the long lead times associated with aircraft development. Obsolescence associated with tougher environmental standards (e.g. noise and emissions) are, again, usually predictable because of the long period over which such standards are proposed, debated and implemented. Occasionally, however, an accident may point to a weakness in aircraft design which is expensive to fix. This expense will add to the cost of operating a specific aircraft type and is likely to impact its value adversely.

234

The value which will be accorded to relative fuel efficiency will depend on the level of fuel prices and the strength of competing advantages in other models such as capacity, reliability, range and convenience of maintenance.

A precise value in the future for a given model will depend on a complex interaction of general factors, viz economic conditions, inflation, fuel prices, and availability of slots at airports together with the range of specific issues outlined above but it should be possible to establish a range of values to cover hard and soft market conditions based on differing assumptions.

The various organisations specialising in aviation information mentioned in 6.1.1 will provide on request a study of the strengths and weaknesses of a specific model and its likely range of future values as a check for the financier on its own conclusions.

Note also, however, that two virtually identical aircraft, delivered in the same year to different operators, may attract values perhaps 10-20% different on resale after, say, 10 years. The key factors are utilisation and maintenance quality. The major indicator of age in a modern jet aircraft is not chronological age or even hours flown, but rather total cycles flown. One "cycle" is one journey (ie, a take-off and landing). It is on take-off and landing that most wear on an aircraft and its engines occur. A 737-300 which flies 3,500 hours a year on typical journeys ("stage lengths") of 2.5 hours each may, therefore, hold its value better than the same aircraft flown 3,000 hours per year on stage lengths of 45 minutes. The "hour/cycle ratio" in the former case is far preferable. Operation in a corrosive coastal environment may also reduce value by increasing corrosion damage, an airframe's worst enemy. Maintenance needs to be carried out not only on a basis that keeps the aircraft airworthy (ie the standards set by the FAA in the USA or CAA in the UK), but also on a basis which preserves its economic life, with particular attention paid to corrosion prevention. See also 6.5.1. below.

6.3 Transaction Design – Financial Protection
Following the assessment of the operator, the merits of the specific aircraft acquisition and the investment quality of the asset, the financier can look to designing the basic credit aspects of the transaction. The focus

235

will be on both the coverage available from projected operating cash flow and the coverage available in projected future values. For an airline which cannot offer significant financial coverage outside its ability to operate the specific aircraft, it is likely that the financier would be able to consider for a new aircraft the following basic structure:

- an initial advance of 65%–80% of aircraft cost (excluding spares) depending on the perceived risk of the operator, the perceived quality of the asset and the price being paid;

- an amortisation period of 12–15 years with monthly or quarterly payments calculated on a mortgage or equal principal basis; the latter, as demonstrated in Chapter 4, Section 5.9.1, reduces the principal balance outstanding relatively quickly but at the expense of a higher cash flow to the operator – a mixture comprising an initial period of mortgage-style repayments (perhaps 3 years) followed by equal principal repayments is sometimes the most practical compromise;

- both of the above to be in conjunction with a hard-currency debt service ratio which, at its conservatively projected low point, does not fall below 1.20:1; in practice, you may need to demonstrate some flexibility in analysing this ratio, particularly in the first 1-3 years after an aircraft acquisition which is major in the context of the size of the airline — for example, anticipated availability of additional hard currency from the local Central Bank in case of need may enable you to take a more robust view.

First call for the difference between the cost price and the amount of the advance will be the operator. The source of cash may be a sale or trade-in of old equipment or cash built up from trading or raising of equity capital. In some cases, however, airlines do not have access to adequate cash to satisfy this requirement. The difference may then sometimes be made up from one of the following sources of "top-up" funding or security:

- short-medium term (say 2 year) bank letter of credit to secure the excess; failure to renew this support by the operator within, say, 2–3 months before its expiration would constitute an event of default and enable the financier to claim on the letter of credit before it expired and exercise its rights against the aircraft;

- a second mortgage on other equipment operated by the airline in which there is significant equity; this needs careful handling particularly as enforcement would usually require you to buy out the first mortgagee's position before you could act.

- incorporation into the transaction of subordinated debt (often called "mezzanine debt") which, on default by the operator, will rank behind the primary or senior debt for repayment, thereby providing a quasi-equity cushion; providers of such debt are a few, mainly large and experienced, financial institutions who are prepared to include within their portfolios a limited amount of higher risk/higher return loans to improve their average return on assets; two large transactions, involving national carriers in South America, Africa, Asia and Eastern Europe have been completed on this basis.

In the absence of other alternatives, new aircraft acquisitions can sometimes be financed with the benefit of a manufacturer's "deficiency guarantee".

6.3.1   *The Deficiency Guarantee*
The major manufacturers, notwithstanding their limited numbers, compete strongly for most airline orders because the restricted sources of supply are matched, at least in part, by a restricted customer base. Competition is particularly intense for orders accorded any strategic marketing importance.

In this context, manufacturers are sometimes prepared to participate in the financing of certain orders to enable the sale to be completed. The most common form of such participation is the deficiency guarantee, the basics of which are:

- the financier advances in excess of the amount it is prepared to consider as a secured credit risk on the operator (say 90% of cost rather than 70%);

- the manufacturer guarantees that, if the transaction goes into default and the aircraft does not resell for a price sufficient to pay off the remaining principal balance outstanding, then it will pay the first loss thereby incurred subject to a maximum of, say, 20% of the principal balance outstanding on the date of default;

- the manufacturer agrees to assist the financier in remarketing, repairing, storing and maintaining the aircraft after any default.

In effect, therefore, the manufacturer is underwriting the re-sale value of its own equipment – a judgement it is perhaps better qualified than anyone to make. In accepting the guarantee, of course, the financier is exposed to the creditworthiness of the manufacturer and will need to assess that risk as for any guarantor (cf Chapter 5, Section 1.1.1).

6.3.2 Top-Up Security – General Considerations

In considering any top-up security, however, including the deficiency guarantee, I would emphasise two points;

- a sizeable cash contribution from the operator gives it an immediate strong financial incentive to ensure that the transaction works, so that it does not lose the value of that contribution as a result of repossession and forced re-sale at a low price; asset based transactions involving 100% finance are, therefore, relatively unattractive notwithstanding top-up third party guarantees or subordinated debt;

- your security must always be your insurance against failure; as I have emphasised before, do not be carried away by the availability of security to overlook the economics of the proposal and the airline's ability to generate adequate operating cash flow. Adequate cash flow coverage will, of course, be that much more difficult to demonstrate if the airline finances 90% of cost rather than 70%.

6.3.3 Currency

The basic rule for determining currency of repayment is the currency of the repayment source. Prima facie, therefore, an airline with income in a mix of European currencies should finance itself in ECU or one or more of those currencies. The assessment of suitable income for repayment will also need to consider the currency of committed expenditures to arrive at a conclusion as to the currency or currencies in which *net* cash revenues are actually derived.

There is, however, a difficulty in secured transactions for aircraft in this respect. Jet aircraft are priced when new and traded on the second-hand market in US$. Therefore, an airline which finances in £ on delivery at £1 = $1.10 would find itself with a significantly higher debt, expressed in $, if the exchange rate subsequently moved to £1=$1.60. For example, $11 million representing 70% of cost, financed in £ on delivery would be drawn down as £10 million. If £1 million of this were amortised over the first 2 years but the exchange rate changed as above, the debt would then stand at the equivalent of $14.4m or 92% of initial cost. Even if the aircraft value holds up well in $ this is likely to be a debt close to, or in excess of, the re-sale value which considerably limits flexibility for the operator if there is a desire to sell or refinance the equipment. Equally, for the financier, the initial 30% equity cushion in the value of the aircraft has been wiped out.

Going to the other extreme, a financing for a European airline denominated wholly in $ to link into projected asset values may force the airline into default or panic re-sale if the $ appreciates sharply against the European currencies of that airline's income.

The practical solution is often to do one of the following:

- denominate part of the transaction in dollars and part in other currencies to hedge the two exposures, albeit imperfectly; the currency risk thus assumed may require you to reduce the amount you are prepared to finance initially;

- denominate the transaction entirely in other currencies but provide for a security top-up if those currencies appreciate against the dollar to the extent that security cover in the aircraft becomes inadequate; e.g. cash collateral might be required for the additional exposure if both the currency of the financing appreciates by in excess of 15–20% of its exchange rate on delivery and the aircraft is then worth under 135% of the principal balance outstanding;

- denominate the whole transaction in $ and swap part of the payments (say the first 3–4 years) into other currencies leaving time to develop hedging strategies for the later years; the swap risk needs to be addressed in structuring the financing and may again cause the initial amount financed to be reduced.

239

In addition to post-delivery exposure, there is also a pre-delivery risk for an airline whose net cash flow is denominated in a currency other than US$. This arises because a contracted price of $20m for a new aircraft may be, say, equivalent to £12m for a UK charter airline at time of order but the equivalent of £18m by the time delivery occurs. This exposure is particularly acute because of the size of the numbers involved and the lead time between order and delivery (often in excess of 2 years). Forward foreign exchange contracts and currency options can sometimes provide protection to an airline in this respect and should be considered.

6.3.4 *Top-Up Clauses*
In some transactions, it is possible to negotiate all-embracing security top-up clauses which provide that if the value of the aircraft, assessed on say a quarterly basis by independent valuers, drops below a trigger level (e.g. 135% of the principal balance outstanding), then the operator or a guarantor will provide additional security or a prepayment to make up the difference. Failure to do so would give the financier the right to default the transaction and resell the aircraft while its value remains above the amount financed.

The clause, notwithstanding its cumbersome nature to administer, is thus a useful protection and negotiating lever for times when values are under pressure. It is often, however, highly unpopular with operators who can envisage situations where they may be making payments on time and remain able to use the aircraft profitably but find they are deprived of it because they are unable to lodge additional security to cover a situation over which they have no control. In practice, it is unlikely that repossesion would occur as a result of failure to top-up unless the financier believed the operator would soon itself become unviable but it is nevertheless a real and justifiable fear. Many banks, however, have sufficient faith in their ability to assess future asset values to structure transactions without this general provision. They will usually seek specifically to cover any currency risk as described in 6.3.3 above.

6.4 **Transaction Design – Repossession and Legal Protection**
Asset security is clearly valuable to a financier only if:

(a)   until the financing has been repaid in full, no other person or entity can claim a prior right to the asset or the proceeds of sale of that asset; and

(b)   following a default, it can locate and repossess the asset, conclude a sale and re-deliver to a purchaser.

6.4.1 *Developed Countries*

For transactions with airlines in developed countries with long-established and stable legal systems these risks are usually covered by a combination of:

- the financier having legal ownership (and then leasing the aircraft to the operator) or taking a first legal interest/mortgage in the aircraft to secure a loan;

- registration or filing of the financier's interest with the appropriate authorities in the country of the operator.

In certain jurisdictions, notwithstanding that the operator may have economic ownership as defined in Section 3 above, owning and leasing the aircraft will give the financier better legal remedies than lending with a mortgage if the operator becomes bankrupt and better protection through the registration system against the possibility of someone successfully claiming a prior lien. Competent lawyers must, therefore, be closely involved in structuring the legal arrangements to ensure the financier receives the best debt protection available. In others, lenders/lessors may be forced to accept that they may not be able to exercise full control over resale if the operator becomes bankrupt, because of powers accorded to trustees or administrators under applicable bankruptcy regulations (see, for example, the 1986 Insolvency Act in the UK). Again, competent lawyers will be able to advise on mitigation of the consequent legal risks. Beware of legal opinions which state on the one hand that security is enforceable, etc., and, on the other hand, that their opinion does not cover a situation where the airline goes into bankruptcy or administration. Such a 'clean' opinion fails to address the most important questions.

In all cases, financiers will have to accept the practical possibilty that they may have to pay off liens arising from repairs carried out but not reimbursed, landing and navigation fees not paid for etc. before they can take possession of an aircraft following a default. As, for example, the bankruptcy of Hispania in 1989 demonstrated, liens for navigation and landing fees can i) amount to several million dollars and ii) attach to any aircraft in the fleet notwithstanding which aircraft was being operated when the fees were incurred. The financier needs, therefore, to have rights in the documentation to monitor closely the level of such fees being built up and systems in place to ensure that cash-flow problems in an airline are identified early and closely scrutinised.

6.4.2 *Developing Countries*
Transactions with airlines in developing countries where the legal system operates in effect under the control of the government of the day and where the airline is state-owned present different problems. There are risks, however remote, that a government may refuse to allow an aircraft to be re-exported from its country following a default or refuse to de-register it in an attempt to frustrate a re-sale or refuse to recognise a security or ownership interest. Less remote is the possibility that a rescheduling of debt may be sought from lenders to the country generally and that, notwithstanding its security interest and theoretical ability to repossess, a financier may consider that it has no practical alternative but to accept the rescheduling terms; this is a problem especially where a bank has other exposure to a country to protect.

Such risks can be mitigated to satisfactory levels by a combination of some or all of the following:

6.4.2.1 *Selectivity*
* careful selection of transactions so that the aircraft is one which:

  * can fly only internationally

  * generates significant hard currency earnings on the routes it flies

  so that the airline/country concerned will benefit from the aircraft only by ensuring that it can continue to fly internationally to major destinations where a financier could enforce repossession in case of need;

* incorporation into the transaction of a significant down payment by the operator as an immediate investment to protect.

By these mechanisms, the country should have an incentive to co-operate if financial problems occur and, if necessary, prioritise payments to the financier so as not to frustrate its airline's ability to fly the routes which generate the valuable hard currency or so as to maximise the value on a re-sale.

6.4.2.2 *Insulation of Transaction and Government Commitment*

- ensure that the transaction is not one which falls under the category of general country debt by structuring it, possibly, as a lease with ownership of the aircraft outside the country of the operator; to-date offshore leases have not in general been formally included in debt reschedulings;

- avoid transactions where the bank already has a major amount of general country debt to protect, or structure the deal using a creditworthy third party as lessor responsible for achieving repossession in case of need, funded perhaps by you with recourse to the lessor limited to receipts by the lessor under the lease or from sale of the aircraft;

- if a government guarantee would frustrate the objective of isolating the transaction, consider replacing it with a formal undertaking to redeliver, de-register and re-export following default; this will be of particular value if the document includes (i) a pre-signed export licence, (ii) a financial incentive provided by a clause accepting that the government will be liable for damages equivalent to the aircraft's value if the undertaking is not honoured and (iii) a clause that the undertaking is governed by e.g. English Law, albeit that it may not be possible to negotiate such tight protection in all cases.

6.4.2.3 *External Registration*

- reinforce external ownership by registration of the aircraft in a country other than that of the operator, both to protect further against any attempt to lodge prior claims and to avoid any de-registration problems after a default which is followed by repossession outside the country of the operator; this is not always easy or cost effective as aircraft registries in the developed countries are not set up to act as flags of convenience, but can be achieved in certain circumstances particularly for the larger international jets.

6.4.2.4 *Manufacturer Involvement*

- the involvement of the manufacturer as deficiency guarantor will assist a financier both because of the political influence the major companies can exert and the resources they can command should it be necessary physically to arrest an aircraft; such involvement will usually be limited, however, to new aircraft transactions.

6.4.2.5 *Political Risk Insurance*

- Remaining repossession risks can be insured for a maximum of 3 years through the Lloyds and international insurance markets; the cover can be expensive, however, and does not offer complete protection because of:

  - the limited term of the policy (albeit renewal will usually be available) and difficulties in defaulting the lease if renewal cannot be effected.

- The long typical waiting period after the cause for a claim arises before payment becomes due (typically 180 days) during which the commercial policy covering ordinary loss and damage etc. (see 6.5.2) may expire or be cancelled at 7–30 days notice.

- Uncertainties arise from the possibility that it may prove difficult to demonstrate that confidentiality undertakings from the insured lessor/lender have been honoured because of the number of parties involved in a typical transaction; if the airline's government is informed of the existence of the policy, there is a danger it could thereby be invalidated.

- Some of the problems can sometimes be overcome for new aircraft transactions by arrangement of back-up policies from the export credit agency of the country of the relevant manufacturer, which will take effect if renewal of the initial 3-year policy cannot be achieved at an agreed maximum cost. In addition contingency insurance can be obtained to cover any cancellation or expiry of the commercial policy during the waiting period.

In concluding this section, I should once again emphasise that availability of external registration, political risk insurance etc., must not be allowed

244

to cloud your assessment of the integrity of the borrower/lessee and its government and the viability of the transaction; your best protection against loss will always be to choose and structure transactions where the underlying project can be seen to have good prospects of success.

I should emphasise also that properly structured secured transactions involving international aircraft for developing countries represent some of the most attractive business in those nations. The value of jet aircraft as a direct hard currency generator (fares etc.) and indirect hard currency generator (tourist development and improved communications), together with the ability of such aircraft to maintain their investment value, have led several governments to keep payments under financing arrangements related to such aircraft current notwithstanding delays, reschedulings and moratoria on other debt.

6.5   Transaction Design – Asset Value Protection

6.5.1   *Maintenance*

You may have faith in the ability of a specific aircraft model to maintain a reasonable value. The value of an individual aircraft of that model type, however, will be significantly affected by the way it is maintained and operated. For this reason, the financier in a secured transaction should focus with engineering advisers closely on:

* maintenance standards set in the financing documentation;

* who is to carry out the maintenance and the documentation of provisions to ensure that any change in those responsible for maintenance is subject to the financier's approval; major airlines often provide maintenance and spares pooling services to smaller ones;

* the terms of the maintenance programme to be adopted by the airline (focus in particular on whether the programme will promote longevity in addition to airworthiness — cf 6.2.2 above);

* rights for the financier to inspect the condition of the aircraft and its technical records periodically and to require any deficiencies discovered to be remedied;

- ensuring, through assignment, that the financier will receive the benefit of all manufacturer's warranties should it ever repossess the aircraft;

- the possibility of agreeing with the airline that it will contribute cash monthly into a reserve account to pay for major checks and overhauls.

By these means, the financier should ensure that the value of the aircraft is most efficiently protected.

6.5.2 *Insurance*

The airline will be required to maintain commercial insurance to cover both it and the financier against:

(a)   loss of, and damage to, the aircraft through accidents;

(b)   loss of, and damage to, the aircraft from acts of war, nationalisation, formal confiscation, hijacking, etc (usually excluding deprivation of use by the airline's own government, such as refusal to grant an export licence or to de-register etc, which will be covered, if at all, by a political risk policy);

(c)   liability claims from third parties.

The benefits of (a) and (b) will usually be formally assigned to the financier to give him control over application of insurance proceeds. The terms of such insurance should be agreed with the airline in conjunction with competent insurance and legal advisors.

7.   ASSET VALUE RISK

As summarised in Section 5.4 above, Asset Value Risk or residual value exposure arises for a financier in a transaction where the borrower or lessee is not committed to pay the full cost of the aircraft over time but may, after an initial rental or loan period, return the aircraft leaving the financier to recover its remaining investment by re-lease or re-sale of the aircraft.

To some, banking is a business involved with credit risk not asset value risk and some banks will not contemplate assumption of any material

246

exposure of this type. Recent developments have reinforced this view. Furthermore, US banks are restricted in their ability to assume such risk by applicable banking regulations. Airlines, however, continue to look to financiers to assume such risks:

- to enable them to exercise more flexibility in managing the composition of their fleets;

- to reduce capital expenditure requirements and their exposure to possible declines in the value of their equipment; and

- to achieve off-balance-sheet treatment for their aircraft financing obligations.

In addition, lessors often need banks to share the asset value risks which they assume at the end of operating leases. A limited number of banks involved in financing jet aircraft still regard this need as an opportunity and are willing to assume such risks to a limited extent. They, therefore, participate in transactions as asset value guarantors or lessors in non-full payout transactions, or as limited recourse lenders into operating lease transactions. They may be compensated for the additional risk by one or more of i) a premium in the interest rate and/or ii) a share in, or the whole of, any excess in the value of the aircraft at the expiry of the financing period. Asset value risk will arise primarily in two different types of transactions. In the first case, an airline will usually have the option on a given date or series of dates ("Windows") either to return the aircraft or continue with an underlying full payout transaction on pre-agreed terms – this is "Option Financing" and the airline usually is entitled to most of the equity in the value of the aircraft over the financier's outstanding investment. Most banks' involvement in asset value risk is of this type. In the second case, the airline may have no renewal options or a renewal option at prevailing fair market rates – this is "Operating Leasing". A hybrid version is also seen where the lessee has an option to purchase on a specified date or dates at a fixed price which is in excess of the lessor's then capital outstanding. Banks have limited direct involvement in those latter activities as yet but many have become involved as lenders with major non-bank operating lessors (e.g. GPA in Ireland and ILFC in the USA), sometimes with recourse limited to specific aircraft and receivables under operating leases, whilst others have taken equity stakes in such companies. They are, therefore, closely involved with the related risks albeit in an indirect way.

In considering asset value risk, the financier needs to focus on:

7.1 Asset Quality
See Section 6.2 above. The same considerations apply but are brought more sharply into focus as the airline has no obligation to continue to use the aircraft beyond the window date or lease expiry and the financier has no recourse to the airline for the asset value exposure it assumes if the aircraft value on that date is below expectations.

7.2 Likelihood of Return
A transaction which is a non-renewable operating lease and where the airline has no equity interest in the aircraft dictates that the aircraft will in all probability be returned to the financier at maturity; the asset value exposure is thus very real. Certain option lease arrangements, however, are arranged more to achieve off-balance-sheet treatment rather than to achieve the full walk-away flexibility of an operating lease. The airline retains the equity value in the aircraft and may, therefore, accept a degree of asset risk itself on the window dates which would crystallise before the risk assumed by the financiers, or accept that a penalty rental becomes payable if the return option is exercised. If these features are combined with the operator having a clear long-term need for the aircraft in question, then the likelihood of the aircraft being returned is low. For, even if the aircraft is worth less than expected on the window date, the airline may prefer to continue operating in anticipation of an upturn rather than crystallise its own first loss and deprive itself of the use of the aircraft.

7.3 Remarketing Capability
Banks taking an asset value risk must be confident of their own ability to remarket an aircraft in conjunction with technical advisors in case of need, or assume the risk only in a sharing capacity with other banks or operating lessors with such expertise and/or a manufacturer. As with their participation in secured credit risk transactions to achieve sales of their aircraft, the manufacturers may also be prepared to take limited asset value risk in certain circumstances in a higher risk position than the banks, to achieve the same objective. They will then usually be prepared

to act as agent in remarketing the equipment if a return option is exercised, a valuable benefit to others sharing the same risk at lower levels.

7.4 Return Conditions

As emphasised in Section 6.5.1 above, the condition of an aircraft on re-sale will be a key factor in its re-sale value. It is, therefore, crucial that detailed provisions are negotiated with the airline to cover the condition in which the aircraft must be redelivered if a return option is exercised. Banks assuming asset value risk must have familiarity with the factors affecting an individual aircraft's value and use engineering advisers to advise on the specific provisions and the necessary inspection/testing rights to ensure they are complied with.

7.5 Currency

Section 6.3.3 above indicated the need to focus on the fact that jet aircraft are generally traded in US$. Asset Value Risk must, therefore, be assumed in US$. If the underlying financing is in a different currency, then the exposure assumed by the financiers on the return dates has to be converted to $ either by the airline taking the risk or through the swap or foreign exchange markets.

7.6 Return Dates and Notice Periods

Banks and manufacturers assuming asset value risk will wish both to limit the number of return dates, so as to minimise the exposure assumed, and to ensure that they receive sufficient notice that a return option is to be exercised so as to enable them to attempt to negotiate a sale or re-lease before the return date occurs. Return options are, therefore, usually confined to a maximum of 2-3 specific dates in a 12–15 year financing period with a minimum of 6 months' notice required before any such return date can be exercised. A notice period of 12–18 months is preferable to allow time for orderly marketing.

7.7 Asset Value Risk Sharing – Slice Liabilities

Option financing is often structured so that the underlying financing is a full-payout tax-based lease, where the lessor's credit risk on the lessee may or may not be guaranteed by aircraft financing banks.

Linked to this structure are options for the airline to return the aircraft on specific dates and for a syndicate of asset value guarantors then to pay off the lessor or assume the lease obligations and seek to recoup the payment by re-sale or re-lease of the aircraft. The lessor's outstanding capital investment on a return or window date is thus what needs to be covered by the asset value guarantors. Such guarantors may, as indicated above, include the airline, a manufacturer and a group of banks with their respective risks denominated in "slices". Thus, for example, if a return option is agreed for 5 years from delivery and the lessor's termination sum or outstanding capital investment at that stage is to be 80% of cost, it may be agreed that if the aircraft does not resell for that amount then:

(a)   the first loss up to 10% of cost will be borne by the airline (the first slice risk);

(b)   the second loss up to the next 15% of cost be borne by the manufacturer or operating lessor (the second slice risk);

(c)   the third slice being the remaining 55% of cost be borne by a group of banks (the third slice risk).

The banks thus assume the largest risk in absolute terms but in the least risky position.

The return option will sometimes be exercisable only if the airline is not in default under its obligations under the underlying financing and can comply with the return conditions. Any default will cause it to be liable in full for the whole of the lessor's capital outstanding and support (if any) from the manufacturer for this risk will be in the form of the deficiency guarantee described in 6.3.1 above.

As alternatives, asset value risk may be covered by:

(i)   a residual value insurance policy available from a small number of institutions prepared to insure an interested party against failure to achieve an agreed price on re-sale of an aircraft on a given date, or

(ii)   more commonly in certain other industries than the airline industry, a "buy-back" from the manufacturer, or

250

(iii)   a "put" to a creditworthy third party such as an operating lessor at a pre-
        agreed price.

7.8   Pricing

Pure operating lessors take a significant portion of their return in the
upside available to them in the value of the aircraft over their outstanding
capital investment on expiry of a lease. Asset value guarantors in option
financing transactions typically receive a fee for the risk they assume with
the upside retained in whole or in large part by the airline. This fee may
either (i) be paid up-front and expressed as a percentage of the aircraft
cost or value guaranteed, or (ii) be paid as a per annum fee during the
financing period. The level of fee relates primarily to the perceived risk
assumed, but a bank taking the third slice risk described in 6.7 above
might expect to receive the equivalent of between 1%–2% flat on the cost
of the aircraft (or 2%–4% of the risk assumed) depending on the specific
model, the airline and financing structure.

7.9   Conclusions on Asset Value Risk

Pure operating leases have proved especially popular with airlines unable
to finance purchase of aircraft because of the high capital cost involved.
Such leases have enabled them to operate aircraft and pay relatively low
monthly financing charges. Certain larger airlines have also taken advantage
of the low cash flow and low capital commitment to finance part of their
fleet in this way thereby also enhancing their flexibility to adjust their
fleet composition. Lessees under these arrangements will, as mentioned
above, sometimes be granted purchase options to enable them to take an
ownership interest in the aircraft, but usually at a price well in excess of
the lessor's amortised capital investment. It is thus the cash flow, capital
and flexibility factors which attract operators and have resulted in the fast
growth of the market.

Option leasing has been restricted in the main to a few of the more
major airlines looking to combine the advantages of tax-based full-payout
financing with flexibility to walk away and off-balance-sheet treatment,
without sacrificing their interest in the equity value of the aircraft financed.
This market will remain restricted for the foreseeable future.

A strong element of caution is, however, required. The fundamentals
of aircraft values look strong for the reasons I have explained in 6.2.

Nevertheless, no person has a perfect vision of the future and losses could be substantial for those taking high residual value positions if asset values drop sharply for whatever reason for a sustained period and airlines elect to exercise return options. Exposure of this type should, therefore, be strictly limited and closely monitored on both a portfolio and individual transaction basis.

8. TAX BASED FINANCING

Jet aircraft as major capital assets attract tax allowances or credits in various countries as an incentive to purchasers to acquire them and thereby enhance the productive base of the economy. These "benefits" are usually in the form of accelerated depreciation whereby, as described in Chapter 2, Section 4, purchasers are able to set off against their taxable profits in the earlier years of a transaction higher amounts than conventional depreciation would indicate. For example, in the UK aircraft can be depreciated for tax purposes on the basis of 25% p.a. writing down allowances whereas accounting depreciation might be calculated to reflect a useful life of 12 to 15 years. In some countries, "benefits" also include Investment Tax Credits where, in addition to depreciation allowances, an immediate tax deduction of a specific percentage of cost is granted to the purchaser.

Airlines, with their high capital expenditure requirements and fixed asset intensity often do not have adequate taxable profits to take full advantage of available benefits. Tax-based leasing has, therefore, been a common form of financing for aircraft whereby the asset is bought by a lessor able to take full advantage of the benefits who then passes on much of the value of those benefits to the airline in the form of a low lease rate. Such lease arrangements include the famous "*leveraged*" lease structure, available in certain countries (e.g. USA and Japan) but not the UK, whereby a lessor or investor invests only 20% or so of the aircraft cost, with the balance provided by lenders who advance funds without recourse to the lessor/investor. Repayment for those lenders comes in the form of an assignment to them by the lessor of rentals payable by the lessee. The investor receives its return primarily from the tax depreciation it can claim, this benefit being particularly significant because it can be claimed on 100% of cost notwithstanding that the investor's investment is only 20%. This form of financing originated in the USA in the 1970s and remains the most common form of financing for aircraft acquisitions by the major US domestic airlines. Most banks' involvement is as lenders who look to a combination of (i) the airline's ability to pay the committed lease rentals (usually calculated to be adequate to amortise the debt in full with no residual exposure) and (ii) a mortgage over the aircraft leased. Lease terms in the USA have now become as long as 20 plus years for the few major carriers perceived as strong credits. Most banks are unwilling to lend for such a term. Sometimes, therefore, the debt portion is split into tranches with banks taking a shorter term tranche and insurance companies/ pension funds taking a longer term portion.

In some circumstances, lease structures have also enabled a lessor to claim benefits in one country and the lessee or a sub-lessor in another, the so-called "double dip". Such opportunities arise usually from differences in the definition of ownership for tax purposes, some jurisdictions using legal ownership and some economic ownership to determine availability of allowances (see Section 4 above for the difference), enabling "ownership" to be established for tax purposes in more than one country.

Since 1987, many transactions for higher quality airlines have been completed on a "double-dip" basis, using a Japanese Leveraged Lease to add on benefits to tax allowances available to an airline in its own country. Some international airlines have also been able to use US leveraged leases structured through foreign sales corporations (FSC leases). This technique has had limited application because: (i) it can be used only for aircraft manufactured in the USA and (ii) attractive economies can be produced only if the lenders are willing to lend long-term (12+ years) without a mortgage on the aircraft.

The trend around the world is for availability of tax allowances to be reduced and for their value also to be reduced as tax rates on businesses are brought down. The trend is particularly evident in respect of double dip opportunities and cross-border leasing from one country to another, with governments seeking for understandable reasons to restrict the availability of tax allowances to situations where the asset will be used to benefit the economy of its own country.

The Japanese Leveraged Lease remains popular at the time of writing, but is under increasingly intense scrutiny by the authorities in Japan. In

1988, Present Value Benefits of up to 12% were available using this technique, but recent tightening of regulations has reduced this to around 6%. An emerging technique involves utilising certain tax credits available to exporters of US manufactured goods who export through a "foreign sales corporation". These have been christened FISC transactions and, potentially, can yield benefits above those available from Japan depending on the structure. Their application is limited because they can be used only for US-manufactured aircraft exported from the USA and must be structured, to yield the highest benefit, without giving a mortgage over the aircraft to the lenders.

Despite the increasing restrictions on cross-border structures, tax-based leasing still has an important role to play and provides opportunities for financiers with the relevant expertise to achieve good yields through the added value a tax-based structure can bring. Beware, however, in considering any such transaction of the TAX RISKS. Such risks are:

• that the allowances on which the transaction is based will not in the event be available or be disallowed;

• that changes in the tax regime or in the level of tax rates may significantly increase the costs involved in the transaction;

• that withholding taxes may be applied to cross-border payments inherent in double-dip structures.

The likelihood of such tax risks crystallising needs to be addressed. The exposure of the lender into the lease structure will usually be covered by indemnities from the lessee but this then adds to the credit exposure the lender takes on the lessee, which risk again needs to be closely considered.

There may also be other disadvantages in tax-based transactions in the form of reduced flexibility to terminate the deal early for whatever reason, high documentation and legal costs, complexity and restricted availability of currencies. These transactions, therefore, need to be handled with particular care.

9. EXPORT CREDIT FINANCING
As a means to promote exports, the major OECD countries usually have government-sponsored finance packages available to fund exports of capital

equipment. The institutions providing this financial support are commonly referred to as Export Credit Agencies or ECAs. Such financial support has been available to support sales by the various aircraft and engine manufacturers for many years. Non-US buyers of aircraft sold by Boeing and McDonnell Douglas may be able to obtain financial support from the Export-Import Bank of the United States (EXIM). Overseas buyers of Airbus products may be eligible for support from a consortium of ECGD (UK), COFACE (France) and HERMES (Germany). The precise terms and conditions of the financing support available from the individual ECAs differ. The broad parameters, however, are governed by LASU (Long Range Aircraft Sector Understanding) under which the ECAs of the USA, European Community members, Japan, Canada, Sweden and others agreed a set of guidelines for such financing to prevent excessive promotion of exports through subsidised financial packages.

Important elements of the LASU (signed in April 1990) are:

1.   the maximum amount financed may not exceed 85% of the Aircraft Cost (including spare engines and spare parts);

2.   the maximum term of a financing for a jet aircraft may not exceed 12 years with no balloon;

3.   if an ECA provides direct financing, the minimum interest rate is set based on 10-year bond yields for the relevant currency plus a spread. There are, however, no interest rate guidelines for finance provided against a guarantee of an ECA provided that the 85%/12 year rules are not broken.

Although the position appears not to be entirely clear, each ECA does not generally offer finance to a buyer located in its own country or the country of another ECA which is the home country of a rival manufacturer. For example, EXIM cannot provide financial support to British Airways nor can the European ECAs provide financial support to United Airlines. The rationale for this is that, if Airbus, for example, were permitted to offer European ECA finance to United, Boeing and McDonnell Douglas would be disadvantaged because Eximbank can only support exports, not sales by a US manufacturer to a US buyer.

In the 1970s and early 1980s, ECA financing was much in demand because the commercial aircraft finance market was not well developed. In the mid to late 1980s, demand for ECA finance fell away sharply as the ECAs tightened up their terms and conditions in order to reduce subsidies and as the commercial aircraft finance market rapidly developed. During the late 1980s, even middle tier airlines were able to obtain 100% finance on tax-subsidised terms through Japanese leveraged leases and other products. Fifteen year finance terms were common.

Since 1990/1, however, commercial loan finance has become less readily available and more expensive, as discussed earlier. Tax-subsidised transactions are available only to a few top-tier carriers. ECA finance is, therefore, very much back in fashion. Many banks regard an ECA guarantee as equivalent to an OECD government guarantee and weight a loan supported by such a guarantee at 0% for capital adequacy purposes.

Competition to obtain mandates to underwrite and arrange ECA-supported deals is currently fierce. The competition tends to focus on the interest rate to be charged on the guaranteed portion and on whether financing for the 15% non-guaranteed portion can be arranged. A few deals have been done where an EXIM-guaranteed loan has formed the debt element of a Japanese leveraged lease.

ECA finance, however, is not a replacement for commercial finance or operating lease finance. All ECAs have exposure limits and will not be able to fund all deliveries. Each have their own credit criteria and will not accept all airlines. US and many European airlines are not eligible for such finance. Most ECAs tend to prefer government-owned airlines supported by a government guarantee. Current market conditions, however, dictate that we shall see a large number of ECA-supported transactions for the next few years.

10. CONCLUSIONS

Generally, there is no mystery about aircraft financing. Like any other it requires a good knowledge of the industry in which you are operating, the impact of country risk and the needs of, and risks associated with, customers in that field. The more asset-based your approach, the more you need to reinforce this credit and market knowledge with technical knowledge of aircraft and the contacts and expertise to enable you to remarket alongside competent independent engineering and other advisers. This dictates a concentrated and specialised approach to the industry to enable such competence to be developed.

Even a conservative forecast of traffic growth and replacement needs of old aircraft dictate that 5,000 new aircraft will need to be built over the next ten years at a cost in excess of $350bn. Second hand transactions will present further financing requirements. In this situation, the industry is one which provides excellent opportunities for banking business if handled carefully and should continue to be a major market for the foreseeable future.

CHAPTER 7

Syndicated Facilities

by
Peter Wiseman; *updated by* Alby Cator and Chris Porter

1. INTRODUCTION: HISTORY OF THE SYNDICATED LOAN

The features of the euro-market in its infancy were primarily short maturities and relatively modest amounts. Rollover of facilities became a feature, but as in many evolving markets there was scepticism and caution. Eurobonds had emerged as the traditional form of mega-financing and it was to this background that the syndicated facility came into being.

The first syndicated loans appeared in New York in 1967, but the first real impact on European markets was made by Bankers Trust in arranging a euro US$100M loan for Austria in 1968. Two years later I.M.I. of Italy raised a euro US$200M five year loan which, for the first time, reflected the ability of governments and their state owned entities to raise balance of payments finance from commercial banks.

Although the most prominent feature of these facilities was their size, the development highlighted to borrowers in many sectors real administrative benefits. The ready ability to get a group of banks together within the same document, to be able to negotiate only one loan and to be able to have the banks assume much of the administrative burden of operations, attracted corporate and sovereign borrowers alike.

The traditional bond markets now had real competition as the syndicated loan appealed to many potential lenders in the London markets. During the 1960s more and more banks established a London presence, with the American banks particularly anxious to draw funds from the euro-dollar markets and repatriate back to the USA. Following the fall of US interest rates in the '70s this flow was reversed. The syndicated market grew on the back of asset hungry banks and by exported dollars.

In the early days, the arranging/lead management roles and, indeed, the participations, which are explained later, were dominated by the major American banks. But, gradually, the UK and other European banks began looking to the International Sovereign Markets as an alternative to their traditional domestic markets for expansion of their lending. However, it was 1971 before the Japanese banks entered this arena to be followed less than a year later by the first German bank. The level of interest from potential borrowers and lenders in the early '70s fuelled activity in excess of $20bn in 1973, but then the trend of longer maturities and finer pricing which had been a feature was reversed in 1974 largely as a result of a combination of the reduction in supply of off-shore dollars and the collapse of Herstatt Bank. The demise of the latter brought sharply into focus the issues of banking liquidity, the stability of deposit bases and the lengthening of maturities, which had become increasingly exaggerated by the syndicated loan market.

In late 1974 and 1975 there was an erosion of syndicated lending, created by tighter credit appraisal and increased costs to the potential borrowers. Nevertheless, by the end of 1976 the competitiveness and confidence had returned to the financial community and the syndicated loan market flourished until the end of the decade. The market has undergone other temporary reverses notably as a result of heavy exposure to Latin America in the early '80s, when the banking community at large, but particularly the American, was faced with the very real impact of non-performing loans on its balance sheets.

SYNDICATED LOANS
LOANS – VOLUME (1981–1992) ($M)

1981	1982	1983	1984	1985	1986
181,248	152,875	98,629*	194,463	181,048	216,492

1987	1988	1989	1990	1991	1992
334,112	463,693	645,941	590,938	570,495	612,185

*Reflects a downturn in sovereign lending in the aftermath of the LDC re-scheduling. The subsequent increased volumes, particularly in 1987 and 1988, reflect the considerable levels of activity in the UK and USA corporate markets. Depressed figures in 1990 and 1991 reflect banks' capital adequacy concerns and the impact of the Gulf War on confidence.

Having, in these early pages, set the scene as to the origins and capabilities of syndicated facilities, I shall now, in greater detail, describe the salient features today including the roles, the benefits and market developments.

2. MARKETING OF A SYNDICATED FACILITY

In explaining earlier the evolution of the syndicated market two important factors were highlighted, namely amount and administrative saving. These remain key features when evolving a marketing strategy to a potential borrower.

The type of customer seeking syndicated facilities now extends well beyond the sovereign borrower and its related entities, to a wide variety of European, US and South East Asian corporates. A syndicated product is now often a viable option for local authorities, building societies and other financial institutions, and will be employed for purposes beyond working capital/general corporate needs, such as acquisition and project financing, management buyouts and structured transactions including off balance sheet leases and receivables financings.

In the early days syndication was always viewed as the realistic alternative to the bond markets as a means of raising, from financial institutions and investors, large portions of finance not traditionally available from banks on a "one to one" basis.

From a bank's viewpoint, to retain sole banking relationships with all its customers may be an ideal. In reality, however, we have to accept that it is not possible to meet all the financial needs of all our customers and that, in turn, many of our customers believe it healthy to be multi-banked to engender the necessary competitive element in their financings.

How does a banker identify a potential syndicated need? Essentially the exercise is part of the normal research undertaken prior to any marketing call and opportunities will normally arise from the size of requirement. Such opportunities can evolve for a variety of reasons. As facilities are predominantly medium term (between say three and ten years) the shape, structure and strength of a corporate balance sheet or the strength of a sovereign state's economy are paramount.

Whilst the above scenario is constant in all marketing approaches, the key thinking in most cases must be centred on attempting to meet each potential borrower's known or perceived needs. In illustrating this I shall categorise the types of customers and facilities and suggest that certain factors be borne in mind prior to any marketing approach.

2.1 Sovereign or Related Entities

Often, because of the size of the requirement, this type of need can only be met via the syndicated route; for example in 1982 the Republic of France raised $4 billion and in 1983 the Kingdom of Sweden raised $1.6bn. The amount may determine the number and selection of banks a borrower wishes to work together in arranging the finance because many such entities have been regular visitors to the market and they have achieved mature relationships with a large number of financial institutions. In turn these banks will maintain a regular dialogue with, and expect to be approached by, their customers when a borrowing need is evident.

This relationship imposes on the lenders a need to be very up to date in their knowledge of the borrower's financial state, of market attitudes and pricing and to be armed with a good idea of their own institution's appetite for the likely proposition.

Many sovereign borrowers have been able to access the growing number of banks widening their lending base beyond traditional domestic horizons and developing a syndicated market appetite. Traditional euro-dollar financings have been extended to other freely available euro- and domestic currencies and certain deals have emerged in ECUs, primarily in this sector. Many of the sophisticated borrowers have sought more refined hybrid instruments to achieve longer maturities and finer pricing. Sovereign borrowers have used related entities to enable utilisation of tax effective instruments which have become increasingly popular with borrowers and lenders alike. In this regard, banks have been able to reduce interest margins, thereby reducing costs to borrowers, by the utilisation of benefits arising from double taxation agreements, other tax treaties and the increasing use of derivatives.

In spite of the harsh experiences of many lenders referred to earlier relative to Latin America and the rescheduling countries in general, market appetite for sovereign risk has remained high, albeit the lessons learned in the early '80s have resulted in a greater selectivity by the banking community and regular appraisal of country risk.

2.2 Corporate Sector

It is in this sector that the most radical changes have been seen in recent years. A rapidly moving market has made the task of the bank marketeer increasingly difficult. In general, corporate borrowers have become more sophisticated and demanding in their requirements.

An increasing movement away from sole banking arrangements has enabled a more competitive environment to prevail and has heightened the need for marketeers to be more innovative. We shall deal later with the hybrid instruments which have emerged; however, the basic roles and terminology remain common to any syndicated product.

It must be the objective of any lending banker to seek to preserve and expand his customer relationships and, wherever possible, to meet their needs ahead of the competition. Clearly, therefore, syndication, by definition, does contain the inherent threat of competition from rival institutions but conversely it creates new opportunities.

To advocate syndication where the needs of a customer could be met by an individual bank obviously opens up competition; to this extent all marketeers must be satisfied as to the ability of their own institutions to maintain the pre-eminent relationship. From time to time banks will have their own lending and balance sheet constraints which can be circumvented only by involving other lenders. However, it is worth emphasising at this point that syndication should never be used as a means of raising or off-loading finance which cannot be justified on pure risk grounds.

Therefore, in assessing the approach to any corporate, it is important for the marketeer to have an awareness of competitor activities and aspirations and to determine whether syndication poses a threat or offers an opportunity. From the customer's perception, to be multi-banked does create the likelihood of healthy competition and ensures that its organisation is not solely reliant upon the policy or whim of any one bank.

263

Many corporate borrowers will have expanded their panel of bankers as their financial needs have increased and will often feel that a syndicated product offers the opportunity of satisfying the appetites of those institutions seeking to establish or further a relationship. Whereas, in the sovereign market, groups of lead managers/arrangers are relatively common, the sole arranger role has been the most coveted in syndicated facilities within the corporate sector. Expansion, particularly by acquisition, has often created a syndicated loan need and many banks have sought to take substantial underwriting positions in the series of mega-takeovers which have featured in the market. Highly leveraged management buyouts have provided a number of potentially more lucrative lending opportunities both for senior and mezzanine debt to those institutions which have resourced specialist departments to structure and package buyouts/buyins. These opportunities are in addition to debt restructuring which has often been an issue to be considered by borrowers and lenders for syndication.

During the 1980s the corporate syndicated market saw the evolution of a string of hybrid instruments, such as the RUFs, NIFs and MOFs*, which resulted in a continuing erosion of returns to bankers. Declining borrowing margins focus attention on fee income, which, in turn, highlights the enhanced value of an arranging role over that of a participation. This emphasis on fee income has led to bankers, as well as borrowers, looking to other markets, as outlined below, to extend syndicated facilities.

2.3 Project Finance

Globally, this type of finance, by virtue of its size and nature, has been an obvious area of development. Niche expertise has developed within most of the major institutions for handling specialised sectors, notably the oil and gas industries. In recent years the most highly visible UK examples of project financing were the debt raising exercise for Eurotunnel and various project financings for gas-fired power stations. The attendant risks, in what are often limited or non-recourse facilities, reflect in the returns and the preference of most banks to see the risk shared amongst a group of lenders.

*RUF – Revolving Underwriting Facility
  NIF – Note Issuance Facility } Infrequently seen in the 1990s
  MOF – Multi-Option Facility

2.4 Financial Sector

Over the years provision by banks of facilities to institutions which might arguably be viewed as competitors to the banks has been a constant dilemma. However, in the mid '80s many banks, notably the UK merchant banks, saw a lucrative way of satisfying market appetite by involving Japanese banks, which, with their high level of liquidity, had been keen to achieve an expansion of their sterling asset base. The late 1980s and early 1990s saw a spate of UK Building Society (institutions which provide mortgage finance) syndicated facilities, both in sterling and euro-dollars, and many providers of home loan mortgages funded their own book by raising funds from other lenders against packages of the underlying mortgages (see 'Securitisation' – Chapter 13).

2.5 Local Authority Sector

Traditionally, Local Authorities in the United Kingdom have been able to fund themselves through the Public Works Loans Board. However, as the infrastructure in many locations needed the injection of substantial capital, which in many cases had been constrained by legislation, then Local Authorities and their brokers sought the financial assistance of the banking sector to meet this demand.

The emergence of Syndicated Deferred Purchase Schemes resulted in a substantial activity in the London markets in late '85/early '86 and, whilst UK government legislation put a temporary block on such facilities, there is little doubt that this will remain a niche sector of the syndicated loan market.

2.6 Non-Debt Facilities

Whilst the references to date have been to provision of syndicated debt financing, nevertheless, the concept of syndication has extended, and can extend, to bonding, letters of credit and documentary credits. In each case any decision to syndicate would, again, be largely dictated by size. In the USA letters of credit to support corporate commercial paper programmes have often involved the concept of risk sharing amongst a group of banks. Such facilities will often involve a single bank in the role of issuing the letter of credit with the remainder of the syndicate taking risk sharing participations.

Bonding, in particular, does have the inherent difficulty of the acceptability of the beneficiary to potential participants. However, syndication has proved successful in such areas as the Eurotunnel bonding and in supporting major UK exporters.

In the provision of bonding or letter of credit business consideration must be given to the balance sheet costs a bank might incur in fronting the transaction.

3. BENEFITS OF SYNDICATED FACILITIES

Before turning to the various roles which are comprised in a syndicated credit this seems the appropriate point to reflect, briefly, on the benefits to lenders of a syndicated product. On-going interest income represents an important concern. However, the market has now become extremely fee orientated. Originally, those commercial banking institutions with substantial balance sheets had sought rewards from substantial underwritings and loans whilst many of the merchant banks and investment houses had preferred to undertake arranging roles which meant earning fees without assuming a lending commitment. Annual commitment fees have helped the enhancement of returns and, in general, it has appeared that borrowers have been less sensitive to the payment of fees for syndicated, as opposed to bilateral, facilities. The growing strength of many borrowers (particularly the top UK and US corporates) has been further underlined by borrowers seeking to dispense with an arranger and either setting up their own bank lending groups or 'imposing' similar or identical terms on individual banks thereby mitigating or avoiding the need to pay front end fees. Where individual deals are arranged on similar terms and conditions with a range of banks by the borrower itself they are referred to as 'Bi-laterals'.

It is a feature of the syndicated market, as with other aspects of lending, that high commitment produces substantial up front income in addition to high visibility. The income factor must be evaluated carefully by the banker and any bank's final take in a transaction may be determined by its desire to enhance its return on assets.

To underwrite a transaction and then sell down to a target figure does afford an arranger/lead manager or underwriter the potential benefit of an enhanced return on its ultimate participation.

Example of enhancement of return by selling down

Details of a syndicated loan are:

Total amount	:	US$100m
Term	:	10 years
Interest	:	LIBOR (9$\frac{1}{2}$% p.a.) plus $\frac{1}{2}$% mark-up, total 10% p.a.
Fees	:	Front end $\frac{1}{2}$% Facility fee $\frac{1}{4}$% p.a.

N.B. The 'Facility Fee' is payable regardless of the level of utilisation.

If a bank underwrites US$25m of the loan and there is no selling down so that, in fact, it also lends US$25m for ten years, its overall return, i.e. by annualising the fees and adding them to the mark-up over LIBOR, will be:

0.83% over LIBOR (on an annualised basis)

However, if that same bank underwrites US$25m but then sells down to managers, co-managers and participants so that it actually lends only US$5m for ten years, it would have to pass on, say $\frac{1}{4}$% by way of a front end fee to those banks, retaining a $\frac{1}{4}$% flat front end (underwriting) fee for itself. It would, of course, receive the $\frac{1}{4}$% p.a. commitment fee on the amount it was committed to lend i.e. US$5m. Under this scenario the effective, annual return for lending will be:

0.99% over LIBOR (on an annualised basis)

Hence the return on capital employed will be substantially improved and the bank will not be building up its balance sheet but rather leaving capacity for involvement in other facilities.

In the next section we shall illustrate in more detail the other benefits which can accrue from the roles in a syndicated facility.

4. THE ROLES AND REWARDS IN A SYNDICATED CREDIT

Many of the larger facilities are arranged or co-ordinated by a group of banks and a feature of these types of credits is the way in which the various roles are distributed amongst the banks forming the lead group.

Before looking at the roles in more detail it is important to understand the significance and benefits of the various levels of involvement in a facility.

Later in this section under the heading of publicity, two tombstones illustrate typical sovereign and corporate transactions. The Phillips Petroleum Company, Norway facility provides an example of an underwriting and arranging group, where the deal is subsequently syndicated down to participants, designated lead managers and managers. The Irish Permanent Building Society transaction reflects the now more traditional sole arranging role involving selldown to other banks.

The roles normally seen in a syndicated loan are:

Arranger(s): These obtain the mandate from the borrower to put together a syndicate for the proposed facility. They will also possibly underwrite the facility, whilst expecting to be able to "sell down" a large part of their commitment to the Lead Managers, Managers and Participants. The Arranger will take responsibility for the running of the syndication process, e.g. books, documentation, signing, publicity, agent, etc., although if there is more than one Arranger these roles will be split.

Lead Managers/Managers: After the Arranger(s) these banks will take the largest individual lending commitments and, if necessary, may also be underwriters with the Arranging Bank. A minimum lending commitment will be specified in order to qualify for this category.

Co-Managers: Their lending commitment will be less than that of the Managers but there will be a minimum amount required for them to qualify for this category.

Participants: This is the smallest level at which a bank may join a syndicate with each Participant taking amounts as low as $5m.

N.B. The titles used to describe the various levels of participation may be varied according to the preference of the lead/arranging bank.

Producer of Information   Often assumed by one of the Lead
Memorandum: Managers, but see below.

Book Runner: Depending on the size of the loan (and, therefore, the number of banks required) this can be undertaken by a Lead Bank or a number of the Managers. It involves assembling the syndicate.

Agreeing the Documentation: Often undertaken by a Lead Manager but may be delegated to a Manager.

Arranging the Signing: Often undertaken by a Lead Manager but may be delegated to a Manager.

Publicity: Often undertaken by a Lead Manager but may be delegated to a Manager.

Agent: Responsibilities commence after the agreement has been signed. Acts as Agent for the banks in all dealings with the borrower.

Reference Banks: Their function is to provide rates, e.g. LIBOR, at specified times in order to price the facility to the borrower thereby applying identical interest rates to all providers of the funds/services. No fees are received for this function.

Some of these roles will be described in greater detail.

4.1 Arranger/Lead Manager

In addition to being Lead Managers it is quite likely that this group of banks will have underwritten the facility for the borrower. In effect this guarantees the funds to the borrower irrespective of the subsequent success or otherwise of a more general syndication. The alternative to an underwritten situation is a facility provided on a "best efforts basis", which, in effect, means the borrower is prepared to take its chances on raising the sum sought through the syndications market without payment of any underwriting fee.

The ability of a lead manager or group of lead managers to underwrite a transaction has become an increasingly important factor in major corporate credits, particularly in situations such as an acquisition wherein the borrower will require a guarantee as to the availability of the funds.

Where a borrower is anxious to see a transaction syndicated *solely* amongst its relationship banks it is not unusual to find a deal constructed between borrower and lenders as a "club deal". Such a facility will normally be priced and structured to reflect the strength of existing relationships.

In corporate transactions the "sole lead management" designation has been increasingly replaced by the title of "arranger". In the case of a sole lead manager or arranger, clearly, the mandated bank has total discretion as to the roles it wishes to undertake but in joint lead management or arranging roles there are differing views amongst the major players as to the visibility and rewards involved. In looking at the roles in more detail it is important to bear in mind that few transactions are identical and the workload associated with each task will vary according to the size and nature of the deal.

4.2 Information Memorandum

Possibly because it is not common to every facility the role of producing the information memorandum is the least sought after. At the very outset of a transaction the borrower and lead bank(s) involved will discuss the necessity of producing an information package to assist the syndication. To support a sovereign credit such a package would, in the main, represent a financial overview of the country's economic performance and prospects and will often involve the close co-operation of the economic department of the relevant bank and the appropriate arm of the relevant Government.

In the case of corporate credits a number of factors will dictate the need, or otherwise, of an information package. Where a transaction is being syndicated to a group of relationship banks it will often only be necessary to ensure the availability of the latest financial results. Where there is a need for a wider syndication it may be necessary to provide historical and financial detail concerning the borrower's activities. These could be covered by the type of headings seen in a recent UK corporate transaction.

1. History of group.
2. Current ownership and group structure.
3. Activities of subsidiaries.
4. Reasons for facility.
5. Profit trend.
6. Balance sheet trend.
7. Corporate structure overview.

In the case of all historical and current information it would be expected that the borrower would warrant in the subsequent documentation to the accuracy of the content in any such memorandum. Equally, it would be normal for the bank undertaking the role to preface the memorandum with an appropriate disclaimer on behalf of its organisation to the potential participants.

As the borrower is expected to confirm, in material terms, the validity of the information provided there is sometimes a reluctance on the part of borrowers to provide forecasts.

In a term facility many lenders ideally seek some form of projected cash flow and it is in this particular area where sensitivities can exist. Many corporate customers are naturally unhappy about the disclosure of potentially price sensitive information although the use of a "confidentiality letter" may make them more comfortable.

The information package will normally be circulated or made available to banks concurrently with the invitation from the arranger or lead managers to participate in the facility.

The costs associated with the production of any information package will normally be borne by the borrower and claimed as part of the overall expenses at the conclusion of the transaction.

4.3 Running the Books

The role of actually syndicating the transaction to the market place is commonly referred to as "running the books". The bank undertaking this task is responsible for the preparation of the offer either by way of letter or fax to financial institutions and the co-ordination of responses. The invitation will incorporate the terms and conditions under which the facility is being syndicated, including level of participation sought, the returns to lenders and material financial covenants. The magnitude of this role will depend on such factors as the size and complexity of the transaction and the urgency or otherwise of the borrower's requirement. Many larger credits can be syndicated at various tiers, with the bookrunner having initial responsibility for completing or expanding a lead management group and, thereafter, bringing in other banks at various levels of participation as described earlier.

In the case of a global syndication it might be seen as advantageous for there to be more than one bookrunner particularly if funds are being raised in different tranches from various geographical markets, such as for Indian borrowers who have typically borrowed in conventional *and* tax effective tranches. The bank or banks involved are responsible for keeping the borrower and any other arranging banks advised on a regular basis of the progress of the syndication. The bookrunner will also be expected to act as a focal point or filter for any questions on the credit. Many borrowers, particularly corporates, are happy to talk to potential lenders but prefer to see the syndicating bank as a first point of reference.

Where a bank has underwritten the full amount of a credit with a view to achieving a selldown in the market the role of bookrunning assumes an even greater importance. The level of professionalism in pricing and structuring a transaction, together with the standing and reputation of the underwriting bank(s) in the market place will, in addition to the standing of the borrower, all be factors influencing the success of a syndication.

The bookrunner is expected to monitor its own costs for faxes, etc., and would seek reimbursement from the borrower at the conclusion of the transaction.

4.4 Documentation

Arguably, in many deals, the documentation role can be the most demanding and often requires from the institution involved a level of professionalism and commitment.

It is very rare, from the very origins of the market, for a loan agreement or facility agreement to be produced other than by a firm of lawyers. However, such a firm is instructed by, and works for, a financial institution which, in turn, is responsible for ensuring that the terms of the mandate given by the borrower to the syndicate are accurately reflected in the documentation. Many regular borrowers in the market evolve standard documentation which forms the basis of all agreements into which they enter.

However, since the inception of the syndicated product, many changes in a variety of areas have occurred which have necessitated the constant review and updating of many aspects of documentation. Worldwide, all the major law firms have their own style of documentation, but ultimately the banker's responsibility is to ensure that the wording not only reflects the terms of the borrower's mandate, but provides the syndicate with a legally watertight, workable document which will be acceptable both to the syndicate and the borrower.

Whilst a considerable part of many documents is relatively standardised, in areas such as covenants, representations and warranties and events of default (covered in detail in the Chartered Institute of Bankers' examination subject "Practice and Law of International Banking") the banker is required to exercise considerable negotiating skills in recognising the borrower's sensitivities whilst retaining the concepts of materiality to protect the syndicate's lending. As most syndicated facilities involve a medium term commitment it is important that the agreement protects the lenders against changes both in the borrower's circumstances and market conditions.

In general the syndicated facilities to which we refer are unsecured and, therefore, particularly with corporate borrowers, financial covenants become important tools for monitoring the borrower's continuing creditworthiness.

Specifically banks will look to protect themselves against falling net worth and unacceptably high levels of gearing and will seek to ensure that generated cash flow is sufficient to meet the company's interest burden. Ratios applied to different borrowers will often differ widely; however the overall yardstick for financial covenants is that they should be viewed as a package of trigger points so that remedial or protective action can be taken before the loan becomes a bad debt.

In any unsecured transaction bankers will seek to ensure that they are not disadvantaged as against other lenders and facilities by means of a negative pledge and may insist on a cross default clause. Additionally where a facility is based on the strength of the borrower's asset base some form of restriction on disposal of assets will be sought.

Financial covenants, although on-going, are normally capable of being monitored only against the production of financial information. In the case of an interest cover clause, for instance, it is realistically capable of being monitored only against the audited accounts.

Unlike the covenants referred to above the Representations and Warranties will be given on first drawdown and most lenders will seek a renewal of these at subsequent rollovers/drawdowns. These representations and warranties will normally relate to factual matters within the control of the borrower and provide lenders with 'on-going' comfort that the entity is conducting its affairs in such a way as not to threaten the 'legality' of the borrowing.

The negotiation of documentation is a skill developed by study and experience and in the main it is the possible omissions from a document which are as critical as the actual content.

In negotiating this type of documentation the bank undertaking the role must recognise that it is doing so on behalf of a group of banks and should guard against making concessions to the borrower which might be unacceptable to other banks and thereafter difficult to re-negotiate with the borrower.

The documentation role is often not just time consuming but is also the most expensive up front cost for the borrower. Increasingly, borrowers seek to impose a cap on expenses including the legal costs which involve an inherent risk to all syndicate members, in the event of "protracted negotiations". Invariably, in Eurodollar facilities, there is an "English Law" clause.

4.5 **Signing**

The syndicated loan market has traditionally involved high emphasis on status and visibility. The major financial institutions have been seen as large market players, with their considerable human and balance sheet resources. However, at the culmination of any transaction the success, or otherwise, of the deal is often determined by the impact of the signing ceremony.

Many a transaction which has struggled through the syndication and documentation processes has been redeemed by a smooth and prestigious signing. Conversely, a successfully syndicated transaction can be tarnished by a poorly organised ceremony. Although the primary purpose of any signing ceremony is to complete a legally binding agreement between the borrower and lenders it is often the only time in the transaction when *all* the parties are actually directly involved. From the borrower's viewpoint it is important to be able to establish new, and cement existing, relationships. Bankers have traditionally used signing ceremonies to create a presence and follow market trends. The scale of any signing ceremony is normally dictated by cost constraints. Major signings in London often take place in the City Livery Halls or West End hotels and outside the UK the prestigious hotels are the most popular venues, although an increasing number of borrowers are reluctant to pay for an event which they consider is actually giving greater visibility to the lenders.

The venue of the signing ceremony will often be influenced by the borrower, but it is important from an administrative viewpoint that the choice is both suitable in size and location. The role does involve organisational skills and a commitment of resources but often gives that institution the opportunity to promote its senior personnel with those of the borrower.

At the actual ceremony the borrower and banks will be expected to send representatives authorised to sign copies of the engrossments on behalf of their respective organisations. Although legally to have a binding contract it is necessary to sign only one copy, in practice, lawyers normally like to see the borrowers and participants having a signed copy each. In addition to the borrower and banks, the lawyers representing both sides will normally assist in the administration of the proceedings.

4.6 Publicity

Many borrowers consider that the signing ceremony itself can provide the required level of publicity. After all not only does the borrower get its money, but also the unique opportunity to be surrounded by a group of representatives from the world's largest financial institutions. Tombstones, as they became known, appeared in various sectors of the financial press and proved a useful means of promoting bankers' capabilities in the market and the borrower's ability to access the public debt markets.

Although normally prefaced by the words "as a matter of record only" the important factor from a lender's viewpoint is generally how far up the tombstone and in what size lettering its institution appears. This is normally determined by the size of commitment and banks expect to appear alpha-numerically in the category embracing their status, i.e. lead manager, co-manager, participant, etc.

From an advertising angle it is not difficult to see why bankers are keen to see tombstones. However, from a borrower's perception it really does depend on whether or not it wishes to publicise its ability to raise funds in the syndicated markets. Many sovereign borrowers have seen such publicity as a good method of generating lender interest for subsequent sorties in the bond or capital markets. In the main, corporate borrowers are more selective and will have to balance the perceived benefits of, say, a quarter page in the *Financial Times*, against the costs involved.

It is important, when looking at publicity costs, that the issue is addressed in the original offer letter to the borrower from the lead bank particularly if there is any sort of upper limit imposed on expenses to be met by the borrower. The question of who pays for this type of publicity is now largely determined on a case by case basis. If the borrower is reluctant to bear the cost then the arranging bank(s) must decide whether the prestige of the transaction and level of fees generated justifies them paying the bill. At a time when the major financial institutions are competing for sole arranging positions for the top world corporates selective use of advertising space has become a strategic weapon.

In addition to the production of a tombstone, the role of publicity also involves the co-ordination of any press release, normally agreed in advance with the client, any such release normally being dictated by the wishes of the borrower.

4.7 Agent

The agency function, to a very large extent, differs from all the other roles insofar as the primary responsibilities of the Agent do not commence until after the facility has been signed. With regard to this, and the fact that it assures the agent bank of an ongoing relationship with the borrower for the life of the loan, it has been for many years the most sought after function. It is important to recognise that the agent is agent for the banks and not the borrower.

Most major financial institutions have established their own agency sections designed to equip them to handle the administration of all syndicated products. In simple terms the agent is responsible for all the ongoing administration aspects of the facility on behalf of the syndicate. Included in these duties are the collection and making of payments between banks and borrower, calculation, collection and distribution of fees due, circulation of information as prescribed in the agreement, collation of the syndicate's expenses claim and establishment of the syndicate's LIBOR rate as the average of the rates provided by the Reference Banks. It is market practice for the Agent to be remunerated annually in advance for undertaking these tasks. The level of fee will normally be dictated by the size of the syndicate and the level of administrative complexity attaching to the transaction. In many instances, particularly involving a sole arranger, the dual functions will normally be undertaken by the same institution.

The title "Facility Agent" is used in the tombstones in this chapter to indicate the bank fulfilling the Agent's role; the title "Syndication Agent" in the Phillips Petroleum Company Norway tombstone is used to indicate the Book Runner role and will normally only be seen in syndications in which there is more than one Arranger.

The Agent's responsibilities to the syndicate are always comprehensively documented in the main agreement or in a separate side agreement and whilst the Agent continues as a participant in the facility it would normally continue its agency duties for the life of the loan.

June 1992

Phillips Petroleum Company Norway

acting through its Norwegian branch

US $300,000,000
Revolving Credit Facility

Arranged and Underwritten by

National Westminster Bank Plc   **Scotiabank (Ireland) Limited**

Société Générale   **The Sumitomo Bank, Limited**

Lead Managed by

Banque Nationale de Paris	Crédit Lyonnais
Den Danske Bank	The Fuji Bank, Limited
Handelsbanken AS, Subsidiary of Svenska Handelsbanken	National Westminster Bank Plc
NationsBank	Rabobank Nederland, London Branch
Scotiabank (Ireland) Limited	Société Générale

The Sumitomo Bank, Limited

Managed by

Banque Paribas, Copenhagen Branch	Christiania Bank og Kreditkasse
The Mitsubishi Trust and Banking Corporation	Royal Bank of Canada Group

---

Facility Agent	Syndication Agent
National Westminster Bank Plc	NatWest Capital Markets Limited

Exhibit I

278

This announcement appears as a matter of record only   December 1992

IRISH PERMANENT
BUILDING SOCIETY

US $95,000,000
Term Loan Facility

Arranged by
NatWest Capital Markets

Senior Lead Managers

The Bank of Nova Scotia   Irish Intercontinental Bank Limited

WestLB Group

Lead Managers

Bank of Scotland   The Nikko Bank (UK) plc

Managers

Bayerische Landesbank Girozentrale, London Branch   National Bank of Abu Dhabi

NatWest Capital Markets   J. Henry Schroder Wagg & Co. Limited

Facility Agent   Legal Adviser to the Arranger
National Westminster Bank Plc   Allen & Overy

Treasury Services provided by
Ulster Bank Group Treasury

NatWest Capital Markets
NatWest Markets

Exhibit II

279

4.8 Reference Banks

In ascertaining the borrowing costs in a syndicated facility it is normal for the agent to establish LIBOR, or the alternative funding base, by seeking from a small number of banks in the syndicate (known as Reference Banks) their quote (invariably at 11 a.m. London time) for determining the basic funding cost of a particular drawdown. In the case of domestic sterling facilities they sometimes also quote to establish mandatory liquid asset costs. In both instances the ultimate figure is normally averaged and rounded upwards in an agreed manner.

The Reference Banks are usually selected by the borrower on the basis that they constitute a small, representative sample of the mix of banks in the syndicate. For most syndicates there would be three or four Reference Banks. It would be wrong, for instance, for the Reference Banks in a £ sterling syndicate composed of a worldwide group of banks to be drawn exclusively from the main U.K. Clearing Banks or for a similar US$ syndicate to have three Money Centre Banks as Reference Banks.

Fees are not paid for performing this function.

4.9 Fees and Rewards

4.9.1 *Fees*

The type and range of fees payable by the borrower will depend on:

(a) the creditworthiness of the borrower
(b) the size of the facility
(c) the term of the facility
(d) the group of banks in the syndicate
(e) whether the facility is on a fully underwritten or a best efforts basis
(f) the nature and complexity of the transaction.

It is impossible to give a norm for these items as the fees actually charged on a specific deal will be as a result of a mix of all the above factors viewed in the context of the market at that particular time.

Generally speaking the fees will be:

4.9.1.1 *Front End Fee* – Payable at the outset when the facility is arranged. It is usually expressed as a percentage or in basis points and shared between the arranging banks and the committed banks in the syndicate according to their roles and final take (i.e. level of participation).

Any Front End Fee quoted to a borrower will always be a percentage of the total facility amount and comprises two elements; a portion of the Front End Fee will be passed to the participating banks as a Participation or Front End Fee, the remainder will be retained by the arranging bank(s) as an Arrangement Fee.

Thus the borrower would, for example, pay a Front End Fee of 0.25% on the total amount of the facility to the arranger, who would then pay 0.20% on the amount of its participation to any bank that joined the facility, 0.05% on the whole amount of the syndicated facility would thus be the arranging bank's Arranging Fee. In reality banks will be invited to join the facility at various different levels of participation, attracting a sliding scale of fee. The residual that is not paid away as the result of banks joining the facility at the lower levels is called the "pool", and is retained by the arranger.

If the facility is to be underwritten an Underwriting Fee will be paid to the arranging bank(s) who will have to perform this function. Any Underwriting Fee will be a flat percentage of the amount underwritten, which need not be the total amount of the facility, although this is the most common form of underwriting. The fee will be paid with the other Front End Fees. Any underwriting ceases with the signing of the facility.

The borrower and the Arranging Bank may take the view that the borrower's name is so good that the deal can be offered to the market and sufficient banks will respond to enable the facility to be put in place; this is referred to as a "best efforts" syndication. In such relatively rare circumstances the deal would not be underwritten at all and there would, accordingly, be no underwriting fees.

4.9.1.2 *Commitment Fees* – These most commonly take the form of either Facility Fees or Non-utilisation Fees.

(a) *Facility Fee* – expressed as a percentage or basis points per annum and payable pro rata to all committed banks according to their take (participation). The facility fee is payable throughout the term of the facility, usually in arrears on a quarterly/half-yearly basis, *whether or not the facility is drawn.* Again the size of this fee, if, indeed there is one for 'strong' borrowers, will depend on the creditworthiness of the borrower.

(b)　*Non-utilisation Fee/Commitment Fee* – This becomes payable as soon as banks are committed to lend ie usually from the date of signing the documentation, although lenders may agree to pay from the date, prior to signing, when amounts are allocated to the banks for their involvement in the syndicate. It is similar to a facility fee but payable only on the *undrawn* element of the facility and, of course, is calculated either in a percentage or in basis points on a per annum basis throughout the whole term.

4.9.1.3　*Utilisation Fee* – not frequently seen in new facilities but there are many existing syndicated facilities in which such a fee is payable. It is designed to recognise heavy and consistent use of a facility which may have been originally put in place with the expectation of utilisations being of a temporary but frequent basis; it works as a margin enhancement. Thus it would not be uncommon for the fee to be structured in the following way:

Utilisation　0 – 50%　– Nil
　　　　　　　Over　50%　– 3 bp pa

4.9.1.4　*Legal, Stationery and Publicity Fees* – these are payable by the borrower either directly or through the front-end fee and are calculated on a 'cost' basis. The borrower will normally wish to 'cap' such fees. Legal fees are invariably related to the charge made by the independent firm of lawyers which draws up the documentation. Such fees will often incorporate the stationery/printing costs. Publicity fees would cover the cost of publishing tombstones in newspapers/magazines selected by the borrower and the encapsulations of tombstones and any other mementos to be given to the participating banks to commemorate the deal.

The borrower would, of course, incur the costs of its own legal advisers who would be involved in the documentation negotiations.

4.9.1.5　*Facility Agent's Fee* – Although the Facility Agent is the agent of the banks it receives an annual fee from the borrower. This is usually expressed as, for example, 'x per bank per annum'. It is clearly required to cover the administration costs of the Facility Agent bank in fulfilling the role of intermediary between the borrower and the group of banks for the term of the facility.

4.9.1.6 *Evergreen Extension Fee* – At each stage when an evergreen facility is extended then a fee may be payable; it is invariably just a few basis points and frequently reflects the level of the annualised front-end fee.

4.9.2 *Rewards*

Apart from the fees the other, obvious reward for involvement in a syndicated facility is the mark-up over the cost of funds for any lending, i.e. the margin.

For the prominent banks in the syndicate, but especially Arrangers and Lead Managers, other rewards from the borrower may flow from the syndication. This may range from foreign exchange transactions related to the drawdown of facilities, to the transmission business of the company being acquired (if the syndicated loan is to provide acquisition finance), to a greater share of the borrower's existing banking requirements etc.

Furthermore, a successful, skilled syndication perceived by the market as such can lead to enhancement of the reputation of the Arranging Bank leading to the allocation of further arranging roles from the same borrower or from other borrowers.

4.9.3 *Yield Enhancement*

Having described the various roles which are comprised in a syndicated credit and the rewards available this seems the appropriate point to reflect further on certain aspects of the benefits to lenders of a syndicated product. On-going interest income represents an important concern. However, the market has now become extremely fee orientated. Originally, those commercial banking institutions with substantial balance sheets had sought rewards from substantial underwritings and loans whilst many of the merchant banks and investment houses had preferred to undertake arranging roles which meant earning fees without assuming a lending commitment. Annual commitment fees have helped the enhancement of returns and, in general, it has appeared that borrowers have been less sensitive to the payment of fees for syndicated, as opposed to bilateral, facilities.

It is a feature of the syndicated market, as with other aspects of lending, that high commitment produces substantial up front income in addition to high visibility. The income factor must be evaluated carefully by the marketeer and any bank's final take in a transaction may be determined by its desire to achieve a target return on assets.

As explained in Section 3 to underwrite a transaction and then sell down to a target figure does afford an arranger/lead manager or underwriter the potential benefit of an enhanced rate of return on its ultimate participation.

Example of enhancement of rate of return by selling down

Details of a syndicated loan are:

Total Amount	:	US$100m
Term	:	10 years
Interest	:	LIBOR (9.5%) plus 0.5% per annum margin (Total 10% per annum)
Fees	:	Front End 0.5% per annum Facility Fee 0.25% per annum (Note : this is payable regardless of utilisation of the facility)

If a bank underwrites US$25m of the loan and there is no selling down so that, in fact, it also lends US$25m for 10 years, its overall return i.e. by annualising the front end fee and adding it to the facility fee and mark up over LIBOR will be:

Margin	:	50.00 basis points p.a.
Facility Fee	:	25.00 basis points p.a.
Annualised Front-End Fee	:	7.97 basis points p.a.
Yield on US$25m	:	82.97 basis points p.a. over LIBOR

However, if the same bank underwrites US$25m but then sells down to managers, co-managers and participants so that it actually lends only US$5m for 10 years, it would have to pass on, say, 0.25% by way of a front end fee to those other banks whilst retaining a 0.25% flat front end (underwriting) fee for itself. It would, of course, receive the 0.25% per annum facility fee on the amount it was committed to lend, ie US$5m. Under this scenario the effective net annual return for lending would be re-calculated as follows:

Margin	:	50.00 basis points p.a.
Front End Fee (annualised)	:	23.90 basis points p.a.
Facility Fee	:	25.00 basis points p.a.
Yield on US$5m	:	98.90 basis points p.a. over LIBOR

Keystrokes on HP12C calculator

| f | | clear | | fin |

	Display
Front end fee: 0.25 Enter 5 x 0.25 + CHS PV	−1.50
No. of quarters: 40 N	40.00
Equiv. qtly. discount rate: 2.5 i	2.50
Calculated qtly. equiv. rate: PMT	0.06
Annualised rate: 4 x	0.239

N.B. The first line of calculation provides an equivalent front-end fee on a commitment of US$5m when including the praecipuum of 0.25% on the full US$25m facility amount.

Hence the return on capital employed will be substantially improved and the Bank will not be building up its balance sheet but rather leaving capacity for involvement in other facilities.

4.9.4 *Cost to Borrower*
It will be recognised that the yield to the Arranging Bank will be different (ie higher) than that to an underwriting bank which, in turn will be higher

than that to a bank participating at a lower level of lending. This is by virtue of the various fees appropriate to each level which enhance the yield from the lending itself. This means, of course, that the *cost* to the borrower is not the same as the yield to any particular bank but a melding of these various yields.

Example

$750 million 5 year revolving loan

Pricing

Margin	:	0.25% p.a. (25 basis points) above LIBOR
Non utilisation fee	:	0.125% p.a. (12.5 basis points)
Front end fee	:	0.20% flat (20 basis points) – payable to the arranger and distributed as described below

The borrower wishes to have the facility fully underwritten prior to syndication. The arranger will not take the full risk on its own balance sheet and therefore finds two other banks to share this task. These two banks plus the arranger underwrite $250m each.

The two underwriting banks receive a fee payable out of the 0.20% front-end fee of 0.04% flat (4 basis points flat) on the amount of their underwriting.

In general syndication, the arranger invites banks to participate at different levels for which they are paid different rates of front-end fees as follows:

Lead Manager	$75m – 8bp flat
Manager	$50m – 6bp flat
Co-manager	$25m – 4bp flat

The Underwriters will also get a fee calculated on the basis on their final participation level.

Thus the distribution of the front end fee could look like this:

Total paid by borrower: 0.20% on $750,000,000   =$1,500,000

Status	Amount $	Rate	No.	Fee $	Total $
Underwriter	250,000,000	0.04% flat	2	100,000	200,000
Lead					
Manager	75,000,000	0.08% flat	5	60,000	300,000
Manager	50,000,000	0.06% flat	4	30,000	120,000
Co-Manager	25,000,000	0.04% flat	5	10,000	50,000

$ 670,000

Balance retained by the Arranger $ 830,000

The Arranger will provide the balance of $50,000,000, thus this fee of $830,000 represents an effective front end fee, on its final commitment, of 1.66% flat, very different from any ordinary participant's return, and represents the reward for the higher risks and effort involved.

Equally, if the primary underwriters have a final participation level of $50m their total front end fees are $130,000 each, equating to 0.26% flat.

From this we can work out annualised yields both drawn and undrawn, plus the cost to the borrower.

The key strokes using an HP12C calculator are as follows:

Assumptions

Flat front end fee expressed as percentage points: 0.26
numbers of periods: 20 (5 years as quarters)
discounting interest rate to be used as percentage points: 2.5 (i.e. 10% p.a.)

Keystrokes	Display	
f CLEAR FIN		
.26 PV	0.26	Front end fee
20 n	20.00	Number of quarters
2.5 i	2.50	Equivalent quarterly discount rate
PMT	-0.0167	Calculated quarterly equivalent rate
CHS 4 X	0.0667	Annualised rate

287

We can follow this through as follows:

Borrower's annualised cost

Front end fee 0.2% flat discounted		0.0513%
add non utilisation fee		0.1250%
undrawn cost	=	0.1763%

front end fee		0.0513%
add margin		0.2500%
fully drawn cost	=	0.3013%

Yields to Banks

Participant at $25m
Front end fee 0.04% flat   0.0103% p.a.
                         undrawn 0.1333% p.a.
                         drawn   0.2603%p.a.

Co-Manager at $50m
Front end fee 0.06% flat   0.0154% p.a.
                         undrawn 0.1404% p.a.
                         drawn   0.2654%p.a.

Lead Managers at $75m
Front end fee 0.08% flat   0.0205% p.a.
                         undrawn 0.1455% p.a.
                         drawn   0.2705%p.a.

Underwriters
Front end fee equivalent
0.26% flat   0.0667% p.a.
                         undrawn 0.1917% p.a.
                         drawn   0.3167%p.a.

Arranger
Front end fee equivalent
1.66% flat   0.4259% p.a.
                         undrawn 0.5509% p.a.
                         drawn   0.6759%p.a.

Of course some arrangers do not retain a final participation! Hence the deal to them is purely fee earning without the incidence of capital costs on their balance sheets.

Ever conscious of the need to achieve a worthwhile return on Capital Employed lenders will wish to calculate the return to them on a per annum basis assuming nil utilisation (i.e. a committed standby situation) *and also* on a fully drawn basis.

Example:

Terms of a corporate MOF with a 5 year commitment:

Front-end Fee to a participant – 5 basis points
(given a simple annualised calculation this will provide underwriting banks with 1 basis point per annum (utilised or unutilised)).

Facility Fee – 12.5 basis points per annum paid on the underwitten commitment regardless of utilisation.

Therefore the addition of these two fees provides an *undrawn yield* to underwriters/committed banks of 13.5 basis points p.a.

Assuming a committed margin of say 15 basis points and no utilisation fee the *fully drawn return* on the committed facility would then be:

Amortised front-end fee	1.0 bp
Facility fee	12.5 bp
Margin	15.0 bp
Total	28.5 bp p.a.

Furthermore, if the facility includes a typical utilisation fee say:

Utilisation of the committed facility	0–50%	– Nil
	51–100%	– 2.5 basis points

then, with this addition applying only to the fully drawn return, a lender's yield on a *fully drawn* basis would increase to a margin of 31 basis points p.a.

This would be a typical return to an ordinary underwriter. Returns to arrangers can, of course, be enhanced by the retention of a larger portion of the front end fee than that passed on to the underwriters.

289

The *yield* to the banks in turn translates to the *cost* to the borrower.

5. TRANSFERABILITY OF ASSETS

To date, because the emphasis has been on primary market activity, it is almost unavoidable that the syndicated market has been dominated by the world's front line financial institutions. As the evolution of the products has taken place many institutions have sought to concentrate on becoming niche players, preferring to specialise in areas such as project financing, aircraft lending etc. as against supporting pure, vanilla sovereign credits.

With this domination by the top 50/100 institutions it was, perhaps, inevitable that a secondary market would develop to enable the smaller financial institutions the opportunity to increase their asset base through the syndicated market. In fact the motivation for such a development was not entirely at the behest of the smaller organisations as in the early 80s it blended well with the desire of many large market players to offload assets either for balance sheet purposes or purely to generate a trading profit.

Many financial institutions saw considerable potential in reducing levels of exposure to certain borrowers whilst at the same time being able to take advantage of the downward movement in margins by selling off earlier participations and yet retaining a turn for their own book. Each institution may have had its own reasons and objectives for being involved in this market. However, the result was a sharp focus on the question of transferability in syndicated facilities.

Traditionally, it had been felt that for the most part sovereign borrowers were not so relationship orientated, particularly as far as participants were concerned, to worry unduly about the identity of all the lenders. This being so, most facility agreements contained the right of assignability in addition to an inherent right to sub-participate. At this juncture it is perhaps important to establish the difference between these two alternatives and appreciate the impact of each particularly relative to the objectives of the vendor. Sub-participation is essentially a silent method of passing the funding of a loan or fixture from the original lender to another institution whilst retaining the primary obligation and relationship with the borrower. From the borrower's perception it will still be funded by, and pay to, the primary bank. However, the latter must, effectively, take

290

a view on the risk on the sub-participant, as it will require to be funded by that bank.

Assignment or novation by a lender is normally done with the prior concurrence of the borrower. This process does involve the original lender in being discharged from all its rights and obligations. For many borrowers assignability does generate sensitivities, particularly if the underlying transaction is seen as relationship orientated. Indeed many corporate customers are concerned at the possibility of a loan being assigned to an institution with which they do not want a relationship. Such concern is in part created by the necessary levels of disclosure associated with an assignment.

In most corporate transactions the prior consent of the borrower will be required to assignments and always to novations. Nevertheless, with an increasing number of banks feeling the need for balance sheet flexibility the right to assign/novate has assumed considerable importance. Assignment can be achieved by a relatively simple documentation process and does not necessitate a novation agreement.

A number of major financial institutions have developed highly resourced secondary market desks to meet the demand for assets from smaller organisations.

CHAPTER 8

Project Finance

by
Gordon McKechnie

1. INTRODUCTION

1.1 Definitions

The term "Project Finance" is often used to describe the financing of any major capital investment project by whatever external funding sources and through whatever risk assumption pattern. This is a valid use of the term. The discipline of structuring a cohesive capital investment financing package from a variety of funding sources and parties willing to bear risk can often be vital to the successful development of a project. It may involve raising equity and preferred shares as well as debt. The entities participating in the capital structure will include, naturally, those with a commercial interest in the project, such as project sponsor(s), suppliers and purchasers of the project's output. They also include external parties. Examples of these external sources of funds and risk-bearing include:

- commercial banks;

- export credit agencies;

- development agencies and multilateral institutions (such as the European Bank for Reconstruction and Development or the World Bank);

- lessors;

- public and private debt markets;

- a range of equity sources; and

- private, government and multilateral risk insurance agencies.

Each of these entities has its own guidelines, for example the international competitive bidding procurement procedures of the World Bank. A project seeking funding from a particular source will have to comply with the relevant approach.

In this chapter, however, we shall focus more on the analysis of the project itself rather than on the art of organising these diverse sources into a cohesive whole. We shall also adopt a commercial bank standpoint, rather than that of a project sponsor (or its financial advisors) or, indeed, of a development bank which might explicitly take into account in its analysis the project's positive externalities (benefits of the project on economic or social activities outside the project itself). Accordingly, we shall be concerned mostly with the more restricted use of "project finance" in which it is practically synonymous with the expressions "limited recourse financing" and "non-recourse financing" and with the commercial debt provider that bears "project risk" in some form or other.

US Accounting Standard FASB 47 (March 1981) defined the project finance concept as follows:

"The financing of a major capital project in which the lender looks principally to the cash flows and earnings of the project as the source of funds for repayment and to the assets of the project as collateral for the loan. The general credit of the project entity is usually not a significant factor, either because the entity is a corporation without other assets or because the financing is without direct recourse to the owner(s) of the entity."

Note the use of the word "principally" in the first sentence of this definition and the emphasis on "without *direct* recourse" in the second sentence. Completely non-recourse financings, in which lenders look exclusively to the cash flow and assets of the project and have no other form of external support, have been relatively rare. The more typical project financing falls into the category of "limited recourse financing". Here, the lenders have the benefit of some form of support from outside the project or, put differently, indirect recourse – pre-defined and limited in the project contracts and its financing documents – to the project's sponsor(s) and/or third parties. We shall consider some of the forms such support can take in Section 4.

The general characteristic that the lender is, in the first instance at least, dependent on project performance for debt service is central to the project finance concept as used here. Much of this chapter is concerned with the risk analysis a lender undertakes in order to satisfy itself as to the adequacy of debt service capability and the types of protection from the identified risks which it might consider.

1.2 History of the Limited Recourse Concept

The concept that the lender cannot, in certain defined circumstances, rely on the full faith and credit of the project's sponsor or owner has a long history. In the commercial code of classical Athens, for example, a loan secured on a seaborne cargo was not repayable if the ship carrying the cargo was lost at sea. Another example can be taken from the period of expansion of trade and industry in the nineteenth century. One of the key ideas involved in the development of business entities at that time was the limited liability concept: that the shareholders in a company were to be prevented from suffering a loss which exceeded their investment in the company. As such, a lender to the limited liability company could not proceed against the other assets of the company's shareholders in order to recover monies lent unless the shareholder had entered into a contract (or guarantee) in effect permitting it to do so. Although the precise laws surrounding limited liability companies, and the extent to which the corporate veil can be lifted, vary from jurisdiction to jurisdiction, the limited liability special purpose company generally remains the most satisfactory means of limiting a lender's recourse to the project.

Loans which have been made to single project companies over the years have been de facto project financings – whether or not they were seen to be such by the bankers who extended them. In the period since the second world war, many single project companies have been mining entities – set up to exploit a single orebody; others have been single building real estate or property companies. Another strand in the development of project financing in the post-war period lies in the US oil and gas industry. Largely based on tax advantages then available in the US, a number of different limited recourse oil and gas lending structures were developed and widely used, particularly through the 1960s. This process gave the banks involved the experience of assessing individual oil and gas producing fields for their loan value and an increasing familiarity with lending on terms which did not necessarily involve the full faith and credit of the project's sponsor.

1.3 Applications Today

During the 10 years or so immediately prior to the January 1986 oil price collapse, project financing was most closely associated with the petroleum industry. In subsequent sections, we shall use an oil and gas field development loan as the primary example of a project financing. Project financing has also often been used to finance the construction of mines as well as that of mineral processing plants, either associated with the mine or separate from it, property and some industrial and leisure ventures. The privatisation trend of the late 1980s and early 1990s, whether embarked upon for ideological reasons or reasons of budgetary expendiency, has brought project finance to prominence in a number of areas previously generally financed within the state budget. The increase in power plant project financings falls into this category as do financings for toll roads and bridges, rail links and airports. Pipelines have long been the subject of project financing in North America; the privatisation of the gas transmission industry and changes in its integrated structure in Europe are likely to lead to an extension of project financing for European pipelines. Changes in the telecom industry provide project finance opportunities there as well. The Channel Tunnel has been financed using project debt.

The project finance technique has also been applied to aircraft and ship financing. These types of financing are, however, somewhat different in nature from those listed above: an aircraft under the management of Company A and flying between X and Y may run at a loss, but its fortunes may be radically reversed if it were to be sold to Company B and fly the profitable route between Y and Z; an oil field produces oil and change of ownership will not normally produce a radical variation in profitability. These distinctions are not hard and fast ones, but in the context of this book aircraft financing is considered in Chapter 6 on Asset Finance.

The necessary criterion for an economic unit to be amenable to project financing is that it must be possible to isolate the venture's stream of cash flows – both inflows and outflows – in a manner acceptable to both lender and sponsor. As such, project financing need not be limited to asset development or construction projects. As a financing technique it may be applied to the refinancing of existing operations and assets; for example, after their acquisition by a new owner.

1.4 Limiting Recourse – How It Is Achieved

There are basically two ways in which to limit recourse:

(a) by segregating the project into a separate special purpose vehicle company; and

(b) by contract, often the Credit Agreement governing the financing of a project which remains part of a larger corporation.

The former is the more effective route but its efficacy in practice depends on the extent to which the law permits the corporate veil to be pierced. Contractual limitation of recourse is more difficult to draft in the financing documents and may not prove as effective in isolating risk. On the other hand the sponsor may choose to accept these drawbacks for, for example, tax reasons.

1.5 Risk Sharing, "Balance", Commitment and Rewards

In a conventional sovereign or corporate loan, the lender is essentially confronted with a given set of risks and, subject to imposing covenants such as debt : equity ratios and/or varying loan pricing, is faced with the choice of whether or not to take the risks involved. In this respect a project financing is different. Provided one is not dealing with a situation where the project package is coterminous with the wider corporate group, lenders and sponsors can negotiate which risks are to be assumed by lenders within the project package and which are to be supported by one or more other parties outside the project but with contractual relations to it or another interest in it. Risk sharing in a project loan (and, therefore, risk reward) is capable of infinite variation to meet the individual circumstances of the project and the aims and negotiating strengths of sponsor, lender and other parties involved (contractors, operators, offtakers, etc.). Project financiers often look to 'balance' as the hallmark of the ideal structure, where the different elements of risks are borne by the project party who is in the best position to quantify, to manage and to control the particular element of risk.

At Section 1.1 we noted the rarity of true non-recourse financings. Thus, when segregating an entity to be project financed, the sponsoring company can very rarely expect to escape all involvement. At a minimum lenders will usually insist that representations and warranties given be

297

supported by the sponsor as well as the sponsor committing its industrial expertise where the project requires it. Where the project entity retains commercial links with its sponsor, say through the purchase of project inputs or the sale of output, the lender will be actively interested in the ongoing nature of those links. The financing agreements may have to stipulate that transfer pricing (the price at which goods or services are sold by one entity to another) be at independently verifiable market prices or in accordance with a formula agreed in advance by lenders. Equally, in infrastructure project financings based on a concession from (or similar agreement with) the state, the government will have to expect, at a minimum, to create conditions through the concession agreements which are conducive to the project financing being raised. Through this mechanism, some of the contingent risks in the project may in effect be borne by the state.

In addition to looking for "balance", project financiers look to "commitment" from the key parties involved in the project. The lender's analysis of its, and other parties', commitment will include an assessment of what the monetary loss to a party would be if the project went wrong in some way or other. If a key party has little to lose from project failure, a prospective lender should be wary.

Banks lending on project finance terms receive their compensation through front-end fees, commitment fees on the (temporary) undrawn portion of the loan and a lending margin on the advances made. Since the work involved in arranging a project financing tends to be greater than for a normal loan, the front-end fees tend to be higher for a project financing than for a conventional credit facility. Perceived risk in the loan and market conditions also have a bearing on the front-end fees as they do on the lending margins. Traditionally, banks have generally perceived a higher level of risk in project lending than general lending and so require higher levels of remuneration.

Project sponsors sometimes hire an advisor to advise them on raising finance for a project. This may be part of a more general mandate to advise on the development of the project from a financial standpoint. The advisor may also subsequently arrange the finance and participate in the loan facility. Alternatively, the sponsor may preclude the advisor from a subsequent lending role in order to preserve the advisor's position on the

298

sponsor's side of the table in negotiations with the lenders. The advisor will receive separate compensation for his role.

1.6 Balance Sheet Impact

It is a widely held misconception that project financing necessarily means off-balance sheet treatment for the debt. Certain structures, however, have been able to achieve off-balance sheet treatment by auditors.

Accounting standards have changed in different countries over time in recognition of evolving financing structures. For example, in the United States, the oil industry's production payment arrangements (see Section 1.2) were brought onto the balance sheet in 1977 (FASB 19) and the disclosure of take-or-pay obligations (see 2.4.3, below) was dealt with in 1981 (FASB 47).

A project company held by several sponsors, each with less than 50% ownership and none holding overall control, is a common way of minimising the impact of project debt on the respective consolidated balance sheets. However, even this approach must be considered carefully in the light of the specifics of the relevant jurisdiction. EU legislation has evolved in the direction of consolidating accounts not only on strict majority ownership criteria. Thus the 1989 UK Companies Act extends the definition of "subsidiary" to include entities over which the group exercises "dominant influence".

The UK Accounting Standards Board exposure draft on "Reporting the Substance of Transactions" (FRED 4; 1993) continues the trend towards more complete and accurate disclosure in financial statements of transactions which might previously have been accounted for off balance sheet.

1.7 Why Borrow on Project Terms?

A financial advisor or lender to a project should ascertain at an early stage what the motives for borrowing on project terms are and endeavour to develop a list of priorities with the sponsor. The list will affect the shape of the eventual financing package.

Some reasons behind project borrowing are:

(a) Risk sharing. Singly the most powerful motive for borrowing on limited recourse terms. The risk profile of the project may be too high in some respects for a single sponsor to bear in accordance with his desired corporate risk profile. In such a case he will wish to proceed with the project only if the particular risks can be "laid off" for an acceptable cost. The risks a sponsor seeks to lay off may be highly specific, for example a specific aspect of country risk in a developing country project, or a broad range of risks. More generally, project finance arrangements are part of the sponsor's risk/return calculation for the project. Note that project finance is not simply a question of negotiating risk-sharing between sponsor and lender. As noted above, many parties may be involved in sharing risk and may need to be so involved in order to provide an allocation of risk which provides all parties involved sufficient incentive to proceed, as well as assurance of the key parties' commitment to its success.

(b) Presentation in financial statements (see 1.5 above).

(c) Tax advantages. Highly specific in time and jurisdiction.

(d) Restrictions on raising debt. The terms and conditions of existing debt or the relevant regulatory authorities may impose restrictions on raising debt. Sometimes the project can proceed with the necessary degree of leverage to make the equity investment attractive only if it is housed in a special purpose vehicle or if the risk associated with the debt is otherwise effectively removed from the main corporation.

(e) Risk segregation. Management of a sponsor company may have adopted the philosophy that each of its undertakings should be conducted in as great isolation from one another as possible, to avoid problems in one impacting the whole.

(f) Maximising debt capacity. It may be possible to increase the overall debt capacity of a company, by maximising the debt load of each of its individual parts. To arrange project financings, lenders undertake a detailed examination of each individual project and the result may be that the sum of the parts is greater than the whole.

(g) Market testing. Where a project is basically sponsored by government, a policy may be put in place which in effect requires a project to stand financially on its own, not simply within the government's internal financial requirements but also in the private sector financial marketplace. A project financing may be the only (or best) way to develop a project in this type of policy environment.

(h) The only option. In a large number of cases the alternative between project financing and conventional corporate debt does not arise: the aspiring borrower does not have sufficient assets and cash flow outside the project on which its financing could be based. In these situations, though the entire organisation may stand behind the debt, the loan is a de facto project financing and is assessed as such by lenders. An obvious result is that, in such circumstances, the ability to negotiate risk sharing between sponsor and lender is severely curtailed. Other parties may, however, be introduced into the risk sharing equation to good effect.

Some projects are developed by multi-member consortia. A gas pipeline, for example, may be developed under such sponsorship, with gas producers (sellers of gas), and distribution utilities (buyers of gas) participating as sponsors in the project company's equity. The objectives which the participants with different interests bring to the project company will likely be different. Reconciling these differences is important for the project to move forward; this is a task that may fall to the financial advisor or lender.

1.8   Assuming Risk and Providing Funds

We have noted that the commercial risks inherent in a project can be shared among the parties, including the lender. Traditionally, the risk inherent in the loan was assumed by the same entity as provided the funds. In recent years, these two functions have, in certain cases, been separated. The banks which assume the risk may now provide a guarantee (or standby letter of credit) in favour of other entities which are willing to lend on more favourable terms but are not willing to assume project risk. One of the earliest uses of this separation was to structure transactions for projects in Australia which would be efficient from an Australian withholding tax standpoint.

In an alternative structure, instead of issuing a guarantee or standby letter of credit, banks assuming long term project risk have provided a backstop line of credit permitting short term loans to be advanced from other sources, or the sale of short term notes or commercial paper to be made. Such structures have been known by a variety of names, for example, Note Issuance Facilities, Multi-Option Financing Facilities or Backstop Facilities.

Projects often generate tax capacity more rapidly than they can use it against the income generated by the project. In such a situation the post tax returns of the project may be capable of being enhanced through the use of leasing. Lessors, however, while willing to use their tax capacity, are often unwilling to take project risk. In such cases they would require support from other entities which intermediate in the sense of assuming the relevant project risks.

The size of project financings often means that they are raised through facilities syndicated among a number of banks rather than through a single bank facility. The fixed costs involved in establishing a project finance structure can make it prohibitively expensive if the project itself is relatively small. The special characteristics of syndicated loans are considered in Chapter 7. For convenience, however, throughout the remainder of this chapter we refer to the lender in the singular.

2. RISK ANALYSIS

This section reviews some of the specific categories of risk involved in major capital projects which a bank may be called upon to assume, or may be exposed to, in a project financing. Since the risks involved are peculiar to the type of project or indeed the specific project being undertaken, a project lender requires a detailed understanding of the project, of the industry within which it operates, of the motivations of the parties involved in the project and of the relative power between them when the project contracts were negotiated. By way of example we shall focus on a project financing for the development of an offshore oil or gas field, but shall draw occasional examples from other types of project.

302

2.1 Completion and Cost Overrun Risk

In its extreme form, this risk is that the project will not be completed and will, therefore, never generate cash flow. The less extreme form is that more capital expenditure than anticipated will be needed to bring the project to the point of sustainable cash generation, and that this capital cost overrun will be such as to jeopardise the economics of the project and full repayment of the loan.

This risk is common to all loans made for the purpose of project development. It is not usually present in a financing made on project (limited- or non-recourse) terms after the completion of construction, although on a smaller scale it can be. For example, an oil and gas field development plan may envisage a subsequent phase of capital expenditure (the drilling of new wells, the installation of compression equipment or secondary – or tertiary – recovery methods) as part of the planned generation of cash flow on which loan repayment depends. A mine plan may envisage a second capital expenditure phase in the opening of a new pit, which, while lacking some of the uncertainties of the initial capital expenditure phase, resembles a new project.

Generally speaking, completion risk is at its greatest where the technology is new or is being applied in a novel manner or in an untested, possibly logistically remote, environment. Figures taken from the development of North Sea projects show how inadequately the engineering profession initially coped with the budgeting process. This experience accounted for the reluctance of banks to take pre-completion risk in the North Sea; although one must add that this reluctance declined as the engineers' experience with the capital cost budgeting process improved and as other factors made sponsors more cost-conscious.

Sometimes the project being financed is only a part of a system, all parts of which must be satisfactorily built for the project to perform. In such a project the lender should clearly be concerned about the completion of the entire system.

Lenders, of course, have taken completion or cost overrun risk in project lending. However, because the assessment of the risk must be based on a sound understanding of the technology, of the logistics specific to the development and of how (and for what purpose) the budget has been developed, banks have often sought the advice of a

303

construction engineering consultant with experience relevant to the project to be financed. Considerations such as the reputation of the project operator (in the case of most offshore developments) or the project's main contractor (in the case of many land-based projects) are important, but can seldom replace the detailed analysis.

Some projects (notably in the independent power sector) are constructed under "lump-sum" or "fixed price" or "guaranteed maximum price" contracts; in other words the risk of the project costing too much to build is theoretically assumed by the contractor rather than by the owners and operators of the project (and hence the banks financing them). It should be emphasised that fixed price construction contracts cannot be regarded as a universal cure for completion/cost overrun risk.

Where fixed price contracts are available, the detailed contract terms need to be examined. For instance, how are interruptions to construction brought about by strikes handled? The treatment of "change orders" is also very significant. Most major projects are not fully engineered when the main construction contract is let. A fixed price contract is generally only fixed in price for a set programme of work. To the extent that the set programme changes (as, for example, detailed engineering progresses) the price can change. It is not beyond the bounds of possibility that a contractor losing money on a contract might try to make up some of that loss in negotiating the price of change orders or even through litigation. Finally, even if a contract were to be perfect, the project sponsor and his banker would not have eliminated completion/cost overrun risk. The risk of contractor performance, both technically and from a creditworthiness standpoint, remains to be assessed. Contractor performance risk, clearly, is not limited to lump sum contracts, but in those conditions it usually bears closer examination because of the reliance that may otherwise be placed on the contract.

While serving to shift risk to the contractor, a full project or "wraparound" fixed price contract can be costly to the project since the contractor will seek to charge for assuming these risks. The excess cost will vary from project to project but can be as much as a 25% premium. Project sponsors who can capably manage the construction process may wish to assume, and manage, this risk themselves.

Apart from considerations of the contracts and details of the construction programme, a lender's decision on whether to accept completion risk depends fundamentally on how robust operating phase project economics are. To what extent could capital costs overrun before the operating phase cash generation capacity of the project was jeopardised? This type of question is applicable to each risk considered in this chapter. Some of the tools used in its analysis are reviewed in Section 3.

Handling completion risk in loan documentation (as opposed to contract documentation) is considered in Section 4.

2.2 Reserve or Feedstock Risk

A loan supported only by the assets and future cash flow of the project exposes the lender to the risk that an operating phase input to the project may not be available as, or at the price, forecast.

This category of risk takes on different forms depending on the type of project. For a mineral extraction project it involves an assessment of the relevant hydrocarbon reservoir, coal deposit or ore body. Such an assessment may also be an integral part of projects where the main component, in terms of relative capital cost, is an industrial processing plant; for example a lignite mine-mouth power station or an LNG (liquified natural gas) project. For other types of processing plant (e.g. a refinery not specialised in a certain type of crude oil feedstock or a chemical plant) where the input is, or can be made, available from a variety of sources, the feedstock risk largely becomes one of the price of the relevant input under varying market conditions.

To illustrate in more detail the nature of this risk we shall again take the example of an offshore oil field. The assessment of petroleum reserves – how much oil is in the reservoir and how much of the oil-in-place can be produced (the recovery factor) – is the province of petroleum engineering. So important is this assessment to a bank making a petroleum production based loan that many banks actively involved in this type of financing employ a team of petroleum engineers on their staff. Because they are also used by oil companies themselves, equity investors, government authorities and so on, a community of independent petroleum engineering firms has grown up and is well established. A report by one of these firms often supports the analysis by the bank.

305

The relationship between the maturity of a field and the degree of certainty about recoverable reserves is essential for a banker to the industry to understand. While there are significant variations from field to field, the relationship is essentially one of increasing confidence as the field becomes more mature, as illustrated in Fig. 1.

Petroleum engineering is a sufficiently uncertain science that it is often said (by petroleum engineers themselves) that the recoverable reserves in a field can only really be known once the last drop of oil is produced. Oil companies and bankers to the industry obviously have to accept a higher degree of risk than that. But how much higher?

It is important to note that before production begins the degree of certainty can be significantly less than after even a relatively short period of production history. In the appraisal stage, the measurement of reserves is essentially volumetric – based on the results of often widely spaced wells drilled to examine a structure spotted by seismic survey. The reservoir drive mechanism, and hence the recovery factor (the percentage of original oil-in-place that will be capable of being extracted), can only be inferred prior to commercial production and the consequent large scale movements of reservoir fluids and the monitoring of reservoir pressure changes that this permits. This additional uncertainty in the pre-completion phase has added to the reluctance, identified in Section 2.1, of banks to lend on project finance terms in the North Sea before completion. In a typical development plan no significant additional information on the reservoir becomes available between the decision to develop and the commencement of commercial production. Thus, this category of risk does not fundamentally change as the project progresses to the point of completion and commencement of production.

Financings have often been designed on the basis that the lender declines to take pre-completion reservoir risk, but agrees to accept such risk after "Completion". The forms which this can take and the importance of defining "Completion" having regard to the specifics of the reservoir are considered in Section 4.

One further point is worthy of note before leaving this category of risk: recoverable oil reserves are not independent of the price of oil. The terms "economic recovery factor" and "economic life" of a field highlight

306

Figure 1   *Oil Reserves Estimate and Field Maturity*

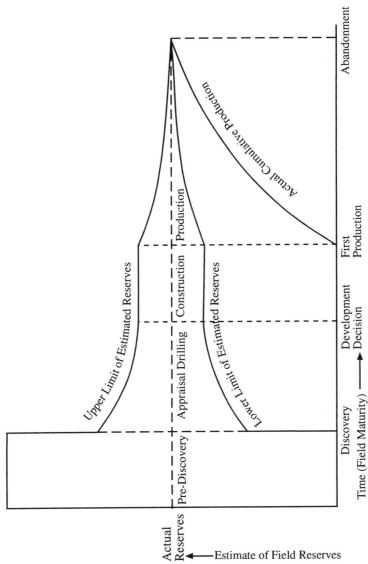

307

this. In a typical oil field the per barrel cost of production (ignoring the depreciation of "sunk" capital costs) rises over the life of the field as the production levels decline. If the variable production costs in a given field were $20.00/bbl (barrel), the field would be generating positive cash flow of $10.00/bbl at an oil price of $30.00/bbl. If the oil price fell to $12.00/bbl, the field would be absorbing more cash than it was generating. Depending on an assessment of abandonment costs and the future evolution of the oil price, the operator will consider abandoning the field before recovering oil which could have been economically recovered (and so formed part of the field's reserves) at $30.00/bbl. Thus, with no change in the field's technical or engineering characteristics, the recoverable reserves fall. This cataclysmic effect (no more production) as well as the more gradual erosion of cash flow through a falling oil price must be considered in assessing how much to lend.

2.3   Production or Operating Risk
Production or operating risk is the risk that the project does not operate as planned or costs more than envisaged to operate at planned levels.

In the example we are looking at, an offshore oil field, this category of risk is largely represented by operating phase reservoir risks. Platform operating costs are not usually a high percentage of overall project costs. But this may not be the case for some types of development nor, as noted in Section 2.2, towards the end of a field's life.

In other types of project, however, operating costs are a very important factor in overall project viability. This is typically the case in a mining project. Here, the ratio of planned annual operating cost to construction cost is far higher than in an offshore petroleum project. As a result of this and of the fact that technology and equipment are mostly standard off-the-shelf products, sponsors and project lenders are often more concerned about operating cost excesses than about capital cost overruns. Project finance completion tests for mine developments usually place heavy emphasis on mine operation costs in the test period.

The analysis of operating cost involves a review of the full process from initial extraction of the ore or coal to its point of sale, or use. The issues to be addressed include: cost of labour, history of industrial action, labour productivity, size of trucks or shovels, distance trucks have to travel, fuel costs and the cost of supporting infrastructure.

308

In some limited recourse loans direct production and operating cost overrun risks are absent. This would typically be the case in asset financings such as a property loan, the financing of an aircraft leased out on a dry lease or of a ship under bareboat charter. Operating costs are not absent in these circumstances, but are shifted to the user by the terms of the contract between the owner and the user. The risk assessment shifts to the terms of the contract, the underlying market and the standing of the user.

Two further elements of operating costs (defined widely) deserve special mention: transportation costs (see 2.3.1) and taxes (see 2.6).

2.3.1 *Transportation Costs and Tariffs*

For a commodity with a low value-to-bulk ratio such as coal or iron ore, and particularly when the product of the mine competes in the international market, transportation costs are of vital importance. For these commodities, transport makes up a significant portion of the delivered cost of the product.

For example, coal from Australian and from western Canadian thermal coal mines compete in the Japanese market. Both have comparable FOB mine costs and similar ocean freight charges. But Australian coal mines are relatively near to the coast while the Canadian coal has to be transported across several mountain ranges before shipment. These inland transport costs proved a decisive factor in the relative competitiveness of coal from these two sources.

Transportation costs are also important to natural gas projects.

Sometimes a new natural gas exploitation project requires that a new pipeline be built. Often these pipelines are dedicated to the gas reservoir they serve. Unless more gas is found and developed in close proximity to the pipeline, it will cease to be a useful asset when the original gas field is depleted. In these circumstances, the transportation system is usually considered as part of the development project in question. And, because pipeline operating costs are low, the main risk involved in the pipeline element of the overall project is a part of the completion and capital cost overrun risk.

In the case of other natural gas production projects, the gas is transported to market by an independent system which charges a tariff to the users. In many cases, there may be no alternative means of transport (and as such the pipeline may be subject to monopoly-type regulation).

When examining a project which needs to pay a tariff to transport its product to market it is important to understand the transportation contract and the elements that make up the tariff. The transportation cost can be a variable charge on the project which varies with elements outside the control of the user project. The tariff may vary with the pipeline's operating and maintenance costs, though these typically are low. The depreciation component and the return on equity components are usually known, but the interest element can vary with the floating market rate of interest depending on contract terms. Pipelines which gather gas from a number of fields have been known to draw up their contracts on the basis that the total tariff is divided among the cubic feet of gas transported; this means that if production from another field were to fall, the tariff per cubic foot could rise. In this case, a lender to a given gas production project might have to form a view as to how likely it was that production from other gas fields would be maintained at forecast levels. This would entail reservoir assessments related to those other fields.

2.3.2 *Relative Project Competitiveness*

A project will, in principle, continue to operate for so long as the gross revenue which it generates exceeds its operating costs. To the extent that two or more producers compete with one another, if the price of the product – thermal coal in the example in 2.3.1 – falls, it will be, all other things being equal, the mine with the highest operating costs (including associated transport costs to market) that is forced to close first. A project lender would, therefore, be well advised to make an assessment as to where the mine being financed fits in a ranking of competing mines by operating cost per unit of production. In the absence of an overriding reason (of which there can be many), it would be prudent to finance the lowest cost producers. When financing producers at the higher end of the cost scale on project financing terms, the structure of the loan would ideally be designed with this in mind; the extent of risk assumed by the lender might, for instance, be reduced.

The project lender also has to bear in mind the debt burden of the project under construction which he is financing. As with many of the points raised in this chapter, this point is not unique to project financing, as was illustrated in the vulnerability of many highly leveraged companies in the recession of the early 1990s. Although the project's operating costs (before debt service) may be low on the scale, when debt service requirements are added the project may compare unfavourably with projects which have repaid their initial debt and not been refinanced by debt. As the lender wants his loan repaid in full with interest, a straight operating cost comparison may not be sufficient. If the comparative competitiveness analysis is to be undertaken, an attempt must be made to assess the likely reaction of the sponsors of competing projects to a price fall.

This analysis will need to include consideration of the willingness and ability (financial and market strength) of those with a commercial operating interest in each relevant project to weather the storm as well as of their different opinions as to how severe the storm will be. (Is the cost of mothballing the project greater than the loss that would be incurred by running it through the period of soft prices?)

While relative production costs are the essential determinant of relative project advantage, what makes relative project competitiveness an issue is the uncertainty surrounding the future price at which the product can be sold – the interaction of supply and demand for the product in question. The sales risk is examined in the next section.

2.4 Marketing and Sales Risk

The marketing or sales risk is that the project's product cannot be sold at a price sufficient to cover all the essential costs of the project (including, of course, taxes and interest) and to repay the debt in full. Although in each of the previous categories of risk, we had to consider risks arising from outside the project itself, the sales risks category is for every project* a much more fundamental interface with the outside world.

The marketing process and the determination of price in the market are so different for each product that they are best considered individually.

Oil is normally sold under relatively short term contract. The details of how the terms of oil sales contracts have changed as the balance of power in the marketplace has swung – from the international integrated companies, to OPEC, to the consumer – is a fascinating study in itself. In general, however, where the contract extends over a period of time, the price at which the oil is sold is subject to change. Depending on the contract, the engines of change have been, for example:

(i)   changes in the official selling prices of the producing governments,

(ii)   changes in spot market oil prices, or

(iii)   changes in the price obtained for a range of products produced by the refiner of the oil ("net back" or formula contracts).

Thus, in a financing of an oil production project the analysis of the marketing/sales risk pays little heed to the sales contract and focuses on price. This emphasis arises because of the nature of the commodity: oil is easily handled, transported and, although within strict quality limits, is an interchangeable commodity on a worldwide basis.

Price forecasting involves predicting supply and demand over the years ahead. It is, as everyone – including the forecasters – appreciates today, an exercise fraught with difficulties. The history of the oil price over the past twenty years provides a prime example. At the height of the OPEC decade at the end of the 1970s, energy economists argued that the price of oil would continue to rise. This seemed self-apparent: oil reserves were limited; like land, no more was being made; the history of the previous 35 years showed growing demand linked to growth in GDP – a link which to that date had been only marginally impacted by the 1973–4 price increase. The only debate was around the rate at which the price rise would take place. On this basis, a number of costly alternative energy projects were planned. Costly offshore oil field developments were financed on limited recourse terms that assumed that the oil price in a "worst case" (see Section 3.4) would drop to no less than $20/bbl. We all know what happened: between November 1985 and April 1986 the spot price of the North Sea marker crude, Brent, fell from $28/bbl to

---

* I exclude here projects spun off into special purpose vehicles selling their product back to the sponsor – or other captive purchaser – under a formula contract. See 2.4.3.

312

nearly $10/bbl. Since then the date at which a return to high prices will occur has regularly receded further into the future.

Yet in spite of the difficulties in forecasting price, each project financing proposal must, implicitly or explicitly, assume a price forecast. Lenders have often, themselves, assumed the risk of price variations adversely impacting cash flow available for debt service. Borrowers interested in maximising the debt a project can carry have often inquired early in discussions as to what future oil price assumptions a prospective lender is using: the lender's response is seen as giving a good indication of the relative eventual amount of limited recourse loan that will be offered.

A project's gross revenue comprises the price it can obtain for its product(s) multiplied by volume of the product(s) it sells. An oil project's oil production volumes, though they may be constrained by some of the technical factors discussed in foregoing sections, are not directly constrained by the market.This is because the oil market has, in the "spot market", a clearing price mechanism. Government interference can alter this. The oil glut in the US which followed the discovery of the East Texas Field in 1930, combined with the effects of the Depression on demand, led first to a fall in the price of oil from the $3.00/bbl level to the $0.10/bbl level and, in turn, to government "prorationing" regulations, through which the output of each producer was restricted. A more recent example can be found in the lifting restrictions imposed by OPEC in an attempt to maintain or increase the oil price. The imposition of a government depletion policy could similarly reduce the amount of oil a project could sell and thus the cash flow available for debt service.

The natural gas price environment contrasts markedly with that for oil. Because gas is a vapour under normal temperature and pressure conditions, expensive, specialised installations (pipelines or liquefaction plants, LNG carriers and regasification plants) are required for its handling and transport. This tends to dedicate gas to a given market, although the single market feature can be mitigated where the market is large or interconnected through a grid. The potential market flexibility of liquified natural gas sales has, in practice, not yet developed to any significant extent.

The result of this difference is that wide variations have existed between markets and projects for the price of like quality gas. Similarly, sales contracts (see 2.4.3) are a more important feature of natural gas project financings than they are for oil. Examination of the sales contract and an analysis of the dynamics of the specific market into which the gas is being sold becomes important to the banker financing a natural gas development on project terms. Government regulation of the gas market must be considered as part of this analysis. If current (1993) EC proposals allowing consumers to buy gas from any EC supplier become law, European gas projects and gas sales contracts will have to be assessed in the light of new market reality. The prospect of this market change is already a risk that needs to be considered.

As part of the market assessment, transport systems must also be considered. Inadequate systems can lead to the problem of "shut-in" gas, i.e. gas which cannot be produced and sold, even though there may be an ultimate market at the existing price (or at a lower level where the producer would still be a willing seller), because it cannot be moved to the market.

2.4.1   *Traffic Risk*

Infrastructure or leisure projects rely on attracting a sufficient custom (or, put differently, selling sufficient product) at a price to generate revenue. By their very nature, the product (e.g. a day at a given theme park, a toll bridge crossing, use by passengers of a certain airport) is unique, although it may compete in some respects (ferries will offer an alternative to crossing the Channel after Eurotunnel opens; one can drive on free roads instead of the toll motorways). One of the most fundamental risk asessment areas for such projects is, therefore, that of sales volume or traffic. How many people are expected to buy the product? And the related issue of what is the price-elasticity of demand (if the price rises or falls what is the effect on sales)? If the product is relatively price-inelastic (e.g. airport charges), such an infrastructure project may be subject to government regulation.

Independent traffic studies generally form part of the economic feasibility study for such projects. However, a wide range of variables may affect demand for such product and, as a result, traffic studies tend to be somewhat soft in reliability terms, particularly where a competing alternative is readily available (e.g. to the light rail link between Paris and Orly).

314

2.4.2 *Commodity Price Hedging*

The commodity derivatives market has developed in recent years. In this market, through a variety of hedging instruments (swaps, options, caps, collars), a commodity-producing project can have its exposure to variations in the price of its product hedged. For example, a project company developing an oil field can enter into an oil price swap under the terms of which it would pay the floating (spot market) price of oil and receive a pre-agreed fixed price over an agreed period for an agreed monthly volume of oil.

The depth of the market and the period over which price risk can be hedged varies with market conditions and the type of commodity. The ability to hedge effectively may also vary depending on the pricing formulae in the sales contract. For example, the future price risk of gas sold on an oil-based price index can be hedged. If the index were coal-based, it could not be so readily hedged.

Companies whose main business is oil may consider the taking and managing (independent of the paper market) exposure to the oil price as a part of their business. As such, they may be disinclined to hedge in this way. However, project lenders or producers whose main business is not oil may place a higher value on price certainty and thus be more inclined to mitigate commodity price risk through the derivatives market.

2.4.3 *Contracts*

All projects earn their revenue by selling their product and such sales are invariably governed by what would technically be described as a contract. Even the payment of a toll in return for the right to drive across a bridge represents a contract. But the project financier's interest in the contract is greatest when the term of the contract is long, when it covers repeated product deliveries and, particularly, when the market for the product functions in such a way that competing consumers are scarce or would be scarce at the relevant price level. We have already noted the relative lack of importance of oil sales contract terms to project financiers. But this is not the case, for example, for gas or electricity.

The clauses in the sales contract which govern payments can vary from very favourable to the seller to granting great flexibility to the buyer. In general, the type of clauses reflect the balance of supply and demand in the commodity at the time the contract is negotiated.

In times of tight supply, a purchaser may be willing to sign a contract on "take-or-pay" terms. Under such a contract, the purchaser is obliged to pay for a pre-agreed volume of product (or the service in the case of, say, a pipeline where such clauses are reasonably common) whether or not he is in a position to take the product*. Beyond that common element a wide variety of possible clauses can be subsumed in the colloquialism "take-or-pay". The price which the purchaser pays under a take-or-pay contract is sometimes directly related to an independent market price for the relevant product. In other take-or-pay contracts the price is established through the application of a formula and may bear little resemblance to a market price. Some take-or-pay clauses base the price on the cost of producing the product for sale such that the risk of cost overruns or higher operating costs would be borne by the purchaser through the sales price formula. Usually take-or-pay clauses only become operative if the project can make the product available. If the gas, say, is made available, is not taken, but is paid for, it would likely be held as inventory in the reservoir to be supplied (on an agreed basis) when the buyer was in a position to take it. In an extreme form of take-or-pay contract, payment would be made even if the product could not be made available. In these circumstances, through the contract with the purchaser, the project sponsor (and hence its financiers) could lay off completion and reserves risks.

When a market is in oversupply, the sales contract is generally, from the project's or seller's standpoint, far less strong. The seller then, typically, does not control price setting and the buyer may even interrupt purchases for a wide variety of reasons. In North America, some producers have supplied gas under a contract containing a so-called "market-out" clause, by which the buyer can opt to suspend his purchase. This clause, particularly if it is not also present in the sales contracts of competing suppliers, can render a project financing virtually impossible.

---

* In a sense this is analogous to time use contracts in property, aircraft or ships. Once he has entered into a contract, the charterer pays (absent default) for the use of the ship regardless of whether or not he is actually in a position to use it.

While an analysis of sales contracts is necessary for the project lender, it is not sufficient. The supply-demand balance can change and economic (and political) pressure can build up for a renegotiation of contract terms. The binding nature of contracts – always a stronger concept in some cultures than others – was universally called into question in the 1980s through changing market conditions. To continue with the natural gas market example, as the US gas market moved into oversupply in the early 1980s, some purchasers of gas suspended their take-or-pay payments and invited suppliers to sue them. If the result of either course of action were to be bankruptcy for the purchaser, the invitation to sue at least had the merit of postponing the day of reckoning, given the likely time the case would take to wend its way through the courts. This possibility makes it imperative that the prudent project financiers understand the economics of the market underlying what, on the surface, looks like a very favourable sales contract for the project. The parties to the contract (beyond a straightforward assessment of their creditworthiness for the obligations they have undertaken through the contract) and their reasons for entering into the contract are important.

2.4.4 *Contract Lending*

Project finance structures have been developed, particularly in the independent power sector, which rely on a network of contracts. These contracts serve to pass many of the individual risk elements to appropriate parties. For example the main contractor building the power plant may bear the cost overrun risk through the terms of the turnkey construction contract (see 2.1); the purchaser of electricity, under the power purchase agreement (usually the key agreement in such structures), may assume the risk of higher fuel costs. The project company's sponsor itself may contribute nothing more than some initial equity and its development and operating expertise. Bank lenders have become comfortable with these structures. They are now being introduced in the bond market.

By way of a simplified example, the sponsor of a hypothetical private sector, coal-fired power plant might endeavour to arrange the following contracts for the project company it sets up.

(i)   Construction contract. Fixed price except for specific overrun elements. The contractor is obliged to deliver a plant which operates to established specifications;

(ii) Coal supply contract. Price of coal fluctuates with a market indicator. If the supplier cannot supply the required volume of coal a penalty is paid;

(iii) Debt financing agreement. Floating interest rate. 15 year repayment. Plus a small overrun financing tranche repayable over 10 years;

(iv) Operating contract. A third party with experience in the industry operates the plant on a fee basis. There are fixed and variable elements to this charge;

(v) Power Purchase Agreement. Price paid for the electricity is based on a formula covering:

   (a) debt principle repayments (base debt and overrun);

   (b) interest on debt, floating with the interest rate;

   (c) operating costs;

   (d) cost of coal;

   (e) element for return to equity; and

   (f) if electricity cannot be supplied because, say, coal is not available, the purchaser pays the fixed elements of the charge (i.e. (a), (b), the fixed part of (c) and possibly part of (e)) less the penalty paid to the sponsor by the coal producer for not supplying coal.

Although the lender can take comfort from a contract structure of this sort, the quality and motivation of the parties to the contracts and the underlying markets still need to be examined.

2.5 Interest Rate and Currency Risk

Projects which borrow on floating rate bases can be adversely affected by a rising interest rate environment, particularly if highly leveraged.

A lender may seek to limit leverage for these reasons. He may also require that the project (or its sponsors) hedges itself against these risks. If the hedge is closely tied to the project, it will likely be a highly structured transaction in its own right.

Currency risk arises when there is a mismatch between the currency(ies) generated by the project and the currency of debt. In structuring the financing, the lenders and sponsors should seek to eliminate this mismatch by appropriate choice of lending currencies. Currency hedges may also play a part in executing the currency risk minimisation strategy, to the benefit of debt or equity, or both.

The risk of currency inconvertibility (or availability of foreign exchange from the central bank of the host country) is different in nature, falling under the category of political risk.

2.6 Political or Legislative Risk
This category covers the risk that action by government (or events within the host country of a broadly political nature) leads to a diminution of debt service capacity.

It is important from the outset to distinguish political risk in a project context from the more general concept of political or sovereign risk. While revolutionary social disruption, a restriction on the availability of foreign currency, or debt rescheduling can indeed impact the viability of a project financing, other types of action – that occur regularly even in the most highly rated of countries – can also be harmful to projects. For instance, the rate of tax on petroleum production may be increased to the point of jeopardising planned project debt repayment. But this action, by increasing government revenues, may be potentially beneficial to sovereign debt holders. Nor, as the example of a tax increase indicates, is political risk in a project context confined to an analysis of cross-border risk.

A long list of potential events that would constitute political risk could be produced. Any such list merely serves to emphasise that a project lender must seek to understand the political and legislative environment in which the project operates.

The other side of the coin is that government support to projects cannot necessarily be assumed to continue throughout the life of the project or the loan made to finance it. This relates to host government support (such as the US refinery entitlement programme in the 1970s) as well as that in effect provided by other nations, or cartels of nations – as the collapse of tin and oil prices in 1986 illustrated.

Changes in government policy can also create the opportunity for projects and hence their financing. The lifting of the prohibition on burning natural gas to generate electricity was essential to the series of gas-fired power station project financings in the UK in the early 1990s. The other essential ingredient, also government induced, was the change in the structure of the UK electricity industry associated with its privatisation.

Where a project is being developed in an unfamiliar jurisdiction or a developing country with a low credit standing, sponsors may seek a project financing to cover country risks. Commercial banks are often no more willing than sponsors to assume these risks. In Section 1.5 we identified the concept of balance in a project financing. The idea is that elements of risk should be borne by the party best able to quantify, manage and control the particular risk element. For developing country risk, this entity may be a multi-lateral agency which is set up to assist the development of such countries. These agencies enjoy preferred creditor status and have programmes which allow other lenders to benefit from this status when lending under the agency's umbrella.

2.7   Concession-based Project Financings

The political re-emphasis on the private sector through the 1980s has given rise to greater possibilities for project financing in infrastructure developments. Some of these projects – or proposed projects – are built within a concession structure. This may be known as a BOOT (Build-Own-Operate-Transfer) scheme. Other acronyms are used to describe variations on this quasi-privatisation arrangement. A concession based project might involve:

(i)   the government grants a concession to a private sector entity to construct and operate, say, a toll road.

(ii)   the private sector entity is granted the right to collect user charges, on a basis agreed with government, over an agreed period of time, or until an agreed return on equity is obtained. The private sector entity bears the commercial risks of the operation within the agreed parameters.

(iii) on the basis of the projected project cash flows, the private sector entity raises construction finance. This may include equity as well as debt. The debt is likely to be on project finance (limited recourse) terms.

(iv)   at the end of the concession, the asset reverts to the government. The reversion terms need to be designed carefully to ensure that the concessionnaire has an incentive to maintain the project towards the end of the concession's life. In certain cases the government may re-bid the concession, awarding it for a further period of time to the highest bidder.

The role of government in these arrangements is of fundamental importance. The concession structure created by the government must be designed to attract potential concessionnaires from the private sector. This will be reflected in the economic regulatory structure (if there are monopoly elements) and possibly in specific changes in otherwise applicable rules to permit the project to be financed. For example, lenders dislike lending on limited recourse terms to projects where equity holders and government (through taxes) earn significant returns before their project debt has been repaid. To create an incentive for the project, the authorities may need to defer tax receipts through, for example, a tax holiday or allowing a more rapid depreciation for tax purposes (higher capital allowances) than had applied to such assets under a pre-privatisation regime. On the other hand the government must also concern itself with public policy considerations and, as a result, may wish to impose specific conditions on the concessionnaire, for example regarding access, quality of service and safety.

Where monopoly elements are present, and as a result economic regulation is appropriate, limitations on abuse of monopoly power through the imposition of a cap on prices and other public policy considerations must be balanced by the need to make the project sufficiently attractive to investors and lenders. Lenders and investors should generally find the existence of an appropriate regulatory structure to be a positive feature of a project with monopoly elements. It shows that the issues have been considered by the authorities, that rules have been developed and that the project is, as a result, less likely to suffer from subsequent arbitrary changes imposed by the state.

In political environments where the private sector is considered to have intrinsic merits over the public sector in the delivery of goods and services, the concession concept can be extended to projects which have a social value (high positive externalities) and are thus worthy of state subsidy. In these cases, the project concession could be awarded to the private-sector bidder seeking the lowest subsidy. Although, at the time of writing, not yet applied to capital projects, this structure has close precedents in the purchaser/provider model developed in the late 1980s and early 1990s in UK local authorities.

A lender to concession-based projects must take into account the risk and consequences of a change in the project's basis from renationalisation under a future government or a change in the terms of government support.

2.8 Insurance

Finally, there is a series of relatively remote risks to which a project is subject, such as physical loss or damage, terrorism, war and suit from third parties. Many of these, usually non-financial*, risks are commercially insurable.

A properly structured project financing will address these issues and seek to have them insured in the market or to be satisfied with the sponsor's capacity for self-insurance. The terms of the Credit Agreement and/or the Security Agreement should address the interest of the lender(s) in the relevant insurance mechanism. Since insurance is a specialised field, project lenders often employ an insurance adviser to act on their behalf in ensuring that the project is properly insured in accordance with the best practice in that market.

---

* Although the insurance markets have from time to time strayed from the principle, generally financial risks such as the future price of commodity X or asset Y or a future exchange or interest rate have not been insurable risks.

Political risk insurance can also be available in the insurance markets and could be used as part of a project financing. In current insurance market conditions political risk policies are generally not available for periods in excess of three years. Most project financings are of longer duration. Business interruption risk cover is also obtainable in some circumstances. Such policies pay out, on an agreed basis, for the loss of revenue consequent upon the happening of an insured event, such as damage to production facilities.

3. CASH FLOW LENDING

It should be apparent from the preceeding sections that project financing is cash flow lending. The lender is relatively unconcerned with the balance sheets and income statements of the project company*. Often, where a start-up project in a special purpose vehicle company is involved, there are, in fact, no relevant historical financial statements. The project lender's focus is on the projections of future cash flow expected to be generated by the project. This type of analysis is also applied to financings (such as leveraged buy-outs) which cannot strictly be called project financings.

3.1 Cash Flow Models

In the following sections we shall consider cash flow projections and sensitivity analyses as tools to assist the lender in making his lending decision and subsequently in monitoring the project loan.

Until recently the mechanical exercise of building up cash flow projections and testing the sensitivity of cash flow to changes in key variables was very time-consuming and tedious. The wide-spread use of personal computers and user-friendly programs has changed that. It is important to realise, however, that the analysis of the risks has not fundamentally changed. No number of computer-generated sensitivity analyses are of any use if one does not know how to apply them, if one does not understand their significance nor have a view as to the likelihood of the

---

*The lender will, of course, be concerned with the financial accounts of the sponsors and other parties to the project as he assesses the ability of these parties to bear risk and meet commitments.

scenarios described coming about. Properly used they are a valuable analytical tool.

3.1.1 *A Simplified Project Cash Flow Projection Line-by-Line*

Table 1 is a very simplified project cash flow projection. The model was developed and run on LOTUS-123. In this section we shall consider of what it consists. The project illustrated by the model is an oil field.

Table 1 is the Base Case, the case the lender considers most likely to obtain. The lender's Base Case may be more conservative than the sponsor's – or equity holder's – most likely case, and almost certainly more conservative than the business plan. This is because equity holders have upside potential as well as downside risk. Unless he has negotiated a sharing in equity returns in return for extending the loan, the lender will not benefit from a better than expected project outcome but will be exposed to worse than expected scenarios.

Line 1 ("YEAR") is time, starting with the present and divided for these purposes into six month periods.

Line 2 ("Oil Production (MMBBL)") is the oil that the project is expected to produce, expressed in millions of barrels (MMBBL), during each six month period of the life of the field. This is an input line and is established on the basis of the data developed by, essentially, reservoir engineers (see 2.2. above). Note that for the first four periods no oil is produced: a pre-start-up development loan is being examined in this analysis. Note also that production peaks relatively soon after the project starts producing oil and then declines for the rest of the field life. This type of pattern is typical of many oil production projects.

Line 3 ("Oil Price ($/BBL esc @5% from 1990)") is the price (expressed in dollars per barrel) at which it is expected oil can be sold. Again, this is an input line based on the forecaster's view of the future development of the oil price (see 2.4 above). In the example, the price of oil is assumed to remain constant in nominal dollar terms until the end of the third year and, thereafter, to increase at a rate of 5% per annum. As with the oil production forecast this may or may not be a reasonable assumption. The cash flow projection is only as good as its input assumptions.

324

Line 4 ("Gross Revenue") is derived by multiplying Line 2 by Line 3. It is in millions of dollars.

Lines 5, 6 and 7 ("Capital Costs", "Operating Costs" and "Taxes") are a simplified representation of the costs, or cash outflows, associated with the project. Because, as project lenders, we are interested in the amount of cash the project needs to pay out and in how much cash the project will have available to pay interest and repay the principal amount of the debt, these are cash items. In generally accepted accounting practice, capital costs would be capitalised and depreciated over the life of the project.

Capital costs and operating costs are input assumptions based on what it is estimated it will cost to build and run the project. Notice that Operating Costs are assumed to increase at a rate of 10% p.a. This is faster than the escalation rate applied to the oil price, a conservative assumption.

Taxes are derived, based on the tax regime that is expected to prevail over the life of the project. Because the tax regimes applicable to projects are often complex, the formulae needed to derive expected taxes accurately are complex. A simpler hypothetical formula has been used in this model to derive taxes. Taxes in any six month period are calculated in the model as 55% of Gross Revenues less Capital Costs and Operating Costs with any tax losses incurred in any period accumulated and carried forward indefinitely until used.

Line 8 ("Net Cash Flow Pre Debt Service") is Line 4 minus Lines 5, 6 and 7. In its construction phase this is the amount of cash the project requires and in its operating phase it is the amount the project is forecast to generate without taking into account the means by which the project is financed and the cost of money.

The next five lines – lines 9 – 13 – model the project loan. For the purposes of this simplified illustration it is assumed that a fixed percentage (here 85%) of capital costs are being debt financed and that interest (at an assumed 10% per annum on the opening loan balance for any period) is capitalised (in the sense of being paid by further drawings on the loan) during the construction period*.

It has been assumed for the purposes of the model that the loan is repaid in eight equal semi-annual instalments, beginning in 1996 (when oil production is forecast to be approaching peak rates) based on the loan outstanding at the end of 1995. While such repayment patterns are common in term lending, they are not always wholly appropriate to a Project Financing because of the potentially uneven or, indeed, unpredictable nature of the revenue stream. Repayment terms are considered further in Section 3.5.

* Although not relevant in considering Table 1, the model logic pays interest from sponsors' cash flow after completion if cash flow before debt service is insufficient to pay interest.

Table 1

BASE CASE PROJECT CASH FLOW MODEL

	YEAR :	1993.1	1993.6	1994.1	1994.6	1995.1	1995.6	1996.1	1996.6
1									
2	Oil Production (MMBBL) :	0	0	0	0	3	3	8	10
3	Oil Price ($/BBL esc.@ 5% from 1996) :	15	15	15	15	15	15	15.4	15.8
4	Gross Revenue :	0	0	0	0	45	45	123	158
5	Capital Costs :	60	75	100	95	10	10	0	0
6	Operating Costs (esc. @ 10%) :	0	0	0	0	15	16	16	17
7	Taxes (55%) :	0	0	0	0	0	0	0	0
8	Net Cash Flow Pre Debt Service :	(60)	(75)	(100)	(95)	20	19	106	140
9	Initial Loan Balance :	0	52	120	213	306	306	306	268
10	Loan Drawdown :	51	64	85	81	0	0	0	0
11	Loan Repayment (equal s.a. 4 yrs) :	0	0	0	0	0	0	38	38
12	Interest (10%) :	1	4	8	12	15	15	14	12
13	End Loan Balance :	52	120	213	306	306	306	268	230
14	Cash Flow to Sponsor :	(9)	(12)	(19)	(22)	5	4	54	90
15	PV @ 10% Net Cash Flow Pre Debt Service :	315	406	525	646	658	670	597	486
16	Cover Ratio (PV NCF/End Loan Balance) :	6.03	3.38	2.47	2.11	2.15	2.19	2.23	2.11
17	IRR to Sponsor : 33.3%								

326

Line 14 ("Cash Flow to Sponsor") shows negative figures during the construction phase. These are the sponsor's equity contribution to the project, the remaining 15% of capital costs. After project start-up Line 14 shows the cash available to the sponsor after servicing debt.

At this point, we have examined a simple cash flow projection for a project. Before considering the last three lines in Table 1, we shall step back to review the discounted cash flow concept.

3.2 Discounted Cash Flow

Discounted cash flow is a means of expressing in a single figure the value of a payment or a series of payments received at a future date or a series of future dates. It is based on the time value of money: the concept that a pound received today is worth more than a pound received at some future date because one can earn interest on the pound received today

Table 1 (continued)

1997.1	1997.6	1998.1	1998.6	1999.1	1999.6	2000.1	2000.6	2001.1	2001.6	2002.1	2002.6
10	10	9	9	8	8	7	6	5	4	3	2
16.1	16.5	16.9	17.4	17.8	18.2	18.7	19.1	19.6	20.1	20.6	21.1
161	165	153	156	142	146	131	115	98	80	62	42
0	0	0	0	0	0	0	0	0	0	0	0
18	19	20	21	22	23	24	25	27	28	29	31
18	76	69	72	65	67	59	49	39	29	18	6
125	70	63	63	56	56	48	40	32	24	15	5
230	191	153	115	77	38	0	0	0	0	0	0
0	0	0	0	0	0	0	0	0	0	0	0
38	38	38	38	38	38	0	0	0	0	0	0
10	8	7	5	3	1	0	0	0	0	0	0
191	153	115	77	38	0	0	0	0	0	0	0
77	24	18	21	15	17	48	40	32	24	15	5
384	332	285	236	192	145	104	69	40	19	5	0
2.01	2.17	2.49	3.08	5.01	0	0	0	0	0	0	0

between now and the future date. Over several periods, the interest received would be compounded, i.e. the interest received on today's pound would be reinvested and itself earn interest for the remaining periods.

It is important to recognise that the time value of money concept is independent of inflation or inflationary expectations.* The time value of money concept is not itself a correction for inflation.**

The future value (FV) is equal to the initial investment (PV, present value, the principal sum) plus the interest earned.

A simple expression of the concept diagrammatically could be:

$$\text{———|———————————|————————} \longrightarrow \text{time}$$

PV ← investment period → FV

@ rate of interest (r) per period

Expressed algebraically:

FV = PV + (PV × r)

or

FV = PV (1 + r)

Determining the future value (FV), or "going forward" in time, is known as "compounding". Determining the present value (PV) or "going backwards" along the time line is known as "discounting".

---

* Except insofar as inflation or inflationary expectations influence the rate of interest.

** Because the loan is made in today's pounds and repaid in tomorrow's pounds it is usual for lenders to assess project cash flows based on the monetary values expected after taking into account the forecast effects of inflation. There can, however, often be merit in examining projects assuming a zero inflation rate. Such projections are referred to as being in "real" — as opposed to "nominal" — terms.

328

The foregoing compounding equation can be rearranged as a discounting equation:

$$PV = \frac{FV}{(1 + r)}$$

These equations cover one interest period. For two interest periods, the equations would look like this:

$$FV = PV + (PV \times r) + (PV + (PV \times r))(PV \times r)$$

or

$$FV = PV (1 + r) (1 + r)$$

or

$$FV = PV (1 + r)^2$$

and

$$PV = \frac{FV}{(1 + r)^2}$$

Work through these equations using numbers until you are comfortable with them. Once you have done this you should be able to recognise the formula for compounding over twenty periods as:

$$FV_{20} = PV (1 + r)^{20}$$

And the formula for discounting a cash flow occurring twenty periods in the future as:

$$PV = \frac{FV_{20}}{(1 + r)^{20}}$$

Generalised formulae for compounding or discounting single cash flows can be expressed as follows (where 't' is the number of periods):

$$FV_t = PV (1 + r)^t$$

and

$$PV = \frac{FV_t}{(1 + r)^t}$$

With this concept, we can return to Table 1.

Line 15 is the present value (PV) in the relevant period of Net Cash Flow Pre-Debt Service occurring after that date (a series of future values: FVs) discounted at 10% p.a. (r, expressed on an annual basis). In other words, it shows the present value at each six month period of the project's then future cash flows before interest payment and principal repayment.

3.2.1 *Cover Ratio*

Line 16 ("Cover Ratio") compares the present value figure in the previous line to the amount of the debt oustanding. At any time after the project is complete the Cover Ratio is a measure of how comfortable the lender is that the debt will be repaid. The higher the ratio the more comfortable the lender is. A cover ratio of 1:1 implies that if the forecasts are met the loan will just repay, with all interest paid, with no margin for error and no return to the sponsor. With a cover ratio of less than 1:1, the loan will not be fully repaid.

There is no mechanistic way of determining how far above 1:1 a cover ratio for a project must be to provide an adequate degree of comfort to a lender. It depends on how conservative the input data used in the projections are and it depends on the characteristics of the project itself. We shall return to this question at 3.3 below.

Other cashflow based ratios are also used in assessing the margin of comfort in the loan, e.g. life of loan cover ratio (as opposed to the life of reserves ratio illustrated in Line 16) and annual interest or debt service cover ratios (Net Cash Flow Pre Debt Service to either interest or interest plus scheduled debt repayment).

330

3.2.2 *Internal Rate of Return*

The internal rate of return of a series of cash flows is derived from the time value of money formulae examined above, assuming the present value to be nil and solving the equation for the rate of interest or discount rate. In other words:

$$PV = 0 = \frac{FV_t}{(1 + r)^t}$$

For a series of cash flows, as we have in a project situation, the equation to be solved for r is:

$$PV = 0 = FV_0 + \frac{FV_1}{(1+r)} + \frac{FV_2}{(1+r)^2} + \frac{FV_3}{(1+r)^3} + ... + \frac{FV_t}{(1+r)^t}$$

The calculation of the internal rate of return is normally very difficult and, like the easier calculation of present or future values, is as a rule performed using a program.

The internal rate of return in the model shown in Table 1 (Line 17 "IRR to sponsor") is calculated on the cash flow stream represented as "Cash Flow to Sponsor" in line 14. It takes into account both the negative cashflows at the beginning of the project and the positive ones later on. The sponsor's equity injections (the initial negative cashflows) can be regarded as the amount required to purchase the subsequent positive cash flow stream. Is it a good purchase, a good investment? If the return to equity – the internal rate of return on the sponsor's cash flow stream – is greater than the returns available elsewhere or greater than the investing firm's risk weighted cost of capital (the "hurdle rate"), then the investment is a good one and one the sponsor should make. An internal rate of return of 33.3% is available in this project based on the assumption that the inputs are valid. If the appropriate hurdle rate is, say, 18% the investment should be made*. Since the lender seeks sponsor

---

* A substantial body of theoretical literature exists on the subject of the appropriate hurdle rate or weighted average cost of capital. This is not our immediate concern in the context of project lending.

commitment to the project, he would be wary of a project that showed inadequate returns to equity, even if debt were well covered.

The internal rate of return is a commonly used tool in assessing the comparative merits of alternative investment possibilities. It enables a ranking of alternatives to be drawn up on the basis of a single, easily understood rate which is not distorted by the size of the investment.**

3.3 Sensitivity Analyses

Projections do not always materialise in reality. The real world is subject to change, a project to the risks reviewed in Section 2. Sensitivity analyses quantify the effect on the project (and, in the case of a project loan, the effect specifically on cash flow available for debt service and on loan repayment) of a change from the base projections in one or more of the input variables.

Sensitivity analyses were performed on the case set out in Table 1 (the "Base Case"). Three tables of sensitivity analysis results, expressed in terms of change in the cover ratio, are set out as Table 2. The cover ratio adopted for this purpose is the ratio at the point oil production begins (here end 1995.6). The input variable which is varied in each of the three tables in Table 2 is the oil price. The first line in each table shows the effect on the cover ratio of a change in the oil price in 1995 assuming no other input assumptions are changed.

If the project lending officer is more comfortable with an oil price of $10/bbl in 1995 (rising at 5% p.a. thereafter), he can determine what the cover ratio under such circumstances would be. From the table one can see that it is 1.46:1.

Suppose that the lending bank's engineering advisers think that the production rate is overstated in the Base Case, that they wish to analyse the project at 30% less production. Reading down the vertical columns of the first table we see that the Cover Ratio under such an assumption (with no other input assumptions changed) would be 1.51:1.

** Internal Rate of Return calculations implicitly assume the reinvestment at the IRR of cash flows generated for the remaining period. This is likely to be unrealistic in many cases and improvements on the calculation are possible which adjust for this feature. They are not considered here.

332

Table 2

SENSITIVITY ANALYSES OF COVER RATIO IN 1994.6

BASE OIL PRICE (1995)	15	14.5	14	13.5	13	12.5	12	11.5	11	10.5	10	9.5	9
0	2.11	2.05	1.98	1.92	1.85	1.79	1.73	1.66	1.60	1.53	1.46	1.39	1.32
5%	2.01	1.95	1.89	1.83	1.77	1.71	1.65	1.58	1.52	1.45	1.39	1.32	1.25
10%	1.91	1.85	1.80	1.74	1.68	1.62	1.56	1.50	1.44	1.38	1.31	1.25	1.18
PERCENTAGE REDUCTION IN OIL PRODUCTION 15%	1.81	1.76	1.70	1.65	1.59	1.54	1.48	1.42	1.36	1.30	1.24	1.17	1.11
20%	1.71	1.66	1.61	1.55	1.50	1.45	1.39	1.33	1.28	1.22	1.16	1.10	1.04
25%	1.61	1.56	1.51	1.46	1.41	1.35	1.30	1.25	1.19	1.14	1.08	1.03	0.97
30%	1.51	1.46	1.41	1.36	1.31	1.26	1.21	1.16	1.11	1.06	1.00	0.95	0.89
35%	1.40	1.35	1.31	1.26	1.21	1.16	1.12	1.07	1.02	0.97	0.91	0.84	0.76
40%	1.28	1.24	1.19	1.15	1.10	1.06	1.01	0.97	0.92	0.87	0.79	0.71	0.63
45%	1.16	1.12	1.08	1.03	0.99	0.95	0.91	0.86	0.79	0.72	0.65	0.57	0.50
50%	1.03	0.99	0.96	0.92	0.88	0.83	0.77	0.70	0.63	0.57	0.50	0.44	0.37

BASE OIL PRICE (1995)	15	14.5	14	13.5	13	12.5	12	11.5	11	10.5	10	9.5	9
0	2.11	2.05	1.98	1.92	1.85	1.79	1.73	1.66	1.60	1.53	1.46	1.39	1.32
5%	2.04	1.98	1.91	1.85	1.79	1.73	1.67	1.61	1.54	1.48	1.41	1.34	1.27
10%	1.97	1.91	1.85	1.79	1.73	1.68	1.62	1.56	1.50	1.43	1.37	1.30	1.24
PERCENTAGE INCREASE IN CAPITAL COSTS 15%	1.91	1.85	1.79	1.74	1.68	1.63	1.57	1.51	1.45	1.39	1.33	1.27	1.20
20%	1.85	1.80	1.74	1.69	1.63	1.58	1.52	1.47	1.41	1.35	1.29	1.23	1.17
25%	1.80	1.74	1.69	1.64	1.59	1.54	1.48	1.43	1.37	1.32	1.26	1.20	1.14
30%	1.75	1.70	1.65	1.60	1.55	1.50	1.45	1.39	1.34	1.28	1.22	1.17	1.11
35%	1.70	1.65	1.61	1.56	1.51	1.45	1.41	1.36	1.30	1.25	1.20	1.14	1.08
40%	1.66	1.61	1.57	1.52	1.47	1.42	1.38	1.32	1.27	1.22	1.17	1.11	1.06
45%	1.62	1.58	1.53	1.48	1.44	1.39	1.34	1.29	1.24	1.19	1.14	1.09	1.03
50%	1.58	1.54	1.50	1.45	1.41	1.36	1.34	1.26	1.22	1.17	1.12	1.06	1.01

BASE OIL PRICE (1995)	15	14.5	14	13.5	13	12.5	12	11.5	11	10.5	10	9.5	9
6%	2.13	2.07	2.00	1.93	1.87	1.80	1.73	1.67	1.60	1.53	1.46	1.39	1.32
7%	2.13	2.08	2.00	1.93	1.86	1.80	1.73	1.67	1.60	1.53	1.46	1.39	1.32
8%	2.12	2.06	1.99	1.93	1.86	1.80	1.73	1.66	1.60	1.53	1.46	1.39	1.32
INTEREST RATE 9%	2.12	2.05	1.99	1.92	1.86	1.79	1.73	1.66	1.60	1.53	1.46	1.39	1.32
10%	2.11	2.05	1.99	1.92	1.85	1.79	1.73	1.66	1.60	1.53	1.46	1.39	1.32
11%	2.11	2.04	1.99	1.92	1.85	1.79	1.73	1.66	1.59	1.53	1.46	1.39	1.31
12%	2.10	2.04	1.98	1.91	1.85	1.79	1.72	1.66	1.59	1.53	1.45	1.38	1.31
13%	2.10	2.03	1.97	1.91	1.85	1.78	1.72	1.65	1.59	1.52	1.45	1.38	1.31
14%	2.09	2.03	1.97	1.91	1.84	1.78	1.72	1.65	1.58	1.51	1.44	1.37	1.30
15%	2.08	2.03	1.96	1.90	1.84	1.78	1.71	1.64	1.58	1.51	1.44	1.37	1.30
16%	2.08	2.02	1.96	1.90	1.84	1.77	1.70	1.64	1.57	1.50	1.44	1.37	1.30

Combining these two variations in input assumptions, we find a cover ratio of 1.00:1. If both these assumptions proved correct, the loan would only just pay out with no margin for error. The lender would not make the loan unless he regarded these assumptions as a "worst case" i.e. that the chances of events turning out even worse were absolutely minimal.

The remaining two tables in Table 2 perform sensitivity analyses with respect to increased capital costs and interest rates. It is interesting to note the relative insensitivity of this hypothetical project to interest rate volatility. Brief tables such as those in Table 2 give general guidance as to the impact of changes in input assumptions. To see what the effects of different assumptions are on other elements of the cash flow projections than the cover ratio at the point of production start-up, a project lender would re-run the full case with a new set of input assumptions. A full print-out of such a sensitivity case is set out in Table 3, below.

Table 3

"WORST CASE" PROJECT CASH FLOW MODEL

1	YEAR :	1993.1	1993.6	1994.1	1994.6	1995.1	1995.6	1996.1	1996.6
2	Oil Production(MMBBL) :	0	0	0	0	2	2	6	8
	Oil Price								
3	($/BBL esc.@5% from 1996) :	10	10	10	10	10	10	10.2	10.5
4	Gross Revenue :	0	0	0	0	24	24	66	84
5	Capital Costs :	72	90	120	114	12	12	0	0
6	Operating Costs (esc. @ 10%) :	0	0	0	0	15	16	16	17
7	Taxes (55%) :	0	0	0	0	0	0	0	0
8	Net Cash Flow Pre Debt Service :	(72)	(90)	(120)	(114)	(3)	(4)	49	67
9	Initial Loan Balance :	0	63	147	264	383	383	383	335
10	Loan Drawdown :	61	77	102	97	0	0	0	0
11	Loan Repayment								
	(equal s.a. 4 yrs) :	0	0	0	0	0	0	48	48
12	Interest (15%) :	2	7	14	23	28	28	26	23
13	End Loan Balance :	63	147	264	383	383	383	335	287
14	Cash Flow to Sponsor :	(11)	(16)	(25)	(31)	(31)	(31)	(25)	(4)
15	PV @ 10% Net Cash Flow Pre								
	Debt Service :	46	139	265	392	414	438	411	364
16	Cover Ratio (PVNCF/End								
	Loan Balance) :	0.73	0.94	1.01	1.02	1.08	1.14	1.23	1.27
17	IRR to Sponsor :	-6.8%							

3.4 Loan Values: How Much to Lend

Determining how much to lend against a project is ultimately a subjective judgment. It is closely linked to the decision as to which input variables to focus on. The base case and sensitivity analyses can provide a useful tool in reaching the decision.

Because the Credit Agreement often stipulates monitoring of the project loan on the basis of a set of Base Case assumptions, agreed (in one way or another) from time to time on the basis of the then prevailing conditions between lender and borrower, a project's loan value is often determined by applying to the Present Value of Net Cash Flow Before Debt Service a Cover Ratio that is deemed to be acceptable. Using Table 1 as our example, P.V. N.C.F. Before Debt Service in 1995.6 (just before oil

Table 3 (continued)

1997.1	1997.6	1998.1	1998.6	1999.1	1999.6	2000.1	2000.6	2001.1	2001.6	2002.1	2002.6
8	8	7	7	6	6	6	5	3	3	2	2
10.8	11.0	11.3	11.6	11.9	12.2	12.5	12.8	13.1	13.4	13.7	14.1
86	88	81	83	76	78	70	61	39	43	33	23
0	0	0	0	0	0	0	0	0	0	0	0
18	19	20	21	22	23	24	25	27	28	29	31
0	0	0	0	0	0	0	20	7	8	2	0
68	69	61	62	54	55	46	16	6	7	2	(8)
287	239	192	144	96	48	0	0	0	0	0	0
0	0	0	0	0	0	0	0	0	0	0	0
48	48	48	48	48	48	0	0	0	0	0	0
19	16	12	9	5	2	0	0	0	0	0	0
239	192	144	96	48	0	0	0	0	0	0	0
1	6	1	6	1	5	46	16	6	7	2	(8)
314	260	211	159	113	64	21	6	1	-6	-8	0
1.31	1.36	1.47	1.66	2.36	0	0	0	0	0	0	0

production, and hence repayment, begins) is $670 million*. A range of possibly acceptable cover ratios would yield the following loan values:

Cover Ratio	Loan Value ($ million)
1.5	447
2.0	335
2.5	268

The cover ratio selected must be sufficiently high to protect the bank against the possible downside risks. No single cover ratio is appropriate to all projects, just as the set of risks involved in each project differs and the environment in which each operates is different**. Note for instance that, all other things being equal, a loan to a project subject to a high rate tax regime (and which is, in fact, paying tax) can tolerate a lower cover ratio than an identical project in a low tax environment. This apparent paradox is explained by the fact that a deterioration in project performance will only partly be reflected in post tax cash flow available for debt service, the other part being absorbed by a reduction in taxes paid.

The cover ratio, then, must act as proxy for the downside risks (or downward movement from Base Case input variables) to which the project is subject.

Another approach to determining loan value is to construct the "worst case" scenario, i.e. to develop a sensitivity analysis reflecting the lender's judgement of the worst possible combined set of circumstances that might afflict the project.

Let us assume that the lender determined that the appropriate worst case input assumptions were:

*This pre-debt service line is the appropriate one to discount for this purpose because the discounting process in effect takes into account the payment of interest. Similarly, the present value at the time interest ceases to be capitalised (and debt is likely at its maximum) is the most useful one in this type of analysis.

**We have noted, above, the influence of the conservativeness or otherwise of Base Case parameters.

- oil price: $10/bbl esc. at 5% p.a. from 1996
- oil production: Base Case less 20%
- capital costs: Base Case plus 10%
- interest rate: average 15%

The resulting sensitivity analysis is shown in Table 3.

Using the same principles for loan draw down as in the Base Case, a loan of $383 million is outstanding at the end of 1994. A cover ratio at this date of 1.02 indicates that a loan of this magnitude can just be serviced in accordance with its terms. However, a closer look at the numbers shows that the sponsor had to contribute equity to the project after start up to meet interest and principal payments to the bank as scheduled for two years. In such circumstances, there is the risk that the sponsor would not make the required contribution; that, holding the lender to the non-recourse nature of loan agreement, he would walk away from the project. The internal rate of return facing the sponsor at the end of 1994 is 0.7%*. If, by the end of 1994, the worst case had become the base case, the investor, unless induced by other factors, would be unlikely to support the project. On this basis, a loan of $383 million is excessive. Depending on the circumstances, the potential lender can approach the problem with several solutions. Among these he could consider (a) requiring greater equity to be injected into the project at an early stage** or (b) requiring a completion guarantee or other form of completion support (see Section 4.1.1) from the sponsor to meet capital costs arising above an amount that can be repaid from operating phase cash flow without further recourse to the sponsor.

---

*Not shown in the table and calculated only through June 2002. The figure shown of -6.8% is the IRR of the cash flow stream starting at the beginning of 1993. Neither rate of return is attractive and a sponsor facing them on base case assumptions would rationally not make the investment. However, as a worst case analysis as one of a range of scenarios including upside possibilities, they might be acceptable to the investor.

**Note that early equity injections reduce the IRR to sponsor and hence the attractiveness of the project to him.

At this point, we have run up against the constraint in our simplified model that was built in by using standard term loan repayment terms (8 equal semi-annual instalments). To establish the appropriate parameters for the worst case used in determining the loan value we need to alter the repayment structure we have been assuming.

3.5 Repayment Terms

Most corporate or sovereign loans that are not repaid in their entirety on the maturity date ("bullet" or "balloon" repayment) are amortised in a series of equal annual, semi-annual or quarterly repayment instalments. It is this type of repayment structure which has been adopted in the cash flow projections set out (Tables 1 and 3) and, indeed, it is often adopted in the Credit Agreements governing project loans. It is not, however, always entirely appropriate. Table 1 shows that cash flow to sponsor totals $144 million in 1996 and $101 million in 1997. While such early returns clearly improve the sponsor's position, they leave a loan (in the Base Case) of about $200 million outstanding when taxes begin to be paid. If circumstances then deteriorate, the lender will have lost the opportunity to capture the cash that the project has paid to the sponsor. Clearly a compromise position is required between the sponsor's desire for early cash flow and the lender's desire to minimise risk through early loan reductions. One solution is to stipulate a repayment schedule of absolute dollar amounts derived from dividing free cash flow between loan repayments and cash for the sponsor, using the Base Case. This will result in uneven repayment instalments but ones which reflect the expected revenue generation pattern of the project. This approach will not, of itself, give flexibility to cope with changing circumstances in the project. Another approach is to structure the repayment clause such that each repayment is calculated as a fixed percentage, say 85%, of net cash flow after interest for the preceding calculation period. The repayment instalments, then, will be variable depending on project performance. Sometimes the two approaches are combined. For example, on each repayment date the borrower will repay the greater* of $38 million and 75% of net cash flow after interest for the preceding period. Project loan agreements customarily further stipulate that in certain circumstances short of an event of default debt service can be increased to 100% of cash flow. Often one of the events that would give rise to such an increase would be the cover ratio

*"the greater" here is in the lender's favour, "the lesser" would be in the borrower's favour.

338

falling below a stipulated level. As a result it is wholly appropriate to run the worst case analysis using the 100% dedication assumption. For consistency of treatment, and because it is cumbersome to change the model for different cases, this approach is often used in all sensitivity analyses, even though it may not model the repayment terms of the loan accurately. Models, of course, can be developed which accurately reflect the repayment terms including a 100% dedication rate if the cover ratio falls below, say, 1.5:1.

4. DOCUMENTATION

A project is defined legally by a series of contracts or agreements. These may include, for example, a licence or concession agreement, construction contracts, feedstock purchase agreements, labour contracts, product sales agreements, insurance policies and export permits. Many of these documents have been considered in previous sections.

The project lender is interested in all the contracts but is likely to be a party only to the credit agreement (considered in Section 4.1), possibly other financial agreements such as a swap agreement (see Chapter 16) and the agreement granting him a security interest in the project assets and agreements (see Section 4.2).

4.1 Credit Agreement

A project loan is a form of term loan. The basic, legal document evidencing the contract between lender and borrower is a Loan Agreement or, as it may sometimes be called, a Credit Agreement. Standard Credit Agreement clauses are generally found (though sometimes in modified terms) in Credit Agreements governing limited recourse loans.

In project loans, however, there are also a number of clauses which are not found in a standard term loan Credit Agreement or which are quite different. Variations on the repayment clause for instance, as considered at 3.5 above, may be appropriate. There will also, likely, be a number of clauses related to the project itself, such as physical maintenance and standards of project operation and covenants to preserve the licence or other entitlement to operate the project. In the oil field development project loan example we have examined, the treatment of completion risk (see Section 2.1) may give rise to some very specific Credit Agreement clauses. These are considered in the next sections.

4.1.1 *Forms of Pre-Completion Support*

Assuming that the lender is not comfortable in accepting the completion risks inherent in the project to be financed, what forms of external support are possible?

Where a source of external support such as a willing creditworthy parent company is available a range of options can be considered and negotiated.

- Corporate guarantee of the debt until "Completion". This guarantee could be designed to encompass the full faith and credit of the guarantor or the guarantee itself could contain a limitation on recourse, limiting recourse in the event of a call on the guarantee to, say, the cash flow and assets of an already producing field.

- Corporate guarantee of a portion of the debt until "Completion". A partial guarantee leaves the lenders with the risk of project non-completion on the unguaranteed tranche of the loan. However, as only a portion of the loan is unguaranteed, pressure on banks to fund cost overruns is likely to be reduced. A partial guarantee, as distinct from a full guarantee, means that the minimum amount of post-completion non-recourse debt is determined at the outset rather than at "Completion". In an oil and/or natural gas development project financing, the reservoir analysis and minimum production profile based on appraisal drilling (see 2.2) are important elements in setting the relative sizes of the guaranteed and unguaranteed tranches.

- Covenant to complete the project. This type of covenant usually involves both the expenditure of physical and technical resources as well as the injection of subordinated debt or equity to bring the project to "Completion". Because a lender's rights under a guarantee and pursuant to a breach of covenant differ, this form of pre-completion support is, for the lender, slightly weaker than the guarantee.

- Limited equity subscription agreement. Under such an agreement the amount of subordinated funds the sponsor covenants to inject to bring the project to completion is contractually limited. If overruns beyond the set limit occur, the sponsors, the lenders and any other interested parties will have to negotiate how to meet them.

340

- Drawdown controls. Many project financings include strict drawdown controls. Where external pre-completion support is absent or limited, drawdown controls can give lenders the option of halting advances (and possibly thereby writing off funds already advanced) if it becomes apparent that the operating phase economics of the project are deteriorating. Where there is outside support, drawdown controls can be designed to introduce funding from the external source at an early stage rather than at the tail end of the construction period when the lender could have more to lose than the sponsor from the failure to inject external funds. Drawdown controls are also used to ensure that funds are spent for the purpose of constructing the project.

Other interested parties could also, in specific circumstances, provide pre-completion support. Possible candidates include government, a strong project operator or joint venture partner and interested takers of the product. In the case of the last of these, the support could be structured through a "take-or-pay" contract (see 2.4.3). In Section 2.1 we saw the possible role of a contractor in providing completion and cost overrun support.

4.1.2 *Completion Test*
In Section 4.1.1, we saw the concept of "Completion" as the date on which the external support may be released. Defining "Completion", or setting the Completion Test, is clearly important. The design of the Completion Test involves criteria which, when met, give lenders adequate comfort in those risk areas for which pre-completion support was sought. Each Completion Test, it follows, is as unique as the loan and relevant set of project risks themselves. A typical Completion Test would cover several categories:

- Physical Completion. The lenders will want to be shown that the physical assets have been built to plan and are capable of sustained production at planned levels.

- Sales contract specifications. If a sales contract only comes into full effect when certain specifications are met, the Completion Test should include comparable criteria.

341

- Reservoir performance or production test. The production test is designed taking into account, for an oil or gas project, the specific reservoir characteristics and the amount of production history engineers believe they need to be adequately assured as to future production profiles (see 2.2).

- Operating Costs. For projects where the level of on-going costs to operate the project is critical to its competitiveness in the market (see 2.3), the Completion Test should provide for a demonstration over an appropriate period of time that the project can operate at acceptable cost levels.

- Economic Test. A typical economic test involves a cover ratio (see 3.2.1) set at the time of loan negotiation. Input parameters to be used in the calculation of the project's discounted cash flows are likely to be established in accordance with prevailing conditions at the time of Completion and to be based on data which have become available with the commencement of production. Formulae for resolving disputes over the input parameters to be used may have to be negotiated as part of loan documentation. As the range of uncertainty in input parameters is likely to be less on commencement of production than it would have been when project construction began, a lower cover ratio should be applicable at this juncture than the one on which the initial decision whether to assume completion risk was based. Where the form of pre-completion support is capable of partial release (e.g. a full or partial completion guarantee), the cover ratio concept can be used to determine the proportion of the loan which should thenceforth be unguaranteed. Similarly where the form of pre-completion support adopted is capable of partial release and where the type of project warrants it, the release of pre-completion support can be staggered over time as the project meets a series of completion tests.

4.1.3 *Other Forms of External Support*

Besides the completion risk, any other risk or variable can be supported by parties external to the project. For example an external party could agree to a floor price on the product which the project is to sell. If the floor price is X and, in a certain period, the product sells for less than

342

X, say Y, then the provider of the support will be liable to make a deficiency payment equal to

$$\text{Actual Production} \times (X-Y)$$

The agreement could also contain a clause whereby deficiency payments made could subsequently be recouped to the extent the actual sales price exceeded the contracted level. A sponsor may be willing, by way of another example, to "underwrite" the current tax regime by agreeing to make deficiency payments if actual taxes payable exceed those that would be paid under the regime current when the lending decision is taken.

What can be negotiated by way of external support depends on the relative concerns of lender, sponsor and third parties over the relevant variable, on the motives of the sponsor in seeking a project financing, and on the relative negotiating strengths of those involved.

4.2 Security

Project Financings have been, whenever possible, secured loans. Whatever the governing law* of the Credit Agreement may be, it is usual for the security to be governed by the law of jurisdiction in which the assets are situated or based ("lex situs"). In English law, project security over, say, an offshore oil project would typically involve a fixed and floating charge over the borrower's percentage interest in the physical assets, including the oil produced until sold and receivables from the sale of the oil (and possibly a fixed charge over the bank account through which the Credit Agreement stipulates sales proceeds must flow); and assignment (by way of security) of the borrower's interest in all licences, rights, contracts and agreements necessary to the orderly operation of the project. Because licences issued to more than one party are issued to the licencees on a joint and several basis, the joint operating agreement between the licencees usually provides for a cross-charging of interests. In such circumstances, lenders must generally accept that they rank behind the other licencees as well as behind any creditors preferred in law. A lender will also seek to have the insurance policies assigned to him and to be named as loss payee

*Not all jurisdictions are equal. For example, English law tends to be pro-lender and French law tends to be pro-borrower.

on the policies. If the lender felt that the support from outside the project for the covenant to maintain the insurance in place was inadequate, he might consider taking out mortgagee's interest insurance cover.

A distinction can be drawn between security that has a value more or less independent of the cash flow from which the lender would normally expect debt service and security where the value is closely tied to the loan in question. Project security taken in a mine or offshore petroleum project loan falls at the dependent end of the spectrum. Except in special circumstances, it is unlikely that a bank could make a better job of mining and selling coal to service a loan than a coal mining company. In such circumstances, the primary purpose of taking project security is defensive: to prevent another party being placed in a preferred position. Circumstances (e.g. failure of the borrower's parent resulting from causes outside the project) can be envisaged, however, where the lender may wish to take over the project or to sell it to recoup part of the loan. Good security assists in accomplishing this.

Security taken in asset financing, where the asset is mobile (ship, aircraft) or capable of alternative use (property) is somewhat further from the dependent end of the spectrum than that over a copper mine or oil field. An aircraft may be operating at a loss on a certain route operated by a certain carrier and may, as such, be unable to service its debt fully. At the same time, however, there may be a market shortage of that particular type of aircraft such that it could be sold to another operator at a price that would pay out the loan.

The ideal form of external support in a project loan is that which is not impacted by the factors that could cause the project loan to suffer. This, however, is not the type of security normally found in a secured project loan.

5. SUMMARY

Project Finance refers to a corpus of financing techniques in which the lender looks principally to the cash flow from the project as the source of loan repayment. In a project loan, the project financier's credit assessment focuses on the risks involved in the project. Project Finance is distinguished from conventional corporate or sovereign lending primarily by the assumption of specific project risk by the lenders rather than by a particular

344

lending structure. Project Finance can, but does not necessarily, mean off balance sheet treatment of the debt incurred for the sponsor of the project.

The petroleum and mining industries have historically made most use of the project finance technique. However, it can also be applied to any capital project or economic unit where it is possible to isolate the cash flows satisfactorily. Particularly with the advance of privatisation a wider range of projects is amenable to this type of financing approach. Such projects include electricity generation plants, toll roads, rail links and airports.

The risks which the project financier has to analyse are specific to the individual project being financed. In general, however, project risks can be conveniently grouped and analysed in categories such as the following:

(i)   Completion or Cost Overrun Risk – the risk that more capital expenditure than anticipated will be needed to bring the project to the point of sustainable cash generation and that these overruns will be such as to jeopardise project economics.

(ii)   Reserve or Feedstock Risk – the risk that an operating phase input, either purchased or a mineral extracted by the project, will not be available as, or at the cost, forecast.

(iii) Production or Operating Risk – the risk that the project does not operate as planned or costs more than envisaged to operate at planned levels.

(iv) Marketing or Sales Risk – the risk that the project's product cannot be sold at a price sufficient to cover project costs and repay debt. In the case of an infrastructure project, an analogous form of risk is traffic risk – the risk that at the necessary price the project cannot attract adequate customers.

(v)   Political or Legislative Risk – the risk that government action leads to a reduction in the project's debt service capacity.

Not all risk categories are present to the same extent in each project financing.

To assist in determining the capacity of the project to generate cash and repay debt, in quantifying the effect of an identified risk (e.g. a drop in the price of the product to be sold), and in designing appropriate financing terms and conditions, the project financier builds a cash flow forecast model of the project. The Base Case is constructed using likely or expected values for the various parameters. Sensitivity analyses are produced by varying these input parameters. As the lenders have little to gain from an improvement in project economics, unless a specific agreement has been reached to share in the upside, their position in the project dictates that they will focus on downside sensitivities, i.e. analyses of the effects on projections of cash flow and loan repayment of a deterioration in one or more variables from their expected levels.

Based on the analysis of project risks, the project financier may decide that certain aspects of the risk are unbankable. This does not mean that a project financing is impossible. A financing can still be structured on a project financing basis if acceptable third parties are prepared to support certain identified risks. The Credit Agreement and other documents will specify the terms of such outside support.

346

CHAPTER 9

Banks' Lending Based on Withholding Tax

by
Allen P. Hing

1. INTRODUCTION

1.1 Definition of Withholding Tax

Several types of lending rely on a bank's ability to lend where a withholding tax applies. It is therefore essential to understand initially what withholding tax is. In general, it can be defined as a tax whereby if one party is to pay money to another party, which is income in the second party's hands, then the first party is required by law to deduct tax and account for it to the Revenue Authorities in the country of the first party.

Example (1)

Company A in Country X borrows US$100m from Bank B in Country Y

Interest payable is at a rate of 10% p.a.

Country X taxation rates include Withholding Tax of 15% p.a.

Therefore, at the end of the first year, interest of US$10m is due. However, *before* payment this will be subject to the local 15% p.a. withholding tax.

Accordingly, Company A will:

(a) Pay US$10m less 15% to Bank B, i.e. US$8.5m.

(b) Pay US$1.5m to its Revenue Authority.

Thus, Bank B receives interest at an effective rate of 8.5% p.a.

This method of collecting tax by the Revenue Authorities can be best described as *deduction of tax at source*.

Examples of this type of deduction can be found quite readily in many countries, e.g. income tax deducted by an employer from an employee's monthly salary; income tax deducted by companies from dividends; payments made by deeds of covenant; etc. All these result in a "net" payment, rather than a gross payment, being made.

The reason for such action by Revenue Authorities is simple. It is more efficient for collection purposes in that the obligation is placed on the payer and if any repayment is due then the Revenue would have the cash flow benefit until any claim for a refund is processed. It would be particularly onerous for the Revenue Authorities to collect the tax from all the overseas recipients of the income if it was paid gross.

The types of income which are subject to a withholding tax at source are numerous and include the following, which is not an exhaustive list:

Interest, dividends, royalties, technical aid fees, profits, etc.

When considering whether any particular type of income is subject to a withholding tax it is much safer to assume that all countries operate a system which requires the deduction of tax of some sort at source. However, the rates in some cases may be nil.

The rates applicable to any particular form of income, therefore, will vary dependent upon the following factors:

1. Whether the recipient is a resident or a non-resident in the country of the payer.

2. If the recipient is a non-resident, then where he is resident.

3. The type of income to which the withholding tax is to be applied.

4. The country in which the payer of the interest is resident.

5. Whether any specific exemptions exist under the legislation of the payer of interest when the proceeds of the loan have been used for specified purposes.

In many instances, a bank will not wish to suffer the withholding tax and will require a borrower to "gross-up" the payments such that, *after* the deduction of the withholding tax, the bank will receive the same amount of income as if no deduction for withholding tax had been made. It must be stressed that the wording in documentation must be extremely clear on this point if future difficulties with the Revenue Authorities, both of the borrower and the lender, are to be avoided.

Example (2)

Company A in Country X borrows US$100m from Bank B in Country Y.

Interest payable is at a rate of 10% p.a.

Country X taxation rates include withholding tax of 15% p.a.

Therefore, at the end of the first year, interest of US$10m is due. However, before payment this will be subject to the local 15% withholding tax.

Accordingly, under the terms of the loan documentation, Company A will:

(a) Gross up the payment by the following formula:

$$\frac{\text{Amount Due}}{(100\% - \text{Rate of Withholding Tax})} \times 100 = \frac{10m}{(100-15)} \times 100 = 11.765m$$

and pay US$11.765m less 15% to the bank, i.e. US$10m

(b) Pay US$1.765m to its Revenue Authority.

Thus, Bank B receives interest at an effective rate of 10.0% p.a.

Borrowing on this basis is more expensive for the borrower. It has cost an additional US$1.765m over and above the cost as shown in example (1). Accordingly, the borrower may not wish to agree to borrowing on this basis unless he has to for his own reasons. These may include the following:

(a) If the borrower is a government agency it may not be required to account to the Revenue Authorities the US$1.765m but may be able to issue a receipt as if it had done so.

(b) The borrower may be able to obtain some benefit from the lender if the lender can obtain some benefit from its Revenue Authorities for the certificate evidencing tax paid (albeit in the country of the borrower).

This particular point will be more fully explained in the Section entitled "Grossing Up Loans."

If a borrower is prepared to borrow only on the basis as explained in example (1), then the lending bank could suffer a considerable cash loss where a withholding tax is deducted at source from its interest income which it is not able to recover:

	US$
Gross interest	10,000,000
Less withholding tax at 15%	(1,500,000)
Cash received	8,500,000
Funding cost, say	(9,800,000)
Total cash loss to the bank	(1,300,000)

As can be seen, if a bank is unable to recover the tax deducted at source, then lending on this basis is unprofitable. The bank, therefore, needs to consider the way that it can minimise or eliminate this loss. To do this it will firstly look at double tax agreements and consider the protection that these afford.

2. DOUBLE TAX AGREEMENTS

First however, perhaps we should consider what a double tax agreement is. A double tax agreement, which may also be known as a Convention to Avoid Double Taxation, is an agreement between two countries setting out the manner in which the income of a resident of one country arising in the other country is to be taxed in that other country.

As mentioned earlier in the chapter this income can come in many forms. The agreement follows a fairly standard format and the details are negotiated between the Revenue Authorities of the two countries concerned on the basis of considering the revenue lost to each of the countries for any particular concession given to the other country. Finally, a position will be reached which is considered to be acceptable to both countries and this agreement then needs to be ratified by the governments of the respective countries. In the United Kingdom this is ordinarily done by introducing a statutory instrument in Parliament.

A double tax agreement will be useful to a lending bank as it will provide for a rate of withholding tax to be applied that is usually lower than the general rate in the country of the payer; further, the rate may even be reduced to nil. It may also state the basis on which the lender is able to claim double tax credits in respect of the foreign withholding taxes suffered and details of tax-spared lending to a country may be included.

If a double tax agreement does not exist between the country of the lender and that of the borrower reliefs may still be available. (But see Section 4.4 regarding "Tax Spared Loans").

In these circumstances it would be necessary for the bank to investigate the tax laws of its own country enabling reliefs to be claimed. Such relief

351

is partially available in the UK, but following the restrictions incorporated in the Income and Corporation Taxes Act 1988, Sections 797 and 798 a UK bank will not generally be able fully to recover any withholding taxes suffered.

Relief obtained under a double tax agreement is called *double taxation relief* whilst that obtained under, for example, UK law, is known as *unilateral relief*. The calculation of the relief is the same, the distinction mainly being that each type of relief is available under a different section of the Income and Corporation Taxes Act 1988.

2.1   How Is the Relief Obtained?

A lender must fulfil certain conditions before it may be able to obtain the relief that it seeks. Generally since the relief is obtained by way of offsets against the profits taxes payable to its own Revenue Authorities, the relief cannot usually exceed the tax payable by the lender.

In many countries restrictions apply to the offsets known as "Double Tax Credits".

For example, in the UK, Belgium, Canada, West Germany and France such tax credits cannot be carried forward or back. In some cases neither can they be surrendered to other companies, even in the same group. In these circumstances it is important to ensure that the lending bank has sufficient tax capacity.

In the US these credits may be carried forward five years or back two years; other restrictions are in effect, though, which make this country unsuitable for tax absorption loans following the restructuring of the US tax code.

Specific examples of how credits are calculated in various countries are included in Appendix D.

Further, any claims of credit must not exceed the treaty rates, it being up to the lender to obtain a refund in respect of the excessive deduction from the borrower's Revenue Authorities. As a final restriction the maximum credit relief that is allowable to a lender may be restricted under its domestic law.

A second way that relief may be obtained is where the overseas tax suffered is deducted directly from the income of the lending.

A further important point to consider here is that, given that the lender is receiving less money than it should, when can it recover the shortfall? Will the amount received be sufficient to recompense it for the cashflow shortfall?

Effectively, a lender is able to obtain the relief only when it pays its tax. This could be after a considerable passage of time following the initial deduction suffered. Clearly, therefore, there is some need to consider the cost to the lender of the delay in receiving the reimbursement.

2.1.1 *Calculating the Double Taxation Relief*
The double taxation relief claimable will be, subject to domestic law, the amount of foreign withholding tax deducted at source. *The rate of exchange* to be used in determining this in the functional currency of the lender is the rate ruling on the day that interest becomes receivable.

2.2   When Can a Bank Claim the Double Tax Credits?
In countries throughout the world rules exist regarding the tax payment dates. For example, in the UK companies pay their UK taxes nine months after the accounting year end and so, effectively, cannot claim the tax credit until nine months after the end of the accounting period to which it relates. This means that withholding tax certificates may be held for anything between nine months and twenty-one months (average fifteen months) before they can be claimed. To compensate for this delay, it is normal for banks to charge an additional margin to borrowers purely to compensate for the cash flow loss of funds. In calculating this additional margin individual banks will need to consider many factors giving a varied interpretation and different costs, e.g. different gearing or risk asset ratios; protection of pre- or post-tax income.

Unfortunately, the need for this additional margin places UK banks at a competitive disadvantage to banks of other countries which may not need to wait as long before they obtain credit, e.g. the United States pays its taxes quarterly in arrears whilst in Belgium taxes are paid quarterly in advance.

3. WHAT IS TAX CAPACITY?

It has been stated that a bank requires tax capacity in order to obtain an offset of the foreign taxes suffered at source. Tax capacity was then defined as the profits tax that a bank will have to pay to the Revenue Authorities. It is not, unfortunately, a simple matter of looking at the accounting profits of the bank and applying the rate of profits tax to them to discover the amount of tax that a bank may have to pay to the Revenue Authorities. There are many additions and deductions which can affect the accounting profits in order that profits taxes can then be assessed.

Every country will have its own particular requirements for calculating these additions and deductions.

Example (3)

The following is a simplified example of a tax computation showing major additions and deductions which are applicable in the United Kingdom.

		£m
PROFIT PER ACCOUNTS		100
ADD:		
Depreciation	2.0	
Non-Specific Provisions	10.0	
Disallowed Special Provisions	15.0	
Tax-Spared Credits	3.0	30
LESS:		
Capital Allowances	30.0	
Restriction under S.798 Income and Corporation Taxes Act 1988	2.0	(32)
LESS:		
Other Items (Net)		(12)
TAXABLE PROFIT		86

354

Notes:

(1)   It can be seen from the above that there are several areas where adjustments are due. The above are only indicative and do not comprise an exhaustive list of adjustments. Some banks may deliberately distort deductions to decrease their tax liabilities; this would be known as tax planning.

(2)   Ordinarily, specific bad and doubtful debt provisions are fully deductible in the year in which they occur and *do not* give rise to any add backs. In recent years, however, the Inland Revenue has increasingly challenged provisions charged against profits leading to add backs for tax calculations. In the event that these amounts actually become deductible in the future they will lower future taxable profits.

Upon receipt of a claim for double tax credits from a bank, the Revenue Authorities may call for proof that these taxes have, indeed, been suffered. The claims are, therefore, supported by withholding tax receipts. These are receipts issued by the Revenue Authority which has received the withholding tax at source. Without these receipts the Revenue Authority of the bank may reject any claim for credit and, as shown earlier, this could cause the bank a considerable cash loss.

Documentation must, therefore, ensure that the receipt will be received by the lender.

Should the receipt not be received within the time scale envisaged in the documentation then it should be asked for from the borrower.

Generally, claims can be made only against the year in which the rollover occurs. Strictly speaking, credits should be claimed on an actual basis. That is to say the tax credits are calculated by reference to interest actually received during the taxation year of the bank under examination by the Revenue Authority.

Example (3) continued

Having established the taxable profit of the bank it is necessary to consider ways in which the resulting liability may be settled.

USES OF TAX CAPACITY	£m
TAXABLE PROFIT	86.0
CORPORATION TAX PAYABLE AT (SAY) 35% *LESS :*	30.1
(1) DOUBLE TAX RELIEF (WHT paid on loans made)	15.0
Corporation Tax Payable	15.1

3.1 Withholding Tax Receipts

For the receipts to be satisfactory evidence to the Revenue Authority of the bank there are various details that need to be included. Each Revenue Authority will, of course, have its own requirements but as a guide they may include the following:

(a)   The name of the borrower;

(b)   The address of the borrower;

(c)   The interest payable subject to the withholding tax;

(d)   The rate of withholding tax to be applied and the amount of tax deducted;

(e)   Details of any reduction due to double tax agreements;

(f)   The dates between which the interest is payable. (Usually the date of lending to the next rollover);

(g)   The name of the lender. In the case of syndicated loans this is usually the Agent Bank. The Agent Bank should then supply each participating bank with a further certificate indicating how much of the withholding tax receipt is applicable to the participating bank's lending;

(h)   The address of the lender ;

(i)   An official stamp of the issuing Revenue Authority.

In the United Kingdom the Inland Revenue would expect the above information to be available upon request together with a reconciliation between the withholding tax deducted as per the certificate (which would ordinarily be in the local currency of the borrower), the currency of the lending and pounds sterling.

(Appendix A shows, by way of example, a withholding tax receipt of Spain).

356

In conclusion, if a bank follows the rules correctly, then it will no longer suffer a funding loss and Example (1) would become:

	US$
	US$
Gross interest	10,000,000
Less withholding tax	(1,500,000)
Cash received	8,500,000
Funding cost	(9,800,000)
Cash flow loss	(1,300,000)
Double tax credit*	1,500,000
Cash profit to the bank before profits taxes	200,000

However, several countries have made concerted efforts to prevent banks from lending on this basis and have introduced rules which effectively prevent the lender from obtaining credits for the full amount of overseas taxes paid. Please see Appendix D.

Remember, the bank can claim only on certificates received. Therefore, certificates are effectively worth up to their face value in cash to the lending bank.

4. TYPES OF TAX-BASED LENDING

Many countries around the world have negotiated double taxation treaties with each other. These agreements, in conjunction with the local legislation of the lender and borrower, govern the availability of tax relief in respect of foreign taxes, enabling the lender to offset foreign withholding taxes suffered against its liability to profits tax.

Examples of the various tax-based loans are given in Appendix C.

The restrictions applicable in the UK are:

1. Sufficient tax capacity must exist in that year;
2. The tax cannot exceed the treaty rate, where applicable;
3. The tax credit is limited to a maximum of 15% of the gross interest income, or the UK tax payable on the profits generated by the lending

*Usable after appropriate period after accounting year end.

whichever is the lower. Any excess overseas tax over 15% will be deducted in calculating that profit.

4.1 Withholding Tax Absorption Loans
This type of lending is described in Example (1).

Under this method the bank will receive interest, net of foreign withholding tax, together with a tax receipt, evidencing payment of the tax, which is then used to support the bank's claim for credit relief against profits tax.

In practice, this type of loan creates a cash flow deficit for the bank and, in order to compensate for the delay in rectifying this position, the bank will probably wish to charge an additional interest margin. The bank will also have to consider for the period of the lending its ability to claim double credits against its forecast tax capacity.

UK banks will not be able to make a profit from this type of lending unless the interest physically received plus the UK tax payable on the margin over cost of funds is in excess of the cost of funds.

4.2 Loans Made on a "Free and Clear of All Taxes" Basis
This type of lending was described in Example (2).

If a bank considers that it wishes to make a lending overseas then it could stipulate to the borrower that it is to receive its interest without deduction of local withholding tax. Of course, it is quite possible when the borrower makes the interest payment that he has to deduct and account for withholding tax. That is to say that the borrower will have to gross up payments to be made to such an extent that, after deducting any withholding taxes due, the bank is able to receive its interest without deduction of tax from its point of view. This treatment, however, increases the overall cost to the borrower.

4.3 Grossing Up Loans
Following on from the position described in "Loans made on a free and clear of all taxes" basis, if the documentation is structured in the manner that the interest receivable includes the grossed up element in support of

358

the tax deduction then the bank may legitimately claim that the interest received for tax purposes includes that grossed up element of the interest thus enhancing the bank's income.

Taking, for example, the figures shown in Example (2) from the bank's point of view, then the following would be expected.

	US$
	US$
Interest received	10,000,000
Funding cost	9,800,000
Profit before taxation	200,000

If the wording of the documentation is such that the grossing up element is an additional amount of interest receivable then the loan could be accounted for on an ordinary absorption basis as follows:

	US$
Interest receivable	11,765,000
Less, withholding tax at 15%	1,765,000
Interest received	10,000,000
Funding cost	9,800,000
	200,000
Double tax credit	1,765,000
Cash profit to the bank before profits taxes	1,965,000

Under certain circumstances the lending bank may negotiate with the borrower to reimburse payments to the borrower. The effects of any such reimbursements, however, must be carefully examined to ensure the bank does not suffer further, eg. is the reimbursement tax deductible? What will the Revenue Authorities' reaction be, etc.?

4.4 Tax-Spared Loans

These loans are possible only where the relevant *double taxation treaty enables credit relief to be obtained against profits tax in respect of foreign withholding tax* which, although normally deductible from interest paid by the borrowing country, will be waived or "spared" under certain specified provisions in the local legislation of that country, which grants an exemption from withholding tax on loans to certain defined sectors of industry for specific purposes.

Ordinarily, these exemptions are granted to loans for infrastructure improvements, flag carrying activities (airlines etc) and activities considered vital to improve the borrowing country's economic position. It is, thus, the authorities in the borrower's country which rule whether a financing warrants a tax spared loan.

In these instances, the bank will receive interest, either free or at a reduced rate of withholding tax, together with an official tax exemption certificate which is used to support the bank's claim for credit relief. Effectively, therefore, the bank is able to claim a credit relief for a withholding tax not actually suffered.

Example (4)

Company A in Country X borrows US$100m from Bank B in Country Y
Interest payable is at a rate of 10% p.a.
Country X taxation rates include withholding tax of 15%.
The lending is exempt from withholding tax under the law of Country X. Additionally this law is included in a Double Tax Agreement between Country X and Country Y as enabling the Bank B in Country Y to claim a double tax credit as if the withholding tax had been suffered.

Then, subject to any further restrictions applicable to Bank B under the laws of Country Y, the following applies:

	US$	
Interest payable	10,000,000	
Withholding tax at 15%	NIL	(exempt under local law)
Interest received by B	10,000,000	
Funding cost	(9,800,000)	
	200,000	
Double tax credit claimable	1,500,000	
Cash profit to the bank before profits taxes	1,700,000	

360

Tax-spared lending is possible from many countries to other countries which would normally be described as Lesser-Developed or Newly Developing Countries.

4.5 Fall Back Rates

Revenue Authorities view lendings under these arrangements with concern and it would always be considered prudent to ensure that a "fall back rate" clause is included in the documentation. This has become necessary because market pressures have reduced the margins chargeable on this type of lending below that which would apply to a normal eurocurrency loan. Ordinarily, therefore, facilities would be negotiated on the current market rates for tax-spared facilities with a fall-back rate equal to the market rate for ordinary eurocurrency lendings.

It is essential, therefore, to have a minimum margin that would be charged not only because Revenue Authorities may act to negate the benefits but because, with declining interest rates, the returns to banks are being diminished. For example, if the interest rate in Example (4) is reduced to 6% p.a. and cost of funds is reduced to 5.8% p.a. the following position arises:

	US$	
Interest payable	6,000,000	
Withholding tax at 15%	NIL	(exempt under local law)
Interest received	6,000,000	
Funding cost	5,800,000	
	200,000	
Double tax credit claimable	900,000	
Cash profit to the bank before profits taxes	1,100,000	

4.6 Countries Involved

Tax spared lending is possible by many lending countries to borrowing countries and below are lists of countries which would lend and borrow on a tax spared basis:

Lender	Borrower
Belgium	Cyprus
Canada	India
France	Malaysia
Japan	Pakistan
United Kingdom	Singapore
	Spain
	South Korea

4.7 Sharing the Benefits

It is common for some of the benefit derived from tax spared loans to be passed back to the borrower in the form of lower interest margins.

With regard to tax-spared lending by UK banks the Inland Revenue became incensed by what was considered an abuse of the tax credit system in operation in the UK. The reason for this was that some banks began to lend at rates below the cost of funds. This gave the Government two problems:

(1) Loss of revenue
(2) Loss to the UK balance of payments

To overcome this problem two major restrictions were placed upon tax spared lending:

(a) The tax-spared credit became taxable income of the bank, and
(b) No credit in excess of 15% of the interest received could be claimed.
(c) The tax credit must not exceed the UK taxes payable on the margin inclusive of any grossing up required in (a).

Accordingly for a UK bank, Example (4) would become:

	US$	
Interest payable	10,000,000	
Withholding tax at 15%	NIL	(exempt under local law)
Interest received	10,000,000	
Funding cost	9,800,000	
Accounting profit	200,000	
Taxes spared	1,500,000	
Taxable income	1,700,000	
U.K. tax payable at 35%	(595,000)	
Double tax credit (limited to the lower of £1.5m or £595,000)	595,000	
Cash profit to bank after profits taxes	200,000	

It is essential to include, within the documentation, clauses to protect the bank by enabling a predetermined margin to be applied should the benefits of tax sparing, for one reason or another, no longer be available.

Appendix A   Spanish W. H. T. Certificate

Nº Expediente 30288	IMPUESTOS SOBRE LA RENTA DE LAS PERSONAS FISICAS Y SOBRE SOCIEDADES	210
DELEGACION O ADMINISTRACION DE HACIENDA DE MADRID	DECLARACION DE NO RESIDENTES (no a... establecimientos permanentes) Periodo impositivo del 1/1/1986 al 31/12/1986	**EJEMPLAR PARA LA ENTIDAD DELEGADA** COD.CO.DELEGACION/ADMINISTRACION DE HACIENDA

DATOS DE IDENTIFICACION

Representante

F/J	C I / D N I	Nombre o razon social	Anagrama
J	A-28-005171	... ESPAÑOLA, S.A.	HIDROLA

Sg C/	Nombre de la via publica	Num	P	L	C.P.	Telefono
					1	402.10.20

Provincia	PR	Municipio	C. Mun º
Madrid	28	Madrid	

Sujeto Pasivo (no residente)

Nombre y apellidos o razon social

Direccion completa: Threadneedle Street, London EC2

Pais	Ci Pais
REINO UNIDO	006

Pagador (cuando no sea el representante)

F/J	C I / D N I	Nombre o razon social	Anagrama

Sg	Nombre de la via publica	Num.	P	L	C.P.	Telefono

Provincia	PR	Municipio	C. Mun º

DATOS DE LA OPERACION A LA QUE SE REFIERE LA DECLARACION

TIPO DE RENTA		DOCUMENTACION	
SIN CONVENIO A) Dividendos y participaciones en beneficios	☐	I Copia de contrato y/o factura	☐
B) Intereses (Bonif. ✗NO)	☒	II Declaracion de pagos al exterior por operaciones invisibles corrientes (TE)	☐
C) Servicios y gastos generales a filiales y sucursales	☐	III Declaraciones de inversion y desinversion extranjera	☐
D) Servicios con deduccion directa de ciertos gastos	☐	IV Declaraciones por I R P F	☐
E) Rendimientos producciones cinematograficas	☐	V Acreditacion de la representacion	☐
F) Otros rendimientos	☐	VI Fotocopia concesion bonif.	☐
G) Incrementos de patrimonio	☐	VII Otros documentos Certificacion residencia (Convenio)	☐
CON CONVENIO P) Dividendos y participaciones en beneficios	☐	Autorizacion declaracion trimestral	☐
Q) Intereses	☐		☐
R) Canones	☐		☐
S) Otras rentas sujetas	☐		☐
X) Operacion no sujeta	☐		

DESCRIPCION SUCINTA DE LA OPERACION ... millones de dolares de fecha 17 de febrero de 1981 (Contrato suplementario de fecha 31 de julio de 1980). Vencimiento 30 de agosto de 1986.

CARTA DE PAGO
JUSTIFICANTE DEL INGRESO EN LA ENTIDAD COLABORADORA O EN EL TESORO

	Sello	Clave Entidad	Fecha	Numero
INGRESO		... TIENDA U42940	12.09.86 *1.052.128	2808 SOCI

EDITADO Y DISTRIBUIDO POR EL COLEGIO DE HUERFANOS DE HACIENDA (O. M. DE 10 DE AGOSTO DE 1953)

CALCULO INCREMENTOS DE PATRIMONIO	Importe de la enajenacion							01	
	Valor de adquisicion				02				
	Mejoras				03				
	— Amortizaciones				04				
	Valor neto de adquisicion							05	
	Incremento de patrimonio (01 - 05) expresado en divisas (a expresar tambien en casilla 14)							06	

SERVICIOS CON DEDUCCION GASTOS DE PERSONAL			Div	CI		Importe Div		Cambio			
	Ingresos integros	07			08		·	09		10	
	— { Gastos de personal declarados a efectos del I.R.P.F., Seguridad Social española y suministros deducibles									11	
	Bases de gravamen (10 - 11) a expresar en cas 16									12	

AUTOLIQUIDACION			Div	CI		Importe Div		Cambio			
	Base de gravamen	13			14		·	15	=	16	5.845.156

Interest Payable

A CUMPLIMENTAR CUANDO SE TRATE DE RENDIMIENTOS BONIFICADOS	Tipo efectivo de gravamen (%)	17 18 %
	Rate of Withholding Tax	
	CUOTA A INGRESAR	18 1.052.128
Tipo de gravamen (%) 23		
Parte no bonificada (%) 24	Recargo de prorroga	19
Reconocida segun		20
Art 25 c)L 61/78 25		
D Tr 3 2L 61/78 26 (marcar con una -X-)		21

Withholding Tax Payable

	TOTAL DEUDA TRIBUTARIA	22 1.052.128

DECLARACION DEL REPRESENTANTE	DILIGENCIA
Declaro que los datos contenidos en la presente declaracion y la documentacion aportada se corresponden fielmente con la realidad de las operaciones realizadas por el sujeto pasivo y entre si.	Examinada la presente declaracion y la documentacion complementaria aportada
	a) Se presta conformidad, con caracter provisional a la presente autoliquidacion, a los efectos previstos en el articulo 305 del Reglamento del Impuesto sobre Sociedades.
...ulo, 23 de agosto de 1986	b) Se remite el expediente a la Inspeccion de Hacienda, para su comprobacion preferente
Fecha y firma	
P. P. & A.	Fecha
...	EL JEFE DE LA SECCION
(nombre y calidad con que actuan de los firmantes)	GESTION TRIBUTARIA REGIMENES ESPECIALES 5 SET. 1986 MADRID-ESPAÑA DELEGACION DE HACIENDA (firma y sello)

Official Stamp Validating the Receipt

Appendix B

COUNTRIES WITH WHICH THE UK HAS DOUBLE TAX AGREEMENTS AND WHERE TAX-SPARING MAY BE APPLICABLE FROM THE UK

Bangladesh	India	Singapore
Barbados	Israel	South Korea
Belize	Indonesia	Spain
Botswana	Jamaica	Sri Lanka
China	Kenya	Sudan
Cyprus	Malaysia	Thailand
Egypt	Malta	Trinidad and Tobago
Falkland islands	Mauritius	Tunisia
Fiji	Morocco	Zambia
Gambia	Pakistan	
Ghana	Portugal	

OTHER COUNTRIES WITH WHICH THE UK HAS DOUBLE TAX AGREEMENTS

Antigua	Guernsey	Norway
Australia	Hungary	Poland
Austria	Ireland	Romania
Belgium	Isle of Man	St Christopher (St Kitts) & Nevis
Brunei	Italy	St Lucia
Burma	Japan	St Vincent
Canada	Jersey	Sierra Leone
Denmark	Kiribati & Tuvalu	Solomon Islands
Dominica	Lesotho	South Africa
Faroe Islands	Luxembourg	Swaziland
Finland	Malawi	Sweden
France	Monserrat	Switzerland
Germany	Netherlands	Uganda
Greece	Netherlands Antillies	USA
Grenada	New Zealand	Zimbabwe

Appendix C
(Example 1)

A comparison of tax based loans where full tax credit relief is available

Assumptions
(1) Ignores additional margins for cash flow delays
(2) Principal £1,000
(3) Period one calendar year
(4) Interest payable annual in arrears on 31 December
(5) Interest Rate 10% pa
(6) Cost of Funds 9.5% pa
(7) Withholding tax rate 15.0%

	Net Rated Loan	Absorption Loan	Grossed up Loan	Tax Spared Loan
Cash Flow				
Interest paid by customer	117.6	100.0	117.6	100.0
Withholding tax suffered	(17.6)	(15.0)	(17.6)	0.0
Interest received by the Bank	100.0	85.0	100.0	100.0
Cost of funds	(95.0)	(95.0)	(95.0)	(95.0)
Cash flow profit/(loss) A	5.0	(10.0)	5.0	5.0
Taxation				
Taxable income	5.0	5.0	5.0	5.0
Grossed up element	–	–	17.6	–
Taxable profit	5.0	5.0	22.6	5.0
Tax payable @ say 33%	(1.65)	(1.65)	(7.46)	(1.65)
Double tax credits	0	15.0	17.6	15.0
Taxes (payable)/repayable B	(1.65)	13.35	10.14	13.35
Bank's post tax retention A + B	3.35	3.35	15.14	18.35

Appendix C
(Example 2)

A comparison of tax based loans by a UK bank

Assumptions as in example (1)

	Net Rated Loan	Absorption Loan	Grossed up Loan	Tax Spared Loan
Cash Flow				
Interest paid by customer	117.6	100.0	117.6	100.0
Withholding tax suffered X	(17.6)	(15.0)	(17.6)	0.0
Interest received by the Bank	100.0	85.0	100.0	100.0
Cost of funds	(95.0)	(95.0)	(95.0)	(95.0)
Cash flow profit/(loss) A	5.0	(10.0)	5.0	5.0
Taxation				
(1) *Credit Version*				
Taxable income (100-95)	5.0	5.0	5.0	5.0
Grossed up element	0.0	0.0	17.6	0.0
Overseas taxes spared	0.0	0.0	0.0	15.0
Taxable income	5.0	5.0	22.6	20.0
UK taxes payable @ 33% Y	(1.65)	(1.65)	(7.5)	(6.6)
Double tax credits	1.65	1.65	7.5	6.6
(lower of X or Y except for Tax Spared Loans when it will be Y)				
UK taxes payable B	0.0	0.0	0.0	0.0
(2) *Expense Version*				
Taxable income (100-95)	5.0	5.0	5.0	5.0
Grossed up element	0.0	0.0	17.6	0.0
Overseas taxes suffered	0.0	(15.0)	(17.6)	0.0
Taxable income	5.0	(10.0)	5.0	5.0
UK taxes payable at 33% C	(1.65)	3.3	(1.65)	(1.65)
Bank's post tax retention				
Credit version (A+B)	5.0	(10.0)	5.0	5.0
Expense version (A+C)	3.35	(6.7)	3.35	3.35

NB   Whilst the above is an indication of which is the most profitable method to use, it is only a guide and the full calculation must be carried out in each instance to prove the most beneficial method. Additionally, relevant rates and regulations are subject to change. Accordingly, detailed up-to-date research must be undertaken when calculating specific double tax credit claims.

Appendix D
(Example 1)

A comparison of loans

Withholding Tax Absorption Loans

Assumptions
(1) Ignores additional margins for cash flow delays
(2) Principal £1,000
(3) Period one calendar year
(4) Interest payable annually in arrears on 31 December
(5) Interest Rate 10% pa
(6) Cost of Funds 9.5% pa
(7) Withholding tax rate 15.0%

	CANADA	UK	FRANCE	BELGIUM
Cash Flow				
Interest paid by customer	100.0	100.0	100.0	100.0
Withholding tax suffered	(15.0)	(15.0)	(15.0)	(15.0)
Interest received by the Bank	85.0	85.0	85.0	85.0
Cost of funds	(95.0)	(95.0)	(95.0)	(95.0)
Cash flow profit/(loss) A	(10.0)	(10.0)	(10.0)	(10.0)
Taxation				
Taxable income	(10.0)	(10.0)	(10.0)	(10.0)
Grossed up element	15.0	15.0	0.0	15.0
Taxable profit/(loss)	5.0	5.0	(10.0)	5.0
Taxes payable at local rates	44% (2.2)	33% (1.65)	33.3% 3.3	39% (2.0)
Double tax credits	6.6(i)	1.65	10.0(ii)	15.0(iii)
Tax (payable)/refundable B	4.4	0.0	13.3	13.0
Post tax retention A + B	(5.6)	(10.0)*	3.3	3.0

Note * See also appendix C example 2

(i) (a) In Canada, the funding cost for tax purposes is on a fungible rather than matched basis. This has been assumed to be at 95% of costs on a matched basis for the purpose of this example:

ie Income	100
Funding 95% of 95	90.3
Tax Profit	9.7

Tax credit is higher of 9.7 @ 44% or withholding suffered (15) at 44%.

(b) The tax credit must not exceed the Canadian tax payable on the income on a country by country basis.

(c) The rate of 44% quoted is an example and consists of Federal Tax and Provincial Tax. The effective rate will, therefore vary from province to province.

369

(d) Whilst the above are correct at the time of going to press, individual circumstances will affect the relevant regulations. Additionally, regulations are subject to change.

(ii) The tax credit is calculated as the withholding tax suffered less the tax payable on the withholding tax:

i.e. $15.0 - (15.0 \times 33\,^1/_3\%) = 10.0$

(iii) The tax credit is 15% of the cash received grossed up for witholding tax

i.e.

$$\frac{15}{100} \times 100 \times \frac{85}{(100 - 15)} = 15$$

**Appendix D
(Example 2)**

A comparison of loans

Grossed up Loans

Assumptions
As in example 1

	CANADA	UK	FRANCE	BELGIUM
Cash Flow				
Interest paid by customer	117.6	117.6	117.6	117.6
Withholding tax suffered	(17.6)	(17.6)	(17.6)	(17.6)
Interest received by the Bank	100.0	100.0	100.0	100.0
Cost of funds	(95.0)	(95.0)	(95.0)	(95.0)
Cash flow profit A	5.0	5.0	5.0	5.0
Taxation				
Taxable income	5.0	5.0	5.0	5.0
Grossed up element	17.6	17.6	17.6	17.6
Taxable profit/(loss)	22.6	22.6	22.6	22.6
Taxes payable at local rates	44% (9.9)	33% (7.5)	$33^1/_3$% (7.5)	39% (8.8)
Double tax credits	7.7(i)	7.5	11.7(ii)	17.6(iii)
Tax (payable)/refundable B	(2.2)	0.0	4.2	8.8
Post tax retention A + B	3.8	5.0*	8.2	13.8

Note * See also appendix C example 2

(i)   (a)   The calculation is as in appendix D example 1 but the tax credit cannot exceed the withholding tax suffered at 44%:
i.e. maximum $17.6 \times 44\% = 7.7$

        (b)   If tax capacity on a country by country basis then the tax credit will equate to the overseas taxes paid, i.e. 17.6

        (c)   The rate of 44% quoted consists of Federal and Provincial Taxes and will vary from province to province.

(ii)   The calculation is as in appendix D example 1:
i.e. $17.6 - (17.6 \times 33^1/_3\%) = 11.7$

(iii)   The tax credit is equal to the cash received grossed up for WHT i.e.
$$\frac{15}{100} \times 100 \times \frac{100}{(100 - 15)} = 17.6$$

(iv)   See also note (d) of Appendix D (Example 1).

Appendix D
(Example 3)

A comparison of loans

Tax spared loans

Assumptions
(1) As in example 1
(2) That the withholding tax is fully spared

	CANADA (a)	CANADA (b)	UK	FRANCE	BELGIUM
Cash Flow					
Interest paid by customer	100.0	100.0	100.0	100.0	100.0
Withholding tax suffered	0.0	0.0	0.0	0.0	0.0
Interest received by the Bank	100.0	100.0	100.0	100.0	100.0
Cost of funds	(95.0)	(95.0)	(95.0)	(95.0)	(95.0)
Cash flow profit A	5.0	5.0	5.0	5.0	5.0
Taxation					
Taxable income	5.0	5.0	5.0	5.0	5.0
Grossed up element	0.0	0.0	15.0	0.0	17.6
Taxable profit	5.0	5.0	20.0	5.0	22.6
Taxes payable at local rates	44% (2.2)	(2.2)	33% (6.6)	$33^1/_3\%$ (1.7)	39% (8.8)
Double tax credits	6.6(a)	15.0(b)	6.6	10.0(ii)	17.6(iii)
Tax (payable)/refundable B	4.4	12.8	0.0	8.3	8.8
Post tax retention A + B	9.4	17.8	5.0*	13.3	13.8

Note * See also appendix C example 2
(i)   (a) The tax credit is calculated as in appendix D example 1
      (b) Assumes that sufficient Canadian tax payable on income arising on a country by country basis.
      (c) The rate of 44% quoted consists of Federal and Provincial Taxes and will vary from province to province.
(ii) The tax credit is calculated as the withholding tax spared less the tax payable on the spared tax, i.e. $15-(15 \times 33^1/_3\%) = 10$
(iii) The tax credit is equal to the income received grossed up at 15%, i.e.
$$\frac{15}{100} \times 100 \times \frac{100}{(100 - 15)} = 17.6$$

CHAPTER 10

Currency Exposure Management

by

Andrew Higgins; *revised by, and with additional material from,*
Brian Terry

1. INTRODUCTION

Ever since trade between areas with different currencies commenced, problems have arisen as to the value of currencies in terms of other currencies. It is not the object of this chapter to chart or explain these fluctuations in value, if indeed fully convincing explanations are possible, but instead to outline the impact on treasuries of exchange rate movements and the options which they have available to them to remove all or part of that risk.

Three factors have accentuated the impact of currency exposure in recent years:

- the continuing increase in world trade, particularly in manufactured goods but, also, in services. In the UK and other Western European countries increasing exports to the USA in the 1980s represented a major factor in the recovery and further growth of companies from the problems of the late 1970s. To succeed, these exporters had, by and large, to invoice their US customers in US dollars.

- the growing volatility of some significant exchange rates to the extent that values can now change quite sharply over relatively short time periods of a week or even within one day. For example, between September 1949 and November 1967, the sterling/US dollar exchange rate fluctuated between 2.78 and 2.82 US dollars to the pound. In 1992 alone the same rate of exchange fluctuated between 1.8680 and 1.5140, a dramatic change. For a UK exporter with US dollar income the consequence of such exchange rate changes is that the sterling value of such income has also fluctuated sharply in recent years.

• the interest of companies in investing overseas has meant that the performance of the new overseas subsidiaries can have a significant impact on overall company financials, in terms both of the profit and loss account and the balance sheet.

As a result of these developments, currency exposure management has become a core treasury activity with the requirement to identify areas of risk, define objectives and implement policies. At the same time, financial institutions have developed hedging instruments to meet the treasurer's needs. Successful marketing of these instruments requires an understanding of what these needs can be.

2. THE NATURE OF FOREIGN CURRENCY EXPOSURE

As a general rule, currency exposure exists if changes in exchange rates impact either directly or indirectly on a company's balance sheets or profit and loss accounts. Three different types of currency exposure are normally identified:

(a) *Transaction exposure* – foreign currency income and expenditure items will change in value between recognition and maturity i.e. receipt or payment, if exchange rates fluctuate. This category also includes such passive items as dividends, interest, lease or rental payments and royalties.

(b) *Translation exposure* (also known as accounting or balance sheet exposure) – at regular periods a company must revalue its accounting items which are denominated in foreign currency. In the case of foreign currency net asset positions, these revaluations with changing exchange rates will produce adjusting items which will need to pass either through the profit and loss account or through the balance sheet directly.

(c) *Economic exposure* (also known as competitive exposure) – such exposure can be either active or passive. In the active circumstance, corporates rely on raw materials from a certain country or are exporting to another, with costs/market share reliant on a certain

374

exchange rate. If that exchange rate changes adversely, then strategic management decisions may be necessary e.g. to relocate production from one country to another. Economic exposure can also arise passively where a purely domestic producer finds his market share falling as an overseas competitor, with lower local costs, benefits from a change in exchange rates and lowers his prices.

Of the three broad types of currency exposure, transaction risks are the most commonly recognised and generally receive the most attention. Translation problems are often considered within the context of financing decisions on overseas investment, while economic exposure can be a major factor in deciding the location of manufacturing facilities.

2.1 The Significance of Currency Exposure

For an exporter or an importer, even a relatively small currency movement can have a disproportionate impact on profits. If, for example, an exporter's margins were 20% of the total price, then a 5% fall in receipts in his home currency would mean a 25% drop in profits. Such an impact will obviously have serious consequences for any company and corporate treasurers will be expected to counter the impact of such events by dealing in the financial markets and, where possible, enable benefit to be obtained from favourable exchange rate movements or neutralise the impact of unfavourable exchange rate movements. A close analysis is necessary, therefore, of the characteristics of each type of currency exposure and the hedging instruments available.

3. TRANSACTION CURRENCY EXPOSURE

3.1 Identification

As soon as a company enters into a commitment to pay or to receive a foreign currency amount then transaction exposure can be said to exist. Identification is possible at four stages:

Budget – estimates or forecasts of currency sales and purchases are relied on for costing and profit calculations or, alternatively, price lists are prepared which will be binding for a period of time.

Committed – goods are ordered and price agreed in foreign currency terms with a sales invoice to be issued or received at a later stage.

Invoice – goods or services are sold and invoiced in foreign currency or conversely an invoice is received for goods purchased.

Payment – matters are crystallised and the exposure is determined as payment of the currency amount in question is either made or received.

Only invoiced items must be formally recognised for accounting purposes, but changes in currency values can impact on the exposure at an earlier stage. Indeed, as these earlier stages must necessarily involve longer time scales before payment, the notional exchange rates relied upon are more likely to vary substantially when compared to the rates available on the day of payment. On the other hand, prior to invoice there is a degree of uncertainty as to whether or not the exposure will actually materialise. The level of probability which will increase as currency exposures move through this cycle of budget/committed/invoice/payment must be borne in mind in any hedging strategy.

Where companies in the same group are carrying out transactions with one another in various currencies, it is important to identify any net group exposures overall which the individual companies may miss. Here, for example, one subsidiary may be selling in a foreign currency to another subsidiary which in turn on-sells to a customer in that same currency. The first subsidiary considers that there is not a currency exposure that needs action as any reduction in proceeds it might suffer from adverse exchange rate movements would generate an equal gain for its fellow subsidiary. The second subsidiary on the other hand believes that no action is necessary as it has a matched position with no net exposure. Overall though the Group is at risk from exchange rate movements if the transaction is viewed from the initial expenditure in one currency through to the final receipt of funds in a different currency.

It is vital in any hedging activity to be confident about the data on the exposure. Information must be comprehensive, up-to-date and accurate. If currency sales are from price lists, with considerable lags before precise data is available, actions may have to be based on rolling forecasts which are adjusted as the actual sales materialise.

376

3.2 Valuation

Traditional practice for most companies with the agreement of their auditors has been to value short term currency assets and liabilities for accounting purposes at the spot conversion rates at the date of their creation. They are then revalued at the appropriate spot conversion rates at maturity as well as at any intervening balance sheet closing dates.

However for transaction exposure management purposes it is more logical to value currency assets and liabilities at the appropriate forward foreign exchange rate for the period up to payment. The forward rate represents the item's opportunity value, the only rate at which the currency amount could actually be determined in value and a good means of judging the effectiveness of any hedging activity.

3.3 Impact

A corporate treasurer must decide the significance of the impact of changes in currency values on his company's business. While a 5–10 year view might be that exchange rate changes will balance out with relative price levels in each country, this is of little use if, in the meantime, the company is in liquidation due to adverse changes in vital exchange rates.

On the other hand, while currency items may appear to form a major part of a balance sheet, factors may, on closer inspection, reduce the actual significance e.g.

(i)   The company may have opposing long and short positions in particular currencies, so exchange rate changes impact only on the net position.

(ii)   When a company has currency payables and receivables, albeit in different currencies, a depreciation of the home currency will generate both profits and losses, so that again it is the net position which is of concern.

3.4 Currency Hedging Strategies

For any strategy to succeed, it must be clearly defined, acceptable to, and understood by, all concerned with treasury matters. If this is not the case, corporate treasurers who are, for example, operating on the basis of hedging everything will face questions as to why the company, with sales in the USA, has not, say, gained from a recent appreciation of the US dollar.

Three alternative hedging philosophies can be adopted:

3.4.1 *Hedge Nothing.* This may be a conscious decision by companies which are prepared to accept a potentially high element of risk in the expectation that the optimum values of exposures will be achieved only at maturity (i.e. between recognition and maturity, currency receivables will appreciate and currency payables will depreciate in base currency terms). Equally consciously, the company may hold a fundamental belief that the taking of forward cover is "speculative". Alternatively, the policy may be due to the company's failure to recognise the inherent risks and the options available.

3.4.2 *Hedge Everything.* This is a typical response by companies which have identified the potential risks and are prepared to forego possible opportunity gains in return for certainty of value. Such companies are usually risk averse and may hold the view that to leave exposures open is to "speculate".

3.4.3 *Hedge Selectively.* Representing a course between the two extremes, the object is to hedge only those exposures where the perceived risk of loss exceeds the perceived opportunity for gain. To be successful, however, this requires the devotion of executive and operational resources to distinguish currencies according to their relative strength and weakness over time and to adopt appropriate hedging strategies. For example, the view may be taken that the US dollar will remain firm for the next three months but weaken thereafter. Consequently USD receivables maturing in less than 90 days may be left unhedged, whereas those maturing beyond would be sold forward according to their maturity probability (e.g. a committed exposure may be considered to be 70% certain as to amount and/or timing but a budget exposure only 40%).

Where currency exposures arise in a variety of relatively weak and strong currencies, statistics suggest there is little difference over time in the results from policies of hedging nothing or hedging everything since

378

neither takes account of opportunity gains or losses. Selective hedging, however, provides an opportunity to preserve or enhance the value of currency receivables and to contain or reduce the cost of currency payables, albeit by accepting a certain degree of risk.

For most companies the overriding aim will be to hedge transaction exposures progressively as their probability increases over time (i.e. Budget – Committed – Invoice – Cash) and their view will be that activity over and above this (i.e. opening unnatural positions or re-opening positions previously closed) to take advantage of market conditions will not be undertaken.

3.5 Internal Hedging Techniques

Using various operational techniques a company can significantly influence its overall transaction exposure to foreign currency risk and, allied to this, improve the cost effectiveness of its collection and disbursement procedures for currency amounts. These techniques are as follows:

3.5.1 *Currency of Billing*

Currency exposures arising out of third party trade could be avoided if a company sourced its raw materials or stock-in-trade and sold on entirely in its base currency. Frequently, however, for competitive reasons, an overseas supplier, say in Italy, may insist on billing in Lire, or even in a third currency (e.g. US Dollars). Interest in billing in US Dollars may come from, for example:

(a) a desire to match dollar payment obligations; or

(b) the fact that the commodity is priced internationally in US Dollars.

Conversely an *exporter* may need to bill in the *importer's* currency if the foreign market is particularly price sensitive or "inelastic" (i.e. price rises cannot be passed on quickly for competitive reasons), the exporter is better placed to deal with the attendant exposures because of exchange control regulations in the importer's country, or simply that the foreign market e.g. the USA, requires pricing in its own currency.

For cross-border, intra-group transactions the choice of currency will determine *where* the exposure arises but not change overall Group exposure. It will usually be preferable to ensure that the exposure rests with the

379

affiliate best placed to deal with it for reasons such as currency management expertise, relative freedom from exchange controls, access to international currency markets or that the residual foreign exchange gains or losses can be used more tax effectively.

3.5.2 *Matching, Leading and Lagging*

One of the simplest exposure management tools available to the corporate treasurer is the technique of matching existing currency commitments not only between affiliates but also with third parties. For example a Swiss Franc 100,000 receivable may first be matched against any payables in the same currency maturing at the same time, before any external hedging is undertaken for the residual, unmatched position.

In practice, however, the timing of currency receipts, especially from third parties, will rarely coincide exactly with intended payment dates. Flexibility of timing is needed, therefore, to optimise flows by:

- delaying (lagging) collection/conversion of strong currency receivables

- accelerating (leading) disbursement/conversion of strong currency payables

- accelerating (leading) collection/conversion of weak currency receivables

- delaying (lagging) disbursement/conversion of weak currency payables.

Particular care must be taken, however, not to antagonise trading partners since, whereas several days' or even weeks' delay in settlement of trade payments to affiliates may be acceptable, significant delays in payments to third parties might well impair trading relationships.

The corporate treasurer should also be alert to the opportunities allowed by different countries to accelerate or delay ("lead" or "lag") payment to beneficiaries. Although frequent changes to settlement terms, particularly intra-group, would probably attract the attention of taxation, exchange control or other regulatory authorities, the delaying of payments from a country where borrowing is difficult or expensive may well allow a company and its affiliates to redeploy existing liquidity or borrow in a more convenient location.

380

3.5.3 *Currency Hold Accounts*

The use of currency accounts, or hold accounts as they are commonly termed, is essential to the efficient management of foreign currency flows. Used as currency denominated ordinary current accounts they fulfil two prime functions:

● the collection of receivables and disbursement of payables in foreign currency

and

● the reduction of gross foreign exchange needs by:

either matching receipts and payments arising in the same currency at approximately the same time; or

permitting cross deals from one long foreign currency to satisfy a short position in another currency without the need to trade both against the base currency.

The decision on whether to locate currency accounts overseas or locally must rest on a careful review of the relative advantages. A major factor here will be the transaction volumes envisaged – high volumes will enhance the possible advantages of transmission cost savings from locating accounts overseas.

The matching of receipts and payments through the use of currency hold accounts thus provides an operationally convenient means of reducing foreign exchange needs, and the corporate treasurer has only, then, to manage actively the residual net currency positions, with consequent savings in dealing and transmission costs.

3.5.4 *Multilateral Netting*

The prime purpose of multilateral netting is to reduce group foreign exchange dealing requirements and money transmission between the participants by enabling each entity to make or receive one remittance only on a common settlement date in satisfaction of all mutual indebtedness.

In its simplest form netting can be adopted by any pair of companies or autonomous units provided there are regular two-way cash flows between them. The technique involves no more than periodically offsetting mutual indebtedness prior to the net debtor initiating a transfer for the balance outstanding. For example, in Figure 1 below Company A owes £100 to Company B but is, in turn, owed £200. By use of netting, gross payables of £300 can be discharged by a remittance of £100 by Company B.

Figure 1
Simple Netting

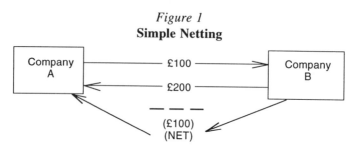

The arrangement can be extended to embrace any number of participants provided there are significant reciprocal cash flows. Where these exist in different currencies it will be necessary for the underlying natural currency balances to be converted, notionally at least, into a common reference currency by the use of exchange rates acceptable to all the participants. This is illustrated in Figures 2 and 3 where, by the use of Sterling as the reference currency, gross payables have been reduced from eq. £560 to eq. £270 net.

Figure 2

Illustration of Multilateral, Multicurrency Netting

Gross Payments

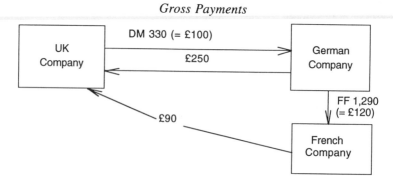

Figure 3

Net Payments

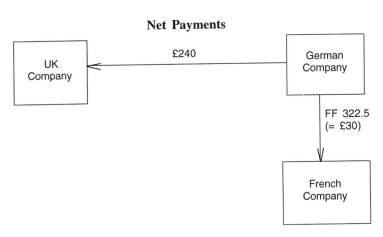

The operation of netting procedures invariably requires the intervention of a Control Centre to collate details of all intercompany payables and receivables and to co-ordinate settlement at maturity; this is the fundamental role of the control centre. The extent of the control centre's further involvement in the netting sequence can vary considerably, according to the relative autonomy of the participants and in particular, whether foreign exchange transactions are to be initiated centrally or by the participants.

3.6 External Hedging Techniques
The principal hedging methods likely to be appropriate to most companies' needs in dealing with *transaction exposure* are as follows:

3.6.1 *Forward Exchange*
Forward foreign exchange is the most commonly used technique for hedging currency transaction exposures. By selling currency receivables forward an exporter fixes the amounts he will receive in his own currency. Similarly, an importer can buy currency forward to determine the cost now of his future currency payable. In both cases, the trader is then protected against any future changes in exchange rates as he has a contract with his bank to buy or sell the currency involved at a fixed price.

The forward market in foreign exchange is possible not because the bank buying or selling the currency is guessing what the rate will be at the time of delivery (banks are as keen as anyone else to avoid currency losses) but because forward rates are, basically, determined by the spot exchange rate adjusted according to interest rate differentials.

Imagine two currencies where the spot rate of exchange is 4 units of currency B to 1 unit of currency A; and one year interest rates are 5% p.a. for currency A and 10% p.a. for currency B.

Ignoring the spread between bid and offered rates (for simplicity), a bank (or anyone else in the market) borrows 400 B and converts them to 100 A, which it then deposits.

At the end of the year, it will owe 440 B and have 105 A, i.e. principal plus interest.

If it has sold 105 A forward at a rate of 1 A: 4.19 B (440/105), it will have a completely hedged position. This explains how a bank can quote forward exchange contract prices to its customers and (in theory at least) cover its exposure. Whether it does cover or not will depend on many factors such as the state of its book, its view of the markets or the ability to 'lay the contract off' by entering into a similar, covering transaction with another bank. It would be rare for a bank actually to borrow, deal at spot and then deposit for this would mean there would be no profit in the deal as this would be the exact basis on which the forward price for the customer was calculated.

Forward rates are said to be at a premium or a discount to the spot i.e. the forward rate negates the interest rate differential advantage. In the example above currency B is at a discount to the spot. If interest rates had been reversed (10% p.a. currency A and 5% for currency B), currency B would be at a premium and the forward rate would be 3.82.

The currency with the *higher interest* rate is always at a *discount* in the forward market. Or, expressed the other way, the currency with the *lower interest* rate is at a *premium* in the forward market.

Anyone wishing to find out the forward rates for *indication* purposes can turn to the financial press and see the previous day's close of business rates of exchange. For example, the Deutschemark against Sterling rates are shown in the paper as follows:

Spot at close of business   *One Month*   *Three Months*
DM 2.3655 – 2.3825   .0037 – .0062 Dis   .0112 – .0137 Dis

Dis = discount.

Forward premiums will have a higher figure followed by a lower figure, which we deduct from spot. Forward discounts will have a lower figure followed by a higher figure and these are added to spot (as in the DM example).

Bearing in mind the discount is added to the spot rate and that two spot rates are quoted the reader wishes to know at which rate a bank would buy or sell Sterling in exchange for Deutschemarks. Given that a bank, wishing to make a profit out of foreign exchange is acting logically, this can be easily worked out. The bank in question will wish to buy Sterling for the minimum amount of Deutschemarks and sell Sterling for the maximum amount. In this particular situation it will buy Sterling spot (i.e. sell Deutschemarks) at DM2.3655 : £1 and sell Sterling spot (i.e. buy Deutschemarks) for DM2.3825 : £1.

If an importer wished to calculate a £/DM three month forward rate, the bank to buy Sterling, sell DM, the above example would give us a spot rate of DM2.3655 plus the discount of 0.0112 making a forward rate of DM2.3767.

Other forward rate examples

Spot rate – Deutschemarks/Sterling 2.3830 – 2.3860
1 month forward + 0.0045 to + 0.0052 (discount)
3 months forward + 0.0125 to + 0.0140 (discount)

Thus the bank sells Dms spot	at 2.3830 and buys at 2.3860
1 month forward: bank sells Dms	at 2.3875 and buys at 2.3912
3 months forward: bank sells Dms	at 2.3955 and buys at 2.4000

As an example, if the bank sells Dms against Sterling for one month forward it takes the spot selling rate, 2.3830, and, in this case, *adds* one month discount (the left hand side of the swap rate) i.e. 0.0045, to produce an outright forward rate of 2.3875.

Spot rate – US Dollars/Sterling 1.4550 – 1.4560
1 month forward – 0.0038 to – 0.0036 (premium)
3 months forward – 0.0105 to – 0.0102 (premium)

Thus the bank sells US$ spot	at 1.4550 and buys at 1.4560
1 month forward: bank sells US$	at 1.4512 and buys at 1.4524
3 months forward: bank sells US$	at 1.4445 and buys at 1.4458

Spot rate – Swiss Franc/Sterling 2.2050 – 2.2080
1 month forward – 0.0020 to – 0.0010 (premium)
3 months forward – 0.0040 to – 0.0030 (premium)

Thus the bank sells Swiss Fcs spot	at 2.2050 and buys at 2.2080
1 month forward: bank sells Swiss Fcs	at 2.2030 and buys at 2.2070
3 months forward: bank sells Swiss Fcs	at 2.2010 and buys at 2.2050

Spot rate – French Fcs/Sterling 8.0880 – 8.0980
1 month forward + 0.0380 to + 0.0420 (discount)
3 months forward + 0.1170 to + 0.1225 (discount)

Thus the bank sells French Fcs spot	at 8.0880 and buys at 8.0980
1 month forward: bank sells French Fcs	at 8.1260 and buys at 8.1400
3 months forward: bank sells French Fcs	at 8.2050 and buys at 8.2205

Spot rate – Italian Lire/Sterling 2282.00 – 2286.00
1 month forward + 9.80 to + 10.80 (discount)
3 months forward + 30.50 to + 32.00 (discount)

Thus the bank sells Italian Lire spot	at 2282.00 and buys at 2286.00
1 month forward: bank sells It. Lire	at 2291.80 and buys at 2296.80
3 months forward: bank sells It. Lire	at 2312.50 and buys at 2318.00

Where the interest rate of the counter value currency is higher than that of Sterling, the forward rate of that currency will also be higher, i.e. at a discount.

386

It is sometimes suggested, particularly when the forward rate is apparently less favourable than the spot rate, that the difference between the two rates is a *cost of covering*. This pre-supposes that the spot rate can, in some sense, be used to value the future currency payable or receivable. However, the forward rate should always be used to value a currency item as it is the *only* rate that can actually be obtained *now* for an amount which will be paid or received *at some date in the future*. To talk of the premium or discount as a "cost of covering" is, therefore, misleading.

It is possible to take a view on future rates, of course, and leave a currency exposure open with the expectation that the eventual spot rate will be more favourable than the forward rate now. This is adopting a policy of hedging selectively and any trader considering such a policy must bear in mind the risks he is accepting, i.e. he could be wrong and the spot rate in the future could be less favourable.

A practical problem does often arise from the difficulty of forecasting exactly when a future receivable will arrive or a future payment will be required, bearing in mind that a forward foreign exchange contract is binding. The currency in question must be paid or received on the due date as far as the importer's or exporter's bank is concerned. If the actual commercial payment, say a currency receivable, is not received as expected, there are two ways to provide the currency due to the bank and continue the hedge. The first possibility is to close out the forward contract by an equal and opposite spot foreign exchange deal and take out a fresh forward deal maturing on the new date of payment. The alternative is to borrow the currency to meet the requirement at the maturity of the forward exchange deal; in due course the currency receivable repays the borrowing.

Another possible solution is to enter into an option forward exchange contract – not to be confused with currency options, a different hedging technique which we shall discuss later in this chapter. The option forward exchange rate will give the flexibility that the customer can take up the contract at any time between two specified dates at the rate agreed. Generally, option forwards will give a worse rate than a deal for a single specified forward date, as banks quote the least favourable exchange rate as far as the customer is concerned for the period, to cover themselves against having to deliver at any time. Some improvement in the rate can be obtained, however, by restricting the period of the option as closely as possible.

For example, say a currency payable is due between five and six months in the future and the forward rate is at a discount compared to the domestic currency. In these circumstances a forward contract with an option to take delivery at any time during the six months will produce a significantly worse rate than an option allowing delivery (i.e. the customer buying DM to make the payment) only in the sixth month.

If this were a DM payable, an option forward contract to buy DMs with the option for the full 6 months would be priced at 2.3655 (the spot rate) while an option limited to the last month would be priced at 2.3840 (spot plus five months forward), not as good as the outright 6 month rate of 2.3880 but considerably better than the first quote (i.e. spot).

A forward foreign exchange contract is a binding commitment and the customer must either take or make delivery of the currency or close out the contract with an opposite deal at the spot rate ruling at maturity. Any corporate entering into a forward foreign exchange deal gives up, therefore, the opportunity to take advantage of movements in the market in its favour although it protects itself from adverse market movements. However, contracts are 'off balance sheet' and do not tie up liquidity unnecessarily. The bank will usually wish to negotiate a limit, though, to accommodate the customer's projected requirements.

While the effect of taking out forward cover is to determine now the exchange rate applying to a future currency payment or receivable, strategies can be applied to produce a more sophisticated result, e.g.

- selective hedging, with determined target exchange rates and an attempt to achieve a closer to optimum result

- partial hedging of currency liabilities/assets e.g. say hedge 50% of currency receivables, but leave 50% uncovered to obtain gains from favourable market movements, accepting that adverse market movements will create losses

- "synthetic" options in which cover is taken if the market rate falls below a floor rate, but reopening the position if the market rises again.

3.6.2 Currency Borrowing/Deposits

The second major hedging technique is to use currency loans or deposits to lock in a value now for a future currency cash flow in the same way as a forward sale or purchase does. For a currency receivable, this involves borrowing the foreign currency, converting it at spot into the domestic currency and repaying the borrowing in due course with the receivable. For a currency payable, the opposite action of buying the currency required and depositing it until the date of payment will have to be taken.

To illustrate how this form of hedge actually works, using the £/DM exchange rate above, say a UK exporter has DM 1.25m receivable due in three months' time. In anticipation of receipt, he borrows DM1,223,990 at 8.5% p.a. which he immediately converts into sterling at a rate of 2.3825. Liquidity of £513,742 is generated which replaces a sterling borrowing costing 6.5% p.a. The DM borrowing plus interest is repaid on the due date by the receivable and it is possible to calculate an effective forward rate to compare this technique to forward exchange as follows:

Currency borrowed		Sterling replaced
DM1,223,990	@ 2.3825 replaces	£513,742
26,010	8.5% p.a. for 90 days 6.5% p.a. for 90 days	£8,234
DM 1,250,000	@ DM 2.3948 = £1.00 = (contrived forward rate)	£521,976

This contrived forward rate compares closely with the forward exchange rate of 2.3962 available as an alternative. Differences will arise where the interest rates obtained vary from those of the interbank market on which forward rates of exchange are calculated. Also, if the borrowing or the deposit are at variable rates e.g. overdraft rates, upwards or downwards movements in interest rates will affect the value obtained through the hedge. In most circumstances, however, the effect of movements in interest rates will be much less than the potential effect of movements in exchange rates. Late receipt or payment can be dealt with in a similar fashion to forward contracts by borrowing or depositing the currency for a further period.

The use of this hedging technique as opposed to forward exchange contracts must depend on the individual circumstances and preference of the corporate. Generally, if this hedge involves borrowing in one currency and depositing in another, the negative spread in the interest rates will make forward exchange a much better method. Again, borrowing in this case will use up credit lines and inflate balance sheets. There is the possible attraction of this technique though, that if the domestic borrowing is at variable rates of interest, then currency borrowing at a fixed rate enables you effectively to fix a rate of interest for the borrowing in your own currency. Greater flexibility as far as dates of receipt/payment are concerned is also obtained – important where these dates cannot be forecast or where a lot of small payments/receipts are concerned.

Where currency loans are being used to hedge forecast currency flows it is necessary to match drawdown and repayment to, say, monthly totals. If term loan facilities are utilised, certain problems will arise depending on the particular policy adopted e.g.

- *Principal of loan equates to forecast annual currency flows* – A view is being taken here that translation adjustments on the principal of the loan will net out against transaction changes in value in base currency terms. This policy does not create a fully effective hedge, as translation adjustments will be determined by exchange rates ruling at the beginning and the end of the period while transaction flows will be determined throughout the year on receipt. Gains or losses are unlikely, therefore, to have an opposite loss or gain through the hedge. Different tax treatment of the various profits and losses could also cause problems.

- *Debt servicing matches annual currency flows* – Hedging activity here depends on matching debt servicing to forecast income flows as far as possible i.e. if income is expected to be relatively uniform, debt servicing should be spread evenly through the year. This solution creates a major problem in that the corporate has large currency liabilities in terms of principal amount for which it has no currency fixed assets. Very large translation adjustments may well occur, therefore, which are unwelcome as they impact on profit and loss and/or equity.

From this it can be seen that if term loans are being used for currency hedging, careful consideration must be given to the implications of such a policy. When the corporate is, for example, matching debt servicing to income flows, then as a consequence it is, as a matter of policy, creating substantial unmatched currency term liabilities. Active management is required to avoid substantial increases in liabilities in base currency terms.

3.6.3   Currency Options

Since their introduction in 1982 currency options have generated growing interest as an alternative means of hedging currency exposures. They provide the right, but not the obligation, to buy (if it is a 'call' option) or sell (if it is a 'put' option) one currency for another at an agreed rate (called the strike or exercise price) either on (European option), or at any time up to (American option), an agreed date. Both forms are available in most developed financial centres.

Currency options may either be "traded" options provided through a financial futures exchange where amounts, strike prices and maturing dates are standardised (i.e each instrument having a fixed size and a range of specified strike prices and expiry dates), or "over the counter" options where all terms are freely negotiable directly with a bank. Currency options have a cost represented by the premium payable to the seller, or writer, of the option. This cost is made up of a charge for two factors:

(i)   intrinsic value which is the benefit to be gained if the option were to be exercised immediately and the proceeds sold back through the cash markets, and

(ii)   time value, the benefit the holder of the option obtains of having the *opportunity* during the remaining life of the option to gain intrinsic value; i.e. it is the amount by which the option's total premium exceeds its intrinsic value.

391

At any given time a contract, viewed from the position of the corporate, will be:

(a) At the money – where the strike price is equal to the current cash (or spot) market price

(b) In the money – where the strike price is more advantageous to the buyer of the option than the current cash price

(c) Out of the money – where the strike price is less advantageous to the buyer of the option than the current cash price.

Thus, a corporate treasurer would exercise an option which is "in the money" at the exercise date but would let one lapse if it was "out of the money" and deal, instead, in the cash market. He neither gains nor loses by exercising the option if it is "at the money". Bearing in mind that a premium has been paid then "in the money" contracts are worthwhile exercising only if the exercise price exceeds the current market price by the amount of the premium.

An option normally has the largest amount of time value premium when it is "at the money". That is, when the spot price is equal to the strike price. An option which is either deep "in the money" or a long way "out of the money" will command virtually no time value.

An "out of the money" option has no intrinsic value and only time value. The further "out of the money" an option becomes, then the less likely is it to be able to "recover" and be exercised. The time value, therefore, decreases as the option moves further "out of the money" and the premium, naturally, becomes cheaper.

"In the money" options have both intrinsic value and time value. The further "in the money" the option becomes, then the greater the intrinsic value it will contain. However, the greater the intrinsic value an option attains, so the time value it has reduces because the probability that the option will be exercised has increased.

Intrinsic value is the amount by which the strike price betters the spot rate, and represents immediate benefit to the purchaser.

392

Hence, an option which is "out of the money" will have no intrinsic value as there is no benefit immediately available. The option consists of time value only. Similarly, an option which is "at the money" will have no intrinsic value whereas an option "in the money" will have intrinsic value.

It should now be appreciated that the time value of an option erodes; it decreases over the life of the contract and will fall off sharply as the option approaches expiry.

There are various models used for valuing options with the basic model having been produced by Professor Black and Professor Scholes in 1973 (not originally for pricing options!). Such models are abstract principles used only as a guide to market makers who may, or may not, choose to use such a model. The general market rules of supply and demand still apply as to what a participant is prepared to pay.

Currency options have a particularly useful application in hedging contingent exposures which can arise, for example, in the classic "tender to contract" situation in which a company does not know if it will need to buy or sell currency at the time it is tendering for a contract. They can also be used by corporate treasurers who seek to insure against a fall in value of, say, a currency receivable but would wish to gain the benefit from market movements in their favour. It is obviously necessary here to accept the premium cost for an instrument that may, or may not, be used.

An example of the use of currency options in the classic "tender to contract" situation is a UK exporter (whose costs are in sterling) who has to tender in US dollars at a time when the forward rate to the date when the proceeds are expected to be received, if the order is won, is £1.00 = US$1.50. If the exporter is confident he will know the result of the tender within say, six months, and is prepared to take the risk of the rate going to £1.00 = US$1.55, he can buy a six month option to sell dollars at 1.55 (the further away the strike price is from the current price, the lower the premium). As there are two variables (the result of the tender, and the movement of the exchange rate) there are only four possible outcomes:

(i)   He wins the tender: the dollar weakens. He exercises the option and protects his desired proceeds by taking a profit which will offset the loss he will make by selling the dollars forward for a lesser amount;

(ii)   He wins the tender: the dollar strengthens. He abandons the option and sells the dollars forward for a greater amount than originally expected;

(iii) He loses the tender: the dollar weakens. He buys dollars in the market, exercises the option and takes a profit. It should be noted that certain banks are now selling options specifically for "tender to contract" situations where, in exchange for a lower premium, the option cannot be exercised if the tender is lost.

(iv)   He loses the tender: the dollar strengthens. He abandons the option, at the maximum cost of the premium.

At a maximum cost of the premium the exporter is protected from adverse exchange rate movements but left able to take advantage of favourable exchange rate movements. The premium, like an insurance premium, is a true cost and is paid to the seller of the option to compensate him for the risk which he now takes. It is sometimes suggested that currency options are too expensive, but the risk assumed by the seller, although not open-ended as there are ways of hedging an option with greater or lesser degrees of certainty, is a real one.

3.6.4   *Participating Forward Foreign Exchange Contracts*
A particular problem corporate treasurers have in using options is the need to pay a premium at the inception of the deal. A number of hybrids have been developed to overcome this problem and one product which is of particular interest meets the objection by combining an option with a forward foreign exchange contract. The option premium is paid through the calculation of the participating forward rate and the benefit for the customer is an agreed percentage of the amount by which the spot rate at maturity is better than the participating forward rate.

For a customer of a bank the participating forward foreign exchange contract would work as follows:

- the customer is quoted the normal outright forward rate.

- the customer decides the participating percentage it wishes to obtain.

- the outright forward rate is adjusted in the bank's favour in return for incorporating the customer's participating percentage in the contract.

- at maturity of the contract the difference between the ruling spot rate and the participating forward rate is calculated.

- the customer's benefit is calculated, representing the participation percentage of the difference in the two above rates.

- this benefit is added to or deducted from the original participation forward rate to determine the actual foreign exchange rate at which the customer carries out its transaction with the bank.

It is important to note here that the participating forward contract is a firm contractual obligation which the customer must perform. The only variable is the rate at which the customer will buy or sell its foreign currency.

To illustrate further how this product would work, the following is an example where a customer wishes to purchase US dollars three months forward:

Spot rate at date of agreement	1.5705
3 months premium	0.0120
3 months forward rate	1.5585
Selected participation	50%
Created participating forward rate	1.5350
Spot rate at maturity	1.6350
Difference	0.1000
Benefit for customer (50%)	0.0500
plus original participating forward rate	1.5350
Final exchange rate achieved	1.5850

The extent to which the participating forward rate will vary from the original normal forward rate when the bank is quoting will depend on the participation percentage selected by the customer. The higher the percentage the further away the participation rate will be from the outright forward rate.

Participating forwards have proved attractive to a number of companies which are not prepared to pay premiums. Availability will depend on the underlying option market and will tend to be limited, therefore, to the major convertible currencies.

3.6.5   *Currency Baskets*

Currency baskets allow the spreading of the risk of adverse exchange movements over a range of currencies. Currencies such as the Special Drawing Right (SDR) and European Currency Unit (ECU) are composed of baskets of currencies. The number of currencies involved greatly reduces the risk of adverse movements against any single currency (and reduces the prospect of large gains, of course, from beneficial movements), which makes such composite currencies particularly popular for invoicing in countries where strict exchange controls render other hedging techniques difficult or impossible.

3.6.6   *Currency Futures*

Currency futures differ from forward exchange contracts in that they are standardised contracts for specific amounts and for specific dealing dates. The contracts are tradeable on an exchange such as the London International Financial Futures Exchange (LIFFE) and the International Monetary Market (IMM) of the Chicago Mercantile Exchange.

Whereas, in the forward foreign exchange market, the counterparty will be an individual bank, in the futures markets all deals are settled with a clearing house, which will require margin payments (usually deposits which fluctuate in line with the prices of contracts), to secure the performance of all contracts. Because they are standardised contracts currency futures lack the flexibility of the forward exchange market and are relatively little used, in the UK at least, for the hedging of transaction exposures.

4. TRANSLATION CURRENCY EXPOSURE

4.1 Introduction

Translation exposure for a corporate arises from the need for periodic revaluations in the Company's reporting currency of those assets and liabilities and income and expenditure streams which are denominated in foreign currency, especially on consolidation of the accounts of foreign subsidiaries. Under SSAP 20 or SFAS 52 (see Section 6), the adjustments necessary following revaluations can be taken directly through a separate equity account and will not affect the income and expenditure figures unless there is a sale or liquidation of the foreign investment. An example of such an adjustment would be a UK company with share capital and assets of £4,000 which purchases a US dollar denominated asset costing US$3,000. The dollar asset has been financed by sterling borrowing at a current rate of £1.00 = $1.25 and the balance sheet would appear as follows:

	£		£
Share capital	4,000	Sterling Assets	4,000
Translation gain (loss)	—	US Dollar Asset	
		(US$3,000 @ £1.00:	
Sterling debt	2,400	$1.25)	2,400
	6,400		6,400

If, in this example, the dollar weakened to say £1.00: $1.50 then the revised balance sheet would appear as follows:

	£		£
Share capital	4,000	Sterling Assets	4,000
Translation loss	(400)	US Dollar Asset	
		(US$3,000 @ £1.00:	
Sterling debt	2,400	$1.50)	2,000
	6,000		6,000

A number of companies find the prospect of such adjustments unattractive and have sought to remove the risk by hedging their translation risks.

4.2 Internal Hedging Techniques

The corporate can consider taking a number of actions internally to reduce or eliminate the net asset value of the subsidiary and thus the currency risk such as:

- subsidiary can be undercapitalised by the parent which probably means the subsidiary has to borrow in lieu of having adequate capital. However, if the subsidiary is subject to thin capitalisation regulations the local revenue authorities may deem the loan to be "quasi capital", disallow interest payments on loans for tax purposes and rule that the interest (whether payable to a parent or a third party) is treated as though it were a dividend. In such circumstances withholding tax could be payable on the interest/dividend.

- reduce net asset position of subsidiary by it paying dividends in excess of its retained annual profits (this would create a position similar to the above).

- encourage financing by a foreign subsidiary in local currency to repay original capital or loans injected by the parent (but care re. thin capitalisation).

- the overseas subsidiary may hold assets expressed in the currency of the parent company.

However, it should be borne in mind that the above activities may impact on profitability of the overseas subsidiary and may well also break exchange control and other regulations. The corporate may well have to consider what external action can be taken in the UK to counter translation exposures overseas. There could, also, be tax implications.

4.3 External Hedging Techniques

4.3.1 *Currency borrowing*

The traditional, and most used, means of hedging this type of risk, is to match currency assets as represented by the net worth of overseas subsidiaries by currency liabilities, i.e. currency borrowing. This form of translation hedging is described as a "natural hedge". The impact of any exchange rate movements in the group consolidated accounts in a

398

revaluation is cancelled out if the adjustment for the currency asset is matched by a similar adjustment for a currency liability. Currency borrowing by one means or another is relatively straightforward and the rapid growth of international financial markets has meant that the range and amounts of currencies available has expanded considerably. Several aspects should be borne in mind:

- Any acquisition may require a substantial proportion of the cost to be in consideration of a purchase of intangible assets. If the corporate either wished or was required to write-off these intangible assets up front then the amount of new net currency assets in the consolidated balance sheet would be substantially reduced. Such an event would, given that the total cost had been financed in currency, mean that a translation exposure consisting of a net currency liability would have been created. It is important, therefore, to determine, prior to the completion of the purchase, the expected overseas balance sheet after the acquisition in order to estimate the currency net asset position requiring hedging.

- A currency loan will require payments of interest in currency and the corporate should consider whether currency income will be available to meet these costs. If this is not the case, separate hedging activity may be necessary to cover the transaction currency risk.

- A number of companies have found that when translation exposure has been fully hedged by currency debt then currency movements can materially impact on the ratio of term debt to equity, i.e. gearing, as surplus resources are in the home currency while currency debt changes in home currency terms. For example, say a company has share capital of £5 million and US dollar borrowing of US$3 million which is shown at eq £2 million at a rate of £1.00: $1.50, the dollar borrowing having been taken to hedge US$3 million of assets. If the exchange rate changes to £1.00: $1.25 then there is no net translation exposure impact, but gearing increases from 40% to 48% with borrowing now representing eq £2.4 million.

- Acquisitions are often made on an open-ended basis without any fixed ideas on future sale or liquidation. Loan facilities, on the other hand, do require an agreed maturity date. The corporate should look for medium/long term finance facilities with bullet repayments, therefore, and bear in mind the need to arrange a replacement borrowing facility when the original borrowing must be repaid if he wishes to continue with this "natural hedge".

- Borrowing in a number of currencies can require the payment of high interest rates compared to, say, US dollar rates. In essence this cost factor cannot be avoided but the present rate of interest must be assessed as to whether it is an acceptable cost to create the hedge; i.e. is the balance sheet being hedged at the expense of a large hit on the profit and loss account?

- The currency net asset position will change over the years as, for example, profits are retained or assets revalued. It will be necessary for the hedge to be changed pro rata to avoid a currency exposure arising once more.

- If the parent company is in a position under which its deposits expressed in its domestic currency could easily be used to finance an overseas acquisition, then by raising currency finance and keeping the equivalent home currency deposits, there is a net cost of the difference between a bank's bid and offered rates plus the bank's lending margin but the currency exposure has been eliminated.

- Tax considerations should be borne in mind when deciding which operation within the group should borrow the funds if there is a preference to ensure that full tax benefit is obtained for the interest costs. Structures such as Dual Resident Companies have, in the past, offered considerable advantages but the US Tax Reform Act has removed these benefits.

4.3.2 *Currency Swaps*
For a detailed explanation of Swaps see Chapter 18.

A currency swap is, amongst other things, a useful technique for hedging a foreign asset into the home currency. It is an alternative to hedging by taking out foreign currency borrowings but need not involve raising new money.

400

For example, assume a UK company has invested $45 million in the USA, and the £/$ exchange rate is 1.50. The company wishes to hedge against a devaluation of its asset which would result from sterling strengthening against the US dollar.

The company arranges a $45 million/£30 million currency swap, agreeing to pay US dollar interest at 8.75% per annum on $45 million, and receive sterling interest at 10% per annum on £30 million.

On commencement of the swap the notional principal amounts are agreed, usually by reference to the spot exchange rate. An initial exchange of principal is optional, and, in the circumstances we are discussing, would probably not be required by the company if it is hedging an existing asset.

Throughout the life of the swap, the interest flows would be:

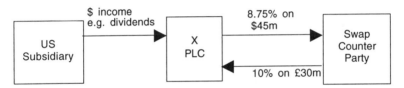

Suppose, on maturity of the swap, the exchange rate is 1.75 and the US subsidiary is not sold. The company would buy $45 million for £26 million in the spot foreign exchange market in order to settle the final exchange of principal on the swap, resulting in an exchange gain of £4 million to off-set the devaluation of £4 million of its asset at the time of the maturity of the hedge.

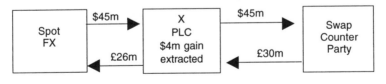

The effect of this hedge is as follows:

● dollar income has been hedged into sterling. Annual dollar interest of $3,937,500 (8.75% of $45m) has been exchanged for sterling income of £3,000,000 (10% of £30m), thus hedging this part of the dollar income into sterling at an effective exchange rate of 1.3125

- the value of the overseas asset has been maintained at £30 million. At the time of maturity of the swap it will be revalued to £26 million, but there is an offsetting exchange rate gain of £4 million, resulting in no net movement in reserves.

Whilst the swap is in place it is effective in hedging the balance sheet translation exposure, i.e. it is not just at maturity of the swap (when a cash gain or loss materialises) that the hedge works. At the interim stages, as each balance sheet is struck, the assets will need to be revalued in the way established by the company (i.e. at year end spot rates/average rates). At the same time the swap will be marked to market and any gain or loss thereby revealed against the swap rate at maturity will neutralise the loss or gain as a result of revaluing the asset. There will, accordingly, be a net nil movement in reserves.

Possible drawbacks in using swaps include, in particular, potential accounting problems as symmetrical tax treatment of assets and liabilities is necessary to avoid increased tax obligations. The present UK tax law in this area is unsatisfactory and unlikely to be clarified until case law determines the position. Against this, though, is the advantage that swaps are off-balance sheet and that the considerable size of the market has provided liquidity in a number of currencies. Liquidity is presently affected, however, due to the capital adequacy requirements of the Basle agreement which incorporate considerably higher weightings for currency, as opposed to interest rate, swaps.

4.3.3 Forward Foreign Exchange Contracts

Such contracts are, occasionally, used to hedge translation exposure, usually on one year forward foreign exchange contracts which are closed out on maturity and then fresh one year contracts taken out. However, the closing out generates a profit or a loss in the Income and Expenditure accounts and requires a cash settlement, while the new contracts establish new rates of exchange for the hedged position.

Forward contracts for longer than one year can also be used but in the intermediate years at balance sheet dates the foreign assets or liabilities have to be revalued at spot (or average depending on company practice)

402

and the forward contract is marked to market. The difference between the mark to market value and the forward value will then appear in the Profit and Loss account as compensation for the entry in reserves as a result of the revaluation of the asset or liability.

4.3.4 *Currency Options*

These instruments at present can offer facilities in only a relatively limited number of currencies and periods and there is the lack of attraction in paying substantial premiums up-front. To date this seems to have been a relatively unusual route for corporates to take in hedging translation exposure.

5. ECONOMIC CURRENCY EXPOSURE

Economic exposure is the most difficult of risks to quantify and manage but is one which can have a very serious impact on any corporate as businesses either see market share disappear or profit margins shrink in order to be able to match overseas competition. Corporates can react effectively to medium/long term adverse changes in exchange rates only by restructuring their operations with changes in sourcing, product or, in extreme circumstances, switching production from what has become a high cost country to one with lower costs. Given that, in a number of industries, there is a considerable lead time between perception of a change in competitiveness and start up of production facilities in another country, it is obviously vital that management should be fully aware of the implications of exchange rate trends and react earlier rather than later. Economic currency exposure can be identified as one of the factors that reduced the UK industrial base in the early 1980s and had a similar impact in the USA in the mid 1980s. The subsequent recovery of manufacturing in both of these countries as their exchange rates weakened again illustrates the impact of economic currency exposure.

Companies can experience economic exposure in several different ways and the following are but two examples.

Company A manufactures in Germany for sale of its products in Germany for DMs. All its sourcing requirements, i.e. labour, raw materials, power, are within Germany and paid for in DMs. On the face of it, therefore, it has no currency exposure.

However, if the competition for the sale of similar products in Germany comes from a foreign company which exports into Germany from a country in which labour and/or raw materials and/or power are cheaper than in Germany, and, furthermore, the currency of that foreign country is weak against the DM, then the German manufacturer has an economic exposure. Due to the commercial factors which benefit the foreign manufacturer it could well be that it will be prepared to sell in Germany much cheaper than the German manufacturer.

The German manufacturer, therefore, needs to be aware of the price of the competitor's goods and needs to monitor the exchange rate between the DM and the foreign currency. This is because any further weakening of the foreign currency against the DM could give the foreign manufacturer opportunities to reduce his German selling price.

Similarly, if there are two German manufacturers, one of which sources its raw materials in Germany and the other of which sources abroad from a weak currency country, there could easily be a disparity in the respective production costs and, therefore, selling prices.

In such circumstances companies which are vulnerable to foreign competition will need to consider moving their manufacturing operations to countries offering low cost opportunities or, at least, source raw materials from the low cost country and seek to reduce their existing costs of production, e.g. by automation.

6. ACCOUNTING TREATMENT OF CURRENCY ITEMS

In both the USA and the UK in the late 1970s there was growing dissatisfaction with the existing treatment of foreign currency items in companies' accounts and in particular with the accounting treatment of the effect of changes in exchange rates. The increasing volatility of exchange rates highlighted, of course, the inadequacies of the previous systems. As a result, in the early 1980s the Financing Accounting Standards Board ("FASB") of the United States issued the Statement of Financial Accounting Standards ("SFAS") No. 52, Foreign Currency Translation, while the Accounting Standards Committee of the United Kingdom issued the Statement of Standard Accounting Practice ("SSAP") No. 20, Foreign Currency Translation.

404

While each standard differs on certain points and there is the major distinction that SFAS 52 is mandatory while SSAP 20 is optional, both had similar aims and features. The objectives of translation treatment under SSAP 20 were explicitly as follows (SFAS 52 has similar objectives):

> "the translation of foreign currency transactions and financial statements should produce results which are generally compatible with the effects of exchange rate changes on a company's cash flows and its equity and should ensure that the financial statements present a true and fair view of the results of management actions. Consolidated statements should reflect the financial results and relationships as measured in the foreign currency financial statements prior to translation."

Major points of interest in the standards for bankers interpreting the audited accounts of their corporate customers are:

(a) Accounts of overseas subsidiaries should normally be translated for consolidation purposes using either the closing or average rate of exchange for the profit and loss accounts (SFAS 52 specifies the average exchange rate *only*) and closing rates for the balance sheet. The exchange movement on opening share capital (the net investment) should be dealt with through consolidated reserves.

(b) If an investment and/or a financial liability e.g. loan, is denominated in a foreign currency, exchange differences resulting from translation should be taken to reserves.

(c) SFAS 52 provides explicitly for forward exchange contracts or other foreign currency transactions to be designated as a hedge subject to certain conditions. SSAP 20 refers only briefly to forward foreign exchange, stating that it may be used for the translation of trading transactions at the individual company level.

The correct accounting treatment of the more recently introduced hedging instruments such as currency swaps and currency options is still under debate. This is a matter of some significance as tax authorities may attack treatment which offsets losses against profits and claim increased tax as being payable. In the UK, at least, it may be that only case law will clarify the situation in a fully satisfactory manner.

7. TAX TREATMENT OF EXCHANGE GAINS AND LOSSES

Exchange gains and losses which arise from commercial foreign currency transactions can be broadly classified under two main headings in the UK (US treatment is similar):

Capital Transactions – normally relate to the financing structure or fixed asset base of the company. For tax treatment they are regarded as fixed or long term items.

Revenue or Trading transactions – arise from day-to-day trading activities and current assets/liabilities of the company. For tax treatment they are regarded as circulating or short term items.

Some transactions cannot be easily categorised under either heading and debate inevitably arises as to the correct treatment.

Exchange differences from trading transactions will be included in overall trading income assessable and subject to corporation tax. For capital transactions, on the other hand, exchange differences will not form part of trading income but will, instead, be assessed for capital gains tax or may, in fact, be tax free. Trading exchange differences cannot simply be set against capital exchange differences as the possibility exists of taxable gains and non-tax relievable losses. Pre-tax the position may be fully hedged, therefore, but post-tax gains will not equal losses due to the different impact of tax.

An example of such tax asymmetry would be a UK company with considerable sales in US dollars which hedges such exposure with a five year US dollar loan (by using the US$ sales income to repay the loan). While gains from exchange rate changes in a year would be part of assessable trading income, translation losses from the US dollar loan (assuming sterling weakens against the US dollar) could not be used to reduce trading income.

It is also important to bear in mind that gains or losses will not normally be considered to arise until realisation and that accounting

406

treatment acceptable to a company's auditors is very significant in the UK, as tax treatment will tend to follow accounting treatment.

Another example of the problems and anomalies possible is the well known case of Pattison (the Inland Revenue) v Marine Midland Ltd (a bank) decided by the House of Lords. Here, this UK based bank raised US$15 million in unsecured loan stock and made a number of short term US dollar loans to its customers. In due course the customers' loans and the unsecured loan stock were repaid and throughout the life of the transaction Marine Midland believed it had a matched position and that no net exchange gains or losses would arise. The Inland Revenue contended, however, that the exchange gain on the repayment of the customers' loans (sterling had weakened against the US dollar during the period of the transaction) represented taxable revenue profits on trading income while the loss on the loan stock was a capital loss and not tax deductible. The House of Lords decided in favour of Marine Midland on the grounds that there could be no exchange profit or loss where no currency conversions had been made (the loan stock proceeds had remained in US dollars) and clear steps had been taken to avoid exchange exposure by ensuring a fully matched position. Subsequently, in 1987, the Inland Revenue issued a Statement of Practice which attempted to clarify the tax situation for cases such as Marine Midland and currency hedging activities. Notwithstanding this statement, however, UK tax law remains unsatisfactory on the subject of tax treatment of exchange gains and losses.

8. CENTRALISED/DECENTRALISED TREASURY OPERATIONS

8.1 Introduction

Companies vary in their structures and in the amount of autonomy individual units, divisions or subsidiaries are allowed, and it is common that treasury responsibilities are centralised or decentralised in line with corporate policy. However, in recent years, there has been a trend for companies to centralise treasury responsibilities both as a reaction to risks and problems arising in such areas as currency exposure with volatile exchange rates and as a perception of the opportunities available to reduce costs/increase income. The possibilities of degrees of centralisation are broad, ranging from establishing a liaison/advisory centre which supplements, assists and monitors local treasury operations up to the creation of a central finance company which incorporates the fullest degree of authority possible. The greater the degree of centralisation introduced the larger the potential benefits possible but equally the greater the internal and external problems which can be encountered. The ultimate choice by any company must depend on the objectives which it seeks to achieve and its identification of the internal and external criteria and constraints which apply.

8.2 Centralisation Objectives
These can include all, or any, of the following:

- to improve funds management

- to reduce finance costs

- to make more effective control of group units

- to apply a higher level of financial sophistication

- to improve foreign currency exposure management

- to rationalise banking relationships

- to improve intra-group communication

- to reduce tax burden

- to reduce administration costs

- to take advantage of electronic banking services

- to treat the treasury operation as a cost centre *or*

- to treat the treasury operation as a profit centre

8.3 Internal and External Criteria and Constraints
- The nature, size and number of units involved in the centralisation exercise

- Group structure and underlying philosophy

- Internal resources available, particularly personnel

- Existing sophistication of financial management at the operational level

- Government regulations, in particular exchange control regulations

- Tax, both defensively to avoid incurring additional tax and aggressively to reduce overall group tax charge

8.4 Areas Where Benefits can be Obtained by Centralising Treasury Operations

8.4.1 *Foreign Currency Exposure Management*
In this area, which has formed the subject of this chapter, a number of advantages can be obtained from centralisation as follows:

- Easier to institute an internal management information system to identify and measure foreign currency exposure

- Hedging policy can be formulated which will be followed consistently for the company

- Currency resources arising in one part of the company can be matched elsewhere i.e. netted against requirements elsewhere with the consequent savings in foreign exchange dealings or hedging activity

- Higher level of expertise can be applied to treasury operations plus improved rates for dealing in larger amounts

- New treasury hedging instruments developed by the financial markets can be investigated and appraised as a matter of course by the central treasury operation for possible applications

8.4.2 *Cash Management*
A range of cash management services are now available both within any particular country e.g. use of lock boxes and zero balancing accounts in the USA and set-off between accounts in the UK, to achieve substantial

savings by more effective use of funds. Electronic Cash Management services such as balance reporting and money transfer have, in particular, become more and more widespread in recent years. A central treasury operation can investigate and utilise appropriate services in each country where the company operates. Inter-Country Cash Management through say multilateral netting services can also be introduced with a central treasury operation.

8.4.3 *Finance*
Possible gains in this area are:

* Higher levels of skills and knowledge applied to negotiation of facilities

* Use of internal cash surpluses to meet other parts of the company's borrowing requirements resulting in a lower external borrowing requirement

* Lower costs of borrowing when taken centrally or through possible utilisation of new financial products

* Control of raising of finance to ensure proper justification

* Rationalisation of banking relationships can reduce administration necessary and result in a closer working relationship with the company's remaining bankers. It is possible to negotiate umbrella facilities providing finance in one package in a number of countries from one banking group

* Release of resources at the local level for other activities such as production and marketing.

8.4.4 *Tax*
The centralisation of treasury operations should provide the possibility of applying a higher level of expertise to tax planning. For a corporate three basic objectives in this area are possible:

* to reduce or eliminate tax liabilities

410

- to defer tax liabilities e.g. by deferring recognition of income

- to change the character of income so a different and more preferable tax rate applies

With these basic objectives in mind, there are a number of areas where the central treasury can plan to the company's benefit e.g.

- minimise cost of capitalising operations

- remit profits without additional tax costs

- mitigate effects of exchange control

- use foreign and local tax charges to maximum advantage

- obtain full relief for financing costs

- avoid double taxation

- utilise foreign tax credits

- maximise deductions in high tax areas

- consider possible utilisation of tax havens

It should also be borne in mind that tax regulations change, often relatively quickly, and constant attention is necessary by a company to ensure that its tax objectives continue to be met. Again, dedicated resources through a central treasury unit are best able to maintain this ongoing review process.

N. B. It is the practice in certain circles to categorise currency risk as relating to "flow" or "stock" rather than transaction or translation. For the purposes of this chapter flow can be taken as the equivalent of transaction and stock as the equivalent to translation.

CHAPTER 11

Interest Rate Exposure Management

by
Chris Mitchell

1. INTRODUCTION

The management of interest rate exposure has been a major growth area during the 1980s and early 90s primarily because of its significance to cash flow and profitability. The continued high volatility of interest rates in most countries and wider liquidity and understanding of capital market instruments, has meant that many treasurers are under shareholder and analyst pressure to "de-sensitise" their companies. This chapter seeks to show the impact of interest rate movements and to provide a pragmatic approach to managing or "hedging" interest rate risk, highlighting the various stages involved. It discusses the features and benefits of the various types of risk management instruments and how they can be used, before focusing on ways of combining the instruments to achieve a company's required objectives.

1.1 Importance of the Problem

The importance of managing interest rate risk has increased as the volatility of interest rates has surged dramatically. One of the primary causes has been the easing of restrictions on the movement of capital between countries which has allowed vast speculative flows of capital to influence exchange and interest rates. In addition governments increasingly favour the use of interest rates to help control their economies by changing the level and direction of movement in interest rates. This volatility can be seen in Figure 1 which shows UK interest rates over the period 1970-93. Focusing on the last five years, three-month LIBOR interest rates virtually doubled during 1988/89 as the Conservative government tried to suppress consumer spending with high interest rates. Rates fell from their highs in

413

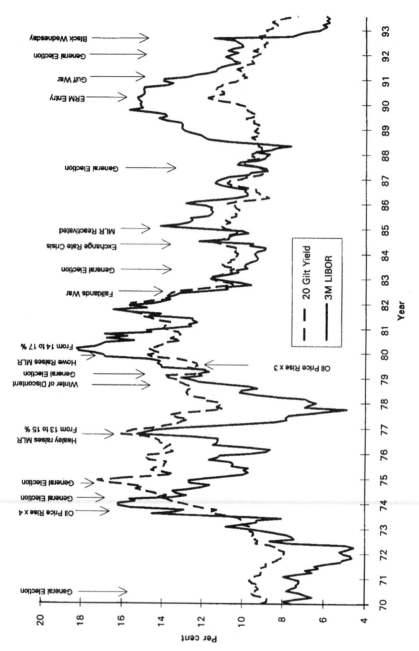

Figure 1   U.K. Interest Rates 1970–1993

414

1990 after the UK's entry into the ERM semi-fixed exchange rate system, but subsequently, during 1990, were kept artificially high to support sterling within its ERM band. This came to an end on "Black Wednesday" when LIBOR rates rose to support the pound before falling sharply as sterling was withdrawn from the ERM. Following this, rates continued to be reduced in an attempt to boost the flagging economy and to emerge from recession.

It can be seen that in the period May 1988 to October 1989 interest rates varied from 7.75% to 15.81%. This represents a virtual doubling of interest costs in just over a year so that the cost of a £10m loan for three months would have increased from £193,750 to £395,250. This increase in volatility has meant that previously unimportant exposures now require sophisticated risk management. Failure to hedge a future large interest rate exposure can lead to an unplanned disastrous effect on corporate cash flow and profits which in some circumstances can be life threatening to a company.

Banks and corporates have responded by devoting a great deal of time and expertise to this problem, developing new products and techniques to manage and transfer the risk. This effort has been helped by improvements in technology which now allow sophisticated risk management systems to be run on personal computers. It has also been stimulated by the increased demand for non-interest income by banks as they look for more off balance sheet activities to improve their capital ratios.

Hedging instruments are now so widely accepted and understood due to their liquidity and ease of use, that a strategy of not hedging exposures can be taken to be speculative in itself. This fact is not lost on board members, or shareholders, who are less likely to tolerate poor results due to unforeseen interest rate movements. These losses are now more transparent than ever and are often widely publicised making an even greater impact.

2. DEVELOPING A RISK MANAGEMENT STRATEGY

There are many risk management instruments available to the corporate treasurer which allow a multitude of differing strategies. However, before any instruments are considered, there are various actions that a company must undertake if it is to manage its interest rate exposure successfully and consistently.

415

2.1 Identify Interest Rate Exposures

The first stage is to identify the anticipated magnitude of interest rate exposures, as without a clear understanding of the company's present and anticipated exposures the treasurer cannot begin to implement any meaningful hedging programme. Timing and term of exposures should be established as well as the probability of the exposure occurring. For example, if a company is bidding for a contract, it may not materialise. The analysis should include a detailed breakdown of future expected cashflows to ensure cash liquidity is maintained.

2.2 Consider the Likely Course of Interest Rate Movements

A view will need to be taken by the organisation of the economic scene and the likely or possible movement of interest rates. Factors to take into account will include relevant exchange rates, monetary policy, economic statistics, political factors, one's own experience and contacts in the market and the views of professional forecasters. Whilst the latter receive much prominence, it should be remembered that their track record is not very good and that forecasting is not an exact science. Hence the objective here is to set the scene of the perceived likely course of movements and the possible variations that could occur.

Once the interest exposures and possible interest rate scenarios have been identified the treasurer should run a series of sensitivity analyses or "what ifs" on the exposures at the various interest rate possibilities. This will enable the treasurer to decide on the exposure's significance to the company's well-being and evaluate an appropriate strategy to be developed.

2.3 Define a Clear Risk Management Policy

Once the risks are known, the company must introduce a clear risk management policy which is relevant to the company's particular exposures. This policy should set clearly defined objectives and risk versus reward parameters. It should be flexible enough to respond to a changing interest rate scenario and the company's own requirements. The policy should be documented together with the factors determining the policy. It is then vital that this is monitored and updated to respond to the company's current objectives. The policy should define the levels of discretion and authorisation afforded to individual staff.

Some companies are either totally risk averse and wish to neutralise interest rate risks completely and some take a conscious decision not to hedge anything. As long as these policies have been carefully considered and are reviewed regularly, both can be appropriate, however they are at the two extremes. Most companies prefer an active risk management policy of selective hedging in an attempt to minimise interest risks and potential hedging costs simultaneously. This strategy could establish a series of target interest rate levels for a particular level of exposure to be covered, as well as stating the required ability to benefit if the interest rate view taken is incorrect. These targets should be regularly reviewed.

2.4   Evaluate the Available Hedging Instruments

Having identified the exposures and defined the company's hedging policy and objectives, the treasurer must identify and evaluate the various methods of achieving the objectives. This should include a review of any natural hedges that exist within the company as well as the array of modern day risk management instruments. It is important to keep abreast of the wide variety of instruments available which can be tailored to ensure exact hedging objectives are met. It is often a good idea to obtain independent advice from a bank at an early stage. The bank may be able to shed new light on a problem, or devise a bespoke strategy by combining instruments to suit the circumstances.

2.5   Implement and Monitor

Once the appropriate strategy has been determined it must be implemented – details, such as obtaining board approval and documentation, should be completed as soon as possible. This releases time to monitor the markets and execute the hedge when the prevailing conditions are favourable. The hedging strategy should not end here as the hedge should be reviewed on a regular basis. It may be appropriate to unwind the hedge and replace it by a more favourable one as individual and economic circumstances change.

3.   INTEREST HEDGING TECHNIQUES

We shall now look at some of the hedging techniques, reviewing their individual features and considering how each allows a treasurer to reduce risk without necessarily sacrificing the opportunity for gain. Initially, the treasurer should look for any internal hedges such as repaying some borrowings with existing or anticipated deposits. If this is not possible it may be beneficial to ensure that both loan and deposit rollover dates coincide to reduce interest rate mismatches. More likely, the treasurer will turn to risk management instruments to hedge exposure. This section will initially introduce Forward Forwards and Financial Futures before progressing to the more sophisticated over-the-counter (OTC) instruments such as FRAs, Options and Swaps which are more readily used by treasurers. Hybrid strategies are examined which combine the products to match exactly the requirements of an individual client.

Throughout this chapter it should be noted that:

(i) To aid comparison, the chapter is written from a borrower's perspective, however all the products can be used to hedge investments.

(ii) Most examples are in sterling and relate to UK market conditions. However, the products are used in all major currencies.

(iii) For simplicity, generally, loan margins have been ignored.

(iv) The hedging properties of each instrument will be expressed pictorially in the form of a risk profile (see Figure 2). This allows a simple and effective comparison of the instruments to be drawn.

Figure 2   Example of a Risk Profile

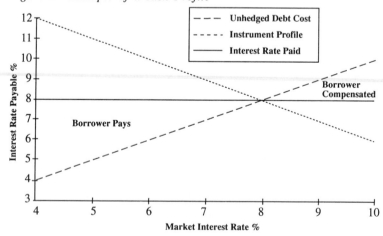

The unhedged debt line shows the variable rate of interest that could be payable in the market at the time of the exposure. The instrument profile shows the offsetting effect of the particular hedging instrument chosen and the solid line indicates the effective interest rate paid as a result of the unhedged debt cost combined with the hedging instrument. In the above example, the variable market interest rate is assumed to be offset exactly by the hedge, giving an effective net 8 per cent payable, irrespective of the market rate

3.1 Forward Forwards
This method of hedging interest rate exposure, whilst used in the past, has largely been relegated as a hedging strategy. In comparison with newer instruments it carries with it many disadvantages and therefore would rank very low, if at all, on any list of techniques utilised by today's treasurer. It is covered here to illustrate the fundamentals of forward hedging and represents a building block on which later generations of products are based. It is best illustrated by way of an example.

A corporate treasurer wants to fix the cost now of borrowing in the future, and decides to cover a three month borrowing requirement that will occur in three months' time.

To achieve this via a forward forward the treasurer will have to borrow for six months and lend for three months. Both transactions would be carried out at the same time and the structure is illustrated below:

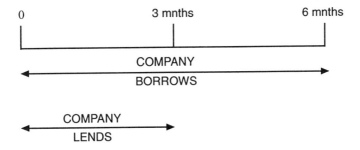

Forward forwards lock in the borrowing rate today for the future period of time, therefore it is irrelevant if interest rates change during this period and the risk profile is a flat line at the appropriate borrowing rate.

This form of hedging is, at best, a cumbersome method of covering forward commitments and has many disadvantages which include:

(i)   **Inflating the Balance Sheet** – especially if the treasurer wishes to reverse the position at a future date and could do so only by means of a deal mirroring the original.

(ii)   **Excessive Use of Credit Lines** – in the example, the corporate treasurer is drawing down for six months what is, in actual fact, only a three month borrowing requirement.

(iii) **Increased Loan Costs** – there is an additional cost as the bank's bid/ offer spread, of approximately 1/8%, between its lending and borrowing rates, is incurred.

3.2   Financial Futures

3.2.1   *Development of the Financial Futures Market*

The financial futures market developed as demand for managing interest rates increased and because the forward market did not provide the flexibility required. In May 1972 the International Monetary Market (IMM) in Chicago began trading the first foreign exchange futures, but it was not until 1975 that the first interest rate contract was introduced by the Chicago Board of Trade (CBOT).

Known as the "Ginny Mae" (GNMA – Government National Mortgage Association) Contract, it represented the first opportunity to hedge interest rate exposure through the medium of the futures market. This contract was quickly followed by the Treasury Bill contract in 1976 on the IMM and in 1977 the Treasury Bond contract was introduced by the CBOT. Since that time, further contracts have been introduced by both exchanges, the most notable of these being the Eurodollar contract traded on the IMM.

In September, 1982 the London International Financial Futures Exchange (LIFFE) began trading a total of seven contracts. The new exchange offered the opportunity to hedge not only dollar interest rates but also sterling rates, as well as several major foreign currencies. Both Chicago and London are able to offer contracts which cater for both the long and the short end of the maturity cycle through such UK instruments as the

420

three month short sterling contract or the Long Gilt contract and in the case of US interest rates, contracts offered include the three month Eurodollar contract at the short end and the US Treasury Bond contract at the long end.

Such has been the rapid pace of development of financial futures that the market is now truly global with markets in Singapore, Montreal, Tokyo, Amsterdam, Paris, Zurich, Sydney, Toronto, Hong Kong, Philadelphia, etc.

3.2.2 *General Description and Definitions*

A financial futures contract is a standardised binding agreement between two parties to buy, or sell, a standard quantity of a financial instrument at some future date at a pre-arranged price from an exchange. It can be used to hedge an expected interest rate exposure by taking a position in the futures market that is opposite to an existing, or anticipated, position in the cash market.

In the majority of cases, the delivery stage of the futures contract does not actually take place as few contracts actually run to maturity. This is because the buyer, or seller, usually establishes an offsetting and nullifying contract before the original futures contract matures.

There are two types of futures contract – short and long term. Short term futures reflect interest rate movements based on a three month deposit rate. Long term (or bond) futures are based on long term bond prices. Both have only limited delivery dates and are traded in three month periods ending in March, June, September and December. Short term futures generally have a specified delivery date and are usually settled in cash, whereas some long term futures can be delivered at any point during the delivery month.

The types of futures contracts should not be confused with "short" or "long" hedges.

A "short" hedge is used to protect against *rising rates* or to protect the capital value of a fixed interest investment such as gilt-edged securities. The term "short hedge" refers to the *sale* of futures contracts whose value will *fall* if *interest rates rise*. These contracts can then be repurchased at their new lower levels to secure a profit which will compensate for the movement in rates that has taken place in the cash market.

A "long" hedge is used to protect against falling interest rates or to fix the price of a planned investment. The term "long hedge" refers to *the purchase* of futures contracts whose value will *increase* if *interest rates fall*. These contracts can then be sold at a profit to compensate for the movement in rates that has taken place in the cash market.

The contracts are highly standardised and both the nature and size of the underlying cash market instrument to which each futures contract is related, are carefully defined. The futures contract states the quantity to be delivered. For example, the Short Sterling Contract is traded in units of £500,000 nominal value and the German Government Bond (Bund) future is traded in units of DM250,000. This ensures that there can be no misunderstanding as to the exact nature of each unit traded. It is important to check the precise contract specification prior to the transaction and details of these can be obtained from the futures exchange selected.

3.2.3 *The Pricing of a Futures Contract*

The price of a futures contract is determined by the underlying market interest rate. For short futures contracts this price is stated as an index of 100 minus the relevant three month interest rate. For example, an interest rate of $6\frac{1}{2}\%$ p.a. is translated to a futures price of 93.50. Therefore there is an inverse relationship between futures prices and interest rates; when interest rates are high the futures price is low and vice versa. This preserves the old adage of "buy low – sell high". On the last day of trading the contract is settled against the three month cash market offered rates, therefore the futures price must eventually converge on the underlying cash market price.

Short interest rate contract movements are priced with a tick (the minimum fluctuation permitted) reflecting one hundredth of one per cent movement in interest rates, i.e. a basis point. The value of a tick depends on the size and term of the contract. If we consider the three month Short Sterling LIFFE contract which has a nominal face value of £500,000, the one basis point movement equates to:

$$\text{Principal Amount} \times \text{Period} \times \text{Basis Point Movement} = \text{Value of Tick}$$

$$£500,000 \times \frac{3}{12} \times \frac{1}{10,000} = £12.50$$

To compute the profit or loss on a futures position you simply multiply together the number of contracts bought or sold by the number of basis points profit or loss and by the value of each basis point movement.

Thus a trader who has a 10 contract short sterling position which is showing a 34 basis point profit will have earned a total of:

$$10 \times 34 \times £12.50 = £4,250$$

Long term interest rate contracts are priced in the same way as the bond market, as a percentage of par. The exchange allows a number of bonds all with differing coupons and delivery dates to be tendered for delivery. As expected the futures price reflects the "cheapest to deliver" of the allowable bonds. In the UK and US each percentage point is divided into 32nds, or ticks, which is the minimum price movement allowed for a futures contract. A price of 98.20 means $98 \frac{20}{32}$ and **not** $98^{1}/_{5}$.

3.2.4 Margins

With the commencement of a contract and the opening of a futures position comes the need to make a payment of a deposit in respect of the position. These monies can be viewed as a "good faith" payment and are referred to as the "initial margin". The three month short sterling contract on LIFFE currently attracts an initial margin of £625 per contract, this margin being set by the Clearing House and liable to change as market conditions dictate. The margin is calculated to reflect the maximum expected daily movement, thus hopefully limiting the potential loss to the margin deposited. One of the attractions of the futures market is the customer's ability to control a high level of contracts in face value terms compared to the initial deposit payment required.

There is a second margin requirement associated with futures trading known as the "variation margin". This arises from the process of daily

423

revaluation of existing open positions and is sometimes known as "settling to market". If, as a result of the daily revaluation, the open position shows a loss, then it is beholden upon the holder of the position to make good that loss. Conversely if the position, after revaluation, shows a profit then these monies will be credited to the position account, where they may be withdrawn by the client if so desired. If the monies are retained in the account then agreement may be reached whereby interest will be paid to the customer on the retained balances.

3.2.5 *Uses of Interest Rate Futures*

Futures can be used for an almost limitless number of interest rate risk management strategies. It is this flexibility that has attracted many building societies, banks, insurance companies and investment companies into being heavy users. However, as previously stated, users must have clear objectives of what they are trying to achieve.

Two common situations where futures can be used are given in Example 1 and Example 2.

Example 1: XYZ Company – Three Month Borrowing

The corporate treasurer of XYZ Co. has identified the need to borrow £10m on 15 August for three months. The treasurer agrees with the lending bank to borrow at a rate of three month LIBOR plus a lending margin. It is now 15th May and the treasurer is concerned that UK interest rates will rise over the three month time period and would like to lock in to current future rates for the three month borrowing. The target borrowing cost is 6.25% (or £157,534 for the three months – 92 days).

Let us first of all look at the position diagrammatically.

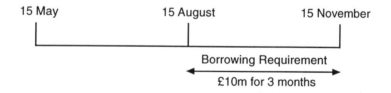

The treasurer immediately sells £10m (20 contracts) of the September sterling futures contract at 94.00. This equates to an implied future interest rate of 6.0% (100-6.0%) and interest cost of £151,233. On 15 August the treasurer's fears are confirmed and cash market LIBOR rates increase to 7.0%. Also on that day the treasurer buys £10m September sterling futures at 93.10 (100-6.90%). The final result is that the underlying debt at 7% costs £176,438 for the three month period, which is in excess of the target. However, a profit of 90 ticks on the futures contracts has been generated. This equates to a cash gain of:

No. of ticks profit × No. of futures × Value of tick = Gain/Loss

$$90 \quad \times \quad 20 \quad \times \quad £12.5 \quad = £22,500$$

The net cost is, therefore: £176,438 − £22,500 = £153,938

The higher interest cost (£25,205) resulting from the increased cash market rate (7.0% vs 6.0%) was partially offset by the gain on the futures position (£22,500) when the contracts that were initially sold were bought back at a cheaper price. This is called a short hedge as the treasurer initially sold (or went short of) futures. The profit on the futures did not fully cover the cash market loss as the price of the futures contract does not always perfectly track the price of the underlying instrument in the cash market. This is called basis risk. The two markets are very closely correlated but under certain circumstances the basis risk can widen to make the hedge less than effective. Basis risk can move either way and can also cause a windfall gain on the futures side of the hedge.

If market interest rates had actually fallen below 6.0% on 15 August, the treasurer would still have paid 6.0% overall (ignoring basis risk), as the lower cost of the borrowing would have been offset by a loss on the futures.

The risk profile of this hedge via futures (again ignoring basis risk) is shown below in Figure 3.

Figure 3   Risk Profile of Short Interest Rate Future

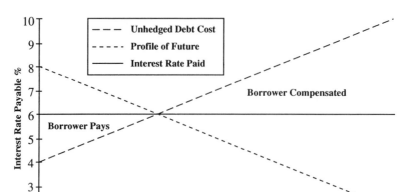

Example 2: ABC Company – Long Term Borrowing

The corporate treasurer of ABC Co. is planning to issue a long term US$ bond to finance its US assets as US long term interest rates are at attractive levels. The treasurer has estimated that it will take two months to prepare the issue and is worried that interest rates for the required maturity will have risen prior to the issue. In such circumstances the treasurer will sell an appropriate number of the most relevant US Treasury Bond futures. If rates rose during the interim the futures could be liquidated for a profit which should approximately offset the increased cost of the long term debt. If the reverse is true and long term yields fall then there will be a loss on the futures position offset by the lower long term debt rates achieved. If however the debt is never issued the corporate may be facing either a windfall gain or a real loss.

3.2.6   Advantages and Disadvantages of Financial Futures
A full discussion of financial futures is outside the scope of this chapter. However, they can be summarised by examining their advantages and disadvantages.

Advantages of Financial Futures:

(i)   **Little Counterparty Credit Risk** – the credit risk is virtually eliminated as futures are executed via a clearing house, which in turn is protected by deposits of futures margins.

(ii)   **Good Liquidity** – the contracts are traded in open outcry with liquidity provided by traders allowing hedgers to establish, or close out, positions at any time. Futures generally provide the price and liquidity benchmarks for the given market.

(iii)   **Low Trading Costs** – as the contracts are traded in standardised contracts on an open market there is transparency and immediate availability of the finest prices. There are no premiums payable.

(iv)   **No Credit Lines Required** – therefore the company is free to use its credit lines for other purposes.

(v)   **Balance Sheet and Working Capital Efficient** – they are off balance sheet contracts which allow an exposure to interest rates without ever owning the underlying instrument. As futures are heavily geared compared to the margins deposited, they allow less working capital to be tied up than would be the case with other hedging techniques.

Disadvantages of Financial Futures:

(i)   **Opportunity Losses** – by using futures, the company is unable to take advantage of any favourable movement in the underlying transaction.

(ii)   **Fixed Contract Sizes and Settlement Dates** – thus the ability to tailor the hedge to a precise cash market exposure is restricted.

(iii)   **Basis Risk** – as mentioned, this can lead to the hedge being less than perfect, as the gain or loss on the futures contract may not be an exact match to the corresponding cash position.

(iv)   **Administration and Daily Payments** – profits and losses are settled to market every day into the margin account which if not established correctly can be time consuming. The monitoring of margins, accounting procedures and basis risk also ties up valuable resources. Daily payments can create cash flow mismatches.

(v)   **Limited Maturities** – futures are only available for limited maturities of up to two and a half years for sterling and seven years for US dollars.

Financial futures do have considerable benefits over forward contracts but they also have significant drawbacks, which have made them unpopular with corporates. Section 3.3 will examine Forward Rate Agreements (FRAs) which were developed to overcome the drawbacks of futures.

3.3   Forward Rate Agreements (FRAs)

3.3.1   *General Description and Definition*
A Forward Rate Agreement (FRA) is the "over the counter" version of the short interest rate future described above. It has become a popular alternative to a future as it is tailored to the user's specific requirements. It provides most of the benefits of a forward forward and financial future with less of the technical and administrative problems.

The FRA is a contract which guarantees a rate of interest that will apply to a notional loan, or deposit, of an agreed amount which is to start on an agreed future date for a specified period. The starting date can be anywhere from one day to 21 months forward, with the period covered usually from three to 12 months. There is usually no premium, margin requirement or brokerage cost when an FRA is obtained via a bank.

The FRA does not involve any exchange of principal between the two parties but is a contract in which the gain, or loss, resulting from a change in market interest rates is paid in cash. The principal is a notional sum which is used only in the calculation of the settlement amount. This reduces the credit risk between the parties. The only risk of loss to the bank is if interest rates move against the customer's FRA position which would result in the customer being required to pay to the bank an amount in settlement. The credit risk criterion adopted by the banks for such contracts is correspondingly small – with credit lines usually below 5% of the principal sum.

When the start of the contract period is reached, a settlement rate will be decided, based upon current market rates for the contract period. The cash payment to be made is determined by the difference between the FRA contract rate and the settlement rate. The settlement rates for those contracts which are for a standard time period, e.g. three months, six months, one year are usually based upon the British Bankers Association (BBA) composite rate ruling for that particular period. This rate is arrived at by the averaging out of the rate supplied by several banks to the Association based on their 11.00 a.m. LIBOR fixing rate. These settlement rates are displayed daily and the majority of contracts are settled in this fashion. For those contracts falling outside the time periods covered by the BBA service, the basis of the settlement rate will be agreed beforehand between the two parties involved.

A company that is using FRAs to hedge its underlying future borrowing would *purchase* an FRA to protect against a *rise* in rates, and *sell* an FRA to protect against a *fall* in rates. (Note that this often leads to misunderstanding as *buying* a future is protecting against a *fall* in interest rates, and *selling* a future is protecting against a *rise*).

At the settlement of the FRA, if market interest rates have risen the seller of the FRA has to compensate the purchaser by an amount equal to the present value of the difference between the initial contract rate and the market settlement rate multiplied by the principal sum. The purchaser of the FRA receives the payment from the seller but, if the purchaser has underlying debt, the principal amount has to be borrowed from the underlying cash market at the higher settlement rate. Therefore the gain from the FRA is cancelled by the increased interest costs. If rates have fallen the purchaser of the FRA would compensate the seller, so that the net cost/receipts generated are always equivalent to the contract rate.

Before an example is given to show the mechanics of the FRA, it is important to explain the terminology.

The **agreement date** is the day the FRA is traded and the terms fixed.

The **contract rate** is the rate agreed at the outset upon which settlement will be based.

The **settlement date** is the day when settlement takes place, and is the first day of the contract period.

The **contract period** is the duration of the interest period covered.

The **settlement amount** is the sum paid between the two parties in settlement of the FRA.

The **maturity date** is the last day of the contract period.

This is shown diagrammatically:

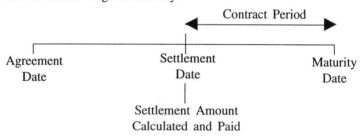

FRA quotations are based on the first day of the contract period to the maturity date. Therefore an FRA covering a six month loan beginning in four months' time is referred to as a "4s vs 10s" FRA.

The mechanics of an FRA can be seen if we look at an example. To aid comparison with futures, the same example, XYZ Co., is used.

Example 1: XYZ Company – Three Month Borrowing

The treasurer of XYZ Co. has identified the need to borrow £10m on 15 August for three months. The loan interest rate will be three month LIBOR plus loan margin. It is now 15 May and the treasurer is concerned that UK interest rates will rise and would like to lock into current future rates for the three month borrowing.

The treasurer immediately approaches the bank to purchase a £10m FRA contract for the period of 15 August to 15 November (i.e. a 3s against 6s FRA). The bank quotes the customer an FRA rate of 6% p.a. for the contract (based on a forward/forward calculation), and the customer,

430

wishing to cover the interest rate exposure, accepts the rate and "purchases" the FRA contract. No funds change hands at this stage – even for a "purchase" of the FRA.

On the starting date of the borrowing (15 August) a settlement rate is established based upon the three month LIBOR. As in the futures example, this rate is 7% p.a. and the treasurer's concern that interest rates would rise has been realised. By means of the FRA the original exposure has been protected, thus the bank pays the settlement amount to the XYZ Co. based on 1% (i.e. the difference between the settlement rate and the FRA rate) on £10m for 92 days (15 August to 15 November). Because the settlement amount is paid at the start of the period (15 August) rather than at the end (15 November), the interest differential payment is discounted to its present value (on 15 August).

If interest rates had declined by 1% p.a., XYZ Co. would have been required to make suitable payment to the bank in settlement of the maturing FRA contract. The formula for the settlement of the FRA contract is shown below. When the figure is positive, the amount is paid to the buyer of the FRA; when it is negative, the amount is paid to the seller.

$$\frac{(L - R) \times D \times A}{(B \times 100) + (L \times D)}$$

Where: $L =$ Settlement rate (expressed as a number and not a percentage)

           $R =$ Contract rate (expressed as a number and not a percentage)

           $D =$ Days in contract period

           $A =$ Contract amount

           $B =$ 365 except where the contract currency is based on a 360 day count convention.

If we now apply this formula to the example above our settlement amount will be as follows:

431

$$\frac{(L - R) \times D \times A}{(B \times 100) + (L \times D)} = \frac{(7-6) \times 92 \times £ \ 10,000,000}{(365 \times 100) + (7 \times 92)} = £24,768.47$$

As the figure is positive, XYZ Co. will receive from the bank the sum of £24,768.47 in settlement of the FRA contract. With this compensation the borrower achieves an effective borrowing rate of 6% per annum despite actually having to pay 7% p.a. on the underlying borrowing. Ignoring the basis risk involved with financial futures, the risk profile of FRAs is the same as futures and is as shown in Figure 3.

3.3.2 Uses of Forward Rate Agreements

FRAs are used to hedge interest rate exposures in the same way as short interest rate futures. They will cover maturities from one month out as far as the relevant futures exchange, as FRAs are usually hedged by banks via futures. In effect, FRAs are a user friendly variation of futures, which can be tailored to suit the company's exact requirements and are therefore more popular with corporates.

3.3.3 Advantages and Disadvantages of Forward Rate Agreements

Advantages of FRAs:
(i) **Improved Flexibility** – FRAs achieve approximately the same result as forward/forwards or futures but offer much greater flexibility as they can be exactly tailored to suit the treasurer's specific dates and amounts.

(ii) **Reduced Administration** – as FRAs are neither traded nor settled via a futures exchange there is no requirement for margin deposits, or margin variation calls, which therefore saves on administration. Also they require less monitoring and management than futures.

(iii) **No Fees Payable** – there are no premiums to be paid.

(iv) **Balance Sheet and Working Capital Efficient** – they are off balance sheet contracts which allow an exposure to interest rates without ever owning the underlying instrument.

(v) **Credit Risk Low** – the exposure to the FRA counterparty is limited to interest rate movements and not the underlying capital transaction.

432

Disadvantages of FRAs:

(i)   **Opportunity Losses** – the holder of an FRA is unable to take advantage of any favourable rate movement in the underlying transaction.

(ii) **Cash Flow Mismatch** – all payments under an FRA contract are paid on the settlement date and not the end of the rollover period when the loan interest is paid. This produces a cashflow mismatch which, if the FRA payment received cannot be invested at the rate at which it has been discounted, would produce a reinvestment exposure.

(iii) **Counterparty Credit Risk** – as the trades are completed directly between companies and banks and not through an exchange, there will be a credit risk to the other party not performing its obligations. Therefore, a bank will normally require a credit limit to be put in place with its counterparty prior to dealing.

(iv) **Limited Maturities** – FRAs are only usually available as far out as the relevant futures exchange, as banks who provide FRAs generally hedge themselves via the futures market.

(v)   **Price** – compared with financial futures the bid/offer spread is typically four to five basis points compared to one or two with futures. The greater the tailoring of the FRA to the exact client specifications, generally the wider the price, as the bank's exposure becomes more difficult to manage.

Corporates use FRAs far more than futures. This is generally because of the bespoke nature of FRAs, the reduced administration and the fact that corporates generally do not trade in and out of the market on an intra day basis and so do not require the ultra fine pricing of futures. FRAs have limited maturities and cashflow disadvantages. The next section examines Interest Rate Swaps which do not suffer from these disadvantages.

3.4   Interest Rate Swaps

Swaps have revolutionised financial risk management and have been proclaimed as one of the greatest innovations in financial history, such that by December 1992 there was US$4.6 trillion of swaps contracts outstanding globally. In this section we will briefly discuss the principles of interest rate swaps and their use in managing interest rate risk. Further treatment of interest rate swaps is given in Chapter 18, which examines their history, mechanics, pricing, risks and regulatory and tax issues in detail. Currency swaps which allow treasurers to fund in the overseas market of comparative advantage and exchange the funds to their required currency are also covered in detail in Chapter 18 and therefore they are omitted from this section.

3.4.1 *General Description and Definition*

An interest rate swap is a contract between two parties to pay each other interest on a notional principal amount calculated on two different bases (i.e. fixed to floating) for a stated period. No exchange of principal is involved; only the difference between the agreed interest rates, or indices, is exchanged. The difference, as with most loans, or deposits, is settled at the end of the rollover period. Note that it is also possible to have floating to floating interest rate swaps, called basis swaps, which are transactions between different floating rate indices (e.g. three month LIBOR against six month LIBOR or LIBOR against commercial paper).

Swaps can be used to hedge interest rate mismatches which arise, for example, where the assets of a company yield a fixed rate income stream while its cost of servicing liabilities is based upon floating rates, or vice versa. A swap can be used to change the borrowing cost to correspond with the income stream. Swaps allow treasurers to create the right mix between short and long term assets and liabilities without affecting the underlying balance sheet.

The mechanics of a swap can best be seen if we look at an example. Although swaps are generally for longer periods than three months, the same example, XYZ Co., will be used to aid comparison with futures and FRAs.

Example 1: XYZ Company – Three Month Borrowing

The treasurer of XYZ Co. has identified the need to borrow £10m on 15 August for three months. The loan interest rate will be at three month LIBOR plus loan margin. It is 15 May and the treasurer is concerned that UK interest rates will rise and would like to lock into current future rates for the three month borrowing.

The treasurer immediately approaches the bank to enter into a £10m swap and is quoted a swap rate of 6% p.a. for the period. The customer accepts the rate and enters into the swap. On 15 August the three month LIBOR fixing rate is 7%, therefore the company will pay interest of 7% plus the loan margin to the lending bank. Under the swap, XYZ Co. is due to receive 1% (i.e. 7% – 6%) from the swap bank in the form of a netted payment. All payments of interest are made on 15 November, i.e. the end of the period.

The details of the swap can be demonstrated by using a cashflow diagram. The cashflows are indicated by arrows showing the direction of the interest payments. The bank loan is shown as a single line away from XYZ Co. to the lending bank and the swap is shown as two arrows in opposite directions, between XYZ Co. and the swap bank.

Figure 4   Interest Rate Swap for XYZ Co.

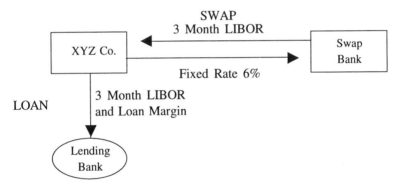

The payments, ignoring the loan margin, are:

XYZ pays lending bank:

$$7.0\% \times \frac{92}{365} \times £10m = £176,438$$

XYZ receives from the swap bank:

$$(7\% - 6\%) \times \frac{92}{365} \times £10m = £25,205$$

XYZ's actual payment is therefore equal to 6% or: £151,233

The important point to note is that swaps match the underlying loan exposure exactly as all payments are made on the interest payment dates. With FRAs, the payments are received in advance which may lead to taxation or reinvestment risks where the money cannot be deposited at the same rate at which it has been discounted.

Another point to note is that as the swap and the loan are separate transactions, the bank which provides the loan does not necessarily have to be the bank that enters into the swap.

3.4.2 Pricing of Interest Rate Swaps

Pricing of interest rate swaps is covered in greater detail in Chapter 18.

The basic principle behind the initial development of the swaps market was the exploitation of the principle of comparative advantage. For interest rate swaps, this lay in the different pricing of credit risk between the normal bank loan market (variable rate LIBOR) and the bond market (fixed rate). For example, the table below shows the relative pricing in the bond and loan markets for 10 year money for two companies, one AAA rated and the other BBB rated.

Table 1 – Theoretical Bond and Loan Pricing of 10 Year Facilities

Company Rating	AAA	BBB
Bond Pricing	Gilts + 30bp *	Gilts + 150bp *
Loan Pricing	LIBOR + 20bp	LIBOR + 90bp

The AAA rated company has a relative advantage over the BBB company in both markets – 120 basis points in the bond market and 70 basis points in the bank loan market. Although the AAA company has a relative advantage in both markets, there is an arbitrage potential of 50bp if the AAA company wanted to borrow floating rates and BBB company wanted to borrow fixed. To exploit this arbitrage, the companies initially borrow in their market of the best relative advantage, i.e. AAA issues a bond at Gilts + 30bp and BBB raises bank debt at LIBOR + 90bp. The interest payments are swapped between the companies, via an intermediary

---

*   In the above "Gilts" is a fixed rate which is equal to the appropriate gilt maturity yield at the start of the transaction.

436

bank which takes the credit risk on both counterparties. The payments are shown below:

Figure 5   Pricing of Interest Rate Swaps

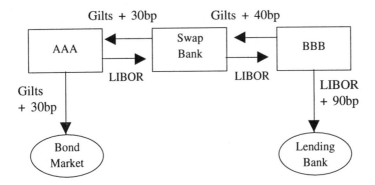

In this example the 50 basis points arbitrage is shared: 20 basis points to each of the borrowers and 10 basis points to the swap bank. The effective costs of borrowing are the AAA rated company pays LIBOR flat and the BBB rated company pays at a fixed rate of Gilts + 130 basis points, i.e. both companies are borrowing at cheaper all-in costs than would have been the case had AAA borrowed a LIBOR linked loan and BBB had issued a bond.

It was matched transactions between counterparties which exploited comparative advantage that helped the swaps market develop in its early stages (see Chapter 18). However, as the market has grown, the increasing volume of business has reduced these arbitrages. Banks have now standardised their pricing and can take on unmatched swaps with single counterparties rather than only acting as intermediary between two borrowers.

Swap positions are often now absorbed into the bank's overall swap portfolio or "warehoused" as the bank is confident that if required, it could reverse the position without much difficulty.

Interest rate swaps are normally quoted now in the same way as a commercial bond issue, as a spread over an equivalent maturity benchmark government security, i.e. Gilts or US Treasuries. A "bid and offer" spread is quoted. The "bid" is the rate at which a bank will pay a fixed rate in order to receive the floating index, usually LIBOR. The "offer" is the rate a bank will receive fixed in order to pay the floating index. In the above example, the "bid" where the bank would pay fixed to receive LIBOR from AAA was gilts + 30bp. The bank's "offer" to receive fixed from BBB was gilts + 40bp in order for it to pay LIBOR. Therefore the bank's swap price was gilts plus 30 to 40bp and its "bid/offer" spread was 10bp.

Following the increase in unmatched trades, swap spreads are determined by supply and demand, an increase in the number of participants wanting to pay fixed ("payers") will increase the spread, and an increase in participants wanting to receive fixed ("receivers") will reduce the spread. It is generally the case that when interest rates are low, and expected to increase, swap spreads will rise as a greater number of borrowers will want to fix their interest costs at the low rate and fewer investors will want to receive a fixed rate. Therefore, demand to pay fixed will outweigh demand to receive fixed and swap spreads will increase.

It is important to note that it is the expectation of interest rates that is the key. If interest rates are low but participants believe they will fall further, then spreads will still be relatively low.

3.4.3   *Uses of Interest Rate Swaps*

(i)   **To Obtain the Lowest Possible Funding Cost**

As shown above, an interest rate swap allows companies to raise funds in their domestic market of relative advantage and swap the interest cost into their preferred basis, the final cost being lower than if they had funded directly from their usual source.

Currency swaps which are covered in Chapter 18 can be used by companies to raise funds in virtually any currency and then swap the proceeds into the required currency and interest basis. This provides them access to different investor groups all over the world and allows companies to fund in their market of relative advantage.

(ii) **To Provide Access to Fixed Term Debt**

Interest rate swaps can also be useful to raise fixed term debt that would not normally be available from traditional banking and bond sources. A company with a poor credit rating will generally not have access to raising fixed term debt via the bond markets, but should be able to raise floating rate funds from the banking market at a competitive rate. This can then be swapped into a fixed rate to provide fixed rate funding without changing the structure of its balance sheet. Even for a company with a high credit rating, raising fixed rate debt via the bond market can be expensive for a one off transaction because of the underwriting fees, disclosure costs, or the high risk premium that a relatively unknown borrower would have to pay.

(iii) **To Restructure Debt or Investment Portfolios**

Swaps allow debt portfolios to be restructured without the need to disturb existing borrowing, or obtain new finance. This gives a much greater freedom and versatility for companies to manage their balance sheet. For example swaps can be used to effectively pre-pay, non-callable fixed rate debt by converting it to floating rate. This enables it to be matched with floating rate assets if required. This method is often used by banks.

Swaps can also be used to convert a portfolio of fixed rate debt into floating rate debt to meet an expectation of a reduction in rates and the swap can be reversed when rates are expected to stabilise or rise again.

In the same way that debt portfolios can be altered so investments can be changed via asset swaps. Essentially, these are swaps where the counterparty is receiving, for example, a fixed income stream via a bond and by means of a swap changes the income to a variable rate without affecting the original investment.

Although borrowers and investors will normally swap against specific assets and liabilities and match the cash flows and maturities of the underlying transaction, this is not always necessary. As they are separate contracts, swaps can be executed, if required, on a more general, non-specific basis, not matching the specific cash flows of a particular asset or underlying transaction at all.

(iv) **Other Uses**

There are many other uses for swaps such as allowing firms to lock in funding rates for borrowing they are certain will take place at a later date. They allow views on interest rates to be taken without restructuring a company's balance sheet. They can be used to hedge a spread over a bond at an attractive rate for an issuer prior to the bond issue taking place. There are also many variations of the standard swap, which will be covered in Chapter 18. These all have various additional uses.

If a swap is no longer needed, it can be terminated and a payment made or received dependent on market rates. A swap can be reversed by using another swap with opposite characteristics or can be transferred to another counterparty. The liquidity for removing a swap is therefore good, however each of the above methods will have differing cashflow or tax implications which have to be taken into consideration.

3.4.4   *Advantages and Disadvantages of Interest Rate Swaps*

Advantages of Interest Rate Swaps:

(i)   **Obtain Lowest Possible Funding Cost** – by exploiting comparative advantage. This original benefit has been steadily eroded by competitive pressures.

(ii) **Access to Low Cost Fixed Rate Funding** – which otherwise might not be available to a low creditworthy company.

(iii) **Flexible** – can be tailor-made to match exact exposures and basis risk is eliminated. There are no cashflow mis-matches as with FRAs or Futures. They also allow hedges against unusual indices such as UK Base Rate, or commercial paper, thus providing the perfect hedge.

(iv) **Good Liquidity and Term** – there is a flourishing and liquid swaps market in most major currencies, usually out to at least 10 years and exceptionally to 25 years. Futures and FRAs can only be used for up to the maximum period at which the futures are traded.

(v)   **Little Administration** – once put in place and the documentation completed, there is little additional administration as payments can be made or claimed automatically on the interest payment dates.

440

(vi) **No Fees Payable** – there are no margin payments, or premiums payable, under normal swaps.

(vii) **Balance Sheet and Working Capital Efficient** – they are off balance sheet contracts which allow an exposure to interest rates without ever owning the underlying instrument.

Disadvantages of Interest Rate Swaps:

(i) **Opportunity Losses** – the user of a swap is unable to take advantage of any favourable rate movements in the underlying transaction.

(ii) **Counterparty Credit Risk** – as the trades are completed directly between corporates and banks and not through an exchange, there will be a credit risk to the other party not performing its obligations. Banks therefore normally require a credit limit to be put in place prior to dealing.

(iii) **Price** – as the contracts are usually tailor-made the bid/offer spread is wider than for exchange traded contracts, but for a standard period this is usually no more than 5-7 basis points for companies with a good credit rating.

(iv) **Documentation** – Interest Rate Swap transactions are governed by a standardised swap contract known as the ISDA agreement (International Swap Dealers Association). This is separate from the underlying loan agreement (if there is one). As amendments to the ISDA agreement are sometimes added by banks, independent legal advice is often required to check documentation which can be expensive and time consuming if relatively few trades are envisaged. The advantage of the documentation is that it is a master agreement so that once it is signed it covers all transactions between the two counterparties.

This section has briefly looked at interest rate swaps which have been developed to provide a flexible risk management tool to overcome many of the problems of futures and FRAs. There are several other different types of interest rate swaps, many of which are described in the later chapter.

3.5 Interest Rate Options

3.5.1 *General Description and Definition*

Interest rate options, like all the instruments described previously, offer protection against unfavourable movements in interest rates but, unlike the others, they also allow the user to gain from beneficial movements. Thus an option provides aspects of hedging and position taking and is probably the most versatile of hedging instruments.

An option on interest rates (or more correctly an option on underlying fixed interest instruments) is a contract giving the buyer the right but not the obligation to fix the rate of interest at an agreed rate (the strike rate) on a notional loan, or deposit, for an agreed period on a specific forward date. In return for this right the buyer will pay a premium to the seller.

Thus the important things to note are:

(i)   The buyer of the option has no obligation to complete the deal, in which case the maximum loss faced is the original cost of the option (the premium).

(ii) On the expiry date, if the buyer chooses to exercise the right to take up the option, the seller has an obligation to make a payment to the buyer to compensate for the extent (if any) to which the strike rate is more advantageous to the buyer than the prevailing LIBOR rate.

Therefore, in effect, the option buyer pays the premium to insure against interest rate risk. The option seller in return agrees to guarantee a fixed rate of interest, if and when it is required by the buyer. The buyer's risk of adverse interest rate movements is eliminated while at the same time the potential to benefit from favourable interest rate movements is retained, since the option can be allowed to lapse if interest rates move in the buyer's favour. The option can also be sold back to the seller at any time for its residual value if it is no longer required.

(i)   Exchange Traded Options

There are two main groups of options. The first group is called "exchange" traded options and as the name implies the options are

442

listed on and traded through one of the several recognised futures exchanges. As with all futures instruments they trade for specific delivery dates, have a notional face value and do not offer the flexibility in terms of precisely matching hedge to exposure. Also the exposure on an exchange traded option needs to be constantly monitored which can tie up valuable management resources.

(ii)   OTC Options

The second type is the "over the counter" or OTC option contract. These are where a bank has written (or has written to it) a customised and tailored option, to their customer's exact specification. As the OTC options are specifically designed with the buyer's individual needs in mind, the marketability of the option is reduced. However, as the option market's liquidity has improved this is now much less of a problem for options dealt in the major trading currencies. This section will concentrate on the OTC options as their advantages over exchange traded options from a corporate perspective far outweigh the disadvantages.

An option can be either a call or a put option. A call option gives the purchaser the right but not the obligation to pay the fixed strike rate, whereas a put option gives the purchaser the right but not the obligation to receive the fixed strike rate, over the option period.

As with currency options, there are European and American interest rate options.

With OTC options, not only can a bank write the options but it can also have them written to it by a company (the company would receive the premium but would also accept the potential of unlimited losses). This aspect of companies writing options is important because it allows complex option strategies to be established, which gives the required protection against adverse movements in interest or exchange rates and can reduce the premium payable. These "low" or "zero" cost options are discussed in Section 4 on Combining Instruments.

The mechanics of a call option can best be seen if we look at an example. To aid comparison with futures, FRAs and swaps the same example XYZ Co. is used.

Example 1: XYZ Company – Three Month Borrowing

On 15 May the treasurer of XYZ Co. has identified the need to borrow £10m in three months' time. The treasurer wants to protect against the possibility of rates rising, but this time it is believed there is a good chance that rates will fall. The treasurer requires the flexibility to be able to take advantage of any reduction and therefore does not want to fix or "lock in" a rate.

The treasurer immediately purchases an interest rate call option at the exercise (strike) rate of 6% p.a. for 2.5 basis points or £2,500 (i.e. £10m x 0.00025 = £2,500). This ensures that the treasurer can borrow the funds at 6% for the period of the option as the writer of the option is committed to compensate the buyer for the extent that the three month LIBOR is above 6.0% p.a.

The treasurer would only exercise the option if rates rose above 6%, however if rates were below 6%, the treasurer would simply abandon the option and borrow in the cash market at the prevailing rate. The treasurer has paid the option writer an upfront premium of £2,500 which, if amortized over the option period, equates to an interest rate of approximately 10 basis points.

Figure 6   Risk Profile of an Interest Rate Call Option

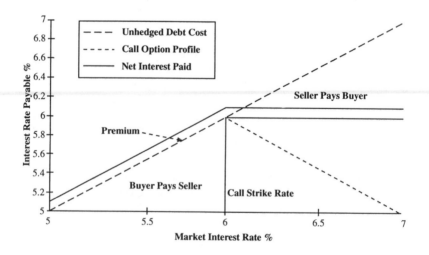

Once the cost of the option premium is taken into account, an all-in interest cost is calculated which, in this example, will mean that the maximum cost to the treasurer will be approximately 6.1% p.a. This is shown in Figure 6, together with the effect of the premium for LIBOR rates below 6% when the option is allowed to lapse.

3.5.2 Pricing of Interest Rate Options
The price of an option is its premium which is influenced by four factors: intrinsic value, time value, the expected market volatility and market conditions.

(i)   Intrinsic Value

The difference between the strike rate and the current interest rate is termed the intrinsic value of the option.

The strike rate for a call option is referred to as:

"at the money"	– the strike rate is equal to the current interest rate.
"in the money"	– the strike rate is more favourable to the customer than the current market rate. The premium is higher than for an "at the money" option.
"out of the money"–	the strike rate is less favourable to the customer than the current market rate. The premium for this is lower than for an "at the money" option.

The intrinsic value is the profit that the holder of an option can realise by exercising the option immediately; therefore an option which is out of the money will have no intrinsic value. At expiration, the value always equals the intrinsic value. The intrinsic value of the call option is shown diagrammatically in Figure 7.

(ii)   Time Value

The longer the maturity (time to expire) of the option, the higher the probability of larger interest rate movements and hence of profitable exercise of the option by the buyer. The option is thus more valuable to the buyer and the risk to the option writer is greater, so the premium is higher. The factor is often referred to as an option's "Theta".

445

Figure 7   Intrinsic Value of a Call Option

Strike Rate 6.0%

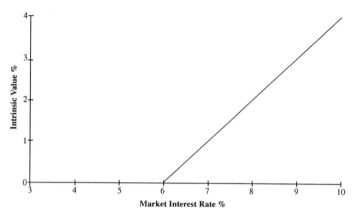

(iii)   Expected Interest Rate Volatility

The higher the volatility of interest rates, the greater the probability of profitable exercise of the option by the buyer, hence the premium is higher. The factor is often referred to as an option's "Vega".

The relationship between intrinsic, time value and expected interest volatility is shown in Figure 8.

Figure 8   Intrinsic, Time Value and Expected Interest Rate Volatility of a 6% Call Option

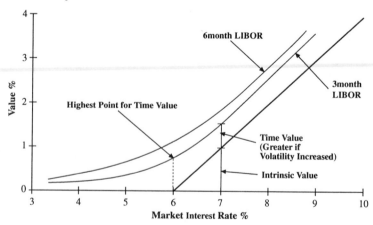

446

As the option period increases, the value of the option also increases, i.e. a change in value from the three month option line to the six month option line shown above. Also the greater the volatility the higher the premium cost.

(iv)   Market Conditions

Various market factors may lead to an increase in the option premium and these include events such as government intervention into the markets or the possibility of the imposition of withholding taxes or exchange controls which will affect the liquidity of the markets.

The pricing of option models is therefore extremely complicated as it has to take all these factors into account.

3.5.3   *Interest Rate Caps*

An Interest Rate Cap is simply a series of interest rate call options. A cap is essentially an insurance policy for a company wishing to protect itself against a rise in short term floating interest rates above the capped level for a specified period, whilst retaining the ability to benefit from any future fall in rates. The option writer agrees, in consideration of the premium, to compensate the company to the extent to which the reference interest rate (usually three or six month LIBOR) exceeds the cap rate on the pre-determined rollover dates.

In effect, the purchaser continues to pay interest at the rate of LIBOR (plus any loan margin) to its lender, with the knowledge that if rates rise above the cap rate on any of the rollover dates, it will be reimbursed by the seller of the cap. It is important that the underlying interest rate index is specified and that the cap rollover dates coincide exactly with the loan rollover dates so that there are no interest rate mismatches. An example of an interest rate cap can be seen in Figure 9.

Interest rate caps should begin at the next rollover date of the loan and any settlements due are paid at the end of the rollover period. The settlement amount paid is calculated by:

$$\text{Cap Principal} \times \frac{\text{Number of Days in Rollover}}{365 \text{ or } 360 *} \times (\text{LIBOR Rate} - \text{Cap Rate})$$

* Depending on the currency

Figure 9   Interest Rate Cap

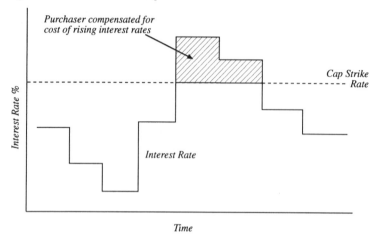

Time

The mechanics of a cap can best be illustrated by looking at an example:

Example 1: X plc – Three Year Borrowing

X plc has an ongoing requirement to borrow £20m over the next three years and is keen to quantify its borrowing cost on a worst case basis at a budget rate of 7.5% p.a. Although a fixed swap rate is available at 6.5%, the treasurer thinks that interest rates (currently at 6%) will fall and therefore would like to benefit from any fall in rates. The treasurer purchases an interest rate cap for three years at a rate of 6.8% p.a. and pays a premium of 185bp or £370,000 (i.e. £20,000,000 x 0.0185) to the cap seller. This premium when amortized across the three years, equates to an additional funding cost of 70bp, making the effective maximum interest payable 7.5% p.a., i.e. the budget rate.

The treasurer is now able to budget at a known worst case of 7.5% as in effect a string of call options on interest rates has been purchased. If rates fall on any rollover date in the next three years, X plc will let the particular call option lapse and pay the market interest rate and therefore benefit fully from any interest rate reduction.

It is worth remembering that, as with any insurance premium, the purchaser hopes that a payment will never be necessary from the seller of the insurance. The person who buys house insurance would prefer the house not to burn down but if it does, the insured is at least covered. Likewise, the purchaser of the above cap would prefer interest rates to fall and to be paying LIBOR interest rates of, say, 5%, rather than the 6.8% maximum possible under the cap.

3.5.4 *Interest Rate Floors*

A floor is a similar instrument to a cap except that it is a series of interest rate put options, i.e. it protects floating rate investment income rather than borrowing costs. A floor is an agreement which can be used to protect against falling interest rates whilst allowing the investor the ability to benefit from rising rates. Like a cap, a premium is payable. The purchaser of the floor is reimbursed by the writer if the market interest rate is lower than the floor strike rate on any of the rollover dates of the floor. Caps and floors can be combined and these are examined in Section 4.

3.5.5 *Advantages and Disadvantages of Interest Rate Options*

Advantages of Interest Rate Options:

(i) **Ability to Benefit from Favourable Movements in Interest Rates** – unlike all the other instruments described previously, options provide protection from adverse interest rate movements whilst allowing the purchaser to benefit from favourable movements.

(ii) **Flexible** – they can be tailor-made to match exact interest rate and cashflow exposures. The premium can either be paid upfront, or spread across the option life. They can be purchased at various rates and periods including borrowings or investments starting in the future. Options are available in most major currencies out to a maximum of approximately 10 years.

(iii) **Attractive to Hedge Uncertain Future Commitments** – if a future commitment does not materialise, the option can either lapse or be sold, there will be no additional costs.

(iv) **Little Administration** – all administration is usually completed by the writer of the option. Payments can be made automatically.

(v) **Documentation** – for one off deals, a simple agreement can be signed.

(vi) **Credit Lines** – as soon as the option premium is paid the purchaser does not have any further commitments to the writer, therefore if a bank sells an option to a company it will not reduce the company's credit line.

Disadvantages of Interest Rate Options:

(i) **Premium Required** – an option requires a premium which is usually paid up front, creating a cashflow disadvantage. This option can readily lose all its value if it is out of the money, at, or near, its expiry date. This can be offset by entering into a zero premium combination (see Section 4 below).

(ii) **Price** – as the contracts are usually tailor-made the bid/offer spread is wider than for exchange traded contracts. The liquidity of the market is not as good as with other instruments and this also increases the bid/offer spread.

4. COMBINING INSTRUMENTS

Futures, options and swaps can be viewed as the building blocks of the current and future generations of derivative products. Each company's hedging requirements are different and the instruments can be modified and combined to achieve varying levels of protection, cost and flexibility to match exactly a company's required objectives.

Some examples of simple combinations of instruments are discussed below:

Collars: Cap and Floor Combined
Double Floor Collars
Swap and Floor Combinations
Participating Swaps
Swaptions

450

The first four combinations are very similar. They will be compared with the help of the same example – X plc.

4.1 Collars

The best known example of combining instruments is the interest rate collar, which is a combination of an interest rate cap and a floor. A borrower would purchase a cap to protect against a rise in interest rates. The premium cost of this cap would be partially, or totally, offset by the borrower simultaneously selling an interest rate floor. Therefore, the collar limits the maximum and minimum rates between which the borrowing costs may vary.

The collar is usually used when a borrower wants to obtain protection against adverse interest rate movements, and wishes to reduce the premium payable. A common strategy is the use of a zero premium collar where the cap and the floor premiums cancel each other out. If market interest rates are higher than the cap level, the borrower is compensated for the increased borrowing costs by the seller. If interest rates are below the floor level, the borrower pays the difference between LIBOR and the floor rate. If rates stay within the band, no exchange is required.

The floor rate will be lower than the comparative fixed rate and is generally lower than floating levels applicable at the time of the deal, therefore allowing the borrower the ability to benefit, to a limited extent, from falls in interest rates. The workings of a zero premium collar can best be seen by looking at the example X plc.

Example 1: X plc – Three Year Borrowing

As before X plc requires protection at a worst case of 7.5% p.a. for its borrowing over three years but is unwilling to pay a premium for a cap. For a zero premium collar, the cap for the collar can be set at 7.5%, i.e. the budget rate and which has a cheaper premium than the cap in the previous example at 6.8%. The benefit of this lower cap premium is reflected in the level at which the floor rate is set and the floor is therefore set at 6.0%.

The following collar can be achieved:

X plc purchases cap at 7.5% p.a.	£ 100,000	premium
X plc sells floor at 6.0% p.a.	(£ 100,000)	premium
Overall Cost:	£ Zero	premium

X plc has established protection against interest rates rising above 7.5% p.a., but has foregone the ability to benefit from a fall in rates below 6.0% p.a.

Figure 10   Risk Profile of X plc's Interest Rate Collar

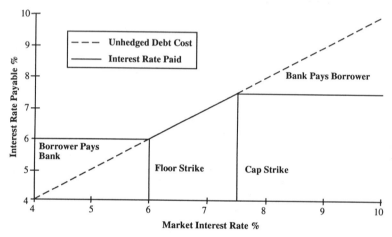

This structure is useful when X plc. believes that interest rates will stay in the bands of the collar but requires the certainty that it is protected if rates rise sharply.

Collars are extremely flexible and can be structured to mirror the company's perception of interest rates. Instead of being a flat band between which interest rates can vary, the collar can be stepped at different pre-determined levels over the life of the interest exposure. This can allow the company to have a lower, or tighter collar, initially and a higher or wider collar in the future at no upfront cost. This can be beneficial for borrowers who are, for example, experiencing short term cashflow disadvantages.

The two main disadvantages of collars are that a credit line is required as the company sells an option to the bank and there may be a potential close out cost should the deal be cancelled. Also if interest rates fall sharply during the period of a collar, then the company is left paying interest at the floor rate, not the lower market rates. This has been a serious problem in the UK as corporates have been entering into collars at levels that were attractive at the time, only to find rates falling rapidly below the floor level. One simple method to reduce the amount payable under the floor is the "Double Floor Collar" as described below.

4.2 Double Floor Collar

A "Double Floor Collar" is designed to provide the same protection as a normal collar, but it allows the purchaser to benefit if interest rates move significantly in their favour. With a normal collar a cap is purchased and a floor is sold to offset the premium to give zero premium payable, however the borrower cannot benefit if rates fall below the floor. If the borrower purchases another floor at a level below the first floor, which is relatively cheap as it is so far "out of the money", the borrower can then benefit if interest rates fall below the second floor.

Again this is best illustrated by looking at how X plc would use a double floor collar to hedge its exposure over a three year time horizon.

Example 1: X plc – Three Year Borrowing

X plc requires protection at a worst rate of 7.5% p.a. for its borrowing over three years but does not wish to pay a cap premium. The treasurer is concerned that interest rates may fall sharply and if they do does not want to be left paying interest rates at the floor level of the collar shown above, i.e. 6%.

The following Double Floor Collar can be achieved:

X plc purchases Cap at 7.5% p.a.	£ 100,000	premium
X plc sells Floor I at 6.25% p.a.	(£ 130,000)	premium
X plc purchases Floor 2 at 5.0% p.a.	£ 30,000	premium
Overall Cost	£ Zero	premium

The advantage of this structure is that a cap has been purchased at 7.5% p.a. without paying an upfront premium, i.e. the collar has been structured so that there is no upfront premium payable. X plc will avoid any payments to the bank if LIBOR remains above 6.25% p.a. Should LIBOR fall below 6.25% p.a. then the maximum amount payable to the bank would be 1.25% p.a. (the difference between the two floors) which would be more than offset by the overall reduction in the cost of the funds below the budgeted 7.5% p.a.

Figure 11   Risk Profile of X plc's Double Floor Collar

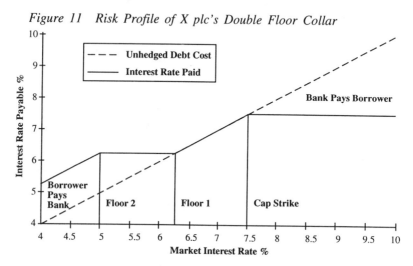

The disadvantage of this strategy is that the floor sold by the company is slightly higher than in a normal collar, so if rates fall the company starts paying sooner. Also as the company sells an option to the bank a credit line is required, i.e. the bank would have a potential credit exposure to the company if rates fell below 6.25%. There may be a potential close out cost should the deal be cancelled.

4.3   Swap and Floor Combinations

Swaps and Floors can be combined to provide a borrower with most of the advantages of option and swap products, with few of the disadvantages. One simple combination of a swap and floor entails a borrowing company entering into an interest rate swap to pay fixed whilst simultaneously purchasing an interest rate floor at a lower strike rate than the swap for the same period. This provides the company with a known worst rate and allows it to benefit if interest rates fall below the floor. The cost of the

454

floor can be incorporated into the swap rate, i.e. increasing the rate, so that no upfront premium is paid. This can best be seen with the help of the example X plc.

Example 1: X plc – Three Year Borrowing

As before X plc requires protection at a worst rate of 7.5% p.a. for its borrowing over three years but prefers not to pay a cap premium. The treasurer believes interest rates will fall sharply and would like to benefit from any falls. The current three year swap rate is 6.5% p.a., but if X plc enters into a higher swap rate of 7.0% p.a., it is effectively paying the bank 0.5% which enables it to purchase an interest rate floor at 5.5%. Therefore, if interest rates fall below 5.5% p.a., the company would be paid the difference between the LIBOR rate and 5.5% p.a.

The net effect is that X plc will never pay more than 7.0% p.a., which is 50 basis points lower than its budget rate, and it will also receive the benefit of interest rates falling below 5.5% p.a.

The risk profile for the swap and floor combination is illustrated below:

Figure 12   Risk Profile of X plc's Swap and Floor Combination

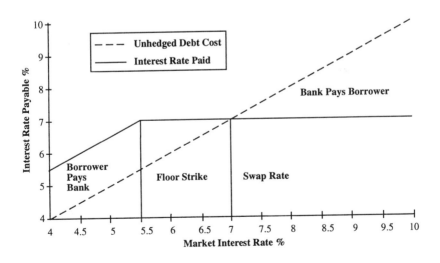

The advantage of this structure is that it provides a known worst case funding rate at no upfront cost, whilst still allowing the ability to benefit from falling interest rates if they fall below the level of the floor. It should be considered if X plc is extremely optimistic about interest rates but still requires protection against interest rate rises and does not want to pay the premium for the cap. The disadvantage is that X plc has to pay for the floor via a higher swap rate, therefore if rates are between 5.5% and 7.0%, X plc will have to pay 7.0%.

4.4 Participating Swaps (also known as Participating Caps)

A participating swap provides protection from rising interest rates and also allows the purchaser to participate immediately in any falls in rates. It is a logical extension of the swap and floor combination described above. A participating swap is where the borrower varies the amount of the floor purchased so that the strike rate can be raised to the same level of the swap, all for no premium cost.

With a participating swap, the higher the strike rate of the swap/floor relative to current interest rates, the higher the "participation" when rates fall below this strike rate and vice versa. The cost of the floor is embedded in the swap rate which is correspondingly higher than a normal swap. This can best be seen with the help of the example X plc.

Example 1: X plc – Three Year Borrowing

X plc requires protection at a worst rate of 7.5% p.a. for its three year borrowing. The current three year swap rate is 6.5% p.a. A participating swap can be established if the swap rate is increased to 7.5%. The income generated by the raising of the swap level is enough to purchase a floor at 7.5% p.a. for 70% of the principal amount (i.e. with £20m this would equate to a floor on £14m). This then allows X plc to participate in 70% of any fall in rates below 7.5%. The further interest rates fall, the lower the overall interest cost. The risk profile is shown in Figure 13.

This combination is attractive when a borrower who does not want, or is unable, to pay a premium for a cap but believes interest rates will be volatile so requires protection from rises in interest rates, and would also like to benefit if rates fall.

4.5 Comparison of the Products

A simple comparison of the swap, cap and floor combination strategies
for X plc can be seen at various levels of interest rates in Table 2 below.

Figure 13   Risk Profile for X plc's Participating Swap

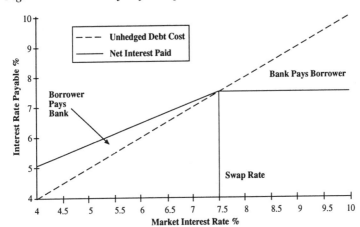

Table 2 Comparison of Risk Management Strategies for X plc

LIBOR	Swap	Cap*	Collar	Double Floor Collar	Swap & Floor	Participating Swap
%	%	%	%	%	%	%
8.0	6.5	7.5	7.5	7.5	7.0	7.5
7.5	6.5	7.5	7.5	7.5	7.0	7.5
7.0	6.5	7.5	7.0	7.0	7.0	7.15
6.5	6.5	7.2	6.5	6.5	7.0	6.80
6.0	6.5	6.7	6.0	6.25	7.0	6.45
5.5	6.5	6.2	6.0	6.25	7.0	6.10
5.0	6.5	5.7	6.0	6.25	6.5	5.75
4.5	6.5	5.2	6.0	5.75	6.0	5.40
4.0	6.5	4.7	6.0	5.25	5.5	5.05
3.5	6.5	4.2	6.0	4.75	5.0	4.70
3.0	6.5	3.7	6.0	4.25	4.5	4.35

* including amortized premium

457

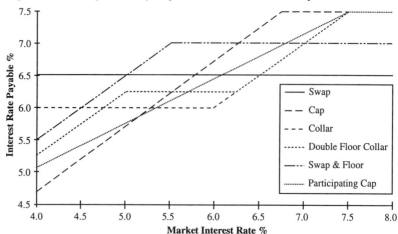

Figure 14   Comparison of X plc's Instrument Risk Profiles

Each strategy provides a worst case interest cost of 7.5% p.a., or better, but different levels of benefit at lower rates. It depends on the treasurer's view of interest rates as to the best strategy to choose. If the treasurer believes interest rates will fall sharply and stay low, a cap may be best. If it is believed rates will rise a swap would be better. If the treasurer thinks rates will fall only a little way then one of the combination strategies should be considered.

4.6   Swaptions

A swaption is simply an option to enter into a swap. As with other option type products a premium is payable. The buyer has the right, but not the obligation, to enter into a swap at an agreed rate on a specified date in the future. If interest rates move in the buyer's favour the option can lapse and a swap can be entered into at the more favourable market rate.

The swaption has two main uses:

(i)   To provide protection against an uncertain interest rate exposure. The swaption allows a treasurer to fix a funding cost on borrowing connected with, say, a proposed acquisition, or project, providing certainty of future interest costs without having the obligation to borrow at the fixed rate should the proposed acquisition, or project, not proceed.

458

(ii)   To hedge a loan, or deposit, that will start in the future whilst obtaining the ability to benefit from favourable rate movements. As with any option transaction the term of the option period and the term of the actual transaction have to be specified.

It is possible for the swaption to be either "swap settled" or "cash settled".

With a swap settled transaction the buyer has the right to enter into an interest rate swap. In these situations it is important to understand that an appropriate credit limit is required for the underlying swap transaction. This may tie up the company's existing credit line.

With a cash settled swaption the bank will simply pay the buyer a cash sum in settlement representing the "value" of the swaption compared to the market rate. The benefit of the cash settled route is that credit risk is entirely eliminated (when the customer is buying the option) and the premium is correspondingly cheaper for the customer. The mechanics of a swaption can best be shown with the help of an example.

Example 1: Y plc – Uncertain Borrowing in Three Months' Time

Y plc has a potential five year borrowing requirement in three months' time. The exposure is uncertain but the firm seeks to hedge its exposure to a possible adverse movement in interest rates. The five year swap starting in three months' time is 7.25% p.a. and the cost of a three month swap settled swaption at this strike is 70bp which, amortized across the five year loan, is equal to 17bp per annum. Y plc requires a swap settled swaption as it actually may want to enter into a swap.

There are four potential outcomes:

(i)   Five year swap rates rise to, say, 8.5% p.a. and the loan is required. Y plc exercises the swaption to fix the interest cost at 7.42% p.a. (i.e. 7.25% + 0.17% which includes the amortized premium). The borrower saves 108bp per annum.

459

(ii) Five year swap rates rise to, say, 8.5% p.a. and the loan is not required. The swaption will still have value even though there is now no longer any debt. This value can be realised by either selling the swaption prior to expiration, or by obtaining a cash settlement on exercise.

Y plc makes a cash gain from the swaption if rates rise, however this gain is less than if it had entered into the original swap at 7.25% as there would have been no swaption premium payable. The advantage of the swaption becomes apparent if rates had fallen.

(iii) Five year swap rates fall to 6% p.a. and the loan is required. Y plc allows the swaption to lapse and the all in funding cost is 6.17% p.a. (i.e. 6.0% + 0.17% which includes the amortised premium). This results in a saving of 1.08% p.a. versus the forward swap.

(iv) Five year swap rates fall to 6% p.a. and the loan is not required. The swaption is allowed to lapse and although Y plc has lost the premium of 70 basis points, it has not locked in at 7.25% p.a. and faced a cost for breaking the swap of over 5.0% (the net present value of 125bp per annum over five years).

The user of the swaption can therefore reduce the risk to adverse movements in interest rates whilst retaining the ability to benefit from favourable movements.

5. LATEST GENERATION OF PRODUCTS

The derivative market is continually evolving and over the last few years a new generation of products has been created. These instruments, which are a natural extension of simple interest rate swaps, have been developed mainly due to demand from investors who are looking to increase returns by exploiting their particular view on the direction of interest rate and yield curves.

They have also been used by borrowers with strong views of interest rate movements and by those borrowers who are particularly badly hit by recession. This latter group have used the new products, not as a specific interest rate hedge, but as a means of minimising short to medium term interest rate payments by taking the potential risk of paying more in later years when hopefully the recession will have ended and revenues increased.

460

This new generation of products typically incorporates one or both of the following features.

(1)   The currency of the index used to calculate interest rate payments does not necessarily correspond to the currency in which it is paid.

(2)   The underlying frequency of the interest index does not always match the frequency at which it is paid.

There is an increasing number of product variations emerging from this generation but most can be broken down into either Differential or Yield Curve Swaps.

5.1   **Differential Swaps**

Differential swaps, which are also known as CRIB or Quanto swaps, were the first in this generation of products. They allow the exchange of interest payments indexed to the LIBOR of two different currencies, with all payments being calculated on the same notional principal in a single base currency and paid in that base currency. Therefore they allow users to take advantage of the yield curve differences between the two currencies to achieve a higher yield or to lower borrowing costs. Typically, a borrower would pay interest linked to a low coupon interest index which has a positive yield curve (i.e. long term interest rates are higher than short term), such as six months dollar LIBOR, against receiving a high coupon interest index from a relatively flatter or negative yield curve. This can best be explained with the help of an example.

Example 1: Diff S.p.A. – Differential Swap

An Italian company, Diff S.p.A., has borrowed 10bn Lira linked to Lira LIBOR. Diff S.p.A. sells a high proportion of its goods to America but does not have any US debt, so it is unable to get "compensation" from low US interest rates if the US recession continues and therefore demand for its products is low. The treasurer believes that over the next two years Lira interest rates will remain high and that US rates will stay low, because the US economy will fail to pick up as fast as the market anticipates. A differential lira/dollar swap would allow the company not only to pay lower immediate interest charges but also to gain economic protection from the US economy, as its payments would be linked to US

461

dollar LIBOR. Thus, if the US economy remains depressed, reducing sales in the US, this should keep US interest rates at a low level.

If the US economy recovers, the increase in sales revenue would more than offset the likely increase in interest charges as US LIBOR increases. The mechanics of a two year Lira/dollar differential swap are shown in Figure 15.

Figure 15   US Dollar/Lira Differential Swap

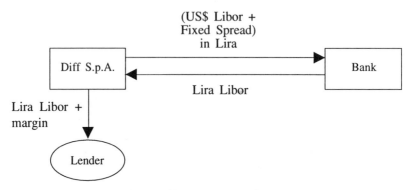

Ignoring loan margins, Diff S.p.A. has effectively switched its debt obligations from six month Lira LIBOR (9.0%), to six month US dollar LIBOR (3.4%) plus a fixed differential spread of 4.0% which is determined by the term structure of interest rates in the two currencies. Although the two LIBOR rates refer to different currencies, all payments are calculated on 10bn Lira and paid in Lira, thus avoiding any currency risk. The rationale for this strategy is that Diff S.p.A. not only obtains a known saving in the first period ($ LIBOR 3.4% + 4.0% is less than Lira LIBOR at 9.0%), but also it obtains further savings during the life of the transactions if the spread between $ LIBOR and Lira LIBOR does not move as much as the respective yield curves imply. If future interest rates correspond exactly with the current market implied forward rates then the differential swap would show neither a profit nor a loss over its life.

The risk occurs if the spread between US dollar and Lira LIBOR reduces by more than the yield curve suggests, but this risk can be limited to a maximum exposure by embedding a US dollar cap into the structure. Therefore the worst case basis is known from the outset. The cost of the

462

cap is usually embedded in the structure, i.e. the spread over US dollar LIBOR increases.

5.1.1   *Medium Term Note Differential Swap*

The differential swap can be used, as above, on its own to allow companies to benefit if their views on the yield curve are correct. However, more commonly they are used with an instrument vehicle such as a Medium Term Note (MTN). This has allowed both borrowers and investors to come together to put their yield curve views into practice. However, the main reason for using an MTN with a differential swap is the regulatory and tax benefits. This is particularly so in the Far East where the stringent regulatory conditions disallow many, such as the Japanese investment trust and management companies. (ITMs) and, until quite recently, life insurance companies, from entering into any derivative transactions.

Also by using an MTN, the bank would have no credit risk against the investor, only the borrower, so that providing the borrower's credit rating is of adequate quality the transaction can still take place. This has been a useful feature as many of the investors are not of sufficient credit quality for derivative business.

The following is a common example of how a differential swap can be embedded into an MTN structure.

Example 1: Invest Company – Reverse Floater Differential Swap Medium Term Note

A dollar based investor, Invest Co., has a view that peseta LIBOR will fall. It would thus be attracted to a yield enhancing scheme which would allow it to benefit if short dated peseta interest rates were to fall. There is also a borrower who wishes to issue an MTN and structure a transaction that would enable it to borrow funds at attractive sub-LIBOR levels. The two parties could both satisfy their objectives via what is called a reverse floater (i.e. the investor gains if interest rates fall) differential swap MTN issue.

An example is shown below in Figure 16.

Figure 16   Reverse Floater Differential Swap Medium Term Note

(i)   Invest Co. purchases MTN

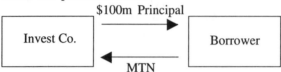

(ii) Borrower Swaps Coupons with Bank

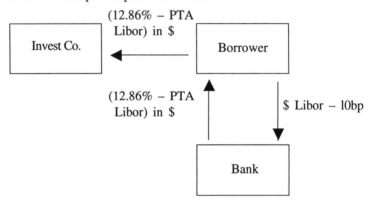

(iii) At Maturity the MTN is Redeemed

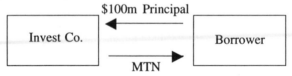

In the scheme illustrated above, Invest Co. purchases a $100m MTN with a five year maturity which has been structured to pay a coupon of 12.86% p.a. minus peseta LIBOR in dollars. The coupon increases if six month peseta LIBOR falls over the life of the transaction, thus crystallising the medium term view of Invest Co. Just in case this view is dramatically wrong and peseta LIBOR rates rise above 12.86%, there is normally a guarantee that the coupon cannot fall below zero. Finally, because of the swap that the borrower enters into with the bank, the borrower ends up paying a sub-LIBOR interest rate on $100m for five years. On maturity the full face value of the MTN is redeemed.

5.2 Yield Curve Swap

As soon as banks were comfortable with being able to price and hedge their own exposure obtained from selling differential swaps, they began to explore new variations such as the Yield Curve Swap. These are basis swaps whereby swap rates rather than LIBOR rates are used for interest rate calculations. This can be explained with the help of an example.

Example 1: Yield Company – Yield Curve Swaps

Yield Co. may have the view that the UK yield curve which is already positive is likely to steepen further, i.e. short end rates may fall or long end rates may rise. Yield Co. could enter into a yield curve swap to pay the two year swap rate, and receive the ten year rate less a fixed margin of say 90bp, say over a period of two years. Thus, every six months the prevailing two and 10 year swap rates would be used to calculate interest rate payments on each leg of the transaction. If two and 10 year swap rates were currently 5.9% and 7.2%, Yield Co. would make a gain of 40bp in the first rollover. See Figure 17.

Figure 17 Sterling Yield Curve Swap

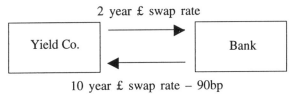

2 year £ swap rate

Yield Co. → Bank

10 year £ swap rate – 90bp

Yield Co. will benefit if the yield curve steepens between the two to 10 year maturity. However, if there is a parallel shift either upwards, or downwards, in the yield curve, it will not have any material impact on the increased cost as the two year rate will be offset by the increased yield on the 10 year position. The risk is that the yield curve flattens and Yield Co. ends up paying out more than it receives. It is therefore essential that Yield Co. has a strong view on the direction of the yield curve.

As with differential swaps, yield curve swaps have also been further developed and are incorporated into MTNs. One such idea is the leveraged yield curve MTN which allows investors to take a view on longer term interest rates but only ties up their cash for a relatively short period of time. This can best be explained with the help of an example.

Example 2: Leverage Company – Leveraged Yield Curve Swap Medium Term Note

A US investor, Leverage Co., has a view that the five year Deutschemark swap rate will fall below its current level over the next twelve months. One way Leverage Co. could benefit from this view is to buy, say, $10m of a one year leveraged yield curve swap MTN. On redemption, for every $100 invested it would get back $100 + 10 x (6.50% – 5 year DM swap rate), where the five year swap rate at maturity is used. For example, if the swap rate closes at 6.00% in a year's time the investor would obtain a total of $105 (i.e. 100 + 10 x (6.5 – 6.0)), which, if Leverage Co.'s view is correct, will allow considerable yield enhancement through a leverage factor of 10. If Leverage Co's. views are incorrect, and the five year swap rate increases, the worst position is that all its principal of $10m is returned, i.e. it loses any potential interest since the coupon on payment cannot fall below zero.

Figure 18   Leveraged Yield Curve Swap Medium Term Note

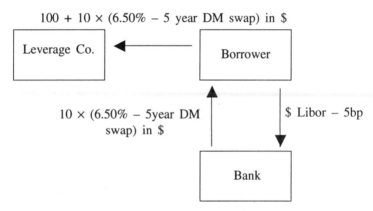

100 + 10 × (6.50% – 5 year DM swap) in $

The diagram above illustrates once again how a borrower could swap out its structured obligation and achieve sub-LIBOR funding level without any direct derivative risk.

466

The above are just a few of the many examples that are possible to take advantage of investors' or borrowers' individual views of the market or hedging requirements. Indeed, these products can now be structured so that the index on which the payments are made can be linked to any other index which would better fit a company's requirements.

6.   TAX TREATMENT OF INTEREST RATE HEDGING INSTRUMENTS

Traditionally, tax legislation has been relatively slow in reacting to the growth in the market for interest rate hedging instruments. As a result, it is necessary to interpret existing, and sometimes inadequate, rules to accommodate transactions not contemplated when they were drafted and it is not possible to state categorically how they will be treated by the respective tax authorities. The main difficulty is that although payments and receipts under such instruments will be calculated by reference to an interest rate, there is sometimes no underlying debt involved and so the associated cash flow will often not qualify for treatment as interest. Additionally, the treatment may be different depending on whether the claimant is a financial trader (e.g. a bank) or some other enterprise. For the former, income and expenses under financial instruments are likely to be part of trading income, for the latter, the nature and purpose of the hedge will need to be examined. To illustrate, the following give an indication of the main features of the treatment for non-financial traders in the UK:

(a)   If the instrument hedges trading income or expenses, or interest expense on a loan funding capital items employed in the company's trade (e.g. a loan to purchase a factory used in the manufacturing business), then it is likely to receive revenue treatment, even if the loan is on capital account. In these circumstances, there is unlikely to be any difficulty in obtaining a deduction for payments made.

(b)   If such a trading connection does not exist, then the instrument is likely to fall within the capital gains tax regime. Not surprisingly, it is likely that all inflows will be taxed. However, it will be more difficult to secure a deduction for outflows:

(i)   Premiums on quoted options, or other options granted by market professionals, are likely to be relievable under capital gains tax

467

rules but need to be carefully analysed to establish whether they should be treated as the cost of acquisition of the option or of the asset acquired under the option.

(ii)   Premiums on other interest rate options will be treated as wasting assets under the capital gains tax regime and so, if the option is taken to maturity, will not qualify for a tax deduction. If an in-the-money option is closed out or sold before maturity, then deduction for part of the premium paid may be available.

(iii)   Premiums on interest rate caps, floors and collars are unlikely to gain full relief under capital gains tax rules and may even go completely unrelieved if there are no receipts under the instrument.

(iv)   Interest rate swaps: no treatment is specified for swaps under statute. However, equalisation payments and receipts are likely to be treated in the same way as if they were interest by virtue of an extra statutory concession. Payments to enter into, or to terminate, a swap are not subject to the concession and so are unlikely to be deductible.

NB: Swap payments between commercial counterparties without a UK bank, or recognised swap dealer, as an intermediary may be subject to withholding tax.

(v)   The settlement on maturity of an FRA will give rise to a capital gains tax gain or loss.

NB: Under forward/forward contracts real interest is received, and so would receive revenue treatment.

It should be emphasised that the UK treatment of these instruments is particularly arcane and other jurisdictions may adopt accounts based rules which are more equitable. Indeed, the UK Revenue have recently proposed a new system for the treatment of payments and receipts under interest rate contracts and options. Broadly, the proposals advocate an accounts based treatment for all companies, be they entering into the instrument for trading purposes or not. For trading transactions the treatment will be largely unchanged but for non-trade transactions a revenue treatment will be adopted although it will only be possible to gain a deduction against a general taxable income in the period to which the expense is attributed.

These new rules remain complex, in particular it is possible that the anti-abuse provisions will adversely affect genuine commercial transactions. Furthermore, it is unlikely that the provisions will come into effect until 31 December 1994 at the earliest. Accordingly, the tax implications of an interest rate hedging strategy will remain an important and complex consideration for the corporate treasurer over and above the direct effect of the hedging instrument on his interest rate exposure. This will invariably involve obtaining the appropriate professional advice.

7. CONCLUSIONS

In this chapter we have outlined the steps that should be taken to develop a strategy for managing interest rate exposure, examined some of the instruments currently available in the market and highlighted the rapid recent developments taking place.

Successful management of interest rate exposure will depend upon:

(i)   An accurate assessment of the current and future interest rate exposure and its nature.

(ii)   The organisation's perception of economic conditions and the likely or possible movement in interest rates.

(iii) Setting an appropriate risk management policy with clearly defined objectives and risk versus reward parameters.

Choice of hedging instruments to meet these objectives will depend in part on:

(i)   The exposure to be hedged. Is it certain and is it short or long term in nature?

(ii)   The cost that the treasurer is prepared to pay to achieve the objectives, whether this be an upfront premium, spread over the term of the borrowing or offset by sacrificing potential benefits.

(iii)   The perceived need, or desire, for flexibility in the organisation's strategy. Thus, if a treasurer wishes to unwind any hedge that is in place, can this be accomplished and at what price?

(iv)   Taxation considerations (as covered in Section 6).

In brief, despite innovations in the markets, three primary hedging choices remain; leaving the exposure open or using internal hedges, fixing the interest rate, or insuring the rate using options. All other strategies are combinations of these three choices and in every instance altering a pure option will mean giving up some of the benefits.

There are, inevitably, other considerations to be taken into account but suffice it to say that the treasurer of today can really have no excuse or good reason for not being able to hedge the monetary liabilities or assets of the organisation against adverse interest rate movements.

We have examined the basic instruments and some of the latest products that are currently available in the market. There is little doubt that these instruments will continue to form the foundation for further complex and innovative funding and hedging techniques that will be developed in the next few years. Already the availability of strategies is complex and the wise treasurer of today needs to make maximum use of the available banking expertise to keep abreast of the latest developments in order to determine the best course of action.

CHAPTER 12

Country Risk Assessment and Sovereign Debt Rescheduling

by Michael Stocks

1. INTRODUCTION

The importance to international banks of a capability to assess country risk first became evident in the early 1970s, as the rapid expansion of eurocurrency lending dating from the 1960s began to embrace an ever more diverse range of borrowers. As far as non-OECD borrowers were concerned, this expansion derived initially from the development ethic of the time, namely that economic growth in developing countries should and could be based on inflows of foreign capital which may need to be borrowed. Underpinning this approach was the belief that, other things being equal, the industrial and agricultural capacity so developed would then generate the foreign exchange needed to service the external debt which had been incurred.

Although this proposition remained a constant, a new dimension was added by the well-documented oil price hike of 1973–74, which brought a massive shift of wealth from oil consuming countries to oil producing countries. Many of the former were plunged into large current account deficits, a feature which was especially prevalent among non oil-producing developing countries.

The industrialised deficit countries for the most part responded to the oil price increase by restraining domestic demand, thereby curbing the growth of non-oil imports in order to make room for the higher cost of oil imports in the context of restoring sustainable current account positions. Those that failed to do so voluntarily were eventually compelled to do so under the aegis of IMF programmes, e.g. the UK in 1976. But developing countries tried generally to finance their incremental current account deficits by borrowing from international banks awash with the surplus funds of the nouveau riche of OPEC.

At the time, this approach did not seem unreasonable. Prices of traditional commodity exports from developing countries were generally strong and interest rates were relatively low. The rationale of the moment was that as long as nominal export growth was higher in percentage terms than the rate of interest paid on external borrowing then the debt could be serviced without undue difficulty and indeed it made economic sense to borrow.

The banking community has been criticised for undertaking so much lending to developing countries during the mid to late 1970s. However, if there were not to be a potentially politically destabilising slump in economic activity throughout the developing world, the current account deficits needed to be financed in some way by capital inflows. Ideally, the official sector (governments, the multilateral institutions – IMF, World Bank, regional development banks, etc. – and the aid agencies) should have undertaken the task rather than the commercial banks. But OPEC's surplus was for the most part deposited with the banks and there is little doubt that the official sector in the industrialised world was perfectly happy at the time to let the commercial banking system provide the conduit through which these oil surpluses were recycled. However, as was widely recognised subsequently within the banking community, the banks are open to the charges that risk was not assessed adequately and that they were too ready to lend for general purpose deficit financing rather than for specific projects which would generate foreign currency earnings streams.

The assumption on which lending was based, namely that debt could be serviced relatively easily provided export growth was higher in percentage terms than the rate of interest on the debt, was rudely shattered in the early 1980s. Following the US push for growth in the late 1970s and the outbreak of war between two major oil producers – Iran and Iraq – oil prices again rose sharply in 1979-80, exacerbating the current account deficits of the oil importers. This time, however, the adoption of monetarism in the industrialised countries, and especially in the US, not only pushed up interest rates sharply but slowed economic activity markedly, causing commodity prices to sag.

Between 1980 and 1983, the debt of developing countries rose by almost US$200bn but export earnings rose by only 10% of that amount.

472

The six month Eurodollar interest rate, on which most international bank lending was based, rose to over 17% in 1982, double the average for the 1972-78 period. Annual interest payments for the non oil-producing developing countries exploded from US$13bn in 1977 to over US$60bn in 1982. Unsurprisingly, debt servicing problems ensued.

In the quarter of a century to 1982 there had been some 80 debt relief rescheduling agreements, but most of these were government to government arrangements, with commercial banks involved in only some 13 agreements, mostly with small African and central American countries and for relatively insignificant amounts, the main exceptions being debt rescheduling agreements with Turkey (1979) and Poland (1982). However, in August 1982, Mexico informed creditors of its inability to continue servicing debt on schedule and the debt crisis had begun; within a year some 15 countries with liabilities to international banks of over US$200bn were renegotiating all or part of their debt service schedules.

The following table offers an indication of the magnitudes of the trends outlined above:

Disbursed external medium and long term public debt (US$bn)

	1970	1980	1985	1991
Brazil	5.1	57.5	91.9	95.1
Mexico	6.0	41.2	88.4	83.9
Argentina	5.2	16.8	41.9	47.2
Egypt	1.5	16.5	35.7	37.0
Nigeria	0.6	5.4	14.6	33.6
Philippines	1.5	8.8	16.3	25.9
Developing countries total	61.7	426.8	809.3	1,159.9

Source: World Bank

The fact that such a large number of countries, including many in Latin America and Africa, have been obliged to reschedule their foreign debt does not significantly diminish the need for country risk assessment. First, those countries which have not rescheduled debt service payments continue to require assessment. Second, short-term trade-related lending may still be possible vis-a-vis many countries which have rescheduled their medium and long term debt and the feasibility of such lending therefore needs to be assessed. Third, some of the countries which have

473

rescheduled are now re-emerging as borrowers, having restructured their debt in such a way as to reduce debt servicing due and free capacity to service new debt; a framework for assessing the creditworthiness of these countries is also required.

The remainder of this chapter looks first at the definitions, concepts and methodologies involved in country risk analysis before giving an overview of the foreign debt rescheduling process.

2. DEFINITIONS

2.1 Country Risk
This, in broad terms, and as far as a bank is concerned, is the uncertainty created when funds must cross international frontiers. It is the risk that a foreign borrower will not satisfactorily service its foreign currency debt obligations – for "macro" rather than "micro" reasons; i.e. beyond the usual risks which arise in relation to all lending.

2.2 Sovereign Risk
When the borrower in question is part of the public sector the risk is often known as sovereign risk.

2.3 Transfer Risk
When the borrower is in the private sector the risk may be known as transfer risk. However, the analysis in both cases, i.e. sovereign and transfer, is much the same.

2.4 Public Sector
This comprises all state-owned agencies and institutions. The designation of a borrower as public sector carries with it the implicit assumption that the state will, in extremis, take responsibility for the financial obligations of the borrower concerned. Since this may not always be so, care must be taken when determining whether an asset is public as far as risk management is concerned.

2.5 Repudiation
A borrower ceases to acknowledge its debt obligations.

474

2.6 **Default**
A borrower ceases to service its debt because it cannot or will not pay.

2.7 **Rescheduling**
Implies a reduction or deferment in annual repayments of principal since these are spread over a greater number of years than previously.

2.8 **Renegotiation**
Implies that the lender will receive less income than previously because of, for example, a reduced interest rate being agreed.

3. **CONCEPTS**
It is self-evident that all cross border lending is subject to country risk. What is less clear, however, is precisely which factors should be considered in determining this risk. It is important to be clear as to what should be assessed and how to segregate the various risks with cross border lending. The concepts which are outlined in this chapter are by no means definitive; they offer an approach which can be defended but which is likely to change with circumstances. Country risk assessment is an art and not a science.

The assessment of country risk should be concentrated on the ability of a country to generate (or conserve) the foreign exchange earnings which will allow residents of that country to service their foreign currency debt. Where the borrower is a state-owned entity the assessment of the country risk alone represents the credit assessment that a lender undertakes when considering any lending proposition. When the borrower is from the private sector, an assessment of country risk is only part of the analysis which is required. In addition, the lender must assess the credit risks that apply to that individual borrower as explained in Chapters 1 – 5.

The concept of country risk to a lending bank is thus different from the concept of country risk to a manufacturing company which may be considering direct investment overseas. In the former, the prime concern is the country's overall external financial accounts. With the latter, more detailed attention needs to be given to the practical aspects of operating overseas, e.g. labour regulations, restrictions on the repatriation of profits/ dividends, and the general business environment.

For a lending bank it is important to keep separate, as far as possible, the assessment of country risk from the assessment of credit risk (i.e. when lending to the private sector). Even if a private sector borrower is financially sound and does itself generate sufficient foreign exchange to service its foreign currency debt, it is still subject to country risk, which can manifest itself in the form of severe exchange control restrictions preventing the borrower from fulfilling its obligations. (Hence the use of the phrase "transfer risk" in these circumstances.)

Consideration also needs to be given to determining which is the country of risk. This will usually be the country of residence of the borrower. However, where a loan is guaranteed it may be considered appropriate that the country of risk should be the country of residence of the guarantor. As an example of this, trade finance provided to Ghana but guaranteed by the ECGD would be UK risk. However, it is imprudent to lay down hard and fast rules in this area and each bank should determine its own approach, conditioned inevitably by any guidelines laid down by the regulatory authorities. This aspect is further complicated by cross border exposure to multilateral institutions such as the EU or African Development Bank where it is impractical to identify a sole country of risk. Lending to the shipping industry, in which a mortgage on the ship is often regarded as the lender's main safeguard against loss, presents a similar difficulty.

Traditionally, the assessment of country risk has been aimed at gauging both a country's willingness and its ability to service its foreign currency debt. Historically, it has been taken that a country's willingness could be assessed by analysing political factors; for example, by identifying the risk that a new regime may renege on obligations incurred by a previous regime because of, say, ideological differences. A country's ability, on the other hand, was taken to be a function of economic factors.

However, it is arguable from a practical point of view that the economic factors should take clear primacy. This is not to under-rate the importance of political factors in assessing risk, but the evidence of countries reneging for ideological reasons on debt incurred by a previous regime is very rare. When it does occur, it is usually the case that to have serviced such debt would have imposed a heavy burden on the economy. Similarly, a country may be able, theoretically, to service its debt, but the government decides to seek a rescheduling because debt servicing is leaving too little foreign exchange for imports and thus political stability may be undermined. Strictly, this would be a political decision stemming from a political judgment, but its roots are firmly in economic factors.

4. PURPOSES

The type of country risk assessment which is adopted by any bank will be determined by its own particular needs, depending on the nature of its international business and the organisational structure of the bank itself. There is, thus, no 'best' method of country risk assessment.

Clearly though, a bank must be mindful of the purposes for which it intends to use any system it chooses.

Among the possible purposes are:

4.1 Credit Assessment

Particularly for sovereign risk propositions, where it is at least as important as in private sector lending to be satisfied that the reward is commensurate with the risk.

4.2 Country Limits

In operating a system of country limits, some capacity to establish the relative riskiness is essential. The degree of emphasis placed on country risk in determining a ceiling on a bank's exposure to any given country will vary from one institution to another. Other considerations which may be relevant here are: the bank's marketing strategy; the existence of historical relationships; and the desire to achieve a geographical balance within the bank's international loan portfolio.

4.3 Portfolio Management

Following on from the above, the ability to measure country risk provides a bank's management with the capacity to solve, or at least attempt to solve, the risk/reward conundrum. It makes it possible to assess the aggregate risk of any given portfolio and hence to judge the appropriateness of the income deriving from that portfolio. (It is important to remember that a bank should be concerned not so much with the reduction of risk but with the management of risk.)

4.4 General Provisions

These are a function of risk. If, therefore, it is possible to measure the country risk element of a loan portfolio, it is possible to establish a provisioning policy which is both rational and prudent.

In all the above, prudence is the over-riding objective. While this is in itself virtuous, it must also be recognised that regulatory authorities throughout the world have become increasingly concerned that banks under their jurisdiction have adequate methods for assessing country risk. For purely pragmatic reasons, then, some system for assessing country risk needs to be established by any bank which has cross-border exposure.

5. TYPES OF ASSESSMENT SYSTEMS

There are no hard and fast rules as to what constitutes the "right" system. The size and nature of a bank's international asset portfolio and the purposes for which each bank needs to assess country risk will go a long way towards determining the system it uses and the level of sophistication of that system.

A major international bank which undertakes cross-border lending to as many as 60 to 80 countries will usually employ its own team of economists and will normally have devised a sophisticated system which incorporates the analyses of its economists and uses various sources of information. The system will probably grade countries according to their creditworthiness, using a scoring or ranking system which in turn will be directly related to economic and political scores or rankings produced by the economists. An ability to compare risk is an essential property of any portfolio management system.

At the other end of the spectrum, a small bank with international exposure which is limited and principally consists of short-term trade finance will not require the same ability to assess medium to long-term risk or need as sophisticated a system of portfolio management for its international business. Such a bank may find it acceptable to rely on external analysis.

Thus the first choice which must be made is whether to use a system which ranks countries according to creditworthiness or to assess each credit on a stand-alone basis with no systemic reference to portfolio

478

considerations. In either case it is normal for economists to make a major contribution to country risk assessment, but as far as is practicable a wide variety of skills should be tapped within the bank. Line bankers with practical experience of a country, gained by frequent visits or an overseas tour of duty, should have an important contribution to make, particularly in the assessment of social and political factors. Whichever approach is chosen, two of the most important aims should be to reduce as far as possible the inevitable subjectivity which enters into economic and political risk assessment and to ensure comparability across countries. Each of these objectives is better achieved within a systemic approach rather than through stand-alone assessments, but neither is easy to reach. Subjectivity will never be completely eliminated, simply because individual judgment has to be used at various points in the process. Similarly, an economist or regional specialist may be able relatively easily to rank the creditworthiness of all countries within a continent or region, but it is more difficult to compare, for example, the relative creditworthiness of Colombia and Indonesia. The system should also be as forward looking as possible. The past is an invaluable guide and it is impossible to assess creditworthiness without a knowledge of recent economic and political trends and of a country's economic structure and how it evolved. But the statement, all too often heard, that country X has never failed to meet its commitments, is meaningless with respect to future creditworthiness.

The systemic approach to country risk analysis embraces a wide variety of actual and/or possible types of system, none of which is perfect. Several of the more common are outlined below, together with their main strengths and weaknesses.

A popular method is for a bank's economists to allocate each country a score, perhaps in a range of 1 – 5 or 1 – 10, with the scores signifying varying degrees of creditworthiness. A political risk score may also be used, with the score, to which line bankers may have input, signifying varying degrees of political risk. The two scores might then be consolidated into one composite score. These scores provide the framework for a range of subsequent decisions. For example, the bank may set a maximum country limit for each particular score or group of scores. It also has in place the framework to judge the acceptability of the rate of return on the business in question and may set minimum rates of return in relation to each score. Portfolio management is also facilitated by a scoring system.

If, for example, the scoring range is 1 – 5, with 1 signifying high quality risk and 5 poor risk, a bank may choose to have 50% of its portfolio in countries scoring 1, 25% in countries scoring 2 and so on.

The effectiveness of a scoring system similar to that outlined above ultimately rests on the quality of the economists' assessment of each country, a factor which is discussed in the next section.

A variant which partly circumscribes the reliance on the economists is the "check list" approach. With this, indicators of country risk are allocated points (usually totalling to 100) in line with their perceived significance. For example, economic factors may be given 70 points and political/social factors 30 points. Within the economic factors the 70 points could be allocated thus:

Balance of payments	10
Size of external debt	10
Growth in GNP	10
Inflation	10
Debt servicing burden	20
Structure of exports	10

And a similar allocation could be made for political factors to cover the remaining 30 points (see Section 7 below).

This approach is flexible, in that it allows each bank to decide for itself which are important factors. Moreover, it has the further advantage that it establishes a fixed framework within which the inevitable subjectivity of country risk can be exercised.

A weakness of the "check list" method is that the criteria are selected subjectively, i.e. the factors are those which appear likely to have an impact on the country's ability to service its external debt rather than those which have actually been shown to have an impact. An alternative used by some banks, therefore, is a statistically-based model, where a wide range of variables is considered and set against the external financial experience of a number of countries. Those variables which are proven to be statistically significant in examples of debt servicing difficulties can be identified, and used in a model to predict future difficulties in other countries. This is something akin to the "Z" scores used in corporate analysis to assess the risk of bankruptcy.

This can be a useful tool, but must be used carefully since it assumes that the relationships which existed during the period of empirical observation continue to hold true now and in the future. Many economies, particularly in the developing world and among those which were centrally planned economies, are going through a period of dramatic structural change which is likely to render valueless any system based on extrapolating historical relationships.

It is of course possible to develop a hybrid system of country risk, in which, say, the check list is backed up by a statistical model which acts as a fail-safe indicator, or where a qualitative report-orientated system is supported by a check list scoring system.

Irrespective of the type of system used, there is a range of economic and political factors which are important and these are addressed in the following sections.

6.   ECONOMIC FACTORS*

To recap, the objective of country risk assessment is to assess a country's ability to generate (or conserve) foreign exchange so that it will be able to service satisfactorily its external debt obligations.

The most sophisticated methodology for making this assessment, and one used commonly in major US international banks, is what is known as the Sources and Uses of Foreign Funds approach. Sources and Uses is an attempt to construct a forecast of foreign exchange cashflow. It estimates future outflows, including the balance of payments current account deficit, amortisation of foreign debt and any other relevant outflows. The total of such outflows, forecast year by year, will equate to the country's gross foreign financing needs. Sources of fulfilling these needs are then investigated and inflows are forecast. These sources will include direct investment, medium and long-term borrowing, short-term borrowing and drawdowns of foreign reserves. If the sum of likely available sources of funds is less than the forecast of uses of funds in any one year, the country is likely at this point to encounter debt servicing problems unless

---

* See end of chapter for definitions of GNP, balance of payments and current account.

481

economic policy measures are taken, for example to reduce the current account deficit.

However, many European banks and those without widespread international exposure will prefer to focus on a number of economic variables and ratios. None of these is, in its own right, a firm indicator of creditworthiness, but for most there are what might be termed "warning bell" levels, beyond which it is usually valid to regard creditworthiness as suspect. It is important, though, not simply to look at the latest year's figure for these indicators; a deterioration over time towards warning bell levels can say as much as a single reading above warning bell levels.

6.1 Debt Service Ratios

The most commonly used ratio is that of debt service. This measures the annual payment of principal and interest on the country's external debt expressed as a percentage of the equivalent year's exports of goods and services, in other words expressed as a percentage of the country's earned foreign income. It thus takes account of earnings from services such as tourism, but not of unrequited transfers such as foreign aid and workers' remittances, which are by nature unreliable and potentially volatile. In essence, it indicates that part of a country's foreign earnings which is already spoken for as a result of its existing debt. Normally, repayment of short-term debt is excluded from the calculation, although interest on this debt is included, since short-term debt is usually trade-related and easily rolled over.

Example: external debt maturing in the year = \$5,000m
interest payments on total external debt = \$3,600m
total annual earnings from exports of goods and services = \$26,875m

$$\text{Debt Service Ratio} = \frac{5,000 + 3,600}{26,875} = 32\%$$

Some years ago, a debt service ratio of 20% was regarded as the threshold between medium and high risk countries, but this standard has gradually been pushed up as debtor countries have improved their debt management techniques. A ratio of 30% is now regarded as the threshold, but as noted earlier, this is by no means a cast-iron guide to creditworthiness. Several countries have succeeded in meeting their

482

commitments over a period of up to five years during which the debt service ratio has been 50% or higher, while others have been forced to reschedule despite debt service ratios of only some 20%. The trend of the ratio is also important. A debt service ratio which has climbed from 15% to 28% over the last three years can be a more serious indicator of impending problems than one which has been stable at 35% for three years. A further factor to take into account is that when looking at historical ratios, a sharp drop in the ratio in a particular year may well indicate that a rescheduling took place in that year or towards the end of the previous year.

Debt Service Ratios

	1987	1988	1989	1990	1991
Argentina	74.3	44.2	36.2	39.4	48.1
Brazil	41.9	48.2	34.6	22.6	30.8
Mexico	40.1	48.0	37.9	27.8	30.9
Philippines	35.6	30.9	25.6	26.8	23.2
Algeria	53.7	78.7	71.8	68.4	68.4

All except Algeria have rescheduled foreign debt.

Source: World Bank

6.2 Total Debt Outstanding

Taken as a proportion of a major economic aggregate such as Gross National Product or total export earnings, these ratios provide simple, albeit crude, measures of a country's total debt burden relative to the whole economy.

Example: total external debt $= \$15,000m$
gross national product (GNP) $= \$31,000m$
total exports of goods and services $= \$19,400m$

$$\text{Debt/GNP Ratio} = \frac{15,000}{31,000} = 48\%$$

$$\text{Debt/Exports Ratio} = \frac{15,000}{19,400} = 77\%$$

Typical "warning bell" levels would be a debt/GNP ratio of 50% and/or a debt/export ratio of around 150%.

Gross External Debt (1991)

	as % GNP	*as % of exports*
Argentina	49.2	430.0
Brazil	28.8	333.7
Mexico	36.9	224.1
Philippines	70.2	215.6
Algeria	70.4	199.3

6.3 Debt Maturity Analysis
This is valuable in two ways:

(i)   In predicting year-by-year debt servicing pressures.

Once the maturity structure is known all that is required is an interest rate forecast and some estimate of new debt requirements, for debt servicing costs to be projected. Even if no interest rate prediction is available, valuable sensitivity analysis can be undertaken.

(ii)   Identification of that proportion of total external debt which is short term (i.e. maturity of less than one year) is a useful guide to a country's vulnerability to slumps in confidence in international capital markets. In recent years short-term debt has increased more rapidly because the banks themselves have been reluctant to commit medium-term funds in what has become a more risky environment.

Whatever the cause, the result has been increasing resort to short-term borrowing as a source of balance-of-payments finance and the consequent need for countries to roll over these debts regularly. Hence the susceptibility to reduced market confidence.

It is possible to get a feel for the amount of 'excess' short-term borrowing that has been undertaken by a country by using international bank lending statistics produced regularly by the Bank for International Settlements.

These figures allow a banker to identify the amount of a country's debt to international banks which both falls due within the next 12 months period and which had an original maturity of under one year.

Based on assumptions that such short-term finance ought to be trade related (primarily for imports) and that the usual maturity of these loans would not exceed 120 days it follows that the total of this short-term debt should not exceed the equivalent of four months' imports.

Example: short-term external debt with original
           maturity of less than 12 months   = \$3,000m
           total annual visible imports   = \$11,000m

           proportion of annual imports $= \dfrac{3,000}{11,000} = 27\%$
           financed by short term debt

                                              = 3.3 months'
                                                     imports

Number of months' imports financed by short-term debt

	1987	1988	1989	1990	1991
Argentina	12.2	12.0	13.4	13.9	9.8
Brazil	8.2	9.0	7.9	7.7	7.3
Mexico	7.4	5.3	5.1	6.1	7.2
Philippines	8.4	6.8	5.5	5.1	5.7
Algeria	7.1	7.1	6.9	8.0	9.5

6.4 Debt Type Analysis

In particular this concerns the terms relating to outstanding debt, particularly the interest rate structure and what proportion carries commercial interest rates. From this it is possible to gauge the sensitivity of a country's financing costs to any change in international rates of interest. In general, for poorer countries the proportion of debt on concessionary terms, i.e. long maturity, low and fixed interest rates, will be higher than that on commercial terms. The "softer" the debt structure, the lower will be the sensitivity to international interest rate movements.

6.5 Liquidity Indicators

Further to the debt service ratio as a measure of liquidity it is also helpful to relate a country's reserves to its financing needs. Often reserves are related directly to imports and expressed in terms of months (known as "import coverage"). Thus a country with reserves of $25bn and imports of $100bn would have cover for three months. This is a purely hypothetical indicator since no country is likely to run its reserves down to zero merely to finance imports; additionally, it fails to take account of currency earnings. Nevertheless, it is a useful guide to a country's ability to withstand short-term financial pressures.

On a similar basis, reserves can be related to a country's short-term financing requirements in a given period (i.e. any current account deficit plus maturing debt).

Again this could be expressed in months and gives a theoretical picture as to how long a country could be expected to honour its financial commitments if all external sources of new finance were to dry up completely.

Example:	external debt maturing in the year	= $5,000m
	current account deficit in the year	= $1,300m
	financing requirement	= $6,300m
	reserves	= $2,400m

$$\text{Reserves/financing requirement ratio} = \frac{2,400}{6,300} = 38\%$$

$$= 4.6 \text{ months' cover}$$

6.6 Balance of Payments Figures

The indicators of debt and liquidity outlined above are the result of a country's balance-of-payments performance in recent years.

It is arguably, therefore, not vital to analyse the raw balance-of-payments figures. However, should some indication of a country's overall external performance be required, it may be considered worthwhile relating the current account to either of the two major aggregates used earlier – GNP or total exports.

486

Example: current account balance   = –$1,300m
          GNP   = $31,000m
          exports of goods and services = $19,400m

$$\text{Current Account/GNP} = \frac{-1,300}{31,000} = -4.2\%$$

$$\text{Current Account/Exports} = \frac{-1,300}{19,400} = -6.7\%$$

Average current account balances (1987-91)

	As % of GNP	As % of total exports
Argentina	–1.9	–15.8
Brazil	0	– 1.1
Mexico	–1.9	–11.8
Philippines	–2.8	– 9.6
Algeria	0.8	0

6.7 Balance of Payments Structure

Although the payments figures alone may not add much to the overall assessment of country risk, some analysis of the underlying structure of inflows and outflows is vital – particularly in identifying vulnerabilities. Among the issues that should be addressed are:

6.7.1 *Exports Structure*

How dependent is the country on one commodity or a few commodites or primary products or exports? How volatile are the prices of these exports? To what extent are export prices determined externally? Are the country's exports directed to one or a few markets? Has the country any fundamental competitive advantage with any of its exports?

6.7.2 *Imports Structure*

How vital are the country's imports? To what extent can they be cut back without damaging the economic fabric of the country (often known as "import compressibility"). What capacity is there for import substitution – particularly, in recent years, in the energy sector?

487

6.7.3   *Other Current Account Inflows*

How stable are these? (Both tourism earnings and emigrants' remittances tend to fluctuate.)

6.8   **Other Economic Indicators**

6.8.1   *Gross National Product*

Absolute size per capita can be taken as an indicator of a country's ability to withstand financial shocks. Growth in GNP needs to exceed population growth if per capita income is to rise and thus help avoid social/political problems.

6.8.2   *Inflation/Budget Deficit*

These reflect a government's ability to manage an economy efficiently. (Moreover, excessive inflation may impact directly on a country's export competitiveness.) Rapid inflation will cast doubt on an administration's ability to effect any development plans which are in hand and also on its effectiveness in controlling inflows of capital.

6.8.3   *Infrastructure*

The degree of infrastructure development will contribute to a country's ability to respond quickly to new demands of adjustment. The existence of a sophisticated financial structure will facilitate the channelling of finance into productive capacity.

6.8.4   *Natural Resources*

The availability of a wealth of natural resources may provide comfort for long-term creditors, but care should be taken not to place too much emphasis on this aspect. A country's problems may be such that it cannot exploit such assets in the short term.

6.8.5   *Domestic Savings*

Savings of a high level will normally allow a greater proportion of capital investment to be financed internally, thus reducing the need for external borrowing.

The above list of economic factors is by no means exhaustive. Each bank should decide for itself which are the most relevant for its own purposes.

7. POLITICAL FACTORS

The assessment of economic risk factors involves some subjectivity, but there are numerous statistics on which judgments can be made. This is not the case for political factors. Because of this, it is vital to keep in mind precisely what risks are to be addressed and ensure that they are addressed in as structured a way as possible. The banker is primarily concerned with the risk that a country will be unable to service its external debt satisfactorily. Therefore a political assessment will address the political factors which may contribute to an inability to service foreign debt satisfactorily. In this context, the principal political risks are:

- internal unrest (ranging from industrial strife to civil war)

- external conflict

- imposition of economic sanctions

The first two risks are the most easily assessable and relate, in essence, to the country's stability. When assessing such risk, however, it is important to eliminate as far as possible the intrusion of personal prejudice regarding the political nature of a country's government. This can be achieved by using a questionnaire approach and preferably involving all country experts in the bank.

There is no ideal political risk questionnaire and individual banks will need not only to choose questions but also choose the weights attached to each question. There may need to be scope for flexibility. For example, the vast majority of countries are not seriously at risk of becoming involved in external conflict. Questions thereon should therefore carry a low weight. But there are several countries, e.g. in the Middle East, where the risk of external conflict may be regarded as the most important single factor and allowance needs to be made for this.

A good questionnaire will be one which addresses the factors which contribute to political stability and also allows for a more general appreciation of the country's track record of political stability. Relevant factors may include:

489

Internal Stability

- pressures arising from unequal income distribution

- presence of significant minorities (racial, religious, etc.)

- perceived fairness of legal and fiscal systems

- stage of development of the country's political institutions

- availability of legal channels for expressing opposition

External Stability

- strategic importance of the country, either because of its geographical location or because it possesses important raw materials

- membership of a regional grouping which might deter external aggression

- treaties with other countries and presence of mutual defence provisions

The difficulty of evaluating the risk of economic sanctions precludes it from formal inclusion in a questionnaire and highlights the principal problem of political risk assessment, namely the "unknown" factor. Over the last 15 years there have been several events which not only were unforeseeable even by academic experts, but led to serious economic consequences for their perpetrators and allies:

- The then USSR's invasion of Afghanistan in 1979, followed by the imposition of economic sanctions against Eastern Europe

- Iraq's invasion of Kuwait in 1990, the subsequent imposition of economic sanctions against Iraq and the damage this has done to Jordan's economy

- The crushing of pro-democracy demonstrations in China in 1989, causing a temporary fall in confidence among creditors

It is not possible, therefore, to assess political risk as comprehensively as economic risk. All that can reasonably be attempted is to assess a range of institutional and structural factors as objectively as possible, while remembering that the vital perspective is that of the individual in the country being assessed. The analyst must view issues such as unequal

490

wealth distribution, the fairness of the fiscal system and so on, as far as possible through the eyes of those who are affected directly.

8. SOURCES OF INFORMATION

The basic sources of financial data are readily available, and are not excessively expensive, e.g.:

8.1 International Monetary Fund
- *International Financial Statistics*
- *Balance of Payments Yearbook*
- *Direction of Trade*

8.2 World Bank
- *World Debt Tables*
- *World Development Report*

8.3 Bank for International Settlements
- *International Bank Lending Statistics*
- *Statistics on External Indebtedness*

8.4 OECD
- *External Debt Statistics*

In addition, information can usually be acquired from the individual countries and from financial institutions. Also, many banks in the industrialised world are members of the Institute of International Finance, based in Washington DC. The Institute offers an economic data base on a range of developing countries to which international bank exposure is significant.

There are several country risk analysis services which are available, at a price, but these tend to be aimed more at the non-financial sector and refer more to the risks of direct investment overseas.

The financial press provides another valuable source, and both *Euromoney* and the *Institutional Investor* provide country risk rankings on a regular basis which may be helpful.

491

9. PROCEDURES OF RESCHEDULING SOVEREIGN DEBT

Since 1979 there have been almost 200 rescheduling agreements between over 40 countries and their creditor banks. The amounts involved (in some cases debt has been rescheduled several times) total approximately $875bn. No two reschedulings are ever precisely the same, although certain common factors occur. Each case tends to be looked at on its own merits in order to take account of individual problems. To take an obvious example, oil price fluctuations will have a dramatically different impact on an oil exporting country such as Nigeria or Venezuela than on an oil importing country such as Brazil. However, it has also been the case that an apparent concession negotiated by one country tends to find its way into the rescheduling agreement of the next country to negotiate an agreement; US banks in particular have attached great importance in negotiations to this concept of precedent.

The Mexican request for a moratorium on principal repayments was to become typical of the first step of the rescheduling process, as was the convening of a group of Mexico's major bank creditors to form what is termed an Advisory or Steering Committee. The Committees usually consist of representatives of between 10 and 16 banks with one or more banks acting as chairman. It is desirable to get a geographical spread of creditors to facilitate the contact with all creditor banks worldwide which will become necessary as negotiations proceed. Nonetheless, major US banks hold at least half the places on many Latin American Committees by virtue of their particularly heavy exposure. Elsewhere the position is different, with European banks more strongly represented – the higher proportion of UK and French exposure is reflected in the composition of the Committees for African countries.

Advisory Committees often form sub-committees in order to discuss recommendations for specific subjects (e.g. trade, interbank and private sector facilities) within the overall rescheduling package. The most frequently used sub-committee is an Economic Sub-Committee which may visit the country concerned to collect data first hand and which will also examine the economic information provided by the rescheduling country, the IMF and the World Bank.

The Advisory Committee does not enjoy any formal authority and cannot negotiate arrangements binding on other creditors. It facilitates

492

however the negotiation process by being a body broad enough to be representative of the creditor banks but small enough to be able to sit around a table with representatives of the sovereign debtor in order to formulate proposals. When the terms for the rescheduling have been agreed between the Committee and the debtor (relating to such subjects as interest rates, repayment, grace periods and conditions precedent) they are summarised in what is called a "term sheet" which is despatched to all creditors. Normally Committee banks are then responsible for dealing with queries from banks within their geographical area whilst countries not represented nationally on the Committee are directed to specific Committee banks as a contact point to answer their questions.

One of the first tasks of the Committee will be to identify which debts to restructure, given that the country's debt can encompass tens, if not hundreds, of individual public and private sector borrowers and just as many creditors. The loans may be governed by credit agreements which will vary considerably in their complexity from one paragraph to hundreds of pages. Interest rates, margins and maturities may all be different. The collection of data is difficult. Information from the sovereign debtor may be used, often supplemented by a reconciliation exercise which may involve independent accounting firms. In order to produce consistent and accurate information regarding the amount of debt to be restructured, a "base date" is decided as a cut-off point. This date may also be relevant in deciding New Money contributions as described below.

Categories of debt will be considered and selected for inclusion or exclusion in the rescheduling under definitions of "Affected" and "Non-affected" or "Excluded" and "Included" debt. The most common items for inclusion will be external debt obligations in respect of medium and long term public sector maturities.

Exclusions typically cover such categories as short-term trade debt, leases, bonds and foreign exchange contracts, although trade debt may be rescheduled on a unilateral basis as happened in Nigeria. The maintenance of short term trade and, to a lesser extent, interbank facilities was often a feature of early rescheduling agreements – e.g. Brazil and Argentina. Sometimes private sector maturities are included or separate arrangements may be made, linked to the public sector arrangements. Forfaiting bills have been included in some instances – e.g. Peru and Yugoslavia.

493

10. PARTIES INVOLVED

10.1 Debtors

We now turn to consideration of the parties involved in a typical rescheduling. In the most simple and obvious instance there is only one debtor, the sovereign entity in whose name debts were incurred and in whose name they are to be restructured. However, it is important to ascertain whether the State can/must borrow in its own name (e.g. the Republic of Liberia in December 1982 and the Republic of Peru in the 1983 Restructuring Agreement) or whether the borrowing powers have been delegated to the government through the Ministry of Finance, central bank or other State entity – e.g. Banco Central de Costa Rica and Banco Central del Ecuador. Where the borrowing is direct the central bank may nonetheless give an undertaking to make available foreign exchange (as happened in the 1984 Polish rescheduling) as part of the security offered to creditors. The sovereign borrower's debts will include debts it guarantees, besides wholly-owned government entities and ministries such as health and public works which may borrow in their own name but which will usually be part of the State's obligation. Commercial banks owned by the State and corporations under at least 51% ownership and State control may be involved. Public sector obligors may sign rescheduling agreements concurrently with the State and on similar terms. The rescheduled debt may still be an obligation of the public sector obligor bearing the State guarantee (e.g. Mexico's 1985 agreements which restructured the debt of 35 Public Sector Obligors) or the maturing debt may be taken over as an obligation of the sovereign entity (e.g. Brazil's 1984 Agreement). In this instance the original obligor discharges his debt by the payment of local currency into a deposit account at the central bank in the name of the foreign creditor. The debt is then assumed by the State for eventual repayment in the relevant foreign currency.

10.2 Creditors

The creditors will encompass all international banks having outstanding relevant debt. There will be a vigorous effort by the debtor(s) and the Advisory Committee to persuade the banking community to agree the negotiated package. Presentations and the opportunity to ask questions may be afforded by the use of "roadshows" held in major financial centres where all principal parties evidence their support for the package. Often the central bank of the host country will be present for similar reasons.

494

Acceptance of the package by all affected creditors is of course the aim although a figure rather less than 100% has become increasingly the norm. This prevents one or two banks holding up the effectiveness of an agreement to the detriment of the general good, whereby a structured agreement replaces the disorder which was probably apparent or would become evident if the debtor(s) went into default. The concept of the necessary majority, of which 90% is likely to be the minimum acceptable to the success of the arrangements, may be referred to as the "critical mass". Dissenters have to recognise that they are not going to receive preferential treatment if they hold out against the agreement, and thus some eventually join in the signing.

Most developing countries are not only indebted to commercial banks; they also borrow money from various multilateral agencies, international or multilateral development banks, central banks, export credit agencies and others. Thus the agencies will become involved in the negotiation process when a country encounters repayment difficulties, and we shall next consider the two main supranational agencies, the International Monetary Fund and the World Bank.

10.3 International Monetary Fund

The International Monetary Fund (IMF) was founded in 1945 and now has more than 150 governments as members. Its resources come chiefly from quotas subscribed by members, and these have been increased over the years in order to keep the resources in line with likely commitments.

According to the Articles of Association of the IMF, its main purposes include assisting countries with balance of payments problems and working for an orderly international monetary system. A large part of the IMF's role is, therefore, the promotion of policies aimed at avoiding debt problems through its regular, usually annual, consultations with its members. These include an exchange of views on the country's financial position and its policies followed by discussion of measures which may be necessary to correct imbalances. A precondition of restructuring is normally that the country involved is a member of the IMF.

In response to the need for financing by developing countries of structural balance of payment deficits in the 1970s, the IMF offered a variety of instruments, the most common of which were:

495

1.   the short term Standby Facility

2.   the Extended Fund Facility which provides multi-year programmes in the form of three year credits repayable over 8 to 10 years and

3.   the Compensatory Financing Facility which provides some compensation for developing countries should they suffer a sharp fall in earnings from their main commodity exports.

At the end of 1991, 51 countries had arrangements with the Fund totalling Special Drawing Rights (SDR) 20.8bn. Apart from the amounts lent directly, the IMF has played a very important role as a catalyst in the rescheduling process. Prior to rescheduling, creditor banks normally insist on an IMF arrangement which will involve the IMF making funds available to the country subject to certain structural adjustments intended to rectify some of the economic problems. Targets will be set and must be met before drawdowns are permitted. The first stage of the agreement is a Letter of Intent which details, *inter alia*, the agreed economic adjustments. The managing director of the Fund then recommends the agreed programme to the IMF Board, subject usually to confirmation that a critical mass of commercial banks has committed to the relevant financial package in order to have some degree of certainty that the necessary monies will be available to fund the full programme. It is invariably an Event of Default under the commercial loan agreements if a country fails to meet IMF targets.

10.4   World Bank

The World Bank was created in 1945. Its primary role is to serve as a financial bridge, channelling capital from the industrial countries toward investment that promotes growth in the poor, mainly agricultural, African, Latin American and Asian countries. It consists of two separate institutions – the International Bank for Reconstruction and Development and the International Development Association. There are three main forms of loan:

• project loans

• structural adjustment loans

• sector adjustment loans

The World Bank's role has been inhibited by its restricted capital base and its original focus on project lending. The Bank has two kinds of subscribed capital, paid-in and callable. Paid-in capital has amounted to $4.1bn in the 40 years since it was established whilst the callable capital, which can be viewed as a contingent liability for the country subscribers, now totals some $70.8bn. To help it play a larger role the Bank evolved new mechanisms of which structural adjustment lending was introduced in 1979/80 to provide quick disbursing finance to support policy changes aimed at improving countries' balance of payments by macro-economic reforms.

10.5 Paris Club
The Paris Club is the informal forum in which the governments of debtor and creditor countries have renegotiated the terms of intra-government debt since 1956 when it dealt with the problems Argentina had to face after the fall of Peron. The Paris Club has no fixed members and is not an institution in the same way as the IMF and the World Bank are. The first step of the rescheduling process is for the debtor country to make a written request which will encompass postponement of payments on debts falling due and will outline its economic situation. The subsequent meeting will be attended by the debtor country, creditor countries, the IMF (as observer) and UNCTAD (United Nations Conference on Trade and Development) together with French Treasury officials.

The rescheduling is normally tied to an IMF programme and the rescheduling terms are set out in an Agreed Minute which constitutes the guidelines for the subsequent detailed bilateral agreements. These are intended to give common treatment to each country which is owed money by the rescheduling country and which has been part of the Paris Club discussions. Interest rates are at commercial rates with precise determination done on a bilateral basis. It is usually stated that debt owed to commercial banks must not be renegotiated on more favourable terms than is in the Minutes, with the intention of preserving comparable treatment of creditor groups. Traditionally principal only of currently maturing or recently matured debt on medium term loans up to 85% was rescheduled. Recently more generous terms have become common, with interest frequently included. For the poorest countries the terms offered to Sudan in 1983 would no longer be regarded as exceptional – 100% rescheduling over 16 years with six years' grace. Previously the Paris Club sought to restrict rescheduling to one year only and to avoid rescheduling of previously rescheduled debt. However, increasing flexibility is necessarily becoming more evident. There have been instances of 18 or 24 month consolidation periods, as well as conditional further reschedulings or goodwill clauses making a vague commitment to future rescheduling.

11. DOCUMENTATION

When rescheduling is agreed between the debtor and the Committee the proposals are put to all the creditor banks. The package will usually contain copies of endorsements from the IMF and World Bank as well as the formal request from the debtor and the Committee's own expression of support. There are often problems of recalcitrant banks which do not want to continue to support or to increase their exposure. Pressure is brought to bear where possible on these banks by the Advisory Committee and official bodies such as central banks, whilst the debtor nation itself will endeavour directly to rally support. An initial commitment will usually be requested by telex and, in order to speed up the process, "early bird fees" (0.375% flat) have been used by Argentina and Brazil to induce banks to respond within a short time scale. This "in principle" commitment is given pending execution of satisfactory documentation.

Many of the clauses in the documentation bear a similarity to the standard Eurocurrency syndicated loan agreement – e.g. those relating to reference rates, funding, increased costs, etc. – but some need to be tailor-made for each individual rescheduling.

One protection creditor banks will seek is that of parity of treatment for different categories of comparable indebtedness. This can be achieved by a covenant of the debtor within the restructuring agreement not to repay comparable indebtedness without the consent of the bank creditors. Another means used to reach the same end is by the incorporation of mandatory prepayment provisions within the documentation. A clause will require a pro rata reduction in the exposure of the bank creditors should there be a reduction in the exposure of third party creditors, provided the defined Majority Banks (often 2/3 by amount) so request and the third party payment was made without their consent.

The documentation usually contains a representation by the borrower that the restructured debt ranks at least *pari passu* with the borrower's other external debt. This restricts the borrower from subordinating the restructured debt in favour of third party obligations. Additionally the agreement usually contains a negative pledge provision to the effect that the borrower will not secure any other borrowing without the express consent of the creditor banks. Exceptions such as liens on specific assets, ships, drilling rigs, real estate, short term trade finance and project related loans which capture specific revenue may be made.

A cross default clause will undoubtedly be included which gives the banks the right to accelerate their debt if another loan agreement is in default. Since the cross default may be a double-edged weapon, i.e. if a small item causes many agreements to be in default by the linking of cross default clauses, this right may be restricted to a default of a minimum specific amount.

The agreement must contain provisions explaining the relationship between the creditor banks and the agent bank and generally the agent will be required to perform, in a reasonable manner, only those duties specifically delegated. Responsibility in the event of non-performance will be restricted to that arising from gross negligence or fraud. Difficulties were experienced in agent relationships during the 1981 Iran/US hostage dispute when US agent banks acted politically to protect their own interests. As a result the agent is now commonly required to seek specific authority from Majority Banks before instigating any significant action on behalf of the creditor banks.

Banks will wish to see a broad assignment clause particularly since the expansion of asset swapping (see below). It is normal for notification of assignment to be required to agent and borrower and often the borrower must give approval prior to the transaction taking place. Permission should not be withheld unreasonably and lapse of a reasonable period of time without objection (say two weeks) may constitute approval in the absence of a specific reply being received. On the other hand, the borrower will have no rights of assignment of its rights or obligations.

Choice of governing law is commonly that of the US which is not surprising since the loan currency is most often US dollars. Alternatives have been used – e.g. English law in the Polish rescheduling agreements and French law in the Ivory Coast. A choice of jurisdiction is normal to allow the banks to bring disputes before courts where they hope that any judgment received will be capable of execution.

Sovereign immunity is a well-established principle in international law providing that a State cannot be sued in the courts of another State without its consent. The sovereign debtor will, therefore, undoubtedly be required to waive any immunity which it or its assets might enjoy. However, the US Foreign Sovereign Immunities Act of 1976 and the UK State Immunity Act of 1978 endeavoured to restrict immunity where the underlying transaction was a commercial act. The loan documentation usually, therefore, includes the statement that these are private and commercial acts, not governmental or public acts.

The US dollar was the most usual original currency in lending to sovereign debtors. However, as lenders now become locked-in for ever longer periods, there is an increasing trend for other currency options to be available, either for the full amount or a specified percentage of each bank's contribution. The option may be exercised as a once and for all choice by the lender at the first availability date or, occasionally, at any time during the tenor of the loan provided a specified period of notice is given. This can be advantageous not only by giving latitude to lenders regarding funding in their preferred currency but also in helping some borrowers by not 'having all their eggs in one basket'. Some borrowers, however, have a hard currency income stream heavily biased to one currency and thus may be more susceptible to exchange rate fluctuations in servicing the debt.

12. TYPES OF AGREEMENT AND MECHANISMS

12.1 Rescheduling

The chief assistance to countries with payment difficulties has been that of rescheduling or refinancing – revising the original agreement(s) to allow more time to repay either all principal amounts falling due in a given period (e.g. Chile 1983/84, Uruguay 1985/89) or a percentage only (e.g. the Ivory coast 1986/89 Agreement rescheduled 80% of principal due in 1986, decreasing annually to 50% of principal due in 1989, with the remainder of the debt repayments to be met on their due dates). The revised agreement will specify in detail the new terms including fees, if any, payable upon the restructuring, interest rates, etc. In the first

500

reschedulings the trend was for the revised interest rates to be higher than the original rates, which reflected the risk involved and amounted to a form of 'punishment' for non-adherence to the agreed terms. In more recent times the view has prevailed that it is futile expecting countries which already cannot meet their obligations to be saddled with higher interest margins. The trend on margins has therefore moved downwards. Fees have usually been reduced and sometimes eliminated entirely.

12.2 Multi-Year Rescheduling Agreements

In 1982 the norm was to consider refinancing of the debt for one year only. This was partially because the problem was viewed as a short term liquidity crisis and partially because it imposed discipline on the debtor to make rapid adjustments. However, as one agreement followed another with the ink barely dry on one round of rescheduling before the next got under way, it has become more frequent to find a Multi-Year Rescheduling Agreement (MYRA) under discussion, which was one of the main policy recommendations of the 1984 Western economic summit meeting in London.

A MYRA involves the rescheduling of a number of years' maturities over a longer term, often incorporating a significant grace period. One of the features will be to ensure that covenants, events of default and other clauses link into arrangements with other creditors to build in as much protection as possible. Common requirements for example will be declarations that there must be an ongoing IMF programme and annual certifications from the IBRD that their loans are not in default. The MYRA was intended to give the debtor more certainty to plan for the medium rather than short term and to smooth out a repayment profile which may have had some enormous humps.

12.3 New Money

A request for a 'New Money' facility was common in rescheduling negotiations, designed to adjust balance of payments deficits and to prevent arrears building up in the debtor's financial obligations. The funds were made available, on occasions, for the purpose of financing certain defined development projects in a country. The largest single New Money loan to date was that for Mexico in March 1987 amounting to US$7.7bn and involving banks being asked to contribute 12.9% of their base date exposure to the country. However, some of this was available only if oil

501

prices fell below US$9 per barrel and, in the event, remained undrawn. Smaller loans can nonetheless result in larger individual percentage contributions being required – e.g. banks put up 15% of their exposure to raise a $240m New Money loan for Uruguay in 1983.

Over recent years, banks have become more resistant to New Money requests and the mechanism has now largely fallen away. New Money was also used in the early years of rescheduling as a means of equalising the contributions of the banks and governments. The latter were – and remain – prepared to reschedule interest as well as principal, a concept which was anathema to the banks, and so a New Money call was a means by which banks could contribute without being required to reschedule interest.

12.4 Securitisation/Long Term Instruments

On a modest scale, certain Latin American banks, particularly those in Mexico and Brazil, have sought to convert short term interbank lines into longer term instruments such as Floating Rate Notes, Commercial Paper and Certificates of Deposit. Both debtor and creditor can gain. The insecurity which results from having access only to short term lines is removed from the debtor who gains the greater certainty of longer term funding. Creditor banks earn essentially the same all-in return as on interbank lines and replace the lines with securities which could eventually be traded off their books if an active market develops. Both debtor and creditor avoid time-consuming repeated re-negotiations of rollovers.

Rescheduling proposals often contain options for banks which have become commonly known as a "menu". These may include exit bonds primarily intended for smaller banks, under which they receive a fixed rate of interest (Argentina 4% in 1987, Brazil 6% in 1988) but also with fixed repayments and the assurance that they will not be asked to put up further New Money. Thus far, exit bonds have not been very successful in view of the unattractive interest rates and the fact that free riders can, in any event at present, continue to receive interest in full whether or not they subscribe to New Money.

More innovatively in early 1988, J P Morgan arranged for Mexico an issue of collateralised 2008 bonds in registered form maturing 20 years after the date of issuance and bearing interest, payable semi-annually in arrears, at a floating rate equal to LIBOR + 1.625% per annum. The payment of the principal of the bonds at maturity is secured by the pledge of zero coupon US Treasury Bonds having a face amount equal at maturity to the bond. The bonds were also excluded from future New Money requests. Banks were invited to tender existing Mexican debt at a discount to face value and Mexico indicated it was prepared to use reserves in purchase of the zero coupon although in the event response was lukewarm and US$3.7bn of existing debt was surrendered in exchange for US$2.6bn of bonds at an average discount of approximately 30%.

12.5 Secondary Market

The question of discounts leads us on to the very nature of the secondary market where Third World debt is traded by banks on their own account and by brokers. Some traders publish a regular list of current prices although it is still difficult to estimate the size of, and volume in, the market.

Like any other market, asset swapping seeks to find buyers for a product someone else wants to sell, at a price. Quite dramatic price alterations can occur as perceptions of the creditworthiness of sovereign debtors change, or they afford greater or lesser opportunities for profitable investment. In autumn 1985 Mexico was quoted as 80 cents in the dollar. One year on, with a dramatic crash in oil revenues and protracted discussions in progress on further assistance from creditors, the price stood nearer 55. In the same period Peru fell from 33 to 20 cents on the dollar as its relationships with its commercial creditors deteriorated.

Price of debt expressed as on the US$1

Country	July 1986	May 1989	January 1993*
Argentina	66	13	43-55
Brazil	76	33	30-76
Colombia	83	56	N/A
Chile	67	60	91
Ecuador	65	12	28-30
Mexico	56	40	66-89
Poland	45	39	26
Venezuela	75	36	51-66
Yugoslavia	80	46	N/A

* a price range indicates more than one instrument is traded

What is the attraction and purpose of the secondary market? It enables portfolio adjustments to be made by creditors, be they for tax reasons, to change their private/public sector debt balance or simply to reduce their exposure. It encourages investment by means of the discounted debt as described below and some debtors use the market to retire debt. Some Latin American banks have done swaps to exchange another nation's debt for its own so that the debt is in effect "nationalised" and it no longer represents a drain on foreign exchange.

12.6   Debt/Equity Swaps

Of increasing importance and linking to the discounts applicable in the secondary market have been debt/equity swaps. Conversion of developing countries' debt into equity is a recent and generally welcome development as a means of reducing external debt and attracting investment by both foreigners and residents' assets previously held abroad. Debt/equity swaps involve the debtor country's foreign currency obligations being acquired at a discount abroad, then being exchanged at face value or at a small discount into local currency by the debtor.

For example, a multinational corporation (MNC) asks a broker to structure a complex financing transaction in order to benefit from the conversion scheme of a less developed debtor country (LDC) when expanding the production capacity of its subsidiary in the LDC.

The broker makes a financing proposal detailing procedures and effective cost in hard currency. He offers to carry out the transaction for a fee of 2.5% of assets to be converted. (Under the LDC's debt conversion scheme, only 70% of total project cost may be financed through debt conversion; 30% has to be met by new hard currency inflows.)

The broker (or the MNC itself) submits documentation on investment in the project to the authority supervising foreign direct investment and to the central bank of the LDC for approval.

After their approval the broker approaches a bank holding assets of the LDC eligible for conversion. He acquires the assets for, say, 30% of their face value and offers them to the LDC's central bank for repurchase in the national currency of LDC at a discount of, say, 45%. (Since repurchase

504

is made at a periodic auction the broker incurs the risk that the discount offered might be outbid by other potential investors so that he would hold the LDC asset for an undetermined time during which secondary market prices could drop substantially. He thus might prefer to lease the needed assets and to undertake an outright buy only after his conversion offer has been accepted.)

The central bank converts the foreign-currency-denominated debt at, say, 55% of face value into national currency which is transferred to an account of the broker or directly to the MNC. The MNC has realised a discount of 41% on the part of the investment eligible for debt conversion financing (see MNC discount below) and it has lowered its total project cost in hard currency by nearly 29% (see Project cost in hard currency below).

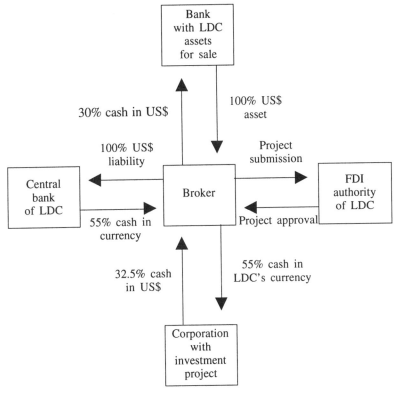

Source: Swiss Bank Corporation/Prospects 1/1989

Investment size is eq. $100m of which eq. US$30m therefore required from new hard currency and eq. US$70m from converted assets (requires purchase of US$127.27m – 55% is to be paid in local currency equivalent).

1. *MNC discount*

    (a) Cost of US$127.27m at 32.5% = US$41.36m (30% for LDC assets + 2.5% broker's fee).

    (b) Investor receives eq. US$70m in local currency. Therefore, saving equals 41%.

2. *Project cost in hard currency*

New hard currency	US$30m
US$127.27m at 32.5%	US$41.36m
	US$71.36m
Investment	US$100m

    Therefore, discount = 29%

This can be advantageous to debtor and investor alike. The debtor retires some of its foreign currency debt and removes the cost of servicing such debt, whilst potential investors acquire local currency more cheaply than would otherwise be the case. Investment can produce a beneficial inflow of technical and organisational knowledge. It can raise the proportion of private enterprise outside the governmental control and improve the prospects for increasing exports.

The debtor country obviously has to be prepared to welcome such foreign investment which has not always been the case. Some countries perceived it as an encroachment on their national sovereignty and there are also concerns that the printing of local currency in exchange for hard currency debt has an inflationary impact domestically, a concern held strongly by the IMF. Nonetheless, many countries have now put programmes in place, including Argentina, Philippines, Mexico, Brazil and Chile.

Debt/equity schemes may inhibit remittance of dividends or repatriation of the new capital for a specified number of years. Likewise, applications to invest in certain sectors with export potential or large industrial projects

506

may be given more favourable treatment or may be more quickly approved.

Additional variations on this theme have emerged, including debt-for-trade swaps and even debt-for-nature swaps. The former are of critical importance to a country such as Peru which, in adopting a desperate programme of curtailing interest payments on its debt, has led to the country's trading partners putting its international business on a cash basis. Conservation organisations are using the debt-for-nature route to finance nature conservation schemes. The World Wide Fund for Nature instigated a scheme in Ecuador at the end of 1987 and Costa Rica had swapped US$5.4m worth of debt for conservation projects by the beginning of 1988.

12.7 The Baker Plan

Proposed solutions to the debt problem are as old as the problem itself. However, in autumn 1985 the debt problem was undoubtedly entering a new phase since the original expectation of a short term liquidity crisis had become potentially a solvency crisis, bringing with it the risk that "debt fatigue" would set in and that the position could deteriorate as both debtors and creditors tired in the search for a solution. A response came from the then US Treasury Secretary James Baker who presented a proposal at the October 1985 IMF/World Bank annual meeting which called for growth orientated adjustment policies, backed by a fresh injection of external finance, to be adopted on a case by case basis by the main debtors. This proposal came to be known as the "Baker Initiative" or "Baker Plan" and a list of 15 potential beneficiaries was identified – Argentina, Bolivia, Brazil, Chile, Colombia, Ecuador, Ivory Coast, Mexico, Morocco, Nigeria, Peru, Philippines, Uruguay, Venezuela and Yugoslavia. Problems were quick to surface. The plan's very informality meant that roles were not clearly defined and there was no real leadership to move it forward quickly. As a US initiative it did not perhaps emphasise enough the full worldwide commitment needed, particularly from those countries achieving vast trade surpluses – Japan and West Germany. Furthermore, it depended upon higher growth rates in the OECD and indebted countries than were actually achieved whilst, within a few months of the IMF/World Bank meeting, the oil price crashed from over 20 dollars to below 10 dollars per barrel throwing many previous predictions into disarray. Thus, whilst we did see further rescheduling packages agreed for Mexico,

Philippines, Argentina, Nigeria and Brazil the so called Baker Plan never took off in the form and to the extent originally envisaged.

12.8 The Brady Plan

Not surprisingly, the debt overhang remained and few developing countries were in a better position in the late 1980s than they were at the time of inception of the debt crisis. Increasingly debtor countries were reacting to the writing down of debts by provisioning in commercial banks' books and in secondary market prices by contending that the lower value is all they could be expected to repay. Ruling out debt forgiveness, which remains anathema to the majority of commercial bank lenders, leaves voluntary participation in debt reduction by banks as the only way to cut down the crippling burden of debt.

Thus, in March 1989, the new US Treasury Secretary, Nicholas Brady, outlined further proposals intended to relieve third world debt problems. Brady's essential premises were that:

(i)   Growth is essential to the resolution of sovereign debt problems.

(ii)   Debtor nations will not achieve sufficient levels of growth without reform.

(iii)   Debtor nations have a continuing need for external resources.

(iv)   Solutions must be undertaken on a case by case basis.

The original plan envisaged that debtor nations would have to adopt policies to encourage new investment flows, strengthen domestic savings and promote the return of flight capital. Specific policy measures in these areas would be part of IMF and World Bank programmes. Meanwhile creditors would have to provide a broader range of financial support. It was suggested banks should negotiate waivers to sharing and negative pledge clauses to permit individual negotiation of debt or debt service reductions. New financing will continue to be required but differentiation should be made between old and new debt. The IMF and World Bank should provide new additional finance to collateralise a portion of interest payments for debt or debt service reduction transactions. Creditor governments in a position to do so should provide fresh funds.

508

The first Brady initiative agreement was reached in February 1990 by, almost inevitably, Mexico. Further agreements have followed, with Venezuela, Uruguay and Nigeria. The Mexican agreement gave bank creditors three options:

- Exchange of eligible debt for 30 year debt reduction bonds at a 35% discount from face value, with principal collateralised by zero-coupon bonds and interest guaranteed for 18 months.

- Exchange of eligible debt for 6.25% interest reduction bonds; guarantees and collateralisation as for debt reduction bonds.

- Exchange of eligible debt for 15 year bonds and provision of new money.

As in the case of conventional rescheduling agreements, no two Brady deals are precisely the same and new options are evolving, including that of a debt buy back by the debtor; the Nigerian agreement of December 1991 included a buy back option at 40% of face value.

The main purposes of the Brady initiative are not only to achieve a positive economic outcome for the debtor country in terms of growth and development, but also to restore the country's creditworthiness. The latter would be signified by the country being able to raise medium-term funds commercially with no compulsion on creditors, i.e. the so-called "return to voluntary financing". Mexico and Venezuela have now achieved this status, both countries having successfully issued international bonds.

CHAPTER 13

Disintermediation, Deregulation, Securitisation and Globalisation of Bond Markets

by
Sarah Scarlett; revised by team from CS First Boston

1. INTRODUCTION

The financial services industry worldwide is going through a period of unprecedented change prompted by domestic and international political and economic influences.

Financial markets are becoming increasingly global in nature, as individual capital markets become more accessible, investors become more international in outlook, and innovation and hedging techniques in the capital markets allow borrowers to create complex financing packages. The increasing sophistication of communication and computer technology has facilitated the process.

Three particular trends are evident in the progression towards a global market place: deregulation, disintermediation and securitisation.

1.1 Deregulation

Significant liberalisation of domestic banking and capital markets regulations has occurred, opening hitherto closed markets to an increasing range of borrowers and offering an expanding variety of instruments.

1.2 Disintermediation

As borrowers move to funding themselves in the capital markets in preference to directly from their traditional banks, banks are finding their intermediary role reduced and need to develop new areas of activity.

1.3 Securitisation

Securities markets have grown as interest rates and currencies have become more volatile. Investors are seeking protection through investment in marketable securities, while borrowers make increasing use of arbitrage opportunities among the various capital markets. The banks themselves, affected by the loss of traditional quality assets, are also investing more heavily in marketable securities.

2. GLOBAL MARKETS

The development of global capital markets can be seen in the following:

2.1 Trading

Advances in computer and communications technology have dramatically changed the trading environment. Communications systems provide banks, brokers and money managers with instant access to market information from around the world. Debt securities such as Eurobonds and US Treasuries are now traded on a 24 hour a day basis as trading books are passed from London to New York, thence to Tokyo or Singapore and back to London. Many equities are also traded on more than one exchange, and electronic links between futures and options exchanges have been, or are being, established, for example between the Chicago Mercantile Exchange and the Singapore International Monetary Exchange, and between the London International Financial Futures Exchange and the Chicago Board of Trade.

2.2 Capital Markets

Although restrictions still exist in some markets on size, credit quality, maturity or timing, issuers can now borrow with relative freedom in most major capital markets and in most major currencies. The innovative ability of the Eurobond market, in particular, provides borrowers with a range of instruments that can, in many cases, be specifically tailored to their needs. Of particular importance have been the liberalisation of the

512

Euro Deutsche mark market, the Euroyen market and the Swiss franc foreign bond market.

2.3 Hedging Techniques

The explosive growth in the second half of the 1980s of the interest rate and currency swaps, futures and options markets allows issuers to take advantage of arbitrage opportunities between capital markets to achieve the funding cost and currency closest to their needs. Financial packages and hybrid securities are increasingly being developed to optimise the borrower's risk-adjusted cost of funds, incorporating options, futures, interest rate caps and other hedging devices. The use of swaps has changed the underlying cyclicality and rhythm of the capital markets, as swap induced management of assets and liabilities triggers new issue volume that is independent of borrowers' net financing needs. The increasing number of issues in currencies such as the Yen, Australian and New Zealand dollars, ECU, Dutch florins, Italian lira, Swiss franc and Deutsche mark is largely the result of swap activity.

2.4 Global Service

The relaxation of controls on foreign institutions operating in the major capital markets, for example, in Switzerland, Germany and the Netherlands, allows banks to offer their clients the full range of funding opportunities with limited need to involve un-related domestic institutions in the transaction.

The increasing globalisation of financial markets has had a significant effect on banks' activities. Disintermediation is causing an erosion of the volume and profit margins of their traditional deposit-taking and lending activities. Deregulation, on the other hand, is expanding the scope of their activities and the markets in which they can operate.

The division between banks and securities institutions is becoming less clear. A growing proportion of banks' assets and liabilities are in marketable form and banks have more scope to manage interest rate, currency and cash-flow exposures through swaps, futures and options. They are, however, not only competing with securities institutions in these areas, for institutional investors and the treasury departments of many industrial corporations have access to the technology and are able to carry out some of these hedging activities for themselves.

Banks have to be able to provide the financial packages now required by sophisticated borrowers. These packages may combine fixed or floating rate obligations, a wide variety of maturities and a broad spectrum of currencies, swaps, futures or options. Banks, too, have to act as principals, a move that started with the introduction of the Eurobond bought deal, and they must have distribution and trading capability. Finally, they must concentrate to a greater degree on fee-earning business to counteract the decline of profitability in their traditional businesses.

In order to survive in the financial markets today, banks have to be able to compete on a broad front, or establish a speciality. Banks are becoming polarised, with the large financial conglomerates at one extreme and small specialised institutions at the other. These financial conglomerates combine the traditional business of a commercial bank with investment banking, underwriting and brokerage skills.

Legal divisions still exist, particularly in Japan and the United States, where commercial banks, in many instances, are not permitted to underwrite most corporate securities. However, no such restrictions exist on securities underwriting offshore and U.S. and Japanese banks have set up underwriting subsidiaries in Eurobond and other domestic markets. In Germany and Switzerland, banks are universal, combining the activities of commercial and investment banks. In the United Kingdom the division between clearing banks and merchant banks has been by custom rather than law, although many commercial banks now have their own merchant banking subsidiaries.

Banks have been evolving into financial conglomerates either by purchasing other institutions or by setting up their own subsidiaries. Among these:

UK: Foreign and domestic banks have purchased stock brokers and jobbers and obtained licenses as primary dealers in gilts.
Many foreign banks have set up subsidiaries to underwrite and trade Eurobonds.

Japan: Foreign banks have been granted securities licences.

USA: Foreign banks have set up or purchased subsidiaries to deal in, and distribute, stock and Treasury securities.

Germany & Holland: Foreign banks have set up or purchased participations in domestic banks to allow them to lead-manage Deutsche mark and Dutch guilder issues.

Australia: A number of foreign banks have set up, or purchased, merchant banking operations.

Banks are also entering into partnerships with banks located in different financial centres for such activities as fund management and venture capital investment.

3. DISINTERMEDIATION AND SECURITISATION

The rising inflation and increasing volatility in interest rates and currency exchange rates seen in the 1970s and early 1980s were the principal macro-economic influences behind the trend towards disintermediation of the commercial banking sector. Higher volatility has led to an increase in the risk exposure of those financial institutions and has necessitated greater attention to matching the term structure of their assets and liabilities. Investing criteria have changed, as investors seek to facilitate risk management by investing in marketable securities. Borrowers, for their part, have had to find ways of alleviating risk through financial packaging and hedging techniques.

3.1 Investment Flows

The changing pattern of investment has been very influential on the structure of the financial markets. Since the first oil crisis in 1973-74 there have been significant imbalances between savings and investment, initially between oil-exporting countries and less developed countries, but latterly between industrialised countries, in particular, between the United States and other OECD countries such as Japan. These imbalances have resulted in large net international capital flows.

On a domestic level, various factors have caused a move away from bank deposits as a satisfactory form of investment. In the United States, depositors became concerned about the credit quality of banks, which

515

had been affected by the risks associated with loans to lesser developed countries, the oil industry, the farming community and the smokestack industries, and moved to investing in higher quality short and long-term bonds. In Japan, the availability of an increasing range of market-sensitive short-term investments has affected the banks' deposit bases. In general, deregulation of deposit rates and greater availability of tradeable securities has caused investors to become more selective. At the same time, individuals are increasingly placing their savings under institutional management, through life assurance, pension funds and investment funds. The institutions are becoming more international in their outlook, and, with access to the same technology and information as banks and brokerage firms, can compete directly with them as investors, moving rapidly to take advantage of new market information, and certainly acting with greater speed and influence than individual investors.

3.2 Raising Funds

These shifts in savings and investment have allowed the capital markets to expand, a situation of which borrowers have been quick to take advantage. High quality borrowers have been able to diversify their funding sources away from the banks. They have also needed effective hedging devices and strategies to counteract interest rate and currency volatility. The capital markets have risen to the challenge in the swap market and by developing new financial instruments to transform and shift the burden of risk. The strength of the stock markets in recent years and their increasing internationalisation has also provided companies with the opportunity to raise equity as an alternative to bank loans or debt.

3.3 Capital Markets

Among the capital markets, two in particular, demonstrate the effects of disintermediation and securitisation. These are the floating rate note market and the euro-commercial paper market. Top quality borrowers, particularly sovereign credits, moved first to the FRN market as an alternative to the syndicated credit market. Investors became concerned by the credit quality of some commercial banks, which had previously been the principal issuers of FRNs, and developed significant demand for high quality sovereign FRNs. Margins and dealing spreads declined in relation to bank FRNs as a consequence and sovereigns were able to borrow at cheaper rates than from their traditional banking sources. This was true even

516

though margins in the syndicated credit market had declined in competition for top quality assets.

The Euro-commercial paper market, which is covered in detail elsewhere in this book, became a second flexible alternative to bank loans.

Banks themselves have had to change their funding and investment patterns. Although banks had always been the major investors in the FRN market, their involvement increased as they sought to replace those assets lost to disintermediation. Similarly, the development of the asset swap market – in which a fixed rate asset is swapped into a floating rate asset or vice versa – has provided banks with alternative high quality investments. It is interesting to note that the market for asset swaps and the euro-commercial paper market have, to a certain extent, been behind the decline in the FRN market. The growing preference for marketable assets has shown itself in another way in the bank credit market, where the inclusion of assignment clauses in many loans has prompted the development of an active market in assignable loans.

Table 1

Comparisons of Eurobonds and Syndicated Bank Loans

Total Eurobond Volume (U.S.$ billions)		*Syndicated Bank Credit Volume* (U.S.$ billions)	
1984	80,315.13	1984	199,279.96
1985	134,246.57	1985	233,166.00
1986	182,477.03	1986	221,289.84
1987	144,366.42	1987	354,051.27
1988	184,803.57	1988	560,327.06
1989	220,691.30	1989	736,246.93
1990	185,651.40	1990	625,003.82
1991	278,187.20	1991	610,887.81
1992	290,573.70	1992	673,699.11

On the liability side, banks have had to find alternative funding sources. FRNs have provided a large part of their funding, but credit concerns, over-supply and restrictions imposed by the BIS capital adequacy

517

rules on banks holding each others' subordinated debt have reduced the attractiveness of the FRN market for banks. More cost-effective has been the interest rate swap market, and many banks have funded themselves by issuing fixed rate debt and swapping it into floating rate debt.

3.4 Asset-backed Finance

The securitisation of the market can not only be seen in the absolute growth of the capital markets, but also in the range of different instruments devised to securitise otherwise illiquid assets. The biggest example of this is the mortgage market in the United States where the market for mortgage backed bonds grew from U.S. $100 million in 1983 to several billions at the end of the decade, while the market for collateralised mortgage obligations grew from U.S. $4.7 billion to over U.S. $50 billion over the same period. These obligations are secured by mortgages on property. The mortgage backed bond is collateralised with a combination of mortgages, government bonds and cash. The market value of the collateral is in excess of the principal amount of the bonds, to ensure that all arrears of principal and interest can be covered if the collateral has to be sold in the event of default. The collateralised mortgage obligation (CMO) is a pass-through obligation, whereby payments of principal and interest on a pool of mortgages are "passed through" to the investor.

Mortgage backed floating rate notes were also issued with success by American savings and loan institutions in the Eurobond market in the late 1980s. The market grew from U.S.$550 million in 1984 to U.S. $2.2 billion in 1986. However, following the deep crisis in the U.S. Savings and Loans industry in 1989/90 this market has virtually disappeared.

Activity in the mortgage backed sector has expanded to non-U.S. institutions. In January 1987, the first issue of sterling pass-through mortgage backed FRNs was launched. The sterling mortgage backed sector has since grown rapidly with outstandings totalling several billions of pounds.

Securitisation of non-mortgage assets has expanded dramatically since 1985. Automobile loans and leases, computer leases, credit card balances, and trade receivables have all been used for ABS issues. The ABS market includes the largest corporate debt issue ever in the US market –

Table 2 – Eurodollar FRN
By Issuer Type
Volume Table

Issuer Type	1987 Amount mm (US$)	Iss.	1988 Amount mm (US$)	Iss.	1989 Amount mm (US$)	Iss.	1990 Amount mm (US$)	Iss.	1991 Amount mm (US$)	Iss.	1992 Amount mm (US$)	Iss.
Central government	50.00	1	2,840.77	7	1,050.00	4	0.00	0	0.00	0	1,700.00	4
Local authority	70.00	1	0.00	0	0.00	0	0.00	0	0.00	0	325.00	1
Supranational institution	0.00	0	0.00	0	0.00	0	110.27	2	0.00	0	1,980.00	11
Public bank	595.00	3	950.00	5	1,265.00	8	1,253.00	10	420.00	5	3,041.50	20
Public finance (other)	0.00	0	0.00	0	0.00	0	700.00	2	150.00	1	1,314.29	11
Public utility	0.00	0	400.00	1	200.00	1	0.00	0	0.00	0	600.00	5
Public corporate	0.00	0	0.00	0	0.00	0	0.00	0	150.00	1	140.00	1
Private bank	997.06	9	2,746.10	9	2,600.00	11	10,090.50	49	2,560.00	28	15,061.50	97
Private corporate	408.00	8	935.00	8	855.00	7	360.75	10	503.13	7	1,214.60	18
Private finance (other)	5,636.55	59	1,690.70	35	2,722.60	48	3,458.88	30	780.00	9	4,718.60	37
Private utility	0.00	0	250.00	1	0.00	0	0.00	0	0.00	0	0.00	0
TOTAL	7,756.61	81	9,812.57	66	8,692.60	79	15,973.40	103	4,563.13	51	30,095.49	205

Iss. = number of issuers

Source: Euromoney Publications Plc.

519

Table 3 – Fixed Rate Eurodollar Market
By Issuer Type
Volume Table

Issuer Type	1987 Amount mm (US$)	Iss.	1988 Amount mm (US$)	Iss.	1989 Amount mm (US$)	Iss.	1990 Amount mm (US$)	Iss.	1991 Amount mm (US$)	Iss.	1992 Amount mm (US$)	Iss.
Central government	4,200.00	14	5,410.00	15	5,715.00	14	5,271.00	9	5,300.00	11	13,509.52	26
Local authority	320.00	2	465.00	3	490.00	3	325.00	2	200.00	1	340	2
State/provincial authority	0.00	0	1,000.00	3	1,020.00	3	0.00	0	2,790.00	5	5,500.00	4
Supranational institution	1,855.75	12	2,356.50	13	3,790.00	12	6,098.00	13	6,900.00	14	7,723.50	17
Public bank	1,685.18	12	2,660.00	18	5,803.53	35	2,556.14	21	5,367.00	24	4,760.00	20
Public finance (other)	1,182.00	10	3,605.00	21	1,854.44	16	1,671.45	10	2,772.00	12	2,810.00	11
Public utility	480.00	4	3,465.00	18	2,580.00	13	1,710.00	9	1,800.00	7	1,680.00	10
Public corporate	385.00	3	580.60	3	880.10	6	420.00	4	1,625.00	8	1,250.00	6
Private bank	3,253.70	23	5,471.31	46	9,690.47	96	3,711.50	25	6,420.31	36	7,242.79	69
Private corporate	26,001.13	218	34,933.60	241	68,061.91	263	24,201.10	144	29,156.55	177	22,175.05	127
Private finance (other)	3,809.68	30	3,254.25	30	5,415.30	28	7,978.30	22	7,864.00	19	5,361.25	38
Private utility	882.75	7	1,800.00	11	4,990.00	16	390.00	3	1,781.55	8	1,800.00	8
Private other	0.00	0	70.00	1	0.00	0	0.00	0	0.00	0	0.00	0
TOTAL	44,055.19	335	65,071.26	423	110,290.80	505	54,332.48	262	71,976.41	322	74,152.10	338

Iss. = Number of issuers

Source: Euromoney publications plc.

520

the US $4bn transaction for Asset Backed Securities Corporation. ABSs, like mortgages, are typically notes backed by the cash flow from the underlying receivables that are either sold or pledged to support the securities issued. Additional credit support is provided by either a letter of credit for a fraction of the initial amount of notes or over-collateralisation with additional receivables. The principal motivations for issuers of ABSs are perfect asset/liability matching, access to a new source of funds, improvement in a variety of financial measures, such as debt to equity ratio and return on assets through structuring transactions as a sale of assets, and the competitive rates provided for these securities, which have generally been rated AAA or AA.

In addition to the dramatic growth in the size of the ABS market, recent transactions have incorporated significant structural innovations. Asset Backed Securities Corporation, for example, issued fixed pay Asset Backed Obligations – the structure allowed the issuer to absorb the risk of varying prepayment speeds on the underlying automobile loans. In addition, this innovative deal adopted elements of CMO technology to allow the issuance of three different classes of obligations with varying maturities. A Bank of America issue transformed short maturity receivables from credit cards into notes with a three year maturity while also obtaining accounting and regulatory sale treatment for the issuer.

4. DEREGULATION

This section reviews deregulation measures in two ways: deregulation trends in the financial and capital markets as a whole, and by country, taking as examples the principal capital markets, the United States, the United Kingdom, Germany, Japan and Switzerland.

Reasons behind deregulation have been varied. In the United States, pressure to deregulate is largely to satisfy the frequently expressed desire to create free markets in which all can participate provided they operate within a regulatory framework in which sufficient protection is accorded to the general public. Artificial barriers still remain, however, such as the Glass-Steagall Act, which prevents commercial banks from underwriting securities, and interstate banking restrictions. In the United Kingdom, the "Big Bang" in October 1986 was the result of a desire to create a competitive, self-regulatory environment, in which London could retain and expand its role as the centre of the international financial markets. In

Germany and Switzerland, the influences were of a more economic nature, while, in the case of Japan, the markets needed to be modernised and the yen made more international. Whatever the reasons, the moves to deregulate have created an environment in which banks can increasingly provide a global banking service to their clients. It should also be recognised that concern about loan losses in the commercial banking sector, and about the fragility in the markets that can be caused by over-securitisation of assets has prompted calls for reregulation of the financial services sector, or at the very least, careful appraisal of any further deregulatory moves.

4.1 Foreign Exchange Controls and Money Markets

A domestic capital market can only expand and eventually become an international financial centre if its activities are not hampered by controls on the movement of its currency. Foreign exchange controls on sterling were removed in the United Kingdom in 1979. In Japan, while the internationalisation of the yen has been taking place gradually since 1978, international trading in yen was permitted in 1985 and, in 1986, restrictions on direct interbank dealing between yen and US dollars were lifted. Japan has also introduced short term money market instruments. With the abolition of exchange controls in Greece in early 1993 the whole of western Europe is now free of exchange controls.

4.2 Capital Controls

Access to capital markets has been enhanced in recent years as capital controls have been lifted or relaxed. Evidence of this can be found in the Japanese, Swiss and German markets in particular. Limitations on the size of new issues have been removed in Switzerland, Germany and Japan, and currency swap markets have been allowed to develop, in part because of specific permission by the authorities and in part because of the abolition of new issue calendars, the existence of which had severely restricted issuing flexibility. Restrictions on the resale of bonds have also been relaxed in Japan.

4.3 Withholding Tax

The removal of withholding tax on payments of interest to foreigners is of major importance in the move towards global markets. If no tax is withheld, domestic capital market instruments become much more attractive to international investors, a large proportion of whom require investments that are free of withholding tax. As a result the potential for competition between domestic and international markets is increased. Of particular importance have been the removal of withholding tax in the United States, where US Treasuries have become a much more important international investment vehicle; in Japan, where removal has assisted in the dramatic expansion of the Euroyen market; and in Germany, where, as in the United States, government securities have become of greater interest to foreign investors. The extent of the removal to date however has not, as might be expected, led to a situation in which relative yield is the sole criterion for investment as between domestic and Eurobond markets. Withholding tax is still imposed on Japanese government bonds and on German domestic corporate securities, and in the United States, domestic bonds are in registered rather than bearer form, requiring identification in order to avoid tax.

4.4 Capital Markets

Significant liberalisation has occurred in the German and Japanese capital markets in terms of the range of instruments that can be issued. Borrowers may now issue zero coupon and deep discount bonds, floating rate notes and dual currency bonds. Credit quality restrictions on borrowers in the Euroyen and Samurai bond markets have been relaxed. In the United Kingdom as well, the range has been extended by the development of a short-term (one to five year) sterling corporate bond market and a sterling commercial paper market.

4.5 Interest Rates

An important influence on banks and their fund raising and investment activities has been the removal or relaxation of interest rate restrictions on deposits, particularly in the United States and Japan. This has led to greater competition and necessitated greater reliance on alternative funding, namely interbank deposits, CDs, floating rate notes and swaps.

4.6 Geographic Restrictions

There has been significant relaxation of the barriers imposed on foreign institutions operating, in particular, in domestic capital or stock markets; the setting up of foreign branches to conduct commercial banking business has been relatively unrestricted. Germany now permits foreign-owned German banks to lead-manage Euro Deutsche mark bond issues and

Switzerland has opened its syndicates to foreign banks. Foreign-owned Dutch banks may also now lead-manage Euro-Dutch guilder issues. In the United Kingdom, foreign and domestic institutions have been allowed to purchase stockbrokers and stockjobbers while Japan has granted securities licences to a number of foreign institutions. In almost all cases the principle of reciprocity between countries is of vital importance in allowing foreign banks to operate.

4.7 Operational Restrictions

Commercial banks in Germany and Switzerland are generally universal banks, operating in the deposit-taking, lending, underwriting and stockbroking businesses. In the United Kingdom institutional barriers were broken down in the 1980s; the separate broker/jobber capacities no longer need to exist; and financial conglomerates have been set up, whose various divisions or subsidiaries can undertake most financial activities. In the United States, the division between commercial banking and securities underwriting is still in force, although a gradual breaking down of barriers is occurring as commercial banks set up discount brokerage businesses and certain commercial banks have recently been awarded permission to underwrite government issues and corporate securities. Interstate banking is also permitted albeit still on a restricted basis.

5. UNITED STATES

The present American financial regulatory system developed from purely domestic economic and political considerations and was created in the 1930s after the stock market crash of 1929. The regulatory environment is uniquely American in its approach; it is intended to create a level playing field and to further the development of the most efficient possible markets.

Although deregulation has been extensive, restrictions continue to be imposed in two important areas: the structural and geographic restrictions of the Glass-Steagall Act and State boundaries and the disclosure and reporting requirements in the US market.

The Glass-Steagall Act (1933) prevents deposit-taking institutions and their affiliates from operating simultaneously as a commercial bank and as an underwriter of securities. State boundary restrictions prevent

524

commercial banks from undertaking commercial banking activities in states other than the one in which they are incorporated. Both restrictions reflect the belief at the time that the more interdependent financial institutions become, the more likely it is that a single failure could result in catastrophic consequences. Until very recently, therefore, commercial banks and investment banks existed quite separately in the American system.

The commercial banking sector consists of the big New York-based money centre banks and of numerous large and small commercial banks throughout the country, limited in their domestic operations by state boundary restrictions. The investment banks underwrite new issues of securities, make markets in, and act as brokers for, bonds and shares, undertake research, act as investment managers and provide the full range of corporate advisory work. The largest of these are known as the special bracket (The First Boston Corporation, Goldman, Sachs & Company, Salomon Brothers Inc., Merrill Lynch, Pierce, Fenner and Smith Incorporated, Morgan Stanley & Co. Inc. and Shearson Lehman Brothers Inc.) and are particularly powerful in bond underwriting and distribution. Others are more specialised, concentrating on merger and acquisition activity, project finance or leveraged buy-outs.

Apart from the commercial and investment banks, an important category of financial institutions is the savings and loan associations, varying in size from the billion dollar S & Ls in California to the small, one town S & Ls scattered throughout the United States. These were established to finance the United States' housing market and are major deposit taking institutions. There are, in addition, many other types of financial institution, providing all types of financial services.

The other important body of regulations is the disclosure and reporting requirements which are designed to ensure that investors are protected by a full and complete disclosure of all relevant information; these are the world's most burdensome and complex initial and on-going disclosure requirements, and have slowed down the development of a foreign bond market (the Yankee market) to the benefit of the Eurobond market where disclosure requirements are far less onerous.

The adoption of Rule 144A of the US Securities Act 1933 in the beginning of the 1990s has, to a certain extent, opened up the US institutional market to non-US issuers (see 'Deregulation' below) who do not wish to go through the full registration process.

5.1 Deregulation

Capital markets: The United States was the first to deregulate brokerage commissions which it did in May 1975. Turnover and competition increased dramatically as commissions fell.

The three key deregulatory measures since then have been the introduction (in 1982) of shelf registration, the removal of withholding tax in 1984 and the introduction by United States Securities and Exchange Commission (SEC) of Regulation S and Rule 144A in early 1990. Apart from disclosure and registration requirements, American capital markets are the most diverse in the world, with a huge variety of short and long-term instruments and an enormous capacity for innovation. In this respect they are perhaps the least regulated of all world capital markets.

The introduction of shelf registration (Rule 415) dramatically reduced the time necessary to bring a new issue to the market. All securities – bonds or shares – have to be registered under the 1933 Act if they are to be offered to the public in the United States. The registration process involves depositing the appropriate disclosure documents with the United States Securities and Exchange Commission prior to formal offers of the securities being made and in the past the time between registration and the offer date could be a matter of weeks. The use of shelf registration statements allows a frequent, good quality borrower to establish a maximum amount of securities that he wishes to issue over a two year period, file a shelf registration statement containing the broad framework for those securities and update it over 48 hours whenever he wishes to issue securities. Hitherto, the speed with which a Eurobond issue could be executed was one of the great advantages of the Euromarket over the domestic market for US issuers or for foreign borrowers who could access the Yankee bond market. With shelf registration, the two markets could be used as directly competitive sources of funds.

The removal of withholding tax on payments of interest by US borrowers to foreign investors opened the government bond market to foreign investors. It also facilitated the access of US corporations to the Eurobond market by avoiding the cost and inconvenience of using a finance vehicle.

Some argued that the purpose behind this action was to help finance the US government deficit; others that it was consistent with the philosophy of developing the most efficient markets.

The impact of removal has led to greatly increased trading of US government securities abroad; on the other hand, continuing regulations concerning the use of bearer and registered instruments and disclosure of investors' identity has meant that the retail sector of the Euromarket, for whom anonymity is a key requirement, still prefer the bearer Eurobond.

The introduction of Regulation S and Rule 144A have opened up a trading market of non-SEC registered securities in the United States among institutional investors. It has also substantially reduced the application of the US Securities Act of 1933 on US persons living outside the United States.

Deposit market: Deregulation in the banking sector commenced with the gradual removal in the late 1970s of controls on deposit interest rates, first for commercial banks and secondly for savings and loan institutions. This led to heightened competition for deposits and with state boundaries limiting expansion of the deposit base, banks moved into the international interbank and capital markets to diversify their funding sources.

Interstate banking: In 1985, the United States Supreme Court decided regional interstate banking was constitutional and many States have now passed interstate banking laws, some of which were national in scope. A number of banks have now moved across state borders on a reciprocal basis.

Glass-Steagall Act: Banks are also developing ways of expanding their range of activities within the confines of the Glass-Steagall Act and encroaching on traditional investment banking areas. Banks have set up discount brokerage operations; state-chartered, non-insured banks have been allowed to underwrite corporate securities; and commercial banks have become increasingly active in the private placement market and in merger and acquisition activity.

The larger commercial banks have also moved into underwriting of securities abroad, through subsidiaries in other major capital markets, and have expanded their domestic activities by purchasing other financial institutions, particularly savings and loan institutions, consumer credit organisations and insurance companies. Several of the New York money centre banks have recently been awarded permission to underwrite issues of government and corporate securities in the US.

6. UNITED KINGDOM

The United Kingdom financial market underwent the most dramatic single restructuring of any of the major capital markets in October 1986, with the passing of the Financial Services Act. Not only did the Act alter the whole aspect of the stock exchange and gilt markets, but it also had a significant impact on the regulation of the Eurobond market, of which London had become the centre. Its effect on the structure of the commercial banking, merchant banking and broking community has been to create financial conglomerates along the lines of universal banks, seen as an essential development in order to compete in all areas of financial service and advice.

The UK clearing banks in particular have been developing securities expertise, either internally or through the purchase of existing stockbrokers, stock jobbers, investment managers and merchant banks. Merchant banks have also purchased stockbrokers and jobbers, but remain smaller, specialised investment banking institutions. With international banks from all over the world present in London, competition among the various institutions is intense and many firms which entered the market in anticipation of the 1986 events have subsequently pulled out or scaled back their operations.

6.1 Deregulation

Options: Recent deregulation in the United Kingdom dates from around 1978, when the traded options market commenced; the London International Financial Futures Exchange was established in 1982.

Bond market: Important to the development of London as a financial centre and to the expansion of the sterling bond markets was the removal of foreign exchange controls in 1979. In 1984, the abolition of withholding tax led to an increasing number of UK companies tapping the Eurobond market. The short-term sterling markets have also been deregulated: in 1985 private sector borrowers were allowed to issue one to five year sterling notes and in 1986 the sterling commercial paper market was started.

Building Societies: Deregulation has also affected the building societies. They may now pay interest gross and have therefore been able to enter the Eurobond market. Since the beginning of 1987, they have also been allowed to borrow in foreign currencies.

Financial Services Act: The progression towards the restructuring of the financial services industry commenced in 1982, when non-stock exchange members were allowed to buy up to 29.9 per cent of stock exchange member firms. This led to a rush of purchases by domestic and foreign institutions in anticipation of eventual 100 per cent ownership, which was permitted in 1986.

Proposals on the restructuring of the gilt market were first made in 1984 and, in 1985, 29 firms (now 19) were appointed as gilt-edged market-makers.

Discussions on the Financial Services Bill itself took place throughout 1985 and 1986. The Act was eventually passed in late 1986 and provided for the abolition of fixed commissions, the introduction of dual capacity for jobbers (market makers) and brokers in the stock market and the establishment of a new supervisory system.

7. JAPAN

The Japanese financial structure, developed immediately after the Second World War, was designed to promote rapid economic growth while protecting depositors' interests, preventing excessive competition and maintaining order. This necessitated strict controls, both on the expansion and creation of institutions, and on interest rates, where a low interest rate policy was applied to stimulate growth.

These inward looking markets operated successfully for 30 years. However, as a result of the 1973-74 oil crisis, the government had to issue significant amounts of bonds to finance the budget deficit, and corporations sustained financial losses. Since banks were required to purchase government bonds, the private sector was deprived of its traditional funding sources; corporations also found themselves to be over-leveraged and began to turn to raising money through fixed rate bonds and shares. At the same time, the Bank of Japan decided to control monetary growth directly, rather than allow it to vary, in order to maintain a fixed relationship between the US dollar and the yen.

Change was gradual but took a dramatic turn in 1980 with the passing of the Foreign Exchange Law, which eliminated ceilings on individuals' holdings of foreign currency, and abolished limitations on the conduct of the financing of foreign trade. The Law also permitted, to a limited extent, the set-off of foreign currency receivables and liabilities.

Although Japan was put under pressure from the West to internationalise the yen, the liberalisation of the domestic markets was necessitated as well by domestic pressures, in particular the detrimental effect on the bond market of Government refinancings.

Deregulation has been extensive and measures have broadly involved: (i) deregulation of deposit rates, the extension of maturities and an increase of the range of instruments in the money markets; (ii) the opening of a foreign exchange market and a gradual increase in Euroyen lending; (iii) the abolition of yen swap limitations; (iv) relaxation of issuing standards in the domestic corporate, Samurai and Euroyen bond markets and an increase in the range of instruments available in those markets; (v) liberalisation of re-sale and trading restrictions in the domestic and Euroyen bond markets; and (vi) increased access for foreign institutions.

Commercial banking and securities activities are conducted by separate institutions, a division that took place in 1948, when the Securities and Exchange Law, modelled on the United States Glass-Steagall Act, was passed. Under Section 65, commercial banks may not underwrite securities, except risk free Government and municipal bonds.

The groupings of Japanese financial institutions are distinct. In the commercial banking sector there are the large city banks, which act as the main banks for private companies; the long-term credit banks which were created to satisfy the long-term (five to seven year) financing needs of Japanese industry; the trust banks, which undertake trust activities and commercial banking; and various smaller regional financial institutions. There are a significant number of foreign banks present in Japan through branches, which undertake commercial banking in a similar manner to the city banks. Securities broking and underwriting are undertaken by the securities houses.

The funding activities of the commercial banks are strictly regulated. With the exception of the long-term credit banks, which may issue five year debentures, the banks are generally limited to funding themselves by short-term (less than two years) deposits. The movement by corporates to borrow away from the banks in the bond and equity markets and the erosion of their deposit base as money market instruments become more broadly available are leading to heightened competition between the institutions. Many are diversifying their lending activities and increasing their international operations as a result.

7.1 Deregulation

Deposit and lending rates: The Bank of Japan is closely involved in determining the deposit rates payable by all financial institutions and they are held well below market rates. Deregulation of interest rates on large deposits took place in 1987 and deregulation of interest rates on smaller deposits is being considered.

Money market instruments: The Japanese money markets are divided into the domestic interbank market, comprising the call market sector and the bills discount sector, and the open markets, which are international, and offer CDs, foreign currency deposits, gensaki (repurchase agreements), bankers acceptances and money market certificates.

By 1979 all interest rates in the bill discount sector (one to four months' duration) had been liberalised. In the call market, comprising demand deposits and deposits with maturities of seven days or less, interest rates have been largely deregulated; interest rates on all but call transactions below yen 3m were deregulated in 1989.

The CD market was opened in 1979, and in 1984 foreign bank and Euroyen CDs were introduced. The minimum denomination was reduced to yen 50m in 1987 and maturities from one month to one year (previously three or six months) are now permitted.

The markets for bankers acceptances and money market certificates (MMC) were opened in 1985. While the bankers acceptance market is not yet well established and sales may only be made to specified institutions, it is viewed as an important potential source of trade finance and a possible link between the bills discount and CD markets.

The gensaki (repurchase) market has never been restricted as to interest rates, although maturities are limited to six months. Constraints on the use of gensaki by financial institutions have been removed and foreign participation was permitted in 1979.

Foreign currency market: Deregulation of the foreign currency market has progressed since 1978, when foreign currency deposit rates were relaxed. In 1984, the foreign exchange market was formed when the real demand requirement was abolished. Yen swap limitations were also abolished that year. In 1985, banks and brokers were permitted to trade yen internationally and restrictions were removed on Japanese participation in syndicated credit facilities. In 1986, direct interbank dealing between yen and U.S. dollars was allowed.

Euroyen lending: In 1983, foreign borrowers were first allowed to borrow Euroyen through bank loans, limited to a one-year maturity. Medium and long-term lending of Euroyen to Japanese residents was permitted in 1986.

Domestic market: Liberalisation measures in the government bond market principally relate to trading. Minimum holding periods have been reduced and full scale trading by Japanese banks and initially five foreign banks was approved in 1985. Later that year a bond futures market was established. The corporate bond market was also liberalised by the relaxation of issuing standards; zero coupon bonds could be issued from 1985 under certain restrictions and in 1986 trading of warrants separately from bonds was permitted.

In the bank debenture market, in 1984, banks were allowed to issue foreign bonds with long-term forward contracts and dollar denominated, yen linked bonds. In 1985, commercial banks issued the first foreign currency convertible issues.

Samurai bonds: In the Samurai bond market, credit standards have been relaxed to permit single A rated bonds, and the ceilings on the size of double and triple A issues have been increased or removed altogether. Restrictions on syndication and distribution methods have been relaxed and the range of instruments expanded to include floating rate notes, zero coupon bonds and corporate bonds with warrants.

Euroyen bonds: Similar liberalisation measures were taken in the Euroyen bond market. Bonds can now be issued by a broad range of borrowers. In 1985, the 20 per cent withholding tax was removed and later that year dual currency bonds, zero coupon bonds and floating rate notes were introduced into the market.

Access for foreign institutions: Foreign banks have been admitted into government bond dealing and the trust banking business. Several foreign banks have been granted licences to deal in securities and Japanese branches of foreign banks will be allowed to manage pension funds in Japan if they have trust licences in their own countries. Six foreign securities firms were admitted to membership of the Tokyo Stock Exchange in February 1986.

8. GERMANY

The Deutsche mark's major role in international finance and trade reflects West Germany's post war economic success, characterised, until recently, by non-inflationary growth, conservative government financing and a relatively stable foreign exchange rate. Monetary control is exercised by the Deutsche Bundesbank, which, although wholly and directly owned by the Federal government, is a separate legal entity whose primary aim under section three of the Deutsche Bundesbank Act of 1957, is the "safeguarding of the currency" through the control of the amount of money in circulation and credit supplied to the economy.

In recent years, however, deregulation in the New York, London and Tokyo markets has caused the Bundesbank to re-evaluate and modify its previously conservative approach to the development of the capital market. In addition to remaining competitive with the other major financial centres, Germany had a further motive for such deregulation: due to higher real interest rates and a rising dollar in the few years just prior to liberalisation, Germany suffered substantial net capital outflows. By inducing international investors to purchase more Deutsche mark assets, this net capital outflow could be lessened, allowing the Bundesbank more freedom to reduce domestic interest rates in the face of high unemployment.

The German financial system is characterised by the strength of its deposit taking institutions, the three main groups being: commercial banks, savings banks and credit co-operatives, all of which are effectively universal banks. In addition, there are the postal savings and giro banks and building and loan associations. The other two main groups of financial institutions are the long-term credit institutions, essentially mortgage banks and the investing institutions, namely insurance companies, pension funds and investment companies.

The commercial banks, and in particular the big three – Deutsche Bank Aktiengesellschaft, Commerzbank Aktiengesellschaft and Dresdner Bank Aktiengesellschaft – are active in all areas of finance, including commercial bank lending, underwriting, distribution and trading of securities, investment management and insurance. The big three have national branch networks and significant international activities. They play particularly influential roles in German industry.

8.1 Deregulation
Deregulation has affected the bond markets rather than commercial banking. The German domestic bond market is the third largest in the world after the United States and Japan. Government entities and banks are the largest issuers, with corporates tending to rely to a far greater extent on bank loans rather than bonds for funding. Foreign borrowers are also active issuers of Deutsche mark bonds, but the Bundesbank does not differentiate between foreign and Eurobond markets; bonds syndicated internationally are viewed as Eurobonds.

Withholding tax: In 1984, the Bundesbank repealed withholding tax on payments of interest on domestic bonds held by foreign investors. This had the effect of increasing foreign demand for domestic paper, making it a feasible alternative to Euro-Deutsche mark bonds. Schuldscheine, a form of assignable loan, which had been free of withholding tax, lost their comparable advantage over domestic bonds.

534

Euro-Deutsche mark market: In May 1985, the Bundesbank significantly liberalised the Euro-Deutsche mark market. It allowed foreign-owned domestic banks in Germany (excluding Japanese-owned banks) to lead-manage Deutsche mark Eurobond issues and expanded the range of instruments that could be issued. The new instruments were floating rate notes, zero coupon and deep discount bonds and dual-currency issues. Interest rate and currency swaps involving Deutsche marks were also allowed for the first time. Finally, the issue queues were abolished, and the Bundesbank only required notification of new issues three days before the beginning of the month in which the issue was to be launched.

In a controversial move in 1988 the West German government decided to re-introduce withholding taxes on bonds issued by German entities. However, the decision was revoked in 1989 following sharp criticism from all parts of the German commercial and investment sectors.

Market diversity was enhanced as a result of these measures and the abolition of the calendar has allowed the swap market to develop. Market development of money market instruments (FRNs and CDs) is however hindered by the stockmarket turnover tax. Furthermore, restrictions still remain on early redemption of public issues (five years) and private placements (three years) since the Bundesbank is unwilling to let the short-term money markets develop at too rapid a pace.

In 1986 the monthly Deutsche mark new issue calendar was replaced by half-monthly notification of new offerings. The Bundesbank also decided that it would no longer announce the volume of proposed issues, but only of completed capital market transactions. Then, in 1989, the notification system was abolished.

Domestic bond market: Liberalisation measures in the domestic market were also taken in 1986. An option market commenced for certain federal government, post office and railway bonds. In addition, 16 foreign-owned banks in Germany were admitted to the consortium which places federal government, post office and railway bonds, for a 20 per cent share. However, the Bundesbank decided it would control the placement of federal government obligations through a system of control numbers.

Finally, foreign-owned banks in Germany were permitted to issue certificates of deposit.

9. SWITZERLAND

Switzerland's emergence as a major international capital market occured during the 1960s as increasing amounts of foreign capital were drawn to the country, attracted by its stable currency, the lack of restrictions on capital transfers, and the reputation of the Swiss banks for efficiency and security, in part the result of their high capital ratios. Bank secrecy laws were an added incentive. The development of a market for Swiss franc capital exports was essential if the currency was not to appreciate to unacceptably high levels, and a foreign bond market was one way to achieve this. Although liberalisation moves have been gradual, the Swiss franc bond market now ranks second in size to the Eurobond market.

Despite this the Swiss franc bond market remains relatively insular. Restrictions remain on market participants and issuing techniques, and secondary market trading is, as yet, not as developed as in the euromarkets. Withholding tax at the rate of 35 per cent is imposed on all payments of interest and dividends by Swiss companies and stamp duty of 0.3 per cent is levied on all transfers of all securities issued in Switzerland or on transactions that take place in Switzerland (there is no stamp duty on transactions with foreign titles between foreigners).

Swiss deposit-taking institutions have the status of universal banks and, although many of them undertake specialised activities, categorisation is generally made by ownership. They include the big three commercial banks (Credit Suisse, Swiss Bank Corporation and Union Bank of Switzerland), private banks, smaller commercial banks, cantonal (state owned) banks, regional and savings banks, foreign and co-operative banks (Raiffeisen).

The big three have branch networks throughout Switzerland and in the major financial centres of the world and are true universal banks. Private banks have traditionally specialised in asset management, particularly of high net worth individuals and estates, and the cantonal, regional and savings banks in mortgage financing. Some cantonal banks have expanded into international activities, commercial lending and portfolio management.

The Swiss capital market has traditionally been controlled to a large extent by the big three. The public market operates under the syndicate system, the most powerful of which has been made up of the big three

536

commercial banks (the lead rotating among themselves), together with groupings of cantonal and private banks. There are, in addition, various more flexible ad hoc groupings of banks. In the early 1990s this syndicate tradition has been gradually liberalised to the point where it hardly exists anymore.

Private placements are not syndicated but placed by the managing bank, which holds the notes on account for investors.

9.1 Deregulation
Deregulation in Switzerland has focused principally on the liberation of capital exports and the bond market.

Capital markets: With the increasing frequency of large taps have come important changes to the S.Fr capital market structure. These have boosted overall efficiency and competitiveness in the foreign and domestic markets and changed government bonds from a relatively illiquid instrument into an effective benchmark (there has been a third re-opening of the nine and 13 year $4^1/2\%$ government bonds recently). This trend towards benchmarks comes about as the S.Fr market undergoes some major changes, the most important of which included the April 1st, 1993 removal of a stamp tax on foreign issuance and the withdrawal of the syndication rule, which required that all banks participating in the syndication group of an issue had to be located in Switzerland. There has been a change to the "Verankerungsprinzip" – the same rule as in Germany (each Manager has to be domiciled in Switzerland).

On the domestic side, the government started scheduling regular monthly debt auctions in 1992. This boosted liquidity and led to the creation of an underlying futures contract shortly thereafter providing, for the first time, an effective market benchmark. Another boost for liquidity is expected in 1995 when the "Electronic Stock Exchange" will be introduced.

Syndication and Marketing: In 1980 foreign banks, governments and central banks were first permitted to purchase Swiss franc notes and to purchase sub-participations in Swiss franc loans. In the same year, the big bank syndicate started to invite non-syndicate banks into the bond syndicate as ad hoc managers.

In 1982, the public calendar for new bond issues was abolished and the quarterly maximum limits on new issue volume were lifted. The only remaining requirement was to notify the Swiss National Bank of the proposed launch date of a new bond issue, although the Bank reserved the right to coordinate launching dates. This internal calendar was abolished in 1984.

Publicity and marketing of Swiss franc private placements was first permitted on a restricted basis in 1982. Also that year foreign banks were first allowed to participate in syndicated Swiss franc loans as sub-underwriters (provided their identities are not publicly disclosed).

The trend towards benchmarks and the removal of size and maturity restrictions have led to an increase in the volume of issues launched, and allow much greater flexibility in adapting to changing market conditions. Zero coupon bonds can now be issued as a result of the abolition of size restrictions and the swap market has flourished. These factors, as well as the gradual breaking down of the traditional syndicates, have caused greater competition among the banks for mandates. The development of secondary market trading in notes and the impact of the purchasing power of the new mandatory pension funds are also having an effect on new issue volume.

Trading: The liberalisation measures with respect to trading all relate to the private placement note market. Trading of notes was permitted on a restricted basis in 1980; all restrictions were then abolished in 1982. Notes originally had to be held in safe custody with the managing bank; this requirement was eliminated in 1986, clearance of notes through the Swiss clearing system, SEGA, having been permitted since 1984.

Pension Funds: In 1985 an Act of Parliament stipulated that companies should establish pension funds. Recent statistics on assets held by Swiss pension funds are notoriously hard to get. The last official figure published by the Federal Office for Statistics is for 1990, when volume stood at S. Fr 265 billion, up from S.Fr 198 billion the year before. Industry experts now estimate capital at around S.Fr 265 billion and project it will rise to between S.Fr 433 and 450 billion by 2000. Pension funds are already the largest group of Swiss institutional investors and have already developed significant purchasing power.

10. REGULATION

10.1 United States

10.1.1 *Capital Markets*

Capital market activitives within the United States are principally regulated under the Securities and Exchange Act of 1933, which concerns itself with the primary distribution of securities and under the Securities and Exchange Act of 1934 which covers disclosure requirements. The provisions of the 1934 Act apply both at the time of issuing bonds or shares (also regulated by the appropriate stock exchange) and for on-going information, namely annual and interim reports and reports on material events. All disclosure documents have to follow a particular form, the most common of which are the 10K (annual report), 10Q (interim report), 20F (issue of yankee bonds), 6K (material events). The provisions of both Acts are administered by the Securities and Exchange Commission (SEC).

All issues of securities to the public have to be registered under the 1933 Act. In addition to federal securities laws, issuers of bonds to the public in the United States have to concern themselves with the state securities or "blue sky" laws, and appropriate registration procedures have to be undertaken or sales restrictions imposed to comply with these laws.

A further semi-regulatory element of the capital market system is the existence of the rating agencies and the necessity for every issue of securities to be rated according to the credit quality of the borrower and the legal status or security of the issue itself.

10.1.2 *Bank Regulation*

Bank regulation in the United States is conducted on a federal and state level and banks can choose between being federally chartered or state chartered. National banks with federal charters are regulated by the Controller of the Currency and are members of the Federal Reserve System. Deposits below a given size are insured by the Federal Deposit Insurance Corporation (FDIC). The majority of state-chartered banks are insured, but may either be members of the Federal Reserve System, in which case they are regulated by the Federal Reserve Bank, or not, in which case they are regulated by the FDIC. The variety of regulatory agencies has led to a number of distinct and sometimes conflicting

539

patterns of regulation and there is recognition that greater co-ordination of supervision should be developed, particularly as a result of recent domestic and international lending crises.

Areas of regulation cover accounting, disclosure and reporting requirements, specify loan and capital adequacy ratios, and involve evaluation of liquidity and foreign exchange exposure. Particular focus has been paid to the appropriate accounting for overdue and unpaid loans and to disclosure of significant lending exposure to high risk countries. Another area of attention is capital adequacy, and the United States developed the concept of primary capital (common and perpetual preferred stock, capital reserves, mandatory convertibles) as a measure of capital adequacy distinct from total capital. The inclusion of certain types of instrument in the definition of primary capital led to the development of new forms of floating rate note in the Eurobond markets, similar forms to which were then developed by bank regulatory agencies in other countries.

10.2   United Kingdom

10.2.1   *Capital Markets*
Following the 1989 Finance Bill the Bank of England exercises only limited control over the sterling markets and the London CD market, which is the market for CDs issued by English banks or London branches or subsidiaries of foreign banks, regardless of currency.

Controls are, in principle, restricted to CDs, which may not be longer than five years, and to restrictions on which firms can lead manage euro-sterling offerings.

In addition, the structure of all new instruments denominated in sterling or bonds with a sterling content must be notified in advance to the Bank.

10.2.2   *Bank Regulation*
Traditionally, the regulation system in the United Kingdom has been based on co-operation and frequent consultation between the banks and the Bank of England. Supervision has been based on prudential guidelines and extensive reporting requirements rather than specific rules. Criticism of this approach has been made in recent years and the collapse of Johnson Matthey Bankers in particular led to proposals by a Review

Committee set up in 1985 to change some specific areas, while retaining a flexible approach. The changes proposed by the committee led to the creation of a Board of Banking Supervision within the Bank of England comprised of ex-officio senior executives within the Bank and certain other members. The Board provides advice to the Governor on matters such as capital adequacy, liquidity and the evaluation of supervisory policies. In addition, the two tier system of licensed deposit-taking institutions and recognised banks was abolished and rules which regulate banks' exposure to individual borrowers were introduced.

In addition to the Bank of England's large exposure rules (referred to above) supervision currently covers accounting and disclosure requirements and sets guidelines with respect to loan and capital adequacy ratios, liquidity and foreign exchange exposure. Capital adequacy is assessed through a gearing ratio and a risk assets ratio, which are established on a case by case basis after taking into account the circumstances of the bank concerned.

10.2.3   *Financial Services Act*

The Financial Services Act, which came into full force in April 1988, extended the regulation of investment business and was the most comprehensive overhaul of investor protection legislation seen in the UK. The principal areas covered are:

(i)   The prohibition of carrying on investment business other than by authorised or exempted persons;
(ii)   The establishment of a new regulatory structure;
(iii)   The regulation of the conduct of business, and the imposition of minimum capital requirements;
(iv)   The regulation of collective investment schemes;
(v)   Contents of listing particulars for listed securities and prospectuses for unlisted securities;
(vi)   Miscellaneous provisions dealing with such matters as organisational structure and enforcement; and
(vii)   A centralised compensation scheme.

The supervisory system contemplated by the Financial Services Act combines self-regulation and centralised control. At the head is the

Securities and Investments Board which is supervised by the Treasury, and, in turn supervises the regulatory policy of the self regulatory organisations (SROs) of the individual market sectors, as well as the recognised investment exchanges (RIEs). Any person or body wishing to operate in the financial services industry in the UK must be a member of an SRO or a member of a recognised professional body. The most significant SROs are:

(a)   The Securities and Futures Authority Limited (SFA) which regulates dealing and broking in domestic and international securities, related options and futures, money market instruments, corporate finance, etc.;

(b)   FIMBRA (the Financial Intermediaries, Managers and Brokers Regulatory Association) which regulates the activities of investment intermediaries to retail customers;

(c)   IMRO (the Investment Management Regulatory Organisation) which regulates investment managers and trustees; and

(d)   LAUTRO (the Life Assurance and Unit Trust Regulatory Organisation) which regulates life companies and unit trust managers and trustees.

10.3   Japan

The Japanese financial system is heavily regulated by the Ministry of Finance, which has an influence over the activities of all financial institutions operating in Japan. Its activities include overseeing Japan's financial dealings with the rest of the world; licensing and supervising banks and regulating structural changes in the system; regulating and supervising the securities industry; acting as the treasury for the Government; and running the national budget general account and the tax system.

10.3.1   *Securities and Money Markets*

The issuing and trading of securities is regulated by the Ministry of Finance according to the provision of the Securities and Exchange Law of 1948. Subsequent revisions have tightened the regulatory environment which had originally been based on self control and free competition. A licensing system was adopted for securities companies and a registration system for securities salesmen. The law also covers corporate disclosure and securities distribution.

542

In the money markets, the Ministry of Finance regulates interest rates and maturities on deposits and money market instruments.

10.3.2 *Bank Regulation*

The basic regulatory framework relating to the conduct of banking business in Japan is contained in the Banking Law of 1927, as amended in 1981. It covers such matters as supervision by the Ministry of Finance, foreign banks' operations, accounting practices and mergers. Much of the Ministry of Finance supervision has been by way of non-binding administrative guidance, although more formal regulation was contemplated in the 1981 amendments, and the Ministry of Finance does have the right to issue legally binding banking rules. Guidance is provided on appropriate ratios with respect to loans to individual borrowers, capital adequacy, liquidity and foreign exchange exposure and on the treatment of country risk. The Bank of Japan has limited supervisory authority, in part through its operations at the discount window which controls interest rates and lending volume, and in part through examinations of commercial banks every two years.

Foreign banks operating in Japan are also regulated by the Banking Law but the principal of reciprocity is given a great deal of weight in application of the law.

CHAPTER 14

International Capital Markets — Bonds

by
Sarah Scarlett; revised by team from CS First Boston

1. INTRODUCTION

A government, bank or corporation wishing to raise money in the capital markets has at its disposal a broad range of instruments and currencies, whether in its own domestic market or in the Eurobond or foreign bond markets. This chapter focuses on the most important of those markets: the Eurobond market and the domestic and foreign bond markets in the United States, the United Kingdom, Germany, Japan and Switzerland; and describes the principal instruments that are available in these markets.

The term "bond" is used to describe a negotiable security, either in bearer or registered form, evidencing a debt for a fixed term and bearing a fixed rate of interest. As a generic term, it also describes those securities bearing a floating rate of interest or being convertible into equity, as well as perpetual debt. Warrants for debt or equity, which may be attached to bonds or issued separately ("naked" warrants), also form part of the bond market.

The domestic, Euro and foreign bond markets are differentiated by currency, the location of the borrower and the syndication technique. In domestic capital markets the borrowing currency is the local currency, and borrowers, underwriting syndicates and investors are all located within that country. Eurobonds and foreign bonds are international bonds. Eurobonds are issued outside the country in whose currency they are denominated and distributed through international syndicates, whereas foreign bonds are issued in the local currency through a domestic syndicate but by foreign borrowers; underwriting syndicates may also include foreign banks. In general Eurobonds are not subject to volume constraints imposed by national authorities, although timing limitations and the requirement for a domestic lead-manager exist for some currencies.

2. HISTORY AND DEVELOPMENT OF THE EUROBOND MARKET

2.1 History
On 1st July, 1963, the first Eurobond was issued by Autostrade under the guarantee of IRI, a holding company owned by the Italian state.

In the aftermath of the Second World War large amounts of capital were required to rebuild the Western European economies and New York provided a much needed source of funds for foreign borrowers. Most borrowers were government institutions, largely owing to the stringent reporting requirements demanded by the 1933 Securities and Exchange Act which governs all public offerings of securities in the United States and which deterred corporate borrowers. Foreign issues in New York, now known as "Yankee" bonds, were in this period managed exclusively by US investment banks, who underwrote them with an American underwriting syndicate, but large proportions (up to 90% in the case of European governmental issuers) were placed outside the United States. Their attractions for investors were their invariably high quality, their freedom from withholding tax (in contrast to domestic US shares or bonds) and their denomination in dollars.

To accommodate European investor demand a partial infrastructure for a Euromarket existed by the early 1960s. The most important stimulus in the formation and subsequent growth of the Eurobond market was the Interest Equalization Tax ("IET"), which became law in the United States on 2nd September, 1964 retroactive to the previous 18th July. This tax made purchase of foreign bonds by US residents unprofitable, effectively closing the US capital markets to foreign borrowers, except those specifically exempted from IET, such as Canada, Mexico and Finland.

Thus, when the IET was imposed, a non-US placing network for bonds already existed. All that was required to create a truly European capital market was for European bankers to adapt the American bond management and underwriting systems to suit the peculiarities of a market which would be supra-national in that it would not be located in any particular centre.

While the IET was the market's catalyst, another action by the US authorities also did much to develop the Euromarket. Just as the IET was a response to a deteriorating US balance of payments position, so the Voluntary Restraint Programme ("VRP") for US corporations was an attempt to stem the flow of capital exports for investment. The VRP, announced on 10th February, 1965, caused well-known US corporations to turn to the Eurobond market to finance their investments outside the United States. This diversification in the market initially displaced other potential borrowers, but they found that the market subsequently became more receptive to corporate issuers. Indeed in 1967 an impressive list of European companies floated issues for the first time.

In January 1968 the VRP was replaced by a mandatory set of guidelines administered by the Office of Foreign Direct Investment ("OFDI"), the effect of which was to release a flood of American issues onto the Eurobond market that year, many of which were convertible into equity. In early 1974 IET was reduced to zero, and the OFDI guidelines were removed. As these two factors had played so prominent a role in the creation and development of the market, there were many who thought that their disappearance would herald the demise of the Eurobond market. The annual volume of issues in the Euromarket, which had risen from US$148m equivalent in 1963 to US$3.7bn in 1973 did contract in 1974 but by 1975 had recovered to US $8.3bn and almost doubled the following year to US$15.2bn. The universe of institutional and retail investors in Eurobonds continued to expand and new issue volume rose to US$47.5bn in 1983.

Until 1984, the Euromarket developed with little interference from legislative changes, but in that year the removal of withholding taxes imposed on foreign holders of domestic issuers' bonds in the United States, Germany and the United Kingdom had a significant impact on its activities. Because approximately 70% of Euromarket issues were denominated in US dollars, and because one of the major attractions of Eurobonds had always been their lack of withholding tax, the removal of withholding tax in the United States in particular caused many people once again to predict that the Euromarket would lose its attraction for many issuers and investors. Instead, in 1984 volume in the market nearly doubled to US$80bn.

The movement towards liberalisation and deregulation which characterised 1984 continued steadily, marked by further specific measures undertaken in Germany and Japan and new issue volumes in 1992 reached US$326bn.

The Eurobond market has reached maturity on the basis of credibility as a secure investment medium (defaults have been relatively rare even in the early 1990s' recession) and through liquidity in an increasingly sophisticated secondary market. A cross-section of end-buyers of bonds from a new issue today might include a private individual whose money is handled on a discretionary basis by a bank, the pension fund of an international company, an insurance company with long-term foreign currency liabilities and a central bank. While the Eurobond market commenced and grew primarily on the basis of retail investment, in recent years institutions have become major investors in Eurobonds and now form a much greater proportion than the retail sector.

2.2 Currency

Eurobonds have been issued in a broad range of currencies including the US dollar, the Deutsche mark, Pound Sterling, other leading European currencies (excluding the Swiss franc), the Yen, the Canadian dollar, Middle Eastern currencies (in particular the Kuwaiti dinar) and various currency linked composite units such as the European Unit of Account, European Currency Unit and the Special Drawing Right.

The US dollar remains the single most important currency. Its dominance seems likely to persist for two reasons. The considerable volume of US dollars outside the United States provides the liquidity crucial to both investors and secondary market makers who are financing their positions. Secondly, the size and timing of bond issues in the US dollar sector of the Eurobond market are subject only to market forces. Controls imposed by monetary authorities on the timing and size of issues in other currencies have been liberalised in recent years, but still exist to an extent in some sectors, and the depth of liquidity available in the US dollar sector has yet to be developed.

Table 1 shows the development of the market since 1985, by currency.

Liberalisation of borrowing regulations and the growth in the interest rate and currency swap markets have been the principal causes behind the increasing number of borrowings denominated in Deutschemarks, Japanese Yen, ECU, Sterling, French francs, Australian dollars and New Zealand dollars. It is estimated that by the end of 1992 there were approximately US$3.1 trillion interest rate swaps and US$1.6 trillion currency swaps outstanding and that approximately two thirds of international bond issues during the course of the year were swap-related. As a result new issue volume in certain currency sectors became increasingly dependent upon the right swap opportunities being available. The emergence of the Australian and New Zealand dollars as Eurocurrencies has been caused almost entirely by the attractive opportunities in the swap market provided by these currencies.

A further sign of the extent of the currency swap market was the dramatic increase in the number of US corporations which raised capital in the non-US dollar markets, particularly the Swiss franc foreign bond market and the Yen market.

2.3 Euroyen Market

Volume in the Euroyen market increased from US$197m equivalent in 1979 to US$1.1bn equivalent in 1984 and US$21.8bn in 1987, following deregulation in 1984. In 1992 volume reached US$35bn. The first Euroyen bond was issued in 1977. Until March 1979, borrowers were limited to international organisations such as the World Bank and the Asian Development Bank. Regulations were then further relaxed to allow Euroyen issues by governments and government agencies, with priority being given to those borrowers which had already issued at least three Samurai bonds and were rated "AAA". New MoF guidelines, effective 1st December, 1984, allowed a wider group of issuers to borrow in Euroyen, including governments, government agencies, foreign corporations and a limited number of Japanese corporations. Non-Japanese issuers which are public entities must have a rating from one of the United States agencies of "A" or better while private entities must either be rated "A" or better or meet the financial criteria for issuing in the Samurai market, namely certain minimum size requirements and financial ratios (previous use of the Samurai market is no longer a prerequisite). The issue of Euroyen bonds is subject to approval by the Ministry of Finance.

Table 1
Eurobond New Issue Volume
1987 - 1992 Volume Table

Currency	1987 Amount mm (US$)	Iss.	1988 Amount mm (US$)	Iss.	1989 Amount mm (US$)	Iss.	1990 Amount mm (US$)	Iss.	1991 Amount mm (US$)	Iss.	1992 Amount mm (US$)	Iss.
US dollar	61,289.66	501	76,929.84	512	121,134.30	601	71,427.87	379	80,014.41	418	107,354.00	566
Sterling	14,922.46	120	24,746.50	142	20,316.23	113	21,634.82	95	26,551.38	132	24,682.05	124
Deutsche Mark	14,606.05	127	23,771.98	198	16,301.10	147	19,493.40	125	40,337.55	215	34,516.92	195
European currency unit	7,439.71	70	11,210.76	92	12,354.79	116	17,714.83	84	32,282.86	116	22,372.34	106
Japanese yen	22,345.13	161	16,148.03	222	17,238.00	332	23,378.80	307	35,619.14	225	34,911.28	170
French franc	1,656.41	17	2,504.70	20	4,532.56	46	9,177.54	53	17,268.21	87	24,180.46	113
Australian dollar	8,912.02	193	8,214.51	151	6,738.25	120	5,007.58	95	4,453.16	59	4,960.75	57
Dutch guilder	2,419.03	31	3,606.20	43	2,066.11	25	1,402.46	11	3,799.08	25	7,466.57	47
Danish kroner	1,398.64	34	985.94	23	211.43	5	180.71	4	321.97	7	356.40	8
Canadian dollar	5,925.15	94	13,034.70	164	12,757.04	114	6,341.92	55	22,482.35	165	16,284.94	90
Italian lira	720.42	10	1,529.46	16	3,671.51	31	5,894.28	35	9,090.79	59	7,826.38	37
New Zealand dollar	1,488.61	27	818.71	20	692.09	21	527.86	13	325.10	10	148.98	4
TOTAL	143,123.30	1,385	183,501.00	1,603	218,013.50	1,671	182,182.10	1,256	272,545.80	1,518	285,060.80	1,517

Iss. = Number of issuers

Source: Euromoney Publications Plc

The Euroyen market had an erratic start after liberalisation; an excess of issues was brought to the market and soon exhausted demand for the paper outside Japan and the availability of attractive swap opportunities. After about two months, new issue activity virtually ceased. In 1986, however, the Euroyen market continued to mature and was, in 1992, the third largest sector of the eurobond market.

2.4 Deutschemark Market

Prior to May 1985, issue activity in the Deutschemark market was restricted to fixed rate and convertible bonds and a strict calendar of issues applied. Furthermore, only German-owned domestic banks could lead-manage issues.

In May 1985 and 1986 the market was deregulated to permit the issue of Floating Rate Notes, warrants, zero and deep discount bonds and dual currency bonds. Issuers could enter into interest rate and currency swaps, and foreign-owned German banks could lead-manage issues. Growth of the market had been hampered to a certain extent by the new issue calendar, which required lead-managers to advise the Bundesbank of the intention to do an issue and its proposed launch date twice monthly.

2.5 ECU Market

Bonds denominated in ECU were first launched in 1981 and attracted issuers and investors because of their inherent diversification of interest rate and currency risk. Traditionally dominated by supranationals and public institutions, borrowers have included sovereigns, government agencies, banks and corporations. Individuals, particularly in the Benelux group of countries, were the principal investors in the early stages of the market. Although they have remained major investors, institutions are increasingly active. Recently the Swiss market has provided substantial placement for ECU denominated bonds which has further increased the importance of the ECU sector. The market grew from a volume of equivalent US$6.6bn in 1986 to equivalent US$32.3bn in 1991. The ECU bond market suffered a major sell-off as a result of the upheavals within the ERM commencing in mid-1992 and issuing volume has since been dramatically reduced.

2.6 Eurosterling Market

Although the first Eurosterling issue was launched in 1972, the market is generally thought to have come into existence in 1977. Since that time, the market has grown substantially and is now the second largest sterling debt market.

The market's growth has, over the years, been significantly affected by legislative changes. The abolition of exchange controls in 1979 was the first in a series of such measures. Changes introduced in the 1984 and 1985 Finance Acts, including the removal of withholding tax, generated explosive growth in domestic issuance of Eurosterling bonds.

The market's investor base was initially dominated by non-UK investors, but Eurosterling bonds have become increasingly accepted by domestic institutions.

The Bank of England still demands to be notified prior to the launch of any sterling or sterling-linked eurobond issue.

2.7 Reflows

The flow of funds from interest and principal repayments, the latter arising from redemptions and sinking or purchase fund payments, now amounts to billions of dollars per annum and the availability of this cash flow for reinvestment should provide long-term support for the market. In general, however, it is thought that interest payments are less likely to be reinvested.

2.8 Issuers

Eurobonds have been issued by supra-national organisations, governments, government agencies, banks and private sector corporations. The common factor shared by these issuers is a high credit standing. While there have been exceptions in buoyant markets and for those issuing equity-related instruments, the Eurobond market is generally limited to issuers which, should they be rated by the US rating agencies, would be rated at least BBB. There are many occasions when investors will accept only paper rated A (or an implied rating) or better.

Until 1965, almost all Eurobonds were issued by public sector entities. In that year, after the introduction of the VRP, US corporations became an important category of issuers in the Eurobond market; other corporations, obliged to find funds offshore, soon followed. Comparisons of issuers by geographical area and by category are set out in Table 2.

Table 2
Geographical Spread 1989–1992
(in US$ millions)

Area	1989	Iss.	1990	Iss.	1991	Iss.	1992	Iss.
Supranational	14,790	104	21,612	99	30,903	112	37,571	132
USA and Canada	23,357	212	24,893	151	37,835	217	35,234	153
Western Europe	85,012	799	87,315	638	136,211	748	144,734	793
Far East	83,357	406	43,016	318	63,090	472	55,020	392
Australasia	7,583	87	3,353	52	3,144	37	3,541	37
Others	6,590	92	5,460	60	7,001	57	14,471	154

Iss. = Number of Issuers

Source: Euromoney Publications Plc

3. DOMESTIC BOND MARKETS

3.1 Japan

The bond market in Japan can be divided into the long-term domestic securities market, the short-term domestic market and the Shogun bond or Samurai bond market. The issue and trading of bonds is supervised by the Ministry of Finance.

The market has undergone significant liberalisation in recent years and has expanded and developed rapidly as a result.

3.1.1 Medium/Long-Term Domestic Securities

The long-term fixed rate securities market in Japan includes a wide variety of public bonds issued by the government or government-related bodies and private bonds issued by domestic and foreign entities such as banks, utilities and industrials.

553

Table 3
Japan - Volume of Bonds Outstanding at Fiscal Year End
(in billions of Yen)

Category	1989	1990	1991	1992
Government Bonds	1,609,101	1,663,380	1,716,474	1,783,682
Municipal	70,822	72,702	74,470	78,703
Government Guaranteed	195,132	195,944	197,343	195,376
Corporate Bonds	88,886	99,001	112,465	142,968
Bank Debentures	594,375	676,628	743,601	766,340
Samurai Bonds	49,549	59,798	63,270	68,730

Public Government bonds: Bonds of five, 10 or 20 years' duration are issued monthly by the government through a syndicate composed of financial institutions and securities companies, of which the latter provide broad distribution to institutional and retail investors in Japan and around the world.

Government Agency bonds: Government agency bonds are issued by corporations which are wholly-owned by the government, and are sometimes guaranteed by the government. Issuers are corporations such as Japan National Railways, Nippon Telegraph and Telephone Public Corporation and Japan Housing Corporation. Maturities are of seven to 10 years.

Municipal bonds: Municipal bonds are issued by local governments through public offerings and private placements. Maturities are mainly of seven to 10 years.

Financial debentures: Financial debentures are debentures issued by co-operative banks, the long-term credit banks and The Bank of Tokyo Ltd. They are issued monthly and can be of one year without coupon or of three or five years' duration with coupon.

Corporate bonds: Corporate bonds are issued by private business corporations, electric power companies and others, such as the Japan Broadcasting Authority and Teito Rapid Transit Authority. Corporate bonds have maturities of six to 15 years, whereas convertible bonds are generally of four to 15 years' duration. Corporations are also able to issue bonds with warrants for shares attached. As a rule corporations wishing to offer bonds to the public must be of a certain size and meet certain minimum financial ratios.

3.1.2 *Short-Term Domestic Securities*

The short-term, yen-denominated, fixed rate market in Japan is comprised of securities yielding administered rates of interest, and securities providing market sensitive returns. Finance Bills, for example, are issued at submarket rates, primarily for purchase by the Bank of Japan. Short-term repurchase ("gensaki") transactions and bank certificates of deposit (CDs), in contrast, provide competitive rates of return.

Gensaki: The gensaki market in Japan is a market in which medium- and long-term debt securities are sold with a repurchase agreement that specifies the date and price of the obligatory repurchase. The opposite transaction, that is, purchase of securities for mandatory resale, is called a "reverse gensaki". Started in the late 1950s, the gensaki market provided the earliest means of market sensitive short-term financing in Japan. The gensaki market was opened to foreigners in 1979.

Gensaki transactions are available for any maturity up to one year, with most agreements extending three months or less. Gensaki transactions have, at times, constituted a significant portion of the secondary market trading volume of government bonds, although recent expansion of the professionally traded secondary government market has resulted in a smaller percentage of trades representing repo transactions.

Certificates of Deposit: The domestic yen CD market was opened in 1979 for Japanese and foreign banks to raise short-term yen funding through the issuance of negotiable fixed rate instruments. CDs mature in three to six months and are quoted on a money market yield basis, i.e. with a coupon.

3.1.3 *Samurai Bonds*

Samurai bonds are yen-denominated bonds with maturities of three to 20 years issued by foreign borrowers in the domestic Japanese market. The

Samurai bond market opened in 1970, when the Ministry of Finance authorized supranational and highly rated foreign government entities to issue Samurai bonds within certain size and maturity restrictions. In 1979, the government expanded Samurai borrowing to include certain private issuers that met rigorous financial criteria. During the 1980s and especially in 1989, the Government of Japan significantly relaxed the restrictions on Samurai issues, allowing slightly lower rated borrowers into the market (at least A rated), abolishing both maturity and volume limits and shortening the issue queue.

Priority for issuance has been given (in descending order) to international agencies, sovereign governments, government agencies and to corporations of the highest credit standing which are also engaged in commerce with Japan.

Samurai bonds have semi-annual coupons, and settlement, clearing and other administrative procedures are more complicated than for Euroyen bonds. For instance, Samurai bonds are issued in registered form, and although they can be exchanged into bearer bonds and vice versa, this is a costly and lengthy process.

Samurai issues have, with only a few exceptions, been lead-managed by one of the major Japanese securities houses although certain foreign houses act and have acted as co-managers or underwriters. Documentation and official filings are lengthy, must be in Japanese and are time-consuming. For these reasons, it is difficult to launch an issue with the speed that is characteristic of the Euromarket.

Despite many efforts by both the government and the Japanese securities dealers to attract foreign borrowers to the Samurai market, recent growth in the market has been slow relative to the explosive growth of the Euroyen market and the recent popularity of this market is drawing issuers and investors away from the Samurai market.

3.2 Switzerland

For many years Swiss Franc ("SFr") denominated securities have been attractive to foreign investors because of the relative strength of the currency. Normally yields are low but this has been found acceptable in

556

view of the generally positive real rate of return. During periods when the Swiss Franc has appreciated sharply against other currencies, the Swiss National Bank has introduced certain restrictions regarding the purchase of Swiss franc securities by investors located outside Switzerland. Currently, there are no restrictions in this respect. Liberalisation of size and maturity restrictions, queuing requirements and syndicate structures in the 1980s allowed the market to expand further and have also led to increased competition among banks for business.

The Swiss franc foreign bond market is the only means for borrowers to raise term Swiss francs (other than through currency swaps) because the Swiss National Bank has not yet permitted a Euro-Swiss franc market to develop.

3.2.1 *Domestic Securities*

The major categories of Swiss franc domestic securities are the "Schweizerobligationen" and "Kassenobligationen". The former are domestic bonds with maturities of eight to 15 years issued by governmental, corporate, financial and non-financial institutions in Switzerland and the latter are medium-term notes which are issued by domestic banks on a daily basis with maturities of three to eight years.

3.2.2 *Foreign Bonds and Foreign Notes*

The foreign bond market comprises either public issues of bonds with maturities typically of eight to 15 years or unlisted private placements of notes issued with maturities typically of 18 months to eight years.

The maximum size limitation on public issues of SFr200 million was eliminated early in 1985; there has been no maximum issue size for note issues since 1980. Notes have been publicly tradeable since 1982 but until 1986 had to be held in safe custody with the lead bank, although they have been tradeable through the Swiss clearing system, SEGA, since 1984. Types of instrument available in the Swiss franc market include fixed, floating and convertible issues, issues with equity warrants and dual currency issues. The following tables show the growth of the Swiss franc foreign bond and note market by type of instrument and by location and category of borrower. Approval for public bond issues must be sought from the Swiss National Bank.

Public bond issues are syndicated through fixed syndicates of banks which are comprised of established groupings of banks, or through ad hoc groups of banks. The largest of the fixed syndicates is led by the three big commercial banks (Credit Suisse, Swiss Bank Corporation and Union Bank of Switzerland), all of which have direct placing power through their branch networks or through management of in-house funds. Foreign-owned Swiss banks may now form part of the syndicates.

Table 4
Switzerland – Volume of Swiss Franc Bonds issued each year
(in billions of SFr)

Category	1988	1989	1990	1991	1992
Government	0.70	0.94	0.82	1.85	7.32
Cantons and Municipalities	1.55	0.58	2.42	3.20	5.98
Banks and Mortgage Associations	7.43	8.23	9.82	9.42	8.84
Non-bank Corporates	5.04	4.50	3.52	3.05	3.57
Foreign Entities		30.16	32.54	28.81	26.30

Private placements are normally fully underwritten by a bank or a limited number of banks residing in Switzerland, including foreign-owned banks.

3.3   United Kingdom

3.3.1   *Domestic Securities Market*
The UK fixed income domestic securities market consists primarily of the following:

- Money market: Discount Bills and Negotiable Certificates of Deposit;

- UK Government Securities (Gilt-Edged Stocks, "Gilts");

- Local Authority Bonds and Stocks; and

- Foreign bonds, i.e. Bulldog bonds.

There is also a long-term corporate bond market, but this has never been a major source of funds for the UK corporate sector, and is currently dominated by secured debt issued by property companies and unsecured borrowing by banks. Both this and the Bulldog market have been gradually superceded by the more flexible and liquid Eurosterling market.

Although new issue volume is still dominated by UK government issues, the diversity of borrowers has dramatically increased in other sterling bond markets and has coincided with greater variety in the structuring of new issues. Many of the novel techniques now being used in other bond markets originated in the sterling bond markets, e.g. partly-paid bonds, convertible bonds and index-linked bonds.

The domestic sterling bond markets are changing dramatically as a result of the abolition in October 1986 of fixed commissions and of the single capacity of brokers and jobbers (market-makers). There have been many new entrants into the market and the amount of capital devoted to market-making has increased sharply.

3.3.2 *Money Market*
The two most important examples of Discount Bills are UK Treasury Bills, (usually maturing in 91 days), and Commercial Bills of Exchange (usually maturing in 90 to 180 days), both of which are issued at a discount from their redemption price of par.

Fixed and floating rate Sterling Certificates of Deposit ("£CDs" and "FRCDs") are issued by UK banks with maturities ranging from three months to five years.

3.3.3 *Gilt-Edged Stocks*
Gilt-edged securities are securities issued by the UK Treasury. The Gilt market is by far the largest of the sterling markets, is extremely liquid and provides a wide range of maturities. Issue maturities range from "shorts" of one day to five years, to issues with no final maturity which are considered irredeemable, such as War Loan issued in the Second World War.

The Bank of England manages all new issues of Gilts and, to the extent that an issue is not completely sold, taps out the balance over a period of time at market related prices through the government broker ("Tap stock").

Gilts are frequently issued on a partly-paid basis, i.e. investors are required to make only a token payment (usually not less than 15% of the nominal amount) on the issue date, with the balance to be paid in subsequent instalments.

Variable rate Gilts have been issued on which interest is paid semi-annually and indexed to the average discount rate of three month Treasury Bills for the relative interest period, which rate is determined by the Bank of England.

The UK Government has also issued index-linked stock, which carries a low coupon of, say 2%, with capital redemption indexed to the Retail Price Index published by the UK Department of Employment.

Throughout 1987-9 the Gilt market contracted following net redemptions by the UK Treasury as a result of the Government's budget surplus. However, plummeting tax receipts as a result of the deep recession in the beginning of the 1990s has forced the Government to borrow significant amounts in the gilts market since 1992.

3.3.4   *Local Authority Bonds and Stocks*

Local authorities in the United Kingdom issue fixed rate bonds and stocks, the distinction between the two being that bonds have original maturities of five years or less, and stocks have maturities of more than five years. Local authorities have also begun to issue floating rate securities, on which interest is payable semi-annually at a margin above the London Interbank Offered Rate for six month sterling deposits.

3.3.5   *Bulldog bonds*

Before the development of the foreign bond market in the United States, when sterling was the world's primary reserve currency, a highly developed foreign bond market existed in the United Kingdom. Issuers were primarily foreign governments or their agencies. A number of these issues are still outstanding and are listed on the London Stock Exchange. With the imposition of Exchange Control Regulations in 1947, new issue activity terminated until October 1979 when these regulations were abolished.

3.4 Germany

3.4.1 *Domestic Securities*

The domestic bond market in Germany comprises public sector bonds, bank bonds, Schuldscheine (which are not strictly speaking securities) and corporate bonds. The latter category is small in relation to the whole because German corporations have traditionally borrowed from banks rather than through the bond market. With the emergence of a large fixed, liquid Euro-DM market in 1992 there will be more segmentation, resulting in more room for the establishment of a corporate market in the future. The foreign bond market has been treated as being part of the Euromarket. The Deutsche Bundesbank does not differentiate between Eurobonds and foreign bonds and the Euromarket has treated any Deutschemark bond issue syndicated through an international group of banks to be a Eurobond. Before 1992 lead-managers had, however, to be German banks. With the liberalisation of 1992 lead managers of foreign banks do not have to be German subsidiaries but may be branches.

The Euro-DM market grew in volume in 1992 and 1993 in a way not previously seen. New issue levels have reached record highs. Effectively, there is no longer a major difference between the Euro DM and the domestic DM markets (apart from the tax grossing up). The lack of liquidity in the domestic market is the most important driving force for borrowers and investors alike to turn to the Euro DM market. Large sized issues of DM1 billion plus and the commitment of the lead managers to make a market with a tight bid/offer spread have made the Euro DM market the leader of the whole DM market.

In maturity terms the German bond market used to be a long-term market, with maturities of up to 40 years. In recent years maturities have shortened considerably, with 10–12 years now seen as the upper limit.

3.4.2 *Public bonds*

Bonds issued by public authorities (the Federal Government and its agencies such as the Federal Railways, the Federal Post Office, the Treuhand, German states and cities) are floated through a fixed issuing syndicate comprising all the major German and some major international banks. In the case of the Federal Government, the Railways and the Post Office, the syndicate is led by the Bundesbank.

In addition to longer term bonds, public authorities also issue notes with maturities of between two and five years by tender. The Government itself also issues five-year bonds on a tap basis and six or seven year savings bonds which, after one year, can be redeemed by the investor at any time at par, plus accrued interest.

In the short-term market, the Government issues discount notes and financing notes with up to a two year life. Discount notes are sold by the Bundesbank in open market operations while financing notes are specifically tailored for institutional investors (other than credit institutions) and are sold through syndicates of banks.

3.4.3 *Bank bonds*

There is a broad range of bank bonds available in the domestic market, comprising mainly:

Mortgage bonds, issued by private mortgage banks, ship mortgage banks and public credit institutions for the purpose of financing mortgage loans, and secured by the relevant property;

Municipal bonds, issued by private and public mortgage banks principally to finance federal or local authority spending, and secured by claims against the appropriate authority;

Unsecured mortgage bonds, also issued by mortgage institutions, but not secured;

Central savings banks bonds, issued by savings banks, and the proceeds of which are used to extend credit to medium sized business or for the financing needs of the German states;

Commercial bank bonds, which are unsecured bonds issued by commercial banks.

3.4.4 *Schuldscheine*
Schuldscheine are assignable large-sized, short, medium or long-term loans. Assignment has to be in written form and the assignable certificates of indebtedness are traded in the German bond market.

Compared to normal loans or bonds, Schuldscheine offer several advantages. They can be issued without Bundesbank approval and are not subject to calendar requirements.

Typical borrowers are public authorities, central savings banks and private and semi-public banks. Over recent years, foreign borrowers, predominantly supranational organisations and the EEC, have tapped the Schuldscheine market as well.

3.5   **United States**

3.5.1 *Domestic Securities*
The US fixed income domestic capital market, centred in New York, is by far the largest in the world. It can be divided into the following six sectors:

- Government Securities;

- Municipals;

- Mortgage backed Securities;

- Corporate Securities;

- Foreign bonds; and

- Money Market Instruments.

3.5.2 *Government Securities*

The US Government market consists of securities issued by the US Treasury (referred to as "Treasuries") and those issued by various Federal Agencies (referred to as "Agencies"). They encompass a wide variety of negotiable and non-negotiable securities with maturities ranging from five days to 40 years. US Treasury debt is backed by the full faith and credit of the United States Government. Marketable Treasury securities are the most liquid and easily traded instruments in any capital market and have a daily turnover of several billion US dollars.

Treasury Bills have maturities of either 13 weeks (three months), 26 weeks (six months) or 52 weeks (one year) and are sold on a discount basis. Three and six month Bills are auctioned weekly while the one year Bills auction normally takes place every four weeks. The Treasury also occasionally auctions Special Bills and Cash Management Bills with various maturities. The Chicago Mercantile Exchange maintains a futures market in Treasury Bills.

Treasury Notes and Bonds carry a stated coupon or interest rate which is payable semi-annually. Treasury Notes are issued with maturities of between one and ten years and are non-callable during their lifetime. Bonds have an initial offering lifetime of between ten and 30 years and occasionally have some form of optional redemption feature, which varies from one to another.

Agency Securities ("Agencies") are issued by US Government agencies. They are not direct obligations of the US Treasury, but involve Federal sponsorship or guarantees. The increased investor interest in these securities is largely due to their investment quality and their expanding secondary markets. Agency securities are available in a wide range of maturities from Farm Credit Consolidated Systemwide Discount Notes maturing in five days to Government National Mortgage Association ("GNMA") Pass-through Securities with stated maturities of 40 years. The most actively traded Agencies securities are those of the Federal Home Loan Bank; Federal National Mortgage Association; Federal Farm Credit Banks; Student Loan Marketing Association and the Federal Home Loan Mortgage Corporation.

564

3.5.3 *Municipals*

Municipal bonds are issued by state and local governments and their agencies to finance both governmentally owned and operated facilities and, in appropriate circumstances, privately owned and/or operated facilities. In order for interest on bonds issued to finance private facilities to be exempt from Federal income taxation, the facilities must be of specific limited types (e.g., solid waste disposal facilities, sewage facilities, certain electric energy or gas facilities, low income housing, small manufacturing facilities, etc.). In addition, such bonds must satisfy a number of additional requirements. Municipal bonds can have maturities of 40 years, although maximum maturities of 30 years are more common. In the case of privately owned facilities, the municipal issuer almost always functions as a conduit, with the bonds payable solely by the private entity. Tax-exempt bonds, even if sold solely on the credit of a private entity, are almost always exempt from registration with the Securities and Exchange Commission and would not result in required periodic filings with the SEC under the Securities and Exchange Act of 1934.

3.5.4 *Mortgage-backed Securities*

Mortgage-backed securities are bonds collateralised with mortgages. These can either be structured as pass-through securities, whereby payments of principal and interest on a pool of mortgages are passed through to the investor, or as general obligations of the issuer, collateralised by a pool of mortgages.

3.5.5 *Corporate Bonds*

Debt issues by US corporate borrowers range from short-term to long-term (30 to 40 years). All issues are priced at a margin over US Treasuries of an equivalent maturity, the amount of the margin varying according to the credit quality of the issuer and market conditions, namely the demand at the time for that maturity and type of borrower. With the liberalisation of regulations allowing US borrowers to issue bonds at short notice, the US corporate bond sector operates in direct competition with the Eurobond market for US corporates.

"Junk" or high-yield bonds are a form of straight fixed rate corporate bonds. A significant number of junk bonds have been issued in recent years. They are issued by low quality corporates of below investment grade and as a result carry high coupons to compensate for the added risk involved. They have been issued (in particular in the late 1980s) as financing for takeover bids and in leveraged management buyouts.

3.5.6 *Yankee Bonds*

Until the introduction of Interest Equalisation Tax ("IET") in 1964 (retroactive to 1963), the Eurodollar bond market did not exist. US dollar denominated issues by foreign borrowers were foreign bonds, although many of these bonds were beneficially owned by non-residents of the United States. The IET effectively eliminated the issuing activity in the US domestic market of non-Canadian, foreign entities. In 1974, when IET was reduced to zero, the foreign bond sector again became an important source of funds for foreign borrowers.

Yankee bonds are securities issued by foreign borrowers under the sponsorship of a predominantly US domestic underwriting syndicate. They are registered with the United States Securities and Exchange Commission, thus allowing them to be sold to the public in the United States. To date, they have generally been medium-term in maturity, ranging from five to eight years, but issues with longer maturities are available. Borrowers in this market have generally been supranational institutions, foreign governments or their agencies, although the market has, in recent years, seen an increasing number of corporate borrowers.

3.5.7 *Money-market Instruments*

There is a broad variety of short-term money market instruments available in the United States, namely, bankers acceptances, certificates of deposit, commercial paper and tax-exempt notes. Futures and options are widely available on money market instruments as well as in the longer-term market.

Certificates of deposit, issued by banks and thrift institutions (savings and loans), are for seven days or longer, with fixed or variable rates of interest. Fixed rate CDs with maturities of over a year are known as term CDs.

Commercial paper is the name for short-term unsecured promissory notes issued by most entities other than commercial banks. Commercial paper is usually backed by unused bank credit lines to repay the notes in the event the issuer is unable to roll the paper over in the market at maturity. Maturities are from one to 270 days.

States, municipalities and other public entities issue various forms of short-term notes of less than one year's maturity, on which interest is exempt from tax, and the proceeds of which are used as interim or project financing or for working capital purposes.

4. CHARACTERISTICS OF EUROBONDS

Fixed rate medium- to long-term straight unsecured debt offerings have constituted the largest part of primary activity in the Euromarket. The Eurobond market is, however, renowned for its innovative ability, and the range of securities available and actively traded includes securities with features such as floating interest rates, extendable and retractable maturities, debt or equity warrants, multiple tranches and deep discounts. Innovation is frequently used to develop structures with features designed to appeal to particular groups of investors. Bonds have been designed to replicate the features of options and futures for investors whose guidelines do not allow them to invest in those instruments directly. Others have been structured to give tax advantages to certain investors.

Eurobonds do, however, have certain key characteristics in common:

* interest payments are free of withholding tax
* bonds are generally in bearer form
* the vast majority are unsecured
* in almost all cases, publicly offered securities are listed on one or more stock exchanges, although issues are generally traded in the over-the-counter market.

Table 5 shows the development of the Eurobond market by type of instrument from 1989 to 1993.

4.1 Maturity

The Eurobond market was, in its early years, a long-term market, with issuing activity concentrated in the ten to 20 year maturity range. In 1973 and 1974, however, under the impact of inflation, high short-term interest

Table 5
Volumes of Euro-Bonds by Category 1989–1993
(in US $ millions)

	1989	Iss.	1990	Iss.	1991	Iss.	1992	Iss.	1993	Iss.
Fixed rate	120,521	1,175	114,591	908	199,805	1,133	218,610	1,099	257,320	1,141
Fixed rate with warrants for equity	67,379	259	19,705	111	27,577	204	12,551	87	10,294	63
Fixed rate with warrants for debt	0	0	0	0	0	0	789	4	862	4
Convertibles	5,249	39	4,281	31	7,420	64	5,382	35	12,254	87
FRN	24,697	180	45,011	234	37,148	141	47,980	341	52,809	382
FRN with warrants for equity	0	0	0	0	131	1	0	0	0	0
FRN with warrants for debt	337	1	0	0	0	0	0	0	0	0

Iss. = Number of issuers

Source: Euromoney Publications Plc

rates and uncertainty about future interest levels, the focus was suddenly shifted to the shorter end of the maturity range – five to eight years. Since then, lingering fears of inflation and other factors have concentrated demand on medium-term bonds, although the best quality borrowers have once again been able to obtain long-term finance.

Table 6
Types of Eurobonds Issued

	1989 %	1990 %	1991 %	1992 %
Fixed rate	55	63	80	76
FRN	11	23	7	17
Warrants for Equity	31	11	11	4
Convertibles	3	3	2	3
	100	100	100	100

Table 7 shows a breakdown of the maturity at issue; some bond issues (in particular FRNs) have optional or mandatory early redemption. Bonds without redemption features (other than for tax reasons) are known as "bullet" bonds.

4.2 Redemption

4.2.1 *Redemption at the option of the issuer:* Many bonds (but in particular, FRNs and convertibles) may be redeemed at the option of the issuer in whole or in part after they have been outstanding for a specified number of years. In the case of fixed rate bonds, the optional redemption price is usually at a small premium to par until the last year, to compensate the investor for the loss of yield caused by the early redemption of his bond. Floating rate notes may be redeemed at par, but only on interest payment dates, to avoid any loss caused in respect of the unmatched funding positions that would result if the note was called for redemption during an interest period. Optional redemption is also permitted in the event of certain changes in the tax treatment of the bonds (see "Withholding Tax" below).

Table 7
Issue Volume 1987–1992
(in US $ millions)

	1987	Iss.	1988	Iss.	1989	Iss.	1990	Iss.	1991	Iss.	1992	Iss.
1-5 years												
Fixed	72,197	754	111,873	1,077	133,549	1,100	90,401	782	115,219	821	111,247	659
Floating	8,586	80	7,684	76	8,025	80	14,062	85	26,314	69	22,657	180
6-10 years												
Fixed	39,120	348	39,032	301	50,903	344	41,515	240	103,296	531	104,782	534
Floating	4,327	36	7,671	47	8,659	53	21,969	118	5,455	41	19,347	129
11-15 years												
Fixed	824	10	853	7	2,387	20	2,123	15	6,795	41	14,450	64
Floating	734	5	1,260	4	1,133	21	2,804	11	243	3	2,237	12
16-20 years												
Fixed	1,711	11	713	5	698	3	1,178	7	4,878	16	1,616	11
Floating	–	–	1,982	3	725	4	999	6	331	2	621	4
21-25 years												
Fixed	73	2	360	2	1,926	7	765	4	828	9	2,095	9
Floating	57	1	–	–	–	–	–	–	–	–	–	–
Above 25 years												
Fixed	168	3	757	5	663	4	267	4	2,468	19	2,839	7
Floating	2,879	20	6,988	37	6,769	25	5,281	15	4,935	27	3,294	17

Iss. = Number of issuers
Source: Euromoney Publications Plc

4.2.2 *Redemption at the option of bondholders:* This provision, known as a put option, allows the bondholder to require the issuer to redeem its bond on a specified date prior to maturity, or, occasionally, if certain events of an adverse financial or legal nature occur. Many long-term floating rate note issues have puts, generally at intervals of five or less years, enabling certain institutional investors, such as central banks, which are limited to five-year investments, to purchase them. Certain convertible issues may also have provision for a bondholder's put often set at a premium.

4.2.3 *Mandatory redemption:* Mandatory redemption provisions are designed to reduce the average life of a bond, making it more attractive to the investor, and thereby supporting the price in the secondary market. A sinking fund provides that a certain proportion of the bonds be redeemed each year, in quarterly, semi-annually or annual instalments. The redemption price is generally par and the bonds to be redeemed are generally selected by drawings. In some instances the borrower is allowed to apply bonds purchased in the secondary market towards satisfaction of the sinking fund or may be permitted to double the amount of bonds to be applied to the sinking fund in any redemption period.

A purchase fund, in contrast, only operates through purchases in the market at prices below par, thus providing a more direct support to the secondary market price of the bonds. Since a specified amount of bonds must be purchased each year, the task of a purchase fund agent, whose role is to purchase the necessary paper at the lowest price, is a skilled one.

4.3 Size

The sharp increase in the aggregate volume of new issues over the last several years does not convey the dramatic increase in the size of individual financings. In contrast to the beginning of the 1970s, when the average size of a Eurodollar bond issue was in the $20–25m range, fixed rate issues of US$100m and above are now the norm whereas in the floating rate note market it is rare to find an issue of less than US$200m. Convertible or equity-linked issues tend to be smaller and an issue of US$50m is still considered to be reasonably large. The largest fixed rate issue was a US$3bn issue for the United Kingdom, and the largest floating rate note issue was a US$4bn financing for the same borrower;

the largest convertible issue was US$1bn for Texaco, Inc. The largest bond issues with equity warrants were for US$1.5bn each in the names of Mitsubishi Corporation, Toyota Motor Corporation, Mitsubishi Heavy Industries and Sumitomo Corporation.

While individual issues in the convertible market may not be large, the use of syndication techniques allows significant aggregate amounts to be placed at any one time. An example of this was the simultaneous offering in 1986 of four convertible issues for Elders IXL of US$175m, £40m, DM200m and Sfr200m, a total of approximately US$455m.

4.4 Coupon Payments
Coupons in the Eurobond market are paid in arrear. Fixed rate and most convertible bonds pay interest annually; and interest is accrued on the basis of a 360 day year of 12 months of 30 days. A number of convertible bonds (predominantly denominated in £ or US$) pay interest semi-annually, accrued in the same manner. Interest accrual periods for floating rate notes can be of one, three or six months' duration, with interest paid at the end of the period. Interest on FRNs accrues on the basis of the number of days in the interest period concerned divided by 360 or 365 days in the case of sterling FRNs.

4.5 Listing
All public bond issues are listed on a major stock exchange, generally London, Luxembourg, Frankfurt or Amsterdam. Although issues are traded in the over-the-counter market, some institutions, particularly in Germany, are limited as to the amount of unlisted paper they can hold, and a listing therefore broadens the investor base.

4.6 Withholding Tax
It is an essential feature of the Eurobond market that payments of interest, principal and premium (if any) are made free of withholding tax imposed by the country of the borrower. In countries where withholding tax is imposed on direct issues of debt, the entity wishing to raise funds does so through a finance subsidiary located in a country where payments are free of withholding tax, and guarantees payment by the finance subsidiary. Typical locations for finance vehicles are the Netherlands, the Netherlands

Antilles and the British Virgin Islands. It is important in choosing the location of a finance vehicle that a tax treaty exists between that country and the parent company's country so that payments of interest from the parent to the subsidiary on the latter's loan of the proceeds of the bond issue are free of withholding tax.

Virtually all Eurobond issues contain a "grossing up" provision whereby, if withholding tax is imposed, the issuer will pay such additional amounts that the investor will receive, net, the amount it would have received had no withholding tax been imposed. Since "grossing up" would impose significant extra cost for the issuer, it is entitled to redeem all the bonds at par (or, in the case of certain puttable convertible bonds, at a premium to par), plus accrued interest, if withholding taxes are imposed on its payments.

4.7 Form of Bonds

It is still an important requirement of the Eurobond market that bonds be available in bearer form with interest coupons attached. Eurobonds are most frequently issued in the denominations of US$1,000 or US$5,000. Over recent years, bonds of larger denominations (from US$10,000 to US$500,000) have become more common for those issues which are designed to be placed principally with institutional investors. Alternatively, bonds can be issued in two or more denominations, for example, a combination of US$1,000 and US$10,000.

Present tax legislation in the United States (the Tax Equity and Fiscal Responsibility Act (TEFRA)) provides that interest on, and, where a US company is the issuer, principal of, bearer bonds may no longer be paid either in the United States or to US persons. Until amended regulations were published in September 1983, this meant that if secondary distribution into the United States was envisaged, some provision had to be made to exchange bearer bonds for registered bonds. Regulations now permit US investors to hold bearer bonds without incurring penalties as long as certain conditions are met. However, if a bond is to be placed privately in the United States in the initial distribution then registered bonds are required for delivery to the investors.

4.8 Status

The majority of Eurobonds are senior unsecured obligations of the issuer or guarantor, if appropriate.

The terms of the bonds generally contain a pari passu clause, stating that the bonds will rank equally with each other and with other indebtedness of the borrower of the same class. They will also frequently contain a negative pledge clause, which requires the borrower equally and rateably to secure the bonds if it issues secured indebtedness in the future. Negative pledge clauses often contain various exceptions, for example, limiting them to external indebtedness or quoted indebtedness, or excluding mortgages on certain assets, if the funds being raised are to be used specifically for the purchase of those assets.

Bonds sometimes rank as subordinated debt in liquidation. Subordinated, in the case of corporations, to senior debt and, in the case of banks, to deposits. Subordinated corporate debt is rarely issued in the public market, except in the convertible bond market. Banks, on the other hand, frequently issue subordinated debt as a form of capital even though such issues became less frequent in the late 1980s as a result of increasing investor concern over the credit quality of banks and the penalising effect that the Bank for International Settlements' rules have on banks holding other banks' subordinated obligations. The extent of subordination will depend on bank regulations in the country concerned and what type of capital treatment of the debt that the bank in question is seeking.

4.9 Events of Default

Virtually all bond issues contain events of default (except certain subordinated issues for banks) for non-payment of principal, premium or interest, breach of any other covenant or term of the issue, and liquidation or bankruptcy. Many include a cross-default provision, operational if the borrower goes into default on other debt issues. If an event of default occurs and is not cured within a specified time frame, the bonds may be accelerated and become immediately due and payable.

4.10 Trustee or Fiscal Agent

Bond issues are constituted either by a trust deed or by a fiscal agency agreement. Under the former, an independent trustee company acts as representative of the bondholders on all matters affecting their interests, including deciding on action to be taken in the event of default. A trustee has discretionary powers and can agree to changes to certain minor terms on the bondholders' behalf; changes of a material nature require resolution at a meeting of bondholders. A fiscal agent, on the other hand, is the agent of the issuer, and has no fiduciary responsibility towards bondholders. Under a fiscal agency agreement, bondholders can take action directly against the issuer in the event of a default.

4.11 Regulation

The Eurobond market is renowned for the absence of regulation governing its activities, although some regulations are imposed by central banks on the turning of issues in certain currencies or on the banks which may lead-manage such issues. These restrictions have been significantly reduced and few remain. Other regulations relate to listing requirements with respect to prospectus contents.

The main area of regulation is that of selling restrictions, imposed on offers or sales of bonds into, or to residents of, certain countries. The most pronounced of these is a restriction on sales of bonds, whether denominated in US dollars or not, into the United States or to US persons.

Under the provisions of the Securities Act of 1933 all issues of securities which are intended to be distributed to US persons must be registered with the United States Securities and Exchange Commission ("SEC"), a process which involves approval by the SEC of the prospectus prepared in connection with the bond issue. Since the principal market for Eurobonds is normally not in the United States, there is no need to register the issue with the SEC; however, restrictions have to be imposed on the sale of Eurobonds in the United States or to US persons.

All Eurobond issues, therefore, contain a restriction that the bonds may not be offered or sold in the United States or to US persons as part of the initial distribution; and that bonds forming part of the issue (whether or not acquired during the initial distribution) may not be offered or sold in the United States or to US persons until 40 days after closing. Bond issues on which the US sales restriction period is over are known as seasoned bonds.

575

An important exemption from the SEC registration requirements relates to the so-called private placement rules, the most important of which is Rule 144A of the Securities Act of 1933, pursuant to which Eurobonds can be offered in the United States in the initial distribution to "qualified institutional buyers" (QIBs). Since the introduction of Rule 144A in 1990 an increasing number of Eurobond issues now have provisions for a private placement in the US and a significant portion of some issues are now placed with QIBs.

N.B. Rule 144A can also be applied to domestic US bond issues. In such instances the investors are restricted exclusively to QIBs in view of the fact that as such issues do not have to conform to all the requirements of a conventional bond issue as specified by the Securities Act it is a condition that only "professional" investors may buy the bonds. The concept here is that if an issue is made available to professional and non-professional (e.g. members of the general public) investors all relevant information about the issuer and the issue must be made available so that even the non-professional investor can make an informed judgment on the merits of buying the bonds. As Rule 144A requires only restricted information to be available then such issues can only be taken up by QIBs.

Restrictions are also generally imposed on offers or sales of bonds or on distribution of documents to non-professionals in Great Britain (or, if the lead-manager is not located in Great Britain, in his jurisdiction as appropriate) and on offers and sales of bonds to residents of the country of the issuer. Apart from restrictions on offers and sales in the US, Great Britain and the issuer's location, which are spelt out in detail in the offering documents, syndicate members and investors are required to investigate for themselves restrictions on sales in any other jurisdiction where they might offer or sell bonds.

4.12 IPMA

The International Primary Market Association was established in 1985 by the major participants in the Eurobond primary market. Its membership is limited to banks which have lead-managed at least nine issues in the preceding three calendar years or six in the preceding two calendar years. The IPMA issues recommendations rather than rules. Its recommendations have covered such matters as early disclosure of commercial and non-commercial terms of issues at the time of launch, conduct of stabilisation transactions, payment of commissions, allotment procedure, protection and execution of agreements.

4.13 ISMA

Participants in the secondary market are generally members of the International Secondary Markets Association, which was set up by its members to provide a forum for joint discussion and examination of questions relating to the international securities markets, and to provide services and assistance to participants. ISMA also maintains committees and proceedings for conciliation and arbitration. Rules and recommendations cover such matters as dealing practices, settlements, accrued interest calculation and delivery practices.

5. TYPES OF EUROBOND

5.1 Fixed Rate Bonds

Table 8 shows the development of the fixed rate Euromarket by currency between 1987 and 1992. The broadest range of currencies is found in the fixed rate market, although some have been used to a very limited extent.

5.1.1 *Straight bond:* The "plain vanilla" fixed rate bond has a series of annual coupons, and may have optional redemption provisions prior to maturity.

5.1.2 *Zero coupon:* The zero coupon bond pays a single amount at maturity. It has no intermediate interest payments and is priced at a discount such that the compound annual yield to maturity is at a market rate. The attraction of this instrument for the investor lies in its guaranteed return, with no reinvestment risk, and in the way in which the accrual of the unpaid interest is treated for tax purposes, that is to say whether it is considered to be income or capital gain.

5.1.3 *Deep discount bonds:* The deep discount bond pays an annual coupon but is similar to the zero coupon bond in that the coupon is below prevailing market rates and the issue must therefore be priced at a discount to achieve a market return.

577

Table 8
Fixed Rate Euromarket Issues by Currency
1987–1992

Currency	1987 Amount mm (US$)	Iss.	1988 Amount mm (US$)	Iss.	1989 Amount mm (US$)	Iss.	1990 Amount mm (US$)	Iss.	1991 Amount mm (US$)	Iss.	1992 Amount mm (US$)	Iss.
US dollar	44,055.19	335	65,071.26	423	110,290.80	505	54,332.48	262	71,976.41	322	74,152.10	338
Sterling	8,837.96	75	11,592.38	77	10,542.65	64	9,104.87	49	16,770.40	86	19,361.34	96
Deutsche Mark	13,520.89	117	22,337.50	191	12,589.53	126	9,227.58	82	17,822.83	185	31,185.65	149
European currency unit	7,278.30	67	10,804.34	90	11,784.52	111	15,054.90	72	30,664.07	107	19,441.75	94
Japanese yen	19,312.41	143	14,629.79	192	16,358.10	302	20,749.98	278	34,661.02	217	29,772.14	134
French franc	936.86	10	1,852.40	16	4,185.82	42	7,309.19	44	16,578.12	82	23,175.53	101
Australian dollar	8,111.18	185	7,342.25	141	6,654.10	119	5,007.58	95	4,453.16	59	4,960.75	57
Dutch guilder	2,352.29	29	3,606.20	43	2,018.98	24	1,402.46	11	3,696.30	24	6,865.21	45
Danish kroner	1,293.45	32	985.94	23	211.43	5	180.71	4	262.01	6	356.40	8
Canadian dollar	5,854.12	91	13,034.70	164	10,934.75	108	6,341.92	55	22,350.99	163	15,460.00	82
Italian lira	559.74	9	1,115.37	12	2,420.37	25	4,702.02	31	8,939.76	56	6,785.25	34
New Zealand dollar	708.48	21	692.79	18	692.09	21	527.86	13	325.10	10	148.98	4
Finnish marks	181.09	3	447.18	6	0.00	0	882.31	15	729.58	13	22.97	1
Austrian schilling	720.09	6	0.00	0	0.00	0	143.52	3	88.19	1	0.00	0
Kuwaiti dinar	374.72	5	0.00	0	0.00	0	0.00	0	0.00	0	0.00	0
Swedish kronor	0.00	0	78.65	1	1,371.52	25	336.33	6	1,299.92	21	893.99	13
TOTAL	114,096.70	1,128	153,590.50	1,397	190,054.60	1,477	135,303.80	1,020	230,617.90	1,352	232,582.00	1,156

Iss. = Number of issuers

Source: Euromoney Publications Plc

5.1.4 *Retractable/extendable bonds:* Retractable or extendable bonds have a long (12–15 year) final maturity, but the initial coupon is applicable for a shorter period, say three or five years. At the end of the period, the issuer refixes the coupon in accordance with market conditions or establishes a formula according to which the coupon will be determined. The period during which the next coupon will apply is either specified under the terms of the issue, or established at the time by the issuer. The same process applies at the end of that period and continues until maturity. The issuer also has the option to call the issue on the coupon refix date, and investors, if they do not like the rate at which the coupon has been refixed, can put the bonds back to the issuer at par. On the assumption that the bondholders' put is not exercised, the issuer obtains long-term funds, through a series of short-term bonds, but only pays commissions once, at the appropriate level for the period during which the initial coupon applies.

5.1.5 *Partly paid bonds:* Only a portion (15–50%) of a partly-paid issue is paid to the issuer on closing with the balance to be paid at a later date, say after six or nine months. If investors do not pay the balance, they forfeit the initial payment. This structure has leverage benefits for investors, for which they are prepared to receive a lower yield than on a fully paid bond.

5.1.6 *Medium-term Notes:* Medium term notes are a relatively new development in the Euromarket. The issuer sets up a programme whereby he is able to issue short to intermediate-term (typically one to five year) bonds on an agency basis. The bonds themselves generally have all the characteristics of straight Eurobonds. MTNs are principally designed to meet investors' specific portfolio requirements where liquidity is not a main consideration and allow issuers to satisfy particular funding needs in circumstances where the amount required is too small or the maturity or issue structure inappropriate for a fully syndicated public issue.

Typically, bonds with imbedded options such as those whose principal repayment is at maturity and is linked to a stock market index, are issued off MTN programmes. In the early 1990s issuers set up MTN programmes which provide for syndicated issues based on the MTN documentation being made.

5.1.7 *Dual Currency Bonds:* The initial, principal amount of a dual currency bond is payable in one currency, while the denomination of the bond, and therefore the interest payments and redemption, is in another usually weaker currency. The exchange rate between the two currencies is fixed for the life of the issue. A variation in this structure gives the issuer the option to redeem and pay interest in either the weaker or the stronger currency. As compensation the investor will receive an above-market coupon.

5.2 Floating Rate Notes

Floating Rate Notes ("FRNs") are bond issues on which the coupon is re-fixed at regular pre-established intervals at a margin usually over rates for the relevant period and currency in the London interbank market. The traditional FRN was a bond of a fixed maturity with an interest rate re-fixed every three or six months and linked to the rate for deposits in the appropriate currency in the London interbank market.

The FRN was developed in the Eurobond market in 1970 as a financial instrument combining elements of medium-term syndicated bank credits and long-term Eurobonds. At that time, it gave a borrower a longer maturity than was available in the syndicated bank credit market, while reducing an investor's exposure to capital depreciation resulting from a rise in interest rates.

Initially most Euromarket participants regarded FRNs as specialised bonds which offered protection, to both issuers and investors, against volatile interest rates. Since 1980, there has been dramatic growth, both in depth and size, in the FRN market and in 1983 the FRN market truly came of age with the launching of "jumbo" issues (US$500m or greater) by sovereign and supranational borrowers of the highest credit standing. Issues by the EEC, French guaranteed agencies, Sweden, Italy, Belgium and Denmark, resulted in an important increase in secondary market liquidity and consequently in a marked narrowing of interest margins paid by the issuers in relation to LIBOR. The size and liquidity of these issues also began to have an effect on spreads in the secondary market and secondary market-makers were able to narrow the spread between their bid and offered prices.

The following table shows the development of the FRN market since 1987 and the extent to which the US dollar has been by far the major issuing currency. Banks have traditionally been the principal investors in FRNs, funding their investments through matching interbank deposits and, since a very large and liquid short-term European interbank market in the currency of denomination is a prerequisite to the issuance of FRNs, the instrument cannot easily be extended to other currencies. Deutschemark FRNs have been permitted since May 1985.

Significant developments in the FRN market have been the narrowing of interest margins in relation to LIBOR and the lengthening of maturities. Several issues have been launced at LIBOR or below and, whereas in 1982–83 the longest readily available maturities were 10 to 12 years, 1984 saw a number of issues with maturities of 15 to 20 years; more than 60 undated/perpetual issues were launched in 1984–86.

In 1987, new issue volume declined sharply as FRNs competed for investor interest with other products such as Euro commercial paper and asset swaps and as borrowers could achieve floating rate funding through the fixed rate market in combination with the swap market. Later in the 1980's the concerns about credit quality of banks and the new BIS rules further reduced issuance of traditional FRNs. As a result FRN issuance in the 1989-91 period was fairly limited and consisted mainly of various types of asset backed securities such as CMO* issues and issues backed by credit card or auto receivables. 1993 saw a reopening of the traditional FRN market with both sovereigns and banks coming back to the market as issuers.

5.2.1 *Types of Issuer*

Prior to 1975, the FRN market was tapped almost exclusively by industrial and governmental entities as an alternative to fixed rate finance. In August 1975, the first issue was made for a commercial bank, Banque Nationale de Paris. This opening of the FRN market for prime international bank credits gave rise to a significant expansion and for a time the market was dominated by large international banks. Since 1982, governmental and supranational issues have again played an increasingly important part in the market whilst banks continue to tap the market as a source of capital rather than funding.

* Collateralised Mortgage Obligations-see page 518.

Table 9
FRN Issues by Currency
1987–1992

Currency	1987 Amount mm (US$)	Iss.	1988 Amount mm (US$)	Iss.	1989 Amount mm (US$)	Iss.	1990 Amount mm (US$)	Iss.	1991 Amount mm (US$)	Iss.	1992 Amount mm (US$)	Iss.
US dollar	7,756.61	81	9,812.57	66	8,692.60	79	15,973.40	103	4,563.13	51	30,095.49	205
Sterling	2,157.20	12	10,815.89	49	7,854.76	38	10,488.35	35	7,464.03	39	4,938.95	25
Deutsche Mark	742.38	5	1,361.85	5	2,922.03	16	10,265.83	43	22,514.73	30	3,331.28	46
European currency unit	161.41	3	0.00	0	501.24	4	2,659.92	12	1,248.05	6	2,294.62	9
Japanese yen	3,032.71	18	1,518.23	30	879.90	30	2,628.82	29	958.12	8	4,140.70	34
French franc	719.55	7	147.03	2	175.06	2	750.53	3	86.13	1	852.54	10
Australian dollar	501.57	5	509.63	7	84.16	1	0.00	0	0.00	0	0.00	0
Dutch guilder	0.00	0	0.00	0	0.00	0	0.00	0	0.00	0	601.36	2
Danish kroner	105.19	2	0.00	0	0.00	0	0.00	0	59.96	1	0.00	0
Canadian dollar	0.00	0	0.00	0	1,792.79	5	0.00	0	131.36	2	824.93	8
Italian lira	160.69	1	321.41	3	1,178.71	5	1,192.26	4	74.74	1	989.01	2
New Zealand dollar	780.12	6	125.92	2	0.00	0	0.00	0	0.00	0	0.00	0
Austrian schilling	467.56	2	974.94	3	1,231.77	3	1,159.16	6	179.99	3	90.40	1
TOTAL	16,584.99	142	25,587.47	167	25,313.03	183	45,118.27	235	37,280.21	142	48,159.27	342

Iss. = Number of issuers

Source: Euromoney Publications Plc

582

In 1984, the FRN market opened up for collateralised transactions. These bonds, issued primarily by US savings and loans institutions, have been backed by US government securities, US mortgage securities and non-securitised mortgage loans and cash and have in all cases obtained a triple A rating from at least one of the credit rating agencies.

In 1987 the mortgage backed FRN market expanded further with the first issues of sterling pass-through FRNs. These are FRNs issued by a special vehicle company and the interest and principal from the mortgages is "passed through" to the investors in the FRNs.

5.2.2 Coupons

FRNs are issued at a margin over the London interbank offered rate (LIBOR), bid rate (LIBID) or the mean between the bid and offered rates (LIMEAN), depending on the credit standing of the issuer, the maturity of the FRNs and general market conditions.

FRNs frequently have included minimum coupons. Initially, they were set at a rate quite close to the then prevailing interest rates; since then minimum rates have tended to be set at around 5% regardless of the prevailing level of interest rates. The reason for having a minimum rate is to attract non-bank investors who may have to depend on the income generated by their savings. Minimum coupons are, however, becoming less frequently seen.

The rate for each interest period is generally set at 11:00 a.m. (London time) two business days prior to (or, in the case of £FRNs on the day of) the start of such interest period. An agent bank is appointed to establish and publish the interest rate for the period by calculating the average of the reference rates, quoted by three to six pre-selected reference banks or from a Reuters or Telerate page and adding the specified margin.

5.2.3 Types of Instruments

(i)   Mis-match FRNs. The "mis-match" floating rate note is an FRN where the coupon is fixed monthly (or sometimes weekly) over three- or six-month LIBID, LIBOR, or LIMEAN, but paid quarterly or semi-annually. In some instances the rate is fixed monthly at the higher of one- and three- or six-month LIBOR, LIBID or LIMEAN. Mis-match FRNs were first issued in late 1979 in response to serious bear market conditions. The mis-match market was then used sporadically until 1984 when a number of US banks came to the market with the formula, and in periods of steep yield curves, mis-match FRNs have been issued by many more borrowers.

(ii)   *FRNs with "Put Options"*. A large number of issues have put options. These bonds give the holder an option to redeem his note at par on a specified date or dates prior to maturity; the most common combination of dates is a ten year final maturity with puts at the end of the fifth and seventh years. They can be attractive to investors who are limited to purchasing five year paper. A variation on this theme was the "flip-flop" formula as issued by the Kingdom of Sweden and Commonwealth Bank of Australia. In these instances investors bought a *perpetual* FRN with annual options to convert into a dated FRN at a lower interest rate, and further options to convert back into the perpetual thereafter.

(iii)   *FRNs with Interest Rate "Caps"*. "Capped" FRNs are issues featuring maximum levels of interest rate. Typically, issuers pass on the cap, at a price, to another party who has a commercial use for an interest rate cap. Proceeds from the cap sale will be applied against the FRN issue, thereby achieving a substantial cost saving for the borrower. FRNs with both a maximum and minimum level of interest are often referred to as "collared" FRNs.

(iv)   *Perpetual FRNs:* Perpetual FRNs are FRNs with no final maturity, although some have call provisions. A few have been issued by sovereign and other non-bank borrowers, but most have been issued by banks for regulatory capital purposes. At the end of 1986, the perpetual market suffered from an acute attack of lack of confidence and has since seen significantly reduced issuing activity.

(v)   *Hybrid FRNs:* Innovations are continually required in the FRN market. In addition to the types described above there have been convertible FRNs and FRNs with warrants, including issues carrying detachable warrants for bonds of a specific fixed rate with either the same, or a different, maturity.

584

5.3   Convertible Issues

A convertible issue is a fixed rate bond which is convertible, at the investor's option into common (or, sometimes, preference) shares of the company issuing or guaranteeing the bond. From time to time, exchangeable issues have been done, whereby the shares for which the bonds are exchangeable are those of a different company.

A convertible bond has all the attributes of a conventional straight bond issue, except that the coupon is lower reflecting the value of the conversion option. The price per share (the "conversion price") at which the bond is convertible into ordinary shares represents a premium to the market price of the shares at the time the terms of the issue are agreed. The level of the coupon and the premium are related, with a lower coupon requiring a lower conversion premium and vice versa. The conversion price will be subject to adjustment to protect the investors' equity interest in the company, for example, if the company issues shares to its shareholders by way of rights at less than the then current market price or if the shares are consolidated or sub-divided. These anti-dilution provisions vary from jurisdiction to jurisdiction, depending on market practice and the company law of the issuer's country.

The so-called "breakeven point" on a convertible issue is reached at the point at which the amount of conversion premium has been covered by the additional yield provided by the coupon, namely the amount by which the coupon exceeds the dividend on the underlying shares.

Many high premium convertibles issued in the mid 1980s included a bondholders' put option, generally in the fifth or seventh year. The price at which the bondholders can put their bonds to the company is generally at a premium to par, providing a yield to put which is close to, but still below, the current fixed rate bond yield for that maturity and credit. The inclusion of a put option provides downside protection for the investor in the event the shares do not perform sufficiently well to make conversion economically attractive by the date of the put.

An essential component of a convertible bond issue is the exchange rate between the currency of the bond and that of the issuer's shares. There is no exchange rate impact for a US borrower issuing $ bonds or a UK company issuing £ bonds, but for convertibles where the currencies

585

of the bond and shares are different, movements between them after the issue date will affect the value of the conversion option.

Specifically, the conversion terms of a convertible bond issue will be defined in terms of both a fixed foreign exchange rate to be applied to the face value of the bonds upon conversion (no matter where the then prevailing foreign exchange rate might be) and a fixed conversion price expressed in terms of the domestic currency.

In order for conversion to occur, the company's share price must, during the term of the bond, increase by at least the amount of the premium, in terms of the foreign currency and not just in terms of the local currency. If the domestic currency weakens against the currency of the bond issue, then the share price would need to rise by more than the amount of the premium in order to ensure conversion. On the other hand, if the domestic currency strengthens, then the share price could increase by less than the amount of the premium in order for conversion to be economically attractive.

Table 10 shows the growth of the convertible market by currency.

5.4 Warrants

Warrants for debt or equity have become an increasingly important, and, in the late 1980s, dominant, part of the Euromarket. The warrants may be issued with a bond, called the host bond, and then physically detached and either exercised or traded separately. Alternatively, the warrants may be issued independently of bonds: these are termed "naked" warrants.

5.4.1 *Equity Warrants*

An equity warrant gives the holder the right to purchase shares of a company at a fixed price (the "exercise price") for a fixed period of time (the "exercise period"). Equity warrants are generally offered as part of a package with fixed rate bonds or common shares but can also be issued as "naked warrants" (see below). The exercise period of an equity warrant is sometimes linked to the maturity of the host bonds.

586

Table 10
Convertible Issues
by Currency 1987–1992

Currency	1987 Amount mm (US$)	Iss.	1988 Amount mm (US$)	Iss.	1989 Amount mm (US$)	Iss.	1990 Amount mm (US$)	Iss.	1991 Amount mm (US$)	Iss.	1992 Amount mm (US$)	Iss.
US dollar	9,477.86	85	2,046.00	23	2,150.97	17	1,122.00	14	3,474.87	45	3,106.38	23
Sterling	3,927.29	33	2,338.23	16	1,918.82	11	2,041.60	11	2,316.95	7	381.75	3
Deutsche Mark	342.78	5	72.64	2	789.54	5	0.00	0	0.00	0	0.00	0
European currency unit	0.00	0	406.42	2	69.03	1	0.00	0	370.73	3	635.97	3
Japanese yen	0.00	0	0.00	0	0.00	0	0.00	0	0.00	0	998.44	2
French franc	0.00	0	505.27	2	171.68	2	1,117.82	6	603.96	4	152.39	2
Australian dollar	299.27	3	362.63	3	0.00	0	0.00	0	0.00	0	0.00	0
Dutch guilder	66.75	2	0.00	0	47.13	1	0.00	0	102.79	1	0.00	0
Canadian dollar	71.03	3	0.00	0	29.50	1	0.00	0	0.00	0	0.00	0
Italian lira	0.00	0	92.67	1	72.43	1	0.00	0	76.29	2	52.12	1
Norwegian kroner	0.00	0	0.00	0	0.00	0	0.00	0	104.09	1	0.00	0
TOTAL	14,184.98	131	5,823.85	49	5,249.10	39	4,281.42	31	7,049.68	63	5,327.05	34

Iss. = Number of issuers

Source: Euromoney Publications Plc

587

Table 11 shows a breakdown of the bond with equity warrant market by currency.

The bond element of a bond issue with equity warrants has all the attributes of a conventional straight bond issue except that the coupon is lower than the coupon required for a conventional straight bond issue, reflecting the value of the warrant.

The key terms of an issue of bonds with equity warrants are the equity content of the issue (i.e. the number of shares which will be issued if the warrants are exercised), the exercise price of the shares, the exercise period of the warrants, and the coupon and issue price of the bonds.

The equity, or exercise, content of the issue can be defined as:

$$\text{Equity Content} = \frac{\text{No. of shares} \times \text{Exercise price} \times \text{Exchange rate}}{\text{Principal amount of bond}}$$

where the exchange rate is the current rate of exchange between the currency in which the shares are denominated and the currency of the bond.

Whilst in general the Euromarket is flexible on the exact terms selected by an issuer, most issuers tend to set their terms with an equity content of between 25% and 100%, an exercise price of between 95% and 115% of the current share price, and an exercise period between three and 10 years from the date of issue. The warrants are usually exercisable at any time, except during the first 30 days after the closing of the bond issue.

As for a convertible issue, the terms of the bond and warrant are interdependent of each other. The equity content, the exercise price and the exercise period will determine the value of the warrant and the coupon and issue price of the bonds will reflect this value. Conversely, if an issuer has a target coupon level, only two of the three terms of the warrants can be pre-set but the other term must then be set to give the warrants the value required by the market.

Bonds with equity warrants vary from convertible bonds in three principal respects. The warrants are exercised in cash, which means that the company obtains new cash when the shares are issued and that the host bonds remain outstanding. On a convertible issue, no new cash is

588

involved because the bonds are cancelled upon conversion. For the same reason, a warrant issue provides the issuer with flexibility as to the equity content of the issue, whereas the equity content on a convertible issue must be 100% because the convertible bond is used to pay for the shares on conversion. Thirdly, the exchange rate risk inherent in a convertible does not exist on a warrant issue, because the equity warrants are priced, traded and exercised in the currency of the shares.

In recent years a number of naked warrant issues have been made in the Euromarket. These issues have typically been done by market professionals and not by the company issuing the shares. These market professionals have typically covered their obligations under the warrants through complex hedging techniques or may have negotiated an option with a major shareholder in the company into whose shares the warrants are exerciseable. Such warrants are referred to as "covered" warrants.

5.4.2 *Debt Warrants*

Debt warrants are options to buy, at a given price during the warrants' life, bonds which mature on a fixed date. The exercise price is usually par plus accrued interest. There have been many types of debt warrants, the principal of which are the following:

- Warrants into host bonds: the warrants are exerciseable into the bonds with which they are issued;

- Warrants into back bonds: the warrants are issued with the host bond but exerciseable into a different bond;

- Naked warrants: the warrants are issued separately from a bond issue. Naked warrants have been issued exerciseable into Eurobonds or into US Treasuries;

- Wedding warrants: the warrants are issued with callable bonds, and may be exercised into a bullet bond with the same coupon and maturity date as the host bonds. From issue until the first call date of the host bonds, the warrants may only be exercised by surrendering the host bond. Thereafter, they may be exercised with cash;

- Dual currency warrants: the warrants are exercised in a different currency from the currency of denomination of the bond.

589

Table 11
Equity Warrants by Currency
1987–1992
(in US Dollar Millions)

Currency	1987 Amount mm (US$)	Iss.	1988 Amount mm (US$)	Iss.	1989 Amount mm (US$)	Iss.	1990 Amount mm (US$)	Iss.	1991 Amount mm (US$)	Iss.	1992 Amount mm (US$)	Iss.
US dollar	52.80	3	128.37	5	210.76	22	993.08	87	821.35	71	1,172.40	96
Deutsche Mark	0.00	0	0.00	0	0.00	0	125.98	3	670.41	45	608.16	33
Sterling	0.00	0	16.71	2	218.79	22	1,513.29	43	2,384.91	68	1,116.96	56
European currency unit	0.00	0	0.00	0	0.00	0	9.66	2	189.00	10	3.78	2
Japanese yen	0.00	0	18.44	32	15.01	2	22.05	4	0.46	1	0.00	0
French franc	0.00	0	0.00	0	95.00	13	620.91	38	761.22	63	417.65	52
Dutch guilder	15.37	1	0.00	0	0.00	0	4.84	2	0.00	0	153.98	4
Austrian schilling	9.61	1	0.00	0	0.00	0	0.00	0	16.47	2	0.00	0
Italian lira	0.00	0	24.07	1	0.00	0	61.71	9	42.27	6	6.58	15
Australian dollar	8.47	1	0.00	0	0.00	0	0.00	0	73.61	2	0.00	0
TOTAL	86.25	6	187.59	40	539.57	59	3,351.52	188	4,959.72	268	3,479.52	258

Iss. = Number of issuers

Source: Euromoney Publications Plc

Other warrant formulations include warrants that can be called at the option of the issuer, warrants which pay a coupon, warrants which permit exercise through delivery of the host bond and warrants which give the holder the right to redeem a bond.

Table 12 shows the growth of the debt warrant market by currency.

6. EUROBOND DISTRIBUTION AND MARKETING

Eurobond issues are distributed in a large number of countries, although the extent of the distribution will naturally vary from issue to issue, depending upon factors such as the nationality and credit of the borrower, the size of the issue, whether the issue is publicly offered or privately placed, the experience of the syndicate members and the market conditions prevailing at the time of the issue. In the case of non-US dollar bonds, the currency denomination will, to some extent, affect the initial syndication and distribution procedures.

6.1 Timetable

The following is an abbreviated timetable of the key dates for a straight, fixed-rate euro-bond issue syndicated among co-managers only which is the most common type of syndicate structure.

Day 0   – Launch.
Co-Managers invited by phone and/or by computer-to-computer messages to participate, confirmed by telex.

Day 1   – Managers to have accepted by 10:00 hours (London time). Allotments made by telex overnight.

Day 8-15   – Signing of Subscription Agreement.

Day 15-30   – Payment by subscribers.

                – Closing and payment to the issuers.

If the issue is open-priced (which is often the case in the equity linked market), the underwriters will have accepted their commitments initially, subject to their approval of final terms. The issue is priced at the close of the so-called selling period of 1-7 days and the final terms are telexed

Table 12
Debt Warrants by Currency
1987–1992

Currency	1987 Amount mm (US$)	Iss.	1988 Amount mm (US$)	Iss.	1989 Amount mm (US$)	Iss.	1990 Amount mm (US$)	Iss.	1991 Amount mm (US$)	Iss.	1992 Amount mm (US$)	Iss.
US dollar	13.58	4	15.80	3	2.00	1	27.25	4	25.10	2	70.38	14
Deutsche Mark	3.14	2	16.10	1	0.00	0	4.85	1	136.84	21	137.84	13
Sterling	55.72	14	0.02	2	0.00	0	0.76	1	17.00	1	28.25	4
European currency unit	2.93	2	0.00	0	0.00	0	52.58	8	29.62	25	33.14	4
Japanese yen	0.00	0	1.22	4	0.00	0	0.00	0	0.01	1	0.20	1
French franc	6.27	3	0.00	0	0.00	0	189.62	14	65.23	7	262.76	30
Dutch guilder	8.66	2	1.00	1	0.00	0	0.00	0	10.85	2	24.79	4
Italian lira	0.00	0	0.00	0	0.00	0	0.00	0	0.00	0	10.28	2
Australian dollar	4.32	4	0.00	0	0.00	0	0.00	0	0.00	0	0.00	0
TOTAL	94.63	31	34.14	11	2.00	1	275.06	28	284.65	59	567.64	72

Iss. = Number of issuers

Source: Euromoney Publications Plc

592

to managers for their approval. Managers can theoretically withdraw if they do not like the final terms, although as a practical matter they would not do so unless the final terms were outside the indicated range.

6.2 Syndicate Members

The parties involved in the syndication and distribution of a bond issue are the managers, and sometimes selling group members, both of whom are usually selected on the basis of their ability to underwrite and/or place the securities in question.

6.2.1 *Managers:* The managers collectively underwrite the issue under the lead of the lead-manager and co-lead managers, if any. Their function is to guarantee, i.e. underwrite, the sale of an issue by agreeing to buy the securities for their own account to the extent that the selling group (on behalf of the investors) subscribe for less than the full amount of the issue, and to participate in the placement or sale of the issue. In the English style of underwriting, their commitment is a joint and several commitment, i.e. if one manager breaks his commitment to underwrite his portion of the issue, the other managers take over his underwriting commitment on a pro rata basis. In the US style of underwriting, the managers' commitments are several, i.e. if one manager fails, the other managers are under no obligation to take up his commitment.

The most important manager is the lead-manager, who "runs the books" on the issue. Once given the mandate by the borrower, the lead-manager negotiates and prepares the documentation and prices the issue together with the borrower prior to launch (or establishes the indicated range of terms for an open-priced issue). The lead-manager selects the management group, in consultation with the borrower, who may have particular relationships that he wishes to be taken into account, and invites them to participate when the deal is launched. During the selling period of an open-priced issue, all indications of demand are addressed to the lead-manager who, when the books close at the end of the selling period, decides how many bonds to allot each member of the syndicate. Allotments can be made up to the amount of each syndicate member's demand, or, if greater, his underwriting commitment.

The lead-manager is responsible for ensuring the orderly distribution of the issue. This he does by controlling the level of allotments and by giving protection, which is a firm commitment to individual syndicate members to allot them the amount for which they are protected. The lead-manager also conducts transactions to stabilise the price of the issue in the market during distribution. He can create temporary short or long positions by over-alloting bonds (alloting bonds in excess of the principal amount of the issue) or by buying and selling bonds in the market. IPMA recommendations stipulate that all such transactions must be completed before 30 days after the signing date. Depending on the type of transaction stabilisation may be effected for the account of the underwriting syndicate, which, within limits, is responsible for losses incurred during stabilisation. Conversely, any profits up to a specified amount are for their account.

A limited number of co-lead managers can also be invited into the transaction, for reasons of distribution capability or because of existing relationships with the issuer. The co-lead managers take a larger underwriting commitment than the other managers and sometimes share a praecipuum (see "commissions" below), but otherwise have the same responsibilities as the managers.

6.2.2 *Selling Group:* The selling group's sole function is to place or sell the bonds. They are under no obligation to indicate demand, but, once having indicated any interest, are committed to accept an allotment up to that amount, unless the terms of the issue have been changed since the initial invitation, or, in the case of an open-priced issue, depart from the terms initially indicated. In recent years separate selling groups have become increasingly rare in the Euromarket.

6.3 Pricing
An issue will be priced in one of three forms, open-priced, pre-priced, or bought deal. With the exception of equity linked issues, pre-priced or bought deals have now largely replaced open-priced issues.

6.3.1 *Open priced issue:* The basic terms (issue price, coupon and, in the case of a convertible, the conversion price and put price, if any) are indicated by a range in the invitations to the syndicate. The final terms are established during, or at the end of, the selling period by agreement between the borrower and the lead-manager, after discussion with the other managers. Factors taken into account, both with respect to the pricing itself and the timing, include the market's reception to the issue and the level of demand, the volatility of the bond and currency markets in general and, in the case of a convertible, movements in the company's share price and in the relevant stock market. Once the pricing has been agreed, it is disclosed to the market; at this point, the underwriters, if any, are entitled to withdraw from their commitments if the pricing is unsatisfactory, although this only happens in limited and extreme circumstances. Also, if rarely, an issue can be withdrawn because the managers and borrower cannot agree on pricing.

In the fixed rate bond market the open priced structure has, in recent years, mainly been used for very large offerings (often in relation to so-called Global Bond Issues) and then often expressed as a spread range related to a benchmark government bond.

6.3.2 *Pre-priced issue:* By 1980, the Eurodollar market had become increasingly volatile and underwriters and borrowers began to look for ways to reduce the risk caused by exposure to market fluctuations during the selling period and prior to pricing, while maintaining orderly and satisfactory distribution of issues. The pre-priced issue was developed in response to these concerns. The price is agreed between lead-manager and borrower immediately prior to launch, and the issue is then syndicated in the same manner as an open-priced issue except that there is generally no, or only a very limited, selling period.

6.3.3 *Bought Deal:* The bought deal is a variant of the pre-priced issue, in which the lead-manager, occasionally with a co-lead manager, commits to purchase the whole issue on specified terms. The risk transfers wholly to the lead-manager at that point, subject to completion of satisfactory documentation and certain closing conditions. The lead-manager can reduce his risk by sub-underwriting it or not as he wishes. Generally the lead-manager of a bought deal insists on total flexibility in the choice of syndication strategy and managers and underwriters.

Because syndication techniques for pre-priced and bought deals are broadly similar once the transaction has been launched, it cannot easily be established whether a lead-manager of a particular issue has in fact entered into a "bought deal" commitment, unless a borrower has asked for competitive bids from a range of banks. In a competitive bid, a borrower invites certain banks to bid for a given principal amount of bonds (with certain other specific characteristics) and the bank making the highest bid wins the mandate.

6.4 Syndication

The lead-manager can select any combination of managers, underwriters and selling group as the syndicate, depending upon his distribution strategy and the need to exercise control over the syndicate.

6.4.1 *Managers only:* The vast majority of transactions are now syndicated solely among the managers, who act as underwriters and selling group. The size of management group is generally 10–12 banks, although management groups of up to 40 banks have been seen, and smaller groups are not unusual. This structure was initially developed in response to the speed with which pre-priced issues had to be syndicated in order to limit each syndicate member's risk as rapidly as possible. A "managers only" issue has the important benefit of allowing the lead-manager to exercise significant control over the distribution procedure and the trading of the issue in the grey market, a task that becomes increasingly difficult as the size of the syndicate grows.

6.4.2 *Managers with Selling or Placing Group:* The lead-manager has the option to invite a separate group of banks to act as selling group members in addition to the managers themselves. This technique is used when pockets of demand are identified with smaller banks, but those banks do not wish to take an underwriting risk. However, their involvement can be important to the success of an issue and, in recognition of their contribution, they are sometimes listed in documentation as placing group members. As indicated above, separate selling groups for eurobond issues are now largely a thing of the past.

6.4.3 *Global Syndication:* The global syndication method was developed in 1985 to syndicate particularly large transactions where more than the usual number of banks need to be involved to ensure broad, firm distribution of bonds, but where control over the syndicate is particularly important

596

if the distribution is to be orderly and the after market trading is to be stable. The technique involves identifying regional areas of demand and appointing a lead-manager for each area, who will be responsible for syndicating a specified portion of the issue in that area. A co-ordinator is appointed who runs the global book, i.e. keeps track of the aggregate demand from each individual syndicate, and manages all stabilisation transactions. Syndicate members typically are not permitted to sell paper into a geographical area other than their own.

Global bonds are often issued in registered form only which allows free trading between bonds initially placed in Europe and in the United States and are cleared through both the Euromarket clearing systems and through DTC, the US system.

A recent development of this structure is the Global Bond Issue. This structure involves the simultaneous issuance of identical bonds in the Euromarket and in the United States (in the US in reliance on Rule 144A (see above) or in an offering registered with the SEC).

6.4.4 *Private Placements:* A private placement is a private issue, not syndicated with a group of banks, placed by one manager. The bonds themselves are often not listed on any stock exchange. The issue will be in large denominations, with relatively few investors, all of whom will be institutional. Private placements generally identify particular areas of demand and are structured to meet the investors' particular requirements. Since they are not publicly announced, there are no accurate statistics available.

6.5 Distribution and Marketing

6.5.1 *Distribution:* Eurobonds are placed through institutions (mainly banks) in various financial centres including London, Brussels, Dusseldorf, Frankfurt, Luxembourg, New York, Paris, Geneva, Zurich, Singapore, Hong Kong and Tokyo. The degree to which any given centre becomes involved in any offering depends upon such factors as the country of origin and the quality of the issuer, the currency in which the issue is denominated and the syndicate of financial institutions through which the bonds are sold. Similar factors determine the even wider distribution to end investors.

Eurobonds are not registered under the US Securities Act of 1933 and may not be offered or sold either in the United States or to its nationals or residents as part of the initial distribution of the bonds subject to certain exceptions, the most important of which is Rule 144A of the Act, which may allow an institutional market for Eurobonds in the United States. In addition, depending on the countries of origin of the issuer and guarantor (if any) and the location of the managers, the distribution of the bonds may be restricted in other jurisdictions.

6.5.2   *Primary Market:* The primary market is the market in which new issues of securities are initially syndicated or distributed. All trading during this period is on a "when-issued" basis, i.e. settlement is made when the securities are issued on closing, and is known as grey market trading. Prices are quoted less a discount or plus a premium to issue price. Issues trading "within the fees" are trading at a price greater than issue price less the gross commissions and are profitable to the extent of the remaining commission. Issues trading "outside the fees" are trading at a price less than the issue price less the gross commissions.

6.5.3   *Secondary Market:* Secondary market trading activity in Eurobonds commences after the initial distribution and continues until maturity. It is conducted on an over-the-counter basis by financial institutions throughout the world. "Market-makers", dealers who actively buy or sell Eurobonds as principals rather than as agents or brokers, form the basis of this market. Lead-managers generally undertake to make a market in those issues they lead-manage; the commitment of a major market-maker is crucial to the strong secondary market performance of an issue and is thus of great importance to issuers as well as investors, since the price of outstanding issues will affect that of any subsequent ones. An issuer with a poor secondary market record for outstanding issues will inevitably find subsequent issues more expensive.

In the fixed rate and convertible markets the spread between the bid and offered prices in the secondary markets is typically 0.5% and 1% of the principal amount of the bonds, respectively. Spreads tend to widen in adverse market conditions. Secondary market spreads in the FRN market are quoted in basis points and can be as narrow as 5 to 10 basis points in good markets.

6.6 Commissions

The members of the syndicate are paid a commission by the borrower for their services. The commission is calculated as a flat percentage of the total issue amount. Generally, the commission is split into management and underwriting commissions but it is also often expressed as a combined commission.

The commission is paid to the managers pro rata to each manager's underwriting commitment. In addition to a combined commission a selling concession is paid to the managers. The selling concession is a compensation for selling efforts and is, therefore, divided pro rata to allotments. For fixed rate and floating rate bond issues both the commission and the concession are deducted from the issue price at closing.

For equity linked bond issues the management fee is paid shortly after closing while the underwriting fee is paid as soon as stabilisation transactions have been completed and the expenses of the issue finalised. This is because for equity linked transactions the underwriting commission is subject to adjustment for profits or losses arising from stabilisation transactions and to deduction for expenses that are not reimbursed by the borrower for straight debt issues. Under IPMA recommendations, unreimbursed expenses may only be deducted to a maximum of the lower of 10% of the underwriting commission and 20% of the managers' expense cap.

In the 1970s and 1980s the fixed rate straight Eurobond market had an established range of commission depending on the maturity of the issue. This commission structure was largely abolished in the late 1980s and commissions are now subject to negotiation on a case by case basis. However, generally, total commissions for a five year issue would amount to 0.30% to 0.35% and for a ten year issue 0.40% to 0.50%.

Commissions on equity linked issues are generally $2^{1}/_{4}\%$ for five year issues and $2^{1}/_{2}\%$ for issues with longer maturities.

There are no fixed commissions on floating rate note issues but, in practice, they are generally lower than for fixed rate issues with a similar maturity.

7. ASSET PACKAGES

Asset packaging is a generic term used to describe the purchase of securities such as bonds which, with, for example, an interest rate/currency swap or option, effectively transforms them into an asset more appropriate to the funding base or specific requirements of the purchaser. Such asset packaging is now commonly done in the secondary bond market.

8. EUROBOND CLEARING SYSTEMS

The major part of Eurobond clearing and settlement is conducted through two centralised clearing systems, Euro-clear (Euro-clear Clearance System Public Limited Company), in Brussels and CEDEL (Centrale de Livraison de Valeurs Mobilieres S.A.), in Luxembourg. The systems were set up to provide an efficient, risk-free settlement system for internationally traded securities, avoiding the costs and delays caused by physical delivery of certificates. Participants in both systems must be institutions.

Euro-clear was established in 1968 and now has over 125 shareholders from among its participants. It is operated by Morgan Guaranty Trust Company of New York. At the end of 1992, Euro-clear had 2,700 participants. CEDEL was established in 1970 by a group of major financial institutions and is independently managed. At the end of 1992, it had approximately 2,980 participants.

The two systems match settlement instructions received by their participants and effect delivery of, and payment for, securities by book-keeping entries in participants' cash and custody accounts. Each issue of securities is identified by a serial number which is assigned during the primary distribution of the issue. All trades which are to be settled through the systems must identify that number as well as the securities account numbers of the parties making the trade.

Transactions between participants in Euro-clear and CEDEL are conducted across an electronic bridge between the two systems, where transactions are netted out at the end of the day and the necessary transfers made. The securities themselves are held at depositary banks throughout Europe.

600

Turnover in the six years 1983–88 is shown in the following table:

Table 13
Turnover 1986 – 1992
(in billions US$)

	Euro-clear	CEDEL
1986	2,280	1,207
1987	3,080	1,560
1988	3,030	1,718
1989	3,570	1,732
1990	4,090	2,430
1991	5,740	3,336
1992	9,780	4,731

In addition to clearing securities, Euro-clear and CEDEL provide a number of other services, such as collection of interest and principal payments, forwarding of redemption, conversion and other notices to participants and borrowing and lending of securities. The range of securities cleared includes Eurobonds, foreign bonds, domestic bonds, certificates of deposit, warrants, US Treasury notes, Euro-commercial paper, and, increasingly, equities.

9. THE PROSPECTUS

A prospectus is prepared for every publicly offered transaction that requires a listing on a stock exchange. The extent of the information it contains is dictated by the rules of the stock exchange on which the issue is to be listed and the need for disclosure of information on the company and securities for marketing reasons or for reasons of providing a complete picture for the investor so that he can make an informed investment decision on the basis of the facts provided in the document.

The issuer takes full responsibility for the contents of the prospectus, although the lead-manager and its lawyers will try to ensure that it is accurate and complete through participation in the prospectus preparation and conduct of due diligence and inquiries with senior management. Issuers should note the responsibility statement in the prospectus which, subject to variations, reads as follows:

"The issuer, in respect of information relating to the issuer and the Bonds, having made all reasonable enquiries, confirms that this document contains all information with regard to the issuer and the Bonds which is material in the context of the issue of the Bonds, that the information contained in this document is true and accurate in all material respects and is not misleading, that the opinions and intentions expressed therein are honestly held, and that there are no other facts the omission of which makes this document as a whole or any of such information or the expression of any such opinions or intentions misleading."

The prospectus would normally contain the following information:

Page 1: The title of the issue, a summary of its terms and the names of the managers.

Page 2: Responsibility statement, summary of sales restrictions and table of contents.

Description of Securities: Full details of all the legal and market terms of the issue, e.g. price, redemption provisions, negative pledge or other convenants and events of default. Although these are sometimes expanded in the relevant constitutional document (trust deed or fiscal agency agreement), the potential investor should be able to find out all he needs to know, or that might affect him, with respect to the securities themselves from this section of the document.

Description of Borrower: A description of the history, business and activities of the borrower, with a capitalisation table showing the capitalisation of the borrower at a recent date, adjusted for the issue of the securities, and details of the Board of Directors and senior management.

Financial Statements: Recent audited financial statements plus an audit report. Unaudited interim financial statements for subsequent periods would be included if available.

Subscription and Sale: A summary of the syndication arrangements for the issue, plus detailed selling restrictions.

General Information required by the relevant stock exchange, such
Information: as details of resolutions passed authorising the issue, and
statements that there has been no material change in its
financial condition since the date of the last audited financial
statements and that there is no litigation that is material in
the context of the issue of the securities. The Euro-clear
and CEDEL reference numbers for the securities are also
found in this section. Under this category, although generally
found in separate sections, can be included subjects such
as exchange control restrictions, if any, or a description of
the taxation laws with respect to the issue, namely under
what circumstances withholding, estate or capital gains
taxes, if any, are imposed on payments or transfers to non-
residents.

The contents of the section relating to the borrower and the audited
financial statements are affected by the rules of the stock exchange on
which the issue is to be listed. However, with the EC Prospectus Directive
coming into force, the requirements on prospectus contents became more
homogenous as among EC stock exchanges.

In a London listing the Prospectus may be substituted by an Extel Card.
Extel Cards are circulated by the Extel Statistical Service, an organisation
which provides information to its subscribers on companies and other
entities the shares or bonds of which are listed on The International Stock
Exchange in London. Information on listed entities is updated at regular
intervals by the Extel Service itself.

The Stock Exchanges' disclosure requirements vary depending on whether
the borrower is an EC or non-EC government or government entity, or
a corporation. Generally, disclosure requirements for equity-linked issues
are more burdensome for issuers than those for straight debt issues.

Although the stock exchanges have become increasingly flexible with
respect to prospectus contents, the lead-manager should always take into
account questions of adequate disclosure or marketing when deciding
what information to put into a prospectus. If the investor community is
not familiar with the borrower or if the borrower is either not a particularly

high quality credit or changes in its financial situation have occurred since an earlier issue, a fuller description is generally provided. The lead-manager also has to decide whether a preliminary prospectus should be prepared for marketing or disclosure reasons, because the final prospectus is only available once the subscription agreement has been signed, seven to 10 days after the issue is first marketed. The preliminary prospectus is "subject to completion and amendment" which allows changes of a minor nature to be made or, if the issue is open-priced, final terms to be inserted. Changes of a material nature, if any, should be disclosed to the syndicate.

10. RATING AGENCIES

The rating of a public bond issue is an established feature of the United States public market and is gaining increasing prominence in the international market. In order to rate an issue, independent rating agencies assess the creditworthiness of an issuer and assign a rating to the issuer or the issue itself which defines its status and differentiates it from other issues. The rating agencies continually assess the credit quality of borrowers through financial and ratio analysis, adjusting accounting practices where necessary to bring them into conformity with industry practice. General and specific economic conditions are also taken into account. The ratings are based, in varying degrees, on the following considerations:

1. Likelihood of default – capacity and willingness of the obligor as to the timely payment of interest and repayment of principal in accordance with the terms of the obligation;

2. Nature of, and provisions of, the obligations; for example, whether it ranks as senior or subordinated debt or whether it is secured or supported by a guarantee or letter of credit from a third party;

3. Protection afforded by, and relative position of, the obligation in the event of bankruptcy, reorganisation, or other arrangement under the laws of bankruptcy and other laws affecting creditors' rights.

Long- and short-term debt are also treated differently for rating purposes. It is important to note that a rating is not an audit nor is it a recommendation to buy.

The principal rating agencies are Standard & Poor's Corporation and Moody's Investors Service, Inc. Both are privately owned.

The rating schedules for debt obligations and commercial paper are as follows and assess the capacity to pay interest and repay principal:

Standard & Poor's

Long-term Debt Obligations

AAA	Extremely strong
AA	Very strong
A	Strong
BBB	Adequate
BB)	Predominantly speculative, to varying degrees
B)	Predominantly speculative, to varying degrees
CCC)	Predominantly speculative, to varying degrees
CC)	Predominantly speculative, to varying degrees
C	Bankruptcy petition filed but debt service payments continued
D	In default

Plus (+) or Minus (−). Relative standing within the categories AA to B may be shown by a + or − sign.

Commercial Paper

A-1+	Extremely strong
A-1	Strong
A-2	Satisfactory
A-3	Adequate
B	Speculative
C	Doubtful
D	In, or expected to be in, default

Moody's

Long-term Debt Obligations

Aaa	Best quality
Aa	High quality
A	Upper-medium-grade
Baa	Medium-grade
Ba	Speculative elements
B	Lacking characteristics of desirable investment
Caa	Poor standing
Ca	Speculative to a high degree
C	Lowest class

Relative standing within the classes Aa to B may be shown by the addition of 1, 2 or 3.

Commercial Paper

P1	Superior ability for repayment
P2	Strong ability for repayment
P3	Acceptable ability for repayment
Not Prime	Outside above categories.

11. BIBLIOGRAPHY

Japanese Finance: *The Impact of Deregulation,* Helen Troughton, Euromoney Publications.

Japanese Finance: *Markets and Institutions,* Euromoney Publications.

Securities Market in Japan 1986, Japan Securities Research Institute.

Handbook of Securities of the United States Government and Federal Agencies 1986, The First Boston Corporation.

Swiss Capital Markets, Henri B. Meier, Euromoney Publications.

Bank for International Settlements, *Annual Reports.*

A History of the Eurobond Market – The First 21 Years, Ian M. Kerr, Euromoney Publications.

CHAPTER 15 (Part I)

The Raising of Capital and Listing of Securities on the World's Stock Exchanges – London

by
Patrick K. F. Donlea

1. INTRODUCTION: THE LONDON STOCK EXCHANGE

The London Stock Exchange* evolved during the seventeenth century from informal gatherings of stock and share dealers in the coffee houses around the Royal Exchange. Records of daily price lists go back as far as 1698, and among the stocks listed then was the Hudsons Bay Company. At this time the government and a number of trading enterprises began to raise money by public subscription, and as securities were issued and subsequently bought and sold on an increasing scale, a regular market began to form.

While the eighteenth century saw the continuance of capital raising for the expansion of trade, the nineteenth century brought change in emphasis as funds were raised for the development of transport, particularly railways. The first half of the twentieth century was chiefly concerned with the raising of capital for the iron, coal and steel companies and the utilities until the advent of nationalisation. Since the Second World War, a large number of private industrial, commercial and financial companies have come to the market, including many of today's household names.

* The full name is The International Stock Exchange of the United Kingdom and the Republic of Ireland Limited.

607

In the last ten years a considerable number of previously nationalised companies have been privatised by the government, raising large sums of capital. These companies have been listed by way of public and international offers for sale. This has led to the re-emergence of a market in utility stocks.

At the end of 1993, there were over 1,900 UK and Irish registered companies listed on the main market and 256 dealt in on the Unlisted Securities Market (USM). In addition, over 700 foreign companies are listed on the London Stock Exchange, principally US, Japanese, South African Fund and German securities. The total equity market value of the listed company securities was £2,771 billion and for the USM £5 billion.

The first formal rules of the London Stock Exchange were adopted in 1812, but prior to 1921 there was no control over the admission of securities to the market. Since then the requirements for listing have been steadily improved and tightened, while at the same time measures have been taken to improve the efficiency of the market, such as the strengthening of the dealing code, the establishment of greater control over the accounts of member firms and their liquidity margins.

Developments since then include the establishment of the Unlisted Securities Market ("USM") and changes in foreign company requirements. The USM, established at the end of 1980, was formed in order to encourage smaller companies to obtain a quotation for their shares on a formal market, but without the more onerous requirements of a full listing. However, although the USM proved popular during the 1980s, the relaxation of some of the main market requirements and problems of liquidity in small companies led the London Stock Exchange to review the future viability of the USM. These problems were accentuated during a period of contraction in economic activity which was felt particularly keenly by smaller companies. The Stock Exchange has decided that no new companies will be admitted to the USM from the end of 1994 and that the USM will be closed by the end of 1996. Accordingly, USM companies are being encouraged to seek a full listing in the interim.

The changes in foreign company requirements are designed to recognise the domestic listing requirements of foreign exchanges and the adoption of streamlined, continuing obligations for such businesses.

The most significant development in recent years has been the passing of the Financial Services Act 1986 (the "Financial Services Act"), which introduced a new statutory framework for regulating the securities and investment industry in the United Kingdom. The passing of the Financial Services Act coincided with amendments to London Stock Exchange regulations which permitted firms to charge commission on a negotiated basis and act simultaneously as agency brokers and market makers. This change reflected practice in other countries, particularly the USA, at a time when international security dealing had greatly increased in importance. It further coincided with changes in EC and UK legislation designed to harmonise company law and listing regulations.

2. THE LONDON STOCK EXCHANGE: FUNCTIONS

The function of the London Stock Exchange as an institution is to see that a fair, orderly and efficient market-place is provided for the issue and transfer of securities. This means that two fundamental conditions must exist. First, equal opportunity for all to possess the information necessary to make a balanced investment judgment: the more certain the public feels that it will be told all necessary facts at the time of the flotation of companies and thereafter, the less attention it will pay to rumour. At the same time, investors should be able to deal in shares with the knowledge that prices take account of the latest information concerning the security, released in such a way so as to ensure as far as possible that there is no advantage to either buyer or seller at the time of dealing. However, it must be stressed that once the London Stock Exchange has seen that the information is available to all, it is not its function to pass judgment on the merits or value of a security. Secondly, there must be equal opportunity for all potential investors to obtain securities and to deal on the best terms. The public should feel confident that it is not essential to be associated with the sponsors to an issue or to be a member of a special syndicate in order to have a fair chance of obtaining a security when it is brought to the market; thereafter, the public are entitled to expect that the best buyer or best seller will be successful in the market.

The Quotations Department is the arm of the London Stock Exchange which is responsible for ensuring that these principles are adhered to. The London Stock Exchange delegates its powers relating to the listing of securities to the Committee on Quotations. This Committee meets regularly to grant listings and adjudicate amendments to the listing requirements where necessary.

The Company Announcements Department is responsible for releasing press announcements to the market so that share prices can reflect the latest information. Additional sections are responsible for monitoring price movements and in the event of an exceptional change in share price where no announcement has been made, the broker to the company will be asked to provide an explanation.

2.1   The London Stock Exchange and the Law

The London Stock Exchange's legal position is governed to a large extent by the Financial Services Act which provides for a statutory framework for regulating the securities industry. No person can carry on an investment business in the UK without obtaining authorisation under the Act unless that person is exempted.

The Securities and Investments Board ("SIB") was formed to regulate the securities and investment industry and makes rules and regulations which have the force of law. The SIB authorises directly and indirectly certain institutions to carry on an investment business provided that the business is conducted in a manner which complies with the SIB's requirements. Authorisation is normally obtained by membership of a recognised Self Regulatory Organisation ("SRO"). One of the SROs is the Securities and Futures Authority to which London Stock Exchange members belong. The London Stock Exchange is defined as the competent authority in implementing EC regulations or listing requirements for companies applying for listing. The London Stock Exchange can ultimately operate the sanction of refusing a listing to a company which does not comply with its disclosure requirements.

Finally, Section 187 of the Financial Services Act exempts the SIB and SROs from liability for damages for anything done or omitted in the discharge of their functions under the Act unless done in bad faith.

2.2   Basic Legal Requirements for Prospectuses / Listing Particulars

The information requirements for a prospectus are legally governed in two ways. Those companies seeking a full listing or already listed must comply with the rules made in accordance with the provisions of Part IV of the Financial Services Act. Those companies seeking to raise capital by a prospectus issue on the USM will have to comply with Part V of the Financial Services Act and regulations made thereunder.

2.2.1 *False and misleading statements in prospectuses*

Investors are protected by various laws in respect of omissions from, or false and misleading statements in, prospectuses. The main laws are as follows:

(a) Section 19 of the Theft Act 1968 which states that any director of a company who, with intent to deceive its members, publishes a written statement which to his knowledge is, or may be, misleading, false or deceptive in a material particular, is liable to seven years imprisonment.

(b) Sections 166 and 168 of the Financial Services Act provide that if a prospectus includes any untrue statement or omits material information on the company, directors or, *inter alia*, any person authorising its issue may be liable to pay compensation to the subscribers.

(c) Section 47 of the Financial Services Act specifies two criminal offences in relation to the issue of listing particulars. The first relates to misleading statements, promises or forecasts or dishonest concealment of material facts. The second relates to engaging in any course of action creating a false or misleading impression as to the market in or the price of or value of any investments.

(d) Section 2 of the Misrepresentation Act 1967 would appear to allow a claim for damages against the company for any misrepresentation made by or on behalf of the company, whether the misleading statements are made negligently or fraudulently.

In addition to the statutory liabilities above, investors can also have recourse to common law claims for damages.

2.2.2 *Listing rules*

The disclosure obligations for companies listing securities are set out in Part IV of the Financial Services Act with the London Stock Exchange appointed as the competent authority for making detailed listing rules and for their administration. In view of the fact that these rules have statutory force, the London Stock Exchange has limited powers of flexibility but is allowed in certain circumstances to grant derogations from the requirements.

An overriding statutory duty of disclosure is imposed by Section 146 of the Financial Services Act which states that:

"In addition to the information specified by listing rules or required by the competent authority as a condition of the admission of any securities to the Official List any listing particulars submitted to the competent authority under Section 144 shall contain all such information as investors and their professional advisers would reasonably require, and reasonably expect to find there, for the purpose of making an informed assessment of:

(a)   the assets and liabilities, financial position, profits and losses, and prospects of the issuer of the securities; and

(b)   the rights attaching to those securities."

It should be mentioned that the listing requirements referred to above are ultimately the product of directives issued by the European Commission, namely the Admission Directive, the Listing Particulars Directive and the Interim Reports Directive.

Listing Particulars refers to the information document complying with the disclosure requirements of the London Stock Exchange. The requirements for this document include the description of the business, the requirement to give three-year accountants' reports and detailed information on the directors, the articles, material contracts and indebtedness. The emphasis of the information required varies according to the type of issue such as an issue to finance a substantial acquisition, a rights issue, Eurobond issue or an issue of debentures. In all cases a responsibility statement is required by the directors of the issuing company or in the case of Eurobond issues, by the company itself. The listing particulars may not be published until such time as they have been approved by the London Stock Exchange. All listing particulars documents are filed with the Registrar of Companies.

It should be noted that listing particulars are not normally required where the listed equity of the issuing company is increased by less than 10%. In these cases an announcement giving details of the issue is published.

2.3   Principal Conditions for Listing on the London Stock Exchange

2.3.1   *Introduction*

The efficient operation of a stock market depends primarily upon adequacy of information, a quantity of securities whose distribution is sufficiently wide to provide marketability, and certainty of procedures for the settlement of business. Two manuals, "The Rules and Regulations of the London Stock Exchange" and "Admission of Securities to Listing" ("the Yellow Book") lay down the basic requirements to ensure that these principles are adhered to. However, it is clearly stated that the requirements are not exhaustive and that the relevant Stock Exchange Committees may add and subtract therefrom in any particular case, as a variety of conditions may exist which require ad hoc decisions by the Committee; there is, therefore, scope for flexibility in the interpretation of the listing requirements.

2.3.2   *Market capitalisation*

Applications are considered from companies whose listed securities are expected to have an initial aggregate market value of at least £700,000 in the case of shares and £200,000 in the case of debt securities. In practice, the market capitalisation of companies seeking a listing will be much greater than this.

2.3.3   *Shares in public hands*

At least 25% of any class of issued equity capital or securities convertible into equity capital, is required to be in the hands of the public, that is, persons who are not associated with the directors or major shareholders. In normal circumstances, this means that 25% of the company's equity will have to be offered to the public, but in the case of very large issues or where there is already a spread of public shareholders, the London Stock Exchange will allow a lower percentage. As described in greater detail below, the London Stock Exchange expects that companies will obtain a listing by making securities available to the public by means of an offer for sale or public issue, and that only in special circumstances will concessionary methods, such as placings and introductions, be permitted.

2.3.4 *Financial record*

The company is expected to have a financial record of at least three years before applying for a listing, and a company whose assets consist wholly or substantially of cash or short-dated securities will not normally be regarded as acceptable for listing. In certain circumstances, the London Stock Exchange will relax these requirements: in particular, for mineral exploration companies where the existence of adequate reserves of natural resources substantiated by an independent expert can be established, and an estimate of the capital cost, time and working capital required to bring the company into a position to earn revenue can be provided; and also for investment companies, where it can be shown that the directors and investment managers have had satisfactory experience in the management of investment companies, especially those already listed, and where the company is restricted from investing more than 10% of its assets in any one company.

2.3.5 *Accounting requirements*

The London Stock Exchange will not normally grant a listing where the latest financial period audited and reported on by the accountants (who must be independent of the company) ended more than six months before the date of the listing particulars. The accounts must be fully consolidated and a report containing any significant qualification or reservation on the figures would not normally be acceptable to the London Stock Exchange. In respect of UK companies, the London Stock Exchange expects accounts to be prepared in conformity not only with the Statements of Standard Accounting Practice approved by the principal professional accounting bodies in the UK, but also with the International Accounting Standards published by the International Accounting Standards Committee.

2.3.6 *Advertising and availability of information*

In the case of an offer for sale or public issue, the full listing particulars must be published in at least one national newspaper. In the case of placings, introductions and intermediaries' offers the listing particulars

614

need only be published in one national newspaper by means of a formal notice, similar to a "tombstone" advertisement.

2.3.7 *Submission of documents*
All applications for listing must be made by a sponsoring firm (which includes merchant banks and accountants, in addition to stockbrokers). All documents in support of an application must be submitted for approval to the Quotations Department as early as possible. The listing particulars must contain all the information required in the Yellow Book (further details of which are given below). When reading proof documents submitted for approval the prime consideration of the London Stock Exchange is to see that all relevant information is disclosed clearly and accurately so as to enable the potential investor to make a fair assessment of the proposition and the worth of the securities.

2.3.8 *Continuing obligations*
The continuing obligations lay down the requirements to be observed by a company in maintaining its listing on the London Stock Exchange. They are principally concerned with immediate communication of information that is likely to affect the prices of the securities or influence investment decisions (such as announcement of results and dividends, acquisitions and realisations of assets, changes in directorates, etc.); the production of half-yearly profit statements; the inclusion of certain information in the annual report and accounts; and the conduct of certain practices and procedures for the benefit of the investor either in exercising his rights or in the transfer of his securities. The requirements relating to acquisitions and realisations are described in more detail in Section 8.

The London Stock Exchange expects that directors will not divulge price sensitive information in such a way as to place in a privileged position any person or parties outside the company and its advisers, and that such information will be released in such a way that London Stock Exchange transactions are entered into at prices which reflect the latest available information.

The obligations also state that, unless shareholders otherwise permit pursuant to Section 89 of the Companies Act, a company proposing to issue for cash securities having an element of equity must first offer these securities to existing shareholders. This rule does not apply to foreign companies listed on the London Stock Exchange.

Directors must comply with the requirements set out in the "Model Code" for directors' dealings, given in the Yellow Book.

3. METHODS OF ISSUE

There are various ways in which a company can obtain a listing on the London Stock Exchange and the actual method adopted will depend on the size and type of the issue, the spread of existing shareholdings and the state of market conditions. The London Stock Exchange's principal requirement is that securities should be offered for sale to the public, as being the fairest way to ensure that everyone has an equal chance of subscribing and of receiving an allotment. However, the public offer is not necessarily a suitable method for every company and the London Stock Exchange is therefore prepared to consider applications for a waiver from their basic requirement where another method of issue is considered more appropriate. The methods of issue available are set out in the following paragraphs.

3.1 Issue by Public Subscription

The first method which a company can employ is itself to make a direct offer to the public by publishing a prospectus inviting subscriptions for the securities. This method used to be the normal procedure, but in recent years it has become less common in the case of companies, although it is still used by public authorities, the best example being when the steel companies were denationalised and their shares resold to the public in the late 1950s. The reason why this method has declined stems from the fact that it was always necessary to arrange for the issue to be underwritten to ensure its success, which in turn meant that an issuing house was introduced to make the underwriting arrangements, and in these circumstances it was easier for the company to leave the issuing house to organise the whole issue. The only other companies using this method with any frequency were investment trusts during the period 1968 to 1972, when approximately twenty issues were made in this way, the reason being that the management company of the investment trust wished to arrange the issue itself without bringing in an issuing house.

3.2 Offer for Subscription and Sale

This method is the one which is now used by most new companies and involves the company or its existing shareholders either selling securities

616

to the issuing house, which in turn publishes listing particulars inviting the public to purchase the securities from it, or selling the securities to the public using the issuing house as an agent. The detailed procedures by which the public subscription and offer for sale methods are carried out are almost identical, and the main difference is that the issuing house accepts primary responsibility for the sale of the securities. Most of the largest companies which have gone public in recent years have used the offer for sale method.

In certain cases part of the amount offered for sale had been underwritten firm, which means that the firm underwriter (such as an institutional investor) has agreed to subscribe for shares and will automatically be allotted them. However, prior approval must be obtained from the London Stock Exchange to do this, and the amount will be strictly limited, so as to ensure that the public will still have a fair chance of obtaining shares.

There should usually be at least two market makers independent of the sponsoring member firm and normally at least 5% of the shares placed or underwritten firm must be offered to the independent market makers. Where the market value of the equity shares being issued is more than £50m the Exchange may permit a lesser percentage to be offered to the independent market makers, providing such amount is not less than £1.25m.

The most important examples of flotations with special features have been the privatisation of enterprises previously owned by the government such as BP, Amersham International, Enterprise Oil, British Telecom, British Gas, British Airways, British Airports Authority, the water companies and the electricity companies.

These issues, apart from their large size, have included special elements in addition to firm underwriting, such as firm underwriting with clawback, international tranches of equity offered simultaneously in the USA, Japan and Europe and in most cases, partly paid share offers, the balance being callable over a period of 12 months from the issue date.

3.3 Offer for Sale by Tender

A variation on these methods of issue, which safeguards the vendors against a very large premium on the price developing immediately after

617

the issue, is the offer for sale by tender. This method has been used for many years by water companies under the requirements of the Water Act 1945. The shares are offered for sale at a minimum issue price, and in the form of application the subscriber states not only the number of shares required but also the price, above the minimum, which he is prepared to pay. Allotments are then made from the highest price downwards until the issue is fully subscribed. As the securities issued by water companies were fixed interest preference shares and since one water company did not differ vastly from another, there was ample evidence on which to tender and therefore the price difference between the lowest and highest tenders was not very large.

In the late 1960s the tender method was adopted by companies generally in an attempt to ensure that the best possible price was obtained by the vendor and to frustrate the "stags" subscribing for purely speculative purposes. The London Stock Exchange would not allow a method which resulted in different subscribers paying different prices to be used as it wished to avoid discrimination as far as possible and ensure an adequate market in the shares offered. Thus, in these cases, allotment was made at a single striking price with all applications above the striking price being accepted at that price and all those below being rejected.

The London Stock Exchange had to be satisfied with the method of determining the price and the basis of allotment, and it was therefore necessary for the issuing house to be given discretion in determining the basis of allotment, reducing large or multiple tenders and accepting a slightly lower level of price to increase the spread of holders, scaling down all applications accordingly. However, the tender method has certain disadvantages: the public can find the method more difficult to understand and may therefore be reluctant to subscribe, being afraid of paying too much; the tender price gives a theoretically correct valuation and therefore there is no incentive to apply rather than buying the shares in the market; and in some cases, the companies concerned have had a disappointing price performance after the relevant issue.

3.4 Offer to Intermediaries

For smaller issues, where there is likely to be less public interest, an offer to intermediaries may be used. An offer to intermediaries is restricted to marketings of securities with a market value of between £25 million and

£50 million. Up to 75% of the securities being issued, or £25 million, whichever is the less, may be placed with the sponsoring member firm's own clients and the balance of the issue marketed either by an offer for sale or an offer to intermediaries. Intermediaries in this context include member firms of the London Stock Exchange and the public is therefore given the chance of applying for shares through their own advisers.

The sponsoring member firm must allocate securities to at least five placees for each £1 million marketed by it and there must be at least two market makers independent of the firm who must be offered at least 5% of the securities being placed.

This method of issue is comparatively new (1993) but the intermediaries' offers that have been made so far appear to have been well received by the small, independent firms of brokers. Intermediaries are not allowed to allocate shares in the offer to their clients at a price that is different from the offer price, but they may charge their clients a commission.

3.5 Placing

In this method the securities are not offered to the general public through a prospectus but are placed at a fixed price among institutions such as insurance companies, pension funds, unit trusts and investment companies by the sponsor, which has usually purchased the securities from the company or its existing shareholders in the same way as in an offer for sale.

This method is cheaper than an offer for sale since there are no sub-underwriting costs, the advertising requirements are less onerous, and there will be lower receiving bank charges. Nevertheless, exactly the same information on the company must be made available to the placees in the placing document, which constitutes a prospectus.

Because of the limited publicity and the restricted group of purchasers, this method is regarded by the London Stock Exchange as a concession which, in general, is only allowed when it is thought that there is not likely to be a significant public demand for the securities. In these circumstances there are only three instances where the London Stock Exchange will allow placings:

(a) *Small issues* – for issues by a new applicant for securities with a market value up to £25 million. The sponsoring firm must allocate the securities to at least 100 placees and at least 5% of the shares must be offered to an independent market maker.

(b) *Limited public interest* – where it can be proved that the issue or the company itself is unlikely to attract public interest. In this category would fall the issue of fixed interest debentures and loan stocks, and in the case of this type of issue the London Stock Exchange will always give placing permission whatever the size of the issue. The London Stock Exchange will normally be prepared to allow up to 50% of an issue to be placed and may be prepared to allow a higher proportion in issues to raise a large monetary amount or in other exceptional circumstances.

(c) *Market conditions* – If market conditions were poor or if there had been several recent unsuccessful issues, it could be argued that placing firm into institutional hands was the only feasible way of completing the issue successfully.

3.6 Introduction

Although it has been assumed that the application for a listing is linked with an issue or sale of securities to the public, there are cases where a reasonable distribution of shares already exists. The London Stock Exchange will waive its marketing requirements in cases where it can be shown that the securities are already of such a substantial amount and so widely held that their adequate marketability when listed can be assumed and that the normal supply and demand among new and existing holders will provide a satisfactory market. No standard rule as to the number of shareholders or the spread of holdings which will provide eligibility for an introduction can be applied since each case must be judged on its merits. In order to make its decision as to the spread of shareholders the London Stock Exchange will require to know the number of shareholders, the ten largest beneficial holders, and the holdings of the directors and their families. The London Stock Exchange will not allow any special disposal of a large block of shares to coincide with the introduction, as it is felt that this should be effected by the normal methods of issue. The usual circumstances in which the London Stock Exchange would be expected to give consent to an introduction are as follows:

(i)   *Overseas companies* – where the securities are already listed on another stock exchange.

(ii)   *Sufficient spread* – where the company's securities are sufficiently widely held to fulfil the London Stock Exchange's requirements as to marketability (for example, it has a listing on the USM).

(iii)   *Holding company* – where a holding company is formed and its securities are issued in exchange for those of one or more listed companies.

4.   THE FIRST STAGES

4.1   Decision to Go Public

Obtaining a listing on the London Stock Exchange is complex, expensive and for many companies can be a traumatic experience. Any company which is prepared to submit to detailed investigations, to commit itself to extensive disclosure requirements, to open itself to press scrutiny and in some cases to give up family control and become exposed to unknown outside shareholders, must have good reasons for going public. The decision on the part of the owners and directors of a company seeking a listing may be governed by a number of factors. They could be influenced by the need to develop their business by raising further finance which would not otherwise be available from the existing shareholders or from the company's bankers. Alternatively they may consider that the company would benefit if it were able to acquire other companies, using its own shares as consideration for the acquisition. Again from the company's point of view it may be felt that there is some publicity value attached to a listing which may help to increase the status of the company, improve its image, and encourage the sale of its products.

Often, however, the company's financing problems or its own considerations will be of secondary importance, the main object of a listing will be to give existing shareholders the benefit of a ready market for their shares as well as the opportunity to realise a proportion of their investment in the company. Apart from the wish to capitalise to some extent on past labours, there are also tax considerations.

4.2 Appointments of Advisers

As mentioned above, when a company goes public it has to use the services of a member firm, since the London Stock Exchange rules state that "all applications for listing must be made by a sponsoring broker who must be a member of the London Stock Exchange". It will therefore be the responsibility of the broker to submit documents to the London Stock Exchange, deal with any points of principle arising, arrange for formal listing, approach the market and monitor dealings.

After the company has appointed its lead financial adviser to arrange the issue and co-ordinate the activities of all the other professional advisers involved, and has chosen its *Sponsoring Broker,* it will be necessary to consider the appointment of all the other advisers. These will include the company's *Auditors* and its own *Solicitors,* and in addition *Reporting Accountants* and *Lawyers* who will be appointed to act on behalf of the issuing house. It may be necessary to appoint valuers to carry out an up-to-date valuation of property, and consideration must also be given to appointing *Receiving Bankers* to take in applications from the public, *Registrars* who will be responsible for issuing share certificates and effecting transfers, *PR advisers* who will advise on the approach to the press and arrange for the prospectus to be advertised in the newspapers, and *Printers* to print proofs and final documents.

4.3 Preliminary Discussions on Points of Principle

The sponsor would have detailed discussions with the company to see whether or not it would be prepared to sponsor the issue, and in arriving at its decision the following factors would be taken into account:

(a) the abilities of the directors and the management of the company, including provision for management succession;

(b) the company's trade, including likely future trends in turnover and the stability of demand for its products;

(c) the trading results achieved by the company and the directors' projections of the future sales and profits;

(d) the financial position of the company as shown by the latest balance sheet of the company; and

622

(e)   the anticipated financial requirements of the company.

Thereafter there would be further discussions and the sponsor would
then present a memorandum with proposals covering various important
aspects of the issue as follows:

Capital reorganisation – some form of capital reorganisation is almost
always required, and may involve the formation of a new holding company,
the amalgamation of subsidiaries, the splitting of the shares into smaller
nominal values, and a capitalisation issue to the existing shareholders in
order to create additional new shares which can then be offered on to the
public. It will also give an opportunity to simplify the capital structure
and to tidy up the classes of capital which are no longer appropriate, for
example founders' shares, deferred shares and shares with restricted or
multiple voting rights. The essence of any capital reorganisation is to
produce the simplest and most straightforward structure for the issue and
at the same time ensure that the issued share capital of the company bears
a proper relationship to the profits and assets of the business.

Form of capital to be issued – although theoretically the company has
various alternatives, in particular ordinary shares, preference shares,
debentures and loan stocks and convertible stock, in practice the most
likely security to be issued in the case of a new company will be the
ordinary shares, as this satisfies most of the reasons for going public. The
other forms of security would normally be issued by a listed company in
raising further finance. More relevant at this stage is the question as to
whether the company itself requires additional finance at the time of the
flotation. If it does then the company would issue new shares to raise its
money and the remaining shares needed to satisfy the London Stock
Exchange requirements for the amount to be offered to the public would
come from the existing shareholders.

Method of issue – advice would be given on the best method of making
the company's capital available to the public and obtaining a listing. In
giving this advice the sponsor would take into account the points which
have already been referred to above in deciding the various methods of
issue, and also examine the requirements of the company and its existing
shareholders.

623

Terms of issue and costs – an indication of the terms and price will be given, but the fixing of the actual price will be left open until the latest possible moment so that account can be taken of any changes in the general economic and political situation or in the movement of the stock market, all of which will have considerable bearing on the success of the issue.

With respect to the costs involved, it is only possible to give a general indication as expenses vary with the method, size and complexity of the issue and the amount of work carried out by the professional advisers. Furthermore, where existing shareholders are providing shares for the offer to the public it is appropriate that the actual cost of selling the shares

Table 1

Estimated cost of an offer for sale of ordinary shares with a value of £75 million in London in 1994

(Giving a total of market capitalisation for the company of £200 million)

Item	£
Commissions	
Underwriters ($\frac{1}{2}$%)	375,000
Sub-underwriters ($1\frac{1}{4}$%)	937,500
Brokers ($\frac{1}{4}$%)	187,500
Sponsor's Fees	350,000
Broker's Fees	160,000
Advertising/Public Relations	75,000
Accountancy Fees	150,000
Legal Fees	350,000
Listing Fee	37,000
Receiving Banker's/Registrar's Fees	50,000
Printing	75,000
Total	£2,747,000

The expenses exclude VAT which is chargeable on certain items.

In percentage terms, the costs are equivalent on

the £75m. offering to	3.7%
the market capitalisation to	1.4%

and a proportion of the legal charges and any stamp duties payable by the purchasers should be allocated to them, with the balance of the expenses being the responsibility of the company. An estimate of costs for a £75 million issue is shown in Table 1 from which it will be seen that the main items of costs are the commissions of 2%. In the case of smaller companies the percentage costs naturally increase as the basic fixed costs remain much the same, whereas for larger companies the fixed costs are more easily absorbed.

Timing – there are two main factors which will dictate the actual timing of the issue. First the London Stock Exchange rule that audited accounts cannot be more than six months out of date at the time of issue, which effectively means that the company must go public within six months of its financial year end unless it is prepared to have an interim audit. Secondly, the time needed to prepare all the documents connected with the issue and the listing, especially the accountant's report, which in normal circumstances would take at least three months and in the case of larger and more complex groups with overseas subsidiaries throughout the world, would take longer still. Within this framework of timing it is necessary to take into account likely political, economic and financial events which may affect the timing in some way.

4.4 Financial Investigation

The issuing house will require one of the larger firms of accountants (which may be the company's auditors) to prepare a detailed confidential report on the company which will serve as the starting point for the assembly of information and the source document for all financial facts concerning the company. The terms of reference for this investigation will be very wide and will cover the company's record, its forecasts, how accurate its budgets are, its working capital requirements, its liabilities, its dependence on suppliers and on large customers, adequacy of credit control and bad debt provisions, the management structure, labour force and worker relations, its plant and premises – in fact the issuing house will want to know everything about the company, good and bad, and any unusual features or risks. Although this report (which is known as the "long-form" accountants' report) will take some three months to prepare and will be an expensive item on costs, both the sponsor and the company have a great deal to gain from such a report prepared by an independent person who has looked at the company in detail, and a critical examination may well indicate weak spots in the company's organisation or accounting procedures which can be dealt with before the issue.

5. THE PREPARATORY STAGE

It is at this stage that a detailed programme will be worked out with the advisers for the preparation of all the documents required for the listing. There will be frequent meetings to discuss the documents and many revisions of the proofs before they reach the final stage. At the same time all documents will be submitted to the Quotations Department by the sponsor who will be responsible for passing back any comments raised by the Department and dealing with points of principle on any problems arising from the requirements or the comments.

The documents are numerous, but the more important ones are as follows:

5.1 The Prospectus

The legal background to prospectus issues has already been referred to. However, the following major points must be covered:

5.1.1 A statement must be included on the front of the prospectus that "The Directors of the Company whose names appear on page 00 accept responsibility for the information contained in this document. To the best of the knowledge and belief of the Directors (who have taken all reasonable care to ensure that such is the case) the information contained in this document is in accordance with the facts and does not omit anything likely to affect the import of such information".

5.1.2 Prominence must be given to particulars of share capital and details of all indebtedness including bank overdrafts, loans, mortgages, acceptance credits, hire purchase commitments, guarantees and contingent liabilities, at a date within one month of listing.

5.1.3 Information on the trend of the group's business since the end of the year to which the last published accounts relate and information on the group's prospects in the current year.

5.1.4 All special factors or potential risks must be mentioned, and a statement must be made indicating whether or not the company relies on any one customer or any one supplier to a material degree.

5.1.5 A reasonable breakdown by turnover and trading profit must be given of the company's more important trading activities. A geographical breakdown of turnover and profits must also be included.

5.1.6 An explanation must be given for the trend of profits shown in the accountant's report, dealing in particular with the effect of changes in the financing of the company and of the acquisition or disposal of assets.

5.1.7 A statement by the directors that in their opinion the company has sufficient working capital for its present requirements. This statement would not normally be required for a bank or investment trust.

5.1.8 A statement that the company is not involved in any litigation or claims of material importance – if it is, full details must be given and the directors' opinion as to the validity and likely success of the claims.

5.1.9 Full details of main premises (i.e. those that account for more than 10% of net turnover or production), including location, size and tenure. Only summary information need be given about other buildings owned or leased.

5.1.10 Various disclosures by the directors, including details of shareholdings, emoluments, service contracts, interests in assets transferred and contracts of significance between the directors and the company.

5.1.11 Confirmation that taxation clearances have been obtained from the Inland Revenue in respect of past profits, and if not, a statement that indemnities have been given by the existing shareholders covering past taxes and any future inheritance tax.

5.2 The Accountants' Report
The following principal matters must be covered in the accountants' report:

5.2.1 The consolidated audited accounts of the group for the last five years.

5.2.2 The accounting policies followed in dealing with items which are judged material or critical in determining the profits and losses and net assets reported on.

5.2.3 Where a material proportion of the profits or assets are overseas, an indication of the amount and source of such assets or profits must be given, and any restrictions affecting the remittance of profits or the repatriation of capital from the countries concerned must also be explained.

5.2.4 It must be stated that the accounts show a true and fair view of the profits and state of affairs of the company and it is expected that the following points will, *inter alia*, be ascertainable from the report: whether the company has been making proper provision for depreciation and obsolescence; what the practice is regarding the valuation of stock and whether this is properly and consistently carried out; what relationship the value of the fixed assets as shown in the balance sheet bears to current values; whether full provision has been made for all taxation and how capital allowances have been treated for tax purposes.

5.3   Other Documents
In addition the London Stock Exchange require two further documents on accounting matters which the reporting accountants are responsible for producing:

5.3.1   *The statement of adjustments*
This statement reconciles the original audited figures with those appearing in their report, dealing with both assets and profits or losses.

5.3.2   *Profit forecast and working capital documents*
One of the most important parts in the prospectus is the section dealing with the company's prospects and in particular the profit forecast and dividend projection if one is to be given. If the company has published (this can be oral as well as written) a profit forecast for any period for which results have not yet been published a forecast must be included in the listing particulars. This must be reported on by the auditors or reporting accountants and by the sponsor, this will be by way of a statement in the listing particulars. The report by the accountants must include confirmation that the forecast or estimate has been properly

compiled on the basis stated and that it is presented on a basis consistent with the accounting policies of the group. There is a natural tendency to be conservative and allow for a margin in the actual figure disclosed for the forecast profit. However, such profits, when they are announced in the course of time, should not exceed the forecast by more than 10% (except in exceptional and unforeseen circumstances) as the public could justly feel that the tone of the prospectus had been unduly pessimistic about the company's prospects. Special attention will be paid to possible "windfall" profits and the likelihood of extraordinary items arising, and in some cases extra difficulties will result from businesses with short order books or seasonal patterns of trading. Special care would be paid by all the advisers to the wording on the forecast and prospects to be included in the prospectus so that potential investors should not be misled in any way.

The statement on working capital is also very important and requires detailed analysis and checking, especially as the London Stock Exchange looks to the sponsor to provide it with a letter confirming that the statement in the prospectus has been made by the Directors after due and careful enquiry. In order to write this letter the sponsor will have to carry out a careful investigation into the company's cash flow forecast for the next twelve months which will be compiled on a monthly basis so that all the potential troughs in the cash position will be revealed. Where the company has to rely on bank overdrafts or other loans to cover its cash requirements, the sponsor must confirm to the London Stock Exchange that it has seen letters from banks confirming the availability of overdraft or loan facilities. It is normal practice for the sponsor to look to the accountants for comfort on the working capital position prior to writing their letter to the London Stock Exchange.

The sponsor must also provide the London Stock Exchange with two additional letters. The first must state that the sponsor is satisfied that the directors of the (issuing) company have had explained to them their responsibilities and obligations as directors of a company under the listing rules and, in particular they are aware that they must apprise the public of the financial position of their company and so avoid the creation of a false market post flotation. The sponsor will usually inform the company of this obligation both orally and in writing.

The second letter should report to the Exchange that the sponsor has obtained written confirmation from the directors of the (issuing) company stating that they have established procedures which provide a reasonable basis for them to make proper judgments as to the financial position and prospects of their company.

5.3.3 *Articles of Association*
A company cannot apply for listing until it is a public company. In addition, the Articles of Association of unquoted companies often contain restrictions in relation to matters such as share transfers and the appointment of directors, which are not appropriate for a listed company. It will therefore be necessary for the lawyers to draw up new Articles of Association for the company which comply with the London Stock Exchange requirements and for such new Articles of Association to be adopted by the company in general meeting and filed prior to the listing.

5.3.4 *Subscription and sale agreement*
The parties to this agreement will be the vendor shareholders (if any existing shares are being sold), the directors, the company and the sponsor. The agreement, which will be conditional on the grant of listing by the London Stock Exchange, will provide for:

(a)   the purchase of shares from the vendor shareholders and the subscription of shares from the company by the issuing house; and

(b)   the subsequent offer for sale to the public of such shares by the issuing house.

Directors' warranties as to the accuracy of the statements in the prospectus will be included in the agreement, including confirmation that no facts have been omitted which would make any statement therein misleading. The directors will also be required to give warranties in respect of the balance sheet and profit and loss account for the last financial year, disclosure of unusual, long-term or abnormal contracts and litigation to which the company is, or may become, a party, and finally the taxation liabilities of the company. In addition those vendor shareholders who were directors or family connected, in the case of a family company, will be required to give indemnities regarding tax liabilities which may subsequently be levied on the company in respect of the profits or assets of the company existing prior to the listing.

5.3.5 *Directors' responsibility letter*

The directors must also provide the London Stock Exchange with a letter confirming that all information required to be included in the listing particulars by Section 146 of the Financial Services Act 1986 (i.e. to enable shareholders to make an informed assessment of the past, current and future financial positions of the company) is included.

Many more documents must be prepared, including *inter alia*, the application form, renounceable letter of acceptance, underwriting letter, board minutes, service agreements, press announcements, powers of attorney and share certificates.

6. THE FINAL STAGES

6.1 The Approach to Existing Shareholders

Shortly before the issue it will be necessary to send a letter to all the existing shareholders dealing with the following matters:

6.1.1 Convening an Extraordinary General Meeting to adopt the new Articles of Association and to alter the capital structure of the company for the issue. The capital reorganisation will normally involve an issue of shares to the existing shareholders by way of capitalisation of reserves. The capitalisation shares are allotted to the existing shareholders on renounceable letters of allotment and part of them will be sold on to the sponsor. Any shares subscribed for cash by the sponsor in order to provide additional capital for the company would also be allotted on renounceable allotment letters. The shares allotted or sold to the issuing house which are offered for sale to the public are renounced in favour of the successful applicants to whom renounceable letters of acceptance will be posted.

6.1.2 Obtaining confirmation from the existing shareholders that they will sell a proportion of their shares to enable the issue to take place and the listing to be granted. In order to inform the shareholders of the number of shares required from them, it will be necessary for the company to indicate the number of new shares it proposes to issue itself to raise additional funds. In addition the shareholders will want to know the price that they could expect to receive for their shares; as market conditions could change in the following three weeks and affect the price, the usual procedure is to indicate to shareholders a minimum price below which the issue would not take place.

6.1.3 Obtaining powers of attorney from the shareholders authorising the chairman or one of the directors of the company to sign the Subscription and Sale Agreement on their behalf and arrange the sale of their shares.

6.2   Fixing the Price

The value which can be placed upon a company's share capital depends on a number of interrelated factors, including the capital structure, the denomination of the shares, the size of the issue, the forecast earnings and dividends, the net asset value, the quality of earnings and prospects for the industry and general market conditions.

Technically there are four bases which could be used for setting the price. The first is the price at which existing shares have changed hands – however, such prices are unlikely to be a good guide, as the shares will not have transferred that frequently and then only between a limited group of people. A second guide is the value of the net assets of the company, but this too can be misleading since part of the assets can be in at cost while some businesses rely heavily on goodwill. The third is the earnings ratio and dividend yield of already listed companies operating in the same industry and with as many comparable characteristics as possible. It will be necessary to pitch the issue price at a lower level than that of comparable companies, in order to allow for the unfamiliarity of the new company and to attract sufficient investors to take up all the shares being offered for sale. This is of prime importance since the issue must be a success for the longer term interests of the company. Although the existing shareholders naturally want to achieve as high a price as possible for their shares it is important to price on terms to attract new investors to ensure a successful offer, especially as the vendors may still be large shareholders in the company. On the other hand the price must be sufficiently competitive to avoid an unduly large premium arising when dealings commence to the disadvantage of the vendors and the company.

632

The fourth is bookbuilding. This is the description of the technique used in an offering of shares whereby an investment bank collects investors' bids for shares to be issued so as to establish the most appropriate selling price. By matching supply and demand in this way bankers hope to avoid excessive volatility in the shares when they start trading in the secondary market. By bookbuilding it is possible to identify long term investors rather than expose the offering to stags (i.e. those investors who seek to make a quick capital gain by selling their allocation of shares immediately after flotation or an initial public offering (IPO) in the expectation that the market price will rise due to an oversubscription for the shares).

The price has to be fixed some four days before the offer for sale is advertised in the newspapers and applications invited from the public. The responsibility for fixing the price lies with the sponsor, the broker and the directors of the company.

6.3 Underwriting

As soon as the price has been fixed, underwriting proofs of the prospectus will be printed, so that underwriting letters can be sent out that same evening. The reason why the sponsor uses a broker to carry out the bulk of the underwriting on its behalf is due to the fact that the broker is in constant daily touch with the institutions over the buying and selling of securities and is therefore in a position to make an up-to-date assessment of their likely reaction to the new issue, whether they would accept underwriting and, if so, how much. As a result of this constant communication and the experience of previous issues the broker is able to build up an underwriting list (covering insurance companies, pension funds, investment trusts, unit trusts, banks and private clients) which allows underwriting to be completed quickly and efficiently.

The underwriting process is rapid and replies to the underwriting invitations must be given on the telephone by 3 p.m. on the following day, by which time the broker hopes to be in a position to confirm to the issuing house that the underwriting has been completed. Thereafter the institutions must return a letter of confirmation to the brokers as written evidence of their participation in the underwriting, although the oral reply is taken as a firm commitment. With regard to underwriting costs, the underwriters will receive a flat commission of $1\frac{1}{4}\%$ on the value of their underwriting participation, whether or not they will have to take up shares, and the brokers will receive a commission on the value of those shares for which they have arranged underwriting. The sponsor may take an overall underwriting commission of $\frac{1}{2} - \frac{3}{4}\%$, or as an alternative take its commission from the difference in the price at which it buys shares from the company or its shareholders and at which it sells them to the public. Underwriting commission cannot exceed 10% by law (Section 97 of the Companies Act), but in normal circumstances the actual commission will not exceed $2\frac{1}{4}\%$. In addition, fees are charged for advice and services by the sponsor.

6.4 The Completion Meeting, Press Advertising and Listing

The Extraordinary General Meeting and the completion meeting to sign all the documents will be held on the day before the underwriting arrangements are completed. On Impact Day, the company's lawyers will file the prospectus and other relevant documents with the Registrar of Companies and a detailed press announcement on the proposed offer for sale will be released.

The prospectus, together with the application form, will be advertised in at least one national newspaper. Press comment, particularly at the time of advertising the offer for sale, may have a marked impact on the reception given to the company by the public. It is therefore important that the directors and the sponsor should hold meetings with the press and other opinion-formers before the advertising in order to provide summary information to financial journalists.

The formal application for listing will be made by the brokers on the day that the advertisements are published, and all the necessary forms and documents connected with the listing and the offer for sale will be lodged with the Quotations Department. Applications for listing are heard by the Quotations Committee each week on Wednesdays and Fridays, and assuming all documents have been approved in proof form and the necessary documents have been lodged in time, the actual Committee hearing should be a formality. The Committee may require the broker to answer any particular query prior to issuing formal notification that listing has been granted.

6.5   The Opening and Closing of the Subscription Lists, Allotment and Dealings

The form of application will provide that an application, once lodged, cannot be withdrawn until 3 or 4 days after the closing of the subscription lists. This date is usually 3 days after the publication of the prospectus. No allotment of shares can be made until the subscription lists have closed.

The object of this is to give time for consideration, consultation and the study of press comments before submission of applications. In practice, subscription lists will be open at 10.00 a.m. and close on the same day, sometimes at 10.01 a.m. if the offer is heavily oversubscribed. The receiving bankers will then be responsible for counting the applications and thereafter the sponsor must decide on the basis of allotment. The sponsor reserves the right to reject suspected multiple applications so as to reduce the chance that an unduly high proportion of the issue might be allotted to "stags" seeking to make a quick profit rather than to genuine long-term investors. In general, if the offer for sale is oversubscribed, applicants for large numbers of shares will be allotted a percentage of their application and the small applicants will ballot for allotments. Although it is undesirable for the company to have a register with a large number of tiny individual shareholdings, every applicant must be given a fair chance of receiving shares. Preferential consideration can be given to applications from employees of the company, but under Stock Exchange regulations this is restricted to a maximum of 10% of the shares offered for sale.

Cheques from successful applicants will be banked on the same day as the closing of the subscription lists as it takes several days for cheques to be cleared. The purpose of preventing the revocation of applications for a period of time after the opening and closing of the subscription lists is designed to curtail the activities of "stags" who may try to revoke their application if a fall in the price seems likely following a change in market conditions. Assuming the renounceable letters of acceptance are posted to successful applicants promptly there is no possibility of applications being revoked, but thereafter there is a risk for the sponsor especially if any cheques have not yet been cleared.

Renounceable letters of acceptance, together with balance cheques in the case of partial allotment and letters of regret returning unsuccessful applicants' original cheques will be posted as soon as possible, so that dealings can start the following day. The broker will be watching the first dealings very closely and where necessary will try and balance buyers and sellers so as to ensure an orderly early market.

For about six weeks after first dealings shares will change hands on the renounceable letter of acceptance. After the last day for renunciation, a shareholders' register will be made up and definitive certificates will be issued to the final holders.

7. FURTHER ISSUES OF SHARES

Where a listed company requires additional funds, it may obtain these either from its own shareholders or from the public at large. In the case of ordinary shares or loan/preference capital convertible into ordinary shares or warrants to subscribe for ordinary shares, such funds must be obtained (under London Stock Exchange rules) by an issue to ordinary shareholders in proportion to their existing holdings, unless shareholders in general meeting agree otherwise. Loan capital and preference shares, where the rights of the existing ordinary shareholders are not affected, may be offered to the public at large.

In cases where the amount to be raised will exceed £20 million, the Bank of England likes to be informed of the proposed impact day, being the day when the terms are first known, in order to help maintain an orderly queue of issues.

7.1 Rights Issues

In recent years the greater part of additional share capital required by companies already listed has been raised through rights issues.

The normal procedure for a rights issue is that a press announcement would be released at 9.00 a.m. and sub-underwriting letters would be circulated for replies by 3 p.m. on the same day. Thereafter the rights offer is communicated to shareholders in a prospectus circulated by the company. The subscription price of the rights issue is usually at a discount to the existing share price of between 10 and 20 per cent. The London Stock Exchange requires various points to be covered in the rights issue prospectus, the most important being as follows:

(a)   statement confirming the sufficiency of working capital and a schedule showing the indebtedness of the company at a date within one month of the issue;

(b)   details of current trading, future prospects and dividends – where a forecast of profits is made supporting letters from the accountants and issuing house must be included in the circular letter to shareholders; and

(c)   reasons for the issue and the use to which the proceeds will be put.

If the company has sufficient authorised but unissued capital to cover the issue, a provisional allotment letter ("PAL") will be sent out simultaneously with the listing particulars, which constitute the prospectus. Where it is necessary to hold a shareholders' meeting to increase the authorised capital, the PAL will be posted on its own after the meeting has been held. The PAL is a transferable document which may be of significant value (with the rights issue price normally being at discount on the current market price) and is traded on the London Stock Exchange. Dealings in the rights "nil paid" commence on the first dealing day after the despatch of the PALs.

London Stock Exchange regulations require that the offer must be open for three weeks to enable shareholders to consider what action to take. On the expiry of the three week period, the shareholder or person who has purchased the rights must, assuming he wishes to accept the allotment, pay for the new securities. The PAL will then be stamped "fully paid" and remains a transferable document until such time as it has to be submitted for registration when it will be replaced by a definitive share certificate.

Shares not subscribed during the three week offer period are required by the London Stock Exchange to be dealt with by one of the following methods:

(a)   sold for the benefit of the shareholders entitled thereto;

(b)   offered to existing shareholders by the provision of application forms for excess shares; and

(c)   any shares remaining thereafter will be allotted to the sub-underwriters.

The costs of a rights issue can vary depending on the size of the issue, with the main items of cost being the underwriting and sub-underwriting commissions of up to $2\frac{1}{2}\%$.

7.1.1   *Deep discount rights issues*

Rights issues are sometimes made by companies on a "deep discount" basis. These types of issues involve the offering of shares to existing shareholders on a non-underwritten basis at a price which is heavily discounted against the existing market price. One of the advantages to companies in this type of issue is the saving of underwriting commissions. However, part of the effect of such issues is to reduce significantly the existing share price following the issue of new shares as a result of the large bonus element in the rights issue share price.

There are certain disadvantages connected with such issues, the principal one being that existing holdings by shareholders are substantially diluted in percentage terms unless the shareholders subscribe fully for their rights entitlement. For UK shareholders there may be capital gains tax liability in the event of the sale of their nil paid rights. In addition, as a deep discount issue is not underwritten, there is no guarantee to the company that the new shares will be subscribed and, therefore, in the event of an exceptional fall in the existing share price to, or below, the rights issue price, the company risks failing to raise the amount of capital which it has invited investors to subscribe.

7.2   **Placings**

7.2.1   *Equity*

The London Stock Exchange has no monetary or percentage limits on marketings of new equity securities for cash where the company is already listed. The method is to place securities firm with institutional investors at the issue price at a small discount to the current market price.

The ability of companies to issue new equity capital or capital with an equity element such as convertible bonds, direct to third parties for cash is limited. Statutory protection for pre-emption rights for equity shareholders is set out in Section 89 of the Companies Act, 1985. This right can be waived by shareholders in general meeting for a period of up to five years. The five year period is the maximum time that directors, by law, can allot authorised but unissued capital.

Further to this the London Stock Exchange require all listed and USM companies to limit the authority to waive pre-emption rights to a period up to the next Annual General Meeting or fifteen months, whichever is the earlier.

Further limitation is imposed by the Pre-emption Guidelines issued by the London Stock Exchange. These guidelines represent the combined views of the users of the market including professional investment institutions and companies. The Investment Committees representing insurance companies and pension funds will advise their members to approve a resolution for an annual disapplication of pre-emption rights by a company, provided it is restricted to an amount of shares not exceeding 5% of the issued equity share capital. The company should not, without prior consultation with the Investment Committees make use of more than $7^{1}/_{2}\%$ of issued equity capital by way of non-pre-emptive issues for cash in any rolling three year period. Furthermore, the guidelines require that the discount at which non-pre-emptive share issues for cash are made should be restricted to a maximum of 5% of the share price immediately prior to the announcement of an issue.

Assuming shareholders' approval has been given and a listing granted, fully paid renounceable allotment letters would be issued to the placees and dealings would take place in these documents until such time as registered certificates were issued.

7.2.2   Loan capital
Unlike equity issues, no limit is put on the size of fixed-interest issues which are the subject of a placing and there is no requirement under the

Companies Act or otherwise to obtain shareholders' approval, since there is a limited class of investor (primarily insurance companies and pension funds) interested in this type of security. This method of raising finance has considerable advantages: first, in terms of costs (maximum $1\frac{1}{2}\%$); secondly, the terms need not be fixed until the afternoon of the placing by reference to the levels in the gilt market which means that the borrower secures terms more closely in accord with current market conditions; and, thirdly, the funds can be handed over to the company within five or six days of the placing.

Listing particulars have to be prepared for which the directors have to take full responsibility and a copy has to be filed with the Registrar of Companies. The listing particulars will contain restrictions on borrowings, prior charges, sale of assets and change of nature of the business, and will also include enough financial information to enable a subscriber to assess the income and capital cover for the stock and to be satisfied about the indebtedness and working capital position of the company.

The placing operation starts on Day 1 with the terms being agreed with the company, whereupon the sponsor will issue pre-placing letters to institutions for reply by 3 p.m. on the same day. At least two market makers must be included in the marketing on the same terms as all other participants. Listing will be granted the same day.

Formal placing letters confirming the price and requesting payment against delivery of an allotment letter are dispatched on Day 2. A formal advertisement is published in one national newspaper (usually the *Financial Times* or the *Daily Official List*) on this day to advise investors of the new security and the placing price and terms; dealings will also commence on Day 2 on a nil-paid basis, pending settlement and payment three days later.

7.2.3 *Other Methods*
(a) Offer for Sale – occasionally this method is used to raise additional capital but the costs are high due to underwriting and preparation of a full prospectus.

(b)   Open Offers – this is an offer limited to the shareholders of the company but not giving them fixed rights proportionate to their existing holdings.

(c)   Vendor Placings – where the vendor of a business requires cash from the purchaser (which in turn only wishes to issue shares as consideration for the acquisition) it is usual, subject to placing permission being granted by the London Stock Exchange, to place the shares so as to raise the necessary cash for the vendors. In this case there is no requirement to obtain shareholders' approval to the proposal as technically the shares are issued on a share exchange basis and not wholly or partly for cash. Details of the acquisition would be given in a press announcement. Shareholders would only receive details in a circular if the size of the acquisition represented more than 25% of the purchaser's assets or profits, in which case shareholders' approval would be required, or 15% in which case an information circular would be issued to shareholders.

In all cases where more than 10% of the issued equity of the acquiring company is being placed a "100% claw-back" arrangement operates. Under a claw-back arrangement, all the shares placed can be clawed-back by existing shareholders, proportional to their existing interest in the company. This rule, which is a reflection of the formal procedures required by institutional investors, protects pre-emption rights in large vendor placings.

However, placees receive a commitment commission of $\frac{1}{2}\%$ in respect of their commitment together with an additional $\frac{3}{4}\%$ on all their shares liable to be clawed-back. Shareholders normally have three weeks to elect to purchase shares. If the commitment period runs over 30 days, an additional $\frac{1}{8}\%$ commission is paid for every week or part thereof over 30 days until the period ends.

(d)   *Cash underwriting for a takeover* – as in (c) above this is a method whereby the shareholders of a company being taken over are able to sell at a fixed price any shares in the purchasing company offered as consideration which they do not wish to retain. Arrangements are made for the shares to be underwritten in the normal way at a discount on the current price. Commission arrangements are similar to those in Vendor Placings referred to in (c) above.

(e) *Eurobond issues* – These are international placings of, usually, bearer debt securities with a syndicate of international professional investors. The London Stock Exchange accords such issues special treatment in view of the overwhelming professional nature of the market. The London Stock Exchange has published a separate guide to the listing of Eurobonds. (See Chapters 13 and 14.) Bonds may be convertible into the equity of the company or have warrants attached and, as long as the effective dilution of the existing equity does not exceed 5%, there will normally be no requirement to offer the securities to existing shareholders.

8. LISTINGS OF OVERSEAS COMPANIES

In recent years there has been a steady number of overseas companies listing their shares in London, with the greater proportion coming from the USA. Overseas companies must comply with the standard requirements laid down for UK companies seeking a listing, although in practice it is recognised that differences in legal and financial systems will exist and that some compromises may have to be made. The London Stock Exchange have certain concessionary requirements for well established overseas companies listed on a recognised overseas stock exchange for at least two years.

It has to be understood that foreign companies seeking a listing in the UK must issue listing particulars complying with statutory disclosure obligations and therefore, the London Stock Exchange have limited powers of waiver.

8.1 The Procedures for Listing

The first step is for the broker to apply to the London Stock Exchange for permission to "introduce" the shares. An introduction will be allowed if there is a sufficient number and spread of shareholders and provided the company is listed on its domestic stock exchange this will be a formality and there will be no requirement to market any shares. Thereafter an information document must be prepared with one box advertisement being published in a national newspaper. As there is already a market price available for the shares, dealing can commence the business day after listing has been granted.

9. ACQUISITIONS AND REALISATIONS

The continuing obligations for listed companies set out in the Yellow Book include requirements regarding acquisitions and realisations. These are in addition to the regulations contained in the City Code and the Rules Governing Substantial Acquisitions of Shares published by the Panel on Take-overs and Mergers; whilst neither of these is part of the listing rules, the London Stock Exchange encourages listed companies to comply with both.

The Yellow Book rules relating to acquisitions and realisations include acquisitions or realisations by any subsidiary undertaking of the listed company but exclude transactions that are of a revenue nature in the ordinary course of business.

9.1 Classification of Transactions

The classification of a transaction is determined by comparing the size of the transaction with the size of the listed company proposing to make it. The comparison is made using the percentage ratios set out in the next paragraph. The different classifications are:

Class 3 –	acquisition or disposal where all the ratios are less than 5%.
Class 2 –	acquisition or disposal where any ratio is 5% or more but less than 15%.
Class 1 –	acquisition or disposal where any ratio is 15% or more but less than 25%.
Super Class 1 –	acquisition or disposal where any ratio is 25% or more.
Reverse takeover –	an acquisition by a listed company of a business or unlisted company where any ratio is 100% or more, or which would result in a material change of management or change in shareholder control of the listed company.

The percentage ratios are found from the following calculations:

643

Assets –   the value of assets acquired or disposed of divided by the assets of the acquiring or disposing company.

Pre-tax Profits –   the profits attributable to the assets acquired or disposed of divided by the profits of the acquiring or disposing company.

Consideration   the value of the consideration divided by the value of
to assets –   the assets of the acquiring or disposing company. (If consideration is deferred then the consideration for the purposes of this text is the maximum consideration payable under the agreement. If total consideration is not subject to any maximum, the transaction will normally be treated as Super Class 1, notwithstanding the class into which it would otherwise fall.)

Market   the value of the consideration divided by the market
capitalisation –   capitalisation of the equity shares of the acquiring or disposing company immediately before the acquisition or disposal.

Gross capital –   the gross capital of the company or business being acquired divided by the gross capital of the acquiring company. This test is used only in the case of an acquisition.

The gross capital is calculated as the aggregate of the value of consideration payable, the market value of its non-equity share capital and debt capital, all other non-current liabilities and the excess of current liabilities over current assets.

The figures used are those from the latest published audited consolidated accounts, although the assets figure may be adjusted to take account of subsequent transactions in respect of which information has already been published under the listing rules. Where one of the calculations produces an anomalous result, the London Stock Exchange may substitute other relevant indicators of size.

9.2 Aggregation

The London Stock Exchange may require two or more acquisitions or two or more disposals to be aggregated for the purposes of determining the classification of the latest transaction if any of them has occurred within the previous 12 months or during the period since the latest audited balance sheet, listing particulars or circular, whichever is shorter.

Acquisitions or disposals will be aggregated if they are entered into between the company and the same parties, involve the acquisition or disposal of any interest or securities in one particular company, or together lead to an involvement in a business which did not previously form a substantial part of the company's principal activities.

9.3 Class Requirements

9.3.1 *Class 3*

The company must notify the Company Announcements Office where the consideration includes the issue of securities for which listing will be sought, otherwise no announcement is required. However, if an announcement is made, whether it is a requirement or not, it must be made as soon as possible, after terms have been agreed and must include:

- brief details of the assets being acquired or disposed of,

- the effect on the company of any disposal,

- the amount of any securities being issued

and either

- the value of the consideration and how this is being satisfied (including the terms of any deferred consideration and amount of any securities being issued)

- or the value of the assets being acquired or disposed of.

9.3.2 *Class 2*

The company must notify the Company Announcements Office as soon as possible after the terms of the acquisition or disposal have been agreed. The announcement must include:

645

- particulars of the assets or businesses being acquired or disposed of,

- description of the trade carried on by or using the assets, the value of the consideration and how it is being satisfied,

- the value of the assets acquired or being disposed of,

- the consideration and how it is being satisfied,

- the profits before taxation attributable to the assets,

- the effect on the company of the acquisition or disposal including the benefits expected to accrue,

- details of any service contracts of proposed directors of the company,

- the application of the sale proceeds (where relevant)

and, if shares are to form part of the consideration received on a disposal, whether these securities will be sold or retained.

9.3.3 *Class 1*

The company must fulfil all the Class 2 requirements but must also despatch an explanatory circular to shareholders within 28 days of the announcement. The circular must contain the information required for the Class 2 announcement plus the following:

- in the case of an acquisition or disposal of a listed company, a table showing consolidated balance sheet and latest audited consolidated three years' profits or losses after all charges except taxation, the taxation charge shown separately, taken from the published accounts of the company.

- in the case of an acquisition or disposal of an unlisted company or business, a table showing the latest audited balance sheet and the latest audited consolidated three years' profit and loss accounts together with details of the basis of preparation and any audit qualifications.

646

– in the case of an acquisition or disposal of an asset, a summary of the relevant financial information together with confirmation that the directors consider that the value to the company justifies the price paid or received.

– as an appendix, copies of all Class 2 announcements since the publication of the company's latest annual report, or if later, listing particulars or class circular to shareholders.

– in addition various items of regulatory information, including a working capital statement are required.

If listing particulars are required for an acquisition where part or all of the consideration is to be satisfied in shares, these may be incorporated into the Class 1 circular provided they are in a clearly marked section. If listing particulars are to be incorporated, the circular must be submitted to the London Stock Exchange for approval prior to posting. The securities will not be listed until the circular has been despatched.

9.3.4 *Super Class 1*

The company must fulfil all the Class 1 requirements, but in addition must obtain the prior approval of the company's shareholders in general meeting. An agreement effecting the transaction must be conditional on shareholders' approval being obtained.

The Super Class 1 circular must include all the information required for a Class 1 circular, with the addition of:

– in the case of an acquisition, where the latest accounts of the acquired company or business were qualified by the auditors, there must be an accountants' report on the company or business,

– a statement of the effect of the acquisition or disposal on the earnings or assets and liabilities of the company, such as a pro forma statement of assets,

– working capital and indebtedness statements,

647

material contracts, not in the ordinary course of business, entered into during the preceding two years to be on display.

If a profit forecast has been given for any period for which results have not yet been published, a profit forecast must be given in the circular (for more details see Section 5.3.2).

9.3.5 *Reverse takeover*

Upon the announcement of a reverse takeover, the London Stock Exchange will suspend the listing of the company's securities pending the meeting at which shareholder approval will be sought. If approval is given, the listing will be cancelled. If approval is not given, the listing will be restored provided the company continues to satisfy the conditions for listing.

In the event of a cancellation of the listing, if the company wishes to be listed again, it will be treated as a new applicant. In any event, the company will need to prepare a Super Class 1 circular and listing particulars.

9.4 Other Requirements on an Acquisition or Disposal

9.4.1 *Cash companies*

A cash company is one (other than an investment company) whose assets consist wholly or substantially of cash or short-dated securities, because it has disposed of all or a substantial part of its business or otherwise ceased to have a business of sufficient substance to support its market capitalisation.

A listed company which becomes a cash company will not satisfy the listing conditions and will be suspended. It will then be given a period of six months following the date of the general meeting approving the disposal of its former business in which to take the necessary steps to satisfy the conditions for listing. If at the end of this period the company does not satisfy the listing conditions its listing will be cancelled.

9.4.2   *Indemnities*

The prior approval of shareholders in general meeting must be obtained for any arrangement in connection with an acquisition or disposal under which a listed company agrees to accept any liabilities for costs, expenses, etc., incurred by a third party, whether contingent or not, which would be exceptional in the course of such a transaction, and under which the amount is either unlimited or exceeds 25% of the average of the company's profits for the last three years.

9.5   Takeovers and Mergers

If a listed company undertakes a transaction that is subject to the requirements of the City Code, the offer document issued to the holders of securities of the offeree company must contain information in addition to the requirements of the City Code. This information includes details of the precise terms of the securities for which the offer is made (including whether they are "cum", i.e. "with" or "ex", i.e. "without" dividend or interest payment), total consideration offered, how securities issued will rank, how documents of title will be issued, any payments proposed for loss of office, middle market quotations for the securities to be acquired or offered, the nature of the offeror's business and financial and trading prospects, and where an offer involves the exchange of securities a statement indicating the effect of acceptance on the capital and income of the offeree company's shareholders, as well as the effect of full acceptance of the bid on the offeror's assets, profits and business.

Drafts of documents in connection with takeovers, mergers and offers must be submitted to the London Stock Exchange for approval prior to posting. Where the consideration being offered consists of securities for which listing will be sought, listing particulars may also be necessary.

9.6   Transactions with Related Parties

The Yellow Book regulations provide certain safeguards against directors or substantial shareholders taking advantage of their position. Where any transaction is proposed between a listed company (or any of its subsidiary undertakings) and a related party, a circular and the approval of the company in general meeting will usually be required. The related party will not be permitted to vote where applicable.

The circular to shareholders must be produced in accordance with the general requirements for circulars, but in addition must give full details of the transaction, and the nature and extent of the interest of the related party in it. In the case of an acquisition or disposal of an asset, an independent valuation is required and all such transactions must include a statement by an independent adviser acceptable to the London Stock Exchange as to whether the transaction is fair and reasonable so far as the shareholders of the company are concerned.

If the transaction with a related party is one where each of the class tests described in Section 9.1 is less than 5% but one or more exceeds 0.25%, the London Stock Exchange may waive the requirement for a circular provided that an appropriate independent adviser gives written confirmation to them that the terms of the transaction are fair and reasonable so far as the shareholders of the company are concerned, and that the company undertakes to include details of the transaction in the next published annual accounts.

9.7 Model Code

UK companies and overseas companies with their primary listings in the UK must adopt by board resolution, and secure compliance with, a code of dealing in terms no less exacting than those of the Model Code. The code of dealing should cover both directors and those employees of the company and its subsidiaries who, because of their office or employment, are likely to be in possession of unpublished price-sensitive information.

The Model Code imposes restrictions beyond common law and statute (e.g. the Companies Securities (Insider Dealing) Act 1985 and Companies Act 1985) and its purpose is to ensure that directors and persons connected with them do not abuse, and do not place themselves under suspicion of abusing, price-sensitive information that they may have or be thought to have.

The essence of the Model Code is that a director, and those connected with him, must not deal in his company's securities on consideration of a short-term nature, must not deal in his company's securities when he is in possession of unpublished, price-sensitive information in relation to those securities and, where he is privy by virtue of his position to

650

unpublished, price-sensitive information in another listed company's securities, he must not deal in those securities.

In addition, a director must not deal in any securities of his company during the periods of two months immediately preceding the preliminary and interim announcements of the company's results. These prohibited periods are known as "close periods".

A director must not deal in any securities of his company without advising his chairman (or designated director) in advance and receiving clearance to deal. The chairman (or designated director) should receive clearance for his own dealings from the board. Dealings may be cleared in circumstances where a director would otherwise be prohibited to deal in exceptional circumstances at the discretion of the person clearing the deal. Exceptional circumstances would include, for example, pressing financial commitments that could not be otherwise satisfied.

9.8 Definitions

Capital – Authorised: The total amount of shares a company may issue as recorded in the company's Memorandum of Association.

– Issued: That portion of the authorised capital which is issued.

Convertible Preference Shares: Preference shares or loan stock.

Convertible Stock: which, under specified conditions, can be converted into ordinary shares.

Debenture: An instrument creating or acknowledging a debt, which may be secured. It usually bears a fixed rate of interest, and may be bearer or in registered form.

Deferred Shares/Stock: Shares/stock which do not receive a dividend/ share of residual value until prior ranking shares or stock have been paid a dividend/share of residual value.

Limited: (Also Ltd). A private limited liability company the shares of which may not be offered to the general public and may not be quoted on a Stock Exchange.

Loan Stock: See "Debenture". Loan stock is a term used for a debt obligation which is usually unsecured.

Non-voting Shares: A form of ordinary share the holder of which is not permitted to vote at the issuing company's Annual or Extraordinary Meetings.

Ordinary Shares: Usually shares, the holders of which, receive dividends/ capital after all other claims of any other shareholders have been paid.

PLC: Public Limited Company. One whose liability is limited to the nominal value of their shares. Minimum issued capital £50,000.

Pre-emption Rights: The right of existing shareholders to subscribe for a portion of additional shares to be issued to third parties for cash by a company in priority to non-shareholders.

Preference Shares: Shares, the holders of which, are paid dividends/ capital before ordinary and deferred shareholders.

Rights Issue: An additional issue of shares to which existing shareholders have the "right" (which has an intrinsic value) to subscribe on a pro-rata basis according to their existing shareholding.

Scrip, Free, Capitalisation, Bonus Issue: A pro rata application of a company's reserves to an issue of additional shares to existing shareholders.

Shares: The shares into which the capital of a company is divided. They have a "par value", e.g. £1, and can be fully or partly paid. Shareholders have the right to share in profits and residual net value after all prior claimants have been paid. Shareholders are the "owners" of the company. Usually in registered, not bearer, form.

Warrants: An option which entitles the holder to buy a specified number of shares or debentures in a company at a fixed purchase/subscription price; it has an intrinsic value.

N.B. The various forms of shares may be issued in voting and non-voting forms. There must always be some voting shares.

CHAPTER 15 (Part II)

Equities – Switzerland

by Swiss Bank Corporation

1. INTRODUCTION: SWISS STOCK EXCHANGES

There are three stock exchanges in Switzerland, of which Zurich is the most important, followed by Geneva and Basle. They all belong to the Association of Swiss Stock Exchanges, which was founded in 1939. The appropriate cantonal authority regulates the activities of the stock exchanges. Trading follows the "open-outcry" system and takes place on the so-called trading rings. Stocks can also be bought and sold on the over-the-counter market off the stock exchange premises. In contrast to some other countries, banks in Switzerland act as brokers as well. Trading at the stock exchanges lasts from around 10 a.m. to 4 p.m. For 1995, the introduction of an electronic trading system called EBS, which will concentrate trading on one market, is planned.

Switzerland plays a major role in international investment, particularly direct investment. A stock exchange listing, therefore, is attractive for a foreign company because it creates broader access to the Swiss investment community. This includes domestic investors, the vast discretionary portfolios managed by the Swiss banks and institutional funds, such as those of insurance companies and pension funds.

In 1993, total trading volume on the Swiss stock exchanges was SFr 343bn, of which about 10% was due to foreign equities. At the end of 1993, stocks of 215 Swiss and 249 foreign companies were listed on the Zurich stock exchange. Most foreign companies with listed stocks in Switzerland are based in North America, followed by Germany, the Netherlands, Japan and the UK.

American and Canadian companies' shares are traded in the form of certificates registered in a Swiss nominee company. UK company share certificates have a coupon of transfer attached. German and Dutch company certificates are original common stock in bearer form and can be transferred easily in Switzerland or to their home countries.

2. CRITERIA FOR LISTING
Listings for foreign companies in Switzerland are limited to those companies which are already well known to Swiss investors and to companies for which it can be expected that an adequate market for the shares will develop. Specific criteria have been established to satisfy these concerns, based on the market value of the shares held with the three big Swiss banks, namely Union Bank of Switzerland, Credit Suisse and Swiss Bank Corporation, and on the number of custody accounts with those banks in which the shares are held.

For an industrial company, the requirements are a minimum market value of SFr 10 million, deposited in at least 250 custody accounts; for banks SFr 50 million in at least 1,000 accounts; and for investment funds SFr 100 million in at least 2,000 accounts. A security may not be officially traded on the ring without being admitted to the quotations list under the "listing regulations". For foreign securites, the exchanges have agreed to work with a Swiss Admission Board to which the listing application is submitted. The board is comprised of representatives from the Swiss Stock Exchange Association, the Federal Department of Finance and members of the private industry.

An informal and internal listing committee comprised of the three big banks approves the application for listing on the basis of the above criteria, but also takes into account the financial structure, historical performance and management of the company. Banks other than the big banks have also introduced foreign companies to the Swiss stock exchanges. The most common method to place issues is to have them fully underwritten by a banking syndicate.

3. LISTING PROCEDURES
In addition to obtaining approval of the sponsoring bank, a company wishing to list its shares must apply to the Swiss National Bank and the Swiss Admission Board. The company must also approach the stock exchanges on which the shares are to be listed. Finally, the listing

prospectus must be prepared and its content published in the Swiss newspapers. Usually, the sponsoring bank organises a road show with the company before the placing and listing of the stocks in Switzerland. The company's sponsoring bank, usually one of the big three, will initiate the listing-application process and prepare the prospectus. Listing usually takes between one and two months to effect.

Disclosure requirements are less onerous than in most other stock exchanges, and information from the latest annual report serves as the basis for the listing prospectus. For an English company, the body of the prospectus appears in English, with a summary of that information in German, and, also in German, information on listing and delivery of the shares, dividend payment details and notification that the company intends to publish promptly in Switzerland all official communication to shareholders. The body of the prospectus will include a brief description of the company's activities, a description of the rights attached to the shares, an indebtedness statement, corporate details, details of dividends paid in the preceding five years, details of management and the most recent financial statements.

4. TYPES OF EQUITY

Typically the equity of a Swiss company consists of bearer shares, registered shares or non-voting certificates. In recent years the tendency has been to simplify the capital structure to only one or two different stock classes. In particular, the somewhat unpopular participation certificates are disappearing gradually from the market. For example, in 1993 Nestlé converted its bearer shares and participation certificates into registered shares and now has only one share category outstanding. Voting shares frequently have restricted voting rights. A common clause is that an individual or a group can exercise a maximum of 3% of all voting rights. Bearer and registered shares must show a minimum nominal value of SFr 10. Because of the new Swiss Companies' Act, Swiss companies also must permit foreign investors to buy registered shares. As a result, the former price differences between bearer and registered shares have almost disappeared. Preference and cumulative shares may be issued, but they are not as common in Switzerland as they are in the UK or in the US. Companies may acquire up to 10% of their own share capital.

Dealing on the stock exchanges is conducted by member banks at prices fixed on the floor by licensed dealers. The appropriate cantonal stock exchange advisory committee registers these dealers. Prices are published every day in the official lists of the stock exchanges and in the newspapers.

5. CONTINUING REQUIREMENTS

Under the new Swiss Companies' Act, new and important accounting principles have to be fulfilled. Furthermore, Swiss companies have abandoned their tradition of secrecy in favour of disclosure based on international standards.

The profit and loss account, balance sheet, report of the auditors, business report and proposals for the allocation of net profit must be made available to the shareholders at the offices of the principal establishment and branches of the company not later than ten days before the regular general meeting. The accounts and reports must then remain available to the shareholders for a year from the date of the meeting. Each shareholder is entitled to receive a copy of the profit and loss account and the balance sheet at the expense of the company.

CHAPTER 15 (Part III)

Equities – USA

by
Brian J. Terry and Sarah Scarlett

1. INTRODUCTION: STOCK EXCHANGES IN USA
In the USA there are the New York, Philadelphia, Boston, National, American, Cincinnati, MidWest, Pacific, Intermountain, Spokane and Chicago Stock Exchanges.

The New York Stock Exchange, constituted in 1817, is the largest and it lists and trades 1,500 stocks, almost 1,000 corporate bonds, nearly 400 convertible bonds and over 200 convertible preferred stocks. It is, in fact, the world's largest secondary market. During 1992 the NYSE traded an average of 202 million shares daily. At the end of 1992 there was a total of 2,089 issues listed with 116 billion shares having a value of US$4.0 trillion; the value of trading was US$1.75 trillion.

There is also an electronic market (NASDAQ) which is sometimes referred to as the over-the-counter (OTC) market. This is a screen trading system whereby market makers competitively offer and bid, while supplying quotations for the institutions' dealing screens.

The Securities Act of 1933 had, as its two basic purposes, the provision of full disclosure to investors and the prohibition of fraud in connection with the sale of securities. Then, on 6 June 1934, the Securities Exchange Act was enacted providing for the regulation of securities trading and the establishment of the Securities and Exchange Commission.

Just as the London Stock Exchange did in October 1986 the NYSE abolished the fixed commission system in April 1975.

2.   CRITERIA FOR LISTING

A company (listing or) offering its shares to the public in the United States is required to register the shares with the United States Securities and Exchange Commission under the provisions of the Securities Act of 1933 (the 1933 Act). The registration process involves filing a registration statement with the SEC, which must approve it before the securities can be sold. A company issuing or offering shares for the first time to the public is described as making an "initial public offering" (IPO). While an IPO is the usual route, there are some alternatives to issuing stock under a full registration statement, such as intrastate issues and private placements.

2.1   Initial Listing

While each case is decided on its own merits, the NYSE generally requires the following as a minimum:

1.   Demonstrated earning power under competitive conditions of: *either* $2.5 million before Federal income taxes for the most recent year and $2 million pre-tax for each of the preceding two years, *or* an aggregate for the last three fiscal years of $6.5 million *together with* a minimum in the most recent fiscal year of $4.5 million. (All three years must be profitable.)

2.   Net tangible assets of $18 million, but greater emphasis is placed on the aggregate market value of the common stock.

3.   Market value of publicly held shares, subject to adjustment depending on market conditions, with the following limits:

Maximum $ 18,000,000
Minimum $ 9,000,000
Present (12/31/92) $ 18,000,000

The market value requirement is subject to adjustment, based on NYSE Index of Common Stock Prices. The base in effect as of December 31, 1991 is the Index on July 15, 1971 (55.06). The Index as of January 15 and July 15 of each year (if lower than the base) is divided by the base, and the resulting percentage is multiplied by $18 million to produce the adjusted market value standard. The adjustment formula is used only when the current Index is below the base.

4. A total of 1,100,000 common shares publicly held. (If the unit of trading is less than 100 shares, the requirement relating to number of publicly held shares shall be reduced proportionately.)

5. *Either* 2,000 holders of 100 shares or more, or of a unit of trading if less than 100 shares, *or* 2,200 total stockholders *together with* average monthly trading volume (for the most recent six months) of 100,000 shares.

2.2 Non-US Companies—Alternative Listing Standards

To provide an alternative set of listing standards for companies organized outside the United States that meet the normal size and earnings yardsticks for NYSE listings, the NYSE will consider the acceptability of such companies' shares and shareholders on a worldwide basis.

In view of the widespread use of "bearer" shares in other countries, in contrast to the US practice of registered shares, a company would find difficulty in certifying the requirement of 5,000 round-lot shareholders on a worldwide basis. Therefore, the NYSE requires that a member firm attest to the liquidity and depth of the market for the company's shares. These standards would apply only where a broad, liquid market for a company's shares in the company's home market exists.

3. TYPES OF ISSUE

The means of offering stock can be by way of a primary offering of new stock, a secondary offering of existing stock, or a combination of the two, known as a partial secondary offering. Once a company has become a public company, the registration requirements for subsequent issues of stock are simplified. Provided the company is of a certain size, it is able to offer stock by way of a shelf registration statement (rule 415). This is a shorter document which comprises a description of the range of securities the company might wish to offer during a given period and the documents already filed with the SEC such as annual and interim reports. A new offer of securities can be made merely by filing an amendment to the existing shelf registration statement.

Alternatives to full registration include intrastates sales of stock, private placements and regulation A sales. In intrastate issues, the company may sell stock to residents of one state, provided it is incorporated and transacts a significant portion of business in that state. Private placements allow sales to be made to a small number of sophisticated institutional investors (colloquially called Section 144A issues, referring to the 1933 Act), while regulation A offerings involve sales of less than US$1.5 million in any twelve month period. Restrictions on resale of varying degrees are imposed on intrastate offerings and private placements.

American Depositary Receipts (ADRs) are a means by which the shares of non-US companies, which are quoted on an official stock exchange e.g. London, can be traded in US$ denominations in the US domestic market. The shares are bought in the local exchange e.g. London and held by a custodian on behalf of a Depositary Bank which then issues ADRs which may be traded as securities in their own right. The price of ADRs parallels the share price in the original market (with adjustments for currency exchange)(see Section 7 below).

4. LISTING PROCEDURES
In the case of an IPO the registration process can take up to four months. Once the registration statement has been prepared it is filed in preliminary form with the SEC. At this point the initial marketing of the stock can commence on the basis of the preliminary prospectus which forms part of the registration statement. The SEC reviews the registration statement, which may take between four and six weeks. If it has any comments, these must be incorporated into the final version. Once the SEC has approved the registration statement it becomes effective and the stock can be priced and sold. After filing and for a period of 90 days after the effective date, the company and its advisers are restricted as to the amount of information they can provide to the public. New publicity, profit forecasts and the expression of opinions concerning the value of the company are prohibited.

Only those shares that are offered to the public will become registered as a result of the filing of the registration statement with the SEC. If stock is still held in the hands of private shareholders following the IPO, restrictions are imposed on the way in which they may sell that stock.

The registration statement itself falls into two parts. The first part, which is the preliminary and, when completed following pricing, the final prospectus, contains a description of the company, risk factors associated with an investment in the stock, use of proceeds, a capitalisation table showing the capitalisation of the company before and after the issue, and a table showing the dilution of the shareholders' investment in similar manner; a description of the stock and of major shareholders; selected historical financial information and a discussion and analysis by management of that information; financial statements, which must cover three years. Part two, which is available for inspection at the offices of the SEC, contains supplementary schedules, such as the expenses associated with the issue, indemnification of directors and officers, details of unregistered stock during the preceding three years; and exhibits such as the underwriting agreement and any contracts of a material nature.

If a company is selling less than US$5,000,000 of stock, the information that is required is slightly less detailed. Similarly, a foreign company offering stock in the US market may be subject to simplified disclosure rules, depending on the extent of dislosure in its own country.

5. TYPES OF EQUITY

Public corporations issue shares expressed as either common or preferred stock, both types representing fractional ownership of a company. There are no bearer shares – all shares being in registered form. Shares can be of any denomination or of "no par value".

The number of shares a public corporation can issue has to be authorised by its board of directors. The portion sold at any one time is described as "issued and outstanding". Any shares authorised but unissued may later be issued to raise capital, distributed to existing stockholders as a stock dividend or a stock split, presented to employees or issued in exchange for shares of another corporation in a merger, acquisition or as an investment. Corporations may buy back their own shares from third parties which are then held in the corporation's treasury, i.e. not retired. This could be done in order to improve the market value of the company's shares (by reducing the number in the hands of investors) or to defend against an unwanted takeover bid by another corporation or investor.

Non-voting stock is possible but may jeopardise listing with the NYSE.

6. CONTINUING REQUIREMENTS

Once a company has become public, it is required to comply with the provisions of the Securities Act of 1934, under which it must publish and file with the SEC annual and quarterly reports and other reports describing events of a material nature, such as changes in business, mergers and so on.

In addition to filing the registration statement with SEC, the company must qualify its stock for sale under the laws of the various states in which it wishes to sell the stock. These are know as "blue sky" laws.

Share owners are entitled to annual and interim reports and these will be posted to them by the company. Additionally, the company is obliged to disclose publicly most corporate developments that may have a major effect on shareholders or the value of their stock. All recorded shareholders must be given proxy statements explaining issues scheduled for voting on at shareholders' meetings.

7. AMERICAN DEPOSITARY RECEIPTS (ADRs)

If a non-US company wishes to list its shares in the USA it can do one of two things. It can list its shares directly (being prepared to satisfy the disclosure requirements of the Securities and Exchange Commission) or list them in ADR form. If in ADR form it would be a 'Sponsored ADR' in which the non-USA company would appoint an American bank as its sole agent for issuing ADRs. There are, however, a large number of 'Unsponsored' ADRs. These have arisen when there is actual or perceived investor interest in investments in non-US companies so that banks, of their own volition and without the cooperation of the company, have issued ADRs; these are not listed on an exchange. In such circumstances there could be a variety of ADRs from different banks in circulation at a time when a non-USA company decided to have a sponsored ADR. Then it would be necessary for the Agent Bank or the company to pay cancellation costs to the other banks so that their ADRs could be replaced by those of the newly-appointed Agent Bank.

As negotiable instruments ADRs are usually quoted in US dollars and pay dividends or interest in US dollars.

Sponsored American Depositary Receipts would be issued at the instigation of, say, a company with a quotation on The International Stock Exchange in London. Thus, if an American investor wished then, to invest in, say, ICI by way of an ADR the American Agent Bank 'Depositary Bank' of ICI would buy the appropriate number of shares in London and deposit them with the Custodian Bank of the 'Depositary Bank' which, according to Security Exchange Commission requirements, must be a branch of an approved American company (but not the Agent bank itself). An ADR representing those shares would then be issued by the Depositary Bank and traded in the USA.

However, if an American holder of an ADR wished to sell but there was not another American investor willing to buy then the American Broker would sell in London the UK equities backing its ADR, convert the sterling proceeds to US$, repay the US investor and withdraw the ADR. This is described as 'flowback' and it is an unavoidable consequence of limited interest in the shares of foreign companies.

Flowback does, of course, frustrate the objectives of publicly quoted companies of seeking to establish an "international flavour" to their spread of shareholders.

CHAPTER 15 (Part IV)

Equities – Japan

by
Brian J. Terry and Sarah Scarlett

1. INTRODUCTION: THE TOKYO STOCK EXCHANGE

There are eight stock exchanges in Japan (the first was established in 1878) and collectively they carried the listing of 2,106 companies through 346 billion shares as at June 1992.

The principal stock exchange in Japan is the Tokyo Stock Exchange (TSE) which, at the end of 1992, following the decline in the Nikkei index, had fallen to second place after New York.

Japanese enterprises in the post-war period depended heavily upon bank loans for their financing which made them highly leveraged. Many new issues of shares since then have been made in order to repay bank loans and thereby improve the structure of the companies' balance sheets.

2. CRITERIA FOR LISTING

The criteria for listing a foreign company's shares on the TSE have been eased significantly since October 1983, at which time the double auditing system, which required the financial statements to be audited according to domestic and Japanese standards, was abolished, and the volume of documents required for listing was significantly reduced.

Notwithstanding these developments many foreign companies delisted in 1992/3 and there have been few listings. This has resulted from a combination of the decline in the Nikkei index and the strength of the Japanese Yen (which latter point has made it difficult for Japanese investors to obtain capital gains on foreign stocks).

664

A foreign company wishing to list its shares on the TSE must obtain approval from both the TSE and the Japanese MOF. Foreign companies must already be listed on their domestic exchange and the shares must be sufficiently liquid in that market. Foreign companies must have been incorporated and continuously in business for at least five years and must have paid dividends in each of the three years immediately preceding listing, with the expectation of continued payment of dividends following listing. In terms of size, companies must have shareholders' equity at the end of the financial year immediately preceding listing of at least Yen 10 billion and profits before tax in each of the three years prior to listing of at least Yen 2 billion.

No restrictions may be placed on the transferability of shares and the number of shares which must be listed varies according to the size of the unit of shares which is traded.

A company may be delisted for filing false financial reports or for violating the listing agreement.

3. TYPES OF ISSUE
A company that is listing its shares may distribute its shares to the public in one of three ways. In a primary offering new shares are offered to the public at a fixed price. In a secondary offering, shares that are already in existence may be offered to the public at a fixed price. Sales may also be made on a brokerage basis by selling shares that are already listed on the company's home exchange to the public at market prices. Typically, issues are underwritten. The public placement is the only method of issue i.e. there are no sales by tender etc.

4. LISTING PROCEDURES
The listing procedures generally take between seven and nine months to complete, or one month longer if the shares are being listed in conjunction with a primary or secondary offering of shares. In those cases, a Securities Registration Statement (similar to a new issue prospectus) must be filed with the Japanese Ministry of Finance in addition to the Securities Report for the Listing Application. All documents have to be reviewed by the TSE itself and subsequently by the MOF. Listing is granted following approval by both parties.

Numerical Criteria for Stock Listing

As of April, 1992

	Domestic Stock	Foreign Stock
Application	All of the following criteria must be met.	All of the following criteria must be met.
No. of Shares to be Listed	If the issuer is based: (1) In or around Tokyo; 4 million shares or more (2) Elsewhere; 20 million shares or more	If the stock is to be traded in a unit of: (1) 1,000 shares; 20 million shares or more (2) 100 shares; 2 million shares or more (3) 50 shares; 1 million shares or more (4) 10 shares; 200,000 shares or more (5) 1 share; 20,000 shares or more
No. of Shares Held by "Special Few" (i.e., 10 Largest Shareholders & Persons Having Special Interest in the Issuer)	Provisional Criteria: 80% or less of the number of shares to be listed by the time of listing, and also 70% or less by the end of the first business year after the listing.	Not applicable. The stock is instead required to have a good liquidity in the home market.
No. of Shareholders Holding 1 "Unit" or More (Excluding "Special Few")	If the number of shares to be listed is: (1) Less than 10 million shares; 800 or more (2) 10 million shares or more but less than 20 million shares; 1,200 or more (3) 20 million shares or more; 2,000 plus 100 per each 10 million shares in excess of 20 million shares, up to 3,000	Not applicable. The stock is instead required to have 1,000 or more shareholders in Japan.
Time Elapsed after Incorporation	5 years or more with continued business operation	Do.
Shareholders' Equity	¥1 billion or more in total and ¥100 or more per share	¥10 billion or more in total
Net Profit before Taxes	Following (1) or (2) (1) a. Annual total for each of last 3 business years: 1st business year; ¥200 million or more 2nd business year; ¥300 million or more Last business year; ¥400 million or more b. Amount per share ¥15 or more for each of last 3 business years and ¥20 or more for last business year (2) a. Annual total for each of last 3 business years: ¥400 million or more b. Amount per share ¥15 or more for either 1st business year or 2nd business year and ¥15 or more for last business year	Annual total for each of last 3 business years: ¥2 billion or more
Dividends	(1) Dividend record; Paid in cash for the business year ended within the latest year (2) Dividend prospect; Able to maintain ¥5 or more in cash per share after listing	(1) Dividend record; Paid for each of last 3 business years (2) Dividend prospect; Able to pay continuously after listing

Notes: (1) The TSE also has listing regulations for straight bonds, convertible bonds, bonds with warrants, etc.
(2) All numerical criteria above are for a company which provides 1,000 shares as the number of one "Unit" of shares.

666

Numerical Criteria for 1st Section Assignment and Delisting of Domestic Stocks

As of April, 1992

	Assignment of Listed Stock to 1st Section	Delisting
Application	All of the following criteria must be met.	In case of falling under any of the following criteria
No. of Shares Listed	20 million shares or more	Less than 4 million shares
No. of Shares Held by "Special Few" as of Each End of Last 2 Business Years	70% or less of the number of shares listed	More than 70% of the number of shares listed (Provisionally 80%)
No. of Shareholders Holding 1 "Unit" or More (Excluding "Special Few") as of Each End of Last 2 Business Years	If the number of shares listed is: (1) Less than 30 million shares; 3,000 or more (2) 30 million shares or more but less than 200 million shares; 3,000 plus 100 for each 10 million shares in excess of first 20 million shares, or more (3) 200 million shares or more but less than 220 million shares; 4,800 or more (4) 220 million shares or more; 4,800 plus 100 for each 20 million shares in excess of first 200 million shares, or more	If the number of shares listed is: (1) Less than 10 million shares; Less than 400 (2) 10 million shares or more but less than 20 million shares; Less than 600 (3) 20 million shares or more; Less than 1,000 plus 100 for each 10 million shares in excess of first 20 million shares, up to 2,000
Average Monthly Trading Volume	For each period of last 6 months and preceding 6 months: If the stock is listed on; (1) TSE only; 200,000 shares or more (2) TSE and either of Osaka or Nagoya SEs; 200,000 shares or more on any of 2 SEs, or 250,000 shares or more in total of 2 SEs (3) TSE, Osaka and Nagoya SEs; 200,000 shares or more on any of 3 SEs, or 300,000 shares or more in total of 3 SEs	(1) For last 1 year: Less than 10,000 shares, or (2) No trades during last 3 months
Dividends	(1) Dividend record; ¥5 or more in cash per share for each of last 3 business years (2) Dividend prospect; Able to maintain ¥5 or more in cash per share after assignment	No cash dividends paid for each of last 5 business years and excess liabilities continued for last 3 business years

The two most important documents for a listing are the listing prospectus and the Securities Report for the Listing Application. In addition the company must provide copies of preceding years' annual and interim reports, press releases and other documents filed with its domestic exchange, copies of its Articles of Association, Board resolution authorising the listing, a legal opinion, signed audit reports and various documents concerning the listing and trading of the company's shares on its home exchange. The company is also required to sign a listing agreement with the TSE.

The Securities Report and the Listing Prospectus must be prepared both in the listing company's own language and in Japanese. The Securities Report is for the purposes of the TSE and the MOF only whereas the listing prospectus is circulated to all investors and contains all the information given in the first volume of the Securities Report, except certain supporting schedules.

The Securities Report falls into two volumes. The first volume contains an outline of the corporate legal, tax and foreign exchange systems in the home country; an outline description of the company, including a description of the shares and the dividend history; a description of the business and operations of the company and of its production facilities; financial statements; and a summary of the procedures for share transactions and servicing in Japan. The second volume contains a description of the reasons for seeking a listing; a summary of the corporate disclosure and accounting systems in the home country; a summary of the major events in the company's history and a ten year performance record; details of the number of shares held by major shareholders; a description of any stock options or pre-emptive rights; and descriptions of labour relations, competition, sources of raw materials, distribution, related companies and future prospects.

While the criteria for listing and delisting of securities are established by the respective stock exchanges the actual listing or delisting itself requires the approval of the Ministry of Finance.

The Tokyo, Osaka and Nagoya exchanges each have two sections – the "first" and the "second". When stocks are newly listed on these exchanges they must be placed on the "second section" for a stipulated

668

period notwithstanding that they may meet the more stringent listing requirements for the "first section".

5. TYPES OF EQUITY

There is only one type of share – the common stock – and it is issued in registered form.

Most common stocks have a par value of Yen 50, but some have Yen 20 or Yen 500 par values. Under the Commercial Code amendments that became effective on 1 October 1982 a company whose shares are listed on any Japanese stock exchange is required to adopt one "unit" as the basic unit of trading. As as result the basic unit of trading of most Yen 50 p.a. value stocks is 1,000 shares; that of the Yen 500 par values is 100 shares (although notable exceptions to this are Sony and Fanuc with Yen 50 par values which are traded in 100 share units). However, foreign shares listed on the TSE trade in one of four different units – 10, 50, 100 and 1,000 shares – depending on their price.

Certificates for shares representing less than a unit may be issued only in certain limited circumstances. Since the transfer of shares normally requires delivery of the certificates, fractions of a unit for which no share certificates are issued (recorded shares) are not transferable. Thus, a holder of such a fraction of a unit may, at any time, require the issuing company to purchase such shares at their last reported sale price on the TSE. If a certificate has been issued for shares representing a fraction of a unit they continue to be transferable but the transfer can be registered by the issuing company only if the transferee is already a registered shareholder.

While stock dividends are new shares issued out of distributable profits and are rare, bonus issues are new shares issued out of capital reserves and earned reserves and are common.

6. CONTINUING REQUIREMENTS

Following listing, the company is required to file a Securities Report with the MOF and the TSE each year, as well as semi-annual reports and any other information relevant to shareholders. The annual Securities Report contains the same information as the initial Report filed on listing, updated, but need only include two years' financial statements instead of five.

Certain requirements for listing and referred to in Section 2 "Criteria for Listing" have to be maintained after flotation otherwise the shares are delisted.

CHAPTER 16

Commercial Paper

by David H. Wells

1. INTRODUCTION

For borrowers wishing to tap the short term securities markets rather than to draw under one of the variety of bank facilities available, Commercial Paper (CP) can meet a whole range of specific needs. However, there are two related areas to be examined before coming to these markets: firstly, the short versus long term funding decision; and, secondly, the extent to which the funding uses up available bank credit lines (notwithstanding that funds are provided by third party non-bank investors).

Factors likely to influence the first decision fall into five categories:

(i)   the borrower needs only to cover a shortfall of funds for a limited period, given fully fluctuating cash flows;

(ii)   the borrower wishes to fund a long term project, and will utilize short term facilities until a longer structure, such as a bond issue, is in place;

(iii)   by rolling over short term borrowings in a positive yield curve environment, the borrower will achieve lower interest costs than by using a long term fixed interest rate instrument;

(iv)   it may be cheaper as lenders will usually look for lower margins, where they take their risk on board only for short periods, thus having the opportunity to re-assess their investment on each rollover date;

(v)   companies wish to fund working capital and/or trade flows by instruments so flexible as to amounts and dates as to be able to match their own cash flows with borrowings.

Turning to the second question, the principal benefit for borrowers using the CP and Medium Term Notes (MTN) markets is the development of a creditor base outside the banking sector: useful if banks were to suffer from capital constraints or the impact of a credit crisis. However, the provision of back-up lines of credit for CP, and the use of foreign exchange and interest rate swaps to hedge borrowings raised other than in the currency or interest rate form required, also uses up bank capital and credit lines (although of course at a lower rate than if the banks lent to the borrower directly). Consideration must be given to the trade off between the all-in cost of funds, including hedging costs, and the extent to which bank lines are filled up.

For example, if a borrower was looking for three year fixed rate sterling funding, and the all-in cost (including amortized set-up costs) was equal, he would be better advised to issue three year fixed rate MTNs rather than issue CP backed up with a three year bank credit line and swapped to fixed rate funds, since the former would have no impact on bank credit lines. For the CP alternative, both the back-up line and the interest rate swap would have a Balance Sheet impact for the banks providing them.

In addition to lower (or nil) utilization of bank credit lines, funding through CP brings borrowers other advantages:

(i)   lower all-in cost of funds than that usually available through bank lines;

(ii)   securities markets may achieve funding from a source in another financial or geographical sector, when that naturally/normally accessed is unavailable (see below, on the development of CP in the US);

(iii)   sale of paper bearing the company's name may achieve a wider investor appreciation of the name, to be exploited by later equity or debt issues;

(iv)   development of as wide as possible an armoury of funding sources, to increase flexibility in times of unforeseen shortage of funds, and to free up bank lines to leave room for emergency use.

672

2. ORIGIN

CP originated in the US in the 19th century as a means of tapping non-bank sources of funds needed for working capital. The banks were unable to satisfy all the financial needs of industry because of the legal restrictions which prevented them from operating in more than one state: thus in credit-scarce states certain corporations found themselves unable to borrow on competitive terms from local banks, and therefore turned instead to open-market sales of paper to raise funds. Commercial paper has been introduced to other countries with appropriate facilitating legislation being passed in, for example, the UK and France in the mid 1980s, and Germany, Spain and Portugal more recently, and it is one of the manifestations of disintermediation.

3. COMMON FEATURES OF THE CP MARKETS

3.1 Pricing

CP pricing is based primarily on the creditworthiness of the issuer. Investors will draw comparisons with the yield available on CP issued by equivalent credits, and on alternative short term instruments such as certificates of deposit. Peer grouping of issuers is discussed under the section on credit ratings below. Benchmarks vary between the CP markets, and are detailed within the sections on each separate market.

In addition to the benchmark cost plus or minus the margin applicable to each issuer, which constitutes the interest yield on the paper issued, the cost of funds to the issuer of commercial paper will also include:

(i)   printing and other security costs of issuance;

(ii) dealer commissions, which will be taken either as a spread between the price at which the dealer buys CP from the issuer and sells it to investors, or will be collected quarterly in arrears. Dealer commissions vary from 0.03% in the Euro CP market, to up to 0.125% in the USCP market;

(iii) most CP programmes are reinforced by back-up bank credit lines, which will have various up-front, commitment, and utilization costs.

3.2 The Discount Basis

CP is normally issued on a discount basis: that is, on a £1,000,000 principal amount, the investor does not invest £1,000,000 and on maturity receive back that amount plus interest. Rather, he invests less than the face amount of the note and on maturity receives back the full face amount: the difference between the two constitutes his interest. This feature, where all the investor's return is made up by the difference between purchase price and redemption amount, is also referred to as a "zero coupon" or as a "deep discount" (see also Chapter 19).

This type of paper is sold on a yield basis (purchase price being agreed between parties on confirmation of the deal), as follows (for paper of less than one year maturity):

$$PRICE = \frac{FACE\ VALUE}{[1 + (Tenor\ (Days)\ x\ Yield)]/365^*}$$

*365 for £; 360 for most other currencies

3.3 The Credit Rating System

The use of credit ratings, almost a prerequisite in all the CP markets, began in the USCP market following the failure in 1970 of Penn Central, with US$82 million of CP outstanding. At that time, investors switched from name recognition as the principal criterion for issuer selection, to reliance upon the independent commercial rating agencies to establish an assessment of the creditworthiness of borrowers. The only major exceptions have been for brief periods in new CP markets, such as the sterling and French Franc markets in the late 1980s, when investors would buy unrated paper from well-known major domestic issuers, but similar defaults or near defaults by these issuers, and greater market penetration by the rating agencies, has led to the position where unrated paper is estimated to account for less than 10% of global outstandings of CP, and remains on a declining trend.

Of the major agencies, Standard & Poor's issue ratings graded from Al+ downwards, based on the creditworthiness of the issuer and rates the debt programme in question, while Moody's, which grades from Pl down, rates on the basis of the company itself, and the strength of its balance

674

sheet and further debt-raising capacity. Fitch and Duff & Phelps are the third and fourth major rating agencies in the USCP market. Many major investors will not accept paper other than that issued by A1/P1 rated borrowers (or paper enhanced to Al/Pl status – see Section 3.4 below).

In 1991, in response to market concerns over credit quality, the Securities and Exchange Commission (SEC) introduced amendments under Rule 2a-7 of the Investment Company Act of 1940, which forced money funds to restrict to 5% of portfolios their holdings of paper rated less than Al/Pl. Since the money funds hold some 50% to 60% of USCP outstandings, this ruling has further strengthened the role of the credit rating agencies in the USA.

Rating definitions are as follows:

Standard and Poor's

Al	Strong – those issues determined to possess overwhelming safety characteristics will be denoted with a plus (+) sign, i.e. A1+.
A2	Satisfactory capacity for timely repayment.
A3	Adequate capacity for timely repayment.
B	Speculative capacity for timely repayment.
C	Doubtful capacity for payment.
D	In, or expected to be in, default.

Moody's

Pl	Superior ability for repayment.
P2	Strong ability for repayment.
P3	Acceptable ability for repayment.
Not Prime	Outside the above categories.

Fitch

F1
F2 } Approximating to A1, A2, A3 and P1, P2, P3.
F3

The prevalence of the rating system has enabled an easy price-tiering to be effected in the market. Note that there is less than US$1 billion of unrated paper outstanding in the US commercial paper market.

3.4 Credit Enhancement

For a company which wishes to raise funds through the CP markets, but which would be unable to get a good credit rating, there are various ways to enhance its creditworthiness.

A common method adopted is to arrange for a highly rated bank to issue a guarantee, or in the USCP market a letter of credit or insurance bond, to support the programme. This effectively substitutes the credit of the bank for that of the issuer. The guarantee or letter of credit may be attached to, or written on the reverse of, the commercial paper note.

The guarantee or letter of credit can be syndicated by way of private agreement by the "lead" bank and participating banks. Alternatively the credit enhancement can be supplied by the parent of a non-rated subsidiary issuer, or a government for one of its nationalised entities. Furthermore, prime quality assets or receivables may be set off against the programme as backing.

By achieving a prime rating in this way, the issuer can then borrow at the finest interest rates. These methods, however, will all incur some additional cost, and straightforward enhancement by banks is becoming less popular due to the increasing Balance Sheet costs for the banks involved.

3.5 Bank Back-Up Lines of Credit

It is almost a *sine qua non* for access to the market, that the issuer should arrange back-up bank lines of some form, to ensure that if rollover is difficult at some time due to market conditions or the change in creditworthiness of the issuer, funds will be available to repay the maturing paper.

When allocating credit ratings to CP programmes, the rating agencies pay particular attention to the adequacy of back-up lines. They will typically look for the availability of undrawn committed lines equivalent to 100% of the CP it is planned to issue, although levels of availability of 50% can be sufficient if the issuer can show high natural liquidity which could be used to pay maturing CP in need. An example of the latter could be an insurance company holding high cash balances and short term government securities as part of its liquidity ratio requirements.

676

365 day back-up lines have become popular, since they meet the requirement to provide funds for maturing CP while remaining relatively "cheap" because, being of a term up to one year, they carry a zero weighting for the capital adequacy calculation of the banks giving them. However, issuers of CP must balance these cost advantages with the need to match the maturity of assets and liabilities.

4. THE US COMMERCIAL PAPER MARKET

4.1 History

This is the first established and still by far the biggest commercial paper market in the world, with over US$550bn outstanding at the end of 1992.

The exponential growth in the USCP market which has been a feature of the last 20 years was rooted in developments after the Wall Street Crash. The 1933 Securities Act exempted issues of CP from SEC registration requirements provided they conformed to two criteria:

(i)   that issues should be for working capital purposes, and

(ii)   that paper should not be issued with maturities over 270 days.

Having ensured that CP issues conforming to the above criteria would avoid the expensive registration process, "Regulation Q" then produced an environment of regulation which channelled investment demand towards CP by imposing ceilings on the absolute level of interest rates that could be paid on deposit accounts. In 1966 and 1969, as a result of tight credit conditions, open market interest rates in the US rose above the Regulation Q ceilings. In order to avoid receiving the artificially low interest rate on deposit accounts, investors turned increasingly to money market funds to achieve higher rates. These funds, which invested in CP among other money market instruments, saw huge growth in their total funds under investment over this period. At the same time, borrowers were finding credit very tight at the banks and were encouraged to issue CP. USCP outstandings of US$10 billion in 1966 tripled in the three years to 1968.

In the 1980s USCP growth was spurred by worries over the reliability of the US banking system both as debtor and as creditor. The Mexican

Figure 1   Growth in USCP outstandings 1979 to 1992

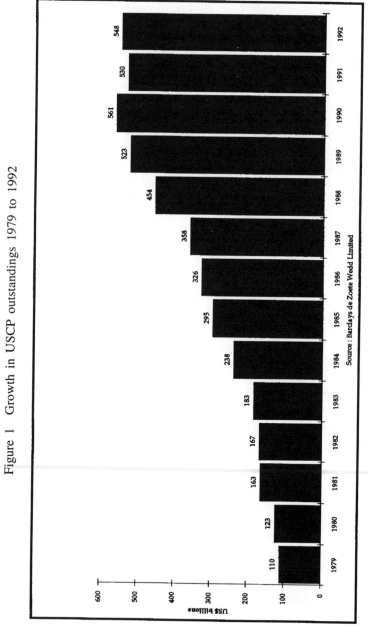

678

debt crisis of 1982, and a series of US bank failures, rendered depositors eager to find an alternative sector in which to invest. At the same time increasing capital costs made bank loans expensive and credit problems made some banks seem unreliable as long term creditors.

Another recent factor has been the steepening of the US$ yield curve, which has forced many borrowers into the short end of the markets.

The ability of finance houses to issue CP, where they cannot issue bills, played a decisive role in the development of the market. Although in terms of numbers, non-financial issuers still predominate, nevertheless in volume terms the financial houses constitute the bulk of outstandings. Three in particular form the nucleus of the market. General Electric Credit Corporation ("GECC") had US$38.2 billion (over 6% of the market) outstanding at the end of March 1993, Ford Motor Credit Corporation ("FMCC") had US$20.2 billion, and General Motors Acceptance Corporation ("GMAC") US$15.1 billion. The volume of outstanding CP has outstripped that of bank credit.

4.2 Parties to a USCP Programme and Sequence of Events

(a) The issuer.

(b) A dealer. Usually this is a major US investment bank. Discussions will take place on a daily basis between dealer and issuer to agree on amounts of finance required and the rates available in the market which are acceptable to the issuer. The dealer will then buy notes from the issuer (in practical terms from the administrative issuing and paying agent) and resell them to investors.

Alternatively, an issuer may sell its paper "direct" to the market, using its own sales team. As a rule of thumb, to justify establishing such a direct sales force, outstandings of around US$2 billion are required.

(c) An issuing and paying agent ("IPA"). This is normally a member bank of the New York Clearing House Association. On issue day the IPA delivers notes to dealers against proof of payment, and at maturity, having received funds from the issuer, it will effect repayment when it receives the notes back from their holders.

(d)   Investors.

It is possible for (b) and (c) to be the same institution.

4.3   Form, Denominations, Maturities and Settlement

Historically, on issue day the IPA would deliver notes by dating and "authenticating" (by its own counter-signature) physical security printed commercial paper notes pre-signed by the issuer and held in stock at the IPA's offices. Increasingly, instead of delivering physical notes, the IPA will arrange issue and payment through the book entry system of the Depository Trust Corporation ("DTC"). By the end of 1993 the DTC expected that the vast majority of USCP would be settled in book entry form, eliminating printing and delivery costs, reducing delays and errors in reconciliation, and improving security.

Most commercial paper issues are in multiples of US$1 million although denominations as small as US$25,000 are possible. It is estimated that the average purchase of commercial paper is US$4 million and that the average outstanding per issuer is US$120 million. The average maturity of outstanding paper is 30 days and most paper falls within the 15 to 45 days range.

Exemption from registration requirements with the Securities and Exchange Commission reduces time and expense for the issuer. The conditions of exemption are:

(a)   The paper has an original maturity of no greater than 270 days.

(b)   The proceeds be used to finance current transactions, i.e. not for capital investment, acquisitions, etc. (see below regarding 4(2) programmes).

Settlement is almost always for same day value, but some issuers will look to issue value spot in order to link issuance with foreign exchange swaps, or to make comparisons with the cost of issuing ECP.

4.4   The Distribution Process

Issuers usually place paper with investors through commercial paper dealers although the very large issuers will have their own in-house sales force. Appointed dealers, typically two or three, sign bilateral Dealership Agreements with the issuer, setting out the forms of note, settlement timetables, and legal background (legal opinions confirm that the CP when issued will constitute legal and binding obligations of the issuer ranking, where the programme is not credit enhanced, *pari passu* with all other unsecured and unsubordinated obligations of the issuer). The documentation is almost industry standard.

Issuers and their dealers will usually be in telephone contact every day to confirm issuing levels and maturities. The more active issuers "post" rates on screen based information systems such as Bloomberg, Reuters, and Telerate.

Dealers generally charge between 5 and 10 basis points commission on the face value of the paper. The leading commercial paper dealers are Merrill Lynch, Goldman Sachs, Lehman Brothers, and First Boston.

There is no active secondary market although dealers and direct issuers may be prepared to buy back paper before maturity in order to provide investors with liquidity.

As explained above, the CP market is for short term funding of working capital needs and is described as a "3(a)3 Programme" because of the section of the Securities Act 1933 under which it is controlled. However, under Section 4(2) of that Act there is an allowance for a *private placement programme* which enables issuers to borrow for non-working capital related requirements. As such there is no time limit for the maturity of the paper but the proposed investors are required to be institutions or otherwise financially sophisticated. While the paper cannot ordinarily be traded in the market, most 4(2) programmes allow for resale of the paper to other institutional investors under Rule 144A. Ratings by the rating agencies are required in the same way as for 3(a)3 programmes.

Funds raised via 4(2) programmes would, normally, be used for acquisitions and capital expenditure.

4.5 Investors

As already noted, the major investors in USCP are the money funds. Other buyers include bank trust departments, state and local governments, pension funds, investment firms and even individuals.

Figure 2

FEDERAL RESERVE statistical release

These data are released each Monday. The availability of the release is announced on (202) 452-3208.

H.15 (519)

SELECTED INTEREST RATES
Yields in percent per annum

For immediate release
July 26, 1993

Instruments	1993 Jul 19	1993 Jul 20	1993 Jul 21	1993 Jul 22	1993 Jul 23	Week Ending Jul 23	Week Ending Jul 16	1993 Jun
Federal funds (effective) [1][2][3]	3.13	3.08	3.36	3.12	2.99	3.09	3.01	3.04
Commercial paper [3][4][5]								
1-month	3.12	3.13	3.15	3.15	3.15	3.14	3.13	3.19
3-month	3.17	3.18	3.19	3.20	3.21	3.19	3.18	3.25
6-month	3.30	3.32	3.35	3.35	3.39	3.34	3.31	3.38
Finance paper placed directly [3][4][6]								
1-month	3.06	3.05	3.07	3.07	3.09	3.07	3.06	3.12
3-month	3.11	3.10	3.12	3.13	3.15	3.12	3.11	3.16
6-month	3.14	3.14	3.14	3.16	3.20	3.16	3.14	3.16
Bankers acceptances (top rated) [3][4][7]								
3-month	3.09	3.13	3.15	3.18	3.16	3.14	3.10	3.16
6-month	3.21	3.27	3.29	3.35	3.35	3.29	3.23	3.28
CDs (secondary market) [3][8]								
1-month	3.08	3.09	3.11	3.11	3.10	3.10	3.09	3.13
3-month	3.13	3.15	3.16	3.17	3.19	3.16	3.14	3.21
6-month	3.30	3.31	3.36	3.39	3.41	3.35	3.30	3.36
Eurodollar deposits (London) [3][9]								
1-month	3.00	3.00	3.00	3.06	3.06	3.03	3.05	3.09
3-month	3.13	3.13	3.13	3.19	3.19	3.15	3.18	3.21
6-month	3.31	3.31	3.38	3.38	3.44	3.36	3.35	3.37
Bank prime loan [2][3][10]	6.00	6.00	6.00	6.00	6.00	6.00	6.00	6.00
Discount window borrowing [2][11]	3.00	3.00	3.00	3.00	3.00	3.00	3.00	3.00
U.S. government securities								
Treasury bills								
Auction average [3][4][12]								
3-month	3.05					3.05	3.04	3.10
6-month	3.15					3.15	3.14	3.23
1-year				3.44				3.40
Auction average (investment) [12]								
3-month	3.12					3.12	3.10	3.17
6-month	3.24					3.24	3.23	3.33
Secondary market [3][4]								
3-month	3.03	3.06	3.07	3.09	3.09	3.07	3.02	3.07
6-month	3.14	3.18	3.19	3.24	3.24	3.20	3.13	3.20
1-year	3.27	3.32	3.36	3.43	3.48	3.37	3.27	3.39
Treasury constant maturities [13]								
1-year	3.42	3.48	3.52	3.61	3.62	3.53	3.41	3.54
2-year	3.99	4.09	4.15	4.22	4.25	4.14	4.00	4.16
3-year	4.35	4.42	4.49	4.59	4.62	4.49	4.34	4.53
5-year	5.00	5.08	5.17	5.24	5.28	5.15	5.00	5.22
7-year	5.37	5.42	5.53	5.60	5.66	5.52	5.39	5.61
10-year	5.71	5.75	5.83	5.90	5.95	5.83	5.74	5.96
30-year	6.54	6.55	6.62	6.65	6.71	6.61	6.58	6.81
Composite								
Over 10 years (long-term) [14]	6.24	6.26	6.33	6.38	6.44	6.33	6.28	6.55
Corporate bonds								
Moody's seasoned								
Aaa	7.13	7.14	7.17	7.18	7.21	7.17	7.16	7.33
Baa	7.88	7.89	7.94	7.96	8.00	7.93	7.90	8.07
A-utility [15]					7.48	7.48	7.36	7.59
State & local bonds [16]				5.61		5.61	5.50	5.63
Conventional mortgages [17]						7.20	7.16	7.42

* The Baa corporate bond rate for July 14 was revised to 7.89 percent.

4.6 Yield Benchmarks

Although issuers and investors focus on the actual yield on the USCP at the time of issue, comparison with the yields available from other issuers is made by reference to the Fed's form H15.

This form (see Figure 2) allows comparison of various current rates/ yields, including those for USCP. The USCP rates in the H15 are known as the Fed "AA" index, or the Fed "Composite" rate.

5. THE EURO-COMMERCIAL PAPER (ECP) MARKET

5.1 History

The US$ CP market moved offshore in the early 1970s, mainly as a result of US restrictions on capital exports. It became difficult to fund US subsidiaries offshore with dollars transferred from domestic financing programmes. Instead programmes were put in place to allow such subsidiaries to tap the enormous pool of US dollars held by non-US investors. This particular window disappeared with the repeal in the US of Interest Equalisation Tax in 1974. Prior to this the market was tapped by about 20 US multinationals, with paper outstanding reaching a peak of US$2 billion.

In 1978, Euronote facilities reappeared as an alternative to syndicated loans, but activity was subdued until 1984, when almost US$20 billion of facilities were arranged. Large borrowers, such as GMAC, had noticed that it was possible to raise funds more cheaply in the Euromarket than in the US, where demand was more easily satisfied.

The growth of the Euronote market through RUFS, SNIFS, NIFs, Bonuses, etc., to a 1986 level of US$25 billion, spawned the dealer ECP market as prime borrowers discarded the need to have their issues underwritten. The move to dealership structures led to more systematic placement of ECP with investors outside the banking system, and the development of true disintermediation in Europe.

Although the yield differential between the US and Euromarkets has been largely eliminated by the arbitrage activity of the big players, the Euromarket is now so firmly established that many borrowers, both US and foreign, have ECP and USCP programmes established alongside each other, to enable them to make use of whichever offers the cheapest funding on a daily basis, and in order to develop global investor recognition in the capital markets. ECP outstandings at the end of June 1993 totalled US$76.1 billion.

5.2 Parties to an ECP Programme
The situation is very similar to that which obtains in the USA. The participants are:

(a)   The issuer.

(b)   The dealers – usually the issuer will appoint a number of dealers, one of which is called the Arranger and will be responsible for the original coordination and documentation of the programme.

There are no direct issuers in the ECP market to date, probably because the investor base is more widespread than in the USCP market (the money funds are not so well developed in Europe), and because very few programmes have achieved the level of outstandings estimated to be necessary to make the exercise pay.

(c)   The Issuing and Paying Agent (the IPA).

(d)   Investors.

The dealer and the IPA can come from one financial group but, if they do, the "Chinese wall" principle applies.

5.3 Form, Denominations, Maturities, Currencies and Settlement
The ECP market was quicker than the USCP market to dispense with the expensive and cumbersome physical ("definitive") notes, and most trades use global notes settled through the book entry systems of Cedel in Luxembourg or Euroclear in Brussels. However issuers have a legal obligation to exchange global notes into definitive notes, either at the bearer's request, or on non-payment of the global note when properly presented for payment at maturity. For this reason, and to cater for those investors who still prefer to hold definitive notes, most issuers still print

a small stock of definitives, or are prepared to print them within a few days.

(Features of security printing include special paper, watermarking, the intaglio printing process, fluorescent colouring and latent image. Definitive notes are in bearer form and, therefore, of value to the holder (or finder), global notes have no intrinsic value.)

Definitive notes are usually in US$1 million and US$500,000 denominations. The average purchase of ECP is about US$5 million, and maturities range from 7 days to 365 days. Like the USCP market, most ECP falls within the 20 to 45 days range.

The US dollar accounts for about 90% of all issuance in the ECP market. Five other currencies that may also be issued are: Deutschemarks, ECU, Lire, Swiss Francs and Yen. The Bundesbank does not permit issues in Deutschemarks by financial institutions, and the Japanese Ministry of Finance must be approached by issuers for a special licence to permit Yen issues.

Almost all issuance is for spot settlement (i.e. delivery two business days from the date of the contract), since this is the minimum timetable which allows settlement within the rather strict advance notice requirements of Cedel and Euroclear.

5.4   The Distribution Process

Historically distribution would take place through a Tender Panel linked to a Multi Option Facility, where lending banks would opt to receive "Euronotes" from borrowers instead of lending cash, with the aim of selling the Euronotes to investors and hence freeing up their own Balance Sheets to permit new lending. The drawback with this approach to distribution was that the Tender Panels were comprised mostly of lending banks, most of which had no distribution capabilities, with the result that most paper stayed within the banking system. Euronotes failed fully to disintermediate the banks from the lending process.

Since the beginning of 1992 almost all new issuers of paper have set up dealership structures, with separate back-up facilities. In this way they

685

distinguish between lending and distribution abilities, with resultant cost savings.

There is no legal distinction, in the hands of an investor, between Euronotes and ECP. The only distinction, one of terminology, relates to the distribution process. Figures from Euroclear for total outstandings across the market as at the end of June 1993 show ECP in issue has reached US$76.1 billion, and Euronotes US$28.4 billion. The figure for Euronotes includes issues of Euro Certificates of Deposit by banks, and outstandings of Euronotes are estimated to be less than US$5 billion and in decline as the maturing Multi Option Facilities are not renewed and are replaced by ECP dealerships.

ECP dealership documentation is identical in effect to that of the USCP market, but all dealers and the issuer sign a single Dealership Agreement, rather than signing several bilateral agreements. Typically three to five dealers are appointed, depending upon the size of the programme.

Two issuing mechanisms prevail in the market:

(a) *Unsolicited bids or direct bidding:* having identified investor demand, a dealer will speak to the issuer and bid directly for a certain amount of notes for a certain maturity at a certain rate. Whilst the issuer may not have signalled his intention to issue he may be persuaded to issue by the amount, maturity and rate contained in the dealer's unsolicited bid or bids.

This is the most common and practical form of issuance, since it promotes immediate distribution to end investors.

(b) *Competitive bidding:* dealers are asked to bid for a tranche of notes which the issuer plans to issue. Those bidding the lowest yield obtain the notes for onward placement with investors.

This is less effective than direct bidding, since maturity and volumes are dictated by the issuer, and may not match investor demand. To this extent paper may need to be warehoused with dealers until investors are found.

The more active issuers "post" rates on screen based information systems such as Bloomberg, Reuters, and Telerate. This acts more as a guide to maturity and yield targets, to help dealers to focus their search for investors, than as a request for competitive bids.

Dealers generally charge between 3 and 7 basis points commission on the face value of the paper, taken at the time of trade or quarterly in arrears.

Like USCP, no secondary market has developed, and dealers prefer to find end investors who will hold the notes to maturity. This is to prevent the problem of an issuer competing with itself by virtue of the fact that paper from a previous issue was still circulating at the time a second issue was made. However, dealers may be prepared to buy back paper before maturity in order to provide investors with liquidity.

5.5 Investors

These are made up of the expected very broad range of investors who are motivated by a need for a relatively liquid investment producing risk diversification and a market rate of return. They do, therefore, cover the whole spectrum of investment funds, pension funds, insurance companies, corporates, and (rarely) banks. ECP investors are concentrated geographically in those countries with developed institutional investors, such as France and the UK. Restrictions in the dealership documentation prohibit the sale of paper to US investors, in order to avoid registration requirements under the US Securities Act, 1933.

5.6 Yield Benchmarks

The Bank of England publishes composite rates for both ECP and SCP. The Bank approaches a panel of dealers each day for rates at 11.30 a.m., and publishes a median rate for each maturity. The rates will normally be based on actual deals in the primary market, i.e. one, two, three and six month maturity paper issued by companies rated either A1 or P1 by the two main US rating agencies. The quotations are ranked and the median rate chosen is representative.

It was intended that this benchmark provide an independent yardstick, similar to the Fed's Composite index in the USCP market, to enable borrowers/issuers to make peer group pricing comparisons. In particular it was hoped that its use would reduce reliance on the interbank cash market as a benchmark.

Nonetheless, the ECP market remains steadfastly focused on LIBID and LIBOR for benchmarking purposes. These London interbank bid and offered rates suffer from uncertain definition, since different banks quote different rates at the same time and spreads between bid and offer rates vary. Interbank rates fluctuate too with perceptions of the credit risks of banks, often irrelevant to issuers and investors in the ECP market. ECP market participants typically watch up to four brokers' screens, taking an average to determine the level of LIBID or LIBOR, and then adding or subtracting the margin appropriate for the issuer to calculate the yield at which paper is to be priced.

6.   THE STERLING COMMERCIAL PAPER (SCP) MARKET

6.1   History
It was not until March 1986 that measures were announced to permit the development of a market in Sterling CP. In order for this to be achieved, issuers had to be exempted from certain parts of the 1979 Banking Act, which would otherwise have left them open to action as unauthorised deposit-takers. Legislation to this effect was submitted by Chancellor Lawson on 20 April 1986.

To ensure an orderly start to the market, the Bank of England laid down strict requirements as to who would be eligible to issue paper, and in what way it might be distributed. These rules were partially relaxed in March 1989, and now state that the following categories of SCP issuer are permitted:

(a)   companies with equity or debt listed on the International Stock Exchange of the United Kingdom and the Republic of Ireland Limited or the Unquoted Securities Market, and which have net assets of at least £25 million, or

(b)   companies under the guarantee of a company complying with (a), or

(c)   UK registered companies with no equity or debt listing, but which have net assets of at least £25 million and which have submitted the relevant details equivalent to those required for a eurocurrency security debt listing to the Stock Exchange (this is called a Schedule 3 application), or

Figure 3

Figure 4

690

(d)   companies with equity or debt listed on any authorised stock exchange
        and which have net assets of £25 million or more and which complete
        a Schedule 3 application, or

(e)   international organisations exempted from the Banking Act 1987 and
        of which the United Kingdom is a member, or

(f)   foreign public sector bodies the debt of which is listed on any authorised
        or official Stock Exchange, or

(g)   banks, building societies and insurance companies.

The market initially feared a shortage of supply of paper due to the
artificially low yields on Banker's Acceptances (caused by extensive
purchases by the Bank of England in the course of monetary policy)
which would keep all but those unable to issue bills, such as property and
investment companies, or those whose bill lines were full, from tapping
the SCP market. This, however, has not been the case. A wide range of
names has come to the SCP market, as SCP has offered a cheaper form
of finance than bills when yields on the latter are not artificially depressed.

The attractiveness of the bill market for borrowers will continue to
restrain growth in SCP outstandings, as will competition from the cash
markets. The latter is an issue because in the sterling markets there is not
the measure of concern over bank risk which has enabled yield levels on
USCP and ECP to be driven substantially below bank deposit rates and
still attract investors. Outstandings in the SCP market have at £5.6 billion
in June 1993 only just regained the levels seen in August 1989.

6.2 Parties to an SCP Programme
The parties to an SCP programme are identical to those of an ECP
programme, although it is worth noting that two dealers (Barclays de
Zoete Wedd and Natwest Capital Markets) account for nearly 90% of
market outstandings. In view of this it is not usual to appoint more than
three dealers to an SCP programme.

6.3 Form, Denominations, Maturities and Settlement
SCP is bought and sold on a same day value basis, and as such cannot
be settled through Euroclear or Cedel due to their advance notice

requirements. Almost all issuance is therefore represented by definitive notes, hand delivered in London against payment by banker's draft or CHAPS (same day electronic transfer using the Clearing House Automated Payments System). In late 1992 the Bank of England introduced a London based book entry system (the Central Money Markets Office or "CMMO") to handle SCP amongst other instruments, but the market has been slow to take advantage of this service.

Definitive notes may be issued in multiples of £100,000, but in practice only £500,000 and £1 million notes are used although some of the larger issuers are looking at the possibility of printing £5 million denominations.

SCP may be issued for any maturity between 7 and 364 days; the majority of paper in the market is issued for between 18 and 35 days.

6.4   The Distribution Process
The comments made in Section 5.4 covering the ECP market apply equally here. The SCP market follows the practices of the ECP market so closely, except for settlement procedures and issuer qualification, that common documentation applies, so that issuers with multi-currency requirements set up a single SCP/ECP, or ECP/SCP, programme.

6.5   Investors
These are made up of the expected very broad range of investors who are motivated by a need for a relatively liquid investment producing a market rate of return. They do, therefore, cover the whole spectrum of investment funds, pension funds, insurance companies, corporates, and (rarely) banks. SCP investors are almost exclusively UK based.

6.6   Yield Benchmarks
Similar to the ECP market, the Bank of England publishes composite rates but issuers and investors compare issuing levels with sterling LIBID and LIBOR.

692

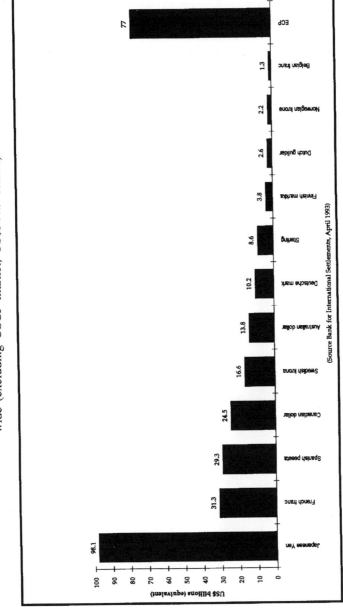

Figure 5   Total outstandings as at 31.12.92. Domestic and ECP markets world-wide (excluding USCP market, US$544.9 billion).

693

7. HEDGED OR SWAPPED CP

The objective here is to produce competitively priced funds for a borrower in a currency other than that of the original CP issued. In effect it requires the combination of two transactions. First is the issue of CP, followed by an immediate spot purchase and forward sale (to correspond with the maturity date of the original instrument) of the currency in which borrowing is actually required. As the base from which this mechanism starts is a funding source which frequently produces finance at a cheaper rate than conventional bank rates, or interbank related rates, it produces borrowing in the second currency at cheaper rates than would be available by borrowing in that currency by a direct route. A "window" is said to exist when the interest rate differentials and the underlying forward margins combine to create the ideal circumstances for this mechanism to benefit a borrower.

8. OTHER DOMESTIC EUROPEAN CP MARKETS

Using ECP/SCP documentation issuers can achieve cost effective funding in US dollars, Deutschemarks, ECU, Lire, Sterling and Yen. By employing the hedging techniques described above in Section 7, issuers can raise any other major currency at will. However, the ultimate cost of funds in the desired currency will depend upon the vagaries of the currency markets, and will be difficult to forecast. Issuers with substantial borrowing requirements in such currencies will therefore look to establish a parallel CP programme in the relevant domestic CP market, relying on cost advantage, volume, or certainty of pricing considerations to outweigh the costs of complying with local legislation, documentation and administration.

Domestic CP markets are well established in the French, Spanish, Belgian and Dutch markets, and to a lesser extent in Portugal, and Hungary. These markets all have domestic language documentation and settlement procedures. There is also a domestic Deutschemark market which developed strongly between January 1991 when DMCP issues were first permitted, and August 1992 when the regulations were further relaxed to permit issuance under ECP documentation and settlement conventions. Most newcomers to CP issuance wishing to issue in Deutschemarks are adopting the more flexible ECP structure.

694

It is logical to expect that over time the authorities overseeing the various domestic markets will embrace deregulation, permitting the establishment of a truly Europe-wide ECP market, where issuance in any freely convertible currency is allowed without restriction.

9. MEDIUM TERM NOTES (MTNs)

9.1 Rationale

MTNs are bonds continuously offered under a dealership programme in a similar way to CP. The original idea behind them was to cut down documentation expenses for regular issuers of bonds, by establishing programme documentation (Dealer Agreement, Agency Agreement, Prospectus) under which the issuer may launch any number of tranches in any permitted currency and for any term, with tranche documentation simplified to a one page Pricing Supplement which made reference to the full terms and provisions of the original documentation. Front-end costs of underwriting and documentation had always confined issuers to minimum bond sizes of about US$100 million, and MTNs have brought the minimum tranche size down to about US$5 million. Investor demand via the dealers can prompt the issue of an MTN tailored to the investor's currency and maturity requirements. Previously the investor would have had to find the closest approximation of his requirements in the secondary market for bonds, sometimes without success.

The MTN markets also captured business from the various private placement markets, as dealers took advantage of the growing derivative markets to produce highly structured products under MTN programmes, offering investors assets linked to variable interest rate, currency, commodity and tax structures.

Many borrowers, approaching the capital markets for the first time, are choosing not to set up CP programmes, but instead to launch MTN programmes with maturities from one month out to thirty years. An MTN with a six month maturity bears the same features, for issuers and investors, as CP.

9.2 The US MTN Market

The market for MTNs in the United States is the deepest and most liquid MTN market. Since its inception in 1983, when GMAC first appointed a dealer group to distribute notes on its behalf, the US MTN market has experienced spectacular growth. Market outstandings are in excess of US$142 billion.

This type of development did not occur overnight. The first group of borrowers to use the MTN market were finance subsidiaries of major US motor manufacturers. These issuers used the market to raise borrowings with which they could accurately match their financing needs in terms of size and maturity. A wider range of borrowers subsequently realised that the opportunities available from the market offered them a flexible means of raising medium term financing. As a result of this increase in awareness the market expanded to include bank, government and corporate borrowers. Structured issues became more popular as the market matured, asset backed programmes were established and investors were attracted on a large scale. It is now estimated that 95% of investors in US capital markets are prepared to utilize MTNs as a component of their investment portfolio.

9.3 The Euro MTN Market

The MTN concept was exported from the US to the Euromarkets in 1986. By 1988, more than 80 programmes had been established, but issue volumes remained small while investors avoided what they regarded as an immature market. In 1989, investor demand increased in response to the participation of active issuers such as the Kingdom of Spain, Kingdom of Belgium and GMAC. This activity has continued and total outstandings continue to grow, particularly in the form of structured issues. Outstandings in 1993 totalled approximately US$95 billion through over 150 active programmes.

Within the EMTN market, issuance in a wide range of currencies is possible, subject to compliance with the relevant domestic regulations. For example issuance in sterling and French francs and Deutschemarks is regulated, while issuance in US dollars, ECU, and Australian dollars is not subject to approvals from the relevant authorities. Altogether a total of 17 currencies have been issued to date.

696

10. SUMMARY

The short term capital markets, in the form of commercial paper or short maturity medium term notes, provide a cost effective and flexible source of funding. Most eligible borrowers, that is those who are of sufficient credit standing to be able to obtain at least Al/P1 credit ratings, have made arrangements to include CP and/or MTNs in their armoury of funding alternatives.

COMPARISON OF FEATURES

	US COMMERCIAL PAPER	EURO COMMERCIAL PAPER	STERLING COMMERCIAL PAPER
Size: (August 1993 outstandings)	$545 billion	$81 billion	£5.7 billion
Currencies	US$	US$, ECU, DM, SFR, A$, Can$, Lire, others through currency swap out of US$	Sterling
Issuer criteria	Ratings a prerequisite. A1/P1 preferred, but A2/P2 does work ($70 billion outstanding as at August 1993).	No regulatory requirements, but minimum of A1/P1 ratings demanded by most investors.	Debt/equity listed in London (or guaranteed by such a company), or complete Schedule 3 "dummy" debt listing. Minimum of A1/P1 ratings demanded by most investors.
Pricing (Typical issue cost for an A1+/P1 rated corporate, including dealer commissions)	FED AA Composite minus 5 basis points. (Note that during 1993 the Fed AA equated to 2bp below LIBOR for 30 day paper, and 5bp below for 90 day paper.)	LIBID to LIBOR	LIBID + 4bp to LIBOR
Set-up costs	$50,000	As for SCP. It is usual to include an SCP option, for no material additional cost.	$36,000
Issue mechanism	Dealer distribution, or direct issuance where the issuer itself sells paper to investors.	As for SCP.	Dealer distribution. Unlike the USCP market there are no non-bank direct issuers.

	US COMMERCIAL PAPER	EURO COMMERCIAL PAPER	STERLING COMMERCIAL PAPER
Dealers	3 dealers dominate with over 75 % of the market (Merrill Lynch, Lehman Brothers, Goldman Sachs).	3 dealers dominate, 3 American, 2 Swiss, 2 UK.	BZW, Natwest, Lloyds dominate.
Maturity	1 to 270 days, average 35 days	1 to 365 days, average 65 days	7 to 364 days, average 27 days
Denominations	Minimum $100,000, no maximum.	No restrictions. Market norm is a minimum of $500,000.	Minimum £100,000, in practice £500,000 and £1m notes are used.
Typical outstandings per issuer	$300 million to $5 billion	$100 million to $2 billion	£50 million to £500 million
Settlement basis	Same day	Spot	Same day
Documentation	Dealer and Issuing and Paying Agency Agreements. Legal Opinions.	As for SCP	Dealership Agreement, Issuing and Paying Agency Agreement, Legal Opinions.
Interest calculations	Interest bearing or discount	Interest bearing or discount	Interest bearing or discount
Form of security	Bearer	Bearer	Bearer
Bank guarantees	Bank back up line normally required	Bank back up line not normally required	Bank back up line not normally required
Minimum net worth of issuer	None specified	None specified	£25m
Purpose of borrowing	Working capital (N.B. see section 4.4 re 4(2) USCP programmes)	No restriction	No restriction

CHAPTER 17

Bankers' Acceptances

by
Brian J. Terry

1. BANKERS' ACCEPTANCES: INTRODUCTION

A banker's acceptance is a time bill of exchange drawn on and accepted by a bank. As far as English Law is concerned the definition of a bill of exchange is contained in the Bills of Exchange Act 1882 Section 3 which states:

> "A bill of exchange is an unconditional order in writing, addressed by one person to another, signed by the person giving it, requiring the person to whom it is addressed to pay on demand or at a fixed or determinable future time a sum certain in money to or to the order of a specified person or to bearer.
>
> An instrument which does not comply with these conditions, or which orders any act to be done in addition to the payment of money is not a bill of exchange."

The person giving the bill is known as the drawer and the person receiving it is the drawee. Acceptance of a bill is the writing, usually across the face of the bill, by which the drawee agrees to the order of the drawer. When the drawee accepts the bill he is called the acceptor. The Bills of Exchange Act states that the mere signature of the drawee without additional words is sufficient and this may be on the front or the back of the bill; usually "Accepted" is added to the signature. However, the acceptance must not express that the drawee will perform his promise by any other means than the payment of money.

Thus, if the customer of a bank, under an agreement, draws a bill on that bank and the bank accepts it the bill becomes a banker's acceptance. The bank will charge an acceptance commission for this service. The drawer then has a "two name bill" i.e. his own name and the bank's, which is a highly creditworthy document. The drawer will then have the bill discounted, invariably by the accepting bank but he may take it to be discounted by another bank if he so wishes. At maturity the holder for value will present the bill for payment to the accepting bank which will be in a position to make payment by debiting its customer's account under the terms of the agreement made between them when the acceptance facility was originally agreed. As explained, the accepting bank will invariably be the discounting bank so it will be the holder for value. However, even in this situation the discounting bank may well have re-discounted the bill, probably with others, to fund itself rather than hold the bill until maturity.

An alternative structure by which a banker's acceptance may be created in order to finance trade may be understood by study of the following example:

A timber company in the USA wishes to finance the import of timber from Brazil by way of a banker's acceptance. It, therefore, arranges with its American bank to issue an irrevocable letter of credit in favour of the Brazilian exporter. This letter of credit specifies the details of the shipment and gives the Brazilian exporter the right to draw a bill of exchange (time draft) for a specified amount and payable at a future date on the American bank. If the draft is then drawn in strict conformity with the conditions of the letter of credit the exporter can negotiate it with its local, Brazilian bank and obtain immediate payment for the discounted value of the bill. The Brazilian bank then passes the bill to the American bank for acceptance. Once accepted the bill is returned to the Brazilian bank which will hold it until maturity or re-discount it in the market (this could be with the accepting bank). In effect the American timber importer has "borrowed" by way of a banker's acceptance. The shipping documents will be released to the American importer against a trust receipt thereby giving it the time to sell the timber and use the sale proceeds to pay the bill at maturity (typically after 90/180 days).

Through this mechanism the drawer of the bill has been able to borrow funds, essentially working capital, until it is "in funds" itself by virtue of receipt of sale proceeds of a trade to which the drawing of the bill was related. This is, however, a sweeping statement as the question of "eligible bills" and "ineligible bills" needs to be addressed; this will be done later under the specific headings of UK, and US, Bankers' Accceptances. Suffice it to say here that if the bill is eligible i.e. technically it may be rediscounted with, say, the Bank of England or the US Federal Reserve Bank, it will attract the finest discount rates thus giving the drawer access to very competitively priced finance. As will be seen this will be below other appropriate, conventional, commercial rates related to LIBOR, UK Base Rates, US Prime Rates etc. However, when making comparisons it is important to remember that the rates normally quoted are as discounts whereas most other short term commercial rates will be interest. For valid comparisons a yield to maturity basis will need to be used and the acceptance commission or the lending margin (as appropriate) must be included in the computations.

Essentially a banker's acceptance facility is one of several by which a bank makes working capital loans to its customers. As such, therefore, a proposition for this type of facility will require the approval of the bank's credit committee or equivalent.

2. THE DISCOUNT BASIS

Bills are issued on a discount basis: that is, on a £1,000,000 principal amount, the investor (lender) does not invest £1,000,000 and on maturity receive back that amount plus interest. Rather, he invests less than the face amount of the note and on maturity receives back the full face amount: the difference between the two constitutes his interest. This feature, where all the investor's return is made up by the difference between purchase price and redemption amount, is also referred to as a "zero coupon" or as a "deep discount" (see also Chapter 19).

This type of paper is sold on a yield basis (purchase price being agreed between parties on confirmation of the deal), as follows (for paper of less than one year maturity):

$$\text{PRICE} = \frac{\text{FACE VALUE}}{\dfrac{[1 + (\text{Tenor (Days)} \times \text{Yield})]}{365^*}}$$

*365 for £; 360 for US$

3. STERLING BANKERS' ACCEPTANCES

Acceptances had their origin in the City of London in the 18th century when it became the practice for traders to obtain the addition of a reputable merchant's name to their trade bills against payment of a fee. Through this and associated financial activities these merchants evolved into fully fledged merchant banks and some have developed further to become investment banks. Those which specialised particularly in acceptances became known as Acceptance Houses.

The principal behind a banker's acceptance remains unchanged to this day. Interestingly, the instrument was given a boost in the mid-and-late-1970s during the time of the Bank of England imposed "Corset" which was designed to restrict, among other things, bank lending. As, however, acceptances were not restricted in the way that straight lending was, they offered a loophole that was exploited by many banks in London.

Accepted bills are classified as "eligible" or "ineligible" with a difference in the discount rate applicable; discounts on eligible bills being the finer of the two. Eligibility means that a bill is available for re-discount at the Bank of England. The rate at which this can be achieved is the Bank of England's intervention rate which it uses to signal to the financial markets what level of interest rates it considers appropriate for the well-being of the economy. The "Base Rate" of individual banks will respond to changes in the Bank of England's intervention rate.

Eligibility for re-discounting at the Bank of England at the finest rates was traditionally restricted to bills accepted by the Accepting Houses, the UK Clearing Banks and a small number of British Commonwealth and other foreign banks.

However, in August 1981, the Bank of England published new guidelines on UK monetary control with the result that a substantial number of additional banks, including US, Japanese and Continental European names now enjoy eligible status.

Purchases by the Bank of England are from the Discount Houses and not the banks. Bills will be priced by the Bank of England according to the band into which they fall governed by the number of days outstanding as follows:

Band 1 = 1 – 14 days
Band 2 = 15 – 33 days
Band 3 = 34 – 63 days
Band 4 = 64 – 91 days

Bank of England intervention normally takes place at 12 noon and 2 p.m. but dealings outside these times are possible. This activity is described as the Bank's "open market operations".

3.1 Parties to a Banker's Acceptance

The parties involved in a banker's acceptance will include some, or all, of the following:

(i)   The Drawer   –   i.e. the bank customer
(ii)   The Acceptor   –   i.e. a bank, Acceptance House
(iii) The Discounter   –   i.e. a bank
(iv)   The Re-discounter   –   i.e. another bank, Discount House,
                                   Bank of England.

A typical banker's acceptance will take the following form:

Figure 1

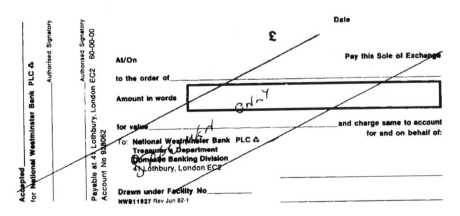

705

3.2   Sequence of Events

Once a bank has agreed to make an acceptance facility available to a customer the sequence of events will be:

(a)   Documentation covering terms and conditions signed.

(b)   Customer advises bank on the day funds are required.

(c)   Customer draws bill, or bills, on bank.

(d)   Bank accepts bill or bills.

(e)   Bank discounts bill(s) and credits proceeds to customer's account (N.B. There is a dealing cut-off time of 12 noon).

(f)   Bank collects the agreed acceptance commission (usually by deduction from the amount credited under (e)).

(g)   Bank holds bill(s) until maturity.

or

(h)   Bank re-discounts bill(s) (perhaps with others discounted for other customers).

(i)   At maturity the holder for value/holder in due course presents the bill to the accepting bank for payment (unless the accepting/discounting bank decided to hold the bill itself until maturity).

(j)   The accepting bank debits the customer's account with the face value of the bill.

(k)   The customer may then draw more bills on the bank if further working capital is required.

In practice a customer will invariably leave a supply of inchoate bills with its bank. An inchoate bill in this instance is one which has been signed by the drawer but the amount and date have not been inserted. Upon the request from the customer for a certain amount of borrowing

706

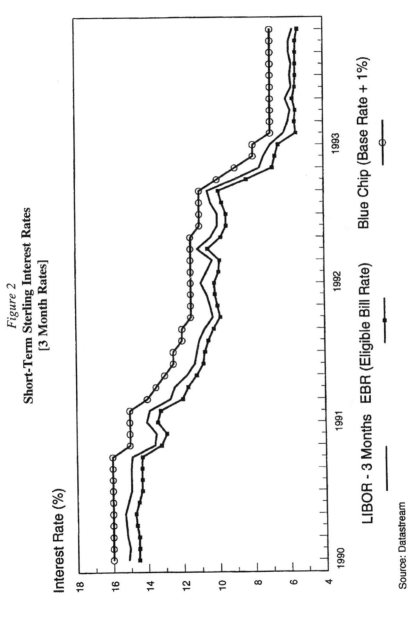

Figure 2
Short-Term Sterling Interest Rates
[3 Month Rates]

Interest Rate (%)

LIBOR - 3 Months   EBR (Eligible Bill Rate)   Blue Chip (Base Rate + 1%)

Source: Datastream

707

the bank will complete the bill(s) as to amount, date it/them and accept it/them. The bank will discount the bill(s) and credit the proceeds to the customer's account.

3.3 Tradeability of Bills

An eligible, accepted bill, once in the market, is a fully negotiable bearer instrument which may be actively traded throughout its life. For example, a Discount House may purchase it, at the appropriate discounted value, for its books as part of its own market operations or on behalf of one of its investment clients which group may include corporates, pension funds and insurance companies. Eligible bills are also lodged by the Discount Houses with the Bank of England or with other banks as security for very short term advances.

Eligible acceptances provide the holders of short term surplus funds with such a secure and liquid investment that the cost of raising finance in this manner is often lower (on a discount to yield basis) than the cost of a loan linked to inter-bank money market rates and is appreciably lower than conventional overdraft facilities linked to Base Rate.

3.4 Eligible and Ineligible Bills

Accepted bills fall into two categories:

Eligible   –   Available for rediscount, i.e. purchase, by the Bank of England.

Ineligible   –   Not eligible for re-discount, i.e. purchase, by the Bank of England. The discount rate in the market is higher for ineligible bills than it is for eligible bills.

The Bank of England views eligible bills as an integral part of its Monetary Control System and thus emphasises its desire to see adherence to its guidelines, thereby preserving the quality of the market. Furthermore, it expects all bills that it purchases from the market to comply with its criteria and in cases of doubt, it may seek evidence of the underlying transactions from the accepting bank, or request the accepting bank to repurchase the bills at current market rates.

In order to achieve eligible status, a bill of exchange must comply at least with the following main criteria:

(i)   the tenor should be a minimum of seven days and a maximum of six months (187 days) – 1 month tenor bills are by far the most common, with 2, 3 and 6 months or other periods in descending order of popularity.

(ii) the underlying transaction should be self-liquidating i.e. items of a capital expenditure nature cannot be financed in this way.

(iii) the bill should be drawn (and claused to such effect) in respect of a trade transaction (not necessarily involving the UK or a Sterling obligation) although for non-UK drawers the underlying trade transaction must be cross-border. The drawer warrants to the acceptor that the transaction has not been financed by any other means.

Examples of acceptable clausing are:

(a)   "Drawn against sales of motor vehicles".

(b)   "Drawn against shipments of meat and meat by-products".

(iv) the bill must be payable in the UK, preferably in London.

(v)   the bill must be drawn on, and accepted by, a bank whose acceptances are recognised as eligible for discount at the Bank of England.

(vi) the bill must not be drawn by a bank or bear the guarantee of a bank.

Individual bills should be drawn in a minimum amount of £50,000 with a maximum of £1,000,000.

Bills which do not satisfy all these criteria are ineligible and, accordingly, will be discounted at less preferential rates. The discounting bank will be obliged to hold them in its own portfolio until maturity, or sell them to a Discount House; they cannot be onsold to the Bank of England.

3.5 Costs

Under an acceptance credit the costs consist of two elements:

(i)   the acceptance commission (per cent per annum).

(ii)   the discount rate (per cent per annum).

The rate of acceptance commission is dependent upon the customer's credit standing and therefore would be similar to the margin appropriate for equivalent lending facilities.

The discount rate for eligible bills varies according to market conditions and the tenor.

As the discount charge and acceptance commission are paid at the beginning of the borrowing period rather than the end, a discount to yield calculation should be made to compare the cost of borrowing via an acceptance credit with alternative forms of short term financing.

Example

A grain importer wishing to finance a shipment draws a bill on 21 July 19XY with a face value of £1,000,000 payable in three months' time on 21 October 19XY (i.e. 92 days). The bill is accepted by the exporter's bank and discounted when the Eligible Bill Rate is 10.25% p.a. and with an Acceptance Commission of 12.5 basis points (0.125%) p.a.

The importer would receive £973,849.32.

This is calculated in the following way:

Face value of bill   £1,000,000.00

Less:

$$\text{Discount} - £1,000,000 \times \frac{92}{365} \times \frac{10.25}{100} = £25,835.61$$

and

$$\text{Commission} - £1,000,000 \times \frac{92}{365} \times \frac{0.125}{100} = £315.07 \qquad £26,150.68$$

£973,849.32

Then a discount to yield adjustment needs to be made using the following formula:

$$\frac{\text{Rate of Discount + Acceptance Commission}}{\left(1 - \dfrac{(\text{Rate of Discount + Acceptance Commission}) \times \text{No. of Days}}{100 \times 365}\right)}$$

Therefore:

$$\frac{10.25 + 0.125}{\left(1 - \dfrac{(10.25 + 0.125) \times 92}{100 \times 365}\right)} = 10.6536\% \text{ p.a.}$$

This rate can then be used to compare with alternative funding sources on which interest rather than discount is paid.

3.6 Other Features
The maturity of bills is usually 1, 2, 3 and occasionally 6 months but with a minimum of seven days and a maximum of 187 days (the odd days on the max. allows for maturities that would otherwise fall on non-business days). Odd days are, however, perfectly acceptable.

There is a minimum denomination of £50,000 and a maximum of £1m although individual banks may deal with specific customers outside this range. Intermediate amounts, including odd amounts e.g. £521,742.09 can be drawn.

It is necessary to have a commercial bank dealing cut-off time of 12 noon so that subsequent rediscounting, if required, can take place.

3.7 Features and Benefits for UK Issuers
(a) Probably the most attractive feature of this market, is that compared to a direct bank loan or LIBOR-based loan all-in borrowing costs for acceptance financing will usually present a considerable saving, often more than 30 basis points.

For this reason it may be a useful basis for raising loans in other currencies (see Section 5).

(b)   Secondly, acceptance financing will be most cost effective if the borrower can specify the duration of his funding needs, and thus the life of the acceptance. However, it should be borne in mind that if the collateral underlying an acceptance transaction is sold early, the borrower would be required to prepay the acceptance, and the associated penalty would raise the effective borrowing cost.

(c)   The nature of the pricing structure is such that the customer is aware of the overall cost at the outset, which is obviously attractive i.e. he is protected against subsequent rises in the Base Rate which would increase the cost of borrowing on overdraft.

(d)   This type of facility may be useful when conditions for obtaining longer term funds are difficult, for example because of high interest rates.

See Figure 3 for comparative rates.

3.8   Attractions for Non-UK Borrowers
The acceptance market also has attractions for foreign borrowers.

Since the removal of UK Exchange Controls in 1979, there have been no legal restrictions on the raising of domestic Sterling finance by non-UK borrowers, and the Bank of England has encouraged foreign use of the Sterling acceptance market, providing there is strict adherence to the criteria governing its operations. It is not a requirement that the UK has to be involved in the underlying trade transaction.

The Bank of England's current guidelines, as explained in Section 3.4, are applicable equally to bills drawn by foreign entities except that the underlying transaction must be:

(a)   cross-border trade (i.e. imports/exports).

(b)   the provision of cross-border services that have already been provided and where there is an unconditional obligation to pay.

712

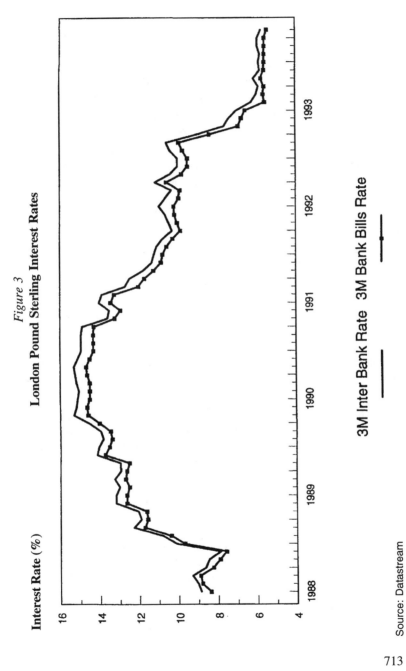

Figure 3
London Pound Sterling Interest Rates

Interest Rate (%)

3M Inter Bank Rate   3M Bank Bills Rate

Source: Datastream

4. US$ BANKERS' ACCEPTANCES

According to the Federal Reserve Bank's "Advances and Discounts, Regulation A" a banker's acceptance is "a draft or bill of exchange, whether payable in the United States or abroad and whether payable in Dollars or some other money, accepted by a bank or trust company, or a firm, company, or corporation engaged generally in the business of granting banker's acceptance credits". See Figure 4.

When the Federal Reserve System was established in 1913, it was felt that a market in Bankers' Acceptances should be developed along the lines of that in London, to improve New York's position as an international financial centre, and to aid both domestic bank business and foreign trade. To this end, national banks were, for the first time, authorised to accept time drafts, and the Fed. itself supported the nascent market both by buying eligible bills for its own portfolio and by rediscounting them through the discount window.

Like the Sterling market, the US$ bill market retains the characteristics of its origins in trade finance. Under Federal Reserve regulations, financial houses may accept bills for the following purposes: to finance foreign trade, domestic shipment of goods, domestic or foreign storage of readily marketable staples, and to provide Dollar exchange credits to banks in certain countries. The foreign trade does not have to include the USA.

When a bank accepts a bill, it will normally require backing for it, in the form of documentation which confirms its character as a trade transaction: invoices, warehouse or terminal receipts, bills of lading, etc. Thanks to the double credit backing which these bills carry, the US BA market has never known an investor lose his money, as has happened in CP, for instance when Penn Central went bankrupt in1970.

After an initial period of growth, the US BA market suffered a setback during the Depression and then the War, but thereafter, as international trade revived, this method of financing grew increasingly popular. Still, it was used mainly to fund domestic imports and exports. In the late 1970s and early 1980s the shape of the market changed drastically. With the sudden huge increase in the price of oil, BAs began to be more widely used, and particularly by the Japanese, to finance oil and other imports.

714

Figure 4

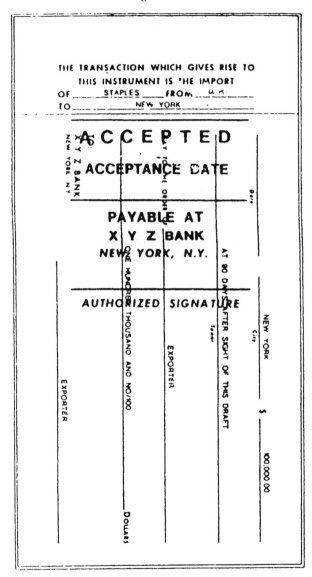

The Federal Reserve's practice of buying acceptances for its own account was ended in 1977, and as of July 1984 it also discontinued use of repurchase agreements on banker's acceptances in its open market operations. It is, however, a frequent participant in the market on behalf of its foreign customers (usually central banks). The Fed. continues to accept bankers' acceptances from member banks as collateral for borrowing from the discount window.

4.1 Eligible and Ineligible Bills

Despite the general withdrawal of the Fed. from the frequent and active participation in the market the Federal Reserve Regulations still specify the types of acceptances that are deemed to be "eligible for discount". These regulations are important to banks and their customers for the following reasons:

Firstly, only an acceptance which meets the conditions as eligible for discount may be sold by the accepting bank without resulting in the proceeds becoming subject to reserve requirements. (This is in marked contrast to the UK where *the acceptance* of a bill incurs reserve requirements). Ineligible bills are a more expensive funding medium because when they are sold in the money market a reserve requirement results and this raises the cost to the customer.

Secondly, the Federal Reserve Act limits the amount of acceptances eligible for discount that a member bank can create to 200% of capital and reserves.

Thirdly, as mentioned above, only eligible bills (rather than ineligible) can be offered as collateral for borrowing at the discount window.

4.1.1 *The Discount Window*

Section 13(7) of the Federal Reserve Act and the Board's regulations specify the requirements necessary for eligible acceptances to be used as collateral for advances from the Fed's "discount window". The regulation of banker's acceptances has evolved around this concept of "eligibility".

The Federal Reserve Bank provides liquidity to banks through these advances of funds. Such advances must be secured to the satisfaction of the lending district Reserve Bank. Summarised below are the criteria for a member bank to present eligible acceptances as collateral:

Eligible Acceptances Under Section 13(7) of the Federal Reserve Act: Shipment or Storage Acceptances

A banker's acceptance is an eligible acceptancc under Section 13(7) of the Federal Reserve Act if (i) it has a term of not more than six months and (ii) it is used to finance:

(a)   the importation or exportation of goods to or from the United States or between two foreign countries;

(b)   the shipment of goods within the United States; or

(c)   the storage of "readily marketable staples" in the United States or in a foreign country, provided that the accepted draft is secured, at the time of acceptance, by a warehouse receipt or other similar document conveying or securing title to the stored goods.

The Board has not prescribed by regulation precise criteria for defining a Section 13(7) acceptance. However, Board interpretations have established the following general rules for the eligibility of acceptances under Section 13(7):

(a)   *Import–Export Acceptances*

(i)   In general, the transaction being financed must be the subject of a firm contract for sale of the goods.

(ii)   In the case of an acceptance to finance imports, the term of the acceptance should correspond to the shipment of the goods* and/ or the period needed for the sale and distribution of the goods into the usual channels of trade.

(iii)   In the case of an acceptance to finance exports, the term of the acceptance should correspond to either the exporter's customary

*   In general, an acceptance satisfies this requirement if it is created up to 30 days before or after shipment begins, and matures up to 30 days after shipment ends.

credit terms or the time required to ship the goods (which may include time needed to assemble goods for shipment) plus more than 30 days.

(iv) Acceptances should not be drawn while other financing for the transaction is outstanding.

(b) *Domestic Shipment Acceptances*

The term of the acceptances must correspond to the shipment of the goods provided that the acceptance may also cover the usual and customary period of credit given in the industry.

(c) *Storage of Staples Acceptances*

(i) The staples must be subject to reasonably immediate sale, shipment or distribution into the process of manufacture and must be held in an independent warehouse.

(ii) There is no precise definition of "readily marketable staples", but in general the term means tangible commodities, including certain manufactured goods stored in bulk form, for which there is a wide and ready market.

An eligible acceptance must have written on it information identifying the basis for its eligibility. Generally this is done by filling in an appropriate eligibility "stamp" applied to the accepted draft.

4.2 The Dealer Market

The market for accepted drafts is provided by 15 or so Acceptance Dealers. They act between the two sides of the market and, because of the broad base of international business financed through bankers' acceptances, a wide variety of principal amounts and maturities are available for investors.

The rates on Bankers' Acceptances will depend upon the credit of the bank both domestic and foreign, but normally the major American money centre banks will command the finest rates. In times of financial stress in the market – e.g. end of quarter days and 31st of December – the rate differential between domestic and foreign banks can, and does, widen considerably.

718

Bankers' Acceptances: Eligibility and Reservability

Type of Banker's Acceptance	Eligible for discount	Exempt from reserve requirements if sold
Export-import, including shipments between foreign countries:		
Tenor – 6 months or less.....................	Yes	Yes
6 months to 9 months.............	No	No
Shipment within foreign countries:		
Tenor – any maturity............................	No	No
Foreign storage, readily marketable staples secured by warehouse receipt:		
Tenor – 6 months or less....................	Yes	Yes
6 months to 9 months.............	No	No
Domestic storage, readily marketable staples secured by warehouse receipt:		
Tenor – 6 months or less....................	Yes	Yes
6 months to 9 months.............	No	No
Domestic storage, any goods in the United States under contract of sale or going into channels of trade and secured throughout its life by warehouse receipt:		
Tenor – 6 months or less....................	No	No
6 months to 9 months.............	No	No
Dollar exchange, required by usages of trade – only in approved countries:		
Tenor – 3 months or less....................	Yes	No
3 months to 9 months.............	No	No
Finance or working capital, not related to any specific transaction:		
Tenor – any maturity............................	No	No

719

4.3 Other Features

Bills for acceptance by banks may be drawn for periods up to six months. They will generally be for amounts of US$1m or multiples thereof; odd amounts can be handled but will be at slightly poorer rates. Dealing cut-off time is 11.00 a.m.

4.4 Finance Bills

Another type of acceptance is the working capital acceptance (or finance bill) such as predominates in the UK banker's acceptance market. With this instrument there is no underlying collateral e.g. warehouse receipt, bills of lading, invoice etc. These were once widely available but outstandings have diminished considerably since the Federal Reserve began imposing reserve requirements in mid-1973 on bank liabilities on such instruments. These acceptances are not acceptable for discount or purchase by the Federal Reserve (unlike the situation in the UK with the Bank of England).

4.5 Advantages to Borrowers

As against other borrowing alternatives, acceptance financing can be an attractive funding option. Compared to a direct bank loan or a LIBOR-based loan, for example, current all-in borrowing costs for acceptance financing present approximately an advantage of 10–15 basis points or more. Figure 5 provides a rate comparison of bankers' acceptances and LIBOR.

The commission charged by a bank for acceptance financing varies according to the quality of the borrower's credit. For top-rated borrowers, acceptance costs are approximately equal to the all-in costs of issuing commercial paper. For lesser credits, however, acceptance financing can present a distinct advantage over commercial paper financing.

Acceptance financing is most cost effective if the borrower can specify the duration of his funding needs, and thus the life of the acceptance. If the collateral underlying an acceptance transaction were sold early, the borrower would be required to prepay the acceptance which would raise the effective borrowing cost.

Another advantage to a borrower using acceptance financing would be the increase in its credit availability from a given bank. Statutory restrictions

720

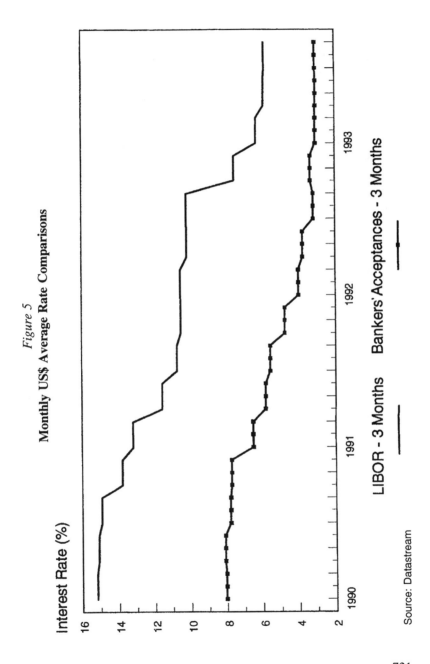

Figure 5
Monthly US$ Average Rate Comparisons

LIBOR - 3 Months   Bankers' Acceptances - 3 Months

Source: Datastream

721

limit the amount of conventional credit that a Federal Reserve member bank may extend to a single borrower. This general lending limit is equal to 10% of a bank's capital stock and surplus. Through acceptance financing, a bank can extend up to a maximum of 10% of additional credit to a single borrower provided that the acceptances are eligible for discount.

5. HEDGED BANKERS' ACCEPTANCES

This mechanism achieves the objective of producing competitively priced funds for a borrower in a currency other than that of the original issue instrument. In effect it requires the combination of two transactions. First is the issue of a banker's acceptance followed by an immediate spot purchase and forward sale (to correspond with the maturity date of the original instrument) of the currency in which borrowing is actually required. As the base from which this mechanism starts is a funding source which frequently produces finance at a cheaper rate than conventional bank rates, or interbank related rates, it produces borrowing in the second currency at cheaper rates than would be available by borrowing in that currency by a direct route. A "window" is said to exist when the interest rate differentials and the underlying forward margins combine to create the ideal circumstances for this mechanism to benefit a borrower.

Example

(a) Customer wishes to raise US$10,000,000 by way of Sterling bankers' acceptances.

(b) Data required in order to calculate the interest rate for the US$.

    (i) Sterling eligible bill rate for the period: 9.8125% p.a.

    (ii) Acceptance commission: 0.125% p.a.

    (iii) US$: £ spot rate (bank buys):   1.5765

    (iv) Forward foreign exchange swap price for period: –0.0121

    (v) No. of days in period of borrowing: 92

(c) Calculate discount price of Sterling
i.e. Discount price = Bill rate + commission
Therefore 9.8125 + 0.125 = 9.9375

(d) Calculate effective yield in Sterling terms

i.e. Effective yield $= \dfrac{\text{Discount Rate}}{\left(1 - \dfrac{(\text{Discount Rate} \times \text{No. of Days})}{36,500}\right)}$

Therefore: $\dfrac{9.9375}{\left(1 - \dfrac{(9.9375 \times 92)}{36,500}\right)} = 10.1928\%$ p.a.

(e) Calculate effective cost of borrowing US$ fully hedged i.e. using Sterling from discounted banker's acceptance to buy US$ spot and contracting to sell US$ forward 3 months to produce Sterling which will be used to redeem banker's acceptance liability.

Effective Cost = Stlg effective yield $\times \dfrac{360}{365} + \left(\dfrac{(\text{Forward Rate} \times 36,000)}{(\text{Spot Rate} \times \text{No. of Days})}\right)$

$\times \left[\left(\text{Effective yield} \times \dfrac{360}{365}\right) \times \dfrac{\text{No. of days}}{36,000} + 1\right]$

= 6.9727% (Cost of borrowing US$ for 3 months).

(f) Assuming customer could otherwise borrow at LIBOR (7% p.a. + $\frac{1}{8}$% p.a.)

cost would be:	7.1250% p.a.
Cost of borrowing US$ by hedged Sterling banker's acceptance:	6.9727% p.a.
saving	0.1423% p.a.

723

CHAPTER 18

Swaps

by
Francis D'Souza and Brian J Terry; revised and with additional material
by Philippa Skinner and Eric Warner

1. INTRODUCTION

In the late 70s/early 80s, swaps began as linkage and arbitrage tools
between the various capital markets, foreign exchange markets and money
markets. It was the tool which helped counterparties use their relative
advantages in their own markets to derive cost savings which were then
shared between the counterparties. This ability to arbitrage investor
preferences in different markets was the driving force for the interest rate
swap business in the early days.

The continuing evolution of the swap market in the 1980s has rendered
what many considered a passing arbitrage "product" of the late 1970s
into one of the most durable and valuable tools available for managing
the financial flows of any organisation. Furthermore, swaps are now
traded as instruments in their own right and a fully-fledged market now
exists in many financial centres.

While volumes stated by market participants are perhaps exaggerated,
a recent study by ISDA (The International Swap Dealers Association)
showed that the notional principal amount of all swaps written in the first
half of 1992 totalled US$1,500 billion. There are as many reasons for the
growth of this market as there have been swaps executed but the key to
the durability of swaps as a financial technique has been the market's
ability to meet the needs of a vast array of potential users in a manner not
quite matched by any other financial instrument. The needs of users, be
they corporate treasurers, bank liability managers, finance ministers or
portfolio managers, have been the main factors behind the growth of the
swap market. The market has responded to those needs in a most creative

and dynamic way. The result has been a closer integration of the world's capital, money and foreign exchange markets, and a significant widening of the options available to users for borrowing, investing, hedging and arbitraging in these markets through swaps.

What then, basically, is a swap? Essentially it is an agreement between two or more parties (referred to as counterparties) to swap (or exchange) the obligations on two or more debt instruments, or the benefits on asset instruments. Thus in an *interest rate swap*, Counterparty A may have a debt instrument, e.g. a bond, on which it has the obligation to pay a fixed rate of interest to the purchasers of the bond. Counterparty B may have a debt instrument, e.g. a loan from a bank, on which it has the obligation to pay a floating rate of interest. Through the mechanism of the swap market it is possible for these two obligations to be exchanged. Each counterparty continues to have its obligations to the third parties (i.e. the bond holders and the bank respectively), under the original instruments but its net payments away, by way of interest, are swapped from "fixed rate to floating rate" or "floating rate to fixed rate".

In the case of Counterparty A its obligation to pay a fixed rate of interest to its bondholders is covered by the swap it enters into with Counterparty B, i.e. Counterparty B pays Counterparty A a fixed rate of interest for the period of the swap agreement. In turn Counterparty A will pay to Counterparty B a floating rate of interest. So, in effect, Counterparty A has swapped from a "fixed rate payer" to a "floating rate payer" by virtue of the fact that its fixed rate payments are covered by the fixed rate payments it receives from Counterparty B and its net payment is the floating rate interest it pays to Counterparty B.

The opposite situation applies to Counterparty B as it becomes a net "payer of fixed rate".

The respective rates of interest need, of course, to relate to the same principal amount i.e. the value of the bond issue must equal the amount of the bank borrowing, but this underlying principal amount is not swapped in an interest rate swap. It would be pointless to do so as it is the same currency and the same amount for both parties. In fact the swapping of the interest payments does not have to be on a gross basis but a single *net* payment can flow from the Counterparty with the higher of the two interest rates to pay.

726

A cross currency swap, in contrast, *does* also involve the exchange of principal because, in this case, two different currencies are involved. At the instigation of the swap the two principal amounts are deemed to be equal at the particular exchange rate agreed upon for the swap. By the same token interest rate payments will usually be made gross as they will be in the two, respective currencies. At maturity the two amounts of principal will be returned to the original holders so that those parties can redeem their third party debts.

A swap counterparty will be referred to in terms of its obligation under the swap agreement. It will be, for example:

Interest Rate Swap
(a)   the payer of fixed rate funds and receiver of floating rate funds; or
(b)   the payer of floating rate funds and receiver of fixed rate funds.

Cross Currency Swap
(a)   the payer of fixed rate US$ funds and receiver of floating rate SwFc funds; or
(b)   the payer of floating rate SwFc funds and receiver of fixed rate US$ funds etc.

As a complication to this nomenclature the counterparties may also be described according to the *principal* that they are *providing* (even though in many cases principal amounts are not exchanged). There can be, therefore,

(a)   The provider of fixed rate US$
(b)   The provider of floating rate Yen.

In these instances the following alternatives are possible:

(a)   The *provider* of fixed rate US$ is the *receiver* of fixed rate US$ (i.e. interest) and the *payer* of floating rate Yen (i.e. interest).
(b)   The *provider* of floating rate Yen is the *receiver* of floating rate Yen (i.e. interest) and the *payer* of fixed rate US$ (i.e. interest).

Whilst, in the early days of the market, some swaps were arranged directly between the two counterparties it was more frequently the case that a bank brought the two counterparties together. By interposing itself between the two counterparties the bank became "the intermediary". The bank then had "risks" against both counterparties and each counterparty then had a "risk" on the bank rather than the other counterparty. The bank took a nominal "fee" (generally a few basis points) from the respective interest payments as they passed through it from one counterparty to the other.

As time went on and the market developed further, the role of the banks as arrangers of swaps became the norm. Increasingly, the bank intermediaries faced the problem of having one swap (i.e. with one counterparty) in place without having arranged, contemporaneously, the immediately offsetting swap. Thus the banks quickly developed skills which allowed them to "warehouse" the first transaction until the offsetting deal could be struck (see section 2.2). Following this development, as the swap market continued to grow in size and liquidity, the intermediaries managed their swap risk exposures on a portfolio basis whereby sophisticated hedging techniques allowed risk to be managed on a net basis, i.e. the net resulting position of all the swaps in a portfolio. This is substantially the situation in banks today.

In the following sections, we shall look at what the basic swap structures are and how they are used. We shall also look at what are the attendant risks on swap transactions, how to evaluate and manage them and we shall also have a look at how the recent capital adequacy regulations have affected the market.

2. BASIC SWAP TYPES

Although knowledge of the underlying assets or liabilities facilitates understanding swaps, it is important to realise that functionally and legally the swap is a totally distinct contract. Furthermore, swaps can be, and are, used as a method of speculating on the markets.

The explosive growth in the swap market reflects, to a great extent, the creativity and the ingenuity of swap market operators in creating and fitting swap structures to meet customer requirements. Underlying all the variations there are four basic swap types.

- The Interest Rate Swap

- The Fixed Rate Currency Swap

- The Cross-Currency Interest Rate Swap or Currency Coupon Swap

- Basis Swaps

2.1 Interest Rate Swaps

In terms of transaction volume the interest rate or coupon swap is by far the most common type of swap; of total swaps of US$1,500 billion in the first half of 1992 interest rate swaps (dollar and non-dollar) accounted for US$1,300 billion representing an increase of 55% over the same period a year earlier. The unprecedented growth in the interest rate swap market since its genesis in the early 1980s is demonstrative in itself of the substantial benefits to be gained by market participants.

The basic structure of an interest rate swap consists of the exchange between two counterparties of fixed rate interest for floating rate interest in the same currency, calculated by reference to a mutually agreed notional principal amount. This principal amount, which would normally equate to the underlying assets or liabilities being "swapped" by the counterparties, is applicable solely for the calculation of the interest to be exchanged under the swap. *At no time is the principal physically passed between the counterparties.* Through this straightforward swap structure, the counterparties are able to convert an underlying fixed rate asset/ liability into a floating rate asset/liability and vice versa.

The majority of interest rate swap transactions are driven by the expected cost savings to be obtained by each of the counterparties.

For example, investors in fixed rate instruments are more sensitive to credit quality than floating rate bank lenders. Accordingly, a greater premium is demanded of issuers of lesser credit quality in the fixed rate debt markets than in the interest rate bank lending market. The counterparties to an interest rate swap may, therefore, obtain an arbitrage advantage by accessing the market in which they have the greatest relative cost advantage and then entering into an interest rate swap to convert the cost of the funds so raised from a fixed-rate to a floating-rate basis or vice versa.

The credit arbitrage available through the use of an interest rate swap may be illustrated by considering two counterparties, Counterparty A and Counterparty B with the following profiles:

Exhibit 1	Counterparty A	Counterparty B	Comparative Advantage
Credit Rating Cost of Raising Direct Fixed Rate Funding	AAA 10.80%	BBB 12.00%	1.20%
Cost of Raising Direct Floating Rate Funds	6mth LIBOR plus$^1/_4$%	6mth LIBOR plus$^3/_4$%	.50%

As expected, Counterparty A with the superior credit quality has a greater relative cost advantage over Counterparty B in the fixed rate debt market, i.e. 1.2% than in the floating market, i.e. 0.5%. Despite the fact that Counterparty A can also raise direct floating rate funds more cheaply than Counterparty B, a potential arbitrage therefore exists whereby Counterparty A and Counterparty B may *both* obtain a cost saving by accessing the markets in which they have the greatest relative cost advantage and entering into a swap to exchange interest obligations.

Exhibit 2

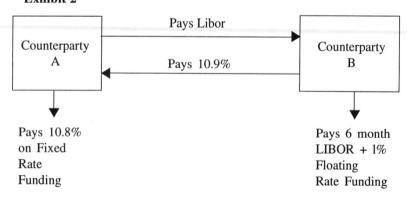

730

(Interest rate swap diagrams always illustrate the interest payments being made and swapped. There is no swapping of principal).

Exhibit 3	Counterparty A	Counterparty B
Direct Funding Cost Fixed Rate Funds Raised Directly by Counterparty A	(10.80%)	
Floating Rate Funds Raised Directly by Counterparty B		(6mth LIBOR+$^{3}/_{4}$%)
Swap Payments Counterparty A pays Counterparty B Floating Rate Interest	(LIBOR)	LIBOR
Counterparty B pays Counterparty A Fixed Rate Interest	10.90%	(10.90%)
All-in Cost of Funding	LIBOR– $^{1}/_{10}$%	11.65%
Comparable Cost of Equivalent Direct Funding	LIBOR+$^{1}/_{4}$%	12.00%
Saving	35 Basis Points	35 Basis Points

This ability to transfer a fixed rate cost advantage to floating rate liabilities has led to many high quality credits issuing fixed rate Eurobonds purely to "swap" and obtain, in many cases, sub-LIBOR funding.

In the typical issue related interest rate swap, the issuer will normally be issuing fixed rate paper but actually wanting floating rate funds. Because of its standing in the market, the issuer is able to issue at a level such that combined with a fixed to floating interest rate swap it can generate very cheap floating rate funds. That is cheaper than it could obtain by going direct to the floating rate market. The counterparty to this swap will probably be a corporate which can access only short term funds through commercial paper or bank borrowings but desires to access fixed term funds. A bank would act as principal and bring these two counterparties together. Originally banks would only do the deals once they had both sides of the transaction in place. However, banks have since developed techniques which enable them to conclude the swap with the first counterparty and then find the second counterparty at a later stage. This is called warehousing and the methods used have been the single most important reason for the success and growth of the swap markets.

2.2 Warehousing an Interest Rate Swap

Exhibit 4

First Step

Swap arranged with one counterparty (i.e. A) and hedged through U.S. Treasuries.

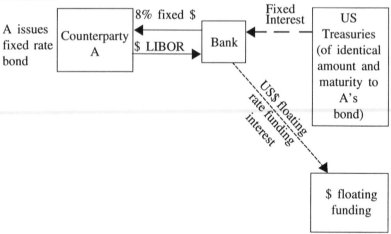

Counterparty A has issued a fixed rate bond issue and then swapped into floating US$ with the bank.

At this stage the bank does not have a suitable counterparty to match the swap so it warehouses the transaction. This means it borrows floating rate US$ funds (interest covered by A's payments) and buys US Treasuries of identical amount and maturity to A's bond issue. Thus it will receive fixed rate US$ from this investment to cover the 8% fixed it needs to pay to A under the swap.

(Assume that the US Treasury is priced at par i.e. 100% and the coupon is 8%).

Second Step

Swap is arranged with Counterparty B but, due to movement of interest rates, B is prepared to pay only 7% fixed and to receive US$ LIBOR. Thus:

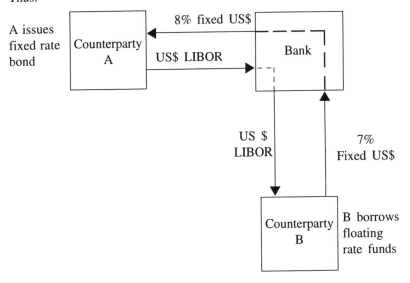

However, because interest rates have fallen (e.g. the fixed has dropped from 8% to 7%) the price of the US Treasuries will have risen to 104.312%. So, the bank, despite having "lost" 1% on the fixed swap payments between B and A, is compensated by the "profit" it makes by selling its hedge (the US Treasuries); with the remaining proceeds of the Treasuries' sale it will, of course, repay its LIBOR borrowing.

The "reverse" hedge may also be created by going short of the hedging instrument i.e. the bank sells U.S. Treasuries which it does not own. Such a hedge may be applied to an interest rate swap in any currency where there is a suitable government bond. The technique has some associated risks and costs which cannot be discussed here but suffice it to say that, provided the hedging instrument is as "risk-free" as possible, these will not be significant and are certainly manageable.

In addition to the cost advantages, interest rate swaps often provide the only mechanism for entities effectively to access markets albeit indirectly which are otherwise closed to them. The ability to obtain the benefits of markets without the need to comply with the prospectus disclosures, credit ratings and other formal requirements provides an additional benefit especially for private companies.

The interest rate swap market also provides Treasurers with a mechanism for managing interest rate costs and exposure whilst leaving the underlying source of funds unaffected. For example, the cost of fixed rate funding may be reduced in a declining interest rate environment through the use of the interest rate swap technique whilst leaving the underlying funding in place. This may be illustrated by considering the actions of Counterparty A, with underlying fixed rate debt costing 9% per annum, during a period of declining interest rates:

(a)   At the beginning of interest rates declining:
      Counterparty A with a fixed rate debt at 9% would swap to obtain LIBOR funding (see Exhibit 5).

(b)   During the period of interest rate decline:
      Counterparty A would leave the swap in place as interest rates decline.

(c)   At the end (or perceived end) of interest rate decline:
      Counterparty A would enter into a second swap to "lock into" the new lower fixed rate of, say, 8% (see Exhibit 5).

The ultimate effect of the above series of transactions is a saving of 1% for Counterparty A as the net cost of funds is reduced from 9% to 8% for the remainder of the borrowing period (assuming this is matched by the term of the swap arrangement).

Exhibit 5

Step 1 – at beginning of declining interest rates:

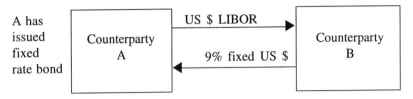

Step 2 – at perceived end of interest rates decline:

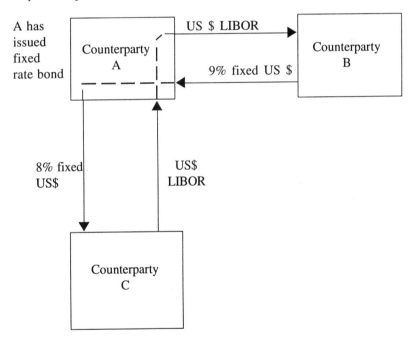

2.3 Fixed Rate Currency Swaps

A fixed rate currency swap consists of the exchange between two counterparties of fixed rate interest in one currency in return for fixed rate interest in another currency. The following three basic steps are common to all currency swaps (see also Exhibit 6):

(a) Initial Exchange of Principal

On the commencement of the swap the counterparties exchange the principal amounts of the swap at an agreed rate of exchange. Although this rate is usually based on the spot exchange rate, a forward rate set in advance of the swap commencement date can also be used. Whilst the physical exchange of principal most commonly takes place, this initial exchange may be on a "notional" basis (i.e. no physical exchange of principal amounts).

Whether the initial exchange is on a physical or notional basis its importance is to establish the quantum of the respective principal amounts for the purpose of (a) calculating the ongoing payments of interest and (b) the re-exchange of principal amounts under the swap at maturity.

(b) Ongoing Exchanges of Interest

Once the principal amounts in each currency are established, the counterparties exchange interest payments based on those principal amounts at the respective interest rates in the two currencies.

(c) Re-exchange of Principal Amounts

On the maturity date the counterparties re-exchange the principal amounts established at the outset.

This straightforward, three-step process is standard practice in the currency swap market and results in the effective transformation of a debt raised in one currency into a fully-hedged fixed rate liability in another currency.

However, it is the principal which is fully hedged not the new currency interest payments which are assumed under the swap. Unless, therefore, the payer has a natural inflow in that same currency it must consider the need to hedge the currency exposure through the instruments available e.g. forward exchange contracts.

In principle, the fixed currency swap structure is similar to a long-date forward foreign exchange contract. However, the counterparty nature of the swap market results in a far greater flexibility in respect of both maturity periods and size of the transactions which may be arranged. A currency swap structure also allows for interest rate differentials between the two currencies via periodic payments rather than the lump sum reflected by forward points used in the foreign exchange market. Readers will understand that in a forward foreign exchange swap (under which one currency is bought at spot with another currency and then swapped back at maturity) the amount of principal expressed in the two currencies at the outset of the deal is *not* the same as that at maturity. This is because a premium or discount to the original exchange rate is calculated from the differential of the interest rates of the two currencies involved and this sets the exchange rate at maturity. In effect this allows the interest rate differential to be "rolled-up" and settled in the final re-exchange of principal. In a currency and interest rate swap, as the *same* exchange rate is used at the beginning *and* the maturity of the swap for the exchange of principal amounts, the interest rate differential of the two currencies must be recognised in interim payments of interest in each currency at the two different, respective interest rates. This enables the swap structure to be customised to fit the counterparties' exact requirements at attractive rates. For example the cash flows of an underlying bond issue may be matched exactly and invariably at much finer rates than those available on the foreign exchange market.

In common with the interest rate swap, a major driving force behind the currency swap market is the cost saving it provides. The swap allows counterparties to arbitrage their relative access to markets in much the same way as the interest rate swap. Thus, a strong borrower in the Swiss Franc market may obtain a finer fixed US Dollar rate by raising funds directly in fixed Swiss Francs and then "swapping" them into US Dollars.

In addition to the cost advantage the currency swap market also enables entities effectively to access foreign capital markets and obtain funds in currencies which may otherwise be unobtainable except at the highest premium. In this way the swap market provides a significant contribution to the greater integration of the world's capital markets.

2.4 Cross-Currency Interest Rate Swaps or Currency Coupon Swaps

The cross-currency interest rate swap is a combination of an interest rate swap and the fixed rate currency swap. The fixed interest rate in one currency is exchanged for floating interest rate in another currency.

A typical example of this would be a British building society issuing fixed rate Dollar bonds when the Dollar bond market looked attractive and swapping the proceeds into floating rate Sterling which it requires to fund its mortgage portfolio.

It is not necessary that e.g. the British building society physically executes a spot sale of US$150m with the intermediary bank for it, then, to execute a spot sale of US$150m for £100m with the counterparty. These transactions can be executed with two entirely separate banks as long as the British building society and the counterparty have agreed the spot rate of exchange, and thus the amounts of principal in the respective currencies, on which the swap of obligations will be based. However, the re-exchange of principal amounts at maturity will have to be made by the counterparties. As has been explained the exchange rate for this re-exchange is the same as that which applied at the execution of the swap. In a sense, therefore, it is a "false" forward rate and would not be acceptable to any source other than the respective counterparties. At maturity, therefore, each counterparty has restored to it the exact amount of the particular currency which it swapped at the outset.

Interestingly, if the counterparties were entering the currency and interest rate swap but had no wish to swap principal amounts in the two different currencies i.e. they both needed the swap to hedge foreign currency cash flows, no exchange of principal at spot rate or any other rate with the intermediary bank or any other bank would occur at the beginning or the maturity of the swap arrangement.

2.5 Multi-Legged Swaps

There are many occasions when an intermediary bank cannot match the requirements of one counterparty with those of another. In such circumstances it may prove to be necessary to involve three or more counterparties.

738

Exhibit 6

Initial Exchange of Principal

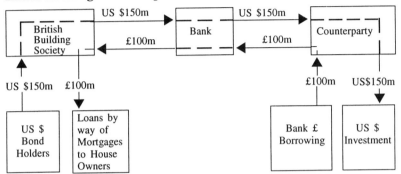

Future, Periodic (Interest) Payments

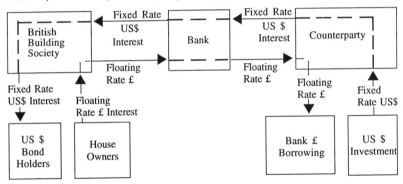

Exchange of Principal at Maturity

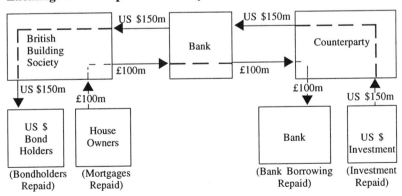

Example:

Company A wishes to borrow floating rate US$, but is advised by its investment bank that, despite its AAA rating, it could not issue such paper in the bond market until some of its existing floating rate US$ bonds mature in two years' time; it, currently, makes full use of its US$ commercial paper programme. It has not previously borrowed in the buoyant, floating rate Euro-Yen market.

Company B is a worldwide, household name with low gearing and is regularly encouraged by a number of banks to make its first entry into the fixed rate US$ bond market; however, it has a need for floating rate Yen in order to hedge its exports invoiced in Japanese Yen.

Company C has made little use of its A1/P1 rating but has a number of long term construction projects for which it has US$ costs and will receive US$ in payment; accordingly, it would like to fix the cost of the US$ it needs to borrow but is not keen to place paper in the bond market for certain strategic reasons.

All parties can take advantage of their respective markets of maximum advantage by the following arrangements:

(a)   The bank makes a Euro-Yen FRN issue for Company A.
(b)   The bank makes a US$ fixed rate bond issue for Company B.
(c)   Company C borrows in the US$ Commercial Paper market.

The bank then acts as an intermediary in the following swaps:

(i)   Company A swaps its floating rate Japanese Yen for floating rate US$.
(ii)   Company B swaps its fixed rate US$ for floating rate Japanese Yen.
(iii) Company C swaps its floating rate US$ for fixed rate US$.

740

Exhibit 7

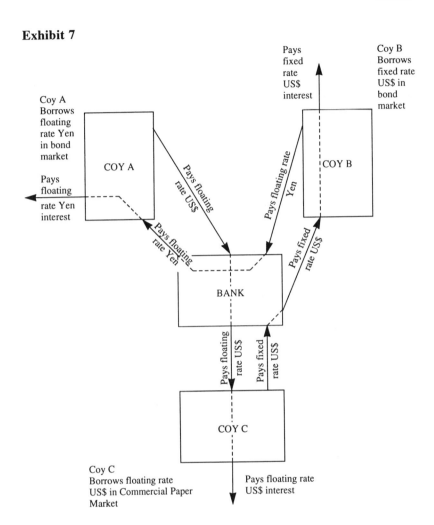

2.6 Basis Swaps

This is also sometimes called the floating/floating swap and typically in this swap floating rate interest calculated on one basis is exchanged for interest calculated on a different basis in a single currency. The forerunner for this swap was the US Dollar Prime rate/LIBOR swap. There are also Treasury Bills/LIBOR and Commercial Paper/LIBOR swaps. The term "basis swap" also applies to cross currency swaps where the interest is on a floating basis in each currency.

The availability of the basis rate swap market provides an excellent method for entities to arbitrage spreads between different floating rate funding sources. More importantly, it provides a discreet and most efficient method, for European entities in particular, to simulate the US Commercial Paper funding market without the necessity of meeting the stringent US requirements for a Commercial Paper programme.

2.7 Pricing

If we revert to the original interest swap example in Exhibits, 1, 2 and 3 it will be seen that Counterparty A can obtain fixed rate funds at a 1.20% advantage over the rate at which Counterparty B can. Additionally, it can obtain floating rate funds at a cost lower by 0.50%. Therefore, the net positive differential which arises out of the swap is 0.70% (1.20% minus 0.50%). In the example these 70 basis points have been evenly shared between the two counterparties. In practice the normal market forces of supply and demand would prevail and the split need not be even. If a bank is acting as intermediary then its fee must also be taken out of this positive differential.

There is such liquidity in the market now that intermediary banks will normally be able to react to target rates required by one counterparty by matching the targets received by another counterparty and this can be achieved whether or not the counterparties are available at the same time.

2.7.1 The Swap Spread

The "price" of a swap generally means the rate on the fixed rate side of the swap, and it is assumed, unless specified otherwise, that the floating rate side is LIBOR flat. In some currencies, the price on the fixed side of a swap is quoted in terms of a spread to an underlying bond yield. The price of a swap being based on the fixed-rate side, reflects the cost of paying or receiving fixed-rate funds. In the major markets (US$, C$ and to a lesser extent, sterling) this pricing is realised as a *spread* over the respective government cost of funds. Thus in the US dollar market, for example, interest-rate swaps are quoted as a spread above the US Treasury bond for a comparable maturity; in sterling markets the spread is above the gilt for a comparable maturity, and so on.

742

In such markets the price of the swap is determined by adding the swap spread to the relevant bond yield. Thus the price will be determined finally only at the execution of the swap as the underlying bond yield is likely to be changing minute by minute. (NB: The swap spread (i.e. over the respective government cost of funds) must not be confused with the normal dealing spread for swaps which is, as with other financial instruments, the dealer's turn between the bid and offered rates).

Example

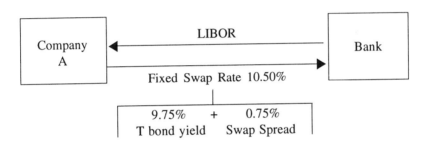

Markets where the swaps are quoted in terms of spreads tend to be those where the underlying bond market furnishes a reliable and liquid method of hedging. In such cases, the bank which makes a market in swaps effectively sees a risk only on the swap spread, which is a more manageable risk than the absolute risks run in unhedged markets.

2.7.2 *Factors influencing the swap spread*

Whereas movements in the underlying government bond yield are affected by macro-economic factors (e.g. the general level of interest rates in the economy and government attempts to influence this) the swap spread is purely a function of supply and demand for fixed-rate funds at any given point in time. Thus if there is considerable demand from fixed rate payers at any one time the swap spreads will gradually rise and vice versa.

743

As a result, a swap spread tends to have an inverse relation to the underlying bond yield. That is to say, when interest rates are high there is less demand to pay a fixed-rate of interest over a long term, and the spread contracts accordingly. Conversely, as interest rates decline there is increasing demand to pay fixed, and the spread widens. Historically, the swap spread in dollars has varied between 20 and 120 basis points, with a mean of about 60 for 5-year swaps.

The same supply and demand influences occur also in markets where pricing is not in spread terms – in any currency significant demand from fixed rate payers will push prices up. However, without the swap spread to separate the movements in the swap market from those in the underlying bond market, the effect is less visible.

The precise degree of any counterparty's advantage in using the swap market, therefore, depends not only on its relative funding advantage in any market, but also on the swap spread level at any time. The volatility and substantial market variations of the latter can reduce or even negate the benefits of the former. Moreover, the phenomenal growth of the market has led to the continued expansion of the number of counterparties seeking to use this valuable treasury tool. In theory at least, the swap spread should be increased (or decreased) depending upon the credit quality of the counterparty seeking to enter the swap but this has not happened extensively in practice. The trend, however, was given a boost by the BIS Risk-Weighted Capital guidelines, published in 1988, which, for the first time, compelled banks to keep a portion of capital against off-balance sheet instruments such as swaps. As the market continues to mature, it is inevitable that this trend will develop further.

2.7.3 *Other pricing influences*

Finally, the all-in cost to any counterparty undertaking a swap is affected by any deviation from standard or "vanilla" terms. Excessively high or low principal amounts (market minimum in US$ is US$5 million), deferred (or forward) start swaps, increasing or amortising principal structures, and long maturities for which markets are thin will cause variations from the generic price quoted as standard in the market. Pricing for such structures is, of course, derived from the quoted generic swap prices. There are several different mathematical methods for pricing, say, a forward start swap, so that two banks may give different prices for the same structure given the same underlying swap prices. Here again, however the fact that the market can cope with such deviations from the norm is a further sign of the enormous adaptability and flexibility which the swap market has shown.

2.7.4 *Floating rate pricing*
The price benefits which accrue to a counterparty in a fixed/floating or floating/fixed swap are reflected in the price of the *fixed* side of the transaction; the floating side is invariably quoted as *LIBOR*. This is not to say, of course, that a counterparty may not judge the merits of a contract by measuring its floating rate cost of funds as so-many basis points *under* LIBOR. This view would require it to consider the swap of the fixed rate obligations at actual cost. The principle involved in establishing the prices, however, is always the same ie based on the fixed rate side.

As explained swaps are normally priced off the fixed rate side but what about those occasions in which both parties are looking to pay a floating rate ie a basis or floating/floating swap? Banks and other financial institutions frequently make use of these structures where one floating rate obligation is swapped for another, different, floating rate obligation e.g. 3 month LIBOR for 6 month LIBOR or 90 day CP. Corporates also use basis swaps in a cross currency situation eg exchanging obligations in US dollar LIBOR for sterling LIBOR. The price for such basis swaps is usually quoted in terms of a margin of basis points over or under one or both floating legs and will reflect the position of the underlying book of the bank treasury at the time of quoting.

For example if a bank is long on sterling loans (as might be the case with a UK Clearing Bank), on which it receives floating rate interest, it might be more prepared to pay away sterling (by way of competitively priced floating rate interest) in order to receive floating rate US$ to cover its US$ deposits (which require the bank to pay away US$ interest to its depositors).

Example of a $ swap dealing screen:

Period	A US Treasury Bond Yield	B Swap Spread	C All-in-rate
2 years	7.90	58/53	8.48 - 8.43
3 years	7.91	70/64	8.61 - 8.55
4 years	7.90	77/72	8.67 - 8.62
5 years	7.87	85/81	8.72 - 8.68
7 years	8.00	87/82	8.87 - 8.82
10 years	7.96	95/90	8.91 - 8.86

NB: In columns B and C the offer price is quoted first and then the bid price.

The figures in Column A show the yield for various maturities of US Treasury Bonds; those in Column B represent the spread above the corresponding T-Bond for each maturity for the highest category of counterparty. The figures in Column C show the bid and offered rates quoted by a bank (whose page this is on Reuters/Telerate etc) indicating what it would pay (bid) or receive (offer) by way of fixed rate interest on a US$ contract. Because the swap spread is the only element of the pricing which is quoted firm by the dealer, the yields and all-in-rates are shown as those prevailing at the time. Therefore provided that the two year treasury is still yielding 7.90% p.a., for a two year contract it would quote 8.48% p.a. to a counterparty for that company to be a *payer* of fixed and 8.43% p.a. for the counterparty to be a *receiver* of fixed.

3. THE MARKET PLACE
Like most other new "products" in international finance, "swap" transactions are not executed in a physical market. Participants in the swap "market" are many and varied in their location, character and motives in executing swaps. However, the sum total of the activities of participants in the swap market have taken on the character of a classic

746

financial market connected to, and integrated with, the underlying money, capital and foreign exchange markets.

The market in swaps, both interest and currency, now goes out to 10 years. Longer swaps can be arranged in exceptional circumstances but these are really only possible for the highest rated companies because of the element of creditworthiness plus the impact of the cost to the bank of capital adequacy on the pricing of the swap.

3.1 The Interest Rate Swap Market

The largest section of the swap market, by far and away, is the interest rate swap market. Though historically it evolved slightly later than the currency swap, the interest rate swap proved far more useful to a wider range of counterparties, and this market's growth throughout the late 1980s and early 90s remained meteoric. In 1993, the interest rate swap market accounted for approximately 60% of all outstandings from all other swap markets. As the largest swap market, interest rate swaps have the characteristics of a well-organised financial market. Continuous markets are made around the globe by most of the large commercial and investment banks. There are also sub-sectors of the market (e.g. basis swaps) in which niche players specialise, and there are a variety of brokers who match intermediaries in the banking sector.

In recent years interest rate swaps in several currencies have gained ground. Among the fastest growing have been European currencies, Sterling, DM, French Franc and Swiss Franc. Liquid markets now exist in all these currencies, as well as in Australian Dollars, Yen and Canadian Dollars. Lately the "minor" currencies have experienced significant growth, with interest rate swap markets evolving in Italian Lira, Spanish Peseta, Dutch Gilder and Belgian Francs.

3.1.1 *The Short Term Market*

This segment of the market is extremely volatile in price (i.e. in terms of spreads versus Treasuries and/or 1/2 year LIBOR) reflecting this segment's close proximity in maturity to the volatile US Dollar money markets and the futures market in Chicago. Market-making or position-taking in this segment is therefore only for the most experienced dealers as timing is critical and markets are extremely volatile. However, in this segment a premium must be placed on the close integration of a bank's overall treasury operations with the swap operations to ensure that the profit potential is maximised and the risks absorbed are both prudent and well-managed.

The centre of this market is New York followed (not too closely) by London and Tokyo. The participants, while principally banks, include a number of brokers who have extended their normal money market dealing activities with banks to include interest swap activities. The most successful of the brokers are undoubtedly a select few US investment banking houses closely followed by the (somewhat obscure) money market brokers. Success as a broker or principal in this segment of the market is dependent not only on close integration of an institution's treasury and swap operations, but also on distribution and, in particular, the ability to move positions quickly due to the price volatility and risks inherent in the market. "Inventory" (i.e. a booked but not closed position) also quickly becomes stale in the short-term market because most transactions are done on a "spot" (immediate settlement) basis; holding a position for any period of time may, therefore, mean one's inventory may not move irrespective of price.

3.1.2 *The Medium/Long Term Market*
As one moves along the yield curve, the interest rate swap market becomes dominated by securities transactions, corporate risk management and, in particular, the Eurodollar bond market. However, this market sector is very large: it is not unreliably estimated that some 75% of all Eurodollar bond issues are swapped. The advent of the swap market has also meant that the Eurodollar bond market now never closes due to interest rate levels: issuers who would not come to market because of high interest rates now do so to the extent that a swap is available. Indeed, the Eurodollar bond market owes much of its spectacular growth in the 1980's to the parallel growth of the swap market. The firms that now dominate lead management roles in the Eurodollar bond market all have substantial swap capabilities and this trend will continue.

Pricing in this segment of the market is exclusively related to the US Treasury rates for comparable maturities (on a "spread" versus Treasuries basis) and is marked by the relative stability of these "spreads" by comparison to the short-term market. Given the size of most Eurobond issues ($100 million plus) and the over-supply of entities able and willing to approach the Eurobond market to swap into floating-rate funds, most major houses in the swap market now enter into swap agreements with an issuer without a counterparty (fixed-rate payer) on the other side. This "warehousing" activity is normally hedged in the US Treasury or financial futures market, leaving the warehousing manager with a "spread" risk, or the difference between the spread at which he booked the swap with the issuer and where he manages to find (over the course of time) a matched counterparty. The relative stability of spreads and a positively sloped yield curve (for funding the hedge at a positive carry) have allowed the market to function reasonably well on this basis with only occasional periods of severe over-supply in any particular maturity. The major houses tend to spread their inventory across the yield curve to reduce risk and to ensure ready availability of a given maturity for particular clients' requirements.

Bids for bond-related swaps tend to differ between the major houses by only a few basis points: the swap market is quite efficient in price given the (still relatively) few houses who deal in bond market size and maturities. Hence, a premium is placed on creating bond structures which offer the fixed-rate issuer a lower cost and, therefore, a better spread (below) LIBOR. Apart from creative bond/swap structures, the key to operating successfully in this segment of the market for the bond/swap arranger has been the development of a highly refined sense of timing for the underlying issue. While finding a "window" in the Eurodollar bond market has always been the "sine qua non" for a successful lead manager, with the advent and development of the swap market the focus of the potential lead manager has shifted from an "investor" window to a "spread" window. Given that the long-term swap market operates on a relatively stable spread level versus US Treasuries, and that the Eurodollar bond market is notoriously volatile versus Treasuries for different types of issuers, a similiar premium to that of creativity applies to the lead manager who can locate a "spread window" for a particular type of issuer. This "creativity" and search for a "spread window" has sometimes led to mispriced and/or virtually incomprehensible bond structures (to the bond investor) but more often than not, the bond/swap structures so created have provided value to both the Eurobond investor and issuer.

749

However, it is clear that (below) LIBOR spreads available to issuers declined as the market became more efficient in pricing the relative value of a given swap: at the outset of the market, a "AAA" issuer could reasonably have expected to achieve 75–100 basis points below LIBOR on a bond/swap; as the market developed this same issuer might expect only 25–30 basis points below on a "plain vanilla" bond/swap. The lower spreads available have gone almost entirely to the benefit of the fixed-rate payer; intermediaries (mostly commercial banks) have seen their profit margins reduced by a very substantial degree in the primary market. This reduced profitability and the lower spreads available has led, in turn, for most bond/swap arrangers to attempt to put potential counterparties in direct contact with each other and eliminate the intermediation of a commercial bank. This can be a difficult process due to timing and credit considerations but there is a strong incentive now among all parties concerned to see whether a "direct write" is possible on a new issue.

This structure may, however, solve one problem and create another. For instance, the payment of interest from a resident in the UK for tax purposes may incur withholding tax if the payment is to a non-resident. Such withholding would be avoided if payments were made to a UK bank or to the UK branch of a foreign bank acting as a principal in the swap transaction. There are possible structures to avoid withholding tax if a "direct write" is necessary or desirable if one of the counterparties is a resident of the UK. They would usually require a double taxation agreement between the UK and the other country concerned but, even so, each structure employed would need to be examined on its own merits and should be arranged only with the benefit of the opinion of tax advisers.

Corporate risk management swaps have provided the "retail" base for banks to produce, or lay off, large positions generated by bond issue swaps. From time to time the supply and demand elements caused by pressure from such end users can significantly move swap rates.

3.1.3 The Secondary Market
The secondary market in long term interest rate swaps is a highly opportunistic segment of the market. As interest rates fluctuate, a fixed rate provider or taker may find that a substantial profit can be realised by

"reversing" (with a "mirror" swap) the original swap or cancelling the original swap in return for an up-front cash payment (see Section 4.1). As dollar interest rates have fluctuated widely since the advent of the swap market, secondary market activity in long-term swaps has grown rapidly.

3.2 The Currency Swap Market

The currency swap market is the oldest and most creative sector of the swap market. Recently it has been the fastest growing market. The currency swap market has even greater potential for growth than the dollar swap market, particularly in light of the growth in local/Euro capital markets in a wide range of currencies.

The most important currencies, after the US$, in the swap market are the Swiss Franc, Yen, Deutschemark, ECU, Pound Sterling and Canadian Dollar. The first four currencies have been popular in the swap market due to their relatively low interest rates (versus the Dollar) and the relative ease of access by a wide range of issuers to private and public debt in the "Euro" and domestic markets of these currencies. Many supranational and sovereign borrowers find their access to the debt markets of such currencies constrained (versus their sometimes quite large requirements) and therefore make extremely active and frequent use of the currency swap market. Such entities either lend in these currencies (and are therefore covering/matching assets with liabilities) or are trying to diversify their debt portfolios away from the Dollar and the costs which vagaries of that currency can impose on national budgets.

The currency swap market is still dominated by the Dollar on "one side" of the swap but many "direct" currency combinations are developing rapidly such as the Yen/Swiss Franc, Yen/ECU, Deutschemark/Swiss Franc etc. The other high-interest rate currencies involved in the currency swap market are viewed as speculative vehicles for aggressive debt portfolio managers or companies in the local market which would have to pay dearly for fixed rate debt. This latter phenomenon accounts largely for the active use of "exotic" currency debt markets by prestigious international issuers. This has occurred recently in a number of (formerly closed) capital markets in which the first few Euro-issues are completed at wide divergence to the domestic market rates. The swaps that are thereby made possible have accounted for the presence of many high-powered issuers in the Danish Kroner, French Franc, New Zealand Dollar and Australian Dollar markets – all within the first six months of 1985. The quality image such issuers have given to these markets has gained acceptance for the "new" markets and, hence, fostered their growth.

4.   RISKS ON SWAP TRANSACTIONS

As the volume of swap related transactions has grown to immense proportions – with tens of billions of transactions completed – many central banks, market participants and users have begun to focus on the credit and non-performance risks inherent to swap transactions.

While "credit", per se, is not extended in a swap transaction, the parties involved assume a "settlement" or "counterparty" risk in the event of default by the counterparty. Settlement risk can be quantified at any point in time as the current "value" of the swap contract. This can be assessed as the amount a counterparty would need to pay/be paid to make the values whole if a contract was unwound. At the inception of any swap, the counterparties' exposure is zero – current market rates will remain in effect. The risk attaching to a swap contract is, therefore, the degree of exposure in the future.

Settlement exposure results from the potential default of a counterparty when exchange and/or interest rates have moved away from those applicable to the swap. This potential exposure is a function of:

(a)   the probability that the other counterparty will default on its obligations ("credit risk") and

(b)   the probability and extent that current market rates will move away from contracted rates in the direction that would cause a loss to the remaining counterparty ("market risk").

The risk of loss to a party entering into a swap transaction is, therefore, a conditional probability where two, not necessarily related, events are required to occur.

To assess the exposure on swap transactions, banks use statistical models to determine potential exposure based on past experience and volatility. On the basis of these models, banks determine the acceptability of the counterparty and may accord the counterparty a "credit limit" by translating the potential exposure to a "loan equivalency" according to predetermined weightings.

If a large player in the swaps market, say the World Bank, were to arrange all its swaps through a single, intermediary bank, there would be substantial exposure by each party to the other and this would clearly need to be measured and monitored. By the same token any bank acting as intermediary and/or principal in a substantial swaps portfolio would have considerable contingent liabilities not necessarily revealed in its balance sheet. This factor has, for some time, been attracting the attention of central bank regulators of commercial/investment banks (see Sections 4.2 and 4.3).

4.1 Measuring Currency Exposure or Mark-to-Market Exposure

This is a fairly straightforward process and is done by discounting future cashflows at current interest rates (either fixed or floating). In the case of currency swaps, the cashflows are discounted at current interest rates and current exchange rates.

The sum of these, i.e. the net present value, indicates the current exposure of the swap and may, of course, be positive or negative depending on the direction of exchange and interest rates since the original swap was concluded. Although, for the purpose of aggregating exposure, only swaps which have a positive, current exposure need to be considered, the measure is used either way for the purpose of terminating or "unwinding" swaps. By following the procedures above, two counterparties can agree a front-end amount payable by one party to the other in return for cancelling all future cashflows. This may be useful for reducing credit exposure or, in the case particularly of end users, of realising any (hitherto) theoretical profit made on the swap. (Equally, it may be tax efficient to unwind a swap which has a positive current exposure and realise the "loss" early on).

Most operators in the swap market, mark their books to market on a daily basis and, therefore, it is a relatively simple job to measure individual and overall current exposure on swaps.

4.2 Capital Adequacy Requirements for Swaps

In recent years the Bank for International Settlements (BIS) in Basle, Switzerland has been engaged in an extended exercise to determine new levels of capital adequacy requirements for banking products. A particular focus has been the voluminous off-balance sheet business in which the world's major commercial banks have become heavily engaged, and this focus has centred on the international swap market. Accordingly, the final version of the guidelines issued in July, 1988 contained detailed, new provisions for the treatment of swaps.

The determination of the amount of capital required to be held by a bank against any particular swap transaction is a two-stage process. First the notional principal of the swap is converted to a *Credit Risk Equivalent*, which effectively translates the off-balance sheet transaction into a balance sheet equivalent. Second, the credit risk equivalent is weighted by one of four *risk factors* - 0%, 10%, 20%, 50% - expressing the credit quality of the counterparty to produce a *Risk Weighted Asset*. Eventually the bank will be expected to maintain a capital ratio of 8% to its total Risk Weighted Assets (or any higher ratio chosen by the appropriate regulator).

Determination of the first stage of this process, the credit risk equivalent of a swap, depends upon the type of transaction and its maturity. The following table summarises this process:

Maturity	*Less than 1 Year*	*Over 1 Year*
Type		
Interest Rate Swaps	0.0%	0.5%
Currency Swaps	1.0%	5.0%

These figures represent the multiple which is to be "added-on" to the mark-to-market value of a swap. The purpose of this "add-on" factor is to capture the potential future exposure of a swap transaction due to movements in interest and exchange rates.

The total amount reached by this process is then multiplied by one of the four risk factors, depending upon the nature and credit quality of the counterparty. Briefly summarised the categories are these:

754

0%   Central Governments of OECD countries.

10%   Certain Public Sector entities of OECD countries, provided that they are located in the *same* country as the bank holding the transaction with them.

20%   Banks incorporated in OECD countries, and Public Sector entities located in other OECD countries. Also banks incorporated outside the OECD provided the maturity is less than one year.

50%   All other counterparties, including corporates, non-bank financial institutions and banks incorporated outside the OECD.

4.3   Other Risks to Intermediary Banks

Apart from the commercial risk of one of the counterparties defaulting a bank acting as intermediary assumes additional risks. These are:

(a)   Market Risk
(b)   Sovereign Risk
(c)   Mismatch Risk
(d)   Basis Risk
(e)   Delivery Risk

4.3.1 *Market Risk*

The greater the depth of the market the less this risk is. The swaps market is deeper at the short end and the opportunities of reversing an existing position decrease as the term gets longer. At the same time the longer the maturity so the uncertainty about future interest and exchange rates increases bringing with it potentially greater adverse consequences of a default.

4.3.2 *Sovereign Risk*

(See Chapter 12). This reflects the potential risks of the future availability of a particular currency which may be affected by exchange control regulations, economic performance, political stability etc.

4.3.3 *Mismatch Risk*

Competition to construct swaps means that many banks take a position i.e. they commit to one counterparty before they have another counterparty in place. Additionally, the precise requirements of two counterparties as to timing (both principal and interest) and amounts rarely match exactly. Therefore whether the counterparties are identified simultaneously, or not, mismatch risk invariably occurs. (See Section 3.1.2 for hedging a warehoused swap).

4.3.4 *Basis Risk*
Another element of mismatch. For example if a swap with Counterparty A is written at 10% fixed against three month LIBOR and the related swap which the intermediary bank arranges is $10^1/4\%$ fixed against six month commercial paper there must be an assumed spread between three month LIBOR and six month commercial paper rates. As this spread converges or diverges so the risk would decrease or increase respectively.

4.3.5 *Delivery Risk*
If there is a cross border payment involved, then, as with any such transaction there will be delivery risk i.e. the payment away is made before there is confirmation of safe receipt of the payment in.

5. RECENT DEVELOPMENTS
There have been several variations on the basic plain vanilla interest/currency swap. This has come about due to the sophistication of players in the markets who are willing to apply other financial instruments as well as accepting mismatch-type risks. Nowadays, virtually any type of cashflow can be swapped into any other type of cashflow and this flexibility is frequently needed to match innovative structures in the securities market.

5.1 Amortising Swaps/Zero Coupon Swaps
Amortising swaps (where the notional amount amortises down) and zero coupon swaps (where no interest payments are made until maturity) are both quite feasible but usually require a bank counterparty to run the risk of this type of cashflow against a conventional "bullet" one. These are examples which illustrate the flexibility of swaps. Indeed, almost any structure of cashflows can be swapped.

5.2 Callable, Puttable or Extendable Swaps
Callable, puttable or extendable swaps are all, as the names suggest, swaps where one or other party has the right to terminate the swap before its maturity

date or to extend that date, on terms agreed at the outset. This is another example of an opportunity to arbitrage between retail investors in fixed rate securities and issuers, as the extra yield demanded by investors in securities which have a "call" is frequently less than the fee paid by a swap counterparty for the right to terminate his swap. The premium paid by the swap counterparty goes to subsidise the investor's cost of funds.

5.3 Swaptions

One of the more interesting developments in the derivative markets in recent years has been the cross-over between swaps and options. The swaps referred to in Section 5.2 above involve option theory in their pricing, since all those facilities have embedded *swaptions* in them. Swaptions, or swap options, are what the name suggests, that is an option to buy or sell a swap. Though the pricing of these instruments involves complex mathematical calculations, the principles are quite straightforward. The "buyer" of a swaption pays a premium for the right, but not the obligation, to enter into a swap contract at some time in the future. As indicated earlier in the chapter, the underlying swap contract over which the option is held can be either as a payer or receiver of a fixed rate of interest. The "writer" of the option receives the premium for taking the other side of the underlying swap contract.

Examples where this facility can prove useful are in corporate finance or project finance applications, where the realisation of the project (and hence the need for finance) is uncertain. However, the project remains at risk to rising interest rates or exchange rates over the period of uncertainty. In such situations a swaption guarantees a fixed interest rate should the project proceed, but without the commitment to a swap which might prove expensive to cancel.

5.4 Cross Index, Quanto or Differential Swaps

In the early 1990s there emerged one of the most significant extensions to the swap market. These were Cross Index Swaps, also known as Diff swaps or Quantos. Essentially these swaps involve the ability to convert rights or obligations based on a normal index, for example Sterling loan index to Sterling LIBOR, to a wholly different index, e.g. US Dollar LIBOR, but with all flows remaining in the original currency. Thus, a UK corporate with sterling borrowings could, through transacting a Cross swap, index his sterling payments to US dollar LIBOR.

At a time in early 1992 when Sterling short term rates were at 10% and Dollar rates were at 4%, this was an attractive proposition for many European based companies. Similarly, Dollar based investors in floating rate instruments saw their yields plummet through the early 1990s and sought to boost their yields by indexing the returns to European short-term rates which remained high. Again the significant point to note is that all flows remain in the original currency, thus removing any exchange rate risk from the purchaser of the swap.

Such swaps involve continuous, dynamic hedging on the part of the bank that writes the transaction to resolve the interest and exchange risks being undertaken. This hedging activity is accounted for in the spread over the index which is charged to the purchaser.

The principle behind quantos has been extended to virtually any asset or liability. For example, it is now possible to take returns on a gilt in Yen, or to take a future oil price in French francs, without exposure to the exchange rate.

6. ASSET SWAPS

The use of swaps to convert the nature of a medium term security to a different type of income has given rise to a whole sub-section of the swap market. Although usually involving plain vanilla currency or interest rate swaps the "asset swap" product has taken off more than any other new application of swaps. The term "asset swap" describes the package of bond and swaps together and because the nature of the asset is changed it is also often referred to as a "synthetic security". Although more or less any type of swap can be applied to any type of asset, by far and away the most common type of asset swap is the combination of a fixed rate Dollar eurobond with an interest rate swap to create a synthetic US$ FRN. (See Exhibit 8). Typical investors are commercial banks seeking to replace dwindling conventional loan portfolios with assets which may be even higher yielding. The timing of the rise in the swap market and the fall in the syndicated loan market means that the volume of asset swaps has risen significantly.

Exhibit 8

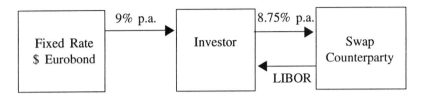

The fixed rate US$ eurobond yields 9% p.a. A $ interest rate swap of matching maturity has a rate of 8.75% p.a. versus US$ LIBOR. By combining the two together the investor has an 'asset swap' with effective yield of LIBOR plus 0.25% p.a.

7. COMPARISON OF YIELDS

It has been explained that one of the attractions of swaps is that both (or all in a three-legged or four-legged, etc., swap) counterparties achieve a lower cost of funding (or a higher rate of return in an asset swap) than would have been possible had the parties gone direct to the appropriate market. However, it is rarely a straight-forward operation to compare one rate with another, one yield with another, or even quotes for swaps from two different banks. There is the need, therefore, invariably to reduce all yields to a common base in order that a valid comparison can be made.

Readers will appreciate that interest can be paid at maturity or on a discounted basis up-front; interest may be compounded and the effect will be different according to whether this is on a monthly, quarterly, half yearly or annual basis; the calculations may be based on a 360 or 365 day year. Most European securities have annual coupons and the yield is, therefore, compounded annually whereas most securities in the USA pay interest semi-annually so the yield is compounded semi-annually. There are, however, four types of yields for fixed interest income investors and lenders:

Annual coupons compounded annually
Annual coupons compounded semi-annually

Semi-annual coupons compounded semi-annually
Semi-annual coupons compounded annually

The following are examples within the differing conventions and instruments extant at the time of writing:

(a) UK securities: On most issues interest is paid semi-annually based on the number of days elapsed divided by a year of 365 days.

(b) Swiss securities: On most issues interest is paid annually based on the number of days elapsed using a 30 day month divided by a year of 360 days.

(c) Yen bond: Interest paid semi-annually with yield to maturity quoted on a non-compounded basis. Interest is accrued on the basis of actual days elapsed in actual months over a 365 day year.

(d) Schuldscheine (Germany): Interest is paid annually and accrued on the basis of actual days elapsed in 30 day months over a year of 360 days.

(e) USA Securities

	Instrument	Interest Pricing	Day Basis
1	US treasury issues	Discount	Actual/360
2	US treasury bonds	Interest	Actual/Actual
3	US treasury notes	Interest	Actual/Actual
4	Federal National Mortgage Assoc. (FNMA) debentures	Interest	30/360
5	General National Mortgage Assoc. (GNMA) bond and participation certificates	Interest	30/360

760

6	Commercial Paper	Discount	Actual/360
7	Corporate Bonds	Interest	30/360

(f) Euro bonds: including US$, DM, Yen and Sterling — Interest normally paid annually and accrued interest calculated on the basis of actual days elapsed in 30 days months divided by a year of 360 days.

(g) Eurodollar FRNs: Interest usually paid quarterly or semi-annually calculated on the basis of actual days elapsed in actual months divided by a year of 360 days.

By way of example the following calculation illustrates the significant difference of quoting under the Euro basis and the US basis in order to achieve the same yield.

(i) Conversion from US to Euro
$$Ya = [(1 + Ys/200)^2 - 1] \times 100$$

(ii) Conversion from Euro to US
$$Ys = [(1 + Ya/100)^{0.5} - 1] \times 200$$

Ya is the annually compounded yield
Ys is the semi-annually compounded yield

Annual Compounding:

If US basis yield = 10.178%
then eq Euro basis yield = 10.437%

Semi-annual Compounding;

If US basis yield = 11.302%
then eq Euro basis yield = 11.621%

Discounted cash flow techniques are used so that comparisons of different yields calculated on different bases can be made. By calculating the Internal Rate of Return decisions can be made as to whether a particular swap will be worthwhile. It is imporant, of course, to understand the basis on which swaps are offered by banks to make sure the calculations have made the same assumptions regarding frequency of interest payment, compounding etc.

8. TAX IMPLICATIONS

It is not possible, within the bounds of this chapter, to go into the detail of the tax considerations of swaps. The tax consequences of many financial arrangements differ from one tax jurisdiction to the next and in many less developed financial centres in which swaps are only infrequently seen at present the tax authority may not have drawn up definitive legislation. There are, therefore, few generalisations that can be made as to the manner in which swaps will be regarded by the tax authorities in the assessment of tax due from a corporate, or individual, counterparty in the annual review. However, there may be the additional complication as to whether or not withholding tax could be payable as and when interest payments are made when such payment is to a non-resident for tax purposes. Furthermore, tax legislation changes frequently making it dangerous for a publication like this book to attempt to summarise current legislation at the time of going to press.

The basic questions often encountered are:

"Do the payments made represent interest?" If they do then they should be tax deductible. However if there is no lending between the two parties does interest accrue?

"Is the foreign exchange premium/discount at maturity when compared to spot or a comparable forward exchange contract regarded as a gain or loss?"

"Is the swap a speculative transaction or is it in the ordinary course of business of the counterparty?"

"Is the swap related to a capital transaction or a short term cash flow?" (In the UK how does the "Pattison v Marine Midland" case affect the situation?).

"Will any tax be at capital gains tax rate or corporation tax rate?"

762

All this can merely serve to emphasise that swaps, as with other financial arrangements, can have significant tax consequences. Any banker constructing or recommending a swap to a client or any company considering a swap must take the necessary professional tax advice in the light of the particular circumstances at the time. It may be prudent for a bank, in the interests of its customers, not to charge fees (which may not be deductible) but rather to wrap up any costs in the overall rates.

9. COUNTERPARTY FAILURE

9.1 Background
Since the last edition of this book the picture has changed dramatically with respect to counterparty failure. In 1989 the swap market experienced its first major series of defaults on swap contracts written with UK Local Authorities. These defaults followed a celebrated legal case, which was taken eventually to the House of Lords, which ruled that under the terms of their incorporating statutes, Local Authorities in England and Wales had no *power* to enter into swap contracts. Therefore such contracts were declared *ultra vires*, or beyond the powers of Local Authorities. For the banks which had entered into swaps with the Local Authorities (on the presumption that they were equivalent to UK government risk), the effect was the same as a counterparty default. The costs ran into millions of pounds, and the legal ramifications still reverberate through the courts.

Since that time there have been other notable defaults (Maxwell Communications, Olympia & York), as global recession took its toll. These have resulted in a series of losses for banks, and thus sharpened the attention both to credit and to market risk on the part of swap risk managers. Also, the events of the last few years have identified a new risk for the swap market: *vires*, or legal risk, being the underlying authority to make valid and binding contracts. This has caused a wide-ranging look at a whole host of counterparties, from US Municipal authorities to UK building societies, as banks seek to satisfy themselves on this issue.

9.2 Interest Rate Swaps
The cost (if any) to the intermediary bank would be that of entering into a new matched position in relation to the remaining non-defaulting party. This will be determined by the interest rate difference between the fixed

rate to which the bank is contractually bound with that remaining counterparty and the fixed rate currently available in the market at the time of the default. Substantially the concern is with the level of the fixed rate of interest for the remaining period of the swap contract as the floating rate will be exposed only for the remaining period of the particular funding base e.g. 6 months LIBOR.

It may be, of course, that a default could work in the bank's favour. If the defaulting party was the payer of fixed rate funds and the "replacement" rate at the time of default is higher than that counterparty's contracted rate the bank will be able to gain by, itself, lending fixed rate funds in the market and receiving a higher fixed rate of interest than it will continue to be obliged to pay to the remaining counterparty. Of course, it will have to borrow at floating rates the funds it will need to lend out at fixed rate but this floating rate cost will be covered by the contractual payments of the non-defaulting counterparty. The bank will, therefore, make a fortuitous turn on the fixed rate transactions.

The corollary to this proposition, however, is that if fixed rates have fallen when the fixed rate payer defaults the bank will incur a loss unless it can find, say, a lower rated (relative to the credit rating of the defaulting party when the swap was set up) counterparty who would be prepared to pay the appropriate fixed rate to match the contracted fixed rate of interest.

If the payer of the floating rate interest defaults the bank would have to borrow at the current fixed rate and lend at LIBOR. Therefore, if fixed rates are lower the bank gets a fortuitous gain but if they have risen it faces a loss unless it, again, can find an appropriately rated replacement counterparty. See Exhibit 9.

9.3 Currency and Interest Rate Swaps

The bank's risk here may be to movements in the particular interest rates of the currencies concerned *plus* the exchange rate between the two currencies as compared with those obtaining under the swap agreement. However, the type of swap determines the degree of exposure. That is to say that a fixed-to-fixed currency swap is exposed to movements in fixed

764

interest rates in both currencies and the exchange rate; fixed-to-floating currency swaps are exposed on the fixed rate currency interest rate and the exchange rate; floating-to-floating currency swaps are exposed only to the exchange rate.

If a counterparty fails the intermediary bank would need either to find a suitable replacement counterparty (which would probably be very difficult to do) or borrow in one of the currencies (that in which it will be receiving interest payments from the non-defaulting counterparty) and deposit in the other currency by converting at spot the borrowed funds. The currency interest then earned will cover the commitments to pay the remaining counterparty. See Exhibit 10.

Exhibit 9

Original interest rate swap structure

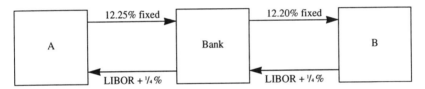

Structure after A defaults

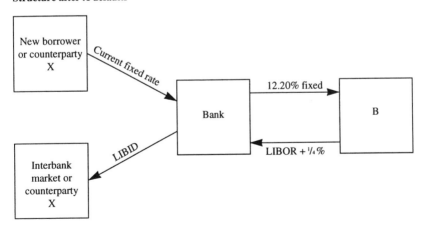

Structure after B defaults

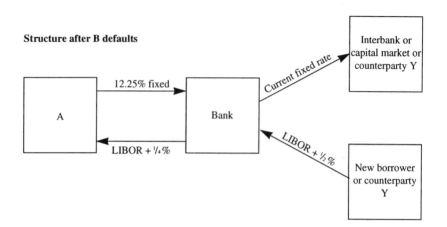

Exhibit 10
Currency and Interest Rate Swap

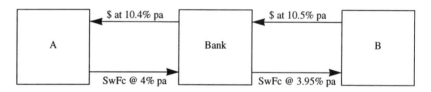

Structure after A defaults

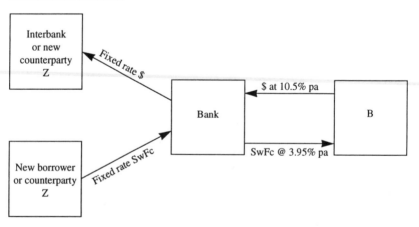

766

10. WHY DO BANKS GET INVOLVED IN SWAPS?

The reasons are many and varied. If a bank is involved in a swap as a principle then it would do so for the same reasons as any other principle as has already been explained e.g. cheaper funds, interest or currency hedging, higher yields, etc.

It would rarely seek to specialise solely as an intermediary as the fee income for this activity, on its own, is relatively low. However, a bank's activities as a bond issuer are enhanced by its swaps capability and it is from the total package of bond plus swap that a worthwhile return may be obtained. An increasing number of banks do make markets in swaps and, with very skilful operators, this activity can be very profitable.

Notwithstanding the variety of rewards in strict monetary terms to banks many will operate in swaps in order to provide a necessary service to their customers. In a sense, therefore, the degree to which a bank regards itself as a relationship bank will influence its philosophy towards swaps activity.

11. BIBLIOGRAPHY

Swap Finance, Vols 1 and 2, edited by Boris Antl, published by Euromoney Publications.
Swap Financing, edited by Satyajit Das, IFR Books, 1989.

CHAPTER 19

Tax-Based Capital Markets Financing Instruments

by
Max Ziff and Brian J Terry

1. INTRODUCTION

A corporate treasurer or finance director faced with the choice of the large number of options available to him in today's complex capital markets, must weigh up the advantages and disadvantages of each particular instrument against that corporate's own parameters.

Some of the most obvious constraints will involve the cost, flexibility and term of a particular structure. However, in today's global markets, an increasingly important consideration is taxation, and not least, the tax implications of different forms of finance.

We discuss below three particular tax-based financial instruments:

1. Deep Discount Securities
2. Coupon Stripping
3. Preference Share Financing.

Each of these instruments has particular appeal to certain categories of borrowers and/or investors.

In the case of deep discount securities the tax-based attractions arise from the fact that the investor obtains a tax deferral benefit which may be shared with the borrower by making the coupon lower than it might otherwise be.

Coupon stripping structures have been used to generate low cost finance by combining a borrowing with a high yielding investment.

Corporates with no corporation tax liability but which, nevertheless, have a borrowing need, may be limited as to the build up of tax losses which would arise if interest (which is a pre-tax deductible) was paid on any borrowing taken. In essence, the raising of funds (i.e. "borrowing") by the issue of preference shares enables the cost of that borrowing (i.e. the "interest") to be paid out of post-tax income (i.e. as a dividend) which has the effect, as will be explained, of reducing the costs of borrowing to the issuing company.

2. DEEP DISCOUNT SECURITIES

2.1 Introduction

The purpose of the first section of this chapter is to investigate the characteristics of deep discount securities. The tax treatment of such securities is of prime interest from both the issuer and investor perspectives. Such treatment differs from country to country, and it is not possible to go into detail here. Instead we shall concentrate on the United Kingdom, where a particular tax advantage is possible.

However the principles of deep discount securities are well established in such jurisdictions as USA, Australia and Germany and the general, but not necessarily particular, taxation concepts explained for the UK will apply elsewhere.

2.2 Background

The UK budget of March 1983 first introduced the tax treatment of deep discount bonds ("DDBs") for UK issuers and investors. In the event, however, the calling of an early General Election in June 1983 resulted in the shortening of the Finance Act, and it was not until the 1984 Finance Act that the legislation was enacted.

2.3 Definition

2.3.1 *Deep Discount Securities*

Schedule 4 of the 1988 Taxes Act defines a deep discount security in its constituent parts as follows:

SECURITY   --   Any redeemable security other than:
                             (A) A share in a company;
                             (B) An inflation index-linked security;
                             (C) A security issued other than for new
                                     consideration.

DISCOUNT   –   Any amount by which the issue price of a redeemable security is less than the amount payable on redemption of that security.

DEEP   –   Where the discount either
(A) represents more than 15% of the redemption value; or
(B) is less than 15% but exceeds $^1/_2$% per annum.

A deep discount security is, therefore, a bond which is issued at a discount to its par value (e.g. issue price £25, par value £100; redemption value £100) for a specified number of years. During the lifetime of the bond either no coupon is paid (a "Zero Coupon Bond") or the coupon is less than the relevant market rate. The element of yield not paid as a coupon is "rolled up" and added to the value of the bond at regular intervals, and in effect, is paid in one lump sum at maturity, together with the original discounted value of the bond when it was issued, so that the investor receives a market-related return for his investment. The effective yield paid to the investor, therefore, compensates him for having to wait for his full return until maturity.

The advantages to borrowers and investors are the different ways in which the timing of such interest paid and received is regarded by the Tax Authorities. This is explained in sub-section 2.4.

2.3.2   Bonds Redeemed at a Fixed Premium
The 1989 UK Finance Act amended the deep discount legislation to include securities redeemed at a known premium in the future. Under this legislation the known premium is taxed in exactly the same way as deep discount and is similarly defined as a premium of more than $^1/_2$% p.a. or 15% overall.

2.3.3   Deep Gain Securities
The 1989 Finance Act introduced special rules for deep gain securities, which it defines as all securities (excluding shares and convertible bonds) which may be redeemed at an unknown future premium. Such securities will receive a most adverse asymmetrical tax treatment in that investors will be taxed as income on a cash received basis, but issuers will receive

771

no tax relief on the redemption premium which will be regarded as capital payment.

2.4   UK Tax Treatment of DDBs

2.4.1   *The Borrower*
Obtains tax relief on any interest coupon paid together with an allowance for the accrual (i.e. the difference each year in the notional uplifted value of the bond – see Section 2.5 below) in the bond for the relevant period.

The relief on the uplift is calculated on an annual accruals basis, unless a coupon is actually paid, in which case the accruals period follows the actual coupon period.

What this means is that although the borrower is not actually paying away cash in respect of interest at the end of each annual interest bearing period, it is able to claim tax allowance as if it had done so by borrowing further amounts at the same original cost and rolling up the principal outstanding.

2.4.2   *The Investor*
The UK investor pays tax on a cash received basis, that is to say either on redemption or sale if earlier.

If held to redemption therefore the entire uplift in the value of the bond is taxed in that year as income.

If sold prior to redemption then the accrued income to that point in time is taxed as income in that year – any difference between actual sale proceeds and the underlying value of the bond being attributable to either a capital gain or loss, as the case may be.

In other words the UK Revenue accepts that, whereas the issuer should be able to claim a tax deduction on the full annual cost of borrowing irrespective of the fact that not all that cost is paid each year in cash, it would be unjust to tax the investor on the income he has not yet received in cash terms, since he does not have the cash to pay the Revenue. Accordingly, the investor is only taxed on the discount when he realises his investment, i.e. on redemption or sale.

2.4.3   *Anti-Avoidance*

Where a DDB is issued by a UK company and held by an associated company (irrespective of residence) there are specific provisions in the legislation to deprive the borrower from obtaining tax relief on an accruals basis. Instead relief is only available on a cash basis to reflect the treatment of the investor and accordingly remove any inherent tax advantage.

Where a DDB is issued by an overseas company and held by a UK associated company, a similar provision applies such that the investing company pays tax on an accruals, not a cash received, basis.

Where the proceeds of an issue are used to invest in "relevant securities" (for these purposes essentially everything except equity, UK corporate bonds, UK government paper or short-term bank paper), then the investor of the DDB is taxed on an accruals basis and not the advantageous cash received basis.

2.4.4   *Investor Risk*

Because the investor pays tax on a cash received basis on all the income earned on the bond to that point in time, he is susceptible to the ruling rate of tax in the year of disposal being higher than that in the intervening period. This is the risk he must offset against the tax deferral benefit enjoyed.

2.5   **The Zero Coupon Bond**

Whereas a DDB is an instrument where the yield to maturity is made up of (i) interest coupons paid, and (ii) the discount, the Zero Coupon Bond ("ZCB") carries no coupon, the entire yield resulting from the discount element.

The cash flow profile of a ZCB is therefore equivalent to a fixed rate instrument with full interest roll-up.

Let us, therefore, examine a bond with a life of ("n"), say 10 years, with an Issue Price ("P") of £38.55 and a Redemption Value ("R") of par £100.

The yield to maturity ("i") can therefore be expressed as:

$$i = [(R/P)^{(1/n)} - 1] \times 100\%$$

Thus,
$$i = [(100/38.55)^{(1/10)} - 1] \times 100\%$$

i.e.
$$i = [2.594^{(1/10)} - 1] \times 100\%$$

$$i = [1.1 - 1] \times 100\%$$

Therefore,
$$i = 10\% \text{ p.a.}$$

This is equivalent to stating that the Internal Rate of Return ("IRR") on the following cash flow profile is equal to 10% p.a. (or using a discount rate of 10%, the Net Present Value ("NPV") = Zero).

TIME	(A) CASH FLOW	(B) 10% DISCOUNT FACTOR	(A×B) NPV OF CASH FLOW
0	(38.55)	1.0000	(38.55)
1	0	0.9091	0
2	0	0.8264	0
3	0	0.7513	0
4	0	0.6830	0
5	0	0.6209	0
6	0	0.5645	0
7	0	0.5132	0
8	0	0.4665	0
9	0	0.4241	0
10	100.00	0.3855	38.55

IRR = 10.00% p.a.   NPV = 0

By taking the issue price of the bond and compounding at 10% on a per annum basis, the accrued value of the bond can be demonstrated thus:

TIME IN YEARS	NOTIONAL UPLIFTED VALUE	ANNUAL ACCRUAL
0	38.55	
1	42.41	3.86
2	46.65	4.24
3	51.32	4.67
4	56.45	5.13
5	62.09	5.64
6	68.30	6.21
7	75.13	6.83
8	82.64	7.51
9	90.91	8.27
10	100.00	9.09

See following graph.

2.6 Advantages of Zero Coupon Bonds

2.6.1 *Reasons for issuing a ZCB:*
• Certainty of cash flow makes budgeting easier;

• Removes interest cost financing exposure (i.e. cost of funding future interest payments);

• Financing projects which do not generate cash in the early years;

• No need to finance interest payments in stages.

2.6.2 *Reasons for investing in a ZCB:*
• Certainty of future investment value if held to maturity;

• Avoids withholding tax timing differences (on domestic sterling instruments basic rate tax is deducted before payment to investors);

• Provides greater price volatility for the speculator by virtue of the implicit gearing in a ZCB;

• Longer average life and duration of investment;

ZERO COUPON BOND

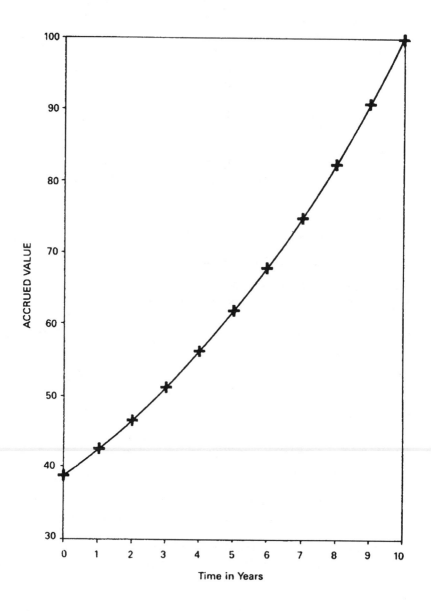

- Tax deferral benefit (available to UK investors and, usually, others);

- Removes re-investment risk associated with conventional bonds.

The rationale for issuing or investing in a DDB as opposed to a ZCB are similar but will hinge on the particular cash flow profile which a DDB affords, which may be more appropriate for different parties than the extreme cash flow profile of a ZCB.

2.7 Stepped Deep Discount Bonds
One variation of a DDB used by Safeway UK Limited is the Stepped Bond. The characteristic of this instrument is an initially low coupon which is increased periodically (every 5 years in the case of the Safeway bond) throughout its lifetime.

Such a structure can be particularly attractive for funding property where initial rental yields are low but subject, to say, 5 yearly rent reviews. These instruments, however, are not popular with investors since for technical tax reasons they cannot be traded other than on interest payment dates.

2.8 Issuance to Date
In reality there have been remarkably few public issues since investors have been reluctant to pass on any tax deferral benefit to issuers in view of the tax rate risk they are running. Instead, it has been common practice for banks to structure such transactions on a private basis where risks and rewards can be shared on a negotiated basis between the parties involved.

3. COUPON STRIPPING

3.1 Introduction
Tax paying companies in the UK have seen a removal of a significant number of the classical ways they have had to shelter their profits from tax such as capital allowances and stock relief, and recent years have seen a resurgence of the quest for financial structures which result in an effective tax deduction not only for interest payments made, but also for capital repayments. Perhaps one of the most successful of these structures has been the Coupon Strip which, as with all clever tax structures, is sure to have a limited life.

3.2 Structure

There are a number of variations on a theme, but the basic idea is that a tax paying UK company issues, say, a £100 million 25 year bond paying interest annually in arrears at a market rate of interest of, say, 10%.

The bond is issued in bearer form and listed on a recognised stock exchange (which would typically be Luxembourg), and soon after issue the bank initially purchasing the bond would strip off, say, the first 10 years' worth of interest coupons.

The bank would sell these coupons for £61.45 million to a syndicate of banks (being the present value of the coupon stream over a 10 year period assuming a rate of interest of 10% throughout the 10 year interest rate horizon) which would simply regard the annual interest coupons as they are received as part interest and part capital repayment of the £61.45 million principal amount advanced.

The bank would then sell the bond (less the first ten years' coupons) back to a UK subsidiary of the issuing company for, say, £40.55 million.

The bank would therefore have made an up front profit on the trade of £2 million, the £100 million used to purchase the bonds as against the £61.45 million sale proceeds of the coupons and £40.55 million resale of the bond to a subsidiary of the company.

3.3 Tax Effect of the Structure

The issuing company will receive a tax deduction in full on the £10 million interest coupon payments made each year through until maturity of the bonds after 25 years.

The subsidiary company will pay tax in full on the coupons received from the issuing company from years 11 through to 25. This tax charge will exactly match the interest deductions by the issuing company during this period.

The subsidiary company has paid £40.55 million for the bonds but receives redemption proceeds of £100 million nominal amount of the bonds in full at maturity after 25 years. This gain of £59.45 million is not taxable under current law since the gain is made on a Qualifying Corporate Bond (QCB) which is specifically exempt from tax under Section 115 of the Taxes Act 1988.

778

3.4 Group Cash Flow Analysis

A cash flow for the issuer's group is shown below assuming a tax rate of 33% and no tax delay built in (in the UK this is usually 9 months after a company's year end).

Year	Bond Principal	Bond Interest Paid	Tax Relief	Subsidiary Bond Purchase	Bond Interest Received	Tax Charge	Total Cash Flow
0	100.00			(40.55)			59.45
1		(10.00)	3.30				(6.70)
2		(10.00)	3.30				(6.70)
3		(10.00)	3.30				(6.70)
4		(10.00)	3.30				(6.70)
5		(10.00)	3.30				(6.70)
6		(10.00)	3.30				(6.70)
7		(10.00)	3.30				(6.70)
8		(10.00)	3.30				(6.70)
9		(10.00)	3.30				(6.70)
10		(10.00)	3.30				(6.70)
11		(10.00)	3.30		10.00	(3.30)	0.00
12		(10.00)	3.30		10.00	(3.30)	0.00
13		(10.00)	3.30		10.00	(3.30)	0.00
14		(10.00)	3.30		10.00	(3.30)	0.00
15		(10.00)	3.30		10.00	(3.30)	0.00
16		(10.00)	3.30		10.00	(3.30)	0.00
17		(10.00)	3.30		10.00	(3.30)	0.00
18		(10.00)	3.30		10.00	(3.30)	0.00
19		(10.00)	3.30		10.00	(3.30)	0.00
20		(10.00)	3.30		10.00	(3.30)	0.00
21		(10.00)	3.30		10.00	(3.30)	0.00
22		(10.00)	3.30		10.00	(3.30)	0.00
23		(10.00)	3.30		10.00	(3.30)	0.00
24		(10.00)	3.30		10.00	(3.30)	0.00
25	(100.00)	(10.00)	3.30	100.00	10.00	(3.30)	0.00
						IRR	**2.24%**

3.5 Conclusion

The net after tax cost of funds of the exercise to the issuer's group can thus be seen to be 2.24% as compared to 6.7% for conventional debt.

It should be appreciated that the above represents an oversimplification of the structure to illustrate the mechanism used, and many banks have their own proprietary variations of the product.

4. PREFERENCE SHARE FINANCING

4.1 Introduction

This section is devoted to corporate financing by way of the issue of preference shares.

Preference shares are a specific class of equity share capital on which the stockholder is entitled to capital repayment and a dividend in priority to shareholders of ordinary share capital, but ranking behind both secured and unsecured creditors.

The tax treatment of such securities, as with deep discount bonds, is of prime interest from both the issuer and investor perspectives.

However, there is no universal system of tax treatment and it is necessary to outline that which obtains in the United Kingdom in order to explain the principles involved. Similar schemes do, however, operate in Canada, Australia and, to a certain extent, in the USA.

4.2 Redemption

Preference shares can be irredeemable or specifically classified as redeemable on or after a specific date.

If issued by a UK resident limited company, redemption can only be effected out of either :

(i)   A new issue of shares; or

(ii)   Effecting a transfer from distributable to non-distributable reserves equal to redemption value of the stock.

This requirement is referred to as "The Capital Maintenance" concept for obvious reasons.

4.3 Dividends and Tax

The financing cost of a preference share issue is represented by a fixed rate dividend payment.

As with all dividends, dividends on preference shares can be paid only out of distributable profits, and are paid in the form of a distribution, on which Advance Corporation Tax ("ACT") is payable.

Such ACT is offsetable against the Mainstream Corporation Tax ("MCT") liability of the issuer. The post-tax cost of such finance is, therefore, dependent on the issuer's tax rate.

The dividend in the hands of the UK corporate investor is regarded as Franked Investment Income ("FII"), i.e. that on which ACT has already been paid. For the corporate investor this income suffers no further charge to tax and indeed the tax credit received can be used to frank the investor's own dividends. For the private investor the dividend is deemed to be received net of basic rate tax. If the individual pays tax at higher rates, then a further liability to tax is due in respect of that higher rate. For the institutional investor, if it is a gross fund (non tax-payer), then the tax credit can be reclaimed; if it is a net fund (tax-payer) then the treatment is the same as for a corporate.

4.4 Example
Take a company with the following financial position:

– Profit before interest & tax		£110 million
– Total borrowings		£600 million
– Shareholders' funds		£1,000 million
– Borrowing cost		10% p.a.
– Advance Corporation Tax (ACT)		$^{20}/_{80}$ of the net dividend
– Corporation Tax		33%
– Ordinary dividends paid	Gross	£20.0 million
	ACT	£4.0 million
	Net	£16.0 million

Assume now that preference share finance is available at the following rates:

	Gross	9.00%
	ACT	1.80%
	Net	7.20%

Let us now compare the position of the borrower if it either finances itself with pure debt of £600 million or alternatively with £400 million of debt and £200 million of preference shares.

		All debt finance		Debt plus preference shares	
		£m	£m	£m	£m
PBIT			110.0		110.0
Interest			(60.0)		(40.0)
Pre-tax Profit			50.0		70.0

Tax:	ACT on Ords	(4.0)		(4.0)	
	ACT on Prefs			(3.6)	
	Mainstream tax	(12.5)		(15.5)	
(Total = 33% on £50/£70 million)			(16.5)		(23.1)
	Distributable Profit		33.5		46.9

Dividends:	Ordinary shares	(16.0)		(16.0)	
	Preference shares	0.0	(16.0)	(14.4)	(30.4)
	Retained profit		17.5		16.5

Key Ratios

Gearing 1
(Debt/Shareholders' funds)   600/1,000 = 60%   400/1,000 = 40%

Gearing 2
(Debt/Shareholders' funds including non-equity capital)   600/1,000 = 60%   400/1,200 = 33¹/₃%

Gearing 3
(Debt including non-equity capital/ Shareholders' funds)   600/1,000 = 60%   600/1,000 = 60%

Interest Cover
(PBIT/Interest)   110/60 = 1.83x   110/40 = 2.75x

Fixed Charge Cover
(PBIT/Interest and pref divis)   110/60 = 1.83x   110/54.4 = 2.02x

Marginal Cost of Debt
(Post tax)   6.70% p.a.   6.70% p.a.

Marginal Cost of Prefs
(Post tax)   —   7.20% p.a.

Therefore, for the tax paying borrower, the cost of preference share finance is more expensive than conventional debt but it may be seen as having a more advantageous visual impact on the company's financial statements.

Let us now look at a company in an overall loss position, say with PBIT of only £40 million, which becomes an overall loss after deducting interest charges.

		All debt finance		Debt plus preference shares	
		£m	£m	£m	£m
PBIT			40.0		40.0
Interest			(60.0)		(40.0)
Pre-tax Profit			(20.0)		0.0
Tax:	ACT on Ords	(4.0)	——	(4.0)	——
	ACT on Prefs	0.0		(3.6)	
	Mainstream tax	0.0		0.0	
(Total = 33% on £50/£70 million)			(4.0)		(7.6)
	Distributable Profit		(24.0)		(7.6)
Dividends:	Ordinary shares	(16.0)	——	(16.0)	——
	Preference shares	0.0	(16.0)	(14.4)	(30.4)
	Retained Profit (Loss)		(40.0)		(38.0)

Key Ratios

Gearing 1
(Debt/Shareholders' funds) $\qquad$ 600/1,000 = 60% 400/1,000 = 40%

Gearing 2
(Debt/Shareholders' funds including non-equity capital) $\qquad$ 600/1,000 = 60% 400/1,200 = 33$^1/_3$%

Gearing 3
(Debt including non-equity capital/Shareholders' funds) $\qquad$ 600/1,000 = 60% 600/1,000 = 60%

Interest Cover
(PBIT/Interest) $40/60 = 0.67x$ $40/40 = 1.00x$

Fixed Charge Cover
(PBIT/Interest and pref divis) $40/60 = 0.67x$ $40/58 = 0.69x$

Marginal Cost of Debt   10.00% p.a.   10.00% p.a.
(Post tax)

Marginal Cost of Prefs
(Post tax)   —   9.00% p.a.

For the non-tax paying corporate the financial ratios are similarly improved as for a tax-payer, but there is an additional funding cost improvement since the gross cost of the preference share is less than the gross cost of conventional debt, and there is no benefit to be derived from offsetting the interest cost against taxable profits, since at the margin there are none.

But why should the investor be prepared to accept a lower gross return for preference shares than for conventional interest bearing debt? If we ignore the effects of quality of security, the answer is simple.

A corporate investor pays tax on interest income at 33%, but on preference dividends, received as franked investment income, he suffers no further tax other than the ACT deducted by the issuer at a rate of 20% on the gross dividend (equal to 25% of the net dividend).

	INTEREST	PREFERENCE DIVIDEND	INTEREST
GROSS RETURN	10.00%	9.00%	10.75%
TAX – CORPORATION @33%	-3.30%		-3.55%
– ACT @ 20%		-1.80%	
POST TAX RETURN	6.70%p.a.	7.20%p.a.	7.20%p.a.

It can clearly be seen above that a gross interest receipt of 10% provides a lower post-tax return than a preference share dividend of

9.00%, and indeed a gross interest coupon of 10.75% would need to be achieved to ensure the same post-tax return of 7.20%.

5 SUMMARY

Preference share finance has been a popular form of finance for many borrowers. For the non tax-payer it may produce cheaper cost of funds than conventional debt whereas for a full taxpaying corporate it may be marginally more expensive.

The key advantages of preference shares for borrowers are that they improve gearing, interest cover and the reported Net Tangible Assets of the company.

For the reasons illustrated above, if the investment is made by a corporate entity then there is a benefit by virtue of the dividend being treated as franked income and not suffering the full rate of corporate tax. This enables both borrower and lender to benefit from the use of the preference share mechanism.

CHAPTER 20

Investors and Investing

by
David P. Hager

1. INTRODUCTION

Investors have a very wide variety of assets from which they can choose when making up their investment portfolios. They need to establish which types and which individual securities will best match their needs, and in order to establish this, each investor needs to set out his objectives, ascertain the types and levels of risk which he can take and ensure that his investment policy is compatible with his liabilities.

There are many different types and sizes of investor and the importance of each will depend on the country or market considered. These range from the private individual to companies with surplus funds, from insurance companies to pension funds, and from central governments and institutions such as the World Bank or International Monetary Fund to investment vehicles such as mutual funds and investment trusts. In the UK it is the pension and insurance companies which are the major force in the equity and bond markets but it is the major borrower in the fixed interest market (the British Government) which is the main influence on the bond market through its ability to adjust interest rates. In Germany the commercial banks have a dominant position whilst in the USA and Japan, the private investor is a major player in the equity markets.

2. THE LIABILITIES

The starting point for formulating investment objectives is the liability profile of each type of investor. It is important to understand how the liabilities of each type of investor will move, both in relation to certain market and economic criteria, and also to non investment events.

For example, a pension fund tends to have liabilities which are related to the salaries received by the members, and usually has, at least for the foreseeable future, an excess of income over outgo. The liabilities are, therefore, likely to grow at a rate in excess of price inflation and there is virtually no need for immediate cash, or indeed marketability of investments. In this case, an investment policy can be tailored towards longer term investments likely to produce growth of income and capital. Conversely, an insurance company writing general business will have claims from a whole variety of sources over a time period of years. An insurance company needs to have adequate reserves available to meet claims expected in the very near future, but also needs to invest to enable it to pay claims which may only be settled several years hence and which will depend on values in the year of settlement. In this situation, the investment policy is likely to be orientated towards a high degree of short term marketable investments often denominated in monetary terms, with much lower levels of long term investment than in the pension fund case. Some investors, such as corporates, may have no particular liabilities as such, but are likely to have specified cash requirements at some stage in the future. For each class of investor it is, therefore, possible to determine the anticipated cash flow pattern in the future, and the extent to which it is related either to monetary values or to real values.

A study of the liabilities will enable the compilation of the least risk investment portfolio. This is the portfolio which would, by using where possible Government guaranteed investments, provide either by income or by capital redemption the anticipated cash flow requirements of the liabilities. This least risk investment profile will only be adopted in cases where an organisation has no reserves of any sort, and investment in this way should produce much lower rates of return than would be available elsewhere, since additional risk over this least risk portfolio should be rewarded by additional return.

3. PORTFOLIO OBJECTIVES

Each investor can decide how much return he wishes to try to achieve from his portfolio, and how much departure from the least risk investment portfolio he can afford to take in order to try to generate any additional return required. Risk can have many definitions, and one of these is related to the liabilities, and measures the chance of not meeting the minimum required return due to a departure from the least risk portfolio.

The objectives can either be complex, quantitative measures or simple qualitative statements, but whatever their form, the investor should clearly know precisely what he is trying to do. For example, an investor in UK shares may set his objectives as the achievement of a rate of return 3% per annum above the FT–Actuaries All Share Index with a probability of 70%. Alternatively, the objective may be stated quite simply as an average rate of return without any severe fluctuations in asset value or too great a dependence on the fortunes of a single investment. For a pension fund or unit trust investor in the UK, it is possible for that investor to measure how other pension funds and unit trusts are performing and hence decide whether his performance is close to average or not. For many classes of investor, the actual performance of others in the same category is unknown and hence the nature of the objective will, to some extent, depend on the general performance measures available. The objectives should not only encompass the anticipated rates of return, but the division of return between capital appreciation and income (if appropriate), the flexibility of the investment policy to meet changing conditions, the level of risk, the taxation environment and a level of overseas investments.

A useful acronym, SYSTEM T, conveniently summarises the main considerations of portfolio construction and security selection:
Security
Yield
Spread
Term
Exchange Risk
Marketability
Tax

3.1 Security
Security can have a number of different meanings, but usually means the preservation of capital in either monetary or real terms over a particular period.

789

Some investors will require almost total security of capital in monetary terms. Such an asset is a short term security issued by the government of a particular country, such as a Treasury bill in the US or a short dated gilt edged security in the UK. A buyer of this type of asset could be a bank which needs to avoid capital changes as its deposits can be repayable at short notice. Other investors, such as private individuals with spare resources or pension funds, can accept the prospect of a very high rate of return, accompanied by the possible loss of the total investment if circumstances were unfavourable on at least part of their portfolio. Capital invested into small fast growing companies, possibly developing new products, falls within this category. Each investor will need to define his level of security and even if he does not do this consciously, the type of investment chosen will reflect this level of security.

3.2 Yield
Yield is used to define the return and this can be in any combination of capital gain or income. Some investors do not mind whether the rate of return is in the form of income or as capital, whilst for others the difference is critical. Returns can either be certain and clearly defined, as on a cash deposit with a bank of high standing, or unknown but estimated, as in the case of an equity or property investment. The rate of return which will be targeted for the overall portfolio will, as mentioned in Section 2, depend on the extent to which the fund can depart from the least risk investment structure.

Investors need to take particular care to ensure that a fair and valid comparison is being made between the yields which are quoted on various types of investment. In the UK yields are quoted using a 365 day year whilst for some non-UK assets a 360 day year (assuming 30 days in each month) is used. A 9% coupon on a bond is worth more if the coupon is paid 4.5% each six months than if it is paid as 9% once a year. Gilt edged redemption yields are quoted as semi-annual rates, so if it is shown as 9.6%, it means an equivalent rate of 4.8% per half year. Hence it is necessary to move these rates onto a similar basis and usually the *equivalent annual rate* is chosen.

Using the 9.6% semi-annual rate above, this is 4.8% per half year.

Hence £100 invested at 4.8% for two half years would become:

£100 x 1.048 x 1.048 = £109.83

i.e. *the equivalent annual rate* is 9.83% p.a.

If a UK investor lends money on an overnight basis for a year and the interest rate is constant throughout that year at 9% the rate per night is:

$$\frac{9\%}{365} = 0.024657\%$$

The interest is paid each day, therefore, the *equivalent annual rate* is:

1.00024657 multiplied by itself 365 times
i.e. 1.0942 or 9.42% p.a.

If an investor buys equities, he needs to ascertain the overall yield (y) taking not only the income received into account but also the capital appreciation or depreciation.

Example

At the beginning of year price of equity	=	100
At the end of year price of equity	=	90
Dividend, gross of tax, paid at year end	=	3

The gross rate of return (i.e. ignoring tax) would be:
100 (1 + y) = 90 + 3
Therefore y = −7%

In practice the calculation would be more complex to take account of taxation and also the payment of dividends through the year. A calculation of this type does not differentiate between capital and income and assumes that it is the combination of the two that comprises the overall return.

Other common terminology includes:

(a)   Current yield; also known as income yield, flat yield or running
      yield.

      This is a simple method of calculating the return of an
      investment but it does not take into account the profit on
      redemption nor does it compound interest payments due during
      the life of the loan. It is calculated as follows:

$$\frac{\text{Coupon rate}}{\text{Market price}} \times 100\%$$

(b)   Redemption yield; also known as yield to maturity or
      bond equivalent yield.

      It is used to calculate the return on bonds with a fixed redemption
      date and which carry a coupon rate of interest.

      It takes account of the interest payments that are receivable from the
      date of calculation to maturity. In essence it gives the internal rate of
      return of an investment based on the current market price, the price at
      which it will be redeemed, the number of years to redemption and the
      income (or interest) payments between the time of purchase and
      redemption. The calculation involves an iterative process to solve the
      equation of r, which is the internal rate of return or yield to maturity.
      The general equation is:

$$P = \sum_{j=1}^{mn} \left[\frac{1/m}{\left(1 + \frac{r^i}{m}\right)} \right] + \frac{S}{\left[1 + \frac{r}{m}\right]^{mn}}$$

Where   P   = price of security at purchase
        m   = number of interest payments per annum
        n   = number of years to maturity
        S   = the par value or value at maturity
        i   = interest payment amount per annum
        r   = internal rate of return or yield to maturity p.a.

(c)   Yield to average life.

This is the same as yield to maturity except the average life term is substituted in the number of periods to redemption.

(d)   The money market equivalent yield (MMY).

Recalculates the discount rate to make it equivalent to a simple interest rate on an interest-bearing instrument. This computation is necessary because discount rates understate the equivalent simple interest rate. The reason is that discount rates are based on maturity value, while interest rates are based on purchase price.

$$MMY = \frac{D}{PP} \times \frac{360}{DM}$$

Where   D   = Dollar discount
        PP   = Purchase price
        DM   = Days-to-maturity

(e)   Yield curve.

A graphic illustration of the relationship between yield and maturity. In normal market conditions, yields should increase as maturity lengthens to compensate the lender for the loss of the use of his money for longer periods. In tight monetary conditions yields on short term securities may be higher than on securities of longer maturity. This produces a downward sloping yield curve known as a reverse or inverse yield curve.

3.3   Spread

One of the fundamental principles of investment is to avoid the vulnerability to a single event. This is because events cannot always be predicted and the unexpected can easily happen! An investor needs to work out his vulnerability to the fortunes of a single company, an industry, an economy, to an acceleration in inflation, etc. Whilst a portfolio can be protected from too much vulnerability to a single event, it is worth remembering that this, in turn, means that in the event of a favourable out turn of a single situation, the impact on the portfolio will also be restricted. This

793

fact limits the extent to which each type of investor finds diversification acceptable and necessary.

3.4 Term

This factor will, to some extent, have regard to the expected cash flow requirements of the investor. For example, if an investor invests in assets where the cash flow from those investments is after the dates on which he requires the cash, he faces the problem that investment conditions may not be good at the time he wishes to sell the investments in order to provide the required cash flows. Alternatively, if the cash flows from the investments occur before they are required, they will need to be invested – even on a temporary basis – at uncertain rates of return. There is, therefore, a need to assess the extent to which the investments should be mismatched to the liabilities by term.

3.5 Exchange Risk

An investor with his liabilities denominated in a single currency will incur an exchange rate risk if he invests in assets of another country. This introduces an additional fluctuation in prices of the overseas assets held, due to exchange rate volatility, above the usual fluctuations from interest rates, company profit expectations, and other economic factors. Each investor will need to assess the level of overseas investment which he can tolerate. In addition, the prices of securities in overseas stock markets and bond markets, are not necessarily correlated with those of the base currency. Where this is the case, the volatility of the portfolio in the base currency may actually be reduced by diversification overseas. Where reliance is made on this reduced volatility by these means, it is necessary to check that the factors resulting in a low correlation in market movements between each overseas country and the base country continues.

3.6 Marketability

Marketability is a name for the ability to sell an asset for cash and the time and complexity involved in making that change. Good marketability may strictly not be necessary for an investor who has no immediate cash flow requirements and where income flows are greater than outgo. However, marketability is very useful if investors wish to change their mind at any time; perhaps when they assess the possibility of a change in the relative pricing of various security markets. A high level of marketability allows the investor the possibility of making changes in his overall asset allocation, but marketability has a price, and one would expect that, all other things being equal, more marketable assets are more expensive to acquire than less marketable assets. The investor needs to ascertain whether the benefits of marketability are worth the price charged.

3.7 Tax

Even if an investor does not pay tax, he is not able to ignore tax considerations when making portfolio investments. This is because other types of investor, who may be investing in the same types of security, do suffer tax, and also because there are often different rates of tax on income, foreign income, and capital profits (or offsets for losses). The prices of various types of asset are distorted by the taxation positions of investors and their preferences for capital or income. This means that it may be cheaper for an investor to purchase a stream of income than to obtain the same expected level of return via capital appreciation. Investors also need to take into account the possibility of payments of withholding tax on certain overseas investments since this tax often cannot be reclaimed. This tax is levied on income payable to investors who are not resident for tax purposes in the same country as that from which the dividend or interest is paid, but certain types of asset do not suffer this tax. Investors need to assess returns after the level of tax which they actually pay, and generally not by reference to gross yields (i.e. yields assuming 0% tax).

3.8 Other Factors

There are many other factors which can be taken into account when making up a portfolio. Legislation or central bank requirements may require certain levels in particular asset classes which would not otherwise have been held as a result of considerations explained above. Political considerations such as the Government attitude to investors holding certain classes of asset can be important, but this can extend to the attitude of shareholders, or customers of the investor in contentious areas.

Competition can have important consequences on investment policy. The ability of an insurance company managed fund to attract new business is usually linked to its recent performance. Hence, the fund usually has an incentive to go for a high risk/high return policy when it commences. If the return is high new business will come, but if it is not then the high risks which have been run will have only affected a few initial investors. This shows how an investor can act in a way where competition is the prime force behind investment policy, whereas logic may have otherwise suggested a much lower risk policy with greater diversification. Accounting requirements can also be important in formulating investment policy. In the USA, the returns on pension fund portfolios have to be reflected in the sponsoring company's accounts with greater linkage than in most other countries. This means that the accounting treatment for the sponsoring company has a very important influence on the way in which the pension fund is invested.

The size of the investor's assets may mean that he has to spread his investments over a much wider variety of categories than he may wish because the size of the market and level of turnover in each category is too small in comparison with his own size.

The prejudice of the individual investor or his employer can also be a material factor in investment selection.

4. RISK

In Section 3 risk was defined relative to the least risk investment portfolio, and was effectively the chance of not meeting the minimum required return from a departure from the least risk portfolio. Risk was also discussed in the context of vulnerability to a single event (Section 3.3) and in relation to currency (Section 3.5). There are many other sorts of risk which need to be taken into account by the investor in addition to the types already discussed.

4.1 Volatility

In the USA it is common to refer to risk as meaning the level of volatility in market price of an asset, and a large volume of statistical techniques based on this meaning are in use there. The concept is that for the same level of overall return from capital and income combined, an investor will prefer the asset whose price is less volatile. Hence return can be traded off against volatility. Concern about volatility will vary from investor to investor. For example, a bank will require a high value of stability in the capital values of its assets as it often has a high level of deposits with it which are repayable at short notice. The bank cannot usually afford

796

substantial movements in prices whereas a pension fund with no immediate cash flow considerations does not need to worry unduly about price volatility as it does not need to realise assets to pay benefits, and can even benefit from volatility by investing its new money at times of temporary depression of market prices.

4.2 Default Risk

Default may occur both on income payments or on the capital redemption of a security. The risk is controlled by diversification of borrower and by careful assessment of the credit rating of the borrower, taking into account the extent to which the credit rating is allowed for in the price of the security.

4.3 Income Risk

Dividend/interest payments may not be at the level anticipated, and furthermore investment conditions at the time of re-investment of the dividend/interest may not be as allowed for.

4.4 Capital Risk

Market conditions may alter so that if an unanticipated cash payment is needed, assets may have to be sold at unfavourable prices.

4.5 Inflation Risk

An asset may maintain its value in nominal or monetary terms but effectively depreciate in real terms due to the impact of inflation on monetary values. This is particularly important where the liabilities are expressed in real terms.

The sophisticated investor using mathematical techniques may try to construct probability distributions of possible outcomes expressed in financial terms and ascertain the present value of each investment by discounting the expected values of all the distributions over the life of the investment. Most investors would not go to this level of calculation – indeed some would argue that it would give a spurious level of accuracy – but they still need to allow for the risks which are important to them in a way which gives as much weight as possible to the maximisation of returns whilst not prejudicing the payment of the cash flows as they are required. Whenever investors look at the price of any asset, they need to ascertain whether the price, allowing for their own tax position, takes into account the risks which are important to them. Is there enough allowance in the price for the level of marketability, risk of default of the borrower, options within the investment either to the advantage or disadvantage of the investor, currency or issue etc?

4.6 Control of Risk

Some types of risk can be controlled by the investor and this can involve an alteration of the level of return which is achieved. For example, if an investor purchases a security, the market value rises if the price increases but the market value falls if the converse occurs. If the investor is concerned at the possibility of a short term market value fall, he can, instead of buying the security, leave most of his cash on deposit and purchase a call option on this security. If the price falls the investor's loss is limited to the amount of the option premium, but if it rises the investor will participate in at least some of the rise. The profit made from a particular price rise may differ if the security is held directly than if the cash plus option route is used. This is one example of the use of options to alter the investor's risk exposure, but other strategies using, for instance, financial futures or forward foreign exchange contracts, can also bring a change in the investor's risk/return profile.

These strategies of hedging the risks in a portfolio using financial derivatives and forward foreign exchange contracts have become increasingly common in recent years. An investor with income or capital denominated in an overseas currency may take out a currency option or a forward foreign exchange contract to reduce or eliminate the effects of currency movements on the sterling value of these items for a defined timescale.

If an investor knows that he will receive a large sum in say a month's time which will need to be invested in equities, he may prefer to take out a financial futures contract now and when he receives the actual cash, he will sell the futures and purchase physical equities. This type of transaction has the effect of allowing the investor to gain the financial effect of investing in equities now, even though he does not have the necessary cash available. The investor will, however, still need to have some assets available now to back up this commitment (called a margin payment), but this is usually only a small percentage of the overall value of the futures contract. A similar overall effect could have been achieved by the purchase of a call option instead of the future. This would have also prevented the investor from losing more than the amount of the option premium if equity prices fell before the cash was invested, but this extra protection also involves additional cost.

Selling a portfolio of UK shares can be similarly accomplished by selling the equity future now equivalent in value to the total portfolio to gain the benefit of today's prices, and then as the individual equities in the portfolio are sold, the original futures position is progressively reversed. Options can also be used to produce fairly similar overall results.

Financial derivatives do allow investors to have exposure to markets of a greater value than the assets which they hold. Therefore, investors can introduce gearing into their portfolios, and hence the risk level can be increased substantially if they so wish. Increased levels of risk may bring higher returns but particular care is needed to avoid savage reductions in portfolio value should adverse conditions arise. As risks are increased, portfolio controls need to be even greater than in normal conditions.

5. PORTFOLIO MANAGEMENT

Once the objectives and risk tolerances have been defined, the investment manager will invest the assets. There are two main types of techniques for constructing portfolios, and these are the "top-down" approach or the "bottom-up" method. The former method is much more popular than the latter, reflecting the much larger number of investors which can use only this method.

Both these methods rely on the evaluation of the values of individual assets based on the anticipated trends for future corporate or economic criteria. Some investors supplement or replace this fundamental type of research with technical analysis which attempts to ascertain future price movements from an investigation into past price patterns.

5.1 The "Top-down" Method

After a thorough appraisal of economic expectations and their impact on various investment media, the manager first decides on the broad areas of investment. The areas for consideration would vary according to the type of investor, but could be domestic equities, overseas equities, property, domestic fixed interest securities, overseas bonds, cash or near cash and index linked bonds. Once the percentage allocation to each broad area has been made, each area is then broken down into further smaller divisions. For example, domestic fixed interest securities for a UK based investor may be divided into gilts, corporate debentures and loans stocks, stocks denominated in Sterling but where the borrower is an overseas government or quasi-government body ("bulldogs"), local authority stocks and others.

Further subdivisions into length to maturity may occur so that, for example, Government fixed interest securities may be placed on 0–5 years, 5–10 years, 10–15 years and over 15 years to maturity categories. Only when the portfolio is split into a number of divisions and the overall characteristics of each are set out is consideration given to individual securities.

The method is particularly suitable for portfolios where it is important to have the portfolio defined by overall characteristics (perhaps because of regulatory requirements) and for security classes where there are not large disparities between the price movements of different securities. The method may be less applicable in areas where security selection can be expected to have a dominant role and where sectors are not homogeneous. Even in situations where investment is undertaken in sectors which are not homogeneous, many institutional fund management organisations still prefer to use the "top-down" method. This is because it enables them to manage portfolios for different clients in a similar way with a common "house" policy for all funds. This structured approach to portfolio management brings a high level of control and the impact of the contribution of any single individual on the performance of a fund is limited.

5.2 The "Bottom-up" Method
This approach says that it is the selection of individual securities that is the most important facet of portfolio construction. The proportions in each sector or type of asset are determined as a by-product rather than as a key decision in the "top-down" approach. This method of portfolio construction is more likely to be appropriate where there are likely to be substantial divergencies of performance between various securities and where the liability profile of the fund does not require specific amounts in particular

800

sectors. This method is likely to find favour with certain types of equity manager where particular emphasis is placed on the added value to be derived from individual security selection. In order for emphasis to be placed on particular stocks the method usually results in fairly concentrated portfolios with fewer securities than in an equivalent fund managed by the "top-down" approach. This is because sufficient weighting needs to be given to a single stock to enable it to have some impact on the overall result. This contrasts with the "top-down" approach where performance is centred on asset categories and where stock selection has a subsidiary role.

5.3 Fundamental Techniques for Security Selection

An investment manager operating either of the two methods set out in 5.1 or 5.2 will use what is generally known as fundamental analysis for the selection of individual securities. In the case of a bond, factors such as for example, gross and net redemption yields, duration, coupon, relative position on yield curve, position relative to equivalent government stock, issuer and term would be analyzed and compared with market price. Comparison would then be made with other similar stocks and the effect on the portfolio of the inclusion of a specific additional stock ascertained. Although a multitude of factors is looked at carefully, managers tend to focus on a few main factors for day to day management purposes.

In the case of equities a similar process is followed. The aim is to identify securities where the market price does not already discount all the known information and where it is possible to purchase an earnings stream that has a greater present value than the current market price. Although equity analysis is more complex than bond investment, greater attention is placed upon features for shares within a single sector such as the price/earnings ratio (P/E), dividend yield and net assets per share than on some other factors.

The P/E ratio is simply the share price divided by the earnings (usually after tax) per share of the company in the current year, but sometimes the prospective P/E (the current share price divided by next year's expected earnings per share) is used or the historic P/E (the current price per share divided by last year's earnings per share) is used. These numbers help an investor to ascertain how expensive the share price is compared to the earnings of the company. If the P/E is 10 on one share and on the other is 20, clearly the company whose share has a P/E of 20 needs to show strong earnings per share growth to justify purchase against the alternative. Managers will compare these P/E ratios between companies in the same sector and will tend to establish buying ranges for shares based on moves in these ratios. Dividend yield and net assets per share tend to be less important in the UK stockmarket, but can be a major influence on prices for some sectors. For example, for property shares the key feature is the relationship of market price to the net assets of the underlying property and property shares rarely trade on income or earnings considerations.

5.4 Technical Analysis

The two methods of analysis in 5.1 and 5.2 use the techniques explained in 5.3 for the selection of individual securities, but technical analysis ignores fundamental security valuation techniques and relies solely on changes and trends in the market prices and other market related factors. Technical analysis is often described as chartism.

Figure 1

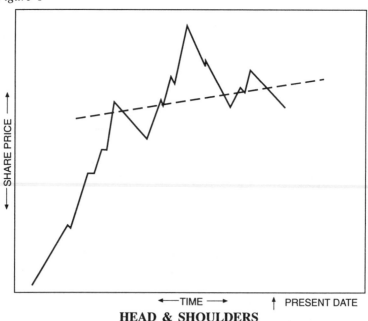

HEAD & SHOULDERS

This method of analysis looks at price movements in absolute terms and relative to an index or a moving average, examines trading volumes, and tries to identify trends in prices. Fundamental analysis (as in 5.1 and 5.2) may be helpful in identifying some trends, but there are many price movements which are difficult to explain on a fundamental basis and which can, at least in the short term, run contrary to this fundamental view. Chartism helps to explain some of these movements and can assist in short term timing.

Some of the predictions for prices are achieved by assessing patterns of share price movements and two examples are given in Exhibits I and II. Exhibit I is a "head and shoulder" pattern whilst Exhibit II is a "double top". Both are examples of patterns which bring expectations of price reversals. There are many other patterns such as "wedges", "diamonds", "flags" and "triple bottoms".

Figure 2

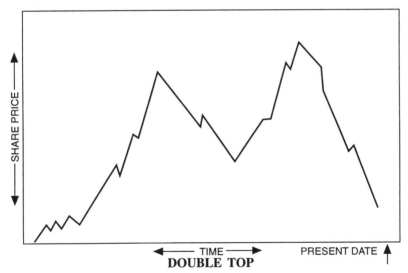

There is a considerable divergence of views on the use of charts. Some investors will use chart information as just another input when making decisions whilst others will base their decision solely on charts. Those taking the latter view may do so because they believe that markets are fairly efficient in adjusting prices to take account of fundamental information and hence it is preferable to concentrate on factors such as chartism where value can be added. The popularity of chartism in a market can also be important. If the practice is widely used, as in the commodity and foreign exchange markets, it is quite likely that investors will buy and sell according to the chart patterns. If the chart predicts a price fall, investors sell and the price will then fall. Hence, a widespread use of charts can make the predictions self fulfilling. In contrast, charts are less widely used in the equity and fixed interest markets and hence less likely to have a major influence on market movements.

Each investor needs to make his own mind up on the value of charts in the particular markets in which he invests.

6. INVESTORS

Investors need to understand the markets in which they operate and their regulatory environments. Some markets (e.g. the London and US stockmarkets) are well developed, with a high level of disclosure of information to investors and are regulated to safeguard investors. Regulation may be by self regulatory bodies (as in the UK) or be by law (as in the United States). Some markets have little central control and minimal regulation, whilst others (e.g. Switzerland) provide a high level of secrecy for investors. Some markets are dominated by domestic investors (e.g. Japanese equity markets) whilst others are strongly influenced by overseas investors (e.g. Swiss bond markets). Institutional investors can be a significant force (e.g. the UK stockmarket) whilst private investors can be the major influence elsewhere (e.g. UK residential property).

Investors will place different levels of importance on each factor influencing the market. For example, an investor who values secrecy and currency stability as a high priority may invest in Swiss Franc denominated investments, whereas an investor wishing to invest exclusively in equities could be expected to invest most of his assets in Japan or the USA or the UK, and perhaps a number of smaller markets.

Some investors will have sufficient knowledge to manage their own portfolios of investments whilst others will use professionals to assist them. The professional managers tend to be concentrated in the main financial centres of the world, and London is the main centre of investors seeking worldwide equity management. For private investors, Switzerland is an important centre, whilst New York and Tokyo contain a large number of managers who invest money mainly domestically. Some investors use investment consultants to help in the selection and monitoring of managers.

Large investors and investment managers can have important parts to play in the efficient running of markets. Their shareholdings mean that they can have influence, if they so wish, in the running of a company. When a company wishes to issue new securities large investors can be requested to underwrite the issue (i.e. guarantee the success of the issue). Most organisations have to have regard to the needs of their likely shareholders if they wish to raise additional finance.

An investor who thinks prices will rise is called a bull, whereas someone who expects prices to fall is called a bear. An investor who purchases a new issue of securities because he believes that the market value will exceed the issue price is described as a stag.

7. PERFORMANCE MEASUREMENT

Once the portfolio of assets has been constructed it is necessary to set up control mechanisms to ensure that the assets are meeting the objectives and risk levels which have been set. The way in which this is done and the frequency of the review will depend on the appropriate time frame for each type of investor. For example a short term orientated investor such as a bank will be monitoring its assets on a very frequent basis and will require asset information on a daily or perhaps weekly basis where the cash flows are low. It will normally be concerned with income levels since the impact of capital values is usually not large as assets are mostly short-dated. On the other hand a long term investor such as a pension fund will tend only to value the assets on a quarterly basis and will usually review performance on an annual basis. Even this annual review will place emphasis on the results over periods of years. This is because it is longer term trends in the prices of equity, property and bond markets, rather than just the income received, which are important to the pension fund, and these trends take time to be established.

Performance measurement techniques have shown substantial advances over the past two decades and sophisticated commercial measurement services are available in both the USA and the UK for certain types of investor. Some investors have developed measures for their own use, perhaps because available commercial products did not meet their needs, or perhaps because no pressure was placed upon them to use anything other than crude measures. Investment managers may have no incentive to introduce realistic measures of the added value that their skills bring to a portfolio, particularly where such figures would not show the managers in the best possible light!

7.1 The Aim

The aim of most performance measures is to produce an overall annual rate of return taking into account both income received and capital changes (either realised or unrealised), based on mid-market prices of securities, and after deducting irrecoverable withholding tax from the gross income received. For an investor subject to tax, it is important to calculate the returns on *an after tax basis,* because it is the size of the return after payment of all taxes that is important and not just the size of the gross return. An appropriate allowance for the costs of investing cash flows may be made depending on the precise method of measurement and the nature of the comparisons which are then made.

Once the overall rate has been calculated, the contribution to the return from income and from capital changes can be shown. Returns are also generally calculated for each sector of the portfolio. The overall return can then be broken down into that due to strategy (i.e. choice of the main market areas), that due to sector choice within each strategy area and the amount due to stock selection. Further analysis can show the contributions from more detailed aspects such as currency changes and market timing. Performance measurement is not just about measuring returns but also building up a detailed knowledge of the reasons behind the result. As discussed in Section 4, returns depend on the risks taken, and hence the risk level should be measured as well as the return. Whilst some investors in the US use quantitative risk measures, particularly where risk is taken to be equivalent to security price volatility, further research is needed in this area and most UK and Continental European portfolios deal with risk in a qualitative way.

7.2 Simple Performance Measures

The approach to performance set out above depends on the availability of market prices for all assets and it also introduces the concept of an annual rate of return. Market prices may not be available and may, in any case, not be important. If market prices are not used, nominal or book prices can be substituted for asset values, and calculations tend then to reflect only income received. This return may be satisfactory in some limited circumstances provided the effect of the underlying assumptions is clearly understood.

Some investors investing in short dated bonds and holding to maturity may just look at current yield, which is just the current income divided by the price. This ignores any capital changes to maturity. Most, however, will look at the redemption yield, adjusted for their own rates of tax on income and on capital, to take account of both income and capital changes to maturity. Redemption yields only apply to bonds, although the current yield method can be applied to a wide variety of assets. The use of the method for assets with wide capital fluctuations may produce answers with little or no practical use.

8. CONCLUSION

The successful investor will not necessarily be the one with the largest rate of overall return on his assets, since to achieve this end product excessive risks may have had to be taken. The successful investor will be the one who has met the investment objectives, and, within the objectives and agreed risk tolerances, has then maximised the return on an after tax basis.

Securities are issued because the borrower requires capital and because the lender wishes to invest. Each party wishes to get the best deal that he can secure for himself and thus the terms will be an amalgam of the wishes of the borrower and those which are likely to be attractive to investors to raise the necessary capital. Hence investors need to appreciate this important compromise between the wishes of both parties when assessing investments, and that investors can influence the terms and type of assets that are issued by the way in which they invest.

Glossary

ABSOLUTE RATE A bid made on Euronotes which is not expressed in relation to a particular funding base, such as LIBOR or US domestic certificate of deposit.

ACCEPTANCE This is the act of a bank adding its name to a bill of exchange drawn on it by its customer and thereby accepting liability to pay the holder at maturity. Accepted bills may be *eligible* (available for rediscount, i.e. purchase, by a central bank) or *ineligible* (not available for rediscounting but, depending on the appetite for the paper of the accepting bank, may be sold in the secondary market). See 'ELIGIBLE PAPER', 'BILL OF EXCHANGE'.

ACCEPTANCE CREDIT This enables a customer to raise short-term finance for international trade transactions inter alia by the drawing of bills of exchange on its bankers. See 'ACCEPTANCE', 'BILL OF EXCHANGE'.

ACCOUNT In the context of the London Stock Exchange an account is a period of two successive weeks during which dealings are put together for settlement on account day.

ACCOUNT DAY/SETTLEMENT DAY The day on which all bargains done for the account are settled; the account day is usually a Tuesday which is seven working days after the end of the account.

ACTUARIAL METHOD A method of repayment where the borrower repays a fixed amount at regular intervals. The interest payable at each interval is calculated on the outstanding amount of the loan e.g. like a repayment mortgage schedule; at the outset of the borrowing, therefore, the repayment amount is composed mainly of interest whereas towards the end, the repayment amount is composed mainly of principal.

ADB (Asian Development Bank) This is an international financial institution founded by the United Nations Economic and Social Commission for Asia and the Pacific (ESCAP) in 1966. Based in Manila, the Philippines, it is owned by the governments of its 45 member countries of which 31 are from Asia and the Far East. Its aims are to generate additional financial resources and to promote investment and economic development in the Asia–Pacific region.

ADBBR (Authorised Dealers Bank Bill Rate) Australian bill discount rate.

ADJUSTABLE RATE PREFERRED STOCK (ARPS) Introduced in the USA in 1982 as a more attractive substitute for fixed interest preferred (i.e.

preference in UK) stock whose value fell as interest rates rose. The adjustable rate was fixed in relation to US Treasury Bill rates thereby ensuring that the stocks traded at close to par. By 1983 this had become distorted by rising interest rates and massive issue volume. Rates were then permitted to be fixed by auction in the form of money market preferred stock, thereby ensuring that the stock could return to trading at par at rate-fixing times.

ADR (American Depository Receipt) A certificate entitling its owner to a bundle of underlying British equities, which are traded outside the London Stock Exchange.

ADVANCES OPTION In a note facility this is the option given to underwriters (who are required to fulfil a commitment to purchase notes at a predetermined rate i.e. the 'maximum margin') to make a short-term advance instead of purchasing the note (usually at the same margin).

ADVANCE PAYMENT GUARANTEE Issued by a bank on behalf of the seller/exporter in favour of the buyer/importer, to protect the buyer by providing for reimbursement of any advance payment made by the buyer, should the seller fail to carry out the contract terms.

ADVISORY FUNDS In the context of the Eurobond market, these are funds left to a bank for investment on a customer's behalf, but only after consultation with the customer. Having such funds at its disposal helps a bank to place new issues of Eurobonds. See 'DISCRETIONARY FUNDS', 'IN-HOUSE FUNDS'.

AFFM (Australian Financial Futures Market) Located in Melbourne and opened in September 1985.

AFTERMARKET – See Primary Market.

AGENCY ARRANGEMENTS Arrangements between corresponding banks inter alia governing the drawing of payment and instruments on each other. See 'CORRESPONDENT (BANK)'.

AGENT BANK (see example of a 'TOMBSTONE').

i)   In the context of the issue of commercial paper, the agent bank administers the issue and retirement of the notes and the reimbursement of funds. The agent bank holds a stock of unissued notes and is advised directly by the dealer of what notes are required, then prepares and validates them and delivers them to the dealers who have purchased the notes as a principal.

ii)   In the context of the issue of Eurobonds, commercial banks are appointed as paying agents in various money centres so that bondholders can cash coupons locally.

iii)   In the context of a syndicated loan an agent bank is appointed to the syndicate. The agent's duties comprise advising the borrower of the rate determined by the reference banks in relation to the funding, distribution of fees, interest and principal, and generally to act as reference point and co-ordinator between the banks and the borrower. The agent usually receives an annual fee for this service.

AGGREGATION The total of the commitments extended to a borrower and/ or its subsidiaries by a banking group to show the group risk/exposure.

AIBD (Association of International Bond Dealers) Founded in 1969 for the establishment of uniform practices in the Eurobond market. Now has over 350 members with varying degrees of involvement in the issuing and secondary markets. See 'EUROBOND', 'ISRO'.

AIBD (interest/yield calculation) This is the Eurodollar bond basis for calculating yields which are on an annual (rather than semi-annual) basis.

AID (Agency for International Development) An office within the US State Department created in 1961 to administer foreign aid, loans and grants.

ALADDIN BOND A new bond issue offered in exchange for an old issue.

ALLOCATION In relation to a Eurobond issue, this describes the amount of the issue allotted by the managing bank(s) to each syndicate member. Also known as allotment. See 'EUROBOND'.

ALPHA SECURITIES Most actively traded shares with 10 or more market makers in each. Market makers are obliged to deal at quoted price.

AMERICAN OPTION An option is said to be 'American' when it can be exercised at any time prior to expiration. See 'OPTION'.

AMEX (North American Stock Exchange).

AMORTISATION When referring to a loan or other term obligation, amortisation denotes a phased repayment programme.

ANSWER BACK A security check whereby a telex operator ensures that the correct answer back code is received from a receiving office before the telex message is transmitted.

ARBITRAGE Buying foreign exchange (or stocks, bonds, money market instruments, metals, commodities, etc.) in one market, and selling an amount to a different party in the same or a different market, for the purpose of gaining profit on the differential, or spread, between the two market prices. The term is sometimes used by continental centres to refer to foreign exchange dealing.

ARPS (Adjustable Rate Preferred Stocks).

ARRANGEMENT FEE A flat fee, usually expressed as a percentage of the total amount of a loan, which is intended to compensate the lender(s) for the notional expenses incurred in arranging the facility. See 'FRONT END FEE', 'MANAGEMENT FEE'.

AT BEST A London Stock Exchange instruction to deal at the best price ruling in the market at the time i.e. the highest price when selling and the lowest price when buying.

AT THE MONEY A warrant, option or similar contract, to acquire a security at a fixed price is said to be 'at the money' when the market price of the underlying security is on a par with the exercise price.

AUTHENTICATION OF EURONOTES The process performed by the issuing and paying agents to give the Euronotes legal effect. This requires the signatures of both the issuing and paying agents and the issuer's facsimile signature on the back of the note.

AVALISATION Undertaking usually given by a bank on a bill of exchange, which has the effect of guaranteeing the instrument. The bank is not normally a party to the bill prior to avalisation but it makes itself primarily liable for payment thereon at maturity. Common in Continental Europe and slowly gaining usage in the UK, often in connection with à forfait business. See 'FORFAITING'.

BACK BOND A Eurobond created out of the exercising of a warrant. Also known as a virgin bond.

BACKSTOP ROLE In the context of a Euronote facility (colloquial). Refers to the underwriter's commitment to purchase notes at a predetermined margin, usually expressed in relation to LIBOR, if notes cannot be placed.

BACK-TO-BACK LOAN When two borrowers, resident in different countries, lend each other matching amounts of their respective currencies for a given period. Interest payable will reflect the differential in the lending rates in the respective markets. The potential for such arrangements exists wherever a major country has exchange control restrictions on investment outflows and/or on the access of non-nationals to domestic credit. Also known as a parallel loan. See 'TOPPING-UP ARRANGEMENTS'.

BACS (Bankers Automated Clearing Services).

BAIL BOND Issued by a bank on behalf of its customer in order to secure the release of a ship which has been arrested as a consequence of a collision or non-payment of repair charges.

BALANCE OF PAYMENTS A country's balance of payments is the record of its transactions with foreign countries. Data is usually presented on an annual basis and expressed in US dollars and/or domestic currency. The balance of payments is in two parts – the current account and the capital account.

The current account is analogous to a profit and loss account, recording transactions in goods, services and transfers. A current account transaction does not create a foreign asset or foreign liability.

The capital account records movements of capital and therefore tracks the transactions which explain the changes in a country's foreign assets and liabilities from one year end to the next.

A typical balance of payments layout follows:

Current account

	Exports of goods
–	Imports of goods
=	Visible trade balance (a)

	Receipts for services, e.g. tourism, banking, shipping, insurance, patents
–	Payments for services, e.g. interest, profits and dividends, etc.
=	Services balance (b)

	Net official transfers, e.g. foreign aid, EU contribution
+	Net private transfers, e.g. workers' remittances
=	Transfers balance (c)

b + c = Invisibles balance
a + b + c = Current account balance

Capital account

	Direct investment, e.g. investment in production facilities
+	Portfolio investment, e.g. purchases of bonds, equities, etc.
+	Other long-term capital, e.g. loans from banks, governments, suppliers, World Bank, etc.
+	Short-term capital, e.g. loans up to one year's maturity
=	Capital account balance

Overall balance: Current account balance + Capital account balance.
Since the balance of payments must sum to zero, balancing items are usually required. These comprise changes in foreign reserves (adjusted for valuation charges) and errors and omissions.

813

BALLOON REPAYMENT A loan repayment programme whereby loan repayments gradually increase in size according to a set formula (hence a "balloon"). The major part of the loan, therefore, is repaid in the later instalments.

BANK BASIS An interest calculation method, also known as CASH BASIS or MONEY MARKET BASIS, actual 365 days basis for domestic £ and domestic Yen and actual/360 day basis for most other currencies.

BANK RISK A term to be used in a Euronote facility, where the credit is guaranteed by one or more banks. The noteholder values *bank* as opposed to *issuer* risk.

BANKERS ACCEPTANCE/TENDER FACILITY A facility, which may be underwritten or not, which allows for tender panel bids on an issuer's bankers acceptances. Available in various currencies. See 'TENDER PANEL'.

BARGAIN Any London Stock Exchange transaction in securities.

BASIS In the context of the futures market this is the difference between the cash price of a financial instrument and the price of a particular financial futures contract relating to that instrument. See 'FINANCIAL FUTURES CONTRACT'.

BASIS POINT

i)   US term for interest rate fractions expressed as decimals, e.g. one basis point = 0.01. Therefore 25 basis points is equivalent to $1/4\%$.

ii)   The minimum price fluctuation allowed for each financial futures contract. Also known as a 'tick'. See 'FINANCIAL FUTURES CONTRACT'.

BEAR MARKET A falling market.

BEARER STOCKS Securities for which no register of ownership is kept by the company concerned. Title is transferred by delivery. The certificates must pass physically from a seller to a buyer.

"BELGIAN DENTIST" A mythical figure, regarded as the classic small investor seeking to invest in Eurobonds in the most tax-efficient way. The Belgian Dentist has a Japanese counterpart in 'Mrs Watanabe'. See 'MRS WATANABE'.

BIBOR

i)   (Brussels Inter-bank Offered Rate). See 'IBOR'.

ii)   (Bahrain Inter-Bank Offered Rate). See 'IBOR'.

BID-BOND See 'TENDER BOND'.

BID DEADLINE The time by which, in the Euronote tender panel facility, the tender panel member must submit a bid to the tender panel agent. See 'TENDER PANEL'.

BID PRICE Price at which buyers offer to acquire securities from sellers. A bid price is always lower than the offered price. Investors will usually trade through market makers. See 'MARKET MAKERS'.

BID QUOTE A trading term used to denote the interest rate at which a trader is prepared to purchase Euronotes.

BID RATE The rate of interest which a bank, when asked to quote, will pay on a deposit from another bank in a particular currency for an agreed amount and period in the inter-bank market. If a bank seeks to place funds then the transaction may well be concluded at another bank's bid rate. See 'OFFERED RATE'.

BIFFEX (Baltic International Freight Futures Exchange).

BIG BANG City slang for the date of 27 October 1986 when all the changes in the dealing system, as well as negotiated commissions and admission of outsiders into London Stock Exchange firms, took place.

BIG BOARD The name by which the New York Stock Exchange is known.

BILL OF EXCHANGE The Bills of Exchange Act 1882 defines a bill of exchange as "an unconditional order in writing addressed by one person (the drawer) to another (the drawee), signed by the person giving it, requiring the person to whom it is addressed (the drawee) to pay on demand, or at a fixed or determinable future time, a sum certain in money to, or to the order of a specified person (the payee), or to bearer".

BIS (Bank for International Settlements) Established in 1930 in Basle to deal with the reparations arising out of the First World War. Played only a minor role in international monetary affairs until the 1960s. Its assets are partly of gold and currencies of the countries whose central banks are associated with it. Monthly meetings are held so that an interchange of ideas can take place between representatives of the central banks. Its traditional role is one of fostering international co-operation.

BLUE CHIP Jargon referring to companies whose shares have the highest status as investments, particularly in the industrial markets.

BOND In the context of investment a bond is a debt instrument, in bearer form and negotiable, containing a promise to pay a specified amount of money at a fixed date and, in most cases, to pay interest periodically at stated intervals during the term of the bond. See 'EUROBOND'. However, see also 'DEEP DISCOUNT/ZERO COUPON BOND'. Bond maturities range from 5 to 20 years, although 5 to 10 years are the most common. See also 'COMMERCIAL PAPER'.

BONUS **(Borrower's Option for Notes and Underwritten Standby)** Synonymous with global note facility. See 'GLOBAL NOTE FACILITY'.

BOOKBUILDING The description of the technique used in an offering of shares whereby an investment bank collects investors' bids for shares to be issued so as to establish the most appropriate selling price. By matching supply and demand in this way bankers hope to avoid excessive volatility in the shares when they start trading in the secondary market. The more traditional method of pricing the shares in an offering is to identify similar companies (as to capitalisation, balance sheet footings, profits, industry, earnings ratios and dividend yield, etc.) and reflect the price of the shares of those companies. By bookbuilding it is possible to identify long term investors rather than expose the offering to stags (i.e. those investors who seek to make a quick capital gain by selling their allocation of shares immediately after flotation or an initial public offering (IPO) in the expectation that the market price will rise due to an oversubscription for the shares).

BORROWING BASE Can have a number of meanings but is generally used in connection with commercial credits and loans to finance companies. With respect to commercial credits, the borrowing base relates to a formula which is allied to eligible assets. E.g. the borrowing base might be 80% of accounts receivable which are not more than 60 days old. With regard to finance companies the borrowing base is broadly defined as tangible working assets less unsubordinated debt i.e. that which is not subordinated (does not rank behind other debt for repayment in the event of a liquidation).

BOUGHT DEAL A bought deal occurs when bankers and brokers take all of a share or bond issue on to their own books. A bought deal can eliminate the cost to the company of the discount to market price at which new shares are sold, if the bank or trading house that is tendering for it thinks it can sell the shares at a higher price.

BRACKET Banks making a new Syndicated or Eurobond issue are grouped into 'brackets' with the lead manager at the top, followed in order by the co-managers, special underwriters (if any), underwriters and other selling group members. Banks in each 'bracket' are listed alphabetically or according to their commitments. See 'LEAD MANAGER', 'SELLING GROUP', 'SPECIAL BRACKET', 'EUROBOND'.

BUCKET ACCOUNT A bank's nostro account in which surplus funds are held.

BULL Speculator who expects a currency to become firmer and buys that currency forward expecting to make a profit on exchange. In the context of the London Stock Exchange the term refers to an investor who believes that the price of a particular share will rise and buys a number of those shares expecting to make a profit by selling them later.

BULL MARKET A rising market.

BULLDOG BONDS Sterling issues *for a foreign borrower* offered for sale to the *UK public market.* Eurosterling issues are those which are placed internationally rather than with the UK domestic institutions/investors.

BULLET A loan which is repaid in one amount at the final maturity date, with repayment of interest only during the life of the loan, or the repayment in "one shot", i.e. capital and interest in one amount at maturity.

BYPASS LOANS These occur when a bank agrees to a commercial facility, presented and guaranteed by a correspondent bank, before the lender knows the name of the borrower.

CABLE A foreign exchange dealing term referring to spot sterling against the US dollar.

CALL A company makes a call when it requests payment by the shareholder of part or all of the unpaid portion of a nil paid or partly paid share.

CALL DATE In connection with the Eurobond market, this refers to the date from which some but usually all the whole outstanding bond issue can be repaid by the borrower, sometimes at a premium. This use contrasts with the widely-known use of the term in connection with calls on partly-paid shares. See 'EUROBOND'.

CALL OPTION See 'OPTION'.

CALL PROTECTION WARRANTS Long maturity, harmless warrants which, during the initial part of their life, can only be exercised by surrendering a host bond, thereby avoiding an immediate call structure on the host bond. See 'HARMLESS WARRANT', 'HOST BOND'.

CALL PROVISION The optional right of an issuer to redeem (i.e. buy) bonds from investors before their stated maturity date, at a specified price, on a specified date or during a given period.

CAP See 'INTEREST RATE CAP'.

CAPITAL GAINS TAX GUARANTEE The French tax authorities require a bank guarantee for an unlimited amount for an unlimited period of time (in

817

practice four years at present) when a foreign subject sells a property in France. This is to cover possible liability for capital gains tax as well as any penalties imposed by the French authorities for infringement of regulations.

CAPPED FRN An FRN with a fixed maximum rate of interest (generally above prevailing market rates). These issues generally offer the investor a more generous margin in return for the cap. See 'FRN'.

CARVE-OUT LOAN A loan secured by an assignment of rights in a portion of a mineral deposit (e.g. an oil field) with repayment coming from the sale proceeds of the assigned minerals. Also known as a production payment loan.

CASH MANAGEMENT Rationalisation of the collection, disbursement, short-term investment and borrowing of funds within and by a company or group, in order to minimise and meet its cash needs at lowest cost. A wide range of traditional and specialised services are offered by banks to assist corporate treasurers in this function.

CASH MARKET The underlying currency or money market in which deals are carried out in the items to which the futures contracts relate or on which option contracts are based, e.g. in the case of a financial futures contract, to purchase a Treasury Bill in six months time, the underlying cash market is in Treasury Bills. See 'FINANCIAL FUTURES'.

CATS (Certificate of Accrual on Treasury Securities) This is a US security representing ownership of interest and principal payments on US Treasury notes and bonds. The instrument is usually purchased at a deep discount to face value and with maturities of 1–22 years. The term is synonymous with TIGERS (Treasury Income Growth Receipts)

CBOE (Chicago Board Options Exchange).

CCIFP (Chambre de Compensation d'Instruments Financiers de Paris). The clearing house for the French Financial Futures Exchange. See 'MATIF'.

CD RATE (Certificate of Deposit Rate) This is the average of bid rates quoted to a lender by the market's CD dealers of recognised standing for the purchase at face value of the lender's CDs of comparative term and principal amount adjusted for reserve costs.

CEDEL (Centrale de Livraison de Valeurs Mobiliers SA Luxembourg) One of the two major organisations in the Eurobond market which clears or handles the physical exchanges of securities and stores securities. Based in Luxembourg the company is owned by several shareholding banks and operates on a non profit-making basis. See also 'EUROCLEAR", 'INTER SYSTEM WORKING AGREEMENT'.

818

CERTIFICATES OF DEPOSIT Negotiable bearer instruments issued by a bank, certifying that a stated sum of money has been deposited with the issuing bank. It can be sold by a holder at any time, providing its holder with greater liquidity than a straightforward bank deposit. Also referred to as CDs. See 'CD RATE'.

CFTC The US Commodity Futures Trading Commision, the official supervisory body for US markets.

CHAMBER OF COMMERCE A body organised to protect the interests of commerce in a town or district. In the UK Chambers of Commerce are independent voluntary bodies, although some foreign Chambers of Commerce are government controlled. See 'ICC (International Chamber of Commerce)'.

CHAPS (Clearing House Automated Payments System) UK settlement banks are linked by computers to despatch and receive sterling payments with same day value, on behalf of themselves, other non-clearing banks and customers. It replaces the "Town Clearing System" by which same day value for sterling items was given for payments between banks operating within defined boundries in the City of London. The Town Clearing System will continue to be used for cheques. See 'VALUE DATE'.

CHINESE WALL This jargon term is used to describe the internal controls considered by securities dealing firms to be necessary to prevent abuses under the dual capacity system, whereby a single firm might act both as broker and dealer/adviser and lender/adviser to both parties in an acquisition situation, etc. causing a potential conflict of interest.

CHIPS (Clearing House Inter-Bank Payments System) Used by US banks and based in New York. See 'CHAPS'.

CHURNING This is defined under the US Commodity Exchange Act as the excessive trading of an account by a broker with control of the account for the purpose of generating commissions, without regard for the investment or trading objectives of the customer. The practice is banned under the rules laid down by the SIB. See 'SIB'.

CIRCUS (Combined Interest Rate and Currency Swap).

CLEAN ACCEPTANCE CREDIT A facility which enables a borrower to draw bills on a bank, upon which the bank undertakes to add its acceptance thus rendering the paper eligible for discount at the finest rates. The bank's remuneration is obtained by way of acceptance commission.

CLEAN UP (30-DAY ANNUAL CLEAN-UP AND WAIVER OF CLEAN-UP) This is a specified period during which there is no short-term bank debt outstanding. This is to ensure that short-term funds are used for short-term purposes. A 30-day annual clean-up means that the borrower must have a 30-day period within 12 consecutive months during which there are no short-term loans outstanding to the bank. Occasionally customers will request a waiver of the clean-up requirement for some special purpose which is granted on normal credit standards.

CLEARING HOUSE FUNDS Funds used on the CHIPS system which are uncleared until the following business day when they will become available for Federal Reserve Transfer or withdrawal in cash. See 'CHIPS'.

CLOSE OUT (CANCELLATION) This is the action taken to complete a forward contract in the event that the customer is unable or unwilling to fulfil his contractual commitment thereunder. The bank assists by providing the customer with appropriate funds at the ruling spot rate only to take them back again at the contracted rate and settle the difference which results. See 'FORWARD DEALS'.

CLOSE OUT AND EXTENSION of a forward exchange contract is the creation of a further period of forward cover at a rate based on the spot price quoted in the close out of the original forward contract. See 'FORWARD DEALS'.

CLUB DEAL A syndicated loan in which the borrower or lead manager approaches other banks well known to the borrower who are prepared to obtain for their own book any amount committed, i.e. there is no "selldown". There is usually no publicity. See 'LEAD MANAGER', 'SYNDICATED LOAN', 'SELLDOWN'.

CME (Chicago Mercantile Exchange).

COCOM (Coordinating Committee on Export Controls) Administers the political decisions of NATO governments as to which items are to be embargoed on strategic grounds for export to the Communist bloc.

COFACE (Compagnie Francaise pour l'Assurance du Commerce Exterieur) French government backed agency which exists to support French exporters. Similar to ECGD.

COLLAR An innovation of the securities market which effectively puts an upper and a lower limit on interest rate exposure.

COLLATERALISED FRN An FRN issue backed by US government securities and thereby effectively having a US government guarantee. See 'FRN'.

COLLECTION A method of settlement whereby banks handle documents (financial and/or commercial) on the instructions of the seller in order to obtain acceptance or payment from the buyer. This method of settlement tends to favour the buyer rather than the seller.

CO-MANAGERS In a syndicatd loan the co-managers fall between the managers and the participants. They are not normally required to give an underwriting commitment, but are invited to participate in the general syndication. For this they obtain a higher proportion of the management fee than that offered to other participants, and more prominent billing on the tombstone. See 'UNDERWRITING', 'TOMBSTONE', 'SYNDICATED LOAN'.

COMEX (New York Commodity Exchange).

COMFORT LETTER See 'LETTER OF COMFORT'.

COMMERCIAL PAPER (CP) This term refers to unsecured promissory notes issued by companies usually at a discount to obtain short-term funds for working capital purposes. In the US banks support customers issuing commercial paper by providing Letter of Credit facilities. This financing method is available only to companies able to command the best credit ratings and paper is usually of 15, 30 or 60 days maturity. Purchasers of commercial paper include banks, other financial institutions, private and corporate investors. Markets exist in Domestic US$, Euro $, Domestic Sterling, Domestic French Francs and Domestic Dutch Guilders. See 'STANDBY CREDIT', 'PROMISSORY NOTE'.

COMMITMENT FEE A bank's consideration for making funds available to a borrower over a period of time. This is a sum (usually expressed as a percentage of the loan) agreed with the borrower at the time of granting of the facility which provides for payment at fixed intervals. The fee is usually levied on the undrawn portion of the facility. A SPLIT RATE COMMITMENT FEE may be included whereby the customer nominates the amount of the facility required during a defined period (usually 6 months). The remainder of the facility (nominated to be 'unavailable') bears a reduced commitment fee.

COMMODITISATION A product becomes "commoditised" as it becomes less profitable and more ordinary.

CONFIRMED LINE OF CREDIT A term used in place of "advised line of credit" in that its availability has been advised to the customer.

CONFIRMING HOUSE An agent in one country for a buyer in another country. The role of the agent is to assist in the trouble-free shipment of goods purchased by the overseas buyer and to pay for them promptly or to underwrite the principal's payment.

CONSORTIUM LOAN See 'SYNDICATED LOAN'.

CONTANGO A London Stock Exchange arrangement whereby settlement for securities is deferred from one account to the next. CONTANGO DAY is the last dealing day of an account, when contangos are arranged.

CONTINGENT SWAP A swap, the terms of which are predetermined but which is only activated on the action of a third party, such as the exercising of a warrant. Also known as an option swap.

CONTINUOUS TENDER PANEL (CTP) In the issue of Euronotes this is a compromise between the sole placing agency and the tender panel. The CTP agent agrees on the issue price (the strike offered yield or SOY) with the issuer, at which price underwriting banks may request protection on their individual allocations. These allocations are calculated pro-rata to their underwriting commitments, but are only exercisable to the extent that the CTP agent has not pre-sold the issue tranche. The SOY can change during the bidding period and underwriters may be able to increase their initial allocations by bidding at, or under, the SOY. See 'EURONOTES'.

CONVERSION PREMIUM Premium over a common stock's market price at which holders of a fixed interest security or warrant may convert it into common stock.

CONVERSION PRICE Option price at which the owner of a convertible bond may convert it into ordinary shares or a floating rate to fixed rate.

CONVERTIBLE A security which can be exchanged for another at some future date or dates at a pre-determined price.

CONVERTIBLE BOND A Eurobond conveying the right to surrender it for ordinary shares at a predetermined fixed conversion price. See 'EUROBOND'.

CORRESPONDENT (BANK) A bank which acts as the agent of another bank, to provide specified services. An account relationship between the two banks involved, though not essential, is often an integral part of the agreement.

COST OF COVERING FORWARD The cost expressed as a percentage per annum, either a positive or negative figure, reflecting the difference in interest rates between two currencies and based on the premium or discount applicable to obtain the forward rate of exchange of one currency in terms of the other. See 'FORWARD DEALS'.

COST OF FUNDS (COF) Cost of funds available to the lender in the market, plus any relative reserve costs. The term is synonymous with Lenders Offered Rate.

COUNTER INDEMNITY When a bank issues a guarantee, it may take a counter indemnity from the customer who undertakes to reimburse the bank in the event of the beneficiary claiming under the guarantee. See 'INDEMNITY'.

COUNTERTRADE This is an international trading transaction where export sales to particular markets are made conditional upon undertakings to accept imports from that market. There are various forms of countertrade:

i)   Counterpurchase (also known as link purchase). The exporter agrees, as a condition of obtaining the order, to arrange for purchase of goods or services from the importer's country. Two separate but parallel contracts are set up.

ii) Barter. This involves a single contract for the simultaneous exchange of goods for goods between two parties. This is fairly rare in practice.

iii) Compensation or buyback deals. Buyback is a form of barter which is favoured by certain countries. Suppliers of capital goods agree to be paid by the future output of the business they are supplying.

iv) Barter by means of trust accounts. This occurs when exports from one country (Country A) are paid for from sale proceeds of local produce from Country B. Payment for goods imported into Country A from Country B is held in a trust or escrow account. The importer in Country B then arranges a documentary credit in favour of the exporter in Country A, which is confirmed by the trust account holding bank. The manufacturer in Country A exports the goods, presents documents and is repaid from the balance of the trust account.

v)   Offset. This is widely used in high technology products. Export orders are given for items such as aircraft on condition that the exporter incorporates components or sub-assemblies manufactured in the importing country.

vi) Switch Trading. This may sometimes be used to arrange payment or part payment for exports by means of a clearing balance which has accumulated with a third country e.g. Country A sells coffee to Country B and instead of being paid builds up a credit balance. If Country A then wishes to import coal from Country C, arrangements can be made to use the credit balance from the coffee sales to pay for the coal. Country B would thus settle with Country C.

vii) Barter by means of an evidence account. Countries with a significant level of continuing business in certain markets may be required to arrange for counterpurchase of goods from that market. It may be practical to balance this kind of trade item by item so the company may maintain an "evidence account" of all transactions. Usually this account must be kept in balance on a year to year basis.

COUNTRY RISK The assessment of risks of doing business in a particular foreign country. The assessment takes into account political factors, import/ reserves ratio, commodity reliance, external debt and sophistication of the country's financial structure.

823

COUPON On bearer securities it is a detachable part of the certificate exchangeable for dividends. Also used generally to denote the rate of interest on a fixed interest security.

CREDIT ENHANCEMENT This is the practice of using a bank's own high credit ratings to enhance the quality of issues from a less attractive lower-rated borrower and sharing the benefit.

CROSS DEAL The sale and purchase of currencies other than the indigenous currency of the originator of the transaction.

CROSS DEFAULT The provision in a loan agreement that default under any other borrowing agreement will also constitute default under this agreement.

CROSS HEDGE This is the offsetting of the risk inherent in one commodity related contract through the use of a contract relating to a different, but price-related commodity. See 'HEDGING'.

CROSS RATE Price of one *foreign* currency in terms of another *foreign* currency. Also referred to as X rate. See 'CROSS DEAL'.

CURRENCY OPTIONS These are forex contracts pioneered on the Philadelphia Stock Exchange whereby the buyer is allowed, without being obliged to do so, to buy or sell a fixed amount of currency at a specified price at any time before the expiry date. The buyer thus enjoys greater flexibility than he/she would have under a formal forex contract. Since May 1985 Sterling/US Dollar option contracts have been offered on the London Stock Exchange in multiples of £12,500. Options can be traded or over-the-counter. Traded options are sold by various exchanges around the world, whereas OTC options are sold direct by banks to customers. An 'American' option can be exercised at any time to maturity whereas a 'European' option can only be exercised at the maturity date.

CURRENCY SWAPS Where two counterparties, sell each other matching amounts of their respective currencies, and usually enter into an obligation to repurchase at a given date of maturity (say after five years). If concluded on the basis of a fixed rate reversal, a contingent liability should be shown in a company's audited accounts, as the deal amounts to a long-term forward transaction.

CURRENCY WARRANT A warrant exercisable by the payment of one currency into a fixed nominal amount of a security in the second currency.

DAWN RAID A sudden, unexpected purchase of a substantial proportion of a company's equity.

DAYTIME BLANK ADVANCE (DBA) This is an overdraft/excess on an account occurring during the course of a business day. The position arises when, from an operational procedure, a payment drawn on the account has to be released before advised covering funds are received.

DEALING DATE The day upon which a transaction has to be contracted for completion on the value date. See 'VALUE DATE'.

DEBENTURE Document issued by a company usually under its seal, as evidence of a loan and of any charge securing it. It is possible to issue "naked" or unsecured debentures (often called "unsecured loan stock") and this is done at times by companies of higher repute; occasionally the debentures or loan stock may be expressed as convertible, i.e. capable of being converted into shares of the company at some future date(s) and at a stated price(s). In practice, most debentures issued to the public, and all those taken by banks as security, are supported by a charge, or a combination of charges, on the assets of the company.

DEBT DEFEASANCE The practice of retiring existing debt early to refinance on a more profitable basis.

DEBT SERVICE RATIO Amortisation and interest payments on a country's external debt expressed as a percentage of total export earnings.

DEEP DISCOUNT BOND A bond issued at a price substantially below face value and a coupon (interest rate) well below market yields. It enables companies to raise funds relatively cheaply on a depressed bond market. The issuer gains the benefit of paying a lower market rate throughout the life of the issue as well as having the ability to amortise the bond discount over the life of the bond. The main advantage to the investor is that the capital appreciation in some countrties, notably Japan, is not taxed as income. The ultimate deep discount bond is a 'zero coupon bond'. See 'AMORTISATION'.

DELAYED CAP FRN An FRN with a maximum rate of interest effective after an initial period. See 'FRN'.

DEPOSITORY RECEIPT Bearer document which is equivalent to, and may be held instead of or exchanged into, multiples of an equity issued through the Euromarket.

DIRECT BID FACILITY (UNSOLICITED BIDDING) A provision in tender panel facilities whereby panel members may make unsolicited bids to the issuer for particular note amounts/maturities.

DISCs (Domestic International Sales Corporations) These were created as an incentive mechanism to promote the export of US goods by deferring the US tax due on export profits if those profits were reinvested in export property. With effect from January 1985 they were replaced by FOREIGN SALES CORPORATIONS (FSCs). See 'FSCs'.

DISCOUNT ISSUE PRICE The issue price of a Euronote either i) on a non-interest bearing basis at a discount to face value or ii) on an interest bearing basis, also issued at a discount. Both to yield the appropriate funding rate plus/minus the appropriate issuance margin.

DISCOUNT ISSUE YIELD The yield on a note at issue date represented by the discount purchase price to face value.

DISCOUNTING The purchase, at less than face value, of an accepted term bill of exchange which is generally retained by the discounting bank until maturity when the full amount is recovered from the drawee.

DISCOUNT RATE Bills are discounted at the prevailing discount rate which varies according to the term and currency of the bill and whether it is eligible for rediscount by the Central Bank. See 'BILL OF EXCHANGE', 'DISCOUNTING'.

DISCRETIONARY FUNDS Funds placed with a bank by customers for investment on their behalf at the bank's own discretion. Such funds are held in particularly large amounts by Swiss banks, and their use for investment in Eurobonds enhances a bank's ability to place new issues. See 'ADVISORY FUNDS', 'IN-HOUSE FUNDS'.

DISINTERMEDIATION Circumvention of the banking system as a source of finance. For example, the trend towards securities in the international financial markets since 1982 at the expense of syndicated bank lending.

DOCUMENTARY CREDITS Essentially documentary credits are a means of settlement in international trade whereby the credit-standing and reputation of a bank substitutes for that of the buyer and offer both parties to a transaction a degree of security. A documentary credit is defined in the "Uniform Customs and Practice for Documentary Credits" as any arrangement whereby a bank acting at the request, and on the instructions, of a customer is to make payment to or to the order of a third party or is to pay, or accept bills of exchange (drafts) drawn by the beneficiary or authorises another bank to effect such payment against stipulated documents, subject to compliance with the terms and conditions of the credit.

DOUBLE TAXATION AGREEMENT See 'DTA/TREATY ACCOUNT'.

DRAWDOWN Full or partial utilisation of a borrowing facility.

DROP DEAD FEE An American term to describe a fee payable by either party to negotiations upon the breakdown of the negotiations and hence the underlying deal.

826

DROPLOCK A droplock is a debt whose interest rate may change on the incidence of some external event, usually a change in market interest rates. A debt may carry a floating rate of interest, for example, until the yield on some market fixed interest security hits a specified rate. At that point the floating rate converts into a fixed rate at a coupon set by reference to the market rate. The actual debt can be constituted in any legal form, the droplock refers to the changed interest rates it may carry over its life.

DTA/TREATY ACCOUNT Double Taxation Agreement applicable where income is collected on securities held abroad to the order of the bank where the owner of the security lives in a country having a reciprocal taxation agreement with the country of origin of the shares.

DTYCSA (Discount to Yield Compounded Semi-annually) This term is used in the à forfait market and represents the return to the lender. See 'FORFAITING'.

DUAL CAPACITY A feature of the deregulation of the London Securities market. All firms are able to operate both as brokers and dealers, previously prohibited. Stock Exchange rules and internal controls have been revised to ensure that conflicts of interest and abuses of the system do not occur. See 'CHINESE WALLS'.

ECP (Euro Commercial Paper) See 'EURO CP'.

ECU (European Currency Unit) A composite currency unit consisting of a basket of ten currencies of EU member countries. In official use it performs the following functions:

i)   It acts as a denominator and an instrument for settling debts between central banks;

ii)   Exchange rate parities for currencies participating in the EMS exchange rate mechanism are set relative to the ECU. Private usage has expanded strongly in recent years.

EDF (European Development Fund).

EFFECTIVE EXCHANGE RATE A measure of a currency's strength against a basket of other currencies. The changes in a currency's value are weighted according to trade flows between the countries in the basket.

EIGHTY TWENTY US tax concession where a US parent has an offshore subsidiary and that subsidiary produce 80% of the group's offshore earnings.

ELIGIBLE PAPER Bank bills payable in the United Kingdom and accepted by those British and Commonwealth banks, the names of which appear on a list published by the Bank of England; the bills are eligible for rediscount at

827

the Bank of England, and qualify as reserve assets for UK banks up to a maximum of 2% of total eligible liabilities.

ELIGIBLE RECEIVABLES Used in connection with accounts receivable financing. It refers to those receivables which, under the term of the credit agreement formula, are eligible as collateral. The position may differ widely from borrower to borrower.

EMS (European Monetary System) This is intended to create monetary stability in Europe, by linking exchange rates and various other budgetary and financial initiatives.

END-END DEALING In the London inter-bank market, a fixture period beginning on the last business day (i.e. working day in London and the overseas centre for the relevant currency) of the month will always end on the last business day of the corresponding later month. Thus a three month fixture period beginning Friday 26 February 19XX will end on Friday 31 May 19XX. One effect of this phenomenon is a tendency for LIBOR to be marginally higher on end-end dealing dates. See 'LIBOR'.

EOE (European Options Exchange) based in Amsterdam.

EQUIVALENT TOTAL MARK UP This is a means of expressing, as an annual percentage interest margin, the mix of fee and net interest income that will be derived from the proposed pricing, drawdown and repayment structures of a lending proposition. Equivalent total mark up figures are used to facilitate the comparison of several possible pricing and lending profiles in order to evaluate and balance the bank's return with the requirements of the potential borrower.

ESCROW A deed, kept in the possession of a third person, which cannot be put into legal operation until the grantee has met certain conditions. When the conditions have been complied with, the document is then delivered to the grantee and takes effect as a deed. It arises in a banking context usually when a bank acts as an independent intermediary, holding funds, between two parties who may be in dispute, or pending the outcome of discussions.

EUA (European Unit of Account) At present this is identical in composition to the ECU. See 'ECU'.

EUROBOND A bond issued in one country and denominated in a currency (or currencies) other than that of the country of issue. This means in effect that the funds are foreign both to the lender and borrower. Bond maturities normally vary between 5 and 20 years. See 'PROTECTION'.

EURO CP (EURO Commercial Paper) A non-underwritten or uncommitted note issuance programme where typically two or three dealers place the issuer's paper.

EUROCLEAR One of the two international Eurobond clearing systems, provided under contract by Morgan Guaranty. See 'CEDEL'.

EUROCURRENCY A freely convertible currency, available for lending, held outside the control of the monetary authorities of the country of origin of the currency by non-residents of the country.

EURODOLLARS See 'EUROCURRENCY'.

EUROEQUITY A form of Eurobond investment aimed at attracting investors' interest in equities rather than fixed-interest bonds, and framed to comply with current US regulations. It is a Guaranteed Convertible Preferred Stock issued outside the USA (just like any other Eurobond) but concurrent with this, there is a domestic common stock issued inside the USA. The Euroequity is convertible at any time (after the first six months) into the domestic common stock on a share for share basis. It carries a minimum annual dividend and dividends can be paid free of US Withholding Tax to non US residents.

EURONOTES These are short-term, fully negotiable promissory notes, usually denominated in US Dollars, occasionally in ECUs and, since March 1985, in Sterling. They are issued at a discount and typically of 1, 3 or 6 months maturity. The promissory notes are issued under facilities which have been given a variety of names of NIF, RUF, PUF. The facilities offered by banks to corporate borrowers often have two elements:

i)   An arrangement to distribute the borrower's short-term notes among potential investors.

ii)   An underwriting agreement whereby if the notes cannot be sold in the market, the borrower will receive the funds from a group of underwriters. This may have the form of a committed back-up standby loan facility.

EUROPEAN INVESTMENT BANK (EIB) The EIB was created in 1958 by the Treaty of Rome with the object of furthering the balanced development of the European Community by making or guaranteeing long-term loans. The EIB lends to public enterprises, public authorities with financial autonomy, financial institutions for projects in member states with three objectives:

i)   regional development

ii)   modernisation and new technology

iii)   projects of common interest to several member countries.

All EIBs loans are vetted by the European Commission to ensure that they are in accord with Community policies.

EUROPEAN OPTION An option is said to be 'European' if it may be exercised only on a specified date. See 'OPTION'.

EUROPEAN WARRANT See 'WINDOW WARRANT'.

EVERGREEN FACILITY A loan facility granted to the customer for a nominal period (say 2 years) but which remains available until the lender requests repayment at which point amortisation commences (over 2 years if that was the nominal period for which the facility was agreed). See 'AMORTISATION'.

EXERCISE PRICE/STRIKE PRICE The price at which the option buyer has the right to exercise the option to purchase or sell. See 'OPTION'.

EXPIRATION DATE In the context of options contracts, it is the last date on which the option may be exercised. See 'OPTION".

FACILITY FEE A facility fee applies throughout the life of the facility, whether notes are issued or the facility drawn down or not. See 'EURONOTE'.

FACILITY LETTER This is drawn up in respect of "one to one" facilities which are not repayable on demand. It conveys the lender's offer of accommodation (i.e. a facility or facilities) to the borrower and when returned with the borrower's written acceptance, serves as a legally binding contract between the borrower and the lender.

FACTORING This is the sale on a continuing basis by one company (the client) of trade debts owed to it by its own customers. The customer of the supplier becomes a debtor of the debt purchasing company (the factor) and has to pay the factor directly in order to discharge the debt.

"FANNIE MAES" US Securities backed by the Federal National Mortgage Association, (FNMA).

FEDERAL FUNDS Shortened form of 'immediately available Federal Reserve funds'. These are the balances of US commercial banks in the Federal Reserve System and can, as such, be transferred with immediate good value, i.e. they are cleared funds.

FEDERAL FUNDS (OVERNIGHT) Cost of overnight federal funds to lender.

FEDERAL FUNDS (USA) Cost of federal funds available to lender in the US Domestic Inter-Bank market.

FIBOR (Frankfurt Inter-Bank Offered Rate). See 'IBOR'.

FINANCIAL FUTURES Financial futures are a flexible and inexpensive means of protecting against the risks associated with violent movements in interest and exchange rates. They operate by means of forward contracts in underlying financial instruments, bank deposits or forward exchange. See 'FINANCIAL FUTURES CONTRACT'.

FINANCIAL FUTURES CONTRACT A financial futures contract is a binding agreement between seller and buyer to make or take delivery of a specified currency or financial instrument at a predetermined future date. See 'FINANCIAL FUTURES'.

FINANCIAL LEASE The full rights and obligations of ownership are passed to the lessee who over the period of the lease, pays rentals sufficient for the lessor to receive substantially the full cost of the asset, plus interest and a profit element. See 'OPERATING LEASE'.

FINANCIAL SERVICES BILL Received the Royal Assent in the UK in July 1986, the bill evolved from a consultative document on investor protection. It updates and extends the regulation of investment businesses with the aims of increasing efficiency, competitiveness, investor confidence and flexibility.

FINEX (New York Financial Investments Exchange).

FIRM CURRENCY A currency which is becoming more expensive in terms of other currencies.

FISCAL AGENT An agent of a bond issuer, primarily concerned with arranging interest and principal payments. S/he may have further discretionary powers set out in the Fiscal Agency Agreement.

FIXTURE A loan or deposit for a fixed period (fixture or interest period) at an agreed fixed rate of interest.

FLEX-LINE A back-up facility available for drawing by an issuer of commercial paper on a regular basis for a limited duration (e.g. for the first 10 days of each month). Commitment fees are only payable for the period the facility is available.

FLIP-FLOP FRN (FLIP-FLOP FLOATER) An FRN with a perpetual maturity and generous margin, convertible into an FRN of shorter maturity (say 5 years) with a less generous margin. See 'FRN'.

FLOATER Floating rate bond, note, certificate of deposit or loan paying a variable rate of interest, though at a fixed margin, often $1/4\%$ over the London Inter-Bank Offered Rate (LIBOR). These bonds usually state a minimum rate, below which their interest rate will not fall (floor coupon). See 'LIBOR'.

FLOATING RATE LOAN See 'ROLL-OVER'.

FLOOR COUPON Minimum rate below which interest rate of floating rate bond will not fall. See 'FLOATER'.

FOREIGN EXCHANGE SWAPS These are the simultaneous and offsetting purchase and sale of foreign exchange in both spot and forward markets, e.g. a purchase for spot and sale in the forwards or the reverse, (or alternatively forward against forward); effectively the two parties are exchanging currencies for a fixed period. Swaps may be used to cover short/medium-term surpluses or deficits in currencies against future requirements.

FOREX Abbreviation for foreign exchange.

FORFAITING This involves the purchase, by discount, of a series of bills or promissory notes in major currencies at a fixed rate, either from an exporter in the primary market or a bank in the secondary market. There is no recourse to the exporter, but the bills/notes must bear the aval of a first-class bank unless drawn on an acceptable government institution. Forfaiting is also known as à forfait' finance. See 'AVALISATION', 'DISCOUNTING', 'PROMISSORY NOTES', 'RECOURSE'.

FORTUNE 500 Fortune is a monthly magazine published in the United States which annually publishes rankings of international companies in terms of sales and net income.

FORWARD DEALS These may be swaps or outright sales/purchases of one currency for another at some predetermined future date. Forward prices are calculated on the basis of current spot rates. Forward rates may be expressed as "premiums" or "discounts" and these express the relative interest differentials between currencies. See 'FOREIGN EXCHANGE SWAPS', 'SPOT DEALS'.

FRANKED INCOME Dividends received by one company from another company whose profits have already borne corporation tax, and which are not subject to further corporation tax. Unfranked income has not borne tax and is subject to corporation tax.

"FREDDIE MAC" US Securities backed by the Federal House Loan Marketing Corporation.

FRN (Floating Rate Note) Security issued on the Euromarket with a floating rate of interest, linked to short-term market rates and fixed at agreed intervals over the life of the issue. They represent an increased proportion of new issues on the Euromarket. See 'FLOATER'.

FRONT BANK Term used to describe a bank which acts as a sole guarantor of a Euronote facility. See 'EURONOTE'.

FRONT END FEE At the outset a flat rate fee is often charged for arranging a managed loan or performing some other function. As payable by the borrower, the fee is normally expressed as a percentage of the amount of the loan; as receivable by a bank it may be expressed as a percentage of such bank's underwriting commitment and/or participation in the loan. Also known as management or arrangement fees. See 'MANAGEMENT FEE', 'ARRANGEMENT FEE'.

FSCs (Foreign Sales Corporations) Within the context of export business from the USA, these have replaced DISCs and tax deferred income accumulated in the existing DISCs will now not be taxed, thereby benefitting US groups which took advantage of the DISC legislation. They were created under the Deficit Reduction Act 1984 with effect from 1 January 1986. See 'DISCs'.

FUTURE (FORWARD) RATE AGREEMENTS (FRAs) FRAs permit banks or corporates to protect themselves against interest rate movements, upwards or downwards, at a specific future date and for a specific period and amount without incurring any commitment to a loan or deposit.

FUTURES A term used to designate all standard contracts covering transactions in financial instruments or commodities for future delivery on an exchange.

FUTURE HEDGING A technique to reduce currency risk by taking a future position equal and opposite to an existing or anticipated position in the cash market.

GATT (General Agreement on Tariffs and Trade) Established in 1947, it is a framework of rules for nations to manage their trade policies. It also provides a forum in which disputes can be negotiated.

GILTS These comprise British Government stocks including issues by the nationalised industries, the local authorities and most public board stocks of Great Britain and Northern Ireland, and the stocks of the majority of Commonwealth governments and corporations.

"GINNIE MAES" US Securities backed by the US Government National Mortage Association.

GLASS-STEAGALL ACT An act of the US congress in the 1930s that prevented commercial banks from conducting investment banking business i.e. underwriting public bond and equity issues.

GLOBAL COMMERCIAL PAPER Non-underwritten Euronote issuance programmes which are sold on a global basis with the book moving between time zones.

GLOBAL NOTE FACILITY A bank's medium-term underwriting commitment which is available to back up both the issue of US commercial paper and Euronotes. Should the issuer be unable to roll over the US CP, this will trigger off a Euronote issuance facility by tender panel. Bridging finance between the time of failed US CP roll-over and provision of funds from the Euronote facility is provided by a swingline. See 'EURONOTE', 'COMMERCIAL PAPER', 'SWINGLINE'.

GNP – GROSS NATIONAL PRODUCT This is the sum of a country's economic output, usually presented on a calendar year basis, though quarterly data are also usually produced for most industrialised economies. GNP may be expressed in nominal terms i.e. at current prices, which enables inter-country comparisons of the size of respective economies to be made (often supplemented by GNP per capita, i.e. nominal GNP divided by the population). The data may also be expressed in real terms i.e. constant prices, using for example 1985 prices. From this, the real growth rate of the economy may be calculated.

GNP comprises:

	Private consumption
+	Public consumption
+	Investment (subdivided into private non-residential, private and public sector)
+	Stockbuilding
+	Exports of goods and non-factor services
–	Imports of goods and non-factor services
+	Net factor income from abroad.

GOLDEN HANDCUFFS In an unsettled and volatile job market golden handcuffs are financial penalties which may be imposed by an employer in the event of a highly paid member of staff resigning, perhaps, after receiving a generous "golden hello". See 'GOLDEN HELLO'.

GOLDEN HELLO In a competitive job market a golden hello refers to financial incentives promised by a prospective employer to attract high calibre and hence highly marketable personnel.

GOLDEN PARACHUTES OR SILVER WHEELCHAIRS Employment contract provisions that may pre-empt a takeover and guarantee substantial severance payments to top management if they lose their jobs after a change of ownership.

GRACE PERIOD In respect of a syndicated loan, the grace period is the period between the signing of a loan agreement and the date fixed for repayment of the first instalment of principal. See 'SYNDICATED LOAN'.

GRADUATED RATE BOND A bond whose coupon changes once or more during the life of the bond. Both the date and level of coupon adjustments are set at the time of issue.

GREENMAIL This is the money a target company uses to buy back shares from a raider who has amassed a block of shares and threatens a hostile takeover. The company buys out the raider at a premium over market price.

GREY MARKET The market in which new bond issues are traded during their initial distribution period and prior to their payment date.

GROSS NATIONAL PRODUCT see "GNP".

"GUBBIES" Jargon word for Australian government debt issues.

GUIDANCE LINE OF CREDIT A line of credit *not* advised to a customer.

GUN (Grantor Underwritten Note) A floating rate note facility akin to a Euronote facility whereby a group of banks (grantors) commit to purchase any notes put back to them by investors on any FRN interest rate fixing date. Put notes are then auctioned out to the market between the grantors.

HARMLESS WARRANT A structure of warrants attached to a host bond that protects the issuer from the potential doubling up of debt in the event of a warrant exercise. See 'WARRANT'.

HEAVEN AND HELL A journalistic term to describe the erratic and volatile nature of the bond market and the varying perceptions of it by its participants.

HEDGING Action taken to offset or reduce possible adverse changes in the value of assets or the cost of liabilities currently held or expected to be held at some future date. See 'FINANCIAL FUTURES CONTRACT', 'FORWARD DEALS', 'CURRENCY OPTIONS'.

HELL OR HIGH WATER LEASE An American colloquialism and not a legal term. It refers to an "iron-clad" lease wherein the lessee has virtually no option but to make timely lease payments.

HIBOR (Hong Kong Inter-Bank Offered Rate). See 'IBOR'.

HOST BOND A Eurobond issue to which is attached a warrant or similar instrument. See 'WARRANT'.

HOT MONEY Vast sum of volatile international money which is available for investment or for speculative purposes always on a short-term basis. When it is used for investment, this money moves from one country to another in order to obtain the benefit of higher interest rates. When used for speculative purposes hot money will flow from a weak currency into a stronger one in the expectation that the stronger currency will increase its value and that a capital profit can be made.

HYPOTHECATION LETTER See 'LETTER OF HYPOTHECATION'.

IBELS (Interest-Bearing Eligible Liabilities). These are interest-bearing sterling deposits of original maturity of two years or less, plus or minus net interest-bearing sterling deposits from UK banks, plus or minus net sterling certificates of deposit.

IBOR (Inter-Bank Offered Rate) The rate of interest at which funds are offered on loan for a specified period in the inter-bank market to first class banks. It may be prefixed by a letter, e.g. BIBOR, indicating the lending centre, in this case Brussels. See 'BIBOR', 'HIBOR', 'LIBOR', 'MIBOR', 'PIBOR', 'SIBOR'.

IBRD (International Bank for Reconstruction and Development) Commonly referred to as the World Bank.

ICC (International Chamber of Commerce) The ICC was founded in 1919 to promote the greater freedom of world trade, to harmonise and facilitate business and trade practices, and to represent the business community at international levels. The ICC is represented by National Committees or Councils in nearly 60 countries and has members in over 40 others. Its International Secretariat is based in Paris. The ICC issues various publications setting down accepted practice and procedures in international trade.

ICCH (International Commodities Clearing House Ltd) A computer system owned jointly by the clearing banks.

ICON (Indexed Currency Option Note)

IDA (International Development Association) The 'soft-loan' arm of the IBRD, aimed at providing assistance to the poorer LDCs. Credits are for 50 years, and carry no interest charges. See 'IBRD', 'LDCs'.

IFC (International Finance Corporation) An affiliate of the World Bank directing finance to stimulate private sector growth in LDCs. See 'LDCs'.

INCOME WARRANT A debt warrant that carries interest on its issue price. In all respects similar to a part-paid issue with a small initial payment. See 'WARRANT'.

INDEMNITY This arises when a bank makes itself primarily liable in respect of a contingent liability entered into by its customer. In this situation it is the Bank's practice to take a counter-indemnity from the customer to ensure reimbursement should it be called upon to make payment. Indemnities may be either:

i)   Terminable a)   valid only for a fixed or determinable time or
                       determinable by giving notice, and –

       b)   fixed or limited for the amount of the liability

ii)   Interminable. See 'COUNTER INDEMNITY'.

INFORMATION MEMORANDUM With syndicated loans, it is common for
the lead manager (or one of the joint lead managers, as the case may be) to
prepare this document. It is based on data provided by the borrower and
contains a comprehensive review of the borrower's operations, including
summarised balance sheets, projections of cash flow, income, profitability,
capital expenditure, future borrowing and annual repayments required to service
existing debt. If the borrower is a sovereign state, the memorandum may lay
greater emphasis on the country's economic and political situation. Also
known as a placement memorandum. See 'SYNDICATED LOAN', 'LEAD
MANAGER'.

IN-HOUSE FUNDS Advisory/discretionary funds which banks invest for
customers. See 'ADVISORY FUNDS', 'DISCRETIONARY FUNDS'.

INTER SYSTEM WORKING AGREEMENT The 'bridge' between Euroclear
and CEDEL, across which payments and deliveries between members of the
two clearing systems are made. See 'EUROCLEAR', 'CEDEL'.

INTEREST RATE CAPS This is a device by which a borrower can "cap" or
limit the interest payable on floating rate debt at a set level. It does not,
however, fix the interest rate until such time as the relative floating rate
exceeds the "cap" so advantage can be taken of lower interest rates should
they occur. Caps can, invariably, be sold independently of the underlying
obligations.

INTEREST RATE SWAPS The market in interest rate swaps has arisen out
of the ability of certain borrowers to access fixed or floating rate money more
cheaply than others. In some market conditions this may result in some
companies not being able to raise funds at all in fixed rates whilst others can
freely do so. Against such an imbalance an interest swap can be arranged to
mutual benefit.

An example of the operation of such a swap would be where one party (A)
raises floating rate debt and a second party (B) raises fixed rate debt in the
same currency. The parties then exchange the interest commitments, enabling
(A) to take advantage of fixed interest rates and to enable (B) to realise a profit
through the additional margins paid to (B) by (A). See 'CURRENCY SWAPS'.

INTEREST – YIELDS See 'YIELDS'.

INTERNATIONAL LENDING AGENCY An official or semi-official organisation whose objects include the provision of loans at favourable rates, particularly to developing countries. Examples include the International Bank for Reconstruction and Development ('The World Bank'), the Asian Development Bank and the European Investment Bank. See 'IBRD', 'ADB'.

IN-THE-MONEY A warrant, option or similar contract to acquire a security at a fixed price is said to be "in-the-money" when the market price of the underlying security is greater than the exercise price i.e. it is already showing a profit. See 'OPTION'.

INTRINSIC VALUE An option is said to have intrinsic value if and to the extent to which the option would currently be profitable to exercise (after allowing for interest). See 'OPTION'.

INVESTMENT TAX CREDIT An allowance in respect of the cost of capital equipment which may be set against corporate tax due to revenue authorities. The amount of the allowance and the period over which it can be carried forward varies depending on the type of equipment purchased and indigenous tax law.

IPMA (International Primary Market Association) The primary market equivalent of the AIBD. See 'AIBD'.

IRON CLAD LEASE See 'HELL OR HIGH WATER LEASE'.

ISDA (International Swap Dealers Association).

ISRO (International Securities Regulatory Authority) Set up as the self-regulatory body for the Eurobond and other capital markets based in London. An SRO under the terms of the Financial Services Bill. See 'FINANCIAL SERVICES BILL', 'SRO'.

ISSUER RIGHT OF REJECTION The right of an Euronote issuer to reject bids from members of a tender panel. Either an absolute right of rejection or a right exercisable only if bids exceed a pre-set margin. See 'EURONOTES'.

ISSUER-SET MARGIN (ISM) In the context of the issue of Euronotes it is similar to the continuous tender panel except that underwriters are guaranteed the protection on their pro rata allocation of paper. Should they opt not to take notes at the issuer set margin, the lead manager will instead.

JUMBO CREDIT An expression used to describe a very large syndicated loan, say US$1,000m or above. See 'SYNDICATED LOAN'.

JUNK BONDS High-yielding, low priced bonds issued by US companies that cannot attract the 'investment grade' classifications of the rating agencies.

These issues range from bottom of the Fortune 500 list down to about the 1500 level in the rankings of the largest US companies. US investment banks have developed this market since the late 1920s and by 1985 junk bonds accounted for about 14% ($60bn) of the total corporate bond sector in the US. See 'BOND', 'FORTUNE 500'.

LDC (Less Developed Country).

LEAD MANAGER The bank or group of banks responsible for the initial contact and negotiation with the borrower to provide a syndicated loan. The term also describes the bank(s) responsible for bringing a new Eurobond issue to the market. See 'SYNDICATED LOAN'.

LEASING A financing arrangement whereby one party (lessor) purchases and provides equipment for use by another party (lessee). Financial advantages can accrue to both parties. Ownership of the leased equipment will often pass to the lessee at the end of the lease or may be purchased for a nominal sum (capital lease). See 'LEVERAGED LEASE', 'FINANCIAL LEASE', 'OPERATING LEASE'.

LETTER OF COMFORT A moral acknowledgement of liabilities incurred and responsibilities, normally by a parent company in connection with a facility to a subsidiary. It usually indicates that the parent will maintain its interest in the subsidiary and is aware of and approves of the terms of the facility in question. A note of caution must be sounded, however. A letter of comfort falls short of a legal guarantee and recent cases have arisen where companies failed to acknowledge their moral obligations towards their borrowing subsidiaries and the lender has been exposed to potential loss.

LETTER OF HYPOTHECATION A trust release or trust letter signed by a customer who has already given a pledge over goods to a lending banker, and who now wishes to obtain the documents of title for the purpose of obtaining the goods, selling them and repaying his debt out of the proceeds. See 'PLEDGE', 'TRUST LETTER'.

LETTER OF POSTPONEMENT This may be obtained by a bank from an existing lender who "postpones" his/her priority right to seek repayment of the existing loan while the bank borrowing is in existence, thereby strengthening the second bank's position as lender.

LEVERAGE An expression common in the USA to refer to the ratio of a company's borrowing to its tangible net worth, or in the case of banks, to the ratio of current liabilities to tangible net worth.

LEVERAGED BUYOUT A situation where a company goes from public to private ownership through the purchase of its own shares prior to refloating

839

them at a higher price. The transaction depends on borrowing most of the purchase price, with a target's assets being used as collateral. Funds for the purchase of the shares are borrowed with the result that the company becomes highly leveraged.

LEVERAGED LEASE A lending arrangement whereby a special 'vehicle' company is formed for the purpose of purchasing and leasing assets. Some 20/40% of the cost of the asset is put up by bankers and other financial institutions in the form of equity in the 'vehicle' company, the remaining 60/80% being provided by medium-term loans by banks. The lease rentals are used first to repay the medium-term debt and interest and second to pay out the equity investors. At the end of the term lease, the lessor purchases the asset for a nominal figure. The equity investors obtain substantial tax credits and allowances which are passed on to them by the 'vehicle' company, which makes this type of financing particularly attractive. The system is used in certain cases to finance aircraft purchases. See 'LEASING'.

LIBID (London Inter-Bank Bid Rate) The bid rate on the London inter-bank market (as opposed to the offered rate) i.e. the rate at which banks are prepared to receive funds from other banks. See 'LIBOR', 'LIMEAN'.

LIBOR (London Inter-Bank Offered Rate). See 'LIBID', 'LIMEAN'.

LIBOR (Lenders Inter-Bank Offered Rate) The offered rate in the particular centre of the lending bank i.e. its cost of funds.

LIBOR (Reference banks) The arithmetic mean of the cost of funds rounded-up, available to the reference banks in the London inter-bank market at a time dictated in the documentation, usually 11a.m. London. See 'REFERENCE BANKS'

LIEN Has numerous meanings, but in banking terms generally refers to a bank's security interest in, or encumberance upon, the collateral. Other liens may result from, inter alia, taxes due and unpaid or court ordered judgements.

LIFFE (London International Financial Futures Exchange Limited) This commenced operations in 1982 and operates on similar lines to established markets in the USA. Financial futures contracts are dealt with exclusively in trading pits by means of "open outcry" on the floor of the Exchange within specified trading hours. Traders register deals with the Exchange Clearing House which guarantees each side of the transaction. See 'FINANCIAL FUTURES', 'FINANCIAL FUTURES CONTRACT', 'OPEN OUTCRY'.

LIMEAN (London Inter-Bank Mean) The mean between bid and offered rates on the London inter-bank market. See 'LIBID', 'LIBOR'.

840

LIMIT ORDER A London Stock Exchange instruction restricting an order to buy or sell, specifying a minimum selling or maximum buying price.

LIMITED RECOURSE FINANCE See 'PROJECT FINANCE'.

LOMI (Letter of Moral Intent) See 'LETTER OF COMFORT'.

LONG A dealer's position is said to be long when his purchases of a particular currency exceed his sales. The reverse position is described as short. See 'SHORT'.

LONG HEDGE This is the *purchase* of a contract e.g. financial futures contracts, swaps, forward deals, options contracts, for hedging purposes. See 'FINANCIAL FUTURES CONTRACT', 'FORWARD DEALS', 'HEDGING'.

LOR (Lender's Offered Rate) Cost of funds available to Lender in local interbank market, plus any relative reserve costs. The term is synonymous with 'COF'. See 'COST OF FUNDS'.

LORO ACCOUNT Refers to the account maintained by another bank for a third party (i.e. their account). Little used by English banks but commonly found in continental payment orders.

MANAGED FLOATING One in which exchange rates are permitted to vary with market forces to some extent, but governments or central banks intervene to prevent undesired fluctuation.

MANAGEMENT BUYOUT This occurs when the management of a company purchases a controlling equity interest in the business from its corporate owners.

MANAGEMENT FEE A flat fee expressed as a percentage of the total loan, which is for the management group of a syndicated loan partly as a reward for, and partly to cover the notional cost of, initial negotiations with a borrower. The fee is also used as an incentive for other banks to join the syndicate, as each manager, co manager and participant is paid a proportion of the total fee, on a sliding scale, commensurate with its respective participation or status. The term can also be used to describe a fee, agreed at the outset between a bank and customer, which is received on an annual basis to cover administration costs in respect of a particular loan. See 'ARRANGEMENT FEE', 'FRONT END FEE', 'SYNDICATED LOAN'.

MANAGER (See example of 'TOMBSTONE') The group of banks which is approached in a syndicated loan after the lead manager(s) has/have received instructions from the borrower to proceed, are known as managers. Managers usually agree to underwrite a proportion of the total loan in order to reduce the underwriting commitments of the lead manager(s). See 'SYNDICATED LOAN', 'LEAD MANAGER', 'UNDERWRITING'.

MANDATE The lead manager(s) in a syndicated loan, having undertaken the initial negotiations with the borrower and having received instructions to proceed with arranging the loan, is/are said to have been awarded the mandate. See 'SYNDICATED LOAN'.

MANDATORY LIQUID ASSETS (MLAs) These are special deposits which UK banks are required to make with the Bank of England. Additional interest is payable by a borrower, calculated in accordance with a prescribed formula on each sterling drawing to offset the Bank of England's MLA requirements.

MARGIN See 'SPREAD'

MARGIN (Financial Futures)

i) INITIAL MARGIN. The deposit which a user of futures markets must make on the initial purchase or sale of a contract. The amount of the deposit represents only a small proportion of the full value of the contract. Sometimes referred to as original security deposit. See 'FINANCIAL FUTURES CONTRACT'.

ii) VARIATION MARGIN. The gains or losses on open contracts in financial futures which are calculated by reference to the market price at the end of each trading day and credited or debited by the Clearing House to Clearing Members' accounts and by members to their customers' accounts. See 'FINANCIAL FUTURES CONTRACT'.

iii) MAINTENACE MARGIN. The minimum margin which a customer must keep in his account with a member of LIFFE in respect of each open contract, normally the same as initial margin, but may be set at a lower level. See 'FINANCIAL FUTURES CONTRACT'.

MARGIN CALL A demand for additional funds because of adverse price movements on an open futures position.

MARGINAL RESERVE REQUIREMENTS A measure introduced by the US Government to contain the money supply and combat inflation. Marginal Reserve Requirements are payable by any bank operating in the USA.

MARK TO MARKET The daily adjustment of an account to reflect profits and losses on financial futures open contracts based on closing market prices at the end of the day. See 'FINANCIAL FUTURES CONTRACT'. Swaps are also marked to market.

MARKET MAKER A dealer (which may be a bank) who trades as a principal and makes a profit on the spread.

MATIF (Marche à Terme d'Instruments Financiers) The French Financial Futures Exchange, in Paris. See 'CCIFP'.

MAXIMUM MARGIN In the context of the issue of Euronotes this is a tender panel structure term meaning both the maximum margin, usually expressed in relation to LIBOR at or under which tender panel bids must be made, and the margin at which facility underwriters commit to purchase notes in the event of insufficient tender panel bids at or under the maximum margin. See 'EURONOTES'.

MAXIMUM PRICE FLUCTUATION On LIFFE, it is the maximum amount the contract price may change, up or down, during one trading session, as fixed by the Exchange. Once the upper or lower limit is reached on a particular contract, further trading may take place at prices within the limit range. Prices may not move outside the limit for a stated period, following which, trade will be without limit for the remainder of the day. See 'LIFFE'.

MIBOC (Marketing of Investments Board Organising Committee) A supervisory board under the City's deregulated structure, to be merged with the SIB. It regulates the marketing of packaged investment products such as long-term insurance and unit trusts.

MIBOR (Madrid Inter-Bank Offered Rate) See 'IBOR'.

MINI-MAX FRN An FRN with both minimum and maximum rates of interest. See 'FRN'.

MINIMUM TURN The turn is the difference between the cost to a bank of borrowing funds in the market and the cost to a customer of borrowing them from a bank, e.g. a bank may borrow six-month dollars at $16^1/2\%$ per annum and on-lend at 17% per annum, giving a turn of $^1/2\%$ per annum. The minimum turn is the minimum percentage gross profit per annum which is aimed at on any particular borrowing. See 'SPREAD'.

MISMATCH FRN An FRN having a coupon structure re-fixed more often and for different maturities than the interest periods. See 'FRN'.

MLAs See 'MANDATORY LIQUID ASSETS'.

MOF (Multi Option Facility) Broader than the classic underwritten Euronote facility (NIF) in that the bank's medium term commitment is to backstop, not only the issuance of Euronotes, but a wide range of other short-term instruments i.e. bankers acceptances and short-term advances in a variety of currencies. See 'BACKSTOP ROLE'.

"MRS WATANABE" The Japanese equivalent to the 'Belgian Dentist'. A mythical figure representing the typical wealthy middle class housewife who, with traditional Japanese conservatism, invests her savings.

MULTI-BANK GUARANTEE A Euronote issue guaranteed by a multiplicity of banks. The noteholder may exercise a put (sale) to the banks in the event of an issuer default. See 'EURONOTE'.

MULTI-CURRENCY OPTION A multi-currency option clause may be added to a loan agreement, giving the borrower the option to:

● switch into another currency listed in the loan agreement, which may cost less to obtain to repay the loan at maturity, if it has in fact weakened against other currencies.

● switch into a lower interest rate currency.

● match assets and liabilities in the same currency, always subject to availablity of such currency at roll-over dates. See 'ROLL-OVER'.

MULTIPLE TRANCHE ISSUE See 'TAP ISSUE'.

NAKED WARRANT An issue of warrants without any host bond. See 'HOST BOND', 'WARRANT'.

NASD (National Association of Securities Dealers) A USA self-regulatory agency for the US securities industry.

NASDAQ (NASD Automated Quotation System) An automatic quotation and information system for the US equity market. It is operated by the NASD. See 'NASD'.

NEGATIVE PLEDGE Pledge not to take any action which would weaken a bank's position as lender e.g. pledge by borrower not to give security to any other lenders.

NEGOTIATION The purchase at full value of financial or commercial documents which are sent abroad for collection and payment at maturity.

NIF (Note Issuance Facility) An umbrella term for the general concept of an underwritten facility for the sale of short-term Euronotes or CDs. But increasingly being used as the generic term for non-underwritten Euronote issuances, otherwise known as Euro-commercial paper. See 'EURONOTE', 'RUF', 'STIF'.

NON-RECOURSE FINANCE See 'PROJECT FINANCE'.

NYCE (New York, Commodities Exchange).

NYMNEX (New York Mercantile Exchange).

NYPLR (New York Prime Lending Rate) A variable interest rate which is determined independently by US banks. It has some similarity to UK banks' base rate.

OECD (Organisation for Economic Cooperation and Development) Members are the major 24 industrialised countries of the world. The organisation exists to help member countries formulate policies for promoting sound growth, and to harmonise assistance to LDCs. See 'LDCs'.

OFFERED PRICE Price at which sellers offer to sell securities to buyers. An offered price is always higher than the bid price. Investors will usually trade through market makers. See 'MARKET MAKERS'.

OFFERED RATE The rate of interest at which a bank is prepared to lend to another bank, in a particular currency, for an agreed amount and period in the inter-bank market. See 'BID RATE', 'IBOR (Inter-Bank Offered Rate)'.

OFFER TELEX The lead manager(s) of a syndicated loan solicit(s) assistance at management, co-management and participant level by sending out to selected banks an offer telex, setting out a summary of the terms and conditions of the loan. The banks approached are usually requested to give an in-principle indication of interest, or otherwise, and whether or not they require an information memorandum. See 'INFORMATION MEMORANDUM', 'SYNDICATED LOAN', 'LEAD MANAGER'.

OPEN ACCOUNT Open account foreign trading takes place when an exporter sends the documents of title for each shipment of goods direct to the buyer with the only condition being that payment be made by a certain date. This method of trading entails the seller, allowing the buyer, in whom he must have complete confidence, control over the goods.

OPEN CONTRACTS These are contracts which have been bought or sold without the transaction having been offset by subsequent sale or purchase, or by making or taking actual delivery of a financial instrument or physical commodity.

OPEN OUTCRY The method of dealing on all futures markets whereby bids and offers are audible to all other market participants on the floor of the exchange. See 'LIFFE'.

OPEN POSITION Dealer's long or short position at any time on which a risk is run. See 'LONG', 'SHORT'.

OPERATING LEASE The Lessor rents the asset to the lessee over a shorter period than its useful life at a rental that does not cover its full cost. At the end of the agreed lease period the lessor then has to sell the asset or lease it for a further period(s) to recoup his outlay or make a profit. He does, therefore, take a risk that the residual value at the end of any given lease period will enable him to undertake further leases or a sale.

OPTION A contract giving the holder the right either to buy (call option) from, or to sell (put option) to, the counter-party a given number of securities at a given price within a specified period. See 'AT THE MONEY', 'IN THE MONEY', 'OUT OF THE MONEY', 'OPTION BUYER', 'OPTION SELLER'.

OPTION BUYER The party who obtains the right, but not the obligation, to buy if the option is a call or sell if the option is a put. See 'OPTION'.

OPTION LINE A facility or facilities to which a bank is not committed but which it might be prepared to make available to a customer upon request.

OPTION SELLER/WRITER The party who is obligated to perform under the terms of the option; i.e. to sell at a stated price if a call is exercised or to buy at a stated price if a put is exercised. See 'OPTION'.

OPTION SWAP See 'CONTINGENT SWAP'.

OTC See 'OVER THE COUNTER'.

OUT OF THE MONEY A call or put option where the exercise price is worth less than the current spot price. See 'OPTION'.

OVER THE COUNTER Trading in securities, shares, options etc., outside the formal exchanges, i.e. all terms, including currency, strike price and premium, are subject to individual negotiation rather than being standard.

PAR
i)   This occurs when the forward rate of exchange is the same as the spot rate.

ii)   The face value at which an issuer of bonds agrees to redeem its bonds at maturity.

PARALLEL LOANS See 'BACK-TO-BACK LOANS'.

PARI PASSU (Latin) The expression means "equally and simultaneously". It is commonly used to provide equal status to a provider of additional finance where finance is already made available through other means.

PARIS CLUB Meetings of Western creditor governments to arrange rescheduling of debts owed by non supplicant (i.e. non problem) debtors.

PART PAID FRN A partly subscribed FRN which can become fully paid at the option of the issuer. See 'FRN'.

PARTIAL SWAP A partial swap involves the borrower of ECUs retaining some components of the ECU while swapping others. The most common form used is to borrow ECU and swap the DM and DFLs elements into either FF, £ or It. Lire.

PARTICIPANTS (See example of 'TOMBSTONE') Participants form the lowest echelon in a syndicated loan, and are approached once the management group has been assembled. They accordingly receive the smallest participation and proportion of fees. See 'SYNDICATED LOAN'.

PARTICIPATION BOND See 'TENDER BOND'.

PAYER In the context of swaps, the payer of the periodic payments e.g. a fixed rate PAYER is someone who pays on a fixed rate basis and receives payments calculated on a floating rate basis.

PAYING AGENT A bank or banks selected by the issuers of a security, responsible for paying principal and interest on an issue, e.g. a Eurobond.

PEG On the London Stock Exchange, to keep the price of shares steady at a given price by buying or selling; on the foreign exchanges, to maintain a country's currency at a fixed rate of exchange by central authority intervention. Crawling is the system for making small automatic changes in adjustable pegs.

PENALTY RATE Charged to a customer who breaks the term of any form of contract, i.e. fixed deposit, forward exchange etc., when, as a result, a bank will incur a loss or loss of opportunity.

PERFORMANCE BOND Issued by a bank on behalf of customers guaranteeing that, having been awarded a contract, they will fulfil the terms and conditions stipulated in the contract.

PHLX (Philadelphia Stock Exchange).

PIBOR (Paris Inter-Bank Offered Rate). See 'IBOR'.

PIP OR POINT One ten-thousandth part of a US$ (the unit varies according to the currency).

PIRATE ISSUE Banks in certain European countries are required by their central banks to issue bonds in a queuing system. A 'PIRATE' issue is one launched outside the queue.

PLACEMENT See 'PLACING'.

PLACEMENT MEMORANDUM See 'INFORMATION MEMORANDUM'.

PLACING or PLACEMENT

i)   A market deal involving the lodgement of funds with another bank or a multinational company. The distinctive feature of such a deal is that the depositor is the party who takes the initiative rather than the borrower.

ii)   An issue of shares or loan stock which is taken up by a deliberately restricted number of investors who have a known desire to invest, as opposed to a public offer for sale to the general investing public.

Provided it is permitted by the London Stock Exchange a placing is much simpler, requiring only an EXTEL card giving information on the shares or stock and financial information on the company. The public offer for sale requires a more voluminous prospectus and will be unattractive for most company issues.

A proportion of the issues is legally required to be allocated to the market to be available to the general public.

PLACING POWER A bank's ability to sell newly issued debt instruments to investors.

PLEDGE A delivery of goods, or their title deeds, by a debtor or borrower to his creditors or lenders as security for a debt or for any other obligation. Legal title remains with the borrower whilst the lender has a lien on the property.

POINTS See 'PIP'.

POISON PILL A right, given by a company to its shareholders to buy preferential shares. The pill's attraction is in its so-called 'flip-over' feature. This allows the 'pill-holder', on a takeover, to buy shares in the surviving i.e. acquiring company, at a discount to market price. That cost to the acquiring company is designed to be prohibitively expensive and so deter unwanted bidders. A similar defensive clause may also be included in a Eurobond issue whereby dissuasively high redemption rates are available to investors in the event of a change of control of the issuer.

POOL Fees shared amongst lead managers in a syndicated loan as a result of participants taking scaled-down fees in respect of their lower proportional participation. See 'SYNDICATED LOAN'.

PRAECIPUUM When arranging a syndicated loan the lead managers invariably retain for themselves a proportion of the management fee, usually justified as the extra reward for the negotiation which led to the award of the borrower's mandate and for co-ordinating the arrangements. The balance of the management fee is available for distribution to other parties in the loan. See 'SYNDICATED LOAN'.

PREDETERMINED RATE In the context of a RUF (also known as a maximum margin). A rate, usually over LIBOR which represents the most an issuer will pay for issuing notes. This will also be the rate at which Euronote facility underwriters will engage to purchase notes. See 'EURONOTE', 'MAXIMUM MARGIN', 'RUF'.

PREFERENTIAL ALLOCATIONS Generic term relating to RUFs, used to describe the practice of allocating Euronotes to facility underwriters at preferential rates. See 'EURONOTE'.

PRE-MARKET See 'GREY MARKET', 'PRIMARY MARKET'.

PRICE/EARNINGS RATIO The current share price divided by the last published earnings (expressed as pence per share). It is used as a measure of whether a share could be considered "expensive", thus a share selling at 50p with a P/E ratio of 10 would be dearer than one selling at 100p with a P/E ratio of 5. It represents the number of years' earnings required to cover the cost of each share.

PRIMARY MARKET

i) In a general context, as distinct from a secondary market where bonds/ securities are first offered for sale.

ii) A term relating to the process of selling a new bond issue. The primary market consists of two stages. The pre-market (or 'grey-market') refers to the period from the announcement of the issue to the date when allotments are made. The aftermarket refers to the period between allotment and payment.

PRIME FIXED RATE Based on Prime Rate, the American term for Bank Rate (the discount rate for prime bills), at drawdown and fixed at that price until the next roll-over period. See 'DRAWDOWN'.

PRIVATE PLACEMENT Similar to a placement although the UK Companies Act 1948 prohibits a private placement being associated with an application for a listing on the London Stock Exchange thereby restricting the shares' marketability. A private placement avoids the requirement for a prospectus.

PRN (Purchase Request Notice) The notice given by the issuer of a Euronote programme to its tender panel agent, (or to its agent within an alternative Euronote distribution structure), an order to initiate a Euronote issue. In a tender panel structure the PRN will be communicated by the tender panel agent shortly after receipt to tender panel members and will initiate the bidding process. See 'EURONOTES'.

PRODUCTION PAYMENT LOAN See 'CARVE-OUT LOAN'.

PROGRESS PAYMENT GUARANTEE Issued to the buyer (beneficiary) confirming that the progress payment made to the supplier, upon completion of certain stages of the contract, is refundable in the event of the supplier failing to fulfil subsequent stages of the contract.

PROJECT FINANCE This can be defined as the financing of a particular economic unit in which the lender is satisfied to look primarily to the cash flows and earnings of that economic unit as the source of funds from which the lender will be repaid, and to the assets of the same economic unit as collateral for the loan.

PROMISSORY NOTE A written and signed promise to pay, unconditionally, to a named person or body, or to bearer, a fixed sum of money, either on demand or at some definite future time, e.g. a bank note.

PROSPECTUS Document giving details of a company, required to support a new issue, and which must be lodged with the Registrar of Companies before any new securities can be offered for sale.

PROTECTION An undertaking given by a managing bank during the selling period of a new Eurobond issue to one or more favoured banks in the selling group that they will receive specified allotments of the new issue in full. See 'EUROBOND'.

PSE (Pacific Stock Exchange) Located in San Francisco and Los Angeles, USA.

PUF (Prime Underwriting Facility) Same as a RUF except that the maximum margin is expressed in relation to US prime. See 'EURONOTE', 'MAXIMUM MARGIN'.

PURCHASE FUND A form of bond amortisation where the borrower is obliged to repurchase a fixed annual amount of its bond issue if the market price falls below a specified level (usually par).

PUT OPTION

i)   the right of an investor to have bonds redeemed (i.e. to sell them back to the issuer) before their stated maturity at a specified price, on a given date or during a given period.

ii)   A contract in the bond share options market allowing the holder to sell a given number of securities back to the writer of such a contract at fixed price for a given period of time. See 'OPTION'.

RAFT (Revolving Acceptance Facility by Tender) An extension of an acceptance facility. To create a RAFT a tender panel and an underwriting group is applied to the acceptance facility, thereby creating a medium-term revolving sub-LIBOR funding instrument.

RAMPING Jargon to describe excessive and unruly price manipulation in the secondary FRN market. It occurs typically when one house buys a significant amount of an issue traded in the secondary market to control the price and force it up in the hope of a quick profit. See 'FRN'.

RATCHET REPAYMENT Repayment of a facility in equal, regular amounts over the whole, or later part, of the term of the lending, usually on an annual or semi-annual basis.

850

RE-ALLOWANCE That part of the selling commission which the selling group member may pass on to his/her clients.

RECOURSE The right, expressly taken by a bank to recover principal and interest from the borrower; it is inherent to most "lending" facilities and certain documentary credit transactions.

REDEMPTION DATE The date on which a security is due to be redeemed by the issuer at its full face value. The year is included in the title of the security; the actual redemption date is that on which the last interest payment is due.

REFERENCE BANKS Reference banks are normally selected from among the lenders in a syndicate and are usually between 3 and 6 in number. The rate of interest to be charged on the syndicated loan is based on the arithmetic mean of the rates at which these banks can obtain funds. See 'SYNDICATED LOAN'.

REPO See 'REPURCHASE AGREEMENT'.

REPURCHASE AGREEMENT (REPO).

i) A trading instrument in the US money market. A REPO exists where the owner of a security agrees to sell that security to an investor while simultaneously agreeing to buy it back at some future date, not later than one year from the original date, or on demand. The price at which the security is repurchased is agreed as an original sale price plus accrued interest, based on an agreed rate of interest for the period of the transaction on a 360 day basis. Typical securities are US Treasury Bills, notes, bonds, 'Ginnie Maes', commercial paper, CDs and banker's acceptances. See 'GINNIE MAE'.

ii) A Euronote trader's agreement to provide liquidity in an issue to an investor by agreeing to repurchase a Euronote at a later date at an agreed price. See 'EURONOTE'.

RESERVE CURRENCY Currency which is widely accepted as a means of international settlement and for the finance of international trade, and which countries are willing to hold in their reserves.

RETENTION BOND Issued by a bank on behalf of the seller/supplier in favour of the buyer who is prepared to release (against submission of a bank guarantee) a certain percentage of the value of the contract normally withheld until the guarantee/warranty obligations under the terms of the contract have been satisfactorily completed.

RETRACTABLE BOND A fixed rate bond issue usually with a long maturity which provides for intermittent coupon refixing by issuer and which gives the investor the right to redeem the bond at each refixing.

REVOLVING LOAN A loan can revolve as to time or amount (within an overall limit). This enables the borrower to drawdown funds, then repay all or a portion of these funds then re-draw. See 'DRAWDOWN'.

REVOLVING UNDERWRITING FACILITY (RUF) A two-tiered financial transaction involving:

i)   The sale of paper to one group of banks/institutional investors.

ii)   A second banking group, standing by ready to support the facility if the first group proves unwilling or unable to take up the paper.

See 'NIF'.

RIGHTS ISSUE When a company, whose shares are already listed, makes a further offer of shares for sale, the London Stock Exchange requires that these be offered to existing shareholders. This is known as a rights issue.

RING FENCE A fiscal term appearing in Government legislation, which means that oil companies' North Sea oil activities are 'fenced off' from their activities both inside and outside the UK, in order that their taxable profits from North Sea oil production are not reduced by reliefs from losses and allowances on other activities.

ROLL-OVER Eurocurrency loans can be made either on a fixed-rate basis or a floating rate. Drawings under such floating rate linked loans will normally be for successive fixture periods of 1, 3, 6, 9 or 12 months, and the maturity and coincidental continuation of such drawings for a further period constitutes a roll-over.

ROUND TRIPPING This term describes the practice whereby companies borrow cheaply and then on-lend in the money markets at a profit. It is a sign of increasing sophistication on the part of corporate treasurers as they have advantage of opportunities to make a profit from their financial activities.

ROUND TURN The total financial futures transaction, in and out, which is completed when the initial long or short position is offset by an opposite transaction or by accepting or making delivery of the actual financial instrument or physical commodity. A single commission may be charged at the time that the total transaction is completed. See 'FINANCIAL FUTURES CONTRACT'.

RUF See 'REVOLVING UNDERWRITING FACILITY'.

SALE RESTRICTIONS Regulatory considerations normally briefly noted on the back of the Euronote restricting and prohibiting the sale of Euronotes to a particular type of investor, e.g. restrictions on sales to US persons.

'SALLIE MAE' US Securities issued and backed by the US Student Loan Marketing Association.

SAMURAI BOND Issues made in the Japanese public market by a foreign borrower. See 'EUROBOND'.

SCALPING To trade for small gains, normally involving establishing and liquidating a position quickly.

SCHULDSCHEINE These are fixed rate promissory notes issued by German banks and corporations, with maturities of one to ten years, rather like CDs. They reflect a real interest rate pegged to current marketing conditions against which German swaps are increasingly being quoted.

SDR (Special Drawing Rights) (composite currency unit). An international reserve asset created by the International Monetary Fund and held mainly by central banks in their accounts with the IMF, but also by commercial concerns, particularly resulting from cash flows from major projects in the Middle and Far East.

SEAQ System (Stock Exchange Automated Quotations System) It shows quotes from competing market makers, details of previous trades, high/low quotes for the day, news items and company announcements. It enables traders to carry out transactions from their offices.

SEC (US Securities and Exchange Commission).

SECONDARY MARKET A market in which CDs, notes, bonds, loan assets, etc., are sold and purchased by those other than the original parties.

SECURITISATION This is the process by which corporations can repackage and sell certain assets as securities (usually representing future income streams, e.g. debtors). These income streams normally have a payment history which can be traced over a period long enough to satisfy a rating agency looking to provide an investment grading to the security, e.g. mortgage loans, car loans, company receivables.

SELLDOWN The amount by which an underwriter's initial commitment (i.e. as given to the borrower in exchange for the mandate) is reduced by the syndication of the loan. See 'LEAD MANAGER', 'MANDATE', 'UNDERWRITING'.

SELLING GROUP Financial institutions marketing a new Eurobond issue. See 'EUROBOND'.

SELLING PERIOD A week or ten days during which managing banks canvass demand for a Eurobond issue among underwriters and other selling group banks on the basis of provisionally indicated coupon and issuing price. See 'EUROBOND'.

SERIAL BOND One issue of a series of bonds with differing terms.

SETTLEMENT PRICE The daily price at which the LIFFE Clearing House clears all financial futures trades and settles all accounts between Clearing Members for each to determine both margin calls and invoice prices for deliveries. The term also refers to a price established by the Exchange to even up a position which may not be able to be liquidated in regular trading. See 'LIFFE', 'FINANCIAL FUTURES CONTRACT', 'MARGIN CALL'.

SHOGUN BOND A non-yen denominated Japanese issue offered to the domestic market by a non-Japanese entity.

SHORT Dealer's position when his/her sales of a particular currency exceed his/her purchases. The reverse position is described as 'long'. See 'LONG'.

SHORT HEDGE This is the *sale* of a contract e.g. financial futures contracts, swaps, forward contracts, options contracts, for hedging purposes. See 'HEDGING'.

SHUNTER A name given to brokers who transact business on an arbitrage basis.

SIB (Securities and Investments Board) The primary regulatory body in the City of London, under the provisions of the Financial Services Bill 1986. It covers investment dealers, investment managers and investment advisors. It has absorbed MIBOR (Marketing of Investments Board Organising Committee) which regulates the marketing of packaged investment products.

SIBOR (Singapore Inter-bank Offered Rate) See 'IBOR'.

SIMEX (Singapore International Metals Exchange).

SINKING FUND Provision by the borrower to amortise debt. See 'AMORTISATION'.

SITC (Standard International Trade Classification) Internationally agreed classification of goods for compiling foreign trade statistics.

SMALL INVESTOR Individual holding less than 10 or 15 Eurobonds, thus having less than $10,000 or $15,000 at stake. Sales to the small investor are sometimes referred to as the retail market.

SNIF (Short-Term Note Issuance Facility).

SOFT LOANS Money lent on favourable terms that would not be obtained by the borrower in the market.

SOLE PLACING AGENCY A Euronote placing mechanism. The sole placing agent sets a fixed Euronote cost over/under LIBOR to the issuer for the life of the facility and has sole distribution rights. See 'EURONOTE'.

SOVEREIGN IMMUNITY This can be claimed by governments or government-owned bodies to avoid court proceedings. Lenders should therefore establish at the outset whether such immunity is waived.

SPECIAL BRACKET When advertisements are drawn up to record details of banks which have participated in a Syndicated or Eurobond issue, the banks are divided into separate brackets. The special bracket is reserved for banks underwriting relatively large amounts of a new issue and often consists of banks which narrowly missed inclusion in the co-managers' bracket. See 'BRACKET'.

SPECIALISED TENDER PANEL (STP) Re Euronotes. Similar to the direct bid facility except that members of the STP comprise a nucleus of houses with perceived note placing strength, who are expected to make a market in the issuer's paper. See 'DIRECT BID FACILITY', 'EURONOTE'.

SPLIT RATE COMMITMENT FEE See 'COMMITMENT FEE'.

SPOT DEALS The sale/purchase of one currency for another, where the exchange rate is fixed immediately for delivery of the currency two working days from the date of the deal.

SPOT MONTH When a financial futures contract is within one month of the delivery date it is referred to as being in the spot month. In London, spot month positions are margined separately from other positions, i.e. they may not be netted or treated as part of spreads for margin purposes. See 'FINANCIAL FUTURES CONTRACT'.

SPREAD This term (which is largely synonymous with 'margin' and 'turn') is used to describe:

i) the difference between the spot and forward prices of a currency

ii) the incremental rate at which banks lend over the cost of matching funds

iii) the difference between bid and offered rates or between buying and selling rates for a currency.

SROs (Self-Regulatory Organisations) SROs are regulatory bodies supervising firms which operate in the investment/security dealing sphere, subject to the approval of the SIB (Securities and Investments Board). See 'SIB'.

STAG A person who applies for a new share issue in the hope of being able to sell what is allotted at a premium when dealing starts.

STANDBY CREDIT Similar in effect to an undrawn overdraft facility, a standby Euro-currency credit is a commitment by a bank to provide funds when called upon to do so at an agreed interest formula. A commitment fee is taken on undrawn funds, usually between $1/4\%$ to $1/2\%$ per annum.

STANDBY FACILITY A RUF where typically the main purpose of the medium term commitment is to act as a standby to the issuance of US commercial paper, to be drawn on only in case of need i.e. where the US market would be unpropitious to an issuer. See 'EURONOTE'.

STARTREK Jargon term for bond priced at a level previously unexplored by the market.

STIF (Short-Term Issuance Facility). See 'NIF (Note Issuance Facility)'.

STIP (Short Term Industrial Paper) An instrument, resembling money market instruments, attracting Sterling funds for up to three months interest rate maturities. The instrument itself may have a life of one to five years.

STOP OUT BID Re Euronotes. A refinement of tender panel bidding whereby one or more of the TP participants have an option to post a bid for all or part of an Euronote issue tranche at a price which other tender panel members must then better. See 'EURONOTE'.

STP See 'SPECIALISED TENDER PANEL'.

STRADDLE The simultaneous purchase and sale of futures contracts for the same type of interest rate on currency futures but for delivery in different months (i.e. a specific type of spread). See 'FINANCIAL FUTURES CONTRACT'.

STRAIGHT DEBT ISSUE Fixed interest Eurobond issue without warrants or any provisions for conversion into another investment. See 'EUROBOND'.

STRIKING PRICE This is the price at which securities are allotted in a tender offer for sale. Everyone tendering at or above the striking price gets some shares at the striking price. Those tendering below do not.

STRIPPED BONDS This innovation allows interest payments to be traded separately from the principal, effectively equivalent to a series of zero coupon bonds.

STUF (Short-Term Underwriting Facility) See 'RUF'.

SUBORDINATED DEBT Debt that can claim, in the event of a liquidation, only after the claims of other (Senior) debts have been met.

SUSHI BOND A Eurobond marketed specially to Japanese investors.

SWAPS TENDER PANEL A further refinement of the tender panel whereby the Euronote issuer can ask for currency and/or interest rate swaps as a particular note issue tranche. See 'TENDER PANEL'.

SWAPTION This represents the combination of an Interest Rate Swap with an Interest Rate Option. Depending upon the terms of the transaction, it will give one party the right, but not the obligation, either to terminate before maturity the underlying swap, or to extend the swap for a further period.

SWIFT (Society for World-Wide Inter-Bank Financial Telecommunication), a co-operative society created under Belgian law and registered in Brussels. It is wholly owned by over 700 of the largest international banks. Its aims are to enable members to transmit between themselves international payments, statements and other messages connected with international banking, and thus to speed up the international settlements system.

SWING LINE FACILITY Where there is an option to drawdown under a facility out of more than one centre, with the agreement of both borrower and lender.

SWINGLINE Used in a global note facility (or BONUS) to allow the issuer to move from the US CP market to the Euronote/Euro-CP market (a type of bridging finance). Typically available from a maximum of seven days and priced over US prime. See 'GLOBAL NOTE FACILITY'.

SYNDICATED LOAN A syndicated loan is arranged when the amount required by the borrower is too large for one bank to provide by itself. Each bank in the loan syndicate agrees to provide a proportion of the total loan.

TAP BASIS A method of issuing Euro CP. The dealer approaches the issuer for paper in direct response to particular investor demand rather than the issuer seeking bids from the dealer. See 'EURO CP'.

TAP ISSUE A financing method where only a portion of the full principal amount is initially issued. The remainder is issued at a later stage depending on market conditions or the need of the issuer. Also referred to as a 'MULTIPLE TRANCHE ISSUE'.

TAX BASED LOANS These are made to borrowers resident overseas whose local laws subject interest to withholding tax (WHT), in respect of which a bank seeks to obtain relief through a tax credit against its own liability to corporate tax. See Chapter 9 re. 'WITHHOLDING TAX AND TAX SPARING'.

Tax based loans may be structured in three main ways:

a) WITHHOLDING TAX ABSORPTION LOANS – a bank receives interest, net of foreign WHT, together with a tax receipt evidencing payment of the tax, which is then used to support the bank's claim for credit relief.

b) GROSSING-UP LOANS – a bank requires the customer to increase the rate of interest payable on the loan so that the bank will receive an amount of interest net of foreign WHT which is equal to that which would have been received had no WHT been imposed, together with a tax receipt to support the bank's claim for credit relief.

c) TAX SPARED LOANS – these are loans to borrowers resident in certain countries with which a country has negotiated a double taxation agreement (DTA) allowing credit relief to be obtained in respect of foreign taxes "spared". Under the law of the country concerned, the loan is granted full or partial exemption from the tax that would normally be deductible from interest payments and the bank will then receive interest gross together with an official exemption certificate used to support the bank's claim for credit relief. See 'DTA/TREATY ACCOUNT'.

TAX SPARING In certain countries where withholding tax (WHT) is levied on interest payable to foreign lenders, there are provisions in the double taxation agreement exempting interest on lendings made available for certain specified purposes from withholding tax.

TENDER ACCEPTANCE FACILITY See 'BANKERS ACCEPTANCE/ TENDER FACILITY'.

TENDER BOND This type of guarantee is issued by a bank in support of a contractor tendering for certain work or for the supply of certain goods or services abroad. The guarantee, issued in favour of the foreign party (beneficiary) is to ensure that the contractor, having gained the contract will accept it according to the terms of his offer and provide any additional bonds called for. Also known as a participation bond or a bid bond.

TENDER DEADLINE Re Euronotes. The time by which tender panel members must submit competitive bids on notes to the tender panel agent. See 'TENDER PANEL'.

TENDER INVITATION Re Euronotes. Communications by the tender panel agent to the tender panel notifying them of the size and maturities required by the issuer and inviting bids. See 'TENDER PANEL'.

TENDER PANEL A group comprised of Euronote facility underwriters, and/ or appointed banks and dealers, who are invited to bid on an issuer's paper in an open auction format. Notes are awarded to bidders in sequential order, from the most competitive bid upwards until the full tranche is allocated. See 'EURONOTE'.

TENDER PANEL AGENT Re Euronotes. The agent is responsible for notifying the tender panel of an issuer's request for bids on notes and for collating and analysing bids and allocating notes to successful panel members. See 'TENDER PANEL'.

TICK See 'BASIS POINT'.

TIG(E)R. (Treasury Income Growth Receipts) Synonymous with CATS. See 'CATS'.

TIME VALUE The amount by which an option's total premium exceeds its intrinsic value.

TOMBSTONE Advertisement placed by banks after a new Eurobond issue or a syndicated loan to record the relative status of the parties involved. See 'EUROBOND', 'SYNDICATED LOAN'.

TOPPING-UP ARRANGEMENTS Common in back-to-back loans. For example, if the £/US$ parity is 2 and £5m is lent back-to-back for US$10m and parity falls to 1.9, the borrower of US$ may be obliged to 'top up' the £ amount to maintain parity with US$10m. Such top-up clauses are usually triggered by parity movements of a given percentage. See 'BACK TO BACK LOAN', 'FOREIGN EXCHANGE SWAPS'.

TRADE-WEIGHTED EXCHANGE RATE See 'EFFECTIVE EXCHANGE RATE'.

TRADED OPTIONS Options which can be bought and sold throughout their life, and exercised by the eventual holder at their expiry date. See 'OPTION'.

TRADING ACCOUNT The 'book' maintained by a Eurobond dealer. It may also refer to the section of a company's annual report in which its trading activities are reported, as well as to the settlement period used for UK Stock exchange transactions.

TRANCHE The drawing of part of a facility granted, e.g. the drawdown of the first tranche (of a loan of $1m) amounting to $100,000 will be on 1 April.

TRI-CENTRALISM Refers to a bank's being represented in the three world financial centres; London, New York and Tokyo.

TRUST LETTER OR TRUST RECEIPT This is a document signed by a customer of a bank, where goods have been pledged as security for an advance and documents of title are held by the bank. To enable the customer to repay the advance by selling the goods, the bank releases documents of title to the customer against his/her signature on a trust letter. The sale proceeds are held on behalf of the bank until the advance is repaid. See 'PLEDGE', 'LETTER OF HYPOTHECATION'.

TSE (Tokyo Stock Exchange).

TURN See 'SPREAD'.

TURNKEY PROJECT Project where the contractor provides all the skills and know-how and masterminds the project up to the point where it is completed and operating and can be handed over to the owners. Normally the finance for the project is provided by the contractor until the commissioning.

UMBRELLA FACILITY An agreement to lend a specified amount which may be utilised either by a parent company or by all/specified subsidiaries. Normally where the balance sheet of a particular subsidiary does not support the level of borrowing requested, a letter of comfort or guarantee is provided by the parent. See 'LETTER OF COMFORT'.

UNCONDITIONAL BOND Commonly known as "on demand". It is payable against the beneficiary's simple statement of claim without the need for evidence of default. "On demand" bonds are a very common requirement of Middle Eastern buyers.

UNDERPINNING In the context of acquisitions and closely related to share underwriting. A merchant bank will underpin an acquisition bid by making an offer to the largest company's shareholders to acquire at a set price (the 'underpinned' price) any of the bidding company's shares to which they are entitled but do not wish to retain.

UNDERWRITING The issue of a Eurobond or company shares is underwritten in case the issue is not fully taken up by investors. With a syndicated loan, to secure the mandate an underwriting commitment is often given. This is an undertaking to provide the full amount or a major portion of the loan. An underwriting fee is payable to lead managers and any other banks involved on a pro-rata basis on the basis of underwriting commitments. See 'EUROBOND', 'LEAD MANAGER', 'MANAGER', 'MANDATE', 'SYNDICATED LOAN', 'RUF'.

UNFRANKED INCOME See 'FRANKED INCOME'.

VALUE DATE Date on which funds are actually available for use by the party entitled to use them. See 'DEALING DATE'.

VANILLA ISSUE Synonymous with a 'conventional' issue in any given securities market.

VENDOR PLACING This occurs when a company makes an acquisition using the money raised by a placing of its shares as consideration.

VRCD (Variable-Rate Certificate of Deposit) The variable interest rate was introduced to improve the CDs marketability.

VRPPS (Variable Rate Perpetual Preference Share) An US instrument used by bank holding companies as a source of primary capital.

860

WAREHOUSING This describes the action of a bank which takes an entire commercial paper issue on to its books before on-selling to investors. Similarly, a swap can be warehoused until a suitable counterparty can be found.

WARRANT A certificate which grants the holder an option to buy a specified security during a given period of time. The warrant may or may not be detachable from another security with which it has been offered. Warrants may be exercised into shares and bonds/FRNs of the same or different currency.

"WEDDING" WARRANT This is an innovative warrant structure. Bonds are callable after the first half of their maturity. The warrants give the holder the option to buy otherwise identical non-callable bonds. For the initial period, however, the warrants are "married" to the original bonds; to exercise the warrant the holder must sell an equal amount of the original bonds back to the borrower. For the second half of the bond's life when the bond becomes callable the warrants are "divorced" and can be paid for in cash in the normal way.

WHITE KNIGHT When a company is the target of an unwelcome takeover bid but is unable to maintain total independence, a merger with another more acceptable company may be a preferable alternative to the takeover. Such a third party company is known as a "white knight".

WHT (Withholding Tax) In many countries a withholding tax is deducted from the gross interest payable on foreign loans made to that country. The interest on such loans is received by a bank after deduction of the withholding tax, together with a tax certificate.

WINDOW WARRANT A warrant exerciseable on particular days or during particular periods. Also known as a European warrant.

WORLD BANK See 'IBRD (International Bank for Reconstruction and Development)'.

WORST CASE COST Term used to denote the worst possible cost scenario to an issuer in an underwritten Euronote facility. See 'EURONOTE'.

YANKEE BOND Issues made in the US public market by a foreign borrower.

YARD OF LIRE Denotes one thousand million Lire.

YIELDS –   Bank discount basis – Bankers Acceptances, Commercial Paper, US$ Treasuries – Interest is *discounted.*
CD or Money Market equivalent yield – Interest paid on Certificates of Deposit, LIBOR Loans.

Coupon Equivalent Basis	) Based on
or	) 365 day
Bond Equivalent Yield	) year.
or	) Interest
Yield to Maturity	) paid twice
or	) yearly *but*
US Basis	) the yield
or	) is
Semi-annual effective	) expressed
or	) as NOMINAL
Nominal annual	) ANNUAL i.e.
	) the first $^1/_2$
	) year's
	) interest is
	) *NOT*
	) compounded.

AIBD Yield – Used for Eurobonds. Interest is paid annually.

ZEBRAS (Zero coupon Eurosterling Bearer or Registered Accruing Securities).

ZERO COUPON BOND See 'DEEP DISCOUNT BOND'.

Index

864

874